BENEATH
THE AMERICAN
RENAISSANCE

BENEATH THE AMERICAN RENAISSANCE

*The Subversive Imagination
in the Age of Emerson and Melville*

DAVID S. REYNOLDS

Alfred A. Knopf, New York, 1988

THIS IS A BORZOI BOOK
PUBLISHED BY ALFRED A. KNOPF, INC.

Copyright © 1988 by David S. Reynolds All rights reserved under International and Pan-American Copyright Conventions. Published in the United States by Alfred A. Knopf, Inc., New York, and simultaneously in Canada by Random House of Canada Limited, Toronto. Distributed by Random House, Inc., New York.

Grateful acknowledgment is made to the following for permission to reprint previously published material:

Harvard University Press: Excerpts from *The Poems of Emily Dickinson,* edited by Thomas H. Johnson, Cambridge, Mass.: The Belknap Press of Harvard University Press. Copyright 1951, © 1955, 1979, 1983 by The President and Fellows of Harvard College. Reprinted by permission of the publishers and the Trustees of Amherst College.

Little, Brown and Company: Excerpts from *The Complete Poems of Emily Dickinson* edited by Thomas H. Johnson. Copyright 1914, 1929, 1942 by Martha Dickinson Bianchi. Copyright renewed 1957 by Mary L. Hampson. Reprinted by permission of Little, Brown and Company.

Owing to limitations of space, acknowledgments for photographs reproduced in the book and on the book jacket may be found on page 627.

Library of Congress Cataloging-in-Publication Data
Reynolds, David S.
Beneath the American Renaissance.
Bibliography: p.
Includes index.
1. American literature—1783–1850—History and
criticism.   2. Literature and society—United States—
History—19th century.   3. Reform in literature—United
States.   4. Radicalism in literature—United States.
5. Historical criticism (Literature) 6. Canon
(Literature) I. Title. II. Title: Subversive imagina-
tion in the age of Emerson and Melville.
PS208.R49 1988 810'.9'003 87-40491
ISBN 0-394-54448-X

Manufactured in the United States of America

FIRST EDITION

To my beloved wife, Suzanne

CONTENTS

Illustrations follow page 340

ACKNOWLEDGMENTS

I would like to thank the National Endowment for the Humanities for awarding me a year-long research grant through the American Antiquarian Society, permitting me to accomplish much of the research required by this book. I am also extremely grateful to the fine staff of the American Antiquarian Society, including Marcus McCorison, John Hench, Nancy Burkett, Keith Arbour, Kathleen Major, and Virginia B. Barnhill. The kind assistance of these and others at American Antiquarian was most useful in the identification of many rare nineteenth-century books and periodicals.

I am grateful to the staffs of the New York Public Library, the Columbia University Library, the Bobst Library at New York University, the New-York Historical Society, the Massachusetts Historical Society, the Library of Congress, the Newberry Library, the Northwestern University Library, the Bancroft Library at the University of California, the Houghton and Widener Libraries at Harvard University, and the Historical Society of Pennsylvania.

Several scholars helped me directly and indirectly. In particular, I want to mention the late Henry Nash Smith, who believed in the project, and Richard Bridgman, who inspired my serious study of American literature.

Rutgers, the State University of New Jersey, aided me greatly by awarding me a Henry Rutgers Research Fellowship, giving me released time and research funds.

I appreciate the encouragement and editorial assistance of Robert Gottlieb, A. S. Mehta, and Jane N. Garrett at Alfred A. Knopf.

My greatest debt is to my family. My little daughter Aline behaved when it counted and cheered me at trying moments. Above all, I thank my wife, Suzanne, who not only understood my long hours in the library and at the computer but also intelligently read the manuscript and made many helpful suggestions.

BENEATH
THE AMERICAN
RENAISSANCE

Introduction

THE OPEN TEXT: AMERICAN WRITERS AND THEIR ENVIRONMENT

The pre–Civil War period, identified by F. O. Matthiessen as the "American Renaissance," has long been recognized as the richest in America's literary history, the period that produced Emerson, Thoreau, Hawthorne, Melville, Poe, Whitman, and Dickinson. This study compares the major literature with a broad range of lesser-known works, combines literary analysis with social history, and discusses writings of various geographical regions and of both sexes. It attempts to bridge the gap between criticism that treats literature as self-referential and cultural history, in which the uniqueness of the literary text often gets lost. American literature was generated by a highly complex environment in which competing language and value systems, openly at war on the level of popular culture, provided rich material which certain responsive authors adopted and transformed in dense literary texts.

Delving *beneath* the American Renaissance occurs in two senses: analysis of the process by which hitherto neglected popular modes and stereotypes were imported into literary texts; and discovery of a number of forgotten writings which, while often raw, possess a surprising energy and complexity that make them worthy of study on their own. An understanding of the antebellum context questions the long-held notion that American authors were marginal figures in a society that offered few literary materials. The truth may well be that, far from being estranged from their context, they were in large part created by it. Each of their careers illustrates in a different way Emerson's belief that the writer "needs a basis which he cannot supply; a tough chaos-deep soil, . . . and this basis the popular mind supplies."[1]

To study the cross-influences and dynamics between the major and minor writers is to participate in the democratic spirit of the major authors themselves, all of whom in various ways expressed their profound debt to lesser writers. As suggested by the above quotation, the relationship Emerson perceived between popular and elite culture was hardly one of hostility or antithesis: rather, it was one of reciprocity and cross-fertilization—almost of symbiosis. Other authors had remarkably similar ideas on the topic. Melville, in his essay on Hawthorne, wrote: "[G]reat geniuses are parts of the times; they themselves are the times, and possess a correspondent coloring."[2] In his semiautobiographical portrait of Pierre Glendinning, Melville explained that even the most apparently trivial literature contributed to his author-hero's creativity: "A varied scope of reading, little suspected by his friends, and randomly acquired by a random but lynx-eyed mind . . . poured one considerable contributory stream into that bottomless spring of original thought which the occasion and time had caused to burst out in himself."[3] Melville himself was a lynx-eyed reader quick to discover literary possibilities in randomly acquired minor literature. Many of his works are heavily indebted to his variegated reading, which seems to have been done in the spirit of a character in *White-Jacket* who says that "public libraries have an imposing air, and doubtless contain invaluable volumes, yet, somehow, the books that prove most agreeable, grateful, and companionable, are those we pick up by chance here and there; . . . those which pretend to little, but abound in much."[4] Hawthorne too was a voracious reader of what he called "all sorts of good and good-for-nothing books," including crime pamphlets, almanacs, and newspapers.[5] He explained his attraction to ephemeral literature as follows: "It is the Age itself that writes newspapers and almanacs, which therefore have a distinct purpose and meaning. . . . Genius . . . effects something permanent, yet still with a similarity of office to that of the more ephemeral writer. A work of genius is but the newspaper of a century[.]"[6] Whitman, whose early fiction and poetry provides a classic example of a writer discovering his powers by experimenting with popular modes, once wrote: "[A]ll kinds of light reading, novels, newspapers, gossip etc., serve as manure for the few *great productions* and are indispensable or perhaps are premises to something better."[7]

To explore the contemporary cultural backgrounds of literary works is to complement the critical literature that focuses on American writers' debt to classic literary sources. One of F. O. Matthiessen's reasons for labeling this period the "American Renaissance" was his perception of extensive borrowings on the part of American writers from the Elizabethans, particularly Shakespeare.[8] More recently, Harold Bloom has described a phenomenon he calls "the anxiety of influence," whereby each major author is described as waging a titanic struggle to get free of the overwhelming influence of classic writers.[9] While such struggles are indeed visible in American writers, it has not been recognized that one of the main weapons wielded by the American writers against oppressive literary influence was a native idiom learned from their own popular culture. The truly indigenous American literary texts were produced mainly by those who had opened sensitive ears to a large variety of popular cultural voices.

Those writers now recognized as "major" had, of course, a profound debt to classic literature; but the key factor to understand is that, unlike some of their contemporaries, they transformed classic themes and devices into truly American texts by fusing them with native literary materials. *Moby-Dick* is a good example of this phenomenon. Melville has often been called America's most Shakespearian writer and *Moby-Dick* his most Shakespearian work. The fact is that *Moby-Dick,* despite certain Shakespearian scenes and characters, is *not* America's most Shakespearian work. That honor goes to a series of forgotten plays written in the 1850s and 1860s by Poe's friend Laughton Osborn, plays that have been deservedly ignored because they sheepishly attempt to duplicate both the form and the content of Shakespeare's plays. *Moby-Dick,* in contrast, gives a fully Americanized version of Shakespeare and other classic sources precisely because it democratically encompasses a uniquely large number of antebellum textual strategies. The anecdotal sermon style, the visionary mode, the Oriental dialogue, dark temperance, city-mysteries fiction, sensational yellow novels, grotesque native humor—these are some of the forgotten popular genres that Melville grafts together to forge symbols that possess stylistic plurality as well as broad cultural representativeness.

The major American writers knew that their compelling metaphysical and artistic concerns—like those of Shakespeare in his day—were produced by a general fermentation of ideas and styles at their unique historical moment. One way to explain these writers' debt to their age is to identify specific "sources." But source study takes us only so far toward comprehending the complex process of literary genesis and flowering, and it does not often lead to larger conclusions about the writer's place in society and history. Emerson perceptively noted that more influential than sources is the temper of the age, which becomes a cultural determinant of the themes and style of great literature. As he writes in *Representative Men*: "[T]he ideas of the time are in the air, and infect all who breathe it. . . . We learn of our contemporaries what they know without effort, and almost through the pores of our skin."[10] Literary genius, in Emerson's view, lies in "being altogether receptive; in letting the world do all, and suffering the spirit of the hour to pass unobstructed through the mind."[11] The present book describes the socioliterary "air" surrounding the major writers and explores the process by which this air seeped through the pores of their skin. Sources do concern me, but only insofar as they illuminate what Emerson called the "spirit of the hour" nurturing the writer's "great genial power." The major texts can be more fully appreciated when considered in the context of the socioliterary factors that suddenly made literary sources, national history, and personal experience available to literary artists as materials for symbolic, timeless literature.

To investigate this subject is to address a central issue of modern literary theory: the bearing that exterior circumstances and the social world have upon the literary text. This book attempts to bring together literary and social analysis by showing that the special richness of major literary works was to a great degree historically determined. It studies literary texts as products of a sudden fluidity of textual modes and strategies perceived and recorded by certain authors, whose special sensitivity to outside forces is heightened by unusual biographical factors. It suggests that certain writers of a specific historical period produced literary texts precisely because of their keen responsiveness to their social and literary environment.

The view of the major writers as alienated rebels has become deeply ingrained in our view of American literature. It has become common to view high literature as an isolated act of rebellion or subversion against a dominant culture. Indeed, several schools of critics have argued that the most distinctive characteristic of American literature is its rejection or transcendence of social concerns. Lionel Trilling in *The Liberal Imagination* (1950) anticipated many later cultural theorists, most notably Richard Chase, by defining classic American literature as an alternate reality distant from social life.[12] Several generations of close readers, from the New Critics through the poststructuralists, have emphasized the supposedly autonomous nature of literary works, placing them at a distance from a popular culture regarded as tame and simplistic. Psychoanalytic critics have typically argued that major authors projected in their works private fantasies and aggressions in reaction against a banal culture that provided no outlet for the tabooed. More recently, with the rise of new historical methodologies in literary criticism, this notion of the alienation of American authors from their society is beginning to be questioned.[13]

The interpretation of the major writers as isolated subversives reifies the existing canon and ignores the open nature of literary texts. It should be recognized that the major writers saw themselves as distinctly democratic artists committed, in Melville's words, "to carry republican progressiveness into Literature" and to immerse themselves so deeply in their time and culture that their works actually became, in Whitman's phrase, "the age transfigured."[14]

This book suggests that during the American Renaissance literariness resulted not from a *rejection* of socioliterary context but rather from a full *assimilation* and *transformation* of key images and devices from this context. Literariness—distinguished by special density and by demonstrable artistry of language or structure—is an intrinsic quality of certain works that can justifiably be called "major"; but it is misleading to remove these works from their context or to ignore unfamiliar writings that in time may also be designated as major.

The emergence of America's national literature in the first half of the nineteenth century resulted, in large part, from a dramatic shift in the rhetorical strategies of popular social texts. Many different kinds of social texts suddenly lost their semiotic equivalences and became colored by a radical infusion of the imaginative. Popular sermons became increasingly dominated by secular anecdote, humor, and pungent images. Popular reform literature moved from staid, rational tracts on the remedies of vice to sensational, often highly metaphorical exposés of the perverse results of vice. Newspapers went through an especially momentous change. The rise of the brash, garish penny papers, supplanting the stodgy sixpennies of the past, brought a new hyperbolic emotionalism and rather amoral exploitation of the tragic or perverse. Even certain papers that tried to remain objective mirrored a society whose republican ideals were mocked by the institution of chattel slavery in the South and wage slavery in the North. On all fronts, it seemed that signifiers were being harshly torn from signifieds, as religious, political, and even journalistic signs suddenly lacked reliable referents.

One outcome of this shift in social texts was an equally dramatic rise in the number and variety of imaginative texts. Since the overwhelming majority of antebellum imaginative texts have been neglected by modern critics, most generalizations about the literary backgrounds of the major literature have been built on shaky foundations. Investigating the total range of fiction volumes, pamphlets, and periodical literature of the day, I have found that the period between 1800 and 1860 witnessed the emergence of two conflicting popular modes, the Conventional and the Subversive, and a third mode, Romantic Adventure, which occupied a kind of middle ground. During the 1830s and 1840s the cultural influence of the three modes grew so enormously that they became a fertile source of thematic conflict and stylistic complexity within the major texts. And the remarkable five years (1850–55) that produced *The Scarlet Letter, Representative Men, Moby-Dick, Pierre, Walden, The House of the Seven Gables,* and *Leaves of Grass* also witnessed the simultaneous crescendoing of the conflicting popular modes, creating a kind of cultural explosion that contributed greatly to the energy and ambiguity of the major literature.

The deep affinities between the major writers and their popular contemporaries may be bypassed in selective readings in the unfamiliar literature of the day, creating a lopsided view of antebellum popular culture, one that greatly exaggerates the importance of Conventional literature while neglecting the immense cultural power of what I call Subversive literature, which was bizarre, nightmarish, and often politically radical. The tendency has been to view the works of writers like Melville and Hawthorne as a revolt against a sentimentalized, optimistic literary culture. A complete review of the volumes listed in Lyle Wright's bibliography of early American fiction reveals that the proportion of Conventional volumes published in the United States, when weighed against the other two modes, actually dropped dramatically after 1820 and remained at a relatively modest level until the Civil War. Before 1800, Conventional fiction constituted nearly 60 percent of the volumes produced, whereas the figure hovered around 20 percent for the 1820–60 period. The proportionate number of Subversive and Romantic Adventure volumes, in contrast, rose from about 20 percent before 1800 to more than 55 percent for the 1841–50 decade.[15] Surprisingly, very little has been written on the Subversive and Romantic Adventure modes, which not only became increasingly influential as time passed but also broke new literary ground that was cultivated by the major writers. As we continue to look for forgotten literature to be added to the growing American canon, a good place to begin our search is among these feisty, sometimes highly problematic novels.

Subversive fiction, which was often highly irrational and rebellious, can be distinguished from the third kind of imaginative text, Romantic Adventure, which was action-packed and sometimes dark but usually stylistically restrained. While the Subversive had roots in eighteenth-century British criminal and Gothic fiction, it took on distinctly American characteristics when reinterpreted by authors who wished to find literary correlatives for the horrific or turbulent aspects of perceived reality in the new republic. The symbolic outcry of Melville's Ahab as he watches the *Pequod* sink—"The ship! The hearse! . . . Its wood could only be American!"—speaks for a whole line of indigenous Subversive texts.[16] There developed an intensifying debate between those who wanted to retain what was regarded as the calmness and polish of British prose and those, on the other hand, who called for a distinctly American wildness, roughness, and savagery, even at the expense of all past literary rules.

Much of this book is devoted to showing the ways in which the social and literary environment became riddled with moral mixtures and ambiguities that prompted various literary responses. Conventional literature tried to avoid or defeat these ambiguities; Romantic Adventure either evaded or objectified them; Subversive literature allowed them to erupt volcanically in often chaotic, fragmented fashion.

When we arrive at the small group of literary texts we find a compact explosiveness of image that occurs because an unusually large variety of cultural codes and strategies are fused. Literary texts brought a measure of self-consciousness and control to the literary response, as certain authors began to manipulate the modes and play them off against each other. The typical literary text of the American Renaissance is far from being a "self-sufficient text," sealed off from its environment. It is indeed what one might call an "open text," since it provides an especially democratic meeting place for numerous idioms and voices from other kinds of contemporary texts. These idioms and voices often conflict to create paradox and irony. But they also *fuse* consistently to create a kind of stylistic implosion resulting in extraordinary compaction of image. Emerson's "transparent eye-ball," Hawthorne's scarlet letter, Melville's white whale, the water of Walden Pond, Whitman's grass leaves—all such complex images represented an enormous compression of varied cultural voices in an explosive center. In the literary text, ambiguity or mystery itself becomes a central issue consciously treated. In Emerson, Thoreau, and Whitman, mystery forms the basis of an exultant individualism and an affirmation of stylistic potency; in Melville, Hawthorne, and Dickinson this potency coexists with more problematic ponderings of ambiguity. It is when each specific contemporary textual strategy is stripped of merely local, time-specific referents and fused with other contemporary textual strategies and classical devices that a new universality is achieved.

The arrival at literariness after an immersion in the popular is repeatedly scrutinized throughout this book. In most cases, it can be said that literary texts were produced only after the major authors had gained firsthand exposure to competing value systems and literary modes. Emerson, for instance, was distinguished from his rather elitist fellow Boston liberals by his rapturous recognition of the rhetorical innovations of the popular preacher Edward Thompson Taylor, the homespun sailors' parson whose poetic sermons epitomized the infusion of the imaginative in popular social texts. Indeed, Emerson's major essays possess native rhetorical fire largely because they are full of the kind of explosive imagery Taylor and others had popularized. Whitman, too, was strongly influenced by the innovative social texts of Father Taylor and other popular speakers. If *Leaves of Grass* has a unique expansiveness, it is because as a popular author earlier in his career Whitman had experimented with every conceivable popular rhetorical voice, from the piously Conventional to the grotesquely Subversive. Similarly, the richness of *Moby-Dick* results largely from Melville's wide-ranging experimentation with popular strategies in his earlier novels.

As will be seen, American writers followed a roughly similar career pattern of early experimentation with popular modes followed by self-conscious mixture of the modes, then stylization of the modes in highly complex literary texts, and sometimes in late career a recoil away from the purely literary toward other forms of expression. In the literary text, which usually is produced in mid-career, we witness a coalescence of competing systems manifested in central images that are irreducible to a single meaning.

To note the unique complexity of the literary text is not to elevate it to the dubious heaven of aporia or indeterminacy. The distinguishing quality of the literary text is not radical subversiveness but unique suggestiveness and great reconstructive power. During the American Renaissance, the proliferation of popular social and imaginative texts was liberating, since it released rich images for literary use, but at the same time it was potentially disturbing, since it threatened to bring about a complete inversion of values and an obliteration of genuine emotion. The major writers sought in their central texts to incorporate as many different popular images as possible and to reconstruct these images by imbuing them with a depth and control they lacked in their crude native state. Uniquely attentive to conflicting voices within their contemporary culture, they transformed a wide array of popular modes and idioms into literary art by fusing them with each other and with archetypes derived from classic literature and philosophy. Their adaptation of an unusual variety of their own culture's popular literary strategies made their works time-specific and culture-specific. Their fusion of these strategies with classical archetypes aided their effort to lend resonance to themes and devices that remained formless or undirected in their popular form. The density of their best works results from this willed reconstruction and intensification of a varied range of popular images.

Exploring the heterogeneous writings that engendered the major literature reveals the inadequacy of hermetic "close readings" that have long dominated analysis of the American Renaissance. The present book rejects the notion of a "definitive" close reading, recognizing that the literary text is a rich compound of socioliterary strands, each of which stems from a tremendous body of submerged writings that have been previously hidden from view. The sections of this book deal successively with religion, reform, sensationalism, women's issues, and humor, tracing the process by which forgotten texts within each dimension were brought to preliterary status and then were assimilated and transformed in literary texts. The writers we have learned to regard as major were those who were particularly attentive to differing socioliterary phenomena and especially inventive in their efforts to reconstruct them artistically. Their full cultural representativeness and simultaneous reconstructive originality become clear when we revisit them several times, from different angles of vision.

Part One

GOD'S BOW, MAN'S ARROWS:
Religion, Reform, and American Literature

1

THE NEW RELIGIOUS STYLE

A CHIEF reason for the rise of literary texts in the antebellum period was a widespread shift in the style of popular religious discourse from the doctrinal to the imaginative. Between 1800 and 1860, popular sermon style, which had in Puritan times been characterized primarily by theological rigor and restraint of the imagination, came to be dominated by diverting narrative, extensive illustrations, and even colloquial humor. In addition, the mainstream churches, knowing they had to compete with novels for the public's attention, began issuing thousands of tracts which increasingly featured moral stories. At the same time, a spirit of piety permeated much secular fiction and poetry. What was once the province of theologians became largely the business of creative writers. By 1841, William Ellery Channing, the leading liberal minister of the day, could concede: "The press is a mightier power than the pulpit."[1]

Critics have long had difficulty locating the major writers in the religious and philosophical context of early-nineteenth-century America. Most have made a strong contrast between the major literature and popular religious writings. A careful look at several major writers' careers, however, suggests that here as elsewhere the standard critical view must be qualified: authors such as Emerson, Whitman, Melville, and Dickinson were in fact distinguished among their literary contemporaries by the breadth and intensity of their responsiveness to experimental developments on the popular religious scene.

The widespread search for replacements for bygone religious texts and dogmas produced a fluidity of genres that contributed directly to the emergence of America's national literature. The gap between sermons and novels, between religious poetry and secular poetry, between sacred allegory and earthly story—in short, the gap between doctrinal social texts and entertaining imaginative texts—suddenly became far narrower than it had been in Puritan times. Previously sacrosanct themes and genres were made available for purely stylized use by American writers. The major literature was produced at this crucial watershed moment between the metaphysical past and the secular future, between the typological, otherworldly ethos of Puritanism and the mimetic, earthly world of literary realism.

The transfer of religion from dogma to the imagination had dramatic repercussions among sophisticated thinkers. Emerson moved from early use of bold illustrations in his Unitarian sermons through a delighted witnessing of even more imaginative sermonizing by evangelical preachers to his final view of the poet as priest. Whitman's famous statement "The priest departs, the divine literature comes" was prepared for by a long period during which he took pleasure in the increasingly secular religious style, a style he often experimented with in his early poetry and fiction. For Hawthorne and Melville, this new style opened up both bygone American Calvinism and sacrosanct texts such as the Bible and *Pilgrim's Progress* for nondogmatic use in modernized allegories and metaphysical fictions. Emily Dickinson, who was extremely sensitive to sermon style and to popular religious literature, discovered psychological, metaphorical reapplications of traditional religious forms and images. Poe progressed from early imitation of popular religious styles (especially the visionary mode) to a nonreligious aesthetic which equated poetic effect with supernal beauty.

Much of the symbolic resonance and thematic complexity of the major texts results from a fusion of elements from two distinctive phenomena of the antebellum religious context: the new sermon style, especially evident in frontier revival preaching; and images from popular fiction and poetry dealing with religion. Stylistic alternatives to threatened faith were being frenetically produced by literally hundreds of antebellum writers. A large floating pool of reconstructive devices were thereby offered to the major authors by their popular religious culture. The major writers distinguished themselves by absorbing a stunning variety of these devices and rechanneling them in literary art.

Emerson's Progress

While Emerson's philosophy and style had a powerful impact upon numerous American writers, it is important to recognize that he himself was the product of a larger change in the style of popular religious discourse. Specifically, a previous change in American sermon style prepared the way for his artistic appropriation of religious imagery.

Colorful illustrations had characterized American revival preaching from the time of Solomon Stoddard's mass religious "harvests" in the 1670s and had become widely used by Great Awakening preachers like Jonathan Edwards and George Whitefield. Edwards's *Sinners in the Hands of an Angry God* (1741), produced by the Great Awakening, became the most famous sermon ever preached by an American precisely because of its extensive use of powerful, horrifying illustrations, such as the comparison of man to "a spider or some loathsome insect" dangling over the pit of hell and of God to an archer whose bow is bent and whose arrow is always ready to be "made drunk with your blood."[2] It should be noted, however, that colonial sermons, including Edwards's, were numerically arranged expositions of biblical passages that followed the traditional Ramist format of "Text," "Doctrine," and "Proof" (or "Application"). Examples were used solely for their didactic message rather than for their entertainment value. Despite the vigor of his images, Edwards was typical in following the tripartite format. In all his sermons he was especially cautious to achieve a tactful synthesis of reasoned doctrine and apt illustrations; he specifically warned ministers to avoid numerous "physical impressions on the imagination" that might lure listeners away from grace into the realm of "mere nature."[3] A hatred of "Romish" impurities, a respect for scholastic authority and doctrinal consistency, and a belief in the depravity of the natural world from which most illustrations are drawn—all of these notions contributed to a generally conservative style even among the most forward-looking colonial preachers.

A truly informal, indigenous preaching style did not begin to emerge until the Second Great Awakening (1798–1815).[4] The earliest and most daring pulpit storytelling in the antebellum period occurred among a group of preachers—Southern blacks—who at first addressed only their fellow slaves but who were destined to attract increasing attention among white mainstream Protestants. We are all familiar with the unparalleled sensation created by Harriet Beecher Stowe's Uncle Tom, whose graphic religious stories showed how, in Stowe's words, "the negro mind, impassioned and imaginative, always attaches itself to hymns and expressions of a vivid and pictorial nature."[5]

What needs to be highlighted is that this innovative use of imagination by black religionists had been an important element in American popular culture ever since the 1790s, when black evangelist Harry Hoosier had accompanied Francis Asbury through the Southern frontier retelling Bible stories in a lively dialect. Even more anecdotal than Hoosier was the

Virginia Baptist John Jasper, who had a remarkable talent for *"stringing together picture after picture"* and for making "a story vivid and familiar to an audience."[6] This typical use of folk storytelling techniques—evident throughout the century in the sermons of black preachers like Lemuel Haynes, Uncle Jack, and Harry Evans—was characterized especially by vernacular dramatizations of the Bible and by secular stories about the conflict between the powerless and the powerful. It is significant that Melville's *Moby-Dick* is full of references to black religious practices, from the passionate black preacher Ishmael witnesses when he first enters New Bedford through the colorful rituals of the humane Queequeg to the entertaining sermon delivered to the sharks by the black cook, Fleece. It is also notable that Whitman developed a powerful fascination with the black preachers and orators who became prominent in New York during the antebellum period. The pictorial style of blacks was an especially creative prototype for American writers who were seeking imaginative replacements for the doctrinal preaching of the past.

An even more important stylistic change during the Second Great Awakening was initiated by white frontier evangelists such as Peter Cartwright, Barton Warren Stone, and James McGready. The fictionalized pulpit anecdotes of these hardy frontier circuit riders and camp-meeting revivalists impelled the rapid growth of the Methodist and Baptist churches. The religious frenzy at camp meetings—manifested in such "exercises" as dancing, barking, shouting, and running—was sparked in large part by emotional, illustrative sermons preached by unlearned ministers to frontier congregations who had little interest in theological niceties. Between 1805 and 1825 the new revivalism was brought to the Northern cities by immensely popular evangelists such as John Summerfield, Lorenzo Dow, and the entertaining "mechanick preacher" Johnny Edwards, all of whom accelerated the general tendency from doctrinal to imaginative sermonizing.

At the same time that American sermon style was being dramatically altered on the popular level, it was also affected by intellectual currents from abroad, most notably European Romanticism and the Scottish Common Sense philosophy. Romanticism helped engender the widespread interest among American preachers (especially Boston liberals) in extemporaneous sermons springing from intuition and punctuated by examples from the natural world and from secular literature. Scottish rhetoricians such as George Campbell and Hugh Blair called for a simplified "popular eloquence" based upon practical example rather than abstruse metaphysics.[7]

Emerson was distinguished among his liberal contemporaries by his openness to *both* the foreign intellectual influences and the new American revival style. A principal element of the complexity of his major writings is the cross-fertilization and, on occasion, the resounding collision between the polished Unitarian style and the vibrant, popularly oriented revival style. He moved from early fascination with the intellectual sources of change to a hearty interest in the kind of torrid popular evangelical preaching that his Brahmin colleagues generally dismissed as crude and chaotic. He produced literary texts precisely because he imported into his prose the warmth and color of a popular idiom that most liberals snobbishly castigated.

The artistic implications of the changing pulpit style were quickly recognized by Emerson, as can be seen in his early journals. His first exposure to the change came while he was a Harvard senior in 1820, when Edward Everett, having just returned from a five-year stay in Germany, where he imbibed European Romantic thought, initiated a revolution in sermon style among Unitarians by delivering a sermon abounding, as Emerson later recalled, "in daring imagery, in parable," giving the young Emerson one of his first lessons in "the magic of form."[8] For a while Emerson was frightened by the prospect of sermon technique becoming more highly valued than religious content. He lamented in his journal in 1823 that "there is a danger of a *poetical* religion from the tendencies of the age," and he expressed fear that soon religion would "consist in nothing else than the progressive introduction of apposite metaphors."[9] Despite these initial reservations, he was coming to believe that his own mental strength was imagination rather than reason, and in 1824 he expressed delight that "the preaching most in vogue at the present day depends chiefly on imagination for its success."[10] By the time he assumed the pastorship of Boston's Second Church in the late 1820s, he was actually prepared to take imaginative flights beyond the sermon form altogether. Only 25 percent of his sermons at Second Church were concerned with doctrinal issues, and his introduction of what he called "new forms of address, new modes of illustration" shocked even the informal Rev. Henry Ware, Jr., who upbraided Emerson for using irreverent imagery in the pulpit.[11] Emerson's reply to Ware shows how crucial his stylistic experimentation was to the expansion of his philosophical vision. "I have affected generally a mode of illustration rather bolder than the usage of our preaching warrants," Emerson explained, "on the principle that our religion is nothing limited or partial, but of universal application, and is interested in all that interests man."[12]

And then came Father Taylor. During the 1830s, the crucial transitional period when Emerson abandoned the Unitarian pulpit and moved to Transcendentalist philosophizing, the maturation of his literary consciousness owed much to the image-filled sermons of Edward Thompson Taylor, the popular evangelical minister of the Seamen's Bethel Church in Boston which Emerson often attended and where he sometimes was a guest preacher. Father Taylor proved to be an important figure in America's literary renaissance. Not only did he profoundly affect Emerson, but he became the prototype for Father Mapple in *Moby-Dick* and was admired by Thoreau and Whitman (who called Taylor America's only "essentially perfect orator").[13]

While Emerson's relationship with Taylor is well known, the social and literary ramifications of this relationship merit further discussion. Taylor's sermons were explosive social texts that fused the mild theology of Boston liberalism with the daring imagery of colloquial revivalism. Taylor had been raised in the streets of Richmond, Virginia, and had sailed before the mast as a privateersman in the War of 1812 before becoming successively a farm laborer, a cobbler, a tin peddler, and at last a Methodist preacher. His unusual rhetoric grew directly from the volcanic soil of American popular culture. Known for his "great hot heart," he brought to the American pulpit a secularized, showmanlike style that would be unmatched in imaginative vigor until the advent of post–Civil War preachers like T. De Witt Talmage and Dwight Moody.

Ushering Southern argot and seamen's slang into the center of the Brahmin establishment, Taylor, who called himself "a Unitarian graft on the Methodist stock," preached extemporaneous, free-flowing sermons filled with racy anecdotes and striking metaphors. In the middle of one typical sermon, tracing the moral descent of a country boy ruined by city vices like gambling and drinking, Taylor lifted his hand and whispered, "Hush-h-h, he is cursing his mother—shut the windows of heaven, *shut* the windows." He treated divine matters with a new familiarity, as is shown by his homely advice: "Don't burn the candle down to the end in sin and then give God the snuff." Taylor became a genuine friend of Emerson, whom he defended against all detractors even after Emerson abandoned formal Christianity. When asked if Emerson was headed for hell, he declared with characteristic jauntiness: "Go there; Why, if he went there he would change the climate and the tide of emigration would turn that way." His images, according to one listener, "went right home like the arrows from the bow of the Conqueror no other man could draw."[14] In the vivid but otherworldly Puritan preaching of Jonathan Edwards, *divine* arrows were thought to be aimed at man's heart. By Taylor's time, it was clear that all the arrows were man-made, and God's bow was firmly held in human hands.

Although Taylor amused and befriended many Boston liberals, Emerson was alone among his contemporaries (Whitman and Melville excepted) in realizing the full significance of Taylor's stylistic innovations. On the most obvious level, Taylor's brash self-confidence pushed Emerson toward his famous assertions of self-reliance. Believing that all other preaching seemed "puny" and "cowardly" beside Taylor's, Emerson said that when you see Taylor "instantly you behold that a man is a Mover."[15] Indeed, it was no very great distance from Taylor's boast: "I am no man's model, no man's copy, no man's agent" to Emerson's advice: "Trust thyself: every heart vibrates to that iron string" or "Whoso would be a man must be a nonconformist."[16] More subtly, Taylor's oratory showed the possibilities of a new *stylistic* self-reliance whereby the emphasis in religious discussion shifted from dogmatic content to creative image, from doctrinal exposition to fluid poeticizing. Taylor's manner, Emerson noted, showed that "Form seems to be bowing Substance out of the World," as "Taylor's muse" is "a panorama of images from all nature & art."[17] Calling Taylor "the Shakespeare of the sailor & the poor," he wrote of a typical Taylor sermon: "The wonderful & laughing life of his illustration keeps us broad awake. A string of rockets all night."[18] Emerson declared that Taylor "rolls the world into a ball & tosses it from hand to hand."[19]

The new sermon manner, as initiated by the frontier revivalists and perfected by Taylor, was simultaneously *all* style and *no* style, and some of the tensions in our major literature derive from this paradoxical combination. The new popular sermons were filled with unusual images that showed the nineteenth-century religionist's search for poetic alternatives to doctrine. These images, however, were usually unpremeditated, unrestrained. This combination of artifice and artlessness was noticed by the major authors. Emerson and Whitman, for instance, called Taylor a natural poet on the level of Robert Burns or the great Renaissance writers; on the other hand, they stressed there was no plan, no reason, no connections behind Taylor's imagery.

An equally important literary manifestation of the new sermon style was a humanization and secularization of religious discourse. Popular preachers like Taylor, Dow, and Summerfield were above all *human* in delivery and message. They not only spoke the language of their congregations but also expressed the universal human feelings of love, friendship, revenge, gaiety, terror. To be sure, emotion had been summoned into American preaching by Edwards, Whitefield, and other eighteenth-century preachers; but even the most colorful early preachers had been careful to warn constantly against confusing religious affection with human feeling. Their nineteenth-century successors were not so cautious. A forcefully *secular* emotionalism had arisen during the camp-meeting revivals of the Second Great Awakening and, despite loud resistance from orthodox theologians and rationalistic liberals, was destined to take on progressively more humanized forms as its influence broadened in the course of the century.

The major literary texts were produced at a moment of cross fire between opposing sermon styles—between the polished but rational style of Boston liberals and the emotional, often wildly imaginative style of the revivalists. Emerson's progression in the 1830s from illustrative but still stodgy Unitarian sermons to the highly imagistic, energetic prose of his major works owed much to his rapturous response to the revival style that liberals like Alcott, Brownson, and Channing dismissed. Having filled his journals and letters of the 1833–36 period with enthusiastic remarks about Father Taylor's preaching, Emerson incorporated both the creativity and humanism of the revival style into his major essays and addresses, produced between 1836 and 1844. His comment on Taylor's ability to roll the world in a ball and toss it from hand to hand was expanded and made universal in *Nature*, in which he says that the imaginative person "tosses the creation like a bauble from hand to hand, and uses it to embody any caprice of thought that is upper-most in his mind."[20] His demand in his 1841 lecture "The Poet" for flexible form, passionate feeling, and native materials in American poetry was linked directly to Father Taylor, for he declared that the poetic genius may be found "in some lowly Bethel by the seaside where a hard-featured, scarred, and wrinkled methodist whose face is a network of cordage becomes the poet of the sailor and the fisherman, whilst he pours out the abundant streams of his thought through a language all glittering and fiery with imagination."[21]

Emerson's mature style was not a duplication of the new religious idiom but rather an adaptation and expansion of this idiom, which in Emerson achieves a special force because it is combined with sophisticated philosophical ideas. Emerson once praised Swedenborg for engrafting high philosophy upon the popular Christianity of his day; Emerson himself did the same with the religion of his period. That the philosophy without the popular idiom was not enough is suggested by the arid, often rarefied prose of most of Emerson's Transcendentalist associates. Only Emerson, who fully recognized the imaginative vivacity of the popular religious style, could write: "The religions of the world are the ejaculations of a few imaginative men."[22] Only he, having responded to the fluid imagery of popular speakers, could declare in a typically homely metaphor that "all symbols are fluxional; all language is vehicular and transitive, and is good, as ferries and horses are, for conveyance, not as farms and houses are, for homestead."[23]

Emerson's Divinity School Address (1838) comes closest, among antebellum social texts about religion, to achieving literary status because it applies inventive imagery (much of it obviously indebted to the popular religious style) to the subversion of the doctrines and forms of traditional Christianity. While preparing the Address, Emerson had expressed disgust in his journals at the frigid sermons of a Unitarian colleague, Barzillai Frost, while he again commended the warm sermon style of Father Taylor, which he said reflected a new vibrant style of American oratory also evident in popular speakers like Daniel Webster. In the Address itself Emerson uses the daringly humanistic popular idiom to undercut the formal, elitist style represented by Frost. The two styles collide most memorably when Emerson tells the story of going one winter Sunday to hear a preacher whose sermon "had no one word intimating that he had laughed or wept, was married or in love, had been commended, or cheated, or chagrined . . . The capital secret of his profession, namely, to convert life into truth, he had not yet learned."[24] "The true preacher," Emerson stressed, "can be known by this, that he deals out to the people his life,—life passed through the fire of his thought."

Throughout the Address, Emerson enacts this enthusiasm for the new secular sermon style by using imagery from the natural world, popular literature, and his own experience, imagery that by turns allures and repels but that always entertains. The above attack on the formal preacher sticks in the reader's brain because it is barbed with a striking image sharper than any of Father Taylor's stylistic arrows: "A snow storm," Emerson recalls, "was falling around us. The snow storm was real; the preacher merely spectral; and the eye felt the sad contrast in looking at him, and then out of the window behind him, at the beautiful meteor of snow. He had lived in vain." This rhetorical use of earthly imagery characterizes the entire Address, from the opening paragraph, in which Emerson invitingly rhapsodizes on "this refulgent summer," to the conclusion, in which he gives the metaphorical mandate: "now let us do what we can to rekindle the smouldering, nigh quenched fire on the altar." At moments, Emerson arrestingly juxtaposes the grotesque and the lovely, as when he says, "the word Miracle, as pronounced by Christian churches . . . is Monster. It is not one with the blowing clover and the falling rain." At other times, he dazzles us with a rapid string of shifting images, as when in three successive sentences he calls the religious sentiment mountain air, the embalmer of the world, myrrh, storax, chlorine, rosemary, and the silent song of the stars. At all points in the Address, Emerson takes the free-flowing sermon style and the humanized religion of his day to its natural conclusion: the subversion of dogmatic Christianity and the joyous assertion of poetic creativity. When he concluded the Address by defining the sermon as "the speech of man to men,—essentially the most flexible of all organs, or all forms," he was taking to a new extreme the imaginative, secular ethos of American public orators. In doing so, he was choosing artistry and humanity above Christianity. It is small wonder that the Address was widely denounced as "the latest form of infidelity" and that Emerson was not invited to address the Divinity School for nearly thirty years. He had been swept by a swelling wave in American popular culture toward new poetic revelations that temporarily alienated him from his more elitist Unitarian brethren but eventually earned him popular favor and enduring fame.

Other Archers

The same popular religious currents that influenced Emerson contributed in different ways to Whitman's *Leaves of Grass,* Melville's *Moby-Dick,* and some of Emily Dickinson's poetry. It might seem strange to mention Melville's "wicked" novel in the same breath as Whitman's expansively optimistic poem and Dickinson's cryptic verses; but the new religious style was adaptable to any metaphysical vision and any genre. As Emerson had noted, preaching had suddenly become the most flexible of forms, available for either affirmative or skeptical use by American writers.

Whitman once declared to his follower Horace Traubel that he could not "have written a word of the Leaves without its religious rootground," a confession corroborated by his statement in the 1872 preface to *Leaves of Grass* that the "one deep purpose" that underlay all others in writing the poem was "the Religious purpose."[25] It is well known that Whitman's Quaker background powerfully influenced his sensibility. In particular, the Quaker belief in spontaneous expression of the "inner light," divorced from creeds or churches, prepared the way for Whitman's poetic singing of himself. It is also well known that Emerson's writings, which Whitman discovered in the early 1850s, gave Whitman a final impetus toward his poem—in Whitman's now famous words: "I was simmering, simmering, simmering; Emerson brought me to a boil."[26] What has been overlooked are the popular religious forces, particularly the evangelical sermon style, that helped bring Whitman to a simmer.

Over the course of the two decades (1835–55) that constituted the "long foreground" of *Leaves of Grass,* Whitman regularly attended the revivals that swept through the working-class districts of New York City during this period. Like Emerson, Whitman was particularly attentive to the *style* of the fiery preachers he witnessed. In New York City, popular sermons were particularly open to specifically stylistic appreciation because they were the product of a new urban evangelism based as much on pulpit showmanship and verbal pyrotechnics as on otherworldly message. This is not to underestimate the seriousness of the revivals for all concerned; particularly in the dark years after the Panic of 1837, evangelical religion reflected very real tensions, frustrations, and hopes on the part of New York's working classes. However, the evangelical denominations, finding themselves in a mushrooming mass market, had to develop new techniques of persuasion. They had to compete against each other, against the popular press, and against secular entertainments like stage melodramas and P. T. Barnum's museum for the attention of a working-class population increasingly made up of rowdies and roughs. By force of circumstances, sermon style was simplified and enlivened, while pulpit performers became more crowd-pleasingly theatrical.

Sources of both inspiration and diversion for the masses, the revivals were for Whitman a schoolroom of popular emotion and of stylized religion. The same boisterous firemen and streetcar drivers that Whitman rubbed shoulders with at the Old Bowery Theater were also frequenters of revivals. They hollered at the entertaining sermons of a preacher like John N. Maffitt with the same frenzy that they hurled rocks and fruit at actors they didn't like at the Old Bowery. The most important of "our amusements" in the late 1830s, Whitman later recalled, were "the churches, especially the Methodist ones, with their frequent 'revivals.' These last occurrences drew out all the young fellows, who attended with demure faces but always on the watch for deviltry." To reach such impish congregations, popular preachers had to fashion especially sharp arrows. As Whitman explained: "The galleries of the church were often sprinkled with the mischievous ones who came to ridicule and make sport; but even here the arrows of prayer and pleading sometimes took effect."[27]

Having abandoned creeds early in his manhood as result of his exposure to radical Quakerism and free thought, Whitman was particularly well situated to view the new sermon style with combined sensitivity and detachment. He developed a lifelong affection for the sermons of such pulpit showmen as Father Taylor, Elias Hicks, Henry Ward Beecher, John N. Maffitt, and T. De Witt Talmage. Because of his broadly nonsectarian outlook, Whitman could revel in the power and style of these sermonizers while discarding their doctrines. He responded with special warmth to what he called the "latent volcanic passion" of Taylor and Hicks. "Hearing such men," he declared, "sends to the winds all the books, and formulas, and polish'd speaking, and rules of oratory." It might seem paradoxical that here he praises Taylor for discarding all rules of oratory, while in the same breath he calls Taylor America's "essentially perfect orator."[28] Once again, we see a major writer learning from popular culture the artful artlessness that is reflected in the writer's own works.

In one sense, *Leaves of Grass* is the nineteenth-century's most stylized, least spontaneous poem, since it was constantly reshaped and amended through numerous editions in Whitman's long lifetime; on the other hand, it is volcanically emotive and "styleless," breaking all poetic rules. Doubtless this studied spontaneity owed much to the crafted carelessness that

Whitman perceived among the new breed of mass manipulators in the American pulpit.

In *Leaves of Grass* itself we see that humanistic religious style and word play (separated from any vestige of doctrine) has become for Whitman its own source of fecundity and regeneration. The popular preachers had begun the secularization of religious discourse that reaches fruition in Whitman's poem, in which the poetic fusion of the divine and the earthly produces combinations that have startling energy. If the preachers had treated the divine with an offhanded familiarity, Whitman outdoes them all by calling God "the great Camerado, the lover true for whom I pine."[29] If they had ushered warm human emotion into sermons, Whitman takes the further step of welding together sacred biblical imagery and common human beings:

> By the mechanic's wife with her babe at her nipple interceding
>   for every person born,
> Three scythes at harvest whizzing in a row from three lusty angels
>   with shirts bagg'd out at their waists,
> The snag-tooth'd hostler with red hair redeeming sins past and
>   to come[.][30]

If Elias Hicks and Father Taylor could fill their sermons with homely nature imagery, Whitman could take such imagery to new extremes, calling a morning glory at his window more satisfying than "the metaphysics of books" and a mouse "miracle enough to stagger sextillions of infidels."[31]

Indeed, *Leaves of Grass* as a whole may be regarded as a sermon—a sermon, that is, of the distinctly experimental nineteenth-century American variety, in which the sacred and the secular, the mystical and the lowly are interwoven with remarkable ease. The poem's prophetic tone, its stately biblical cadences, its numerous references to the soul and to God: all of these religious elements give it a sermonic flavor. But the poem's variety of religious illustrations and applications make it a sermon of the broadest, most comprehensively human kind. Witness the bold reapplications of religious images in the following lines from "Song of Myself":

> Divine am I inside and out, and I make holy whatever I
>   touch or am touched from;
> The scent of these arm-pits is aroma finer than any prayer,
> This head is more than churches or bibles or creeds.[32]

or,

Why should I wish to see God better than this day?
I see something of God each hour of the twenty-four, and
    each moment then,
In the faces of men and women I see God, and in my own
    face in the glass;
I find letters from God dropped in the street, and every one
    is signed by God's name,
And I leave them where they are, for I know that others will
    punctually come forever and ever.

These and many similar inspirational lines in *Leaves of Grass* show Whitman simultaneously adopting and transcending the new religious style of his American contemporaries. As intrigued as were popular preachers by secular alternatives to doctrine, none was so daring as to call armpit odor finer than prayer or body parts greater than bibles and creeds. As inventive as many of them were in coining images, none generated the energy produced by the delightful metaphor of God's letters being dropped daily in the streets. Whitman's lines have universal appeal because they usher the nineteenth-century religious style toward the comprehensively human and the imaginatively poetic.

Whitman's expectation that *Leaves of Grass* would become a best-selling poem was no doubt based partly on his awareness that striking religious imagery had become immensely popular in America. Like Emerson, however, Whitman had been carried by a strong popular impulse to new literary heights that could not be immediately appreciated by the masses. Protestant America before the Civil War was accustomed to mixing religion freely with humanity but was unwilling to go so far as to place armpit stench above prayer or poets above priests. It would take several decades for pulpit discourse to become so secularized that both Emerson's and Whitman's religious images would not raise eyebrows.

It would take even longer for America to accept two other products of its popular religious culture, Herman Melville and Emily Dickinson. The stylization of religion was especially iconoclastic in these writers' works, for it was used to communicate a dark vision that recalled Puritan Calvinism and that appeared at odds with nineteenth-century liberalism. Even though Melville and Dickinson in their characteristic moments seem distanced from the optimistic mainstream, their writings still bear the strong imprint of the new religious style.

Early in *Moby-Dick*, after describing Father Mapple's prow-shaped pulpit, Melville writes: "What could be more full of meaning?—for the pulpit is ever this earth's foremost part; all the rest comes in its rear; the pulpit leads the world."[33] Leads the world, and "leads" *Moby-Dick* too, Melville might have added. Melville's creative exploitation of secularized religious images throughout the novel would almost certainly have been impossible if the "prow" of the popular American pulpit had not broken up the ice fields of doctrinal Calvinism in the decades prior to the writing of *Moby-Dick*. It is significant that Melville devotes three of the first nine chapters of the novel to Father Mapple, who is not only based on the foremost representative of stylistic change, Father Taylor, but whose sermon can be seen as a kind of culmination of the popular anecdotal pulpit style.

While the source for the hymn in *Moby-Dick* has been identified as a hymn of the Protestant Dutch Reformed Church (the church in which Melville was raised),[34] neither the hymn nor Mapple's sermon has been studied in its popular religious context. The most notable aspect of the hymn is that Melville boldly makes several changes in the original hymn, which describes a struggling soul's vision of hell and its subsequent salvation by God. By converting the "I" of the original hymn into Jonah and the surrounding moral terrors into a whale, Melville transforms a rather pedestrian exemplum on hell and redemption into a stirring narrative of capture and escape. Melville's humanization of the divine lends an especially folksy touch, as he has Jonah being rescued by God, who "flew to my relief, / As on a radiant dolphin borne" (in the original hymn, God flies to the sinner on the more traditional "cherub's wings"). By refashioning a church psalm, Melville was following a popular nineteenth-century tendency—the imaginative embellishment of sacred poetry—whose highest product would be Emily Dickinson's poems, almost all of which are structurally adapted from hymns.

Father Mapple's sermon culminates the popular movement toward imaginative pulpit style. The connections between Father Mapple and Father Taylor are obvious enough: both delivered anecdotal sermons to rough sailor congregations while perched theatrically on an elevated pulpit decorated with ship gear and backed by a wall painting of a seascape. A contemporary account of Taylor's preaching is similar in spirit to Melville's description of Mapple. According to the account, Taylor could make his listeners "feel the ship alive under them as he stood on his quarter deck, and the saltness of the sea; could raise the storm and salts would lose track of Sunday in the Bethel, shout 'long boat, *long boat,* and be ready to cast her loose.' "[35] Clearly, this is the kind of overwhelming effect Melville was trying to reproduce in his portrayal of Father Mapple, who spins several sensational "yarns" for his "shipmates" from his lofty prow-pulpit while a storm rages outside. To add even more drama, Melville invents several special effects, such as Mapple's climbing to his high pulpit on a rope ladder.

While the connection between Taylor and Mapple has been recognized before, what has been overlooked is that Mapple's sermon is an improvement on a whole genre of popular antebellum sermons: i.e., fictionalized retellings of the Jonah story. Jonah sermons were in fact very common in popular magazines and tracts written for American sailors. For example, such sermons appeared from 1829 onward as a regular column (titled "Worship at Sea") in the widely read *Sailor's Magazine and Naval Journal*, which Melville mentions in *Redburn*. Contributed to the magazine by popular preachers, these sermons ambitiously wove sailor's slang and creative metaphors into the biblical narrative, thereby producing a mixture of the imaginative and the sacred that directly anticipated Father Mapple's salty sermon. The 1839–40 volume of *Sailor's Magazine* alone contains six separate Jonah sermons filled with colloquial images such as "Carry no leaks out with you; I mean, known sins," or "When the storm breaks in upon you, keep the pump going; I mean repentance," or "If you would be above fear in storms, then commit the helm to him, as your pilot, whom the winds and the sea obey."[36]

Melville's contribution to this popular sermon genre is both an intensification of creative poeticizing and a simultaneous amplification of the brash confidence asserted by Father Taylor and the other popular preachers. Critics have long puzzled over the meaning of Mapple's sermon. In the sermon and in the novel as a whole, however, the precise message is dispersed and deflected by religious symbols whose dazzling verve and multiplicity becomes itself the truest "meaning." The sermon is well positioned at the beginning of the novel, for it enables Melville to rhetorically defeat the doctrinal sermonizing of the past through an exercise in modern-day imaginative sermonizing, thereby freeing Melville to fuse the divine and the earthly with a new boldness throughout the rest of the novel. The colloquial, metaphorical style of Mapple's Jonah sermon is evident from the start: "Shipmates, this book, containing only four chapters—four yarns—is one of the smallest strands in the mighty cable of the Scriptures."[37] Such homely, familiar imagery governs the entire sermon. To be sure, Melville uses the traditional tripartite sermon format of Text, Doctrine, and Application, and a controlling structure is indicated by Mapple's opening announcement of a "two-stranded lesson" to be derived from the biblical story. But the formal sermon outline is adopted only to be transformed, since Mapple's highly embellished retelling of the Jonah story overwhelms clarity of lesson. Most of the sermon reads like an exciting adventure story, with pungent dialogue and graphic descriptions of setting and character—an adventure story with metaphysical overtones, rather like *Moby-Dick* as a whole. Witness the colloquialisms and human touches in a typical passage from the sermon, describing sailors' suspicions about Jonah as he boards the Tarshish ship:

In their gamesome but still serious way, one whispers to the other—"Jack, he's robbed a widow"; or, "Joe, do you mark him; he's a bigamist"; or "Harry lad, I guess he's the adulterer that broke jail in old Gomorrah, or belike, one of the missing murderers from Sodom." . . . Frightened Jonah trembles, and summoning all his boldness to his face, only looks so much the more a coward.

This kind of bold narrative embellishment enlivens the whole sermon, so that when Mapple concludes by praising the person who "ever stands forth his own inexorable self" and who is "only a patriot to heaven," we realize that Melville is asserting a stylistic as well as thematic self-reliance. The popular Jonah sermons had been full of nautical imagery but had always been cautious to note that *God* was the "pilot" and man the common sailor; Mapple, in contrast, calls himself "the pilot of the living God," the "speaker of true things" who "gives no quarter in the truth." The sermon which had begun as an ostensibly structured exposition of a biblical text had become an eloquent exercise in creative imaginings that led to a final declaration of man's capacities as a truth seeker.

It is no wonder that the letters Melville wrote to Hawthorne as he worked on *Moby-Dick* were so full of religious imagery that Melville had to apologize once for "falling into my old foible—preaching" and that elsewhere he could daringly pretend he and Hawthorne were divine: "I feel that the Godhead is broken up like the bread at the Supper, and that we are the pieces."[38] By "preaching" creatively throughout *Moby-Dick* Melville had taken the new humanistic, nondoctrinal style of the popular pulpit to almost Promethean artistic extremes. Like Emerson and Whitman, Melville was liberated by popular embellishments of religion to find a kind of redemption in the very *process* of truth seeking through creative stylization and inventive reallotment of religious symbols. In *Moby-Dick,* the fusion of the divine and the earthly has gone so far that biblical archetypes like Ishmael, Ahab, and Jonah can be imported directly into the modern adventure novel; religious images like hell, devils, angels, and the crucifixion can be connected with all sorts of characters and events; an "ungodly, godlike" whaling captain can be portrayed as a kind of secular preacher aiming both metaphysical and literal "arrows" at a mythic leviathan who seems to embody the living God.

While popular sermon style helped Whitman and Melville produce massively expansive literary texts, it pushed Emily Dickinson toward stylistic concision and metonymy. In a writer like Melville, changing sermon style leaves obvious evidence within the literary text. In Dickinson's highly elliptical, indirect poems, the connections between extrinsic religious change and intrinsic textual performance are less clear. Less clear, perhaps, but no less important. Dickinson's private writings show that, if anything, she was even more attentive to sermon style and popular religious literature than either Emerson or Melville.

Many of the central tensions in Emily Dickinson's poetry result from the collision between the old and the new sermon styles. Dickinson was well positioned to feel every tremor produced by the collision. Her father, Edward Dickinson, was an avowed devotee of the old-style doctrinal preaching: he typically called a well-reasoned sermon by the conservative David Aiken "an intellectual feast," while he branded an imaginative sermon by the more liberal Martin Leland as "Unclean—unclean!"[39] Edward Dickinson also had a puritanical distaste for light literature. Emily recalled that her father read "lonely & rigorous books" and advised his children to read only the Bible.[40]

She had a particularly vivid memory of her brother Austin coming home one day with Longfellow's novel *Kavanagh,* hiding it under the piano cover, and making hand signs to Emily about the book. When the children later read the novel, their father was incensed. While it may seem strange that so apparently innocent a novel as *Kavanagh* should provoke such a storm, we should recognize how revolutionary the novel was, given the strictly doctrinal standards of Edward Dickinson. Longfellow's novel dramatizes the collapse of theological preaching, represented by the departing Rev. Pendexter, and the ascendancy of imaginative religion, embodied in the handsome young preacher Arthur Kavanagh. Kavanagh's piquant pulpit illustrations and stories lead one character to exclaim: "Such sermons! So beautifully written, so different from old Mr. Pendexter's."[41] Emily Dickinson mentioned the novel often in her letters and felt a special kinship with the novel's heroine, Alice Archer, a gloomy, dreamy girl who sublimates her hopeless infatuation for Kavanagh in poetic visions—in much the same way that Emily herself may have been driven to a kind of poetic frenzy by her unrequited passion for a real-life Kavanagh, the Rev. Charles Wadsworth.

Critics have long pondered the Wadsworth-Dickinson relationship, hard evidence of which is frustratingly slim. It is known that while visiting Philadelphia in 1855, during her only trip outside of Massachusetts, Emily most likely was taken to hear Wadsworth preach at Arch Street Presbyterian Church. It is also known that Wadsworth later visited her at least twice in Amherst, that two volumes of his sermons were given to her, that she probably read many of his other sermons in newspaper reprintings, and that she developed strong feelings toward him. Some believe that Emily's great "terror" in 1862 and her incredible poetic productivity that year was a response to Wadsworth's removal to Calvary Church in San Francisco (hence the double pun involved in Emily's description of herself as "the

Empress of Calvary"). Intriguing as the relationship is, the much debated issue of Emily's feelings for Wadsworth is far less relevant than the fact that in the mid-1850s, just at the moment when she was beginning to write serious poetry, she was deeply moved by a preacher who must be regarded as one of the antebellum period's foremost innovators in American sermon style.

Her response to Wadsworth had been prepared for by an increasing preference for imaginative preaching, often against her father's wishes. In 1851 she probably went to hear the popular Henry Ward Beecher, who was visiting Amherst giving a lecture, significantly, on "Imagination." By 1853 she could go into raptures over a notably anecdotal sermon on Judas and Jesus given by the visiting preacher Edwards A. Park, a sermon whose secular emphasis she later described: "It was like a mortal story of intimate young men."[42] The Martin Leland sermon that her father dismissed as "unclean" was imaginatively liberating for her, as she mimicked Leland's theatrical manner and repeated sections of the sermon aloud. Also in the early 1850s, she befriended the popular author and editor Josiah G. Holland, whose liberal religious views were criticized by one conservative paper as "creedless, churchless, ministerless christianity."[43] By aligning herself with several of the most progressive religious stylists of the day, Emily Dickinson was launching a silent but major rebellion against the doctrinal tradition valued by her father.

Her excitement about Wadsworth, therefore, can be viewed as a natural outgrowth of her increasing attraction to the new religious style. One newspaper compared Wadsworth to an earlier pulpit innovator, John Summerfield, but stressed that "Wadsworth's style . . . is vastly bolder, his fancy more vivid, and his action more violent. . . . [His topics are] peculiar, and quite out of the usual line"; he is typically "rapid, unique and original, often startling his audience . . . with a seeming paradox."[44] Mark Twain would also be struck by the uniqueness of Wadsworth's pulpit manner, noting that he would often "get off a firstrate joke" and then frown when people started laughing.[45] In short, Wadsworth's style was adventurous, anecdotal, and very imaginative, with a tendency to the startling and paradoxical. Emily Dickinson once praised his "inscrutable roguery" and seemed to copy his impish style in many poems and in her message to J. G. Holland: "Unless we become as Rogues, we cannot enter the Kingdom of Heaven—."[46] The jocular familiarity with which she generally treats divine and biblical images doubtless owes much to the new sermon style which Wadsworth perfected.

While Wadsworth can be seen as a groundbreaker for Emily Dickinson's imaginative treatment of religion, three other figures on the popular religious scene—Thomas Wentworth Higginson, Sara Willis Parton, and Donald Grant Mitchell—also made important contributions. Higginson has gained notoriety as the rather condescending editor who, despite voluminous correspondence with Emily Dickinson and two visits with her in Amherst, only published a few of her poems and never recognized the immensity of her genius. Although he proved only partly sympathetic, we should recognize the reasons that he was singled out by Emily Dickinson as her literary judge, preceptor, and confidant. He had made a dramatic move from religion to social activism and professional authorship. Beginning as a Unitarian minister devoted to every progressive reform of the day, in the early 1850s he had declared: "We need more radicalism in our religion and more religion in our radicalism."[47] By the early 1860s, when he was editor of *The Atlantic Monthly,* his religious radicalism had brought him to the verge of a devotion to imaginative style that evidently appealed to Emily Dickinson. In the *Atlantic* article appealing to young contributors to which she responded, Higginson endorsed the metonymic imagination by noting that "there may be years of crowded passion in a word, and half a life in a sentence"; he echoed Ruskin's notion of the "instantaneous line"; and he declared that a book is the only immortality.[48] It is little wonder that this man who combined liberal religion, radical activism, and devotion to literature would seem to hold promise to Emily Dickinson, who herself was in several senses influenced by these elements of the American scene. What Higginson did not understand was that she had gone beyond secularized religion to a new form of stylization and artistic manipulation, while he remained in the realm of rebellion and earnest activism. Socially he was far more radical than she precisely because linguistically she was far more radical than he. His religious liberalism had pushed him toward a devotion to metonymy and the instantaneous poetic line but not to an understanding of the weird images, jolting rhythms, and half rhymes that filled her poetry.

The other popular figures, Sara Willis Parton ("Fanny Fern") and Donald Grant Mitchell ("Ik Marvel"), were stylistically closer to Emily Dickinson than Higginson. Although Emily never met or corresponded with these best-selling authors, she loved their writings, which were distinguished by a colloquial freedom with religious topics and a self-consciously quirky style enacting their distaste for the doctrinal preaching of their youths. Parton, who was singled out for praise by Hawthorne and who was the first woman to publicly praise Whitman's *Leaves of Grass,* treated biblical topics with a jaunty zest verging on feminist boldness. Her *Fern Leaves from Fanny's Port Folio,* a book Emily Dickinson read aloud to her family, includes several daring religious passages such as this: "Eve wasn't smart about that apple business. I know forty ways I could have fixed him— without burning my fingers, either. It makes me quite frantic to think I lost such a prime chance to circumvent the old sinner."[49] To many critics, Parton was faulty on both religious and stylistic grounds: one reviewer typically lambasted her "irreverence for things sacred" and her use of "disjointed fragments" instead of continuous narrative.[50] Today we can understand such apparent flaws as products of an antebellum author brandishing her imaginative powers in an effort to subvert the stylistic rigidities of the past. Emily Dickinson would go beyond Parton's disjointed style by making each stanza and sometimes each line an imagistic fragment.

In this regard she also outdid the purposefully disconnected style of Donald Grant Mitchell, whose best-selling novel *Reveries of a Bachelor* (1850) provoked much rapturous praise from Dickinson in her letters. Mitchell's volume is not a story but rather a series of images that float through the mind of an idle bachelor who sits before his fire fabricating thought-phantoms of the past, the present, and the future. Mitchell announces that these images lack "unity of design" since he records them "as they came seething from my thought, with all their crudities and contrasts."[51] This stylistic flexibility is connected with Mitchell's advocacy of a kind of preexistentialist philosophy that dispensed with religious doctrines altogether and placed total faith in an imaginative engagement with the Eternal Now. Emily Dickinson, who more than any other antebellum writer realized the momentousness of the Present, may have been responsive to Mitchell lines such as "Thought alone is delicate to tell the breath of the Present," or "if you bring such thought to measure the Present, the Present will seem broad; and it will be sultry as Noon, and make a fever of Now."

Mitchell, like Sara Parton and Emily Dickinson, had been raised in a conservative religious household where theological preaching was valued, and like them also he quietly rebelled against this stylistic orthodoxy in works filled with completely secularized use of religious imagery. For instance, the traditional Christian notion of the afterlife is demythologized and made psychological when Mitchell envisages "our souls" running "beyond time and space, beyond planets and suns, beyond far-off suns and comets, until, like blind flies, they are lost in the blaze of immensity, and can grope their way back to our earth and time by the cunning of instinct." Reading such a passage, we invariably think of the numerous Dickinson poems which defy all barriers of time and space by soaring freely into the afterlife. Given the imaginative reapplication of sacrosanct themes throughout *Reveries of a Bachelor,* it is small wonder that Dickinson once paid Mitchell one of her highest compliments: she wrote a friend that when Mitchell died she would want to die too, since there would be no one left on earth to interpret her life for her.[52]

It is an oversimplification to say that in her own poetry Dickinson brings

together Wadsworth's humor and energetic paradoxes, Higginson's belief
in the instantaneous line, Sara Parton's pert biblical retelling, and Mitchell's experimental style and philosophy. Still, it is helpful to know that such
imaginative revisions of religion were going on all around Dickinson and
that she was extraordinarily responsive to them. By her own confession,
she came to detest theological preaching ("I hate doctrines!" she declared
after one old-fashioned sermon), and she devoured every example of the
new religious style that came within her rather limited purview. Significantly, the religionists she praised warmly possessed both the modern
stylistic adventurousness and the old concern for ultimate questions such
as Time, Death, the Other World, and so forth. Even in cases (like Mitchell's) where they had rejected formal Christianity, they hadn't become so
secular that they altogether abandoned Puritanism's contemplation of the
Infinite. She once commented that the only way to tell if a poem is good
is to ask whether after reading it you feel like the top of your head has been
taken off. She seemed to apply the same rule to the sermons she attended
and the books she read. A religious work, in her eyes, must possess both
striking imagery and a sense of ultimacy; theology or moralizing is secondary to the work's *effect* upon the imagination. For instance, she disdained
three Baptist tracts about "pure little lives, loving God, and their parents,
and obeying the laws of the land"—purely secular pious stories that, in her
words, "dont *bewitch* me any."[53] In contrast, even though she was skeptical
about Christian doctrines, she could revel in the Rev. Aaron Colton's
"enlivening preaching, . . . his earnest look and gesture, his calls of *now
today.*"[54] Similarly, she could be totally captivated by "a splendid sermon"
from Edwards A. Park, which left the congregation "so still, the buzzing
of a fly would have boomed out like a cannon. And when it was all over,
and that wonderful man sat down, people stared at each other, and looked
as wan and wild, as if they had seen a spirit, and wondered they had not
died."[55] The combined imagery here of the fly, death, and religion seems
to anticipate Dickinson's famous poem "I heard a Fly buzz—when I died."
At any rate, we should note that in both the poem and her letter describing
Park's sermon, it is not theology or Christianity that counts but rather the
existential impact of a momentous situation.

What new religious stylists like Wadsworth and Mitchell had finally
taught Emily Dickinson is that religion could be freely applied to many
secular situations and expressed through startling imagery. Because of
Dickinson's extensive use of witty conceits, many critics have likened her
to the metaphysical poets of the Renaissance or to the American Puritan
poet Edward Taylor. There is, however, a crucial difference between the
metaphysicals and Dickinson that is too often ignored: all the creative
flights of the metaphysicals are finally confined by Christian doctrine,

whereas Dickinson soars adventurously beyond doctrine by mixing the sacred and the secular, the Christian and the pagan. And she had been taught how to achieve this mixture by her popular religious culture.

One of her poetic responses to the new religious style was the redefinition of church, sermons, and worship along totally secular lines. Witness the reduction of religious images to the world in the following stanzas:

> Some keep the Sabbath going to Church—
> I keep it, staying at Home—
> With a Bobolink for a Chorister—
> And an Orchard, for a Dome— . . .
>
> God preaches, a noted Clergyman—
> And the sermon is never long
> So instead of getting to Heaven, at last—
> I'm going, all along.
>
> (#324; c. 1860)

This poem may be regarded as a clever adaptation of the antebellum religious style: not only does it shift worship from the church to nature and sing praise to short sermons, but it actually converts God into an entertaining preacher obviously trained in the new sermon style. A similar fusion of the sacred and the secular is visible in the poem that begins "To hear an Oriole sing / May be a common thing— / Or only a divine," in which the last phrase arrests the reader with its offhandedly casual treatment of the holy. Sometimes this casualness is taken to playful extremes, as when she refers to God as "Papa above!" watching down upon a "mouse," who asks for the privilege of living forever "Snug in seraphic Cupboards." Among the many other Dickinson poems that daringly reapply sacred imagery are "These are the days when Birds come back—," "There's a certain Slant of light," and "Mine—by the right of the White Election!" In these poems such images as holy communion, sacrament, hymns, the doctrine of election are detached totally from their sacred referents and fused with either nature or the human psyche. In still other poems she displays a jaunty freedom with the Bible, as in "The Bible is an antique Volume," which includes a series of secular reenactments of sacred imagery, such as calling Eden "the ancient Homestead," Satan "the Brigadier," and sin "a distinguished Precipice / Others must resist."

While these poems show how Dickinson's religious imagination had been fueled by the ever-broadening applications of secular images in antebellum sermons, their dazzling variety points up the fact that she had been carried beyond mere sermonic breadth toward truth and humanity

in a larger sense. That is, the creativity of the modern sermons she loved
had carried her beyond the sermon form to a total liberated view in which
God and man, the other world and this world could be mutually illuminating and virtually interchangeable. Dickinson always retained her respect
for modern preachers but in time realized how far she had gone beyond
even the most imaginative among them. In a late poem she could indicate
her realization that she had stepped beyond the broad sermon into another
realm:

> He preached upon "Breadth" till it argued him narrow—
> The Broad are too broad to define
> And of "Truth" until it proclaimed him a Liar—
> The Truth never flaunted a Sign—
>
> Simplicity fled from his counterfeit presence
> As Gold the Pyrites would shun—
> What confusion would cover the innocent Jesus
> To meet so enabled a Man!
>
> (#1207; c. 1872)

Here Dickinson uses the tools of antebellum imaginative preaching—
paradox, humor, startling metaphor, stress upon the human Jesus—to
undermine preaching itself. Even the broadest preacher, she suggests, is
trapped somehow by creed, by the belief that truth flaunts "a Sign." In
Emily Dickinson's expansive field of vision, there is no single sign but
rather a rich array of shifting signs, none of which holds the truth but all
of which suggest it. Let us not forget, however, that this very expansiveness
itself owed much to the new religious style. The day she had angered her
father by losing herself in a Longfellow novel about a contemplative girl
infatuated with a creative preacher, her imagination had begun its flight
beyond the boundaries of doctrine toward stylistic freedom.

Heavenly Plots and Human Artifacts

Like sermons, popular religious fiction and poetry were becoming increasingly dominated by imagination and secularism. The genres that were
to affect the major texts most directly were allegory, visionary fiction, and
Oriental tales.

The most traditional religious genre, allegory, was affected by the
general secularizing tendency. Rigorously precise Puritan allegories illustrating Calvinist theology, such as Joseph Morgan's *The History of the King-*

dom of Basaruah (1715), are light-years distant from the scores of popular nineteenth-century allegories that freely treated social issues such as temperance, slavery, and interdenominational warfare. In contrast to Morgan's sober, restrained Puritan allegory, the nineteenth-century ones are enlivened by a relaxed, sometimes colloquial style and a broad range of fiery passions. In Edmund Botsford's *The Spiritual Voyage Performed in the Ship Convert* (1814) an allegorical journey of the ship of faith is modernized by a vernacular perspective; Botsford portrays an ill-spoken crew of genial Christians waging war on the likes of Will All-Joy, Harry Fair-Speech, and Jack Rest-on-Prayer. Hawthorne's college chum George B. Cheever produced numerous updated allegories, most notably the controversial best-seller *Deacon Giles' Distillery* (1835), a kind of popularized "Young Goodman Brown" in which demonic nightly rituals in a distillery produce hellish firewater that threatens to poison the American population. Bunyan's *Pilgrim's Progress,* in the meantime, was updated by several writers of different religious persuasions, from the Calvinist Aaron Lummus in *The Life and Adventures of Dr. Caleb* (1822) to the Universalist D. J. Mandell in *The Adventures of Search for a Life* (1838). All of the popular allegories preached a simplified faith of good works, clean living, and belief in God's goodness and man's perfectibility. Eventually, American allegory would become so secularized that it could be wholly integrated into domestic fiction: witness the use of Bunyanic imagery throughout Louisa May Alcott's *Little Women,* in which each of the four heroines is described carrying her little bundle of sin through her personal Vanity Fair toward a Celestial City that promises to be merely an idealized version of her earthly home. The most important thing to recognize is that by the early 1830s religious allegory, once a quite rigid genre used for illustration of Puritan doctrine, had become a most flexible and adaptable one, fully available for purely literary manipulation by writers like Hawthorne and Melville.

Poe complained that Hawthorne was "infinitely too fond of allegory" and that "the strain of allegory . . . completely overwhelms the greater number of his subjects, and . . . in some measure interferes with the direct conduct of absolutely all."[56] In Poe's eyes, allegory destroyed the verisimilitude, diminished the originality, and exaggerated the didacticism of Hawthorne's fiction. To be sure, a good number of Hawthorne's lesser tales share the preachiness and optimism of most popular pious allegories. "A Rill from the Town Pump" advocates temperance like many of the reformist allegories of the period. "Little Annie's Ramble," "Sights from the Steeple," "The Vision of the Fountain," "The Threefold Destiny," "The Great Stone Face," and "Little Daffydowndilly" are other tales in which Hawthorne uses allegorical elements in tales whose morals sometimes seem embarrassingly conventional. However, even these benign tales are significant because they show Hawthorne participating in the popular movement toward updated allegory. By adapting allegory to suit modern needs, Hawthorne, like lesser authors of the day, was modifying a sacrosanct Puritan form by mixing it with contemporary themes and styles. Hawthorne sounds much like many of the popular allegorists of his period when he introduces "The Threefold Destiny" by saying that the tale is not "a story of events claiming to be real" but rather an allegory like those produced by "writers of the last century," with the crucial difference that "I have endeavored to give a more life-like warmth than could be infused into those fanciful productions."[57] If tales like "The Threefold Destiny" (in which a New England villager wanders for years in search of love, power, and riches only to find them upon returning home) perhaps give more weight to didactically allegorical elements than to human ones, they at least show Hawthorne trying to add even more life and vigor to traditional allegory than his contemporaries were doing. Indeed, Hawthorne's later theory of the romance as a "neutral territory" where the real and imaginary mingle seems to have grown directly out of his many early attempts to make new variations on the combined allegorical and realistic mode of his contemporaries.

We should not be too harsh on Hawthorne, therefore, for his writing a number of rather pedestrian allegories reflecting the simplified liberalism of his period. We should rather take note of the extraordinary range of his lesser tales, which weave allegory into defenses of a large variety of moral causes and viewpoints, including temperance, Sunday schools, the worth of toil, the happiness of home life, nature's beauty, the goodness of children, and so forth. If the cheerful moral of tales like "Little Daffydowndilly" or "Little Annie's Ramble" seems distant from the dark message of "Young Goodman Brown," "Ethan Brand," or "The Minister's Black Veil," we should not charge Hawthorne with prevarication or self-contradiction. Instead, both "Little Daffydowndilly" and "Young Goodman Brown" should be seen as alternate versions of a stylistic exercise in modernized allegory. Hawthorne himself was often unclear about the exact message of his fiction—for instance, as he reread proofs of *Mosses from an Old Manse* in 1854, he wrote his publisher, "Upon my honor, I am not quite sure that I entirely comprehend my own meaning in some of these blasted allegories."[58] His permutations of the updated allegory were so various and mingled that specific meaning was often compromised. Again, we see a sophisticated writer producing complex literary texts because of his enthusiastic response to a popular literary movement, in this case the movement toward secularized allegory.

Henry James noted that Hawthorne had a profound knowledge of such Puritan doctrines as total depravity, predestination, and perseverance of the saints but did not sincerely believe in any of them—he could detach himself from them and handle them objectively. I would add that Hawthorne's very detachment from these doctrines was in large part induced by a popular religious culture that had loosened allegory from its dogmatic underpinnings and had made it available for modernization by nineteenth-century writers. In his best fiction, Hawthorne took the modernizing tendency several steps further than the lesser writers. Certain of his works have gained well-deserved fame because of their success in mixing allegory with New England history in a way that transferred Puritan doctrines from dogma to psychology and Puritan style from religious typology to secular symbol. In other works, Hawthorne applies allegory to nineteenth-century issues in a way that turned contemporary allegory against itself; his ironic updating of Bunyan in *The Celestial Railroad,* for example, satirizes attempts by nineteenth-century liberals to make the passage to heaven smooth and painless. Bunyan's portrait of a lonely pilgrim struggling against countless emblematic perils is overturned in Hawthorne's depiction of a modern railroad train (operated by Mr. Smooth-it-away) that easily carries loads of liberal believers over the Slough of Despond, through Hill Difficulty, and to the gates of the Celestial City. In both his Puritan and his modern works, Hawthorne was using a popular genre (secularized allegory) to achieve nondogmatic renderings of religious topics.

Allegory suited Hawthorne primarily because it provided a safe means of delivering dark, unconventional themes. His manipulation of secularized allegory for new literary ends is most evident in works like "Young Goodman Brown" and "The Minister's Black Veil." By skillfully combining the allegorical and the human in these tales, Hawthorne is able to retain the didactic framework of allegory while at the same time making a universal statement about the darker aspects of human nature. The numerous allegorical elements (e.g., the emblematic character names, the pink ribbons, the snakelike walking stick, the forest, and so forth in "Young Goodman Brown"; or the Rev. Hooper's veil, which is called "a type and a symbol," in "The Minister's Black Veil") would seem to suggest that these tales have some doctrinal message about the revelation of sin, like a Puritan allegory enforcing Calvinism. But because of enlivening realistic and secular elements (e.g., both stories involve tragically strained relationships between a man and his family and friends), the tales are removed from the realm of doctrine and are made thematically dense and universal. The long-standing debate about whether Hawthorne is a Puritan, "Christian" writer, on the one hand, or a forward-looking psychological author, on the other, is really a moot issue. Hawthorne is in fact able to bring together *both* Puritan *and* psychological themes in a creative center because Puritan beliefs had been effectively liberated from theology by the nineteenth-century secular allegorists. The stylistic foundation of Hawthorne's tales, the humanized allegories of his contemporaries, becomes his chief means of reinterpreting past religion. When he wished to probe "the power of blackness," allegory proved a convenient disguise because of its didactic aura. As a professional writer whose tales appeared in many popular periodicals and giftbooks, Hawthorne did not wish to alienate the conventional segment of his reading public with bald expressions of cynical or misanthropic views. As a result, he adopted a favorite device of his religious culture, allegory, so that even when he applied this device to subversive ends, many readers and reviewers were unaware of the subversion. The *Southern Quarterly Review* was typical in commending his tales as "quiet, gentle, fanciful,—clothing naked facts in pleasing allegory, and beguiling to truth and virtue, through labyrinths of fiction."[59] As Melville noted, Hawthorne was generally regarded as "a pleasant writer, with a pleasant style," when in fact a deep gloom often lurked behind his surface cheer.[60]

If secularized religious allegory prepared the way for some of Hawthorne's most intriguing effects, another popular genre, Oriental fiction, had a more widespread effect on the nineteenth-century literary imagination. All the major writers of the American Renaissance at one time or another paid homage to Oriental tales, which they usually praised as philosophically enriching and aesthetically liberating. Emerson typically said that all Oriental tales underscore "the one miracle of intellectual enlargement," revealing "things in their causes, all facts in their connections."[61] One of Whitman's literary goals, as he wrote in "Passage to India," was to "Eclaircise the myths Asiatic, the primitive fables . . . eluding the hold of the known, mounting to heaven!"[62] For both Poe and Emily Dickinson, Oriental fiction was a primary symbol of the unfettered imagination. Hawthorne and Melville often used Oriental motifs as a means of generating artistic and philosophical flexibility.

Ever since its first appearance in eighteenth-century American magazines, Oriental fiction was an important vehicle among progressive thinkers for escaping both the stylistic and doctrinal rigidities of Puritan Calvinism.[63] After the American Revolution, freethinkers such as Thomas Paine had provoked unprecedented wrath among orthodox religionists by arguing, among other things, that Christianity was a man-made religion on the same level as Oriental religions such as Islam and Hinduism. Hoping to avoid the ferocious obloquies hurled upon the likes of Paine, many rationalists and liberals chose to promote their unorthodox views obliquely through Oriental tales, which used the East-West dialogue technique to deny the specialness of Christianity and to promote a nonsectarian faith in human perfectibility and divine benevolence. In Royall Tyler's *The Alge-*

rine Captive (1797) a New England Calvinist, taken captive by Algerians, learns from a Mullah the "gentle precepts" of Islam, including man's perfectibility and God's benevolence.[64] Benjamin Franklin, who learned to be extremely cautious in expressing his deistic views, safely dramatized these views in "An Arabian Tale" (1779), in which an Oriental magician is sorely puzzled about the problem of evil until he is consoled by a beautiful vision of the Great Chain of Being revealed by a kindly angel. Benjamin Silliman in *Letters of Shahcoolen* (1802) underscores the aesthetic appeal of Oriental religion, praising the "rich, brilliant" poetry and "flights of imagination" in Hindu scriptures.[65] Throughout *Salmagundi* (1808) Washington Irving criticizes mainstream religion through the portrayal of an Oriental visitor to America who writes letters home filled with caustic comments such as "into what ridiculous errors these nations will wander who are unenlightened by the precepts of Mahomet, our divine prophet."[66] Likewise, an Oriental visitor in George Fowler's *The Wandering Philanthropist* (1810) is confused by America's baffling variety of sects and promotes a nonsectarian faith in good works. These and many other early Oriental tales exposed the intolerance of most Christians and imaginatively reveled in the lush exoticism of Oriental religions. By the time of William Ware's best-selling novel *Zenobia* (1838)—whose title character is probably the prototype for both Poe's "Psyche Zenobia" and the Zenobia of Hawthorne's *The Blithedale Romance*—Oriental fiction had become philosophically sophisticated and freely mixed with secular adventure. In several of Melville's early novels this combined Orientalism, adventure, and philosophy would be taken toward literary art.

Closely allied to Oriental fiction were visionary tales, or imaginary visions of angels and the afterlife. From the late eighteenth century onward visionary tales offered a means of getting a direct view of the divine, which in Puritan times had been considered ineffable and totally otherworldly. Many popular writers throughout the antebellum period used visionary devices to rhetorically defeat gloomy religion, to enjoy the beauties of celestial bliss, and to generate a spirit of cheer and hope. A typical strategy in visionary fiction, from *The Golden Age* (1785) by "Celadon" through Sylvester Judd's *Margaret* (1845), was to depict a character who is tormented by doubt or by oppressively theological Christianity and who finally is solaced by a reassuring, beautiful angel. Nearly all the major authors would exploit the popular visionary mode, since it allowed the American writer to objectify the divine and apply it symbolically in psychological or realistic fiction.

The redirection of Oriental and visionary devices by two major writers, Poe and Melville, illustrates how such popular devices could lead, on the one hand, to a nonreligious literary aesthetic and, on the other, to broadly metaphysical fiction. The quite different literary ends reached by two authors rooted in similar popular modes suggest the fertility and flexibility that these modes had gained by the 1830s.

Because of the perennial interest in Poe's influence on the French symbolists and decadents, Poe is often portrayed as a lonely visionary who rebelled against a pragmatic, businesslike American society. Baudelaire initiated the myth that Poe launched "an admirable protest" against a utilitarian culture. "The day that he wrote 'all certainty is in dreams,'" declared Baudelaire, "he drove his own Americanism down into the region of inferior things."[67] Baudelaire was unaware that Poe was very much a product of nineteenth-century Americanism in all its complexity. In an early letter to John Neal, Poe enthusiastically quoted Shelley's comment on Shakespeare: "What a number of ideas must have been afloat before such an author could arise!"[68] This comment applies well to Poe himself, since numerous popular literary currents fed into his art. Of all our major writers, Poe was the most obviously engaged in popular culture: he struggled constantly as a writer of fiction and poetry for popular magazines, he reviewed countless popular books, and he dreamed of founding a popular periodical that would make him rich. It is a testament to the fecundity of antebellum popular culture that one of Poe's most sophisticated and influential theories—art for art's sake—was directly related to his adoption of the Oriental and visionary modes that had been commonly used by American writers since the late eighteenth century.

Poe had much firsthand exposure to these modes. It is interesting to note that he had singled out as pioneers three American novelists—Brockden Brown, John Neal, and Catharine Sedgwick—who had themselves in fact made imaginative variations upon visionary devices. Brockden Brown's *Wieland* (1798), in which a visionary religionist murders his entire family at the command of angels, was the first in a line of American novels (later to include Henry James's *The Turn of the Screw*) in which otherworldly visions were stripped of simple cheer and placed in a more ambiguous realm of distorted perception. Likewise, in such Neal novels as *Logan* (1822) and *Seventy-Six* (1823) characters are not only constantly besieged by visions but are carried to irrational heights by explosive passions that distort perception of exterior reality. Catharine Sedgwick's *A New-England Tale* (1822) and *Redwood* (1824) were the first American novels to weave visionary imagery extensively with secular scenes and characters, as Sedgwick realistically portrays angelic "spirit-women" that anticipate some of Poe's heroines. Like such early fiction, much popular American poetry that Poe praised was making innovative secular applications of visionary or Oriental devices. In his most famous critical statement, "The Poetic Principle," the American works he used as models included a Nathaniel Parker

Willis poem about an "unseen company" of spirits that surrounds a poor city girl; Longfellow's "Waif," which envisages human cares stealing away "like the Arabs" folding "their tents"; and an Edward Coote Pinkney poem that sings praise to an angel-woman who is "less of earth than heaven."[69] Critics have long been mystified by Poe's attraction to seemingly ordinary poets such as Pinkney, Maria Brooks, Frances Sargent Osgood, and Estelle Anna Lewis; but when we take note that Poe usually highlights passages in which these poets try to conjure up a sense of heavenly bliss or angelic beauty we understand that his attraction stems largely from the appeal of visionary and Oriental devices.

Significantly, such devices abound in Poe's own poetry. Several poems in his first published volume, *Tamerlane and Other Poems* (1827), show Poe adopting the popular visionary mode and at the same time transforming it, guiding it away from didacticism toward psychological reverie and symbolist aesthetics. In popular visionary poems, dreams of angels or the afterlife had commonly provided respite from life's cares by assuring the dreamer of God's kindness and the beauty of heaven. In Poe poems such as "Dreams" and "Spirits of the Dead," visions are likewise presented as desirable escape mechanisms giving a foretaste of heavenly bliss; but Poe emphasizes the sheer mystical delight of the dreaming *process,* distinct from any clear religious *message.* "Oh! that my young life were a lasting dream!" exclaims the persona of "Dreams," as he rapturously tells of reveling in "dreamy fields of light / ... In climes of mine imagining / ... with beings that have been / Of mine own thought." The speaker goes on to rhapsodize over the "vivid colouring of life" given by dreams "Of Paradise and Love—and all our own!" The visionary mode here begins to be summoned into the human psyche, as dreams are no longer passively experienced for their religious lesson but rather are actively conjured up for their regenerating beauty. This self-conscious manipulation of visionary devices is also evident in "Imitation," in which the speaker says his early life was brightened by the presence of spiritual beings which his spirit would not have seen had he not seen them with his "dreaming eye." "Spirits of the Dead" seems much closer than these poems to the popular visionary literature, since it portrays a graveyard scene in which a depressed person is comforted by spirits of deceased friends who appear in "visions ne'er to vanish." But even here Poe revises the popular mode, as he forgoes the usual concrete descriptions of spirits or heaven on behalf of a delicate atmospheric indefiniteness that leads to the final image of the graveyard mist, which is called "a symbol and a token— / ... A mystery of mysteries!" Similarly, in "Stanzas" nature's mystical beauty is called "a symbol and a token / Of what in other worlds shall be—and giv'n / In beauty by our God."

If in his first poetry volume Poe explored the purely creative and symbolic potential of the visionary mode, in his second, *Al Aaraaf, Tamerlane, and Minor Poems* (1829), he took a further step toward aestheticism by using Oriental devices. Although American writers had long exploited Orientalism as a vicarious source of lushness and beauty, virtually all had mixed aesthetic appreciation with philosophical or religious commentary. Poe's "Al Aaraaf" retains vestiges of the popular religious framework; the title is Poe's renaming of Al Orf, the star of purgatory in the Koran, which Poe describes as "a medium between Heaven and Hell where men suffer no punishment, but yet do not attain that tranquil & even happiness of heaven." This image of an Oriental afterlife is pure fantasy typical of many American popular writers. Where Poe departs from the crowd is his stress throughout the poem upon wild aestheticism (symbolic of poetic rapture) and his complete disregard for the religious comfort predominant in the popular literature. For Poe, Al Aaraaf symbolizes the mediating condition of the poet, who is tied to the earth but always straining toward heaven. On the star lives Nesace, the Spirit of Beauty, along with many other angels, unspoiled by knowledge, who live in a union with beauty that is made intensely blissful because they know it is not eternal. After a certain period everyone on Al Aaraaf dies forever, since, as Poe explains, "an eternity even of bliss" would destroy the angst needed to feel the full power of beauty. Poe here has pushed a common popular mode—fictional rendering of an Oriental afterlife—toward a premodern exemplum that anticipates Wallace Stevens's famous notion: "Death is the mother of beauty."

Poe made further important permutations of visionary and Oriental devices in many of his later poems. In "Israfel" (1831) he again borrows from the Koran, this time singing praise to the angel Israfel, the sweetest singer in the Muslim heaven, whose passionate celestial music embodies Poe's highest poetic ideals. In "The City of Sin" and "The Sleeper" (both 1831) we begin to see Poe's movement toward the arabesque, as horrifying aspects of death (the luridly lit, silent death city; a lover contemplating the decaying corpse of his lovely Irene) are invested with a kind of perverse, ornamental beauty. "The Raven" (1845) and "Annabel Lee" (1849) have become Poe's most famous poems in part because visionary fantasy is combined with arabesque terror and placed wholly in the psyche of a bereaved narrator. "The Raven" gains supernatural overtones from alternating bright and dark visionary images (angels, heaven, hell, demons, God) that are projected on the imperturbable raven by the terrified, increasingly frenzied student. The narrator of "Annabel Lee" explains, in a purely imaginative rather than religious context, that the envious angels in heaven killed his child-love, but that neither heaven's angels nor hell's demons can separate him from her, since he sleeps with her in dreams each night in her tomb by the sea. In each of these poems, visionary devices are skillfully stylized because they are produced by the consciousness of a disturbed narrator.

The centrality of the visionary mode in Poe's work is evident not only in his ubiquitous use of angel or afterlife imagery but also in his poetic theory. Poe defined the poetic sensibility as "no mere appreciation of the Beauty before us—but a wild effort to reach the Beauty above," "an ecstatic prescience of the glories beyond the grave." Poetry, closely allied to music, strikes notes "which *cannot* have been unfamiliar to the angels."[70] It is the Rhythmical Creation of Beauty; its sole arbiter is taste, and it has only collateral relations with the intellect or the conscience. By Poe's time, many popular American writers had separated religion from the intellect and placed it in the realm of the creative imagination, bound to the celestial principally by the secular visionary mode. Poe took this secularizing process to its natural aesthetic ends. Having explored the celestial beauty of both beatific and horrific sensations in much of his poetry, he turned in his theoretical criticism to an equation of poetic effect with supernal beauty. Liberated from dogma by his extensive experimentation with the popular visionary mode, Poe came to the conclusion that beauty had nothing to do with Christian doctrine and was only tangentially related to reason or conscience. For him, poetry was the Spirit of Beauty on a mythological Arabian star; it was the Oriental angel Israfel strumming his lyre in the heavens; it was the pulsating rhythm of a bereaved outcry for the lost Lenore or the distant Annabel Lee. In Poe's eyes, it was indeed very religious, but religious in a completely aesthetic sense, divorced from truth. Poe had arrived at the threshold of a modern poetics as a result of his intimate awareness of the visionary and Oriental devices of his day.

A similar stylization of the visionary occurs in some of Poe's better tales. True, Poe could write rather preachy visionary fiction which shows him directly imitating the more conventional popular writers. Witness his "Conversation of Eiros and Charmion" (adapted from S. Austin's popular apocalyptic tale, "The Comet"), in which two spirits in heaven discourse on the bliss of the afterlife as contrasted with the terrors of a human population doomed by an approaching comet. Also quite ordinary is "The Colloquy of Monos and Una" and "The Power of Words," two more tales in which heavenly spirits converse about poetic and philosophical matters. Another of Poe's religious dialogues, "Mesmeric Revelations," promotes the idea of God as the highest material essence. While these tales reflect the more didactic strain of American visionary fiction, in other tales Poe seems to follow the lead of some of his favorite fictionists, such as Brockden Brown and John Neal, in exploring the visionary not as a vehicle of religious comfort but rather as a product of the irrational mind. The visionary mode becomes truly psychological in well-known works like "Ligeia," "The Black Cat," and "The Fall of the House of Usher." In such works Poe studies the agitated imagination *creating* visions in the heat of passion, opium, or madness. Visions in these tales provoke terror instead of comfort—more important, we are never sure whether the visions are real and the dreamer reliable. Does Ligeia come to life in the body of Rowena? Does Madeleine Usher walk out of her tomb? Does the image of the gallows appear on the black cat's breast? Poe precludes definite answers to such questions, since all visions are filtered through the maddened psyches of flawed narrators. Visionary and Oriental images become thoroughly demythologized and secularized when seen through the haze of the irrational. The narrator of "Ligeia," an old man whose mind has been warped by long opium use, vaguely recalls the loveliness of Ligeia when she became excited: "at such moments was her beauty—in my heated fancy thus it appeared perhaps—the beauty of beings either above or apart from the earth—the beauty of the fabulous Houri of the Turk."[71] It is precisely the uncertainty of visions—the possibility that all visions are "perhaps" merely produced by "heated fancy"—that is the main point of these tales, which call attention to their own artificiality and fictionality. In Poe's hands, the visionary mode is deconstructed just as surely as the House of Usher sinks into the tarn. Visionary devices are no longer used to communicate a religious message; they are coolly manipulated by the creative stylist to illuminate the operations of the subversive imagination.

While Poe developed a nonphilosophical literary theory by observing the purely aesthetic implications of the popular visionary and Oriental modes, Melville produced broadly philosophical fiction precisely because he exploited the other common application of these modes by American writers: i.e., the voicing of progressive ideas through rhetorical accounts of exotic peoples and their religions. Ever since the late eighteenth century, American writers had commonly used fictions about faraway peoples or about angelic visitations as a safe means of airing liberal, sometimes quite skeptical notions. With remarkable frequency, the encounter with foreign beliefs in these popular works creates a *dialogue* that undermines religious certainty by exposing Christianity as just one among many world religions. More often than not, these works criticize American religion as intolerant, gloomy, and corrupt. But the criticism is shielded not only by diverting narratives of exotic adventure but also by passages in which the writer pays obligatory lip service to Christianity. While Oriental devices provided an oblique means of undercutting traditional religion, the visionary mode was frequently used as a reconstructive device. After attacking conventional religious beliefs or practices, the writer could call in an angel or other religious figure to comfort the doubting protagonist and offer a religious alternative, usually a nonsectarian faith of good works and hope.

Melville used both the skeptical religious dialogue and the reconstructive visionary mode in much of his fiction and poetry. Dialogues with foreign religions were common not only in Oriental tales but also in popular travel narratives that influenced Melville. During the two decades before the publication of Melville's first novel, *Typee* (1846), there emerged two contrasting kinds of religious dialogue in travel narratives about voyages to the South Sea Islands. One line of narratives—including William Ellis's *Polynesian Researches* (1829), Frederick Debell Bennett's *Narrative of a Whaling Voyage Round the Globe* (1840), and John Codman's *Sailors' Life and Sailors' Yarns* (1847)—endorsed the efforts of white Christian missionaries to convert and civilize the South Sea pagans. Although Melville lifted much factual information from Ellis and Bennett, he was clearly more powerfully drawn to the more skeptical dialogues in a contrasting line of popular narratives, including Nathaniel Ames's *Nautical Reminiscences* (1832), John H. Amory's *Old Ironside* (1840), Charles W. Denison's *Stories of the Sea* (1844), and George Little's *The American Cruiser* (1846). These works can be viewed as updated Oriental tales because they combined entertaining sea adventure with religious dialogues that exposed the corrupting influences of Christians on simple South Sea Islanders. Amory in *Old Ironside* laments that the peaceful, virtuous islanders have been "contaminated by intercourse with men *called Christians.*"[72] Ames in *Nautical Reminiscences* uses even stronger language, citing the ruination of the South Sea Islanders as evidence that "those who profess and call themselves Christians are by far . . . the greatest scoundrels on the face of the earth."[73] Denison in *Stories of the Sea,* likewise remarking on "the cupidity and cunning of men from christian shores," declares he would rather dwell in the Sandwich Islands "than to be among civilized men, who act like the worst of all cannibals— the cannibals of the human heart!"[74]

It should be noted that such skeptical remarks had to be voiced with extreme caution: Ames's attacks on Christianity in *Nautical Reminiscences* stirred up such a furor in religious circles that in his next novel, *An Old Sailor's Yarns,* Ames announced, "I have studiously endeavored to steer my footsteps clear of the tender toes of every religious sect except the Catholics; whom, in imitation of the Protestant clergy and laity all around me, I have handled without mittens whenever I could get the chance."[75] Melville faced a similar problem in writing his first two novels. Like several travel writers before him, he wished to use the fictional dialogue with foreign peoples as a means of undercutting what he considered corrupt Christianity; but he didn't want to alienate his religious readers. In *Typee* and *Omoo,* therefore, he was careful to dilute his criticism of Christian missionaries with much exotic adventure and with perfunctory paeans to Christianity. The British edition of *Typee* did contain enough bald attacks on the missionaries to induce Melville, at the request of his New York publishers, to excise some thirty pages of potentially sacrilegious material when preparing the American edition. Both the original edition and the expurgated Revised Edition, however, similarly use the popular device of indirectly questioning established religion by studying the customs of foreign peoples.

The contrast in *Typee* between unspoiled, tolerant pagan islanders and vicious, querulous Christians is typical of the sensibility behind popular Oriental tales and travel narratives, as is the ironic exposure of warring Christians and short-lived religious conversion in *Omoo*. Melville knew, as he wrote his publishers about *Omoo*, that his early fiction was "calculated for popular reading, or for none at all,"[76] so he adopted the common device of satirizing mainstream religion through exotic adventure, blunting the edge of the satire by paying occasional lip service to Christianity (e.g., he has the narrator of *Typee* interject pious remarks such as "In truth, I regard the Typees as a backslidden generation. They are sunk in religious sloth, and require a religious revival").[77] His canny use of popular devices paid off, for *Typee* and *Omoo* were generally well received and became his most immediately popular novels.

Just as Poe's early experimentation with visionary techniques led him toward literary aesthetics, so Melville's early adoption of the exotic-dialogue device led him toward a more sophisticated mixture of popular modes in *Mardi*. *Mardi* has been so often viewed as a philosophical work establishing the symbolic-quest motif to be repeated in *Moby-Dick* that we are apt to forget that the novel, which received surprisingly favorable reviews in its day, is heavily indebted to devices that had been commonly used by his contemporaries. As many critics have noticed, *Mardi* is full of references to such elite sources as Plato, Seneca, Rabelais, Burton, Browne, Shakespeare, Montaigne, and Coleridge. What has been overlooked is the fact that all these classic sources are fused and transmuted through Melville's innovative mixture of three popular religious modes of his day: secularized allegory, Oriental fiction, and the visionary mode.

Although, as will be seen, many other popular genres influenced *Mardi*, the religious ones are primarily responsible for the stylistic complexity and thematic density of the novel. Melville outdoes even Hawthorne in the ambitious updating of allegory, for he permits secular adventure to flow into a capacious allegory in which scores of past and present religions, writers, and social movements become successively embodied in a symbolic landscape. As in his first two novels, Melville voices severe doubts about the Christian church here, but he expresses these doubts through a narrative whose fascinations even his harshest critics found hard to resist. Melville's main rhetorical ploy is to air highly skeptical ideas through an Oriental philosopher, Babbalanja, and then to ward off possible charges of infidelity by having this character be converted to a simplified Christianity as a result of an inspiring celestial vision.

Many American fictionists before Melville had similarly expressed unconventional philosophical ideas through the Oriental mode and then recoiled at the end from the skeptical conclusions toward which their narratives seemed to be tending. Frequently in popular literature, a restless doubter is comforted by an angel or a reassuring vision of the afterlife. This is exactly how Babbalanja is converted in chapter 188 ("Babbalanja relates to them a Vision"). Having severely questioned numerous philosophies and religions throughout the novel, Babbalanja dreams of an angel who gives him an inspiring vision of heaven and advises him to seek no more "in things mysterious; but rest content, with knowing naught but Love." Babbalanja, like many a popular hero, adopts a creedless, nonsectarian faith based upon good works. Giving up his fruitless quest, he settles on the island of Serenia and says, "Let us do: let us act. . . . While we fight over creeds, ten thousand fingers point to where vital good may be done."[78] Melville departs from previous American writers in both the depth and the variety of the skeptical questions asked before the doubter's conversion, as well as his refusal to end the novel with the conversion: at the end, the young seeker Taji is still looking for his lost Yillah. But we should note that Taji has not voiced many skeptical views in the novel. The main skeptic, Babbalanja, has been converted and comfortably placed in Serenia, while Taji, who has figured mainly as an adventure hero, can be sent after Yillah without Melville's laying himself open to the charge of utter infidelity. While accepting the basic premises of popular religious modes, Melville is taking them to new stylistic and philosophical heights.

In *Moby-Dick,* the popular Oriental device of replacing church religion with a broad nonsectarianism is treated less artificially than it had been in *Mardi,* as the dialogue between Christianity and paganism becomes fully humanized. The developing relationship between the Presbyterian Ishmael and the cannibal Queequeg is a metonymic enactment of the deconstructive and reconstructive religious dialectic that had governed many Oriental tales and some travel narratives. Numerous writers of exotic fiction had rhetorically shown Orientals or South Sea Islanders to be more virtuous than Christians; Charles W. Denison, as we saw, went so far as to say he would rather live with real cannibals than with civilized "cannibals of the human heart." Melville gives this message a new ironic twist when he has Queequeg, who is dismayed by the iniquities of Christians, reflect: "We cannibals must help these Christians."[79] Just as numerous popular

Oriental tales had rhetorically portrayed fictional pagans pitying unenlightened American Christians, so Melville has Queequeg feel sad that a
sensible young man like Ishmael "should be so hopelessly lost to evangelical pagan piety." Ishmael, too, becomes a genial embodiment of the religious-dialogue theme when he comes to admire Queequeg and to decide:
"I'll try a pagan friend, . . . since Christian kindness has proved but hollow
courtesy."

When Melville seems to be directly borrowing from strictly conventional travel books, he undercuts them. For instance, John H. Amory's
Almonuc: or The Golden Rule. A Tale of the Sea (1840) had described a young
sailor who succeeds in converting to Christianity many South Sea Islanders
and profane seamen (including a tyrannical captain) by always applying the
Golden Rule. Ishmael likewise follows the Golden Rule, but only to end,
ironically, by participating in pagan practices: he knows that as a good
Christian he should do as he would be done by, that he would wish Queequeg to join him in his Presbyterian worship, and that therefore he must
"turn idolator" and join the cannibal in his ritual.[80] Having used the
Ishmael-Queequeg relationship as a dialogic means of breaking down
narrow religious distinctions, Melville goes beyond the most secular of the
religious fictionists by affirming a humanistic spirit of piety. He has Ishmael
inform the bigoted Quaker Bildad that Queequeg is "a born member of
the First Congregational Church . . . of this whole worshipping world."
This catholicity of vision is enforced through the entire novel by the portrayal of the crew of the *Pequod*, a conglomeration of all creeds and races
"federated along one keel" in pursuit of the white whale—that is, humanity
in all its diversity commonly engaged in explaining the infinite.

While Melville in *Moby-Dick* follows the religious-dialogue device to an
inspiringly democratic affirmation of human togetherness and inter-
dependence, there was good reason for Melville to call this novel a
"wicked" book that was broiled in hellfire, since visionary and Oriental
devices, which in *Mardi* had offered solace, are in the end exposed as mere
fantasy and wish fulfillment. True, Melville does still recognize the redemptive possibilities of these devices. As seen, he fully comprehends the
optimistic spirit behind the Christian-pagan dialogue convention. Also, he
twice uses the visionary mode in the usual hopeful way: the angel in the
wall painting behind Father Mapple's pulpit smiles upon a sea-tossed ship
and seems to promise salvation for all persevering humans; and Ishmael,
after tenderly squeezing the hands of his fellow sailors in the sperm vat,
has a comforting visionary dream—"In visions of the night, I saw long rows
of angels in paradise, each with his hands in a jar of spermaceti."[81] Only
a nineteenth-century American like Melville, keenly aware of the colloqui-
ally irreverent piety of Father Taylor and of popular visionary writers like

Sylvester Judd (whose novel *Margaret* Melville owned), could have coined these homely visionary images. Such popular devices, however, can no longer offer lasting consolation for Melville, who is inexorably drawn to the darker side of the visionary and Oriental modes. The visionary mode is darkened through images like the elusive Spirit Spout (the symbol of often glimpsed but never reached revelation) and the insanity that succeeds Pip's vision of "God's foot upon the treadle of the loom" when he sinks deep in the ocean. Similarly, Oriental imagery throughout the book is dark rather than bright: Ahab is called a despotic "sultan" lording it over his "emirs"; the mysterious Oriental sailor Fedallah is revealed as the devil in disguise; reverie on the masthead, a practice Melville says is rooted in ancient Egyptian customs, can lead to self-destruction; a dying whale is said to represent the "dark Hindoo half of nature"; and in his last moment Ahab is shot out of the whaleboat "voicelessly as Turkish mutes bowstring their victim." In this last image, it would seem that Melville is recognizing that one of nineteenth-century America's favorite "arrows"—the Oriental mode—can no longer be "shot" at God but instead has circled back and pierced the religious seeker himself. Ahab's last moment can be regarded as the deconstruction of the Oriental image.

Moby-Dick was Melville's swan song to optimistic use of visionary and Oriental devices until the late resurgence of creativity that produced *Clarel* (1876) and *Billy Budd* (1891). Granted, several of the lesser stories Melville wrote during the 1850s do make conventional applications of visionary comfort. "Cock-A-Doodle-Doo!" ends in redemptively visionary fashion, as the narrator, inspired by the courage of a religious poor family, stares admiringly at their corpses and reports: "I saw angels where they lay."[82] In "The Apple-Tree Table," the rebirth of a bug after years inside a table is said to symbolize human resurrection, and "Jimmy Rose" ends with the hope that the indigent hero, oppressed on earth, will at least find heavenly reward. But these are rather perfunctory visionary moments that occur in lesser tales that seem tailor-made for conventional readers (Hawthorne uses the visionary mode in even more conventionally pious fashion in several of his minor tales). Among the post–*Moby-Dick* works, modern readers have understandably been more powerfully drawn to those in which visionary optimism is undercut rather than affirmed. Visionary images fill the early chapters of *Pierre,* as Lucy Tartan is often called a redemptive angel on earth; but Melville establishes this conventional motif only to subvert it, since both the angelic Lucy and the idealized Pierre are drawn into a poisonous world of urban poverty, shattered homes, and illicit love. The religiously optimistic narrators of "Benito Cereno" and "Bartleby, the Scrivener" project hopeful images upon the mysterious persons and events; but, like Poe and Hawthorne in their best works,

Melville in these stories does not endorse this optimism but rather analyzes it as one of many contortions of the disturbed human psyche when confronted with the inexplicable. Visionary and Oriental devices are notably absent from *The Confidence-Man,* the bitterly tragicomic novel in which sincere religious truth seeking is virtually abandoned on behalf of a highly stylized linguistic shell game in which conventional images are recognized as totally powerless.

We witness the reemergence of optimistic religious devices in Melville's later works, as evidenced by the sincere use of biblical typology throughout *Battle-Pieces,* the reliance upon visionary and Oriental devices at key moments in the religiously problematic poem *Clarel,* and the mythic reconstruction of biblical, allegorical, visionary, and Oriental images in *Billy Budd.* Even though in these works Melville applies secularized religious devices to a kind of imaginative refurbishment of belief, he still confronts the ironies and ambiguities that had puzzled him in the 1850s. *Battle-Pieces* remains (with Whitman's *Drum Taps*) the most powerful poem about the Civil War precisely because Melville is able to take a broadly sympathetic overview of martyrdom and victory on both sides, and lend some measure of hope through the use of demythologized biblical imagery. In reading *Clarel,* we forgive the quite conventional visionary moments (two troubled truth seekers have consoling visions of angels) and the rhetorical use of redemptive Oriental figures (especially Djalea, the admirably peaceful Druze of Lebanon) because of the poem's honest, penetrating critique of many nineteenth-century religious and philosophical currents. *Billy Budd* still sparks debate in classrooms and in scholarly articles precisely because modern readers cannot decide just how sincere the positive religious imagery is: does Melville here present a testament of acceptance giving total endorsement to his blond "angel of God," or is he drawing an ironic portrait of the ineffectuality of virtue in a satanic world?

This provocative question about *Billy Budd* and similar questions about other problematic works cannot be fully addressed until we study ambiguities in the nineteenth-century socioliterary environment. The religious devices studied in this chapter were, in the main, reconstructive devices used by American writers who sought imaginative relief from both social and metaphysical perplexities. In several key literary texts, however, these perplexities overwhelm any redemptive power religious devices might offer. The following chapters show just how troubled the moral and literary climate was, and how cultural ambiguities gave rise to thematic density and to alternate forms of literary reconstruction.

2

THE REFORM IMPULSE AND THE
PARADOX OF IMMORAL DIDACTICISM

O N E of the most enduring myths about America's major literature
is that its rich imaginativeness stood in opposition to a conventionally
moralistic antebellum society. In 1913 George Santayana exemplified the
reaction that was to become standard when he claimed that the major
nineteenth-century writers found "little digestible material" in their society and therefore "broke away from all conditions of age or country."[1]
This contrast between American writers and their circumstances has variously reappeared in Lionel Trilling's definition of American literature as
a marginal genre distanced from social concerns, in Richard Chase's concept of the mythic American romance (as opposed to the more realistic,
socially textured European novel), and in Henry Nash Smith's distinction
between the introspective major literature and superficial popular writings.[2]

Such interpretations are based on the premise that the ambiguous major
literature was an anomaly in an age whose moral vision was governed by
a faith in progress, Manifest Destiny, and human perfectibility. These
optimistic beliefs, so the argument goes, are especially evident in the
enormous body of antebellum writings dedicated to promoting such reforms as temperance, moral reform (by which was meant the fight against
prostitution and illicit sex), anti-Catholicism, antislavery, and labor reform. It is usually argued that the major writers intentionally tried to
subvert the prevailing didacticism of such popular reform writings. One
recent commentator has called reform literature "an extreme, almost

comic result" of the antebellum period's "conventional insistence on the moral usefulness of art."[3] Another similarly concludes that a writer like Melville purposefully "subverts the ideology of reform."[4] In short, the major literature is most commonly viewed as a direct affront to a homogeneously moralistic culture.

What has not been sufficiently recognized is that moral reform literature offered a wealth of imagery and themes to the major writers precisely because, in its most imaginative forms, it was, paradoxically enough, immoral and ambiguous. To be sure, there was a highly influential body of reform literature, written mainly by Northeastern liberals, that was so stylistically restrained and sober that it often overlapped with or fed into popular conventional writings. It is this conventional reform literature, which is indeed progressivist and optimistic, that most critics have in mind when they underscore the uniqueness of the major literature. But a far more complex body of reform literature sprang up during this period, produced first by evangelicals of the Southern frontier and then by working-class radicals and popular authors of the great North Atlantic cities, especially New York and Philadelphia. A wild subversiveness surged volcanically from below and created an electrically charged moral atmosphere that helped produce, among many other things, Melville's famous assertion of literary protest—"No! in thunder."

Between 1800 and 1850 reform literature was increasingly exploited by popular authors and lecturers who ostensibly aimed to correct human behavior but whose texts show that they were actually engaged in exploring dark forces of the human psyche, in venting subrational fantasies, and even in airing misanthropic or skeptical ideas. Early in this period, reform literature was dominated by the conventional. As time passed, however, there arose a strong subversive element, seen in a succession of vociferous reformers whose loudly announced goal was to stamp out various behavioral sins or social iniquities—intemperance, licentiousness, urban poverty, chattel and wage slavery, poor prison conditions, and so forth—but who described vice in such lurid detail that they themselves were branded as dangerously immoral and sacrilegious. The *immoral* or *dark reformers,* as I call them, used didactic rhetoric as a protective shield for highly unconventional explorations of tabooed psychological and spiritual areas. They were regularly blasted by outraged conservatives and in several cases were taken to court for issuing indecent or subversive literature. These reformers righteously proclaimed that they were wallowing in foul moral sewers only to scour them clean; but their seamy writings prove they were more powerfully drawn to wallowing than to cleaning.

The major writers, therefore, were *not* protesting against contemporary popular writings that were uniformly didactic. Rather, they were commenting upon and textually re-creating deep ambiguities in their moral environment. Often they willfully played off the reassuring idiom of Conventional reform against the wilder idiom of Subversive reform to create dense literary mixtures. For example, Hawthorne in *The Blithedale Romance* views an immoral reformer (Hollingsworth) through the distorting lens of a narrator (Coverdale) who embodies safe Boston liberalism: as a result, the novel powerfully reproduces the fragmentation and vicious hostilities within the antebellum reform climate. The novel was the culmination of Hawthorne's long-standing interest in reform issues, evidenced successively by his early journal entries on reformers, by his popular temperance story "A Rill from the Town Pump," by his association with many leading reformers at Brook Farm, and by his use of problematic reform themes in several of his major works, including *The Scarlet Letter.* As will be seen, for both Hawthorne and Melville contemporary reform devices and themes provided an inroad toward literary ambiguity. Melville's early novels, in fact, were so characteristic of their time that they aroused critical controversies very similar to those provoked by popular immoral reformers. Emerson, Thoreau, and Whitman were all intimately aware of both the moral confusions and the creative possibilities embodied in the reform conflicts of their day; the paradoxical bite and moral breadth of their best work owes much to this awareness. In a different manner Poe and Dickinson present abstract, rarefied renderings of popular reform rhetoric.

While reform writings are significant as a fecund source for the major authors, many of them possess a verve and a complexity that make them worthy of analysis on their own. Since so much of this literature has been ignored, it is worthwhile to examine its evolving social and artistic manifestations. The present chapter uncovers thematic tensions and common textual strategies in a large body of influential reform writings. The next chapter explores the process by which these tensions and strategies were transformed in literary texts by the major writers.

The Darkening of Moral Discourse

The profound dualisms and ubiquitous moral paradoxes in America's major literature have often been pondered but never been adequately placed in their contemporary context. The Russian literary theorist Mikhail M. Bakhtin has suggested that complex literature can emerge only when a culture is suddenly deprived of its naïve absence of conflict, when moral systems are recognized as relative rather than unitary. A fluidity of genres and language systems, Bakhtin argues, occurs in a period of "intense struggle" when "boundaries are drawn with new sharpness and simultane-

ously erased with new ease; it is sometimes impossible to establish precisely where they have been erased or where certain of the warring parties
have already crossed over into alien territory."[5] We have seen how antebellum popular preachers often straddled a precarious line between sincerity
and showmanship, and how the erosion of boundaries between the sacred
and the secular led directly to imaginative reapplications of religion by the
major writers. As notable as such boundary erosion was in the religious
sphere, it was even more pronounced—and more directly generative of
literary art—in the sphere of popular reform.

The antebellum period has long been known as the great era of reform
movements, the time when piety came to be widely equated with puritanical moralism and when scores of societies were organized to combat behavioral vices and social ills. Recent social historians such as Bruce Laurie
and Sean Wilentz have distinguished between two major groups of antebellum reformers, the rationalists and the evangelicals, who often shared
similar goals (e.g., to combat intemperance or to aid the poor) but who
battled bitterly over ideology and tactics.[6] It should be emphasized that
every reform—temperance, antislavery, labor reform, antiprostitution,
and so forth—had both its rationalistic and its evangelical supporters. The
rationalists, based mainly in the Northeast, included Unitarians, freethinkers, and Quakers who promoted education and rational self-improvement
and who were appalled by the increasing zeal of their archopponents, the
evangelicals. At first, evangelical reform was the province of relatively
restrained, wealthy philanthropists, such as the New York Presbyterian silk
merchants Arthur and Lewis Tappan, who in the mid-1820s founded the
first of many moral reform and tract societies. But in the early 1830s
evangelical reform was infused with a new fierceness and vigor primarily
as a result of the kind of militant rhetoric that had rumbled on the Southern
frontier since the turn of the century. Notorious firebrands such as the
antiprostitution reformer John McDowall and the abolitionist William
Lloyd Garrison ushered in an extraordinarily harsh rhetoric that threatened to overwhelm moral statement and even to subvert the very meaning
of vice and virtue. It is no accident that the early 1830s proved to be a
crucial moment in the development of the literary sensibilities of several
major writers, for this was a time of widespread relativization of values in
the surrounding culture.

I am inclined to split reform literature into two aspects: the Conventional and the Subversive. Both were ostensibly based upon an interest in
preserving moral and physical healthiness, a belief in the sanctity of the
home, and an identification of religion with moral practice. But the difference between the two groups lies in emphasis and imagery. Conventional
reform writings, particularly the highly influential lectures and novels of

Boston Unitarians, emphasize the ingredients and rewards of virtue rather than the wages of vice. Typical of the Conventional sensibility are Sarah Savage's domestic novel *The Factory Girl* (1814), the Ohio reform paper *The Moral Advocate* (1821–24) published by the Quaker Elisha Bates, William Ware's *The Recollections of Jotham Anderson* (1824), the reform sermons by leading liberal preachers like William Ellery Channing and Joseph Tuckerman, Catharine Sedgwick's novels *Home* (1835) and *The Poor Rich Man, and the Rich Poor Man* (1836), and the addresses of the abolitionist and education reformer Horace Mann.

Though various in scope and intention, such writings typify the Conventional outlook in their accentuation of hopeful themes or characters, including the blissful home, the nurturing parent, the angelic child, the idyllic village environment, and self-improvement through hard work and moral discipline. Savage's novel says little about the harsh realities of factory work while stressing the bliss of a poor virtuous family. Bates's *Moral Advocate* was a reform periodical of the most sincerely didactic variety, printing many staid speeches and reports condemning slavery, capital punishment, and dueling in language that never became overzealous. Channing, Tuckerman, and Mann, who called for the elevation of the poor and oppressed through self-culture, all retained a rational tone and specifically disparaged the often coarse, violent language of their evangelical opponents. The novels of Ware and Sedgwick are Conventional narratives on the power of family togetherness and active morality in the face of social inequities. Eventually, such themes would gain almost mythic status in such Conventional best-sellers as Susan Warner's *The Wide, Wide World* (1850) and Maria Cummins's *The Lamplighter* (1854).

All these works can be called truly *moral* since they avoid excessive sensationalism and always emphasize the means by which vice can be circumvented or remedied. They are emblematic of the progressive, moralistic antebellum popular culture that has been eloquently described by scholars like Rush Welter, Sacvan Bercovitch, and Ann Douglas.[7] To call such writings Conventional is not to deny their powerful impact on the major literature. We should note that Conventional reformers were in several cases linked with major writers: Channing and Tuckerman were preceptors of Emerson and Thoreau; Horace Mann became Hawthorne's brother-in-law; and Melville, who befriended Catharine Sedgwick in the Berkshires, adapted her *Poor Rich Man* in his story "Poor Man's Pudding and Rich Man's Crumbs." The Conventional reformers, despite their generally restrained style, did sometimes employ imagery that would be picked up by the major writers. For instance, one of Horace Mann's favorite images—the comparison of modern poor people to the indigent Bible character Lazarus, who is saved while the wealthy Dives is damned to hell—appears several times in Melville's fiction, most notably in a long paragraph at the end of Chapter 2 in *Moby-Dick*. In a larger sense, the hopeful myths fashioned by Conventional reformers provided what Roland Barthes would call a *doxa* according to which the major authors could define themselves. "A new discourse can only emerge," Barthes writes, "as the *paradox* which goes against (and often goes for) the surrounding or preceding *doxa*, can only see the day as difference, distinction, working loose *against* what sticks to it."[8] We will see later that several key literary texts incorporate myths of Conventional reform with the conscious intention of subverting them.

What has gone unrecognized is that this subversive process itself had ample precedent in the lectures, essays, and fiction of the hitherto overlooked school of antebellum *immoral* or *dark* reformers. If the most fertile soil for literature is a culture of shifting boundaries when it becomes difficult to decide when certain of the warring parties have slipped into the enemy's territory, antebellum reform was fertile soil indeed. With increasing frequency and purposefulness, popular American lecturers and writers learned to manipulate the rhetoric of reform instead of using it with high seriousness. In contrast to Conventional reformers, the Subversive reformers (often called "ultraists" by their contemporaries) deemphasized the remedies for vice while probing the grisly, sometimes perverse results of vice, such as shattered homes, sadomasochistic violence, eroticism, nightmare visions, and the disillusioning collapse of romantic ideals. Ironically, even the most grossly immoral reformers, such as George Lippard and George Thompson, righteously proclaimed pure moral intentions. Often, indeed, these intentions were accepted at face value, as several immoral reformers became the revered leaders of reform movements. Still, I define these reformers as immoral or dark precisely because they provoked notably divided responses and because their writings are mixed texts that resist straightforward interpretation.

The dark reformers are largely responsible for transforming a culture of morality into a culture of ambiguity. Examining representative reform movements illuminates this process. The investigation of specific minor figures reveals various key Subversive strategies that would be adopted by the major authors of the American Renaissance.

The paradox of immoral didacticism was closely linked to the rise of the mass readership in America, as is evidenced by the experience of Mason Locke Weems, the book-peddling parson who can rightfully be called our first significant immoral reformer. As an Episcopalian clergyman in late-eighteenth-century Maryland, Weems had developed a casual pulpit style which struck some as indecent and which he justified with the remark: "Religion with irregularity is better than no religion."[9] This freewheeling

attitude carried over into his work as a book distributor for the Philadelphia publisher Matthew Carey. Setting out in 1792, Weems traveled in his
horse-drawn cart for more than two decades throughout the South,
preaching and hawking books with a shrewd eye on the popular market.

The adaptation of reform literature to the often depraved tastes of
frontier or lower-middle-class readers is shown in Weems's popular moral
reform tracts, most of which he himself wrote. These tracts display a new
amoral *exploitation* of morality by a book peddler who was attentive above
all to salability. Weems's best-seller in the mid-1790s was a racy tract
against masturbation, *Onania,* whose popularity was quickly thought to be
"rather a matter of diversion than serious consideration." A similar ambivalence surrounded Weems's immensely popular paperback condemning
adultery, *Hymen's Recruiting Sergeant* (1799), which one austere Boston magazine attacked for its odd union of exalted "religious moralizing" with "the
low cant and balderdash of the ranks and drinking table." Between 1800
and 1823 Weems produced several other controversial immoral reform
tracts on such topics as gambling, dueling, and drinking.

Weems's normal strategy in these tracts was to present many grotesque,
blackly humorous examples of the effects of vice and then to recoil to safe
moral ground in a long concluding essay on such remedies as education
and religious conversion. Later immoral reformers would outdo Weems in
the graphic horror of their accounts of vice; many would dispense altogether with the concluding moral commentary. Still, Weems was a stylistic
pioneer who began to tip the balance away from simple didacticism toward
psychologically complex portraits of haunted minds, broken homes, uncontrollable lust or violence, and the mingling of religious and sexual
ecstasy.

The paradoxical combination of the perverse and the prudish is typified
by Weems's tracts *The Drunkard's Looking Glass* and *God's Revenge Against
Adultery.* Both works end with sober essays calling for improved education
and stricter blue laws. The illustrative tales that precede these essays,
however, are so filled with violence and eroticism that we can have little
doubt Weems was fascinated with the abominations he pretended to decry.
Weems loved to portray elite figures like clergymen or lawyers in the last
stages of bestial intoxication. In one typical anecdote, the devil promises
great things to a preacher if he will either rape his sister, kill his father, or
get drunk—the preacher gets drunk and then proceeds to murder his
father, rape his sister, and hang himself. Weems looked forward to Poe in
his many stories of normally rational people driven by the demons of vice
into a madness that distorts their vision of perceived reality. In one characteristic story, a man suffering from delirium tremens chops up his loving
wife and three children with an ax under the illusion that they are vipers.

In another, a drunken man who thinks he is a clock spends days on a wall shelf, swinging his arms and shouting "CLICK! CLICK! CLICK!"[10]

This fascination with the tabooed or the bizarre, deflected in ostensibly moralistic prose, reveals a process of sublimation that would become a common trait among American immoral reformers. Weems once confessed to his publisher, Carey, that writing tracts provided an outlet for vicious impulses: "if I had not a fondness to scribble to divert my thoughts from distraction," Weems asked, "what could possibly have kept me from hard drink, gambling," and cheating Carey of profits?[11] Several critics sensed the insincerity of Weems's stance as a moral reformer. William Gilmore Simms, for instance, branded Weems as a "mountebank" who "had no fear of the vulgar" and in fact was attracted to "the social aspects of a tavern." Like many reformers and writers after him, Weems evidently felt that the puritanical ethos of Protestant America precluded frank, open treatment of the violent or the erotic. As a result, he was among the first to turn this ethos into a kind of self-consuming artifact by exaggerating and universalizing the vices he pretended to denounce.

All the major writers would naturally be familiar with Parson Weems, who was a standard American author. The moral ambiguities he represented, however, did not become a widespread phenomenon until the late 1820s, when the rise of several immensely powerful reform movements made immoral didacticism part of the very cultural air that the major authors breathed. Emerson was right when he pointed to the 1820s as the period when suddenly throughout America there was felt "a certain sharpness of criticism, an eagerness for reform, which showed itself in every quarter."[12] Emerson was hardly alone in recognizing the crucial importance of the reform impulse to the growth of a distinctive national literature: as will be seen, Thoreau, Whitman, Hawthorne, and Melville all paid homage to this impulse as well. It is of course beyond my purview to trace the rise of every reform movement. For present purposes, it is sufficient to investigate the moral and stylistic complexities surrounding the following movements: the fight against licentiousness and illicit love (called "moral reform"); anti-Catholicism; temperance; antislavery; and labor reform.

It should be emphasized that the period when immoral reform became a genuine social force (1830–35) was also a moment of marked deepening and expansion in the moral vistas of several writers. It was during these years that Emerson left the pulpit, Thoreau debated on the efficacy of popular reform movements at Harvard, Poe wrote his earliest tales, and Hawthorne's fiction began to probe moral ambiguities. The subversive sensibility of our great writers was nurtured in a moment of stunningly harsh conflict between opposing moral viewpoints, a conflict that unfastened the terms "virtue" and "vice" from clear referents and made them available for stylistic manipulation by the major writers.

A principal arena for this conflict was the so-called Benevolent Empire, the great network of evangelical reform societies that had been initiated in the 1820s by the New York City Presbyterians Arthur and Lewis Tappan and their followers Charles Grandison Finney and Joseph Brewster. In the decade after the founding of the New York Tract Society in 1825, the evangelicals fanned into the most impious realms—foul city slums, village markets, wild frontier districts—distributing tracts and newspapers and founding branch societies in a nationwide effort to stamp out behavioral vice. They rapidly ran into trouble with their archcompetitors, the rationalists, who insisted that the zealous evangelicals were threatening to extinguish rationality and prepare the American public for submission to would-be moral tyrants. Although such freethinkers and liberals as Fanny Wright, Robert Dale Owen, and Joseph Tuckerman are sometimes remembered today as rabid reformers, these and other rationalists were in fact careful to avoid the evangelicals' often sensational post-Calvinist imagery and to keep their own rhetoric within the restraints of reason. Fanny Wright typified the rationalist approach when she attacked those who "have substituted abuse for advice, and violence for argument"—in outlining a plan for her pet project, a national system of education, she specifically directed her appeals to "the temperate friends of reform" who would "effect a quiet and gradual change."[13] Similarly, the Unitarian reformer Joseph Tuckerman, describing how underpaid seamstresses are often forced into the streets, announced: "I wish to write calmly, dispassionately of these great evils, difficult as it to repress the indignation which they awaken." Stressing the solutions rather than the practice of vice, Tuckerman asked, "Why should we look at the evil at all, if nothing is to be attempted for its remedy?"[14]

The evangelicals, in contrast, felt compelled to stare directly at the Medusa head of vice and describe every one of its grotesque features. Indeed, as time passed it became clear that the evangelicals' biggest enemy was not the rationalists who attacked them from without but rather the morbidness and irrationalism that raged within their own ranks.

The most controversial figure in the early evangelical group was John R. McDowall, New York City's great foe of illicit love, who in the early 1830s became the center of an immoral-reform scandal that rocked the Benevolent Empire. Born in 1801 in Upper Canada, McDowall moved in his late teens to the United States, where he became a Presbyterian minister involved in tract distribution in Rhode Island. In 1830 he moved to New York, where he joined Tappan's evangelical army and began touring the brothels in the city's lower-class districts. Shocked by the extent of prostitution in the city, he founded the Female Benevolent Society and published *Magdalen Facts* (1831), a pamphlet which created a firestorm of controversy because of its revelation of widespread depravity among whores and their often wealthy customers. Despite death threats from those who considered him a crass pornographer, McDowall persevered in his fight to expose illicit love and its literature.

What led to his downfall was his widely read, inflammatory weekly newspaper, *McDowall's Journal* (1833–34), which was distributed nationwide by mainly female evangelicals to more than a hundred thousand subscribers. So graphic were the paper's reports of whoredom, abortion, child murder, assignation houses, venereal disease, and obscene books that McDowall was labeled a horrid infidel and his journal a lazar house of putrid moral corruption. The early 1830s was precisely the period when American publishers learned to capitalize on the public's thirst for the sensational: McDowall and his cohorts in the Benevolent Society were tempting targets for editors of cheap newspapers looking for racy material. The *Morning Courier and New York Enquirer* grouped McDowall together with Arthur Tappan and William Lloyd Garrison as dangerous incendiaries corrupting public morals and threatening to divide the nation. The *Courier* reserved special venom for "that infamous bawdy chronicle called McDowall's Journal," whose editors "believe it a most evangelical application of other people's money, to print and disseminate among our virtuous females, pamphlets and papers containing details calculated to poison their imagination, and make them adepts in all the mysteries of human corruption!"[15] Another New York paper, the *Commercial Advertiser,* declared that *McDowall's* was "the most foul and loathsome journal that ever suffused the cheek of modesty," "a sort of Directory of Iniquity—a brothel companion" which "under the pretence of reforming mankind, excites the imagination of youth by the most glowing pictures of sensual debaucheries."[16] McDowall retorted, with some justification, that papers like the *Courier* that charged him with immorality were themselves "grossly obscene and dangerous" periodicals filled with gory reports of local crimes and so forth.[17] Proclaiming his pure intentions, McDowall compared himself to a bold physician probing hideous wounds.

The physician, as it turned out, should have healed himself. In 1834 McDowall was forced to suspend publication when a New York grand jury ruled that his paper was "calculated to promote lewdness."[18] The next year McDowall was convicted by the Third Presbytery of New York of corrupting public morals, illegally using funds donated to his cause, and doing other "scandalous things, too bad to name" (it was rumored he was sleeping with one of the prostitutes under his care).[19] Eventually he was defrocked and driven to isolation and early death. His followers in the

Female Benevolent Society continued to publish his journal under a different name. In the meantime, McDowall's cause was ardently espoused by other evangelicals throughout America, including one Gallowrake ("rakes must go to the gallows"), an Ohio immoral reformer whose widely reprinted articles stunned the nation with accounts of licentiousness even on the Western frontier.[20]

Like all reforms of the period, this one quickly got into the hands of exploitative publishers trying to cash in on the public's growing curiosity for the racy details of vice among the ostensibly pure and respectable. In a period of sudden genre fluidity, the line between illicit-love tracts and pornographic fiction became dangerously thin. For instance, *The Confessions of a Magdalene* (1831), a lurid pamphlet novel about a woman driven to prostitution after being drugged and seduced by a preacher, is evidently intended as a warning to seducers but comes closer to exploiting their nefarious deeds in titillating fiction. Hawthorne, a close reader of newspapers, may have seen in the *Salem Gazette* for January 29, 1833, a story called "The Magdalene," which recounts a fallen woman's squalid life of sin followed by her penitence (rather like Hester Prynne's) while living in an isolated cottage and doing charity work for a nearby village. A whole genre of sensational antiseduction novels flooded the market in the late 1830s and 1840s. Among the most popular was William B. English's *Rosina Meadows* (1846), which traces the fall of an innocent country girl into depraved whoredom after she is seduced by a rich roué. *Ellen Merton, Belle of Lowell* (1844) was one of several novels that illustrated the moral perils of factory life by showing a club of seducers practicing their wiles on working girls. Melville utilized the protest against illicit love in *Typee*, which begins and ends with antiprostitution scenes containing the titillating/ moralistic rhetoric of popular immoral reform. By the late 1840s the antiseduction novel had soared into sadomasochistic fantasy, as is evidenced by the novels of George Thompson or by A. J. H. Duganne's *Eustace Barcourt,* in which an abandoned woman brains her seducer and then madly bathes her illegitimate child in his blood.

The rhetoric of immoral reform was by no means confined to the fight against illicit love. It was increasingly evident in the literature of other reforms as well. Evangelical foes of Roman Catholicism, for example, produced in the 1830s a series of anti-Catholic exposés whose seaminess quickly earned them notoriety as despicable pornography. Such popular works as George Bourne's *Lorette* (1833), the anonymously published *Female Convents* (1834), Rebecca Reed's *Six Months in a Convent* (1835), and Maria Monk's *Awful Disclosures of . . . the Hotel Dieu Nunnery at Montreal* (1836) were among the most infamous works that pictured alcoholism, flagellation, prostitution, and infanticide within convent walls. The confusion about such literature survives even to this day: in the library of the Kinsey Institute (the world's largest collection of American erotica) the only pre-1860 American work listed as "pornographic" is Maria Monk's *Awful Disclosures*. As will be seen later, there *were* (unbeknownst to the Kinsey Institute) several truly pornographic works produced by antebellum Americans, but Maria Monk's book is not one of them. It is instead a rather typical piece of immoral-reform writing, gotten up by four New York evangelical ministers in coordination with an ex-nun, which uses anti-Catholicism as a pretext for studying hidden lust and sadism. Maria Monk's tale of whoredom and baby murder in a Canadian nunnery captured the imagination of antebellum readers: not only did the book sell more than 300,000 copies before the Civil War, but in the late 1880s it could still intrigue the aged Walt Whitman, who reread it while under Horace Traubel's care in Camden. Neither popular readers nor Whitman seemed to be bothered by the fact that shortly after publication of her book Maria Monk was exposed as a fraud or that she eventually died in prison after she had been convicted of picking the pockets of her companion of the moment in a New York whorehouse. Such behavior among ostensibly pious reformers was becoming too commonplace to prevent readers like Whitman from taking interest in their writings.

Another body of popular reform writings that intrigued Whitman—and that had a notable influence on several other major writers as well—was temperance literature. Although we have histories of American drinking habits and temperance movements, no one has dealt adequately with a topic that Whitman in his last days said should be written about: literary representations of drinking and its opponents. Whitman was not alone in recognizing the literary importance of this topic: Hawthorne wrote a temperance story, Poe used temperance imagery in several tales, and Melville scattered such imagery throughout his fiction. In calling for a study of "the influence of drink in literature," Whitman said the subject "has so many sides, noble, devilish."[21] Whitman was right, for American temperance literature, which began as a rather conventional genre, assumed a notably "devilish," subversive aspect as it fell into the hands of immoral reformers and opportunistic publishers.

Before 1830, temperance literature had been produced in America primarily by two groups: Protestant clergymen from Increase Mather through Lyman Beecher whose works were largely theological, stressing that God will not visit the inebriated person; and rationalists, from Benjamin Franklin and Benjamin Rush through Fanny Wright, who emphasized the harmful effects of excessive drinking on one's intellectual and physical well-being. The feisty, dark reform tracts of Parson Weems were, as mentioned, exceptions to the generally moderate writings of the early temper-

ance advocates. A relatively restrained tone governed even the works of
the fervent evangelicals who promoted the American Temperance Society
(founded 1826). Between 1826 and 1832, a buoyant belief in human perfectibility characterized the outlook of these evangelicals, who thought that
a revolution in morals would automatically accompany their reform work.
The statistics seem to validate their optimism, for during this period the
number of local temperance societies leapt from 1,000 to 5,000, while total
membership in the societies swelled from about 100,000 to more than a
million. Temperance had rapidly become the most influential and most
broadly based reform movement in America.

A deepening pessimism, however, crept into the temperance ranks,
produced both by internal dissension between reformers and by indica-
tions that reform did not produce lasting results. The faith in human
perfectibility was shaken by countless cases of supposedly reformed drunkards resuming their old habits. Temperance essays and fiction began to
take on a note of doom, as more and more writers stressed alcoholism's
ravages rather than its remedies. The dark tone of the new temperance
literature is visible in several 1833–34 pieces in Hawthorne's hometown
newspaper, the *Salem Gazette,* such as a *"Horrid Case of Intemperance"* (describing a drunkard burned to a crisp by a blacksmith's fire) and a speech
by Edward Everett which contained grisly stories about inebriated husbands brutally murdering their wives and children.[22] Mary L. Fox's
popular novel *The Ruined Deacon* (1834) pictures the steady descent of a
Connecticut deacon after he begins drinking; also wretched is the deacon's wife, who becomes at first a gloomy misanthrope, then a philosophical skeptic, and at last a raving maniac as result of her husband's
habit. Fox's next novel, *George Allen, The Only Son* (1835), ends in almost
Hawthornesque gloom, as a man whose son had become a drunken
criminal and whose wife died of grief survives as a stern, melancholy
doubter. Similarly bleak is a best-selling temperance allegory, *Deacon
Giles' Distillery* (1835), by Hawthorne's close friend George B. Cheever,
which stirred up an immense controversy because of its graphic portrait
of devils gathering nightly in a distillery to produce alcohol. The metaphors of temperance writers began to possess both post-Calvinist universality and Gothic savagery, as is evidenced in these verses from "The
Rum Hole" (1835) by McDonald Clark, a New York poet Whitman
warmly eulogized:

> Ha!—see where the wild blazing Grog-Shop appears,
> As the red waves of wretchedness swell,
> How it burns on the edge of tempestuous years—
> The horrible Light-House of Hell.

'Tis built on a ledge of human bones,
Whose cement is of human blood,
And dark winds swell'd with memory's groans,
Are dashing tears there, for its flood.[23]

While popular temperance fiction and poetry became increasingly sensational, it was not until the rise of the Washingtonian temperance movement in the early 1840s that mainstream temperance lecturers adopted a similar style. The Washingtonian movement (which influenced Poe and which produced Whitman's temperance novel *Franklin Evans*) ushered both a feistiness and a new imaginativeness into temperance rhetoric. Like many other popular movements that developed marked subversive qualities, it originated in the South and became most influential in New York and Philadelphia. In an effort to compete with other popular entertainments, the Washingtonians tried to create a sanitized version of rowdy working-class culture, sponsoring temperance saloons, temperance hotels, temperance theaters, temperance picnics, and so forth. The Washingtonians were reformed drunkards who used every trick of moral suasion (in particular, dramatic renderings of their own horrific battles with the bottle) to terrify their weeping audiences into reform, which was signaled by the signing of a total abstinence pledge. "The reformed drunkards," Theodore Parker later recalled, "were violent, ill-bred, theatrical. . . . Many respectable men withdrew from the work as soon as the Washingtonians came to it."[24]

The most notorious of the Washingtonians was John Bartholomew Gough, the "poet of the d.t.'s." The most successful temperance lecturer of the 1840s, Gough was always surrounded by controversy; he was repeatedly charged with tawdry lecture tactics, with excessive emphasis on the grisly details of alcoholism rather than the cure for it, and, most damaging of all, with drinking and whoring on the sly himself. Gough loved to tell horror stories about crazed drunkards, such as that of a drunken man so annoyed by the crying of his two-year-old daughter that he roasted the girl over an open fire. As an alcoholic earlier in life, Gough had suffered often from delirium tremens, and his addresses were filled with reports of his nightmarish visions of terrible faces, bloated insects, oceans of blood, hundred-bladed knives tangled in his skin, and so on. A trained actor and singer, Gough raised many eyebrows with his temperance histrionics and once admitted: "I have been called 'humbug,' a 'theatrical performer,' a 'mountebank,' a 'clown,' a 'buffoon.' "[25] Like other immoral reformers before and after him, Gough seemed drawn to the very vices he denounced. He became the focus of a national scandal in 1845, when, after disappearing for a week, he was found in a New York whorehouse, apparently grossly drunk. Gough denied any wrongdoing, claiming he had been carried unconscious to the whorehouse after he had accidentally swallowed drugged cherry soda, but newspapers throughout the nation discarded his story as a transparent lie and branded him as a dissolute hypocrite. Although Gough continued to be a successful temperance lecturer for several decades, the Washingtonian cause was sullied by the scandal, and temperance as a whole became another reform movement poisoned by the paradox of immoral didacticism.

Temperance fiction, under the influence of the Washingtonians, continued to move increasingly away from the didactic toward the sensational. Earlier temperance novels, such as *Edmund and Margaret* and *The Lottery Ticket* (both 1822), had been characterized by quietness and rationality in their accounts of alcoholics recovering as result of Bible reading and domestic piety. By the early 1840s a school of powerful dark-temperance fiction had emerged. Just as Washingtonian lecturers wallowed publicly in past wrongdoing, so popular temperance novelists stressed the shattered homes, crime, and perversity resulting from their favorite vice. *Letters from the Almshouse* and *John Elliott* (both 1841) contain several sketches of drunken husbands dragging their wives about by the hair, driving their families outdoors, or chopping up family and friends with an ax. Whitman's temperance novel *Franklin Evans* (1842), written on commission for the Washingtonians, created a sensation with its bleak portrait of the countless evils flowing from alcohol. *Confessions of a Reformed Inebriate* (1844) showed the psychological ravages of intemperance, as its author described the loathsome visions endured by a sufferer of the d.t.'s. In *The Confessions of a Rum-Seller* (1845) a drunken man murders his own daughter when she cries; after he is hanged for murder, his wife becomes a raving maniac. Maria Lamas's *The Glass* (1849) gives dark temperance an unusual twist by describing a young boy, locked by his drunken mother in a closet, bleeding to death after having chewed his own arm to the bone in an effort to save himself from starvation. The temperance fiction of Thurlow Weed Brown abounded in such scenes of broken homes, insanity, and bestial violence.

The dark-temperance style illustrates well how the puritanical protest against vice, when carried to an extreme, could in fact turn into its opposite—a gloating over the grim details of vice that signaled the triumph of the Subversive sensibility. Because of this ethical fluidity of immoral reformers, it is small wonder that several of them were friends and inspirers of major writers. The Conventional moralist could, by amplifying the reformist zeal of his age, turn into the brash bohemian. This kind of flip-flop was most evident in the crowd surrounding Whitman and Poe. Whitman himself moved from Conventional reform writing ("The Sun-Down Papers'') through dark temperance (*Franklin Evans*) to rebellious, morally liberated poetry (*Leaves of Grass*). Whitman's close friend Henry Clapp, the leader of a bohemian group that met at Pfaff's saloon in the mid-1850s, had early in life been a rabid temperance lecturer and editor but then became a Fourierist rebel who sang praise to free enjoyment of sensual pleasures. The death of a friend drove Clapp to suicidal drinking—one writer said Clapp "lived to preach in his own life a better temperance lecture than he ever delivered in his younger days."[26] Two other Pfaff bohemians, Fitz-James O'Brien and Fitz-Hugh Ludlow, were driven to write moralistic literature despite their iconoclastic lifestyle. O'Brien loved boxing but wrote a flaming protest against boxing, a reform story called "The Prize Fight," on commission for a New York editor. Ludlow's best-selling record of his drug experiences, *The Hasheesh Eater* (1857), was ostensibly a moral protest against the use of drugs, but its reformist intent was belied by its long, dazzling accounts of marvelous drug visions; Ludlow proved indeed to be an immoral reformer, since he continued to drink and take drugs until his death.

Given the antididactic tendency of immoral-reform writings, it is small wonder that Edgar Allan Poe's fiction, for example, was influenced by the rhetorical changes that were going on around him. Poe is known to have joined the Sons of Temperance and written a temperance article in the last year of his life, and he had developed close connections with reformers long before that. In Baltimore in the late 1830s he befriended the alcoholic and opium addict John Lofland, who wrote popular fiction and delivered temperance lectures even though, like other backsliding reformers of the period, he continued to drink and take drugs in private. Another member of Poe's Baltimore set, Timothy Shay Arthur, went on to produce two of the biggest-selling (and darkest) temperance works of the period, *Six Nights with the Washingtonians* (1842) and *Ten Nights in a Bar-room* (1854). The latter novel sold more than 400,000 copies as a result of its titillatingly horrific portrayal of the collapse of a respectable community into complete moral degradation after the establishment of a saloon and a distillery.

The overall tendency of the dark-temperance mode was to discard moralization altogether on behalf of bold explorations of psychopathic states. The antimoralistic implications of popular dark-temperance literature were evident in many statements made by the reformers themselves, such as the following introduction to *Easy Nat* (1844), a widely read temperance novel: "I will not stay to *preach* to [readers]. I will not tarry even to *point a moral.* There is not time. I will simply and hurriedly inform them of the steps" by which a drunkard descends from falsehood through murder to suicide.[27] In a review of William Leete Stone's *Ups and Downs* (1836) Poe singled out for praise a dark-temperance scene about a drunken man pawning his wife's clothes despite her pathetic lamentations, a scene Poe said was useful "to one who would study human nature, especially in its darker features."[28] Other dark-reform fictionists Poe greatly admired were John Neal, Elizabeth Ellett, and George Lippard. The reformers he admired were precisely those who had initiated a process he would complete: the transference of reform imagery from the didactic to the psychological. Given his attraction to dark-temperance devices, we may surmise that the impulse behind his joining a temperance group was less a sincere desire for total abstinence than an instinctive attraction to a movement that had provided him with images of perversity and terror.

Dark-temperance imagery is scattered throughout many Poe tales, especially those written after 1840, when the Washingtonians notably darkened popular reform rhetoric. In particular, "The Black Cat" (1843) is a tale fully in the dark-temperance tradition, with reform images retained but an explicit moral message now totally eclipsed. Many dark-temperance tales of the day dramatized the shattering of a happy family after the husband takes up the bottle. By exaggerating both the happy prologue and the horrific aftermath of the husband's tippling, Poe converts a popular reform formula into an intriguing study of disintegration of the Conventional sensibility through the agency of Subversive forces unleashed by alcohol. Since youth the narrator has epitomized the Conventional: he tells us he had been famous for his docility, gentleness, humaneness. His good nature is especially displayed by his affection for his pet cat. But he recalls that his temperament—"through the instrumentality of the Fiend Intemperance—had (I blush to confess it) experienced a radical alteration for the worse. I grew, day by day, more moody, more irritable, more regardless of the feelings of others."[29] To describe his mental change, Poe uses dark-temperance metaphors: the narrator says that "my disease grew upon me—for what disease is like Alcohol!" One night, when "a more than fiendish malevolence, gin-nurtured, thrilled every fibre of my being," the narrator cuts out his cat's eye with a penknife. To forget the deed, "I again plunged into excess, and soon drowned in wine all memory of the deed." In the crescendoing perversity that leads to the murder of his cat and finally his wife, the narrator is driven by alcohol to the depths of paranoia, misanthropy, and criminality. The climax of the story, in which the narrator's grisly murder of his wife is revealed to the police by his own perverse game playing and cockiness, has a somewhat moralistic overtone recalling the conclusion of many dark-temperance tales—the drunkard, after all, will get his due and is already crying out in fear of "the fangs of the Arch-Fiend!" But Poe, who in many tales exploited different popular genres purely for the *effect* they could produce, is here avoiding didactic statement and exploring the shattered homes and self-lacerating demonism made available by the dark-temperance mode.

An equally inventive reapplication of dark-temperance imagery occurs in another Poe tale, "The Cask of Amontillado" (1846). It has long been known that the immediate source of this tale was Joel Tyler Headley's article "A Man Built in a Wall" (*Columbian Magazine,* 1844) and that Poe probably also knew of Honoré de Balzac's tale "Apropos of Bores" (*New York Mirror,* 1837). But to compare "The Cask of Amontillado" with these pieces is to recognize how Poe's addition of dark-temperance imagery enabled him to produce a tale far superior to its predecessors. "A Man Built in a Wall" is merely a sketch of Headley's grisly discovery, while touring an Italian church, of the skeleton of a man who had died by suffocation after having been walled up in a crypt. Balzac's "Apropos of Bores" is, likewise, just a sensational story, without much resonance, about two people at a party who tell the story of a time they nearly died while being accidentally locked in a cellar vault. Neither of these tales has the psychological intensity or ironic inevitability of Poe's tale, primarily because Poe alone made use of the dark-temperance mode.

In "The Cask of Amontillado" Poe fused a sensational adventure plot with psychologically suggestive dark-temperance images to produce a classic tale of terror. Unlike either of its lesser prototypes, "The Cask" centers on the diseased psychology associated with alcoholism. Everything in the main narrative pertains to the ill results of alcohol. The object of the descent into the vault is a bottle of wine. Both of the main characters are wine connoisseurs, as is their mentioned friend Luchesi. Although the narrator's exact motive for revenge is unclear, a nineteenth-century reader accustomed to alcohol-related criminality would find in Montresor a familiar kind of vindictive psychopath who boasts: "I was skilful in the Italian vintages myself, and bought largely whenever I could."[30] As for Fortunato, the victim of the revenge plot, the double pun on his name ("lucky" and "fated") had meaning in the dark-temperance sense: from his own viewpoint, the devoted wine lover Fortunato feels "lucky" to have a friend with a valued bottle of wine; from the reader's viewpoint, he is "fated" (in the deterministic symbology of dark temperance) to be sucked to his doom by his affection for liquor. Like many victims of alcohol obsession in dark-temperance stories, Fortunato journeys to his demise with full inevitability. He falls easy prey to the wily Montresor because he maniacally loves wines and takes fierce competitive pride in his connoisseurship. Fortunato is indeed fated by his fascination with the Amontillado. Moreover, he is inebriated at the start and becomes progressively more as the tale proceeds; the more wine he drinks, the more his interest in the Amontillado intensifies. Given the dark-temperance fatalism that governs the story, the narrator, Montresor, is just as degraded as Fortunato. There occurs a kind of evil communion between dissolutes when Montresor breaks open a bottle of Médoc and offers it to Fortunato, who "raised it to his lips with a leer." Poe's contemporary readers would naturally have contemplated the universality of desolation caused by alcohol when they read that the skeleton-filled wine vault showed the Montresors to have been "a great and numerous family"—by implication, a family of wine lovers now reduced to bones scattered amidst wine casks. They would also have felt at home with the symbolic interweaving of alcohol and death images, as when Poe described "long walls of piled bones, with casks and puncheons intermingling." They would have appreciated the coupling of drinking and clown-like stupidity in the portrayal of Fortunato (his eyes sparkling with wine as his cap bells jingle), and they would see the appropriateness in the terse tautological exchange that takes place as soon as Fortunato is chained to the wall:

> "The Amontillado!" ejaculated my friend, not yet recovered from his astonishment.
> "True," I replied; "the Amontillado."

The dreary circularity of this conversation, with the repetition of the wine's name, reminds us that all aspects of this crime—the motive, the criminal and his victim, the foil, the instigation—have been tied closely to alcohol obsession and alcohol expertise. The horrid shrieks of both the victim and the murderer as the deadly masonwork is completed suggest the hellish end to which this misled expertise has led. We are left with a tale so morally complex that a modern Poe expert like Thomas Olive Mabbott can write equivocally: " 'The Cask,' on its surface completely amoral, is perhaps the most moral of his Tales."[31] Actually, when viewed in terms of its contemporary popular culture, the tale is a memorable portrait of amorality precisely because it takes to an innovative extreme the twisted dark-temperance morality of its day. The intensification of dark-temperance themes and images, released by Poe from the vestiges of overt moralization, gives rise to an enduring portrait of psychopathic criminality and self-dooming obsession.

Poe's nondidactic manipulation of temperance images—an improvement upon similar manipulation by popular reformers—suggests that temperance reform was destined to run into grave trouble with Conventional commentators, which it did. The sensational lectures and fiction produced by reformed drunkards prompted a backlash of adverse criticism by those who believed a worthy reform was being ruined by money-making histrionics and gross sensationalism. As early as 1833 one pamphleteer complained: "Temperance societies have become excessively intemperate in their language and aim. . . . The excited imagination of the ultra-moralist . . . fancied and multiplied evil upon evil, until he saw Ossa heaped upon

Pelion."[32] In "A Rill from a Town Pump" (1835) Hawthorne both adopted and modified popular temperance rhetoric, noting the extremely ironic phenomenon of Americans who "get tipsy with zeal for temperance . . . in the style of a toper fighting for his brandy-bottle."[33] Three years later, David Reese in *Humbugs of New-York*, to underscore his argument that this was "the *age of ultraism*," pointed to the "tales of lust, and blood, and murder . . . with which the ultra-protestant press is teeming."[34] The rise of the Washingtonians in the 1840s brought antitemperance paranoia to nearly fever pitch. The liberal leader William Ellery Channing pointed to rabid temperance evangelical lecturers as proof that "a dangerous fanaticism threatens destruction to the world under the name of reform."[35] In *Something for Every Body* (1846) Bayard Rust Hall decried the many "itinerants, who wander about in very eccentric orbits and narrate their *rum* days at so much *per diem.*" America was crowded, Hall complained, with "lecturers who tell what all know and yet find it profitable—with 'moral' play-actors—with 'moral' singers—with 'moral' stages—'moral' ferry-boats—while all the time these 'moralists' are often infidel in sentiment and sometimes licentious in practice."[36]

By 1846 Theodore Parker could make the generalization that there had been "more preaching against the temperance movement than in its favor."[37] This comment might startle those who accept the common notion that temperance literature was conventional moral pablum light-years distant from the dense texts of the major writers. But the fact is that temperance literature, in its dark manifestations, was an energetically subversive mode that had a demonstrable influence upon several major works, including, as will be seen, *Moby-Dick*.

An equally subversive literature also arose around another popular reform: antislavery. In the same breath that he made the above comment on hostility to temperance writings, Parker declared: "I think there has been more clerical preaching against the abolitionists than against slavery."[38] There was, in fact, good reason for discomfort with popular antislavery writing, for much of it contained quite dark commentary on metaphysical and social issues. On the deepest level, the existence of slavery brought into question the veracity of the Bible, the applicability of the American Constitution, and indeed the very existence of God. Several slave narratives and antislavery novels of the period launch a vigorous protest against the slave system, a protest that, in its ferocity, gives rise to savage indictments of the religious and social norms of mainstream America. At the same time, slavery was—horribly enough—exploited for its sensationalism by some reformers and editors who wished to provide arousing, masochistic fantasies to an American public accustomed to having its reform well spiced with violence and sex. By the late 1840s, abolitionism was faced with some of the same problems that confronted anti-prostitution and temperance: a serious reform was threatened with exploitation by sensation-mongering journalists and manipulation by authors. As with temperance, this manipulation of abolitionist images paid high literary dividends: key images in *Moby-Dick*, "Benito Cereno," *Leaves of Grass*, and *Walden* derive from the creative readaptations of antislavery imagery in popular culture. But it also raised a real need for moral anchorage in a culture deeply anxious about the widely discussed Subversive implications of the slave system. By the early 1850s, the American public thirsted for a novel that would give vent to all the Subversive forces associated with slavery and yet would somehow rhetorically overcome these forces and ensure victory for the Conventional. It found this novel in *Uncle Tom's Cabin* (1852).

Stowe's influential best-seller brings together two powerful forces—the Subversive and the Conventional—that had been gathering influence in popular literature and journalism since the 1830s. The germ of *Uncle Tom's Cabin* was Stowe's mental vision, during a church service in Brunswick, Maine, of a chained, weeping slave being whipped to death by a harsh overseer. She immediately went home and wrote down the episode, which became the death scene of Uncle Tom. It is significant that the novel began with a sadomasochistic fantasy, for such fantasies had characterized fervent antislavery writings ever since William Lloyd Garrison published the first issue of his abolitionist newspaper *The Liberator* in 1831. In keeping with his avowed belief that an outraged public would stamp out slavery if "all the horrors of the abomination" were "depicted in their true colors," Garrison from the start ran stories of gross atrocities with titles like "Burning Alive," "Horrible Butchery!!," "Blood! Blood! Blood!," and "A Ghoul in Real Life."[39] Although the sincerity of Garrison's antislavery views was indisputable, Garrison's sensational tactics scandalized many, and his paper rapidly became the center of an immoral-reform controversy. The Washington *American Spectator* in July 1831, despite its own antislavery bias, branded Garrison as a "madman" and an "incendiary" who was driven to gross extremes by the *"wild spirit of fanaticism."*[40] Garrison's most virulent critic was the Washington *National Intelligencer*, which called Garrison "the instigator of human butchery," the circulation of whose paper was a "crime as great as that of poisoning the waters of life to a whole community!"[41] Despite criticism and even death threats, however, Garrison persisted in his vehement way, even though he continued to offend Conventional sensibilities. The pioneering abolitionist Lydia Maria Child broke away from the Garrisonians because she thought "the wild spirit of ultraism" was "driving one of the best causes to its ruin." "They ought to call themselves Destructionists, rather than abolitionists," Child wrote a friend. "I am weary, weary of this everlasting pulling down, and no building up."[42]

Like Lydia Child, Harriet Beecher Stowe had little sympathy for Garrison's violent antislavery tactics. She always remembered her father's comment that Garrison and Wendell Phillips were like arsonists who would burn down a house in order to kill a few rats. Still, her initial sadomasochistic vision and several grisly scenes in *Uncle Tom's Cabin* show that she was, on some level, fascinated by the sensationalism the Garrisonians had popularized. Also, several dark metaphysical moments in her novel suggest that she was aware of other subversive aspects of popular antislavery agitation: underlying doubt, cynicism, misanthropy.

The gloomy themes that she detected had indeed run throughout much dark-antislavery writing. The first full-blown antislavery novel written in America, Richard Hildreth's *The Slave: or Memoirs of Archy Moore* (1836), is a good case in point. Hildreth's tautly written novel is uncompromisingly Subversive, not only in its exposure of the atrocities created by slavery but also in its probing questions about human nature, the Bible, God, and moral certainty. In Hildreth's novel there are no moral exemplars (except rebellious slaves), no Christian consolation, no happy ending. Even the narrator, a mulatto slave who escapes to the North and then England after years of enslavement on various Southern plantations, is in several senses flawed. Hildreth portrays American society as a twisted realm in which the most ostensibly pious people are the most cruel. The savagery of church-going slaveholders leads Hildreth to make several skeptical outcries, such as: "The tyrants of every age and country have succeeded in prostrating christianity into an instrument of their crimes, a terror to their victims, and an apology to their oppressions."[43] Even the often amiable wives of overseers are powerless in this distorted moral world—their ineffectual goodness is best described oxymoronically: "What grosser absurdity than the attempt to be humanely cruel and generously unjust!" While castigating Christians in both the South and the North, Hildreth daringly draws a sympathetic portrait of a vindictive slave who murders the white man who had killed the slave's wife. He also throws many barbs at patriotic ideals, including an ironic reference to America as "land of the tyrant and the slave."

The Subversive spirit that had governed Hildreth's novel became a standard feature of slave narratives and abolitionist speeches in the 1840s and 1850s. For example, Frederick Douglass, who had escaped from slavery in 1838 and became famous for his abolitionist speeches and the popular autobiographical *Narrative* (1845), was often attacked for his impudent assaults on American culture, such as his declaration that for slaves the Fourth of July was "mere bombast and fraud, deception, impiety, and hypocrisy—a thin veil to cover up crimes which would disgrace a nation of savages."[44] Throughout his *Narrative* run razor-sharp ironies which undercut American religion and patriotism. He recalls that one of his masters became worse after religious conversion, since he had found "religious sanction and support for his slaveholding cruelty." His slave experience led him to generalize that "the religion of the South is a mere covering for the most horrid crimes" and that "religious slaveholders are the worst." Ironically, his kindest master is the nonreligious William Freeland. Also ironically, Douglass's own most religious moment is his most rebellious one: after thrashing the cruel overseer Covey, he gains "a glorious resurrection, from the tomb of slavery, to the heaven of freedom." Despite Douglass's inspirational courage and heroism, his view of religion and American ideals is fundamentally cynical. His glum motto, which anticipates the symbolic sign ("NO TRUST") of the barber in Melville's *The Confidence-Man,* is "Trust no man," either black or white. As an antislavery lecturer, Douglass shocked many when he described America as "a sort of sham civilization" that abounds in "strange and puzzling contradictions." Douglass stirred up his own kind of immoral-reform controversy, as the Boston *Olive Branch* wrote that his views were so anti-Christian and anti-American that he should be hanged as a traitor. For his turn, Douglass played his wry immoral-reform role by impugning the *Olive Branch* as a "profanely religious Journal."

When Stowe wrote *Uncle Tom's Cabin,* therefore, she had much more than slavery to contend with: she also had the sensationalism, the sacrilegious speculation, and the anti-Americanism that the public debate over slavery had aroused. She knew very well that this combination of Subversive forces was a highly explosive mixture. As she later recalled: "It was a general saying among conservatives and sagacious people that this subject was a dangerous one to investigate, and that nobody could begin to think and read upon it without becoming practically insane."[45] Throughout her young womanhood, Stowe herself had suffered from manic-depressive mood shifts and occasional suicidal feelings prompted mainly by deep religious struggles as she sought alternatives for the rigid Calvinism of her father, the Rev. Lyman Beecher. *Uncle Tom's Cabin* shows that the slavery issue provided Stowe an opportunity both to purge Subversive impulses and to exercise wish fulfillment in fashioning Conventional replacements for the church religion she had left behind.

Those who call *Uncle Tom's Cabin* a feebly sentimental novel tell only a small part of the story; those who see cultural power and political radicalism in its sentimental themes notice other dimensions but still leave important aspects of the novel open to discussion.[46] The novel is a passionate record of the metaphysical and social tensions of antebellum America. It dramatizes the dialectic between doubt and faith, between rebellion and submission—between the Subversive and the Conventional—that had governed American reform culture for decades. An important mixed text, it misses literary status because its warring elements do not *fuse* to create metaphysical ambiguity or multilayered symbols, as they do in the major literature of the period. Precisely because it lacked literariness, it became an effective reform novel whose immediate public influence had an immensity that no literary text could hope to gain. Instead of allowing the Conventional to be absorbed into or undermined by the Subversive, as do Melville and Hawthorne, Stowe gives full expression to the Subversive but uses every weapon in the Conventional arsenal to defeat it. Reminiscent of Hildreth's and Douglass's works, the novel airs almost every conceivable doubt or cynical reflection prompted by the slavery issue. It even contains several sensational scenes, in the Garrisonian tradition, that surely helped the novel's sale even though they offended several reviewers and laid Stowe open to charges of immorality. While open expression of such Subversive impulses proved both purgative and titillating, Stowe's inevitable recoil to the Conventional, in individual scenes and in the novel as a whole, gave the novel a consolatory structure whereby moral and social conundrums were constantly resolved.

The comfortingly pious aspects of *Uncle Tom's Cabin,* most fully embodied in the angelic Little Eva, have often been described. What are less generally recognized are the deeply skeptical musings, sometimes tending toward atheism and moral relativism, that run as a dark undercurrent through the novel. As in the antislavery writings of Hildreth and Douglass, the contemplation of slavery's horrors here leads often toward doubt and anguish. Several characters—the maltreated slave George Harris, the effete aristocrat Augustine St. Clare, the slave-prostitute Cassy, and even Uncle Tom in his despairing moments—are driven by personal wretchedness or social injustice to ask sharp questions about American ideals and religious norms. George Harris is, at the start, a subversive figure of doubt, suicidal despair, homelessness, and rage against white mainstream society. When told to forget his troubles and trust in God, he pointedly asks, *"Is there a God to trust in? . . .* O, I've seen things all my life that have made me feel there can't be a God."[47] Cassy is the classic example of how a proper, pious woman can be turned into a whore, child murderer, and atheist because of forces outside her control. She is driven by her years of oppression at the hands of licentious slave owners to utter many "dark, atheistic words," as when she tells Tom on Simon Legree's plantation: " 'There isn't any God, I believe; or, if there is, he's taken sides against us. . . . There's no law here, of God or man, that can do you, or any one of us, the least good.' " Tom himself, when faced with Legree's "atheistic taunts," bitterly reflects upon "souls crushed and ruined, evil triumphant, and God silent." The most intelligent character in the novel, Augustine St. Clare, is also the most cynical. In his long conversations, St. Clare voices many highly subversive views. He declares that "the country is almost ruined with pious white people" such as brawling politicians and clergymen. Observing both proslavery and antislavery preachers, he concludes that the Bible is twistable to any point of view. St. Clare exclaims, "What poor mean trash this whole business of human virtue is!" even as Melville's Pierre would find that virtue and vice are "trash." Similarly, St. Clare's relativist belief that virtue is "a mere matter, for the most part, of latitude and longitude" is strikingly similar to the notion of horologicals and chronometricals discussed in *Pierre*. After Eva dies, St. Clare even trembles on the edge of nihilism, as he asks, "Who knows anything about anything? . . . [I]s there no more Eva,—no heaven,—no Christ,—nothing?"

Contrary to critical myth, such skeptical musings were very common in antebellum popular literature, especially in overlooked dark-reform and crime writings that gave Subversive themes full play. The originality of *Uncle Tom's Cabin* lay in Stowe's frank treatment of an especially wide variety of such dark themes and in her simultaneous defusing of these themes through an equally wide variety of reparative devices derived from Conventional literature. These Conventional devices (too evident to dwell upon) include the moral exemplar, the human angel, courageous endurance and heroic action, religious aestheticism, and, above all, the nurturing home. These devices are scattered liberally throughout the novel, and all of them come together in the figure of Little Eva, who is exemplar, angel, little soldier, beauty lover, and home deifier all in one. It should be pointed out that Stowe's other antislavery novel, *Dred* (1856), was far less popular than *Uncle Tom's Cabin* precisely because it pondered relativist and atheistical questions surrounding slavery but did not effectively resolve these questions through powerful Conventional images, as did *Uncle Tom*. Characters throughout *Dred* puzzle over Stowe's nagging metaphysical quandaries: one exclaims that the Christian Church, corrupted by slavery, has produced more infidelity than all skeptical writings ever written; another approaches relativism by concluding: "One might almost imagine that there were no such thing as absolute truth, since a change of temperament is capable of changing the whole force of an argument";[48] several times the world is called "a humbug" filled with cheats and false appearances. All of these notions had been aired in *Uncle Tom's Cabin* but had been rhetorically deflected through a massive array of Conventional devices that are largely absent from *Dred*. *Uncle Tom's Cabin* was the most popular novel of the period not necessarily because it exposed the horrors of slavery— Hildreth, Garrison, and others had done that better than Stowe—but because it provided an outlet for every conceivable Subversive notion associated with the slavery debate and yet managed to invest the Conventional with a mythic sanctity it had never known before. Henry

James shrewdly captured this mythic quality when he wrote that *Uncle Tom's Cabin* "had above all the extraordinary fortune of finding itself, for an immense number of people, much less a book than a state of vision, of feeling and of consciousness."[49]

The massive sales and generally glowing reviews of *Uncle Tom's Cabin* suggest that most of Stowe's readers took comfort in this rhetorical deflation of the Subversive; but a significant number saw through the Conventional veneer and discerned licentiousness and gloom beneath. In some circles, the novel became embroiled in the same kind of scandal that had surrounded immoral reformers from Weems through Gough. Two main sources of contention were Stowe's sometimes titillating pictures of whoredom on Southern plantations and her candid questioning of church religion. George Frederick Holmes in the *Southern Literary Messenger* asked: "Are scenes of license and impurity, and ideas of loathsome depravity and habitual prostitution to be made the cherished topics of the female pen, and the familiar staple of domestic consideration of promiscuous conversation?"[50] This charge of Stowe's morbid interest in illicit sex was also made in an angry letter, written to the New Orleans *Picayune,* claiming that Stowe had "painted from her own libidinous imagination scenes which no modest woman could conceive of." Even more threatening to some reviewers was Stowe's pointedly secular replacements for church religion. In a review of the novel that denounced "Cabin literature" as "corrupt altogether and abominable," *Graham's Magazine* claimed that the devil was abroad among mankind when so many loved Stowe's "sanctified dissertations upon negro carousals, and puritanical eulogies of blasphemous psalm-singing, almost to the exclusion of the Bible."[51] Another reviewer found that Stowe "proves herself to be a reviler of the Son of God, and an efficient enemy to his spirit and his principles." In the meantime, Stowe herself was bombarded with mail, the bulk of it complimentary, but a good portion of it, by her own report, "curiously compounded of blasphemy, cruelty, and obscenity."[52] Stowe thus found herself confronted with the familiar immoral-reform problem: her vivid exposure of vice laid her open to nasty charges of hidden fascination with vice.

Therefore, even *Uncle Tom's Cabin,* which has been sometimes interpreted as the epitome of Victorian piety and sentimentality, possessed enough subversive features to elicit notably ambivalent responses from Stowe's contemporaries. The truth is that Stowe was allowing the moral antipodes of her reform culture to clash in a creative center that pleased most but offended some.

When we turn from antislavery writing to another important antebellum reform genre—labor literature (especially the urban-exposé novel)—the ambivalences surrounding *Uncle Tom's Cabin* seem relatively mild. Critics who have concentrated on Stowe and other antislavery writers to the exclusion of zestful working-class authors have neglected a major nexus of tension and literary ambiguity in pre–Civil War America.

The American labor movement followed the overall rationalist-to-evangelical movement that governed most other popular reforms of the period. Before 1830, the predominant labor writers and activists in America had been rationalists who harked back to the egalitarian republicanism of the Enlightenment. The fiction produced by Enlightenment radicalism was generally moderate in tone. To be sure, Charles Brockden Brown's *Arthur Mervyn* and *Ormond* fused Gothic horror with graphic description of city slums in a manner that anticipated later urban-exposé novels, several of which bear obvious traces of Brown's pioneering explorations of the "urban Gothic" mode. Even though Brown wrote under the direct influence of William Godwin and other radicals, however, his fiction is chiefly important for the grim realism of its urban scenes rather than for any socialist message it may convey. When early American novelists did try directly to promote socialism, the result was a stylistically moderate novel like *Equality; A History of Lithconia* (1802), a deist utopian novel about a model community that has gotten rid of class conflict and inequality by electing enlightened intellectuals who have abolished private property and the institution of marriage. The reasoned tone of *Equality* gave way before a more militant brand of anticapitalist writing in the 1820s, as is evidenced by the trenchant works of Gilbert Vale, George Henry Evans, Robert Dale Owen, Fanny Wright, and Thomas Skidmore. While these rationalists launched vigorous assaults on privileged wealth, they restricted themselves to expository prose and public addresses whose generally reasoned style was purposely designed to enforce the rationalist ideas about education and moral improvement they hoped to inculcate. One of their most important contributions was to popularize the labor theory of value, by which they distinguished between hardworking "producers" (manual workers who alone created wealth) and idle, often vicious "capitalists" or "accumulators," who exchanged wealth but did not produce it.

It was not until the late 1830s that a truly imaginative Subversiveness came to dominate American working-class writing. Because the devastating Panic of 1837 virtually killed off trade-union activity (which would not reemerge in full force until the 1850s), working-class advocates were forced to turn to less "practical," more imaginative means of protest and reform. One outcome of the shift was a widespread interest in the utopian socialism of Charles Fourier, whose ideas were popularized in America by Albert Brisbane's *The Social Destiny of Man* (1840). On the social level, Fourier argued that only when man gives free expression to his natural impulses (including sexual ones) could civilization's deceits and divided interests be overcome. On the industrial level, Fourier claimed that society could be totally productive only if it was reorganized as discrete communities (or "phalanxes") in which each worker was engaged in "attractive industry" of his or her choice. While a few of the more than fifty Fourierist communities that sprang up in America between 1840 and 1860 exercised his notions of "free love," most, including the community at Brook Farm, stressed his plans for industrial reorganization, which came to be known as Associationism.

While Fourierist socialism brought a new creativity to utopian thought, evangelicalism and proletarian rowdiness ushered a new violence into working-class activism. In a time of crushing economic depression and widening class divisions, the great Eastern cities became the sites of frequent nativist riots, fierce gang warfare, noisy revivals, and chiliastic prophecies of doom. The turbulent republicanism of the streets brought about a significant change in the rhetoric of labor advocates. Suddenly there arose a fiery rhetoric filled with grotesque imagery aimed at unmasking "idle" and "depraved" aristocrats. The labor theory of value, which had been discussed rather abstractly by the rational socialists of the 1820s, now was vivified in increasingly lurid exposés detailing the vices of the wealthy "upper ten" and the miseries of the oppressed "lower million." In the 1850s, this dualistic contrast between depraved aristocrats and the struggling working class would feed into Hawthorne's contrast between the Pyncheons and the Maules in *The House of the Seven Gables* and between similar class distinctions in several of Melville's works, most notably "The Two Temples," "Poor Man's Pudding and Rich Man's Crumbs," and "The Paradise of Bachelors and The Tartarus of Maids." These well-known renderings of socialistic themes were outgrowths of a crescendoing spirit of working-class protest that had infiltrated a large body of popular writing during the 1840s.

Typical of the new style were the essays and speeches of Mike Walsh, the pugnacious New York Democrat who quickly rose to fame and political power in the early 1840s as a result of his roughneck tactics. An Irish immigrant who had been weaned in the boisterous world of the Bowery gangs, Walsh flirted with land reform and Associationism (he did a stint at Brook Farm) before establishing himself as a working-class politician and editor in New York. His labor newspaper, *The Subterranean* (1843–47), provoked a string of libel suits because of Walsh's sensational charges of corruption in high places. He typically branded a New York judge "one of the human stink weeds which are nurtured by the moral slime and putrefaction of that sink of iniquity, satirically denominated, the 'Halls of Justice.' "[53] The New Yorkers Whitman and Melville were aware of Walsh. In fact, we may surmise that one reason Melville in his fiction permitted

reform rhetoric to soar to zestfully subversive extremes was that he wished
to beat Walsh at his own game. Melville had a personal reason for doing
so, because Walsh had aimed some of his verbal barbs at Melville's politician brother, Gansevoort, shortly after the latter had been appointed the
Secretary of the Legation in London by President Polk. Apparently jealous
over the appointment, Walsh published several devastating attacks on
"Gansevoort or Gander-brained Mellville [sic]," whom he dubbed an
"empty and impertinent upstart," a "vapid and fulsome mountebank."
Such assaults would have been particularly wounding to Herman Melville,
since Gansevoort fell into a deep depression and died while he was abroad.

The new rhetorical militancy was hardly confined to Walsh's blistering
diatribes: it was equally evident in many other labor writings of the 1840s,
most notably lurid urban-exposé novels about the "mysteries" of American cities. Two very popular foreign novels, Eugène Sue's *The Mysteries of
Paris* (1842) and G. M. W. Reynolds's *The Mysteries of London* (1844),
prompted a whole string of American "city-mysteries" novels that pictured
unbridled depravity among the rich and squalid wretchedness among the
urban poor. The typical American city-mysteries novel was more nightmarish and stylistically wild than its foreign counterpart, principally because,
in America, socialist fervor had by the 1840s become fused with a fierce
evangelical emotionalism and a republican rowdiness unknown in Europe.
It is understandable that the dark city-mysteries genre, portraying the city
as a modern "Sodom" populated by depraved aristocrats engaged in
nefarious doings in labyrinthine dens of iniquity, would arise in the 1840s,
for such novels reflected the profound fears and fantasies of an American
population faced with rapid urbanization and industrialization. Most historians agree that during the 1840s American city dwellers lost social
knowledge and physical contact with each other for the first time. The city
was suddenly an overwhelming place, filled with hidden horrors and savage struggles as fascinating as they were appalling. Although New York
and Philadelphia were the most common settings for exposé novels, there
was hardly a single American city or town that was not thought to be
darkened by horrid "mysteries," as is suggested by the various cities indicated in the following titles of exposé novels: Philip Pendant's *The Mysteries of Fitchburg,* Caroline Hargrave's *The Mysteries of Salem!* (1845), Henry
Spofford's *The Mysteries of Worcester* (1846), Frank Hazelton's *The Mysteries
of Troy* (1847), the anonymously published *Mysteries of Nashua* (1849), and
Ned Buntline's *The Mysteries and Miseries of New Orleans* (1851).

By far the most controversial city-mysteries novelist was the Philadelphian George Lippard, whose seamy novels so often leave reform and
morality altogether behind that they will be more fully discussed later in
terms of sensational literature. Lippard was regularly involved in classic

immoral-reform scandals: most notably, his best-seller *The Quaker City; or, The Monks of Monk Hall* (1845) was widely branded, in his words, as "the most immoral work of the age" and became "more read, and more attacked, than any work of American fiction ever published."[54] Such ambivalence of reader response points to very real tensions within the city-mysteries genre, which more than any other type of dark-reform writing paved the way toward literary ambiguity.

Lippard's *The Quaker City* was provoked by a widely reported illicit-love scandal of the sort that Melville would later dramatize in *Pierre*. Melville, who had Pierre exclaim that it would be "a glorious thing to engage in a mortal quarrel on a sweet sister's behalf" and later showed him being attacked by the enraged brother of the woman he had ruined, almost certainly knew of the notorious seduction case (involving a Philadelphian who in a fit of righteous rage shot his sister's seducer) that prompted Lippard's novel. It is also probable that Melville knew of the novel itself; we shall see that in *Pierre* Melville pursued the same moral ironies, often using the same dark city-mysteries imagery, that Lippard does in *The Quaker City*. At any rate, it is significant that Lippard begins with a common labor-reform motive—the exposure of depravity among the urban elite—but amplifies the ironies and "mysteries" surrounding this issue to such a degree that he often travels into new thematic territory. He transforms a relatively uncomplicated case of seduction and revenge into a fictional plot in which not only the wealthy seducer (Gus Lorrimer) but also the seduced woman (Mary Arlington) and her vindictive brother (Byrnewood Arlington) show various degrees of hypocrisy, masochism, sadism, or incestual devotion. In this topsy-turvy moral world, goodness and virtue remain powerless before the forces of darkness, while religion and social respectability are mere masks hiding inexorable evil. In his depiction of Monk Hall, the towering den of vice where outwardly respectable Philadelphians gather nightly to carouse and consummate seductions, Lippard creates a kind of working-class "Young Goodman Brown" by imagining universal evil among such social paragons as preachers, lawyers, editors, and business moguls.

The city-mysteries novel, of which Lippard's is the preeminent example, was a repository for the intensifying paradoxes surrounding previous immoral-reform writings. It would not be until the 1850–54 period that Hawthorne and Melville would craft long novels probing moral ambiguities which, as we shall see, stemmed in part from dark-reform themes. But before the well-known major fiction of irony and moral fluidity appeared, a preparatory thematic broadening of dark-reform issues had occurred in widely read exposé novels like Lippard's. *The Quaker City* has a breadth lacking in previous immoral-reform works because it gives voice to a wide variety of popular reform motifs and social phenomena. While adding new venom to the protest against aristocrats' depravity commonly made by labor advocates, Lippard also gathers together violent images from anti-prostitution, dark temperance, anti-Catholicism, prison reform, bank clos-ings, gang warfare, race riots, penny newspapers. He does not fuse these images to create memorable literary symbols; nor does he allow the perva-sive ironies to turn inward and consume themselves, as would Hawthorne in *The Scarlet Letter* or Melville in *Pierre*. But he does take steps toward literariness by making the dark-reform novel the dialogic arena for varie-gated reform voices whose intrinsic moral paradoxes sometimes give rise to gloomy generalizations of the sort we find in the major literature. A passage describing the conflicting motives of a prostitute leads to momen-tary musing on "the mass of good and evil" creating "an eternal contest in the self-warring heart of man."[55] The portrait of a corrupt preacher prompts the thought that throughout history religion has made man act like a bloodthirsty devil. A scene in which two deluded lovers embrace leads to the pre-Melvillian comment: "Fools that they were! . . . To think that Fate which drives its iron wheels over hearts and thrones and graves, would turn aside its careers for them!" In this realm of heartless fate and amoral people, one character justifiably says this about life itself: "Every thing fleeting and nothing stable, every thing shifting and changing, and nothing substantial! A bundle of hopes and fears, deceits and confidences, joys and miseries, strapped to a fellow's back like Pedlar's wares." An understratum of doubt runs through the novel and becomes especially visible in numerous instances when disillusioned characters question God's existence and man's goodness. Although Lippard inevitably recoils from such dark moments, the fact remains that *The Quaker City* shows how the mixture of dark-reform themes can carry the popular novelist toward troubled philosophizing.

Preliterary Images and Devices in Reform Literature

How did America's reform culture help to engender the major litera-ture? In what ways did the sudden explosion of reform movements and reform literature feed into the literary explosion we have come to regard as the American Renaissance?

In the largest sense, it should be stressed that the age's dynamic reform impulse helped to sweep away musty conventions and to affirm the creative spirit. When Emerson described a "sharpness of criticism, an eagerness for reform . . . in every quarter" as a chief characteristic of the age, he was underscoring both the subversive and the creative potentialities of the popular reform impulse. This impulse indeed seemed ubiquitous: in addition to the reform movements already discussed, other important movements included naval reform, peace reform, prison reform, opposition to capital punishment, agrarianism, antidueling, education reform. Each of these hotly debated reforms progressively found its way into imaginative literature—Melville's defense of naval reform in *White-Jacket*, Whitman's early tracts against capital punishment, and Hawthorne's caricature of the prison reformer Hollingsworth in *The Blithedale Romance* are only the better-known examples of imaginative treatments of such reform issues. The major writers carefully took note of their age's variegated reforms, experimented regularly with reform rhetoric and imagery, but above all learned to give literary expression to the vibrant reform impulse while they escaped the trap of prolonged dedication to individual reforms. The sheer heterogeneity of reform movements was by turns dizzying and liberating. Among so many recommendations for exposing and extirpating error, which could be believed? Hawthorne shrewdly registered the moral confusion generated by his reform culture when he had Coverdale, the narrator of *The Blithedale Romance,* come to suspect after living with warring reformers that "everything in nature and human existence was fluid" and that one could lose all "sense of what kind of world it was, among innumerable schemes of what it might or ought to be."[56] As will be seen, each of the major authors at one time or another expressed puzzlement and terror over the relativism implied by this fluid reform environment. At the same time, this perception of moral fluidity paid high literary dividends, for it made possible a literature in which mystery and ambiguity became central issues consciously treated. The major writers were those who recognized that no single movement merited undivided devotion but that the reform impulse and popular reform imagery were rich native materials offered to the literary artist.

Each reform was surrounded by a distinct body of imagery which reappeared, divested completely of didacticism, in different major texts. Reform literature exposing illicit love, from Parson Weems's *Onania* through John McDowall's lurid newspaper reports through the sensational anti-seduction novels of the 1840s, featured what I call the voyeur style: that is, an indulgently participatory rhetoric that reveled in titillating descriptions of debauchery and seduction. Temperance literature, in its darker manifestations, featured psychopathic states, perversity, broken homes, nightmare visions—all of which images regularly found their way into major texts. Anti-Catholic stereotypes such as depraved priests or licentious nuns provided another repository of subversive images incorporated by the major writers, as did the dualistic contrast between an aristocratic "upper ten" and a wretched "lower million" in labor literature.

In addition to such distinctive image groups, there were overriding stereotypes and textual strategies that many antebellum reforms had in common. The most significant common denominator among disparate reformers was a conscious impulse to "tear away veils" or "lift up masks" in an effort to reveal hidden corruption. To antebellum reformers (particularly the increasingly prominent Subversive reformers), authority figures such as urban aristocrats, wealthy churchgoers, Catholic priests, landlords, bankers, and so forth were "whited sepulchres" whose inner rottenness could be revealed only through what I term unmasking imagery: violent, often sensational language designed to strip hypocrites of their sanctified cloaks and bring to light the horridness within. In a typical moment in A. J. H. Duganne's city-mysteries novel *The Knights of the Seal* (1845), a callous rich man's private sins are revealed as follows: "[T]errible, terrible will be the reaction, when the veil is torn aside, when the sepulchres, no longer whited, burst forth in their own horror and loathsomeness."[57] Similarly, George G. Foster's *New York Naked* (1850) begins with the assertion: "Let us strip off the mask in which each plays its mummery before the rest, and let us show, . . . each with its name indelibly branded upon its forehead, the demons that guide and direct the game of daily life in our metropolis."[58] Since such unmasking imagery was the single most common image group among reformers of all stamps, it is appropriate that *The Blithedale Romance,* the major novel most directly concerned with reform issues, is governed by images of veils and masks. It is also understandable that Melville, after experimenting extensively with reform imagery in his early novels, would have his maddened truth seeker in *Moby-Dick* dedicated to tearing away the "pasteboard masks" covering perceived reality.

Related to unmasking imagery was a popular character type, what may be called the oxymoronic oppressor, which embodied the moral and social paradoxes that reformers were trying to reveal. Hypocrites or two-faced characters are of course stock figures in all literatures. But the antebellum reform climate brought a fiercely democratic, anti-elitist irony—as well as a unique moral and sociopolitical dimension—to create an indigenous version of the hypocrite. In the eyes of many reformers, America itself was a nation that could be best described through contradiction or paradox: it was a republic that permitted slavery; it was a democracy that was witnessing widening class divisions; it was a land of virgin wilderness but also festering cities; it was a nation of Christians who tolerated the most unChristian practices. Such internal contradictions could be most readily figured forth in representative characters whose divided natures could be expressed through pungent oxymorons. In antislavery literature the principal oxymoronic character was the Christian slaveholder. In the city-mysteries novel it appeared variously as the churchgoing capitalist, the reverend rake, the pious seducer. A typical oxymoronic character is the title character of Joseph Boughton's *Solon Grind; or, The Thunderstruck Hypocrite* (1845). A hard-hearted capitalist who maintains the pretense of piety even while he drives poor families to suicide, Grind is living proof of what Boughton describes as a grim rule of modern city life: "Under the garb of sanctity, what notable schemes of fraud, oppression, extortion, and heartless villainy have been carried out."[59]

The oxymoronic character of reform literature took on a self-consuming irony when reformers themselves (not just their capitalistic opponents) became the targets of satire. When Hawthorne portrayed Jaffrey Pyncheon as a sherry-swigging temperance advocate and Hollingsworth as an amoral reformer, he was vivifying cultural paradoxes which in real life had produced various schools of immoral reformers and which in popular literature had appeared as particularly ironic mixed characters. The fictional satire on moral reformers began in the early 1830s and intensified as time passed. One satirical pamphlet, *Orthodox Bubbles* (1831), described several leading evangelical reformers, including Arthur Tappan, caressing several scantily clad whores who report that they get paid well, "especially when we have *charitable* and *pious* visitors, like some members of the 'Magdalene Society.' "[60] The hero of Henry Junius Nott's "Biographical Sketch of Thomas Singularity" (1834) is a pious Magdalen Society member who nevertheless writes popular pornographic poetry; he is also a temperance advocate who guzzles rum in private. Such immoral reformers became stock characters in American popular fiction of the 1840s. George Thompson's *The Countess* (1849) portrays a great statesman who, even though he is "a great temperance advocate, and friend to the cause of moral reform," never visits the city without enjoying "metropolitan pleasures"—including that of "satisfying his lecherous lust."[61] The hero of Emerson Bennett's *Oliver Goldfinch* (1850) is full of "blackhearted sins" but gives liberally to many reform organizations as a means of "rearing a pinnacle of virtue behind which to screen himself."[62] An intensification of the internal contradictions of such characters occurs in Lippard's *The Quaker City*, which aims to expose, in Lippard's words, "the imposture and trickery of the various copies of Simon Magus . . . whether they take the shape of ranting Millerites, intemperate temperance lecturers, or Reverend politicians."[63] The most fully developed of Lippard's oxymoronic characters is the Rev. F. A. T. Pyne, who is a member of numerous reform groups, an inspirer of the business community, a preacher of "Patent Gospel Grace"—but at the same time an unbridled debauchee who applies the money he earns from reform work to the purchase of brandy, opium, and women at Monk Hall. Among fictional stereotypes of the immoral reformer, Pyne was outdone only by the weird heroine of C. W. Webber's *Spiritual Vampirism: The History of Etherial Softdown* (1853). Etherial Softdown is a "feminine Proteus" who manipulates every reform of the day to corrupt, often licentious ends. A vampirish reformer who brings about the death of a succession of hapless men, she lives up to her goal of going "up and down in the land, seeking whom I may devour!"[64] Given this popular character type, the famous immoral reformers of the major fiction—Jaffrey Pyncheon, Hollingsworth, Plotinus Plinlimmon and his followers at the Church of the Apostles—seem very much reflective of the moral ironies of the period.

The broadening of the oxymoronic character points to another common characteristic of reform literature: an underlying philosophical skepticism. The standard interpretation of the major literature is that its metaphysical ambiguities were unusual and daring in an age of progressivist optimism, reform activity, and rising church membership. It should be pointed out, however, that the widespread displacement of otherworldly religion by a secular faith in good works and social activism threatened to undermine the supernatural doctrines upon which Christianity was based. Moreover, there was a bitter truth behind the fictional stereotype of the oxymoronic character: many of the most pious members of society endorsed the most impious practices. This anomaly impelled numerous reformers to question Christianity and even the existence of God. We have seen that a dark thread of doubt runs through much popular reform literature, particularly antislavery writings and city fiction. Since the world seemed full of pious frauds, religion itself could seem fraudulent. The following passage by Henry Clapp, in an 1844 issue of the reform newspaper *The Liberty Bell,* may be taken as a gloss on the religious viewpoint of many American reformers:

> One may not, in these days, confess Christ before men, without many a careful qualification; for, to be a Christian, in the minds of a large majority of the community, is to be a supporter, directly or indirectly, of every sin within the broad pale of fashionable practice. Nay, more; a conscientious man may well explain, in these degenerate times, his belief in a God, before he asserts it very boldly in the presence of a mixed audience; for the God of *this* nation is a God who has a complacent smile for all degrees of moral obliquity. . . . So inverted an order of things prevails in this country, that the name Infidel has become transfigured from its original and repulsive meaning into a term of the holiest significance. To be an infidel now, is to hide the outcast, to unbind the heavy burthen, to open the prison door, to give wings to the hunted fugitive, to come out from iniquitous institutions, to let the oppressed go free.[65]

Deep metaphysical questions, therefore, were being posed by numerous reformers who were horrified by the distance between the ideals and practices of Protestant America. And it was precisely this nagging doubt about received religion that drove reformers to new extremes to find rhetorical and imaginative replacements for bygone religious certainties. The antebellum reformers were still close enough to the Puritan past to sense the dramatic dualisms and the otherworldly emphasis of Calvinism. At the same time, they were driven by their culture's moral obliquities to question otherworldly faith and to go to any linguistic extreme to expose and extirpate social corruption. They therefore became adept at using horrific Calvinist images to vivify actual social conditions.

As a result, there arose a new brand of post-Calvinist or mythic imagery that prepared the way for the totally demythologized use of such imagery by the major writers. By projecting Calvinist doctrines onto the perceived reality around them, the reformers achieved simultaneously a narrowing of theological message and an intensification of metaphorical energy. Witness the use of post-Calvinist imagery in the following description of whorehouses by John McDowall:

> They are the forts of the devil; the mustering place of Satan's armies; the parade-ground of Beelzebub's legions; the campaign-country of Lucifer's allies; the pest-house of earth—the abode of blood. Over them hover the fallen angels flapping their wings of death. Throughout them shriek the souls of the pit, whose grating teeth, gnawing tongues, glaring eyes, horrify the virtuous spectator. The bursting fires of the nethermost hell light up the features of these caverns of despair, and roast the hearts of once doating parents.[66]

Here the tenor (depravity in whorehouses) is smothered by the vehicle (the multilayered post-Calvinist images), as reform writing becomes an exercise in crude but energetic experimentation with metaphor. If Hawthorne and Melville could artistically sculpt Calvinist imagery in purely secular fiction, it was in part because they were products of an age in which such imagery had been liberated from dogma by popular reformers.

Critics have long puzzled over the origin of larger-than-life, mythic symbols in the major literature such as the white whale and the ocean in *Moby-Dick,* or the raging bonfire in "Earth's Holocaust," or Poe's maelstrom, or the multidimensional scarlet letter. Many would agree that such rich symbols are updated, secular versions of the Puritan typological vision, divested of didacticism and dogma. *This very divestment of didacticism was achieved in reform circles before the great literary symbols were fashioned.* The reformers regularly permitted their imaginations to leave behind moral message and fabricate mythic images possessing some of the ultimacy of the Puritan vision but also the secularism of nineteenth-century social realities. Vice was regularly described as a "monster" stalking over mountains and rivers, or a "whirlpool" sucking helpless victims to destruction, or an "ocean" threatening to engulf the world, or an all-controlling "fate." One 1834 reform tract typically called masturbation "a monster in our midst . . . of whose premeditated attacks no note of alarm can forewarn us."[67] A reform newspaper of the day described licentiousness in similar terms: "No heaven-towering mountains can stay it; it is hemmed in by no oceans; it crosses every sea."[68] The popular novel *Easy Nat* (1844) said that intemperance was "like the deceitful tide in some places, which rises, almost imperceptibly to the wanderer, who, unwarned by the human wrecks everywhere visible around him, lingers upon its beach, until the deceitful waves, gathering double force at every advance, rapidly overtake the victim, and hurry him away, down its remorseless vortex."[69] The popular city-mysteries novelists were especially inventive in fashioning graphic post-Calvinist imagery: poverty was regularly described as a "resistless destiny" driving its victims to despair; the callous rich were sometimes called embodiments of "total depravity"; the city as a whole was viewed as the modern Sodom and Gomorrah best described in imagery of hell and damnation.[70] Such imagery took on a new resonance because it was often darkened by biting social satire and by skeptical musings. Given the ubiquity of secularized mythic imagery in reform writing, it would be surprising indeed if the major writers, all of whom kept a close watch on the popular scene, had not adopted such imagery in their own writings.

The post-Calvinist image signaled a cultural shift away from dogma toward literariness. This shift was indicated also by another common feature of reform literature: what might be called the benign-subversive style—the use of moral pretext as a shield against criticism in depictions of the tabooed or sacrilegious. Many reform writings are preliterary texts, achieving a crude ambiguity, because they vent wildly Subversive impulses but then retreat to the level of Conventional morality. The seamy or skeptical segments of reform exposés reflect the perceived horrors of social or private life; the occasional pious rhetoric and the overall righteous intent are obligatory obeisances to the powerful moral conscience bred by American Puritanism. We have seen that a number of popular reformers, from Parson Weems through McDowall to George Lippard, tipped the rhetorical balance so far toward the Subversive that they were regularly branded as dangerous writers. Still, even the most crassly pornographic reformers were quick to proclaim moral intentions. For instance, George Thompson concludes his highly sensational exposé novel *Road to Ruin* (c. 1850) by stating he has succeeded "if any *moral* has been conveyed, calculated to beget a horror for vice, and a fondness for the paths of honesty and virtue." Likewise, even though Lippard's *The Quaker City* was widely denounced as "the most immoral book of the age," Lippard could declare that it was "destitute of any idea of sensualism."[71] The truth was that Thompson, Lippard, and all other dark reformers were inventing moral disguises for notably immoral, sometimes even sacrilegious ponderings.

The major writers introduced many variations upon the popular benign-subversive style. Emerson's peculiar mixture of rebellious and conservative qualities led one contemporary reviewer to call him "a delightfully dangerous, dangerously delightful" writer. Thoreau could seem at once the subversive misanthrope and the benign nature lover, and Whitman often advertised his highly "moral" intentions despite the undeniable iconoclasm of his poetry. We shall see that Melville's famed ambiguity grew directly out of his early experimentations in the popular benign-subversive style and that most of Hawthorne's fiction, including *The Scarlet Letter*, was especially indebted to this style. In Hawthorne's eyes, this style was part of a moral dualism intrinsic in the American character. Several times, in his journals and in *The Marble Faun*, Hawthorne contrasted the Europeans, who he said give free expression to strong emotions, with the more repressed Americans, in whom such emotions rage inwardly and sear the soul. This peculiarly American combination of *outward innocence and inner demonism* helps to explain not only the benign-subversive style but also such paradigmatic mixed characters as Arthur Dimmesdale, Pierre Glendinning, and the confidence man.

3

THE TRANSCENDENTALISTS, WHITMAN, AND POPULAR REFORM

T H E major writers were distinguished among their contemporaries by the breadth of their awareness of the various popular reform movements and by their success in rechanneling the reform impulse imaginatively in their own works. All of them recognized the immense cultural influence of reform movements and, as part of their effort to create culturally representative texts, they repeatedly used reform images. They were intent, however, on transforming these images in various ways. Emerson, Thoreau, and Whitman forged literary devices that reflected the feisty spirit of Subversive reform while avoiding its excesses and that retained the judiciousness of Conventional reform while avoiding its staidness. For Hawthorne and Melville, reform movements were chiefly important for the cultural ambiguities they reflected and the complex imagery and character types they suggested. All the writers made inventive variations upon the benign-subversive style that had been developed by the popular reformers.

Re-Formed Reform: Emerson and Thoreau

In his address "Man the Reformer" (1841) Emerson made the striking generalization: "In the history of the world the doctrine of Reform had never such scope as at the present hour."[1] In another 1841 address, "Lecture on the Times," he declared that America's multitudinous reform movements embodied the spirit of his age and that "these movements are on all accounts important," they "are all pregnant with ethical conclusions."[2] Throughout his career Emerson had firsthand exposure to reform movements: in 1838 he became involved in the protest against the maltreatment of the Cherokee Indians; in the early 1840s he contributed money to the temperance movement and wrote an essay on the Chardon Street convention of popular reformers; in 1844 he gave an address in Concord on West Indian Emancipation; and, most notably, in the 1850s he was aroused to a white fury by the passage of the Fugitive Slave Law, which he often denounced in vitriolic rhetoric typical of popular abolitionists. Emerson was not blind, however, to the delinquencies and moral contradictions of many reformers of his day. Too often scholars generalize that the buoyancy of Emerson's major works reflected the so-called optative mood of an expansive age whose hopeful outlook was particularly visible in reform movements. Actually, it was precisely because Emerson so shrewdly perceived the *immorality* and *uncleanness* of many reform writings that he responded ambivalently to the reform spirit of his era and tried mightily to redirect it in his own writings.

Like Thoreau and Whitman after him, Emerson compensated for a certain temperamental stolidity and coldness by opening himself up fully to the fiery, cutting rhetoric of popular reformers. He had warm praise for the eloquence of rabid abolitionists, whom he called "wild men" who "reinforced the city with new blood from the woods and mountains" and who "utter the savage sentiment of Nature in the heart of commercial capitals."[3] In time, reformers of all stripes had come to symbolize for him the kind of assertive iconoclasm that he would often idealize in his major writings. He declared in 1837 that the person who "has only a good intention is apt to feel ashamed of his inaction & the slightness of his virtue when in the presence of active & zealous leaders of the philanthropic enterprizes of Universal Temperance, Peace, & Abolition of Slavery."[4]

But it should be emphasized that it was the wicked, savage, even immoral side of the reform impulse that came to be most significant for Emerson. Developing a profound hatred for conventionally proper "goodies," Emerson in "Self-Reliance" wrote: "Your goodness must have some edge to it,—else it is none."[5] This goodness with an "edge to it" was taught to him primarily by the enthusiastic reformers of his day. "Without electricity the air would rot," he wrote; ". . . without a spice of bigot and fanatic, no excitement, no efficiency."[6] Emerson's exposure to fiery ultraists during the 1830s and early 1840s brought about a kind of linguistic conversion. It was also during this period that he began to express appreciation for the pungent imagery of backwoods humorists, the stinging oaths of teamsters, the lively banter of Irish kitchen workers, all of which struck him as infinitely preferable to the staid idiom of Boston liberals, who, he declared, "all lack nerve & dagger."[7] He emphasized that the skilled orator learns his style in the street rather than the college; while walking through Boston he would sometimes go out of his way to walk through the back streets and the slums so that he could overhear gutter slang. Reform rhetoric was even more instructive than slang because it was coupled with a specifically subversive intent. When Emerson asserted in 1841 that he owed much to "reformers of all stripes and qualities,"[8] he was referring both to the linguistic fire and the moral iconoclasm of popular reformers. What better could be said of an era, he asked, than that it "put every usage on trial, and exploded every abuse?"[9] He wrote that temperance, abolition, and other movements were all "fertile forms of antinomianism" that provided "a keener scrutiny of institutions and domestic life than any we had known."[10]

While Emerson absorbed stylistic and thematic verve from popular reformers, he did not sheepishly imitate them; instead, he used reformist zeal to fashion reform anew. On the one hand, the savagery and brashness of modern reformers clearly set an example for his own persona as one who struck an original relation to the universe and who did not shy away from using grotesque, sometimes shocking metaphors. On the other hand, the reformers' increasing negativity led him to establish new humanistic and artistic receptacles for the reform impulse. "A thousand negatives it utters clear & strong on all sides," Emerson wrote of reform in an 1839 letter, "but the sacred affirmative it hides in the deepest abysses."[11]

Although this negativity was to some degree admirable to one who prized above all his era's undercutting of social conventions, Emerson wrote that many rabid reformers used "outward and vulgar means" and "affect us as the insane do. They bite us, and we run mad also."[12] Moreover, his vision was so expansive that it could not rest comfortably in any single movement. Since he perceived that "many a reformer perishes in his removal of rubbish" and that much reform "ends in hypocrisy and sensualism," he was doubly eager to redefine reform as constant moral and intellectual self-renewal.[13]

In his major essays Emerson proved himself the ultimate reformer of the age, one who was ready to dismiss social institutions, past religions, and traditional ways of reading and thinking. There is a strongly subversive edge to his best prose which gives it a bracing, sometimes shocking effect. He was intent, however, upon reforming the very notion of reform. He noted the characteristic intemperance of temperance reformers, the rabidness of abolitionists, the hypocrisy of socialists, and the partiality of all popular reformers. He tried always to move beyond individual reforms toward a larger overarching reform that affirmed primal unities and underlying analogies. His shrewd recognition of the ambivalent nature of popular reforms and the pressing need for a wholly rejuvenated reform is made clear in his essay "The Method of Nature," in which he writes:

> The reforms whose fame now fills the land with Temperance, Anti-Slavery, Non-Resistance, No Government, Equal Labor, fair and generous as each appears, are poor bitter things when prosecuted for themselves as an end. To every reform, in proportion to its energy, early disgusts are incident, so that the disciple is surprised at the very first hour of his first triumphs, with chagrins, and sickness, and a general distrust: . . . [T]here is no end to which your practical faculty can aim, so sacred or large, that, if pursued for itself, will not at last become carrion and an offence to the nostril.[14]

The biting reform rhetoric of the day gave Emerson a tool for undercutting stale institutions; but he recognized that in adopting this rhetoric he had to transform it in order to salvage reform, which he realized could quickly become "carrion and an offence to the nostril." Perhaps his most original contribution to the reform culture of his day was his effort to absorb fully the era's subversive reform spirit but to counterbalance it with powerfully reconstructive philosophical elements. In his essay "The Conservative" he described two great "metaphysical antagonists" in society, Conservatism and Reform, that correspond to the cultural forces I have called the Conventional and the Subversive. Individually, he emphasized, these opposing camps were failures. "Conservatism," he wrote, "makes no poetry, breathes no prayer, has no invention. Reform has no gratitude, no prudence, no husbandry . . . [and] in its antagonism inclines to asinine resistance, to kick with its hoofs[.]" Emerson stressed that these opposing forces gain lasting efficacy only when they are judiciously brought together: "Each exposes the abuses of the other, but in a true society, in a true man, both must combine."[15] Emerson attempted in his own writings to make this creative *fusion* of the opposing forces.

In Emerson's major essays we discover a repeated dialectic of subversive dismissal of revered social norms followed by affirmations of self-reliance, aesthetic perception, and the symbolic imagination. It is this combination of the sharply subversive and creatively reconstructive that marks Emerson's real originality in an age when popular reformers increasingly remained on the level of what he called mere "asinine resistance." His treatise *Nature* begins by denouncing old customs and foreign traditions and then moves in an ever-ascending pattern through various forms of the uses and significations of nature and language. "The American Scholar" starts by firmly exposing the fragmented condition of man in modern society and then outlines various methods of restoring wholeness through right thinking, right reading, right action. The Divinity School Address boldly attacks historical Christianity and offers a humanistic, aesthetic religion to take its place. "Self-Reliance" lambastes imitation of all kinds and makes a virtue of nonconformity and independence. "The Poet" attacks conventional rhymesters and opens the way for a democratic, wholly American poetry by calling for a writer who will traverse the entire range of social life, from the sublime to the common. "Experience" takes a particularly long, agonized look at the Subversive, noting the relativity of virtue and the subjectivity of nature and literature, and makes an appeal for renewed respect for action and for the present hour. "Circles" wholly confronts the Subversive, arguing that it is only in the recognition of the fluidity of virtue and the instability of human life that people can be continually renewed. In "Compensation" the dialectical interchange between opposing forces becomes the basis for a thoroughgoing philosophical dualism by which nature and human life are depicted as operating according to a continual process of opposition and renewal, of subversion and reconstruction.

All of these works can be called *reform writings* since they expose errors and offer solutions. When judged against the other reform writings of Emerson's day, we recognize the reasons for their special richness and their enduring appeal for successive generations of readers. Unlike the group I have called Conventional writers, Emerson embraced the trenchant, militant forces within his contemporary culture. Unlike the Subversive writers, however, he did not merely exercise his powers of invective or wallow in the perverse effects of vice; instead, he offered invigorating alternatives to the errors he perceived.

His reconstructive strategy is visible in the way he redirects specific images from his contemporary reform culture toward the aesthetic and the spiritual. In *Nature* he adopts popular reform images only to point them toward the aesthetic pleasures he is trying to illustrate. For example, to communicate man's delight in nature's beauty, he writes: "It is necessary to use these pleasures with great temperance." Emerson has revised temperance imagery in two senses: the pleasures he refers to are those of nature, not of alcohol; and the temperance he describes is a soberness of spiritual perception, not of physical taste. He has removed temperance imagery from any association with sensationalism and pushed it toward the contemplative. When in *Nature* he generalizes about reform, he purposely allies it with mental processes rather than social ills. The abolitionist movement, for instance, is mentioned as one of the "gleams of a better light" in the contemporary world that he says show the operation of a higher Reason in human affairs. Similarly, the notion of reform is rejuvenated in passages like the following: "The beauty of nature reforms itself anew in the mind, and not for barren contemplation, but for new creation."[16] As the extensive discussion of spiritual laws and symbolism throughout *Nature* makes clear, Emerson is making a powerful effort to identify a moral principle and a comprehensive method for reform underlying all the partial reform efforts of his contemporary culture. He does the same in several other works. In "Heroism" he specifically says that temperance has nothing to do with avoidance of alcohol but rather with simple, elegant living. In "The Over-Soul" he insists that no single reform movement is a final solution but that all such movements, taken together, point toward the holistic virtue underlying all partial virtues. In "Self-Reliance" he directly dismisses the "miscellaneous popular charities" and "the thousandfold Relief Societies" of his era, arguing that virtue should not be mechanical but rather a continual upwelling of fresh, independent thinking.[17]

His overall effort of placing reform in a larger philosophical context becomes explicit in "Man the Reformer," which includes the following passage:

> What is a man born for but to be a Reformer, a Re-maker of what man has made; a renouncer of lies; a restorer of truth and good, imitating that great Nature which embosoms us all, and which sleeps no moment on an old past, but every hour repairs herself, yielding us every moment to a new day, and with every pulsation a new life?[18]

This passage says openly what all of Emerson's essays say implicitly: man as reformer must not only be subversive ("a renouncer of lies") but also reconstructive ("a restorer of truth and good"), and his reconstructive powers should be recognized as organically linked to the ever-renewing powers of nature.

Henry David Thoreau also moved from early contemplation of popular reform to a redefinition of the reform impulse. There was a rough similarity in the career patterns of Emerson and Thoreau. Both had an early perception of the deep ambiguities of their reform climate and then refashioned reform to signify a new heady antinomianism and an almost existentialist self-renewal. Both extracted from their era's fragmented, often contentious reform movements a cuttingly subversive spirit that was always directed toward discarding the old and affirming the new. In the later stages of their careers both were drawn into the antislavery fray, which drew from them bitter invective similar to that of many popular reformers. But there were important differences in the way they acted upon the reform impulse. In reading Emerson's famous obituary of Thoreau, we realize that in a sense Thoreau was the stereotype of the popular reformer, taking to a new extreme his age's puritanical ban against drinking, smoking, meat eating, and so forth. At the same time, we see that

Thoreau shared the reformers' penchant for feisty unmasking—in Emerson's words, Thoreau "did not feel himself except in opposition," he always needed "a fallacy to expose, a blunder to pillory."[19]

It might seem odd to call Thoreau representative of his age. He has long been enshrined as an elite author alienated from popular culture. His philosophical bent has impelled several critics to emphasize his intellectual life. Most commonly he has been placed in the pantheon of so-called mythic and nonrealist writers, from Hawthorne and Melville through Faulkner, whose poetic prose and iconoclastic ideas distanced them from mainstream America. On the surface, Thoreau seems even more rebellious than our other major writers since he purposely isolated himself and wrote slashing indictments of his contemporary culture.

In reestablishing Thoreau's links with his age, we should remind ourselves initially of what is already known but sometimes forgotten: he can be directly connected with other reformers and writers of his time. Other Thoreau-like figures included the notable nineteenth-century individualist anarchists—Josiah Warren, Ezra Heywood, William B. Greene, Stephen Pearl Andrews, and Benjamin Tucker—who were from Thoreau's home state of Massachusetts and were his contemporaries. He was closely associated, of course, with the Boston liberals and the Concord Transcendentalists. Even his most famous act of political rebellion, his arrest for refusing to pay the poll tax, had been anticipated three years before by his fellow Concordite Bronson Alcott, who had been arrested for a similar reason. In addition, his influential notion of civil disobedience was spiritually akin to the civil disobedience agitation of William Lloyd Garrison and others.

Too much has been made of Thoreau's isolation and unpopularity. It is true that, like Emerson, he had a somewhat cold personality and that he courted solitude. Also, *A Week on the Concord and Merrimack Rivers* sold so poorly that it provoked Thoreau's famous quip that after the publisher had sent him the unsold copies he owned a library of nine hundred volumes, over seven hundred of which he wrote himself. Still, Thoreau makes a point in *Walden* to emphasize that naturally he is no hermit and that he would fasten like a bloodsucker to any full-blooded man or outlast any barroom customer under the right circumstances. And those who find it hard to believe that the leading Transcendentalists had an eye on the mass market should be reminded of the time Emerson asked Thoreau, "Who would not like to write something which all can read, like Robinson Crusoe?"; Thoreau at first demurred, but when a girl asked whether his lyceum lecture that night would contain "a nice interesting story" he instantly started making up some diverting anecdotes.[20] Even *Walden* is more of a popular performance than is generally believed. Thoreau began writing it in response to curious questions from his lecture audiences about his two years in the woods. The many successive drafts of the book show Thoreau in key passages catering to popular taste—so much so that when the book was completed Thoreau scolded himself in his journal for "Using current phrases and maxims, when I should speak for myself."[21] Moreover, Thoreau's revisions paid off. Although *Walden* was not a best-seller, it did enjoy a first-year sale (nearly two thousand copies) that in that day was quite respectable for a nonfiction volume. Nor should we forget the popularity of *Walden* in the long run. As an antislavery speaker in the 1850s Thoreau was considered a sufficiently lively crowd-pleaser to be asked once to stand in for the popular Frederick Douglass. Thoreau's impassioned speech on John Brown had obvious appeal for the mass readership, for it was chosen by James Redpath to be reprinted with other popular antislavery writings in *Echoes from Harper's Ferry* (1860), which speedily sold more than thirty thousand copies. Even in the most basic senses, therefore, Thoreau was not as alienated from popular culture as we tend to think.

But in fact Thoreau was closer to the popular mentality in more subtle and significant ways than these. Ordinarily Thoreau is distinguished from his contemporaries because of his harsh social criticism and his quirky paradoxical style, which is often seen as contrasting to a tepid popular style. F. O. Matthiessen typically called him a "violent" imagist who tried to "startle his contemporaries out of their complacent dreaminess."[22] Thoreau's imagistic violence and stabbing irony, however, are precisely what bind him most tightly to his contemporaries, who were hardly complacent dreamers. *Walden* and the John Brown speech were Thoreau's most popular performances *because of*, not *in spite of*, their acidic attacks on conventions. By the early 1850s American readers were almost masochistically attracted to reform-minded writers of all varieties who used every weapon of invective and exaggeration to lay bare social corruption and propose ready-made solutions. Thoreau's contribution was to tighten the irony, sharpen the paradox, exaggerate the criticism, and, especially, broaden the proposed solution.

As for his ferocious stabs at his countrymen, they actually didn't raise many eyebrows in a day when ripping off veils to expose inner corruption was a common reform strategy. In fact, he struck some of his contemporaries as a quite typical unmasking reformer. One review of *Walden* sounded like a comment on any popular reform work: "Penetrating to the very pith and core of modern society, [Thoreau] lays bare the worm of corruption which preys upon its vitals—shows hideous rottenness concealed beneath a fair and alluring exterior."[23]

It is no accident that such common veil-piercing imagery was applied to

Thoreau, for he had long been an alert witness of popular reformers, whose devices he frequently borrowed. At Harvard in 1834 Thoreau was elected a member of a debating society that considered such topical issues as abolition, capital punishment, and anti-Catholicism. One question debated by the society was: "Are temperance societies as now conducted likely to produce more evil than good?" Similar questions were asked of the tactics of antislavery and anti-Catholic writers. There is no record of Thoreau's response, but it is significant that at an early age he was already pondering the ethical ambivalences surrounding his age's reform movements.

Thoreau's journals of the 1830s and 1840s make it clear that he was fully aware of the power of the contemporary reform impulse. He quickly came to believe that he lived in a time when all past customs were being subverted by reform—as he wrote in 1837, "not even Old Books nor Old Clothes have escaped the all-grasping hand of reform."[24] Already he was absorbing the age's zealous reform spirit, the same spirit that would lie behind his famous assertion in *Walden*: "Old deeds for old people, and new deeds for new." Not only was he directly under the influence of liberals and Transcendentalists, but he was also gaining a deep interest in popular evangelical reformers such as the gruff temperance lecturer Daniel Foster, the lively New Hampshire abolitionist Nathaniel Rogers, and the popular antislavery orator Wendell Phillips.

Thoreau's homage to popular reformers as harsh but necessary subverters prepared the way for his own militant attacks on stale conventions. In *A Week* he wrote that "countless reforms are called for because society is not animated, or instinct enough with life."[25] Without zestful reforms, he stressed, virtue itself becomes stagnant, when life should always be fresh as a river. The sensibility behind *Walden* was being nurtured by a reform culture in which violent subversiveness was part of the very atmosphere Thoreau breathed.

At the same time, however, Thoreau saw the dangers of popular reform, which he quickly realized could become muddy and immoral. He often expressed disgust at popular reformers' unclean tactics. Thoreau looked closely at his reform-minded contemporaries—at temperance speakers, at labor activists like Albert Brisbane and Horace Greeley, at the Brook Farm socialists, at popular abolitionists—and discovered no true examples of the subtle combination of razor-sharp criticism and totally pure reform strategies he sought. He did isolate a few popular figures, most notably Nathaniel Rogers and Wendell Phillips, who struck him as offering such a combination. He believed that Rogers was "unlike most reformers" because his style was like his New Hampshire "mountain-torrents, now clear and sparkling, now foaming and gritty, . . . but never dark and muddy." Thoreau prized Rogers as an imaginative, hopeful reformer who believed slavery would be "abolished by other means than sorrow and bitterness of complaint."[26] Likewise, in Thoreau's eyes Phillips had "a sort of moral principle and integrity" that was "so rare in a reformer."[27] But in an era of dark reform, Thoreau knew that such purity was unusual even among the most apparently righteous. He could make the stark generalization in his journal: "The clergy are as diseased, and as much possessed with the devil, as the reformers."[28] In 1848 he wrote a friend: "I love reform better than its modes."[29] Thoreau knew well that the problems surrounding contemporary reform modes compromised the whole notion of active virtue. His major texts contain ironic axioms that summed up the strange symbiotic union of virtue and vice in his era. In *A Week,* shortly after commenting on "the restless class of Reformers," he generalized: "We are double-edged blades, and every time we whet our virtue the return stroke straps out vice. Where is the skillful swordsman who can give clean wounds, and not rip up his work with the other edge?"[30] While he was in the final stages of *Walden* he was visited in Concord by what he called "three ultra-reformers"—popular speakers on temperance and slavery—who disgusted him with what he called their "slimy benignity."[31]

A chief reason that Thoreau became the most compelling reform writer of nineteenth-century America was that he shrewdly recognized *both* the promise and the perils of contemporary reform movements. He admired individual, exceptional reformers but suspected reform societies, which he correctly saw were often impure. Throughout his writings Thoreau demonstrates his awareness that reforms quickly became poisoned, even devilish, unless rigorously practiced by individuals of the utmost morality and integrity. In "Reform and the Reformers," an essay of the early 1840s, he lamented that the average reformer was "the impersonation of disorder and imperfection," and he demanded individualistic, human alternatives to reform societies:

I ask of all Reformers, of all who are recommending Temperance—Justice—Charity—the Family, Community or Associative life, not to give us their theory and wisdom only, for these are no proof, but to carry around with them each a small specimen of his own manufactures, and to despair of ever recommending anything of which a small sample at least cannot be exhibited:—that the Temperance man let me know the savor of his Temperance, if it be good, the Just man permit me to enjoy the blessings of liberty while with him, the Community man allow me to taste the sweets of the community life.[32]

He specified that reformers should try to impart "courage" rather than "despair," "health and ease" rather than "disease," and he asked them to "deepen their speech, and give it fresh sincerity and significance."

Although these admonitions were directed to other reformers, it was left to Thoreau himself to offer the most enduring alternatives to the prevailing immorality of the American reform scene. His commitment to radical individualism and creative image-making was in large part a dialectical response to the disease and insincerity that he saw in organized reform efforts. Trying mightily to retain his age's reform impulse while removing from it the impurities it had gathered in American popular culture, he went to Spartan extremes of individual reform and poetic writing, both of which he hoped would ennoble reform.

Several passages in *Walden* show Thoreau's keen perception of immoral reform. In a passage that seems to be based on his disgust over the "three ultra-reformers" who visited him in 1853, he says that if he heard that a do-gooder was coming to his house he would frantically run away "for fear that I should get some of his good done to me,—some of his virus mingled with my blood."[33] "There is no odor so bad as that which arises from goodness tainted," Thoreau emphasizes. "It is human, it is divine, carrion." It is precisely his knowledge of the widespread perversion of moral standards in American society that leads him to write: "The greater part of what my neighbors call good I believe in my soul to be bad, and if I repent of anything, it is very likely to be my good behavior. What demon possessed me that I behaved so well?" Thoreau had frequently noted in his journals that reformers were "diseased," "stinking," or "possessed with devils"; in *Walden* he sharpens the metaphors so that his private repulsion is transformed into memorable prose.

But Thoreau was unusual in his ability to move beyond mere disgust with reformers toward the discovery of active and literary alternatives to his culture's dark reform. In *Walden* he determinedly incorporates imagery from a large variety of popular reforms, including labor reform, temperance, antitobacco, antilicentiousness, and antislavery, with the intention of reinvigorating these images. He makes clear his determination to revise reform rhetoric from the very beginning of *Walden*. In the second paragraph of *Walden* he mentions that people "have been curious to learn what portion of my income I have devoted to charitable purposes; and some, who have large families, how many poor children I have maintained." He ironically mentions such charitable and reform work here and elsewhere in *Walden* with the specific goal of undercutting it and offering fresh definitions of reform. It is because he knew that aid to the poor, opposition to alcohol and slavery, and other reforms had become so tainted in popular culture that he felt compelled to redefine reform altogether.

While making several sallies at "unclean" reformers in *Walden*, Thoreau suggests what true reform is by adopting many reform images and pointing them toward affirmations of individualism, symbolic perception, and the ideal of living deliberately. He fills the husks of popular reform images with ideas as exhilarating and pure as the Walden water. The temperance reformers' insistence upon drinking only water takes on a new universality when Thoreau writes: "I am glad to have drunk water for so long, for the same reason that I prefer the natural sky to the opium eater's heaven. . . . Of all ebriosity, who does not prefer to be intoxicated by the air he breathes?" Abolitionist and labor-reform rhetoric likewise comes alive when directed to the self: "It is hard to have a Southern overseer; it is worse to have a Northern one; but worst of all when you are the slave-driver of yourself." Noting that the average reformer is saddened by "his private ail," he says his excuse for not lecturing against the use of tobacco is that he never chewed it—"that is a penalty which reformed tobacco-chewers have to pay." One of his central messages in *Walden*—the necessity to keep awake and to deliberately shape one's life—is closely linked to his revised definition of reform. "Moral reform is the effort to throw off sleep," he asserts. While it is good to paint a picture, he continues, "it is far more glorious to carve and paint the atmosphere and medium through which we look, which morally we can do. To affect the quality of the day, that is the highest of arts." The Canadian woodchopper, a model for the unencumbered, primitive life Thoreau values, becomes a central figure in the redefinition of reform. Thoreau recalls: "I loved to sound him on the various reforms of the day," which he always regarded "in the most simple and practical light." When a reformer asked the woodchopper if he didn't think the world needed changing, the man genially chuckled and said, "No, I like it well enough." In all of these instances, Thoreau is offering clean, antinomian alternatives to popular reform movements he knew were often tainted and self-subverting.

Whitman's Moral Broadening

Whereas Thoreau in his masterpiece moved from his culture's ambiguities toward a fresh definition of reform, Walt Whitman in his came closer to reproducing the seamy, morally variegated quality of his environment. Thoreau admired *Leaves of Grass* but came to be disturbed by what he saw as its rough realism and sensualism; he famously complained that Whitman promised wonders but threw in "a thousand ton of brick" and that his poem was written "as if the beasts spoke."[34] Other antebellum readers were similarly disturbed by Whitman's sensualism but were even more outraged by his apparent disregard for moral distinctions. A careful look at Whitman's early career reveals that there was good reason for the seaminess and moral breadth of *Leaves of Grass.* Whitman knew better than anyone the crucial importance of the social and literary background of works of genius. He wrote in the 1876 preface to *Leaves of Grass*: "In estimating my Volumes, the world's current times and deeds, and their spirit, must be first profoundly estimated."[35] Literature, in his eyes, was no more than "a great mirror or reflector. There must however be something before—something to reflect."[36] *Leaves of Grass* did indeed mirror its age, mainly because there *had* been something before, something to reflect. And that something was connected to the popular reform impulse.

Most critics are stunned by the apparent distance between Whitman's early writings and *Leaves of Grass.* The standard view is that Whitman had begun as a conventional hack writer of moralistic fiction and poetry and then experienced some dramatic change that made him a literary iconoclast. The fact is that from the start Whitman had experimented with popular genres which had themselves taken on subversive and progressive qualities. The greatest poetic innovator of nineteenth-century America was nurtured by a popular culture that carried the seeds of a new thematic and stylistic rebelliousness.

Toward the end of his life Whitman told his follower Traubel: "There is an embarrassment of riches in reform."[37] Several decades earlier he had scribbled in his notebook: *"My final aim /* To concentrate around me the leaders of all reforms."[38] His close friend and contemporary biographer John Burroughs summed up well Whitman's inclinations when he wrote: "When scanned closely, he appears in the character of a reformer."[39] Burroughs recognized what later commentators have tended to overlook. Whitman's debt to his reform culture was deep indeed. Like Emerson and Thoreau, Whitman closely surveyed America's fanatical reforms and appreciated the fact that this widespread agitation helped clear the air of musty conventions. Also like them, he moved from this appreciation to a literary performance that was at once scathingly subversive and individualistically reconstructive.

Whitman's familiarity with popular reforms was even greater than Emerson's or Thoreau's. During the 1840s, the decade before he wrote *Leaves of Grass,* Whitman associated with some of the most fiery reformers in New York, which, as he remarked with only slight exaggeration, had become "the most radical city in the world." Critics who concentrate on Whitman's exposure to such writers as Emerson, Carlyle, George Sand, and the Oriental philosophers go only partway in explaining his changes during this period. Whitman himself stressed that all his reading would have "come to naught . . . if a sudden, vast, terrible, direct and indirect stimulus for new and national declamatory expression had not been given to me."[40] This vast stimulus was provided primarily by the fanatical reformers whose lectures he loved to attend at the Broadway Tabernacle. He later specified that he liked not *all* the reformers but only the really rabid ones, especially red-hot abolitionists like John P. Hale, Cassius Clay, and Charles C. Burleigh. He also attended temperance lectures by the famous reformed drunkard John Bartholomew Gough and was appropriately terrified by Gough's vivid enactment of the terrors of delirium tremens. What is most important about Whitman's reform stance is that it was one of deep engagement with the spirit of reform and simultaneous disengagement from its programs for change. Whitman himself was a well-known reform writer, but almost from the start he learned to *manipulate* the rhetoric of a given reform (temperance especially, but also antislavery, labor reform, antiprostitution, and anti-capital punishment) and then to discard it, often with a laugh. Many of the reformers he admired were perturbed by his apparent lack of seriousness—as he recalled, they sometimes became more hot with him than with the subject of slavery. *But he knew the reformers better than they knew themselves.* He was aware that their zeal, when carried to an extreme, subverted the very morality they ostensibly prized. Eventually he would proclaim himself the poet of goodness and of wickedness also, but his road to this moral expansiveness was a long one. As early as 1842, the year he produced his best-selling temperance novel *Franklin Evans,* he had illustrated his awareness that in America moral fanaticism could be *exploited* as an avenue to the tabooed. The daringly experimental outlook of *Leaves of Grass* was shaped by Whitman's developing understanding of immoral didacticism.

Whitman began conventionally enough. His earliest known prose piece, "Sun-Down Papers—[No. 5]" (1838), is temperance writing of the most tame variety. Whitman protests against the excessive use of tobacco, coffee, and alcohol on purely hygienic grounds, citing the ill effects of stimulants on the body. In its factual objectivity, this article manifests the staid rationalism of Conventional reform. More sentimentalized, and still conventional, are Whitman's next temperance works, the poem "The Young Grimes" (1840) and the popular stories "Wild Frank's Return," "The Child and the Profligate" (both 1841), and "Reuben's Last Wish" (1842). These works provide increasingly sensational accounts of the horrid effects of drinking but still feature the rewards of sobriety, such as prosperity and domestic unity. It was not until he wrote *Franklin Evans* that Whitman tipped the balance completely to the side of the Subversive.

Franklin Evans has been a puzzle for critics, even those most inclined to be sympathetic to Whitman. The noted Whitman scholar Thomas L. Brasher typically writes: ". . . it is almost incredible that the man who wrote

Franklin Evans also wrote *Leaves of Grass.*"[41] Everyone who dismisses this temperance novel as moral pablum is quick to point out Whitman's own distaste for the book. He told Traubel that he wrote the novel for cash in three days, guzzling from a bottle of port to keep him going. "It was rot," he said of the novel, "damned rot—rot of the worst sort—not insincere, perhaps, but rot, nevertheless."[42] We should note, however, the ambivalence of this dismissal—the novel is "rot" but still is "not insincere, perhaps." This combination of sincerity and wry detachment shows Whitman absorbing the ironic spirit of many immoral reformers from Parson Weems onward. Even more reflective of this spirit is the novel itself, which epitomizes the popular dark-temperance style at its most manipulatively horrific. In the publicity ads, it was promised that this novel by "a Popular American Author" would "create a sensation," which it did—it speedily sold twenty thousand copies in cheap pamphlet form.[43] The American public, which for more than two decades had gobbled up the spicy offerings of dark reformers, turned with glee to *Franklin Evans,* which pretended to be a Washingtonian temperance tract but was a sensational novel unusual only for the sheer variety of dark-reform images it brought together. Shattered homes; the dark "mysteries" of cities; hellish barrooms and theaters; crushing poverty that leads to crime; the hypocrisy and secret depravity of the rich; delirium tremens with its nightmare visions; the haunted minds of criminals; infanticide; Gothic imagery—all of these standard devices of dark temperance figure in this exemplum on the wages of taking the first sip. Far from being a conventionally moralistic exercise, as it is often called, *Franklin Evans* was Whitman's means of using the popularly accepted mode of dark temperance to free morality from unitary meaning and place it in the flowing stream of human psychology and ironic social realism.

In the decade after he wrote *Franklin Evans* (1842–52) Whitman broadened his experimentation with popular genres. During this time he wrote several grisly sensational stories and poems, some pious visionary pieces, a few ultrapatriotic works, some dark works on death and mutability, some moral and biblical tales, and works dealing with topical social issues. If *Leaves of Grass* was the era's most expansive poem, containing the largest variety of voices and topics, it was largely because it was written by one who had unabashedly tried his hand at virtually every genre that had been popularized by previous American writers. When we realize that Whitman in the 1840s traversed the whole spectrum of popular genres, from the piously Conventional (e.g., "The Last of the Sacred Army," "The Angel of Tears," and "Shirval: A Tale of Jerusalem") through the darkly Subversive (e.g., "Time to Come," "The Spanish Lady," "Richard Parker's Widow," "Resurgemus"), we understand why he would frequently emphasize that *Leaves of Grass* was broadly rooted in the popular culture of its day. No other antebellum author so freely adopted seemingly contradictory popular personae as Whitman. The poet who in *Leaves of Grass* would write "Do I contradict myself? / Very well then I contradict myself, / (I am large, I contain multitudes)" was bred by a literary culture of paradoxes and contradictions.

And nowhere did such paradoxes so influence Whitman as in the area of reform. In the course of the 1840s and early 1850s Whitman wrote on nearly every popular reform: temperance, antiprostitution, anti–capital punishment, agrarianism, labor reform, and antislavery. Although his sympathies generally stood with the radical side on such issues, he continued to explore the *imaginative* rather than the *political* possibilities of reform rhetoric, so that popular reform was chiefly important as a training ground in zestful, defiant writing. Even such direct responses to timely issues as "Resurgemus" (his poem praising the European revolutions of 1848), "Dough-Face Song" (verses denouncing a congressional movement toward compromise on slavery), and "The Eighteenth Presidency!" (his prose tract objecting to Franklin Pierce's favors to slavery supporters) make few original political statements. Their real originality is *stylistic,* as the dark-reform style begins to lead Whitman toward a truly rebellious literary stance. In "Resurgemus," a free-verse poem written in 1850 and incorporated into the 1855 edition of *Leaves of Grass,* subversive political passion seems to explode poetic conventions; Whitman combines Gothicized dark-reform images (e.g., the "bloody corpses" of the world's poor are portrayed rising up against "the appalling procession of locusts," or murderous rulers) with an innovative verse form in a way that anticipates his later poetic iconoclasm. His prose diatribe against Pierce in *The Eighteenth Presidency!* is dark reform of the most savage variety, filled with images of excrement, blood, venereal disease, coffins and hearses, running sores, and so forth. In a typical moment Whitman declares that the President "eats dirt and excrement for his daily meals, likes it, and tries to force it on the States."[44] It might seem surprising, given the apparent earnestness of Whitman's rage at such moments, that he later recalled that in this period he had been interested in "the political movements of the land, not so much as a participant, but as an observer."[45] Detachment was in fact there all along, since Whitman often let reformist vitriol flow from his pen for the sheer subversive delight of it, without much attention to programs for change.

We should therefore not be shocked at apparent inconsistencies in Whitman's attitudes toward current social issues. Some might find it inconceivable, for instance, that Whitman, who in *Leaves of Grass* would offer a warm embrace to prostitutes, actually wrote several newspaper articles decrying prostitutes with a righteous indignation that harks back to John McDowall. How could the liberal poetic defender of whores become so prissy as to devote an 1858 article in the *Brooklyn Daily Times* to denouncing their trade as "the great vice of the age," a "damning plague spot," a "horrid abyss of depravity and disease" that is "all the more awful because the pseudo modesty of this hypocritical age shrouds it with darkness"?[46] Standard definitions of concepts such as "liberal" or "prissy" do not apply to the antebellum reformer. There is no great distance between Whitman the poetic defender of whores and Whitman the enraged indicter of whores. The ultrapuritan and the ultraliberal are bound by their fascination with the tabooed. The driving force of both is a Subversive imagination that inevitably surrounds the tabooed with mythic images. In the hands of the flexible, broad-minded Whitman passionate reform would be transmuted into equally passionate but also sculpted poetry.

The great contribution of reform rhetoric to Whitman was that it contributed to both a stylistic and a moral broadening. It was not so much the moral content as the brash spirit of reform that intrigued Whitman. As editor of the *Brooklyn Daily Eagle* in 1846 he wrote: "The duty of the promulger of all moral reforms" is "to advocate and illustrate, the more enthusiastically the better, his doctrine."[47] As Whitman's writings for the *Eagle* show, it was clear that it was the enthusiasm, rather than the doctrine, that counted most. In the paper Whitman printed many dark-temperance tales with lively titles like "Intemperance and Parricide" or "How Rum Can Change a Young Man into a Brutal Scoundrel," horrid stories about drunken sons killing their fathers with crowbars or besotted brutes knocking down little boys for the sheer sadistic sport of it. Despite his ostensible antislavery leanings, Whitman loved to exploit the purely sensational aspects of the slave system, publishing several articles that describe with relish unbridled licentiousness or violence amidst slaves and their masters. This exploitative sensationalism might seem to compromise reformist seriousness, but here again Whitman was moving beyond reform into a neutral ground in which he could see both sides of political issues and playfully juggle moral standards. His advice to Traubel on social issues would communicate this detachment: *"Be radical—be radical—be not too damned radical."*[48] Although Whitman said this at the end of his life, such two-sidedness had been a primary feature of the sensibility that produced *Leaves of Grass.*

Given the crucial importance of dark reform to Whitman's development, it is understandable that his earliest known jottings in free verse (in his notebook for 1847) are highly paradoxical political and moral statements:

> I am the poet of slaves, and of the masters of slaves. [. . .]
> I am the poet of sin,
> For I do not believe in sin.[49]

Here in the earliest example of the characteristic Whitmanesque poetic voice, we find Whitman starting his flight beyond slavery or antislavery, beyond sin or reform of sin to broader moral regions. Even though he had devoted much of his young literary career to the exposure of sin, he could now blithely announce that he does not believe in sin, for the intensity of dark-reform rhetoric has carried him beyond conventional moral categories altogether. The gross exaggeration of sin has led naturally to the negation of sin. *The poeticization of sin has led toward literariness.* When the liberation from dogmatic moralism, achieved mainly through dark-reform writing, was coupled in the early 1850s with an intense individualism learned in part from Emerson, the result was the indifferent, all-encompassing persona of *Leaves of Grass* (1855) who calls himself "Me imperturbe . . . aplomb in the midst of irrational things."[50]

In *Leaves of Grass* Whitman could at last toss about sin and virtue with total freedom and with complete acceptance of paradox:

> I am not the poet of goodness only, I do not decline to be the
>   poet of wickedness also.
>
> What blurt is this about virtue and about vice?
> Evil propels me and reform of evil propels me, I stand indifferent[.][51]

In this and many similar passages in *Leaves of Grass* Whitman proves that by 1855 terms like "goodness," "wickedness," or "reform of evil" had commensurate import for a writer who began as a popular reformer, who manipulated reform rhetoric to struggle free of conventional moral categories, and who now stood above all moral distinctions or partial reforms. From this objective vantage point, potentially reprehensible characters from American popular culture (e.g., drunkards, whores, criminals of all sorts) can be sympathetically portrayed in compassionate, truly democratic poetry. Since dark reform represented an actual elevation of the outlawed powers it pretended to denounce, it is natural that an especially rabid reformer like Whitman would devote many poetic lines to praising the same kind of vicious types that he had treated harshly in his reform writings. He emphasizes:

> Lusts and wickedness are acceptable to me,
> I walk with delinquents with passionate love,

I feel I am one of them—I belong to those convicts and prostitutes
   myself[.][52]

Elsewhere in the poem, addressing convicts, he says, "Me ruthless and
devilish as any," and of prostitutes: "Who am I that I should call you more
obscene than myself?" Here Whitman is assuming the final immoral-
reform stance: whereas immoral reformers from John McDowall onward
had been charged with obscenity but had religiously denied it, Whitman
honestly accepts the charge and in fact proudly brandishes his lust and
wickedness. With Whitman, the antebellum reformer's transparent veil of
pretended piety is finally removed from hidden subversiveness.
   The most extreme revelation of this open subversiveness occurs in some
poems of the 1855–56 editions of *Leaves of Grass* that are particularly
notable for their extreme moral flexibility. In "Great Are the Myths"
(1855) Whitman baldly expresses his acceptance of moral paradox:

   Great is Wickedness—I find I often admire it, just as
      much as I admire goodness.
   Do you call that a paradox? It certainly is a great paradox.[53]

The same poem makes clear that fanatical reform is closely tied in Whitman's mind with turbulent American society as a whole:

   Great are the plunges, throes, triumphs, downfalls of Democracy,
   Great the reformers, with their lapses and screams[.]

Another poem, "Respondez!" (1856), best represents Whitman's wholesale inversion of moral values, since in this remarkable poem he calls for
a total uprooting of social conventions by imagining the widespread ascendancy of evil, diseased, or corrupt people and things. In a subversive
tirade, Whitman writes:

   Let murderers, bigots, fools, unclean persons, offer new
      propositions! [. . .]
   Let there be no God! [. . .]
   Let the infidels of These States laugh all faith away! [. . .]
   Let the she-harlots and the he-harlots be prudent!
      let them dance on, while seeming lasts! [. . .]
   Let the white person again tread the black person again under his
      heel![54]

Elsewhere in "Respondez!" Whitman demands that women and men think
only obscenely of each other, that they should freely fondle each other's

genitals, that churches should "accommodate serpents, vermin, and the corpses of those who have died of the most filthy diseases!" But it is notable that at about the same time he wrote this quite disgusting poem he was, in essays for a Brooklyn newspaper, denouncing "the cant of reformers" as "barefaced and disgusting" and was also posing as a pious reformer himself in his article decrying prostitution, explaining that it is unpleasant but necessary "to grope among the muck and the slime."[55]

It would seem that in all his 1855–56 poses—as atheistical free-love advocate, as critic of reformers, and as fervent moral reformer himself—Whitman was variously reveling in the sheer rage and ferocity that had been unleashed by his reform culture. Significantly, one of the transpositions he calls for in "Respondez!" underscores the maniacal energy of reformers:

> Let the reformers descend from the stands where they are forever
>   bawling! let an idiot or insane person appear on each of the
>   stands![56]

It is this mad reform impulse, which he sculpts and rechannels in the better sections of *Leaves of Grass,* that he has come to value, without any vestige of specific reform programs. In other words, the reform impulse has been finally divested of all pretenses to didacticism and has been absorbed into the shaping personality of the poetic persona. Whitman asks in the 1855 edition:

> Is reform needed? is it through you?
> The greater the reform needed, the greater the Personality you
>   need to accomplish it.[57]

By 1863, when he was confessing in his notebook that his final aim was to gather around him the leaders of all reforms, he made it clear that it was the reformers' fiery personality rather than their politics that he prized: "We want no *reforms,* no *institutions,* no *parties*—We want a living principle as nature has, under which nothing can go wrong."[58] The last phrase is telling: having learned well from the errors of his reform culture, Whitman is looking for a completely unsullied reform principle with which nothing will go wrong. If Whitman became slightly more conservative as the decades passed, if he willingly exchanged the role of America's brash literary bohemian for that of the Good Gray Poet, it is in part because reform rhetoric had carried him to rather frightening extremes. Whitman certainly was no nihilist, nor was he at heart a political activist. He admitted late in life that although he had surrounded himself with the most out-spoken reformers, he always had a lurking sympathy for the reactionary side. He was what he advised Traubel to be: radical but not too damned radical. His greatest radicalism lay in his penetrating perception of his society's moral paradoxes and in his fluid rendering of them in free verse. He agreed wholeheartedly with his friend Gabriel Sarrazin's remark that "it has remained to our century and to America to erect evil and good upon equal pedestals and read in them an equal purpose."[59] Whitman, having spent much of his early career writing dark-reform literature, could have told Sarrazin just how this moral equalization had occurred. *Leaves of Grass* shows us all how it reached innovative poetic expression. In a later discussion of the sensational, erotic, and humorous images in *Leaves of Grass,* it will be shown just how innovative Whitman was in discovering reconstructive devices that transformed the popular subversive imagination into literary art.

4

HAWTHORNE AND THE REFORM
IMPULSE

F o r Emerson, Thoreau, and Whitman the rhetoric of popular reform
writings provided the basis for individualistic redefinitions of reform
whose refreshing breadth resulted from the fact that standard ethical categories had been erased by the intensifying moral wars in antebellum society. For Hawthorne and Melville, reform had a different signification. Like
the other major authors, they were profoundly aware of conflicting reform
impulses. Unlike them, they were interested less in redefining reform than
in discovering artistic correlatives for its ambiguities. In some of their best
works, they explore the fluidity between virtue and vice, the subtle process
by which the Conventional slides into the Subversive.

The specifically moral dimension of Hawthorne's fiction has long been
recognized but not fully interpreted in the context of its times. Henry
James perceived that Hawthorne demonstrated both a deep knowledge for
human evil and "a haunting care for moral problems."[1] Despite his interest
in the social sources of literature, however, James was unable to explain
how this unique combination was socially determined. Critics since James
have generally attributed Hawthorne's moral gloom to his innovative reinterpretation of dark Puritan doctrines, impelled by his guilt about—and
perverse attraction to—various crimes (from harsh religious intolerance to
incest) among his own ancestors. Such historical and psychoanalytic interpretations are, in the main, illuminating and accurate. But it has not been
recognized that in transforming his private obsessions and historical perceptions into fiction, Hawthorne was greatly aided by an *écriture* provided

113

by his contemporary society—specifically, by the rhetoric of a reform culture whose paradoxes he knew well and often discussed. Hawthorne's son Julian recalled that his father read novels for relaxation but seriously *studied* popular newspapers and magazines.[2] Hawthorne himself wrote that great literature has much in common with the most ephemeral writings and that the only way to produce enduring fiction is "to live truly and wisely for your own age, whereby, if the native force be in you, you may likewise live for posterity!"[3] The Hawthorne tales and novels that have most pleased posterity show that Hawthorne lived truly for his own age and absorbed its native force from the ephemeral writings he studied so closely—writings full of examples of the paradox of immoral didacticism.

Toward Literary Ambiguity

In order to reveal Hawthorne's debt to his reform culture, it is useful to consider his early literary development in the context of other American writers. By the time Hawthorne published his first work, *Fanshawe* (1828), there were two major, conflicting literary currents, the Conventional and the Subversive, which represented alternative views of reality. Conventional writers from the Richardsonian sentimentalists of the 1790s to the popular domestic novelists of the 1820s affirmed the values of family, childhood innocence, patriotism, simple piety, and a benign view of national history. Subversive writers, most notably Charles Brockden Brown and John Neal, offered Americanized renderings of horrific Gothic themes in novels featuring crime and irrationalism in wild modern or historical settings. This bifurcation carried over into much of Hawthorne's early fiction, which manifests an almost schizophrenic split between the Conventional and the Subversive. Works such as *Fanshawe*, "The Hollow of Three Hills" (1830), "My Kinsman, Major Molineux" (1832), and "Roger Malvin's Burial" (1832) exemplify the post-Gothic, Subversive Hawthorne, obsessed by themes like fruitless quests, nagging guilt, crime, perversity, and so forth. In contrast, "Sights from a Steeple" (1831), "The Gentle Boy" (1832), "The Vision of the Fountain" (1835), "The Village Uncle" (1835), and "Little Annie's Ramble" (1835) show Hawthorne using Conventional images such as simplified piety, patriotic history, comforting angelic visions, domestic bliss, and regenerating childhood purity.

Many of the Conventional and the Subversive tales lack the shaping force of mythopoesis, the subtle amplification of theme through symbol, that we find in Hawthorne's best work. It was not until the great tales of the 1835–36 period—"Young Goodman Brown" (1835), "The Minister's Black Veil" (1836), and "The May-pole of Merrymount" (1836)—that

Hawthorne consistently brought together opposing cultural forces. What has not been recognized is that precisely during these years Hawthorne discovered prototypes for literary themes and devices in his contemporary popular culture. As will be seen later, he found sources for gloomy reflection in trial pamphlets and crime literature. At the same time, he discovered in reform writings ways of bringing together the Conventional and Subversive in a symbolic, morally resonant center.

Popular reformers were for Hawthorne primary symbols of his society's moral ambiguities. In one of his very first notebook entries (in September 1835) Hawthorne drew the plan for a "sketch of a modern reformer,—a type of the extreme doctrines on the subject of slaves, cold-water, and other such topics."[4] In his proposed story, an enthusiastic reformer, haranguing before a growing street crowd, is on the verge of winning many converts to his views when his oration is interrupted by the keeper of a madhouse, from which the man has escaped. "Much can be made of this idea," Hawthorne exclaims in conclusion. Although Hawthorne never wrote a tale precisely following this plan, it is notable that a man whose journals are otherwise very sparse in references to real social movements or political events chose to comment upon the ironies surrounding zealous reformers. Several other notebook entries of the 1835–36 period, while not directly mentioning reform, propose several themes that bore striking similarities to those in dark-reform writings. In one entry Hawthorne plans a plot (later used in his tale "John Inglefield's Thanksgiving") of a prostitute returning home for a holiday, enjoying the bliss of her former innocent life, but then drawn inexorably back to her "sin and misery, which had become like a fate upon her," as though "the Devil had let her go back for a little while" but is now summoning her back.[5] In another entry, he imagines a sketch of "various kinds of ruin," including "ruin of habits, as drunkenness and all kinds of debauchery . . . Ruin might perhaps be personified as a demon, seizing its victim by various holds." In yet another notebook passage he proposes to write about a man "living a wicked life in one place, and simultaneously, a virtuous and religious one in another."

While only the first of these jottings directly mentions reformers, all the entries bear the impress of ironies derived from topics (prostitution, drunkenness, hypocritical piety) and images (fate, devils, madness) that had been featured in dark-reform writings since about 1832. These entries alone are not enough to prove irrefutably the influence of reform ambiguities on Hawthorne; but when we turn to the temperance tale Hawthorne wrote in 1835, "A Rill from the Town Pump," the evidence of such influence begins to mount. A lifelong advocate of convivial drinking, Hawthorne had no more devotion to the strict abstinence cause than did Whitman when he wrote *Franklin Evans*. But temperance writing gave to Hawthorne, as it did to Whitman, a socially accepted means of exploring new stylistic and thematic territories. For Whitman it provided a release into the feverish world of dark reform where simple moral standards were obliterated; for Hawthorne it provided a means of perfecting symbolic style, reaching toward thematic universality, and discovering a detached authorial voice.

Even though "A Rill from the Town Pump" was accepted in its day as a standard temperance work, it has several distinctly Hawthornian touches that distinguish it from other reform works and that show Hawthorne using popular devices to move toward literariness. The tale is Hawthorne's version of a popular temperance lecture, as he has a town water pump, calling himself "the grand reformer of the age," brashly vowing to wipe out the many ills—poverty, disease, sin, war, domestic quarrels—associated with alcohol. Turning its attention to other temperance speakers, the pump asks if they think it is decent "to get tipsy with zeal for temperance, and take up the honorable cause of the Town-Pump, in the style of a toper fighting for his brandy-bottle? Or, can the excellent qualities of cold water be no otherwise exemplified, than by plunging, slap-dash, into hot-water, and wofully scalding yourselves and other people?"[6] "In the moral warfare you are about to wage," the pump announces, no better example can be found than "myself, who have never permitted the dust, and sultry atmosphere, the turbulence and manifold disquietudes of the world around me, to reach that deep, calm well of purity, which may be called my soul." In this tale Hawthorne is experimenting with popular reform metaphors to gain a new universality of image. When he has the pump boast he is powerful enough to wipe out all the world's ills from poverty to war, he is testing out the larger-than-life, mythic imagery of the popular reformers, many of whom had made vast claims about the power of alcohol and the need for worldwide purification. When he derides the overzealous rhetoric of reformers, he is establishing his own cool, detached vantage point upon the stormy popular scene. When he notes that many temperance lecturers get "tipsy" with their cause, he is manifesting his keen awareness of the paradoxical fallibility of ostensibly pure reformers. In other words, Hawthorne here is writing a Conventional reform work (stressing the rewards rather than the wages of vice) in which he recognizes the foibles of reformers but also moves toward universalization of symbol and message.

In "Young Goodman Brown" (published the same year as "Rill") he arrives at such universalization. If "Rill" is Hawthorne's version of Conventional reform writing, "Young Goodman Brown" might be called his improvement on the dark-reform style. As was noted earlier, since the early 1830s popular evangelical reformers had filled American newspapers and pamphlets with grim stories about corruption lurking beneath civilized surfaces, about the collapse of romantic illusions, about nightly orgiastic rituals in which outwardly respectable people gather in evil communion, about the inexorable attraction to sin once the first wrong step is taken—all of which was frequently described in vivid post-Calvinist images such as hell, predestination, total depravity, and so forth. In 1834 one popular reformer, in a typical report of "highly influential men" who met nightly in "secret meetings, where they detail to each other their illicit adventures and the success of their new intrigues," had summed up the general reform outlook by exclaiming: "Alas! what is our standard of morality when men, holding the sacred trust of a jealous people, deem it a virtue to conceal their own abominations?"[7] Another reformer, commending a writer who boldly exposed the private misdeeds of pious hypocrites, declared: "We want a host of such writers, all over the country" to do likewise.[8] To many antebellum readers, Hawthorne in works like "Young Goodman Brown" appeared to be heeding such urgent calls for healthy exposure of hidden sin. Even the discriminating Bronson Alcott interpreted Hawthorne as a cleansing reformer who studied evil only to eradicate it. Alcott recalled that Hawthorne was *"great on sin*; he would hunt out a sinner better than any American I know."[9]

Hawthorne was hardly doing the unusual, therefore, in writing a story of a young man who becomes bitterly disillusioned after witnessing revered social and religious leaders consorting secretly with fallen women, criminals, and other outlaws under the direction of the devil himself. Given the fact that Hawthorne was a close reader of popular newspapers who commented on the ambiguities of popular reform in his notebooks and in "Rill from the Town Pump," it is certainly possible that in "Young Goodman Brown" he was probing fully the Subversive implications of his reform climate. We should note that this story, possessing as it does several standard devices of the dark-reform style, carries the reader to the verge of moral relativism when Brown, horrified by his fallen idols, cries: "My Faith is gone! . . . There is no good on earth and sin is but a name. Come, devil! for to thee is this world given."[10] Since Hawthorne had by 1835 become fully aware of the ironies surrounding ostensibly benevolent reformers, we may surmise that he had been carried toward a vision of relativism by the all-negating moral wars of his culture, wars in which the reformers, their critics, and those they hoped to redeem were hopelessly caught in a moral quagmire. For a sensitive observer like Hawthorne, immoral reform created a broadening of gloomy message and an intensification of symbolic style; in "Young Goodman Brown" the entire human race seems given to evil, and post-Calvinist imagery occurs in virtually every paragraph. Hawthorne boldly rechannels reform devices in historical fiction, for the first time unleashing the full terrors of New England's past. In short, his age's favorite strategies for unveiling secret corruption had led Hawthorne toward experimentation in the symbolic style and provocative moral historicism that would become his literary trademarks.

The connection Hawthorne had made between popular reformers and moral ambiguity became even stronger in the early 1840s, with the rise of the Washingtonian movement, with William Miller's terrifying predictions of the end of the world, and with Hawthorne's personal exposure to various movements through his reform-minded Peabody in-laws and through his brief stay at Brook Farm. His fiction of this period leaves no doubt that he understood the reform impulse to be a principal symbol of his culture's complexities. In "The Hall of Fantasy" (1843) he includes a sketch of "the noted reformers of the day," who are called "the representatives of an unquiet period" and "a thousand shapes of good and evil, faith and infidelity, wisdom and nonsense,—a most incongruous throng."[11] This insight into the contradictions of reformers is also made in "The Procession of Life" (1843), in which Hawthorne notes that it is far more difficult to breed friendship between supposedly beneficent reformers than between hardened criminals—a situation, Hawthorne writes cynically, that is "too preposterous for tears, too lugubrious for laughter." "Earth's Holocaust" (1844) shows just how violently destructive Hawthorne thought his reform culture was, as he envisages a tremendous bonfire into which reformers of every kind cast emblems of their despised vices, such as liquor, tobacco, coffee, the gallows, bad books, and so forth until the Bible itself is thrown in. The alarmed narrator exclaims that unless the earth itself is burnt up "I know not that we can carry reform to any further point." The narrator goes on to describe reform as "the Titan of innovation—angel or fiend, double in its nature, and capable of deeds befitting both characters," threatening the very "edifice of our moral and spiritual state." In a memorable Hawthorne touch, the reformers throw into the fire one thing which refuses to burn—the human heart. All of these stories underscore the doubleness of reformers, who are presented as superficially loving and righteous but secretly contentious, disruptive, devilish.

Hawthorne's Major Fiction and Antebellum Reform

Hawthorne's perception of deep moral problems within his contemporary reform culture, therefore, had deepened his early fiction. It should be noted, however, that he remained a somewhat disengaged observer of these problems until the late 1840s, when, just prior to writing *The Scarlet Letter,* he became directly involved in a sensational political scandal in which dark-reform rhetoric was flung by both Hawthorne and his enemies. It is well known that the firing of the Democrat Hawthorne from his job as surveyor of the Salem custom house by the newly elected Whig administration in 1849, coupled with the death of Hawthorne's mother that year, contributed to the gloom of *The Scarlet Letter*. Moreover, in the widely publicized fray over his firing, Hawthorne became both a target of and a participant in dark-reform mudslinging that set the stage for certain themes and strategies within *The Scarlet Letter*.

In the "Custom-House" preface to *The Scarlet Letter* Hawthorne emphasizes that he was swept out of office by "the besom of reform."[12] He goes on to say that his public "decapitation" by his Whig opponents was momentarily shocking but finally invigorating to his literary imagination. In the stolid, materialistic world of the custom house, he recalls, his imagination had become a tarnished mirror, so that had he remained in his job even through ten presidencies, he would never have had the inclination or the capacity to write *The Scarlet Letter*. Both the long preface and the novel itself, he stresses, are not the work of a comfortably settled custom-house chief but are instead "THE POSTHUMOUS PAPERS OF A DECAPITATED SURVEYOR." In other words, it was precisely the excitement created by "the besom of reform," by the venomous interchanges between Hawthorne and his opponents, that aroused his imagination from its long torpor.

If we look at the newspaper reports and letters involved in these battles, we see at once that Hawthorne had been plunged into a moral morass typical of antebellum reformers. While his Whig opponents charged that horrible corruption lurked behind Hawthorne's superficial decency, he and his defenders branded the Whigs as tyrannical oppressors who broke all moral laws under the pretense of righteous indignation.

Actually, Hawthorne had, willingly or not, for years been a party in political highjinks at the custom house. In 1846 he had fired two political enemies and replaced them with Democrats. Later he was involved in a kickback scheme whereby his Democratic custom-house subordinates got higher salaries than Whig workers and were expected to repay some of the extra money as part of their party dues. When the Salem Whigs caught wind of the scheme, they had a glorious time blasting Hawthorne in the local press as an outwardly innocent but secretly depraved Democrat. The Whig *Salem Register* on June 21, 1849, said it could make a shocking "exposure of the rottenness of the Custom House managers," declaring that it would oblige anyone who wished to see Hawthorne's errors "spread out in full, in all their glaring hideousness."[13] In the meantime, Democratic journalists were summoning their liveliest rhetoric to endorse Hawthorne. The *New York Post* called his removal "an act of wanton and unmitigated oppression," the *Albany Atlas* called it disgusting, and the Philadelphia

Evening Bulletin insisted that Hawthorne was "one of those glorious souls," an author, whose pious mission it was to "keep his eye fixed on the angel overhead, and not stoop to rake in the muck underfoot." Hawthorne himself was stirred to a boiling rage by the Whig attacks. Just before the firing, he wrote Longfellow: "I must confess it stirs up a little of the devil within me to find myself hunted by these political bloodhounds. If they succeed in getting me out of office, I will surely immolate one or two of them. . . . I may perhaps select a victim, and let fall a little drop of venom in his heart, that shall make him writhe before the grin of the multitude for a considerable time to come."[14]

Hawthorne's literary masterpiece, therefore, was produced at a volatile moment when the air around him buzzed with dark-reform images of hidden corruption, veiled rottenness, inward venom, and so forth. Since Hawthorne for years had been peculiarly responsive to reform ambiguities, it is not surprising that in the six months after his firing he allowed this rhetorical warfare to expand in his blackly satirical "Custom-House" preface and in his thematically paradoxical novel. The fact that he devotes so much space in his long preface to his custom-house job, its termination, and its scandalous aftermath suggests that he is using his own complicated experience with "the besom of reform" as a means of reactivating his subversive imagination. It is significant that the persona of the preface discovers the tattered scarlet A in the upper story of the custom house, and that he says he never would have been driven to write Hester Prynne's history unless he had been dragged "through the public prints, in my decapitated state, . . . ghastly and grim, and longing to be buried, as a politically dead man ought"—after which he became "again a literary man."[15] Hawthorne's political decapitation, with the Gothicized rhetoric that accompanied it, led to his literary resurrection. Just as the "Custom-House" preface is the reader's passageway to *The Scarlet Letter,* so his custom-house experience and the subsequent scandal was Hawthorne's preparation for his classic study of hidden corruption.

When Hawthorne vowed to drop venom into the hearts of his political enemies, he was obviously gearing himself up for a subversive literary performance. As it turned out, however, the venom he dropped was far more subtle in its operations than any of his enemies, or perhaps even he himself, could have imagined. In *The Scarlet Letter* Hawthorne produced the quintessential, sophisticated benign-subversive text. Like the writings of many immoral reformers, the novel provoked notably divided responses, with several reviewers accepting it as a straightforwardly moral book and others damning it as atheistic pornography. The responses ranged from Edwin Whipple's comment that the novel was "the most moral book of the age" to Arthur Cleveland Coxe's assertion that it smelled "strongly of incipient putrefaction" and belonged in the "Brothel Library" along with other American imitations of racy French novels.[16]

Is *The Scarlet Letter* a work of conventional morality or a dangerous piece of sex and sacrilege? Hopeful jeremiad or gloomy antijeremiad? Even to this day, critics are divided over such issues, some emphasizing the novel's undeniably bright, moral moments and others stressing its equally inescapable ambiguities. Hawthorne himself indicated several times that he considered the novel extremely gloomy, so much so that he begged his publisher to issue it in a volume containing brighter tales as well. Henry James, likewise, called it "densely dark" and believed it would long remain "the most consistently gloomy" novel of the first order in the English language.[17] On the other hand, the novel seemed pious enough to such stodgy commentators as the editor Evert A. Duyckinck, who called it a sound "piece of Puritan divinity," and the clergyman Arthur Dwight Mayo, who said it proved Hawthorne "a religious novelist in a high and peculiar sense."[18]

Such divided reader response springs from the simultaneous operation within the novel of profoundly subversive ironies and strong obeisances to conventional morality, establishing *The Scarlet Letter* as our highest fictional example of the paradox of immoral didacticism, a paradox that Hawthorne had experimented with in his earlier fiction. Since about 1835 (the year he first showed clear signs of understanding the ironies behind popular reformers), Hawthorne had made many variations upon the popular benign-subversive device of sugarcoating dark fiction with conventional moral commentary. Melville famously declared that even Hawthorne's titles were "directly calculated to deceive—egregiously deceive" the average reader. "Young Goodman Brown," Melville noted, sounds like a sequel to "Goody Two Shoes" but in fact is a black tale "deep as Dante."[19] Poe, too, noted the distance between the apparent and the real message of Hawthorne's fiction. Many readers, Poe complained, would be fooled by the moral conclusion of a story like "The Minister's Black Veil" into accepting Hawthorne as a didactic writer calling for honest exposure of sin, when in fact through most of the tale he had underscored the horrific inescapability of sin. Indeed, this strategy of tacking a benign moral conclusion onto a deeply disturbing tale became a standard feature of Hawthorne's fiction from the mid-1830s onward.

If Hawthorne learned anything from his reform culture, it was that surface morality frequently cloaked gloom or sacrilege; he permitted this paradox to be enacted stylistically in numerous tales that seem highly moral but are in fact iconoclastic. For instance, "Wakefield" (1836), the story of a middle-class man who without apparent reason walks out on his wife and lives apart from her for decades until one chilly night he rejoins

her, trembles on the edge of being a dreary portrait of shattered domesticity and human arbitrariness; but these subversive themes are muted by
Hawthorne's concluding moral, which underscores the need of remaining
within established systems. Most of "The Haunted Mind" (1835) is devoted to describing the perverse, devilish thoughts that haunt us when we
wake at night; but the tale ends with the image of "bright sunny visions"
of heaven that lull us back to sleep.[20] "Night Sketches Beneath an Umbrella" (1838) likewise conjures up the terrifying thought of eternal noth-
ingness suggested by a lonely walk on a rainy night, but the concluding
picture of a man walking with a lantern symbolizes, in Hawthorne's words,
"the lamp of Faith, enkindled at a celestial fire."[21] "The Birth-Mark"
(1843), in which a mad scientist kills his wife by trying to cure her of a tiny
physical blemish, explores the murderous results of overzealous perfec-
tionism but ends with the image of her going to heaven and him being
upbraided for not accepting the heaven he already possessed. At the end
of "Rappaccini's Daughter" (1844), in which a woman is the victim of her
father's scientific folly, the scientist's unthinkable perversity is mollified by
his daughter's dying prediction that earthly hatred will "fall away as I
ascend."[22] Examples could be multiplied of other bright story endings that
make the dark Hawthorne seem to many contemporary readers, as Melville
expressed it, as "a pleasant writer, with a pleasant style."[23]

 The Scarlet Letter was his most complex performance in the benign-
subversive style. Hawthorne explores the subversive and then recoils to
the pious, in the novel as a whole and in many individual scenes. The most
wild swing between the perverse and the moral occurs in the last third of
the novel, in which Hawthorne drifts into forbidden psychological and
religious territory but then creeps back to the conventional. The most
subversive moment occurs when Arthur Dimmesdale, experiencing "a
total change . . . of moral code" as he returns to town after his forest
meeting with Hester Prynne, has wicked fantasies about several people he
meets:[24] he wishes to blaspheme against church rituals to a good deacon;
he wants to give an irrefutable argument against the possibility of an
afterlife to a bereaved widow he had previously consoled; he is tempted
to drop a licentious "germ of evil" into the mind of a blooming young
maiden; he would whisper evil things to a group of children; and he wishes
he could join in with a drunken, swearing sailor. Like the scene in which
Hester lets down her hair and tells Dimmesdale, "What we did had a
consecration of its own," this moment provides Hawthorne with a temporary identification with the tabooed which he later retracts when, after
Dimmesdale's confession on the scaffold, he moralizes: "Be true! Be true!
Be true! Show freely to the world, if not your worst, yet some trait by which
the worst may be inferred."

The irony is that this concluding moral, praised by Hawthorne's favorable reviewers, is in fact a nonmoral, given the ambiguities that abound in the rest of the novel. After all, the main characters *have* freely shown to the world some evidence of their sin: Hester wears her badge of shame; Dimmesdale confesses in the pulpit that he is a vile sinner; Chillingworth is widely recognized as a devil. But this openness comes to naught, as these figures are caught in the tragic situation of exposers of hidden sin who are trapped in their own sinfulness. In his previous fiction and notebook entries Hawthorne had often taken note of reformers' doubleness, visible especially in the glaring contrast between their benevolent intentions and their immoral performance. Just prior to writing the novel, he had been thrown into a political muckheap filled with dark-reform images. The personal exposure to immoral reform seems to have been the catalyst he needed to project his long-standing comprehension of his culture's moral tensions in a novel over which readers are still divided.

In addition to fashioning the period's most subtle work in the benign-subversive style, Hawthorne transformed key images and themes of popular reform literature. Contrary to popular belief, Hawthorne in *The Scarlet Letter* was not particularly original in his choice of characters or themes. One reason the novel became one of his most popular works was that the antebellum public felt comfortable with a fictional exposé of hidden corruption involving a hypocritical preacher, a fallen woman, an illegitimate child, and a vindictive relative. By the late 1840s such depraved characters were stock figures in popular American fiction. To give one example, Sylvester Judd's *Margaret* (1845) included a subplot involving an abandoned woman, Rose Elphiston, who is forced to live alone with "a significant red letter" sewed on her clothes and whose haughty, skeptical nature anticipates Hester Prynne's.[25] In the same novel, a little girl gives spirited retorts to her prying catechism teachers, much like Hawthorne's little Pearl. Secret sexual escapades among preachers were such common topics in sensational fiction that in his hostile review Arthur Coxe declared that Hawthorne's tale of "the nauseous amour of a Puritan pastor" was a book "made for the market," like many popular seamy works.[26] Moreover, at several moments in *The Scarlet Letter* Hawthorne seems to be pandering to the many American readers who in the late 1840s had proved themselves voracious for novels about hidden sin among the ostensibly respectable. Witness Hawthorne's use of unmasking imagery, quite typical of the popular exposé-novel: the opening exhibition of Hester on the scaffold is described as "iniquity dragged out into the sunshine";[27] Arthur Dimmesdale publicly enjoins Hester to reveal her fellow sinner "even if he step down from a high place"; the scarlet letter gives Hester a kind of moral X-ray vision (like that of many reform characters who can "see through the veil"), enabling her to perceive secret evil within even the most apparently pious townspeople, teaching her that "the outward guise of purity was but a lie"; on his way back from the forest, the suddenly perverse Dimmesdale feels tempted to whisper blasphemous or dirty things to pious passersby. These and many similar images in the novel would naturally be attractive to a mass readership that loved to hate respectable frauds and to be titillated by its reform literature.

Despite such affinities with popular literature, *The Scarlet Letter* was not just another exposé-novel, precisely because it was the *ultimate* exposé-novel. That is to say, it gave full expression to the intrinsic moral ironies that in the typical dark exposé were temporarily dramatized but finally avoided or squelched. Many popular exposés of the 1840s, from Lippard's *The Quaker City* (1845) through George Thompson's *Venus in Boston* (1849), had been paradoxical and problematic novels, since their moral intent was constantly undermined by their opportunistic sensationalism and prurience. This overweening paradox produced interesting tensions and even a crude literariness in several exposés, but it missed full artistic flowering because it was not treated self-referentially—that is, the moral paradox itself was not made a primary theme. The ironies in a popular novel like *The Quaker City* pile onto each other and collide against each other; but they do not become themselves the main object of the author's attention. They remain, therefore, surface ironies of action and behavior that do not breed truly multidimensional symbols. In *The Quaker City* it is ironic that Byrnewood Arlington taunts Gus Lorrimer into seducing a woman who turns out to be Byrnewood's sister; it is doubly ironic that, despite her reputed innocence, the sister actually invites the seduction; it is triply ironic that Byrnewood righteously pursues his sister's seducer even though he himself is a rake with a checkered past; and so on through the whole book. But Lippard seems to miss the final point: that is, the very process of writing in the dark-reform style is itself the greatest irony; the very endorsement of morality through an immoral mode is a rich topic for the American novelist.

It is this topic that becomes central in *The Scarlet Letter.* We have seen that Hawthorne had long regarded reformers as symbols of doubleness, of man's ability to behave simultaneously as an angel and a demon. In *The Scarlet Letter* Hawthorne examines this doubleness as it by turns consumes itself and projects itself outward. Each of the principal characters is a kind of immoral reformer caught in the highly ironic predicament of trying honestly to probe or expose sin and yet in the very process becoming more deeply entangled in sin. Arthur Dimmesdale attains brilliant popularity by preaching on the secrets of sin, and yet veneration from his congregation only increases his horrified disgust over his own buried corruption. Roger Chillingworth is a combination of the demonic revenge figure and the righteous prober of secret error—we despise Chillingworth and yet are forced to recognize that, after all, he is a wronged individual whose dogged delving at last leads to Dimmesdale's confession. Hester Prynne on the surface is "a living sermon against sin"[28] whose honesty and chastened goodness enable her to help the sick and the needy; but she is privately given to skeptical philosophical musings, and the scarlet letter gives her a frightening ability to spot hidden evil within apparently good people all around her. Pearl has a similar ambivalence, since she is simultaneously Hester's happiness and her torture, characterized by both amoral impishness and deeply moral dedication to the honest exposure of her parents' sin. The complicated status of the reformer is even enacted in the scarlet letter itself, which takes on shifting significations ranging from full embodiment of sin to probing unmasker of it.

In all of these cases we see the complexities Hawthorne had attributed to popular reformers taking life as self-qualifying characters and symbols. The ironies collide against each other, as they do in the popular exposé-novel, but they also turn inward and eat at themselves. The moral ambiguities that in the popular exposés are deflected outward into plot are here interiorized and enacted in psychology and in symbol. This interiorization is greatly facilitated by Hawthorne's use of the Puritan past. Hawthorne tapped the introspective earnestness, the typological vision, and the ultimacy of Puritanism but at the same time dramatized the searing ironies he had witnessed in his contemporary reform culture. Neither the Puritan doctrines alone nor the modern ironies alone would have been sufficient to produce mythic American tragedy. By fusing the two, Hawthorne manages to invest the Puritan past with modern ambiguity and to invest nineteenth-century reform themes with a new symbolic resonance. Hawthorne, who had said that literature endures only if it fully embodies its age, had succeeded in transforming dark reform into literary ambiguity.

It is evident from Hawthorne's letters, however, that he was not altogether comfortable with pondering unresolvable moral problems. While pleased at the book's relatively good sale, he complained to one friend that the novel lacked "cheering light" and promised another that his next novel would be "a more natural and healthy product of my mind," "more proper and natural for me to write, than the Scarlet Letter."[29] *The House of the Seven Gables* (1851), despite gloomy features of its own, is indeed a brighter novel than *The Scarlet Letter*, principally because reform and crime (the two dark-popular themes that most strongly influenced Hawthorne) are now treated in more standard, more manageable fashion than they had been in the previous novel. Dark reform still unleashes subversive forces, but Hawthorne does not allow these forces to turn inward upon themselves, to create aporias of thought as he had in *The Scarlet Letter*.

The reform impulse is most obviously felt in the characterization of

Judge Jaffrey Pyncheon and the popular reformer Holgrave. Pyncheon has been long recognized as one of Hawthorne's great villains, based, as we know, on Hawthorne's political enemy Charles Wentworth Upham. But he is also a titanic version of the pious hypocrite so common in the exposé-novel. He is an ardent temperance advocate, the president of a Bible society, the worthy treasurer of a widows' and orphans' fund, a leading party man, a churchgoer—but he is also unthinkably greedy, cold, cruel, and, despite his temperance principles, he drinks sherry on the sly. In short, he is the standard oxymoronic oppressor reminiscent of many intemperate temperance men, selfish philanthropists, and otherwise unctuously hypocritical characters in popular exposés. What distinguishes him from the popular stereotype is the peculiarly Hawthornesque manner in which his villainy is universalized by being associated with Puritanism. Descended from the harshly intolerant, elitist Pyncheons of Puritan times, Jaffrey is part of a mythic line of corruption that shows how the sins of the fathers taint successive generations.

Still, even such Puritan-rooted corruption is less metaphysically ambiguous here than it had been in *The Scarlet Letter,* for it is connected not with self-consuming introspection but rather with exploitative oppression, especially as evidenced by the Pyncheons' maltreatment of generations of indigent Maules. The Pyncheons' sin is as much economic as it is ethical, as much a result of class prejudice as of moral obliquity. It is, in short, Hawthorne's version of the distinction made commonly in popular exposés between an exploiting "upper ten" and an exploited "lower million." For Hawthorne, it is a more manageable because a less interior sin, one linked with surface collisions between socially distanced families rather than with inner battles between warring parts of the soul. Having plumbed the ambiguities behind certain stock characters and themes in *The Scarlet Letter,* Hawthorne seems to be using other popular elements— the wealthy hypocrite, class warfare—as a means of localizing sin and retreating to the surface. The evil of *The House of the Seven Gables* is more clearly bifurcated (rich versus poor; pious exterior versus depraved interior) than it had been in *The Scarlet Letter.* As many popular reform writers could have taught Hawthorne, social dualisms were far easier to handle than inner moral paradoxes.

Hawthorne's characterization of Holgrave and Phoebe Pyncheon provides yet more evidence that the reform impulse is being here rechanneled to be made manageable. Through much of the novel, Holgrave embodies the Subversive reform impulse, Phoebe the Conventional sensibility that opposes it. We are told that Holgrave associates with "reformers, temperance-lecturers, and all manner of cross-looking philanthropists."[30] Hepzibah reads in a penny newspaper of his "making a speech, full of wild and disorganizing matter, at a meeting of his banditti-like associates." We saw that by the 1850s the excesses of many reformers had become so notorious that reformers themselves were widely satirized in popular novels and newspapers. In his portrait of Holgrave, Hawthorne seems to be pushing the satire on reformers to a negation of the reform impulse itself, perhaps because it had led him to perilous thematic depths in *The Scarlet Letter*. In his conversations with Phoebe, Holgrave at first dominates but is finally won over to her view of things. He makes her dizzy "by his lack of reverence for what is fixed," by his reformist zeal to tear down past institutions and rebuild all anew. But love eventually compromises his reform schemes. As he becomes infatuated with Phoebe while they talk in the garden, Holgrave suddenly says that the world is fine after all and that moonlight and affection are "the greatest of renovators and reformers." By the end, he has given himself to Phoebe, decrying his former radicalism by declaring: "The happy man inevitably confines himself within ancient limits." The former champion of change wants to live with Phoebe in a conservative world of stone houses, fences, wealth, and laws.

The tone of this conservative ending has long been debated: is Hawthorne himself endorsing Holgrave's recoil to the bourgeois, or is he satirizing it? It should be recalled that the safe ending was very typical of Hawthorne, and that even in his darkest works he leaves himself some kind of conventional escape valve. The final conservatism of this novel, then, is a structural element typical of Hawthorne's work and of the benign-subversive mode as a whole. But, really, it would not make a great difference whether we knew for certain how Hawthorne felt about Holgrave's final posture. The key thing to recognize is that throughout the novel Hawthorne is simplifying the terms of moral conflict. To be sure, Hawthornesque ambiguities are perceptible in digressions on death, in the portrait of the effete Clifford, in the coupling of Gothic terror and Puritan gloom in the old house itself. But the polarization between Maule and Pyncheon, between poor and rich, between rebellious reform and social conservatism shows that, at the very least, Hawthorne is redirecting the reform impulse toward conflicts that are less metaphysical and more easily grasped than those in *The Scarlet Letter*.

As Melville was to learn after him, however, there was a new kind of ambiguity of the surface. In *The Blithedale Romance* (1852) the fragmentation and superficiality of modern reform movements becomes not only Hawthorne's main topic but is also embodied in the very style. Puritanism has now been left totally behind, as Hawthorne turns his eyes fully on his own century—but what he sees is in several senses more terrifying than the inner moral conflicts he had probed in *The Scarlet Letter*. If the characters of the latter novel were lost in moral mazes, their tortured struggles at least had the saving grace of being fully *human*; hence the emphasis on Dimmesdale's "anguish," on Hester Prynne's "torture," on the "great and warm heart" of the Puritan multitude. The reformers that populate *The Blithedale Romance,* in contrast, either are heartless from the start or go through a kind of conversion to superficiality. The only fully human character, Zenobia, is crushed by the the inhumanity around her; specifically, Hollingsworth's rejection of her after he learns she is not wealthy drives her to suicide. In *The Scarlet Letter* and *The House of the Seven Gables* nineteenth-century immoral reform was imbued with a certain earnestness and depth because it was associated with Puritanism. In *The Blithedale Romance* this earnestness is lost, as immoral reform breeds murderous and suicidal amorality.

The Blithedale Romance was both Hawthorne's most topical romance, the one in which he most obviously grapples with contemporary social issues, and a powerful, acute record of the troubled moral climate of antebellum society. The novel is loosely based, of course, on Hawthorne's brief stay in 1841 at the Associationist community, Brook Farm, where he became increasingly disillusioned with reform projects and the drudgery of communitarian labor. Two years after he left the community he talked with Emerson about his great desire to write a novel on "the singular moral aspects which [Brook Farm] presents."[31] We have seen that such "singular moral aspects" of modern reform provided the thematic background for much of Hawthorne's fiction of the period, from "Earth's Holocaust" and "The Procession of Life" through *The House of the Seven Gables.* We should not be surprised, therefore, that the Blithedale community bears only a slim resemblance to Brook Farm. In his preface Hawthorne stresses that the novel says nothing for or against Brook Farm and socialism, and in a letter to a friend Hawthorne warned: "Do not read [the novel] as if it had anything to do with Brook Farm (which essentially it has not) but merely for its own story and characters."[32] In reading the novel itself, we realize it is about Brook Farm only insofar as Brook Farm was a symbol of larger moral problems posed by antebellum reform movements and pseudo-science.

A lot of cultural water had gone under the bridge between 1841, when Hawthorne left Brook Farm, and 1852, when *The Blithedale Romance* was published. For one thing, Brook Farm itself, initially a Transcendentalist enterprise led mainly by Boston intellectuals, had turned into a Fourierist phalanx dominated by New York working-class Associationists, before it collapsed like nearly all the ill-fated communitarian projects of the 1840s. The history of Brook Farm was therefore a lesson in increasingly fragmented reform schemes leading to inevitable failure, a lesson repeated during the 1840s by several other movements, including temperance, land reform, and antiprostitution. After several leading movements had proved to be idealistically utopian, in the late 1840s and early 1850s there was a widespread effort to unify fragmented reformers through more "practical" or realistic schemes, such as legal reform in the temperance cause or industrial congresses and union activity in the labor movement. Working-class advocates like Wilhelm Weitling and George Lippard, distraught by divisions and errors among reformers, placed a new emphasis on together-ness, on brotherhood—an emphasis that in the 1860s would culminate in the almost mystical vision of universal brotherhood on the part of Uriah Stephens and his followers in the Knights of Labor.

Writing in the early 1850s, Hawthorne explored the moral and psychological consequences of fragmented reform, while he purposely undercut visions of brotherhood and unity. In addition to reflecting upon the tragic fate of Associationist communities, he may have been consciously satirizing popular novels, such as *Henry Russell* (1846) or Lippard's *Adonai* (1851), in which such communities were idealized. *Henry Russell* is particularly intriguing in this regard, for it pictures a happy Fourierist community where association has replaced competition, where men and women work in jobs of their own choosing, where life in a glorious central phalanx is made even more pleasant by constant music from a huge Aeolian harp. In the community, prisons and gallows have been replaced by schools where criminals are reformed, not punished. The novel ends with an affirmation of universal brotherhood enforced at a World Convention of reformers, who agree to banish war, slavery, and all other types of injustice or oppression.

In *The Blithedale Romance* Hawthorne overturns such blithe pictures of utopian bliss. His self-appointed mission seems to be to rip apart all utopian pretenses to brotherhood and noble purpose. In the early part of the novel, Hawthorne metonymically explodes utopian reform in a succession of ironic moments. In a pretentious show of comradeship Coverdale ridiculously shouts out a friendly greeting to a passerby during a whistling blizzard, and becomes enraged at the "churl" for ignoring "our blithe tones of brotherhood."[33] When the reformers meet they congratulate themselves that "the blessed state of brotherhood and sisterhood, at which we aimed, might be fairly dated from this moment," but soon Coverdale himself gets sick and wishes "the reformation of society had been postponed about half-a-century." Zenobia's voluptuous beauty and magnetic warmth put to shame her shallow political views and make the "heroic [Blithedale] enterprise to show like an illusion, a masquerade, a pastoral, a counterfeit Arcadia." Indeed, virtually every page of the novel gives added examples of the flimsy, empty quality of reform schemes when confronted with human experience.

Hawthorne's interests, however, lie far beyond the mere satire on reform. In a very real sense, he uses the reform impulse to subvert itself, to become the engine of its own destruction. We have seen that this self-subverting process was also central in *The Scarlet Letter,* where it gains universality from the fact that actual reform movements are not mentioned. In *The Blithedale Romance* many specific reform movements (prison reform, Associationism, temperance, feminism, spiritualism, mesmerism) are directly brought into play. If such specificity locates the novel in its era and precludes the kind of universality achieved in *The Scarlet Letter,* nevertheless Hawthorne's analysis of moral motives remains subtle and penetrating. He exposes reform variously as cold monomania (Hollingsworth), changeable costume (Zenobia), or shallow whim (Coverdale, Priscilla). In Hollingsworth, the immoral reformer of antebellum society is heightened until he becomes an amoral monster. An ardent prison reformer, Hollingsworth is generously dedicated to improving the condition of criminals; but, ironically, he is the most helpless prisoner and most hardened criminal of all, locked in his single idea and willing to abandon all conscience in exploiting others to further his reform project. From the characterization of Hollingsworth, we learn why since the mid-1840s Hawthorne had focused on the reformer as a primary symbol of America's moral ambiguities: since the reformer so loudly proclaims his benevolence and justice, the distance is particularly great between his conscious behavior and underlying motives, his surface purity and submerged neurosis. Hollingsworth, as Coverdale says with some justice, has "no heart, no sympathy, no reason, no conscience" and exemplifies "godlike benevolence . . . debased into all-devouring egotism."[34] He wants to appropriate the Blithedale property for his own "School of Reform" for criminals, and he coldly abandons Zenobia when he learns she has lost her inheritance. We tend to agree when Coverdale says that Hollingsworth has been "thrown completely off his moral balance," proving that "the besetting sin of a philanthropist, . . . is apt to be a moral obliquity." Hawthorne has drawn the consummate picture of the antebellum immoral reformer, so devoted to a noble cause that he sacrifices all morality in its pursuit.

If Hollingsworth's moral obliquity lies in overzealous commitment to reform, the obliquity of the other characters results from precisely the opposite—from the *lack* of deep commitment to social activism. Reform, Hawthorne suggests, plays havoc with moral principle in distinct ways. Hollingsworth can be placed in the group of antebellum immoral reformers, from McDowall through Gough, whose publicly proclaimed goals were belied by their secret motives or private behavior. Showing the immoral results of reform fanaticism, Hollingsworth thus represents Subversive reform. On the opposite pole of the reform spectrum is Coverdale, the Boston bachelor, minor poet, clubman, and dilettante reformer. Like Hollingsworth, he is a moral monster, but for different reasons. As he comes to realize: "I lack a purpose. How strange! [Hollingsworth] was ruined, morally, by an overplus of the very same ingredient, the want of which, I occasionally suspect, has rendered my own life all an emptiness."[35] Coverdale reluctantly leaves his warm bachelor suite in order to reform the world, but when he feels threatened by disruptions at Blithedale, he immediately wishes to revisit "the settled system of things," to associate again with "the writers of the North American Review, the merchants, the politicians, the Cambridge men." Coverdale, then, is the Boston liberal who typifies the Conventional sensibility. He evokes increasing wrath from both the committed Hollingsworth and the passionate Zenobia, who disparages him for returning to "the whole series of social conventionalisms" he had supposedly rejected. As it turns out, he desperately needs these conventionalisms as a buffer against the profound ambiguities posed by over-zealous reform. After he comes to understand the various excesses and contradictions among the reformers around him, he is terrified by the feeling that "everything in nature and human existence was fluid," as he begins to lose all "sense of what kind of world it was, among innumerable schemes of what it might or ought to be." Hawthorne here is studying the contortions of the Conventional sensibility when confronted with the Subversive forces of errant reform. If, as several critics have pointed out, the second half of the novel is dominated by images of dream, illusion, masks, theater, it is largely because the world suddenly seems unreal to the conventional Coverdale when he is faced with the moral enigmas of his reform culture.

While Hollingsworth embodies the amorality of the Subversive and Coverdale the vapidity of the Conventional, Zenobia illustrates the capacity to shift whimsically from one side to the other, while Priscilla represents the moral nullity at the heart of it all. Zenobia seems initially revolutionary, making "no scruple of oversetting all human institutions, and scattering them as with a breeze from her fan," but she turns out to be a mere actress in reform, willingly surrendering her feminist principles when Hollingsworth denounces them.[36] Priscilla is, paradoxically, both the weakest and the most influential figure in the book. As mysterious and deep as the purses she sews, she is the passive repository for all the passions that fly around her, and thus operates as the central locus of ambiguity in this world of errant or failed reforms. She is accurately described as "only a leaf, floating on the dark current of events, without influencing them by her own choice or plan," and she rightly says, "I never have any free-will." She is by turns gay, sad, frivolous, spunky, morose—she is the black hole of contrary emotions that underlie and finally negate contending reform schemes. It's no wonder, then, that she finally wins the day: at the end, she survives while the queenly Zenobia has been driven to suicide; the once proud Hollingsworth is leaning weakly on her arm; and even the passionless Coverdale closes by announcing he is secretly in love with her. The "victory" of Priscilla is the victory of ambiguity, inertia, and directionlessness in a society whose moral backbone has been broken by its own internecine conflicts.

Having followed the contradictions of his reform culture to their natural conclusion—the drab purposelessness and relativism embodied in Coverdale at the end of *The Blithedale Romance*—Hawthorne seems to have felt that he had exhausted all possibilities for deep topics relating to America. He explained his choice of Rome as the setting for *The Marble Faun* (1860) by complaining that it would be long before novelists would find "congenial and easily handled themes" connected with America, which he said had no mystery, no shadow, no antiquity, nothing but "a common-place prosperity, in broad and simple daylight."[37] Critics have too often cited this comment as proof that Hawthorne's gloomy fiction was a protest against an optimistic American society. The truth is that since the 1830s Hawthorne had been fully conscious of the moral obliquities of his countrymen (especially his reform-minded contemporaries) and had dramatized them time and again in some of the darkest works in the English language. If from the perspective of several years abroad he could emphasize the prosperity and sunlight of American society, it was in part because he himself had exhausted the richest indigenous themes—Puritanism and dark reform, or combinations of the two.

In *The Marble Faun* itself Hawthorne does not totally turn away from the native themes he had explored in his previous romances. He is still intrigued by the collision between the Conventional and its opposite, though here the opposite is not dark reform but rather, as will be seen in a later discussion of *The Marble Faun*, violent crime and its perpetrators. Indirectly, *The Marble Faun* again dramatizes the dark-reform paradox, for it describes the self-consuming moral conscience of the conventional Hilda after she becomes the unwilling witness to the murder committed by her friends Miriam and Donatello. In this novel, Hawthorne gives clear signs that he hated above all Americans' repression of their guilt, while he envied the open expression of sin made possible in European (especially Roman Catholic) countries. A short time before writing the novel Hawthorne had witnessed an Italian man in St. Peter's sobbing with unleashed wretchedness before a confessional; Hawthorne commented that had the man been a Protestant, "he would have shut all that up within his heart, and let it burn there till it seared him."[38] Previously, while he was in England he had noted the frankness of the British, whose "open avowal and recognition of immoralities served to throw the disease to surface" instead of (as he thought was the case of Americans) "turning its poison back among the inner vitalities of the character at the imminent risk of corrupting them all."[39] Many of Hawthorne's characteristic American characters, from Young Goodman Brown and Ethan Brand through Arthur Dimmesdale, burn inwardly with trapped guilt or sin until they find release at key purgative moments, such as Ethan Brand's infernal shriek or Dimmesdale's scaffold confession. In *The Marble Faun* such a moment comes for Hilda when she confesses her knowledge of her friends' crime to the Catholic priest, after which she feels infinitely relieved. While Hawthorne clearly values such frank exposure of sin, he also feels uncomfortable with a naïve dismissal of sin, an easy passage from ambiguity to blind conventionalism. As a result, he alternates his account of Hilda's struggle to escape sin with the attempt by other characters, especially Donatello and Kenyon, to learn from it, giving rise to the theme of the Fortunate Fall. In *The Blithedale Romance* Hawthorne seems to have reached a kind of moral nadir in which virtue and vice were fluid, relative; in *The Marble Faun* he manifests a desire to make a case for both the expulsion of dark thoughts (Hilda) and the retention of them (Kenyon).

If *The Marble Faun* was indeed an attempt to deflect or rechannel the reform ambiguities he had tussled with in *The Blithedale Romance,* the unfinished novels Hawthorne wrote after he returned to America in 1860 suggest that these ambiguities were inescapable. The texts of these unfinished novels show that to the end Hawthorne was haunted by the connection between reformers and irony. When he was trying to come up with an idea for a hypocritical character in *The American Claimant Manuscripts,* he jotted this note to himself: "He may be a sort of reformer, [who] . . . shall have the fatality of causing death, bloodshed, wherever he goes; and this shall symbolize the strife which benevolence inevitably provokes, because it disturbs everything around it."[40] Similarly, in the final study for the *Septimius Norton* manuscript, he wrote: "One of Septimius' grand objects is to reform the world, which he thinks he can do."[41] In the sketch for the proposed story, Hawthorne has Septimius vow to die only after he has rid the world of slavery, intemperance, crime, war—but his reform schemes are negated by his increasing selfishness, as once again the noble reformer who intends to cure all evil becomes the unwitting agent of evil. Likewise, in his second study for *The Dolliver Romance* Hawthorne planned a reform character who works tirelessly to rid the world of all social life, but the world accomplishes the reform on its own, while the reformer's schemes breed only ill. To the very end, then, Hawthorne was virtually obsessed by the paradox of immoral reform.

Some commentators have lamented Hawthorne's well-known complacency on pressing social issues such as slavery and class conflict. But his contribution was not to advocate specific reforms but to make a sensitive overview of all reforms, grasp fully their moral implications, and transmute their ambiguities into believable self-consuming characters and sophisticated benign-subversive texts.

5

MELVILLE'S WHITED SEPULCHRES

I F Hawthorne's sensitivity to the reform impulse was responsible for key themes and devices of his fiction, it also proved to be a major reason he became a literary catalyst for Herman Melville. The Hawthorne-Melville relationship is perhaps the most famous in nineteenth-century American letters, and this kinship between the two writers was based, at least in part, upon a common devotion to the benign-subversive mode, derived mainly from popular reform writings. Hawthorne, himself adept at fashioning fictional reapplications of morality, praised Melville in his review of *Typee* for his "freedom of view—it would be too harsh to call it laxity of principle—which renders him tolerant of codes of morals that may be little in accordance with our own."[1] Melville, for his part, first paid homage to Hawthorne the popular temperance writer. In *White-Jacket,* momentarily becoming a temperance advocate himself, Melville sings praise to "the much admired Pale Ale" produced by a ship's water pump and expresses a wish that "my fine countryman, Hawthorne of Salem, had but served on a man-of-war in his time, that he might give us the reading of a *'rill'* from the scuttle-butt."[2]

In effect, then, Melville "met" Hawthorne through the avenue of popular reform. Moreover, this meeting of the minds was in large part culturally induced, for, just as Hawthorne had profited from an early perception of the ironies behind popular reforms, so Melville in his early novels extensively used reform devices that familiarized him with the kind of moral complexities that prepared him to appreciate Hawthorne. If when he wrote

White-Jacket (itself a novel in the dark-reform tradition) Melville's appreciation seemed relatively superficial in its emphasis on Hawthorne's temperance work, this very enthusiasm for popular reform carried the seeds of the
passionate admiration for Hawthorne that Melville displayed a year later
in his review of *Mosses from an Old Manse*. Melville's "Hawthorne and His
Mosses" is the quintessential antebellum commentary on the benign-subversive mode. Melville's main point is that Hawthorne seems a gentle,
conventional author but is in fact a subversive one whose surface piety is
a deceptive cover for dark metaphysical probings. If in many of his early
novels Melville had played the part of the social reformer "lifting the veil"
off various vices or iniquities (corruption among Christian missionaries,
naval flogging, slavery, intemperance, and so forth), in "Hawthorne and
His Mosses" he becomes a literary reformer, lifting the veil off his Salem
contemporary in an effort to reveal hidden blackness. In turn, Melville
"reformed" himself accordingly, for the whaling novel he was then writing
took a Hawthornesque turn from mere adventure to gloom and symbolism. Given the subversive implications of popular reform, it is small wonder that the writer who had posed in *White-Jacket* as a temperance man
appreciative of "A Rill from the Town Pump" could the next year uncover
Hawthorne's Shakespearian ambiguities and could write in a letter to Hawthorne: "It can hardly be doubted that all Reformers are bottomed upon
the truth, more or less[.]"[3]

A close look at Melville's fiction reveals that his literary development
was tied even more closely to popular reform than was Hawthorne's.
Because previous critics have wrongly associated antebellum reform with
progressivist optimism, Melville's complex fiction has been commonly
viewed as a rebellious gesture by a dark writer who, in the words of one
critic, intentionally "subverts the ideology of reform."[4] To stress Melville's
supposed distance from his reform culture, however, is to overlook an
important source of his thematic and stylistic breadth. Melville's unique
openness to the rhetoric and spirit of a remarkable variety of reform
currents enriched his early novels and contributed greatly to his major
literary triumphs.

The Deepening of Melville's Moral Imagination

We find in Melville's early novels an ambitious, wide-ranging experimentation with reform devices that directly prepared the way for the
discovery of Hawthorne's and his own subversive identity. In an 1850
comment on *White-Jacket* that could be well applied to several of Melville's
early novels, William Gilmore Simms wrote: "The author's role is that of

the reformer."[5] The *dark* reformer, we would add—or, rather, the creative novelist adopting popular reform ironies and using them, in more subtle and varied ways than previous American writers, to explore unconventional themes.

In his early works Melville manipulated the benign-subversive mode in ways that generated thematic complexities which in Melville's later novels flowered as full-fledged ambiguity. In *Typee* and *Omoo* a fairly standard reform stance (protest against mainstream Christianity, in the person of missionaries on the South Sea Islands) provides a cover for quite subversive commentary on the norms and values of white civilization, and for daring suggestions of debauchery and licentiousness among the sailors. In *Mardi*, such reforms as anti-Catholicism, temperance, socialism, and anti-slavery provide a backdrop to Melville's venturesome pondering of moral paradoxes and social conflict. In *Redburn* Melville brings artistry to the dark-reform mode, as the temperance-loving, nonsmoking protagonist becomes exposed to corrupt forces that create an Americanized version of the tale of initiation. In *White-Jacket* several popular reforms (naval reform, temperance, opposition to war) serve as a pretext for explorations into man's savagery and society's unfairness. Given these experimental reapplications of the benign-subversive mode, it is small wonder that more frequently than any other major antebellum author Melville was surrounded by a controversy similar to that provoked by the most notorious popular reformers.

The controversy began with Melville's first two novels. Like *The Scarlet Letter,* each of Melville's early novels was praised by some as pious and pleasant but lambasted by others as immoral or sacrilegious. Reviewers could not decide on whether Melville was a conventional author exposing vice or a subversive one reveling in it. There was much justification for the reviewers' puzzlement, for at several key moments in *Typee* and *Omoo* Melville follows in the popular immoral-reform tradition of manifesting undeniable fascination with the tabooed topics he pretends to denounce. Indeed, the very first chapter of *Typee* shows Melville writing much like a typical immoral reformer, albeit a rather whimsically detached one. In order to underscore his thesis about the ineffectuality of missionary work in the Marquesas Islands, he tells "a somewhat amusing incident" of a missionary who, hoping that female influence would further his religious efforts, brought to the islands his fair wife, who to her dismay soon was stripped of her clothes by curious natives trying to determine her sex. "The gentle dame was not sufficiently evangelised to endure this," Melville explains, so she and her husband abandon their missionary work.[6] Even more characteristic of the popular immoral-reform mode is the account later in Chapter 1 of the Marquesan girls greeting the ship. After a page of titillating description of the "half-naked" girls with "inexpressibly graceful figures" dancing about the ship with "abandoned voluptuousness," Melville describes the orgiastic scene in typical immoral-reform fashion:

> Our ship was now wholly given up to every species of riot and debauchery. Not the feeblest barrier was interposed between the unholy passions of the crew and their unlimited gratification. The grossest licentiousness and the most shameful inebriety prevailed, with occasional and short-lived interruptions, through the whole period of her stay. Alas for the poor savages when exposed to the influence of these polluting examples! Unsophisticated and confiding, they are easily led into every vice, and humanity weeps over the ruin thus remorselessly inflicted upon them by their European civilizers.

As we have seen, Melville was hardly the first American sea novelist to launch such a protest against alleged corruptions of Europeans on the South Sea Islands: this protest had been commonplace in a line of skeptical works that included Nathaniel Ames's *Nautical Reminiscences* (1832) and *An Old Sailor's Yarns* (1835), John H. Amory's *Old Ironside* (1840), Charles W. Denison's *Stories of the Sea* (1844), and George Little's *The American Cruiser* (1846). What distinguishes Melville's protest from the others is its immoral-reform intensity, as Melville pretends to complain righteously of the sailors' licentiousness but in fact seems to be exploiting the reformist idiom to explore unbridled lust. Punitive, reformist rhetoric ("unholy," "most shameful," "humanity weeps") is a convenient shield as Melville ventures into forbidden psychological territory and subverts the sanctimonious pretensions of white civilization. Significantly, *Typee* ends much the way it began—with a titillating immoral-reform scene. In the "Appendix," which exposes the nefarious trade of Hawaiian officials who serve as pimps for depraved native girls, Melville describes "a Polynesian saturnalia" that occurs when licentious sailors are let loose among the prostitutes. "The spectacle of universal broad-day debauchery, which was then exhibited, beggars description," Melville writes, as "Deeds too atrocious to be mentioned were done at noon-day in the open street." *Typee* begins and ends, then, protesting against illicit sex in the same kind of hyperbolic, voyeuristic rhetoric that had characterized immoral reformers from Parson Weems through McDowall and Lippard.

In the main body of the novel, too, we see Melville using the popular device of pretending to reform civilization's evils while in fact plumbing humanity's capacity for savagery, lust, or violence. In addition to the protest against missionaries and against illicit love, other common reforms he utilizes are utopian socialism, peace reform, and temperance, all of which had by 1846 been widely debated in popular novels and newspapers. At one point, sounding much like an Associationist, Melville emphasizes that "our endless catalogue of civilized crimes" is totally absent in the Typee tribe, which as a classless community is blissfully free of the money-grubbing competition that causes crime. Elsewhere, sounding like a peace reformer, he contrasts the pacific outlook of the South Sea natives with "the fiend-like skill we display in the invention of all manner of death-dealing engines, the vindictiveness with which we carry on our wars," which marks civilized man as "the most ferocious animal on the face of the earth." Briefly using a common popular device he would magnify in his later fiction—the ironic or dark-temperance image—he draws a sketch of the corrupted King Mehevi, who "although a member of the Hawaiian Temperance Society, is a most inveterate dram drinker."

Typee is notable for the sheer variety of its reform voices, from antiprostitution to temperance. In its heterogeneity, it was more broadly inclusive of variegated reform attitudes than any American novel written to that date. This very breadth shows that Melville, like Whitman during his apprentice period, is assuming a variety of popular reform poses without taking seriously their ideological content. More precisely, his contemporary culture offered him various reforms that had already been largely stripped of earnest didacticism, leaving him free to extract from the popular reforms their ironic, subversive force while sidestepping commitment to their political programs. On close inspection, we can already see Melvillian ambiguities emerging from their popular shells. His portraits of oxymoronic characters (the intemperate temperance man, the depraved Christian, the peace-loving cannibal, and so forth) are exercises in popular irony that later would blossom in such mixed characters as the "grand, ungodly, god-like" Ahab and the satanic-Christlike confidence man. In a more general sense, the Typee tribe itself is a kind of immoral-reform society whose interior contradictions, mirroring similar contradictions within American reform societies, threaten all moral standards and raise the specter of relativism. Like Melville's America, the tribe has rigorous codes of decorum and taboos against improprieties; but these codes and taboos are permeated with irony. None of the tribesmen raises an eyebrow when Tommo swims about with naked "water nymphs" who playfully poke and fondle him; but when he asks Kory-Kory for the seemingly innocent pleasure of paddling in a canoe with Fayaway, the "proposition completely horrified Kory-Kory's notion of propriety . . . as something too horrible to be thought of." It is considered proper for bereaved women to leap about "in a state of utter nudity" at funeral ceremonies; but women are said to compromise their "feminine delicacy" when they stray near the Ti, a kind of bachelors' club where the men chat and smoke. Most ironic of all, among the Typees polygamy is the basis of conjugal fidelity and decency. Since Typee women have at least two husbands, none want other men, and "[a] baneful promiscuous intercourse of the sexes is hereby avoided." In all these instances, Melville exposes moral standards as relative rather than absolute by stressing the ironically rigorous moral codes of the Typees, codes whose combined earnestness and immorality differs in substance but not in spirit from similar codes in Melville's America.

Despite the ironic implications of *Typee*, Melville was sufficiently adept in the benign-subversive mode to please many readers. The book sold well and was generally praised as "readable," "pleasant," "entertaining." *Omoo*, though also widely praised, got a more ambivalent response, seemingly because Melville gave greater weight to the gloomy aspects of the dark-reform mode he had cautiously disguised or underplayed in *Typee*. Melville's darker emphasis is apparent from his preface, in which he explains his satire on missionaries as follows: "Nothing but an earnest desire for truth and good has led him to touch upon this subject at all. And if he refrains from offering hints as to the best mode of remedying the evils that are pointed out, it is only because he thinks, that after being made acquainted with the facts, others are better qualified to do so."[7] Here Melville follows the lead of many popular reformers who were more intrigued by the ugly wages of vice than by possible cures. Indeed, *Omoo* does contain more extensive (though less varied and subtle) reform devices than does *Typee*. In addition to his continued protest against missionaries, he makes use of subversive themes relating to two very popular reforms, anti-Catholicism and temperance. A semipornographic note is struck in Melville's portrayal of three wine-bibbing, womanizing Roman Catholic priests on Tahiti whose professed chastity is suspect because of the devoted attention lavished on them by their "set of trim little native handmaidens."

This anti-Catholic theme, however, is only part of a larger pattern, reflective of the immoral-reform sensibility, of exposing both oppressive authority figures and oppressed sailors lost in drunken revelry. We saw that by the mid-1840s popular temperance writings tilted so far toward the sensational that they often explored the irrationalism and perversity associated with drunkenness, saying little about proposed remedies. Much of the dark energy of *Omoo* springs from Melville's adoption of such sensational temperance devices. The narrator's very first action is to get deliriously drunk on Peruvian Pisco given to him by the captain of the *Julia*, while the ship's mate, John Jermin, has "but one failing"—a devotion to "strong drink" that makes him obstreperous and punchy. Nearly every scene that takes place on Tahiti contains some reference to excessive drinking: the sailors get tipsy on the brandy of an Irish priest; Captain Guy, Jermin, and the British consul get drunk together; and the shrewish liquor dealer "Old Mother Tot," catching the consul in his cups, shrieks scornfully at him for secretly drinking after having persecuted her for selling rum. Throughout the novel, Melville sustains the pretense of opposing excessive drinking but still devotes most attention to the distorted perceptions and violence resulting from alcohol.

Despite the generally favorable response to his first two novels, some reviewers charged Melville with secret sympathy for the very vices he pretended to expose. Indeed, in some circles *Typee* and *Omoo* stirred up a classic immoral-reform controversy typical of antebellum popular culture. The novels prompted a long tirade in the *English Review* against Melville's "laxity of moral feeling" and "absence of religious principle throughout both works."[8] Citing the opening chapter of *Typee,* on the sailors' debauchery when greeted by the island girls, the reviewer notes the moral paradoxes of the scene: "The strange mixture of genuine licentiousness and affected morality which this passage exhibits, is both painful and ludicrous." George Washington Peck in the *American Review* saw Melville as the master of the titillating voyeur style: "He gets up voluptuous pictures, and with cool deliberate art breaks off always at the right point so as without offending decency, he may stimulate curiosity and excite unchaste desire. . . . It seems necessary nowadays for a book to be vendible, that it be venomous, and indeed venereous." But the New York lawyer and writer Jerry Auld quickly came to Melville's defense in the *Mirror,* charging that it was Peck, not Melville, who was licentious: "But if Omoo is free from the guilt of pandering to a depraved taste, so is not the reviewer. Finding a fair chance to disgorge on the public a little of his own filth, in the pleasant disguise of a moralist and conservative, he launches forth as much disgusting loathsomeness and personal blackguardism as could be crammed in . . . his few pages. . . . And yet . . . this affected jumble of smutty morality and personal abuse finds favor in an austere paper famous for stern conservatism."

We instantly recognize in this debate over Melville's early works the same internecine mudslinging that had long surrounded American immoral reformers. Indeed, what is most intriguing about the debate is its typicality: just as reformers like McDowall and Lippard were branded as immoral by reviewers who themselves were in turn denounced as depraved, so Melville was decried as depraved by a reviewer who himself was called licentious. At the same time, it should be recalled that many other reviewers of these novels took Melville's announced reform purpose at face value, lauding his exposure of corruption. In sum, *Typee* and *Omoo* show Melville cautiously introducing dark, subversive themes under the guise of reformist intent and succeeding in selling this intent to most, but still provoking some significant immoral-reform battles that point to very real complications within his early texts.

In *Mardi* Melville expands greatly upon the dark-temperance mode he had studied in *Omoo* and broadens his ironic reapplications of several other reforms, including socialism, anti-Catholicism, and antislavery. The ubiquity of drinking and smoking scenes in the novel offended reviewers like William Alfred Jones, who objected to the "frequent turning up of the calabashes" in the book; but, even more surely than in *Omoo,* here portraits of revelry provide an inroad toward deeper literary effects. The oxymoronic character of the intemperate temperance man, lifted directly from popular culture, is expanded in the portrait of Donjalolo, the Prince of Juam, one of the first figures the protagonists meet on their island travels. Like John B. Gough and many other backsliding temperance reformers of the 1840s, Donjalolo vacillates between extreme professions of temperance and private bouts with the bottle. In Chapter 84 we see Donjalolo getting totally drunk but in the next we hear him cursing alcohol as a "treacherous, treacherous fiend! full of smiles and daggers."[9] More strongly than ever, Melville is intrigued by the moral paradoxes suggested by the oxymoronic character. He makes a point of stressing that Donjalolo was "famed for his temperance and discretion" but periodically "burst into excesses, a hundred fold more insane than ever. Thus vacillating between virtue and vice; to neither constant, and upbraided by both; his mind, like his person in the glen, was continually passing and repassing between opposite extremes."

Such fascination with the ambiguities surrounding the intemperate temperance character is linked with a growing interest in the mythic, larger-than-life images associated with revelry scenes. We have seen that many reform writers got swept up stylistically in the irrational vices they described: drunkenness, for instance, was regularly called an "ocean," a "whirlpool," and so forth. Throughout *Mardi* we see Melville, for the first time in his fiction, consistently utilizing such images. Note the energetic metaphors (some of them giving a foretaste of the controlling imagery of *Moby-Dick*) in this account of Donjalolo's drunken feast: "The mirth now blew into a gale; like a ship's shrouds in a Typhoon, every tendon vibrated; the breezes of Omi came forth with a rush; the hangings shook; the goblets danced fandangoes; and Donjalolo, clapping his hands, called before him his dancing women." Here and in several other drinking scenes in the novel Melville gleefully throws aside reform pretenses and allows his imagination to revel in the metaphorical excitement of the moment. In this context, it is significant that his philosophical mouthpiece, Babbalanja, toward the end of the book declares that "a wise man can not be made drunk," and praises wine, which he says opens his heart, brings "glorious visions" to his mind, and stimulates his poetic imagination. It would seem that Melville in *Mardi* is stepping beyond the dark-temperance mode toward a poeticizing of the creative powers this mode releases.

Mardi also marks a deepening in Melville's reflections upon debated social realities such as class divisions, Roman Catholicism, and slavery. As in *Typee,* he echoes the popular socialist complaint against economic inequities by picturing extreme class divisions on Media's island, Odo, where the working poor, who live in squalid hovels, slave endlessly to produce goods and capital that are consumed by the idle rich. This is Melville's enactment of the argument, made often in labor writings and city novels of the period, that the frivolous "upper ten" callously lived off the labor of the "lower million." Writing in 1848, the year of world revolutions, Melville sympathetically describes labor activism in Dominora (England) and the ill-fated revolutions in Franko (France). While repeating the common radical protest against social inequities, Melville in the end uses social activism as an alternative to fruitless philosophizing. Babbalanja, noting that "All round us, Want crawls to lairs; and, shivering, dies unrelieved," decides to abandon his quest and aid the indigent. He thus embraces a kind of Christian socialism that is intended to replace institutional Christianity, represented in the novel by the island of Maramma (the Roman Catholic Church), which is pictured as venal, aristocratic, and changeable in its theology. Although, like many popular authors, Melville finds in good deeds and social work some relief for troublesome issues, one issue he cannot fully resolve is slavery. For Melville, as for many commentators from Richard Hildreth through Frederick Douglass, slavery is dangerously subversive of republican ideals and, in a larger sense, of moral certainty. The slave whom Babbalanja interviews in the South of Vivenza (the United States) seems to have lost the "sense of right and wrong," while his unrelieved wretchedness leads Babbalanja to question God's existence: "Oro! Art thou? and does this thing exist? It shakes my little faith." Furthermore, the defense of slavery by Nulli (John C. Calhoun) and others raises again the disturbing possibility of moral relativism. Although Babbalanja pities slaves, he cannot help reflect: "The soil decides the man. . . . The southern tribes have grown up with this thing. . . . Nor are all their serfs such wretches as those we saw."

It might seem unlikely that Melville, who obviously sympathizes with slaves, would dare to express even mild sympathy with the Southern view. The fact is that his literary dabblings in numerous reforms had carried him beyond monistic sympathies to a broader level of vision that opened him up to metaphysical ambivalences. Just as Whitman in his earliest free verse could announce himself as "the poet of slaves, and of the masters of slaves," so Melville in *Mardi,* his first truly "Melvillian" novel, could air many radical views relating to slaves and the poor but at the same time could include arguments for the reactionary side as well. The final effect of immoral reform is a release from unironic moral or political commitment into a fluid world of shifting moral voices and energetic symbols. The rather frenetic, kaleidoscopic texture of *Mardi,* which always drives forward without truly confronting the social questions it raises, is the natural result of a novelist who is now freely riding the reform impulse instead of pretending to advocate any single reform.

Although in *Mardi* Melville redirected the reform impulse toward myth and symbol, it was not until his next novels, *Redburn* and *White-Jacket,* that his reform imagery would come to be consistently invested with post-Calvinist gloom in a way that directly anticipated *Moby-Dick.* We are all familiar with Melville's famous paean in "Hawthorne and His Mosses" to the "great power of blackness" that "derives its force from its appeals to that Calvinistic sense of Innate Depravity and Original Sin, from whose visitations . . . no deeply thinking mind is always and wholly free."[10] It was the dark-reform rhetoric Melville experimented with in *Redburn* and *White-Jacket* that prepared him to make this statement and to apply secularized Calvinist images throughout *Moby-Dick.* Moreover, this praise of the power of blackness was made only after Melville had consciously attempted to write for the popular market. In the middle months of 1849, under great financial pressure and heavy family responsibilities, he produced both novels at a white heat, writing freely, almost automatically, according to what he perceived to be popular taste. He called *Redburn* and *White-Jacket* "two *jobs,* which I have done for money," but qualified this statement by saying that in them "I have not repressed myself much . . . but have spoken pretty much as I feel."[11] His attitude of combined contempt and acceptance might seem strange, particularly in light of the apparently earnest reform themes of *White-Jacket,* which makes a plea for naval reform. But this ambivalence, like Whitman's toward *Franklin Evans,* underscores his detachment from the reforms he pretends to endorse. The texts of *Redburn* and *White-Jacket* suggest that they were indeed "two *jobs*" written for money but at the same time were quite sincere, since they give vent to powerful subversive forces surging upward from popular culture through Melville's unrepressed pen.

Redburn, a study of the initiation of innocence into evil, draws heavily from antebellum popular culture for the terms of this initiation. Wellingborough Redburn has been raised in the safe world of Conventional reform. When he goes to sea and then London he passes into the turbulent world of the Subversive, symbolized by violent images, many of which spring directly from dark-reform literature. Melville makes it clear that

Redburn has been weaned since birth on reform doctrines of the most staid, sober variety. Redburn explains his "scruples about drinking spirits" by saying, "I was a member of a society in my village where my mother lived, called the Juvenile Total Abstinence Association, of which my friend, Tom Legare, was president, secretary, and treasurer, and kept the funds in a little purse that his cousin knit for him. . . . Tom was a very honest treasurer, and never spent the Society's money for peanuts."[12] This grouping of benign, innocent images—"Juvenile," "village," "mother," "little purse," "very honest"—underscores the fact that Redburn has grown up in the prim, quiet world of Conventional reform. Therefore, he at first demurs when a Greenland sailor offers him spirits to cure his seasickness, explaining that he has signed a total abstinence pledge.

Most of Melville's contemporary readers would have been fully aware that such simple devotion to total abstinence was almost surely doomed to failure. It should be kept in mind that by 1849 nearly 80 percent of those who had signed abstinence pledges in 1840 had resumed drinking, so that pledge signing was widely in disrepute. In dark-temperance literature of the late 1840s and early 1850s alcohol was increasingly portrayed as an overwhelming force resulting in terrible perversity, a kind of updated version of the Calvinist God, driving humanity inexorably to earthly hells. Such dark-temperance images are scattered throughout *Redburn*. Ominously, when Redburn first boards his ship he sees several sailors "very drunk," another insensible, and two more gone below to sleep off "the fumes of their drink." The first token of Redburn's descent into evil is his breaking of the temperance pledge. When he accepts the drink for his illness, he guiltily wishes "that when I signed the pledge of abstinence, I had not taken care to insert a little clause, allowing me to drink spirits in case of sea-sickness." But break the pledge he does, and, as Melville's readers could have predicted, the first sip has dark consequences. As Redburn himself says, violating the pledge "insidiously opened the way to subsequent breaches of it, which . . . carried no apology with them." He has a similar experience with smoking, at first refusing a cigar because he was a member of an antismoking society but then joining the rollicking sailors in their cigar puffing.

Just as many popular novelists in the late 1840s were dramatizing the grim results of vice, so Melville works his way toward ambiguity and secularized Calvinism through the dark-reform mode. *Redburn* possesses a certain depth and richness absent from most popular novels precisely because Melville remains in neither the prim Conventional realm (as did most sentimental-domestic novelists) nor the savage Subversive realm (as did many dark-reform writers) but instead mixes the two. After his first sip of alcohol, Redburn is prepared to associate with drunken sailors, to explore the London slums, to accompany Harry Bolton into a lavish den of vice—in other words, he is plunged into the world of dark-temperance and city-mysteries novels. But Redburn never gives himself up to bestiality or perversity, as do the typical protagonists of dark-reform works. Instead, he remains a sometimes bewildered but usually sensitive and sympathetic recorder of dark-reform horrors. Accordingly, Melville is able to treat these horrors with greater detachment, with more attention to symbolic and psychological implications, than had most popular writers.

For the first time in his career, Melville in *Redburn* extensively applied such Calvinist doctrines as hell, predestination, and total depravity to secular events. It should be noted that such post-Calvinist imagery, though common in dark-reform literature since the 1830s, had particularly wide currency in the 1848–50 period, when a multitude of racy exposé-novels by George Foster, Ned Buntline, Joseph Holt Ingraham, and others exploded on the scene. Nothing was more common in exposé-novels than the projection of Calvinist imagery on social iniquities; this was particularly true of exposés dealing with Melville's New York, where the grimy Five Points area was often described as a "hell," prostitutes as "demons," alcohol and gambling as "all-determining fate," criminals as emblems of "total depravity," and so on. Since he was consciously writing for the mass market, Melville knew he had to fill *Redburn* with diverting dark-temperance and city-mysteries images. The novel contains a good amount of sheer sensationalism that bears obvious traces of graphic dark-reform literature of the crassest variety, such as the account of a sailor who leaps overboard while suffering from delirium tremens or the improbable description of another sailor who is burned alive in flames produced by the internal spontaneous combustion of cheap liquor he has drunk. However, even such meretricious moments are significant, for Melville exploits such horrific occurrences as convenient exercises in post-Calvinist image making. For instance, of the spontaneous combustion scene Redburn declares: "I had almost thought the burning body was a premonition of the hell of the Calvinists, and that [the burned sailor's] earthly end was a foretaste of his eternal condemnation." Elsewhere, he emphasizes that all efforts by temperance societies or tract writers to reform alcoholic sailors are vain, since the sailors are virtually predestined to remain addicted to their vice.

While dark temperance provides an opportunity for post-Calvinist writing, the popular city-mysteries mode offers an avenue to the kind of woeful wisdom that would become central in Melville's major novels. Redburn's shattering recognition of man's inhumanity comes when he realizes the indifference to the poor among London aristocrats. The whole London sequence in *Redburn*—with its picture of squalid slums, frivolous rich people, and huge dens of sin—seems heavily indebted to popular urban-exposé fiction. It is filled with typical urban Gothic images: rich people who ignore the poor are "like people sitting up with a corpse, and making merry in the house of the dead"; a cripple on the street carries a symbolic sign of a "mangled and bloody" man whirled about by the "machinery of some factory"; Redburn exclaims that criminals should be burned out of their haunts "with sulphur and brimstone . . . like vermin"; everywhere, "want and woe staggered arm in arm along these miserable streets." All this misery leads Redburn to question God: "Ah! what are our creeds, and how do we hope to be saved?" The huge Aladdin's Palace where Harry Bolton takes Redburn is a labyrinthine, disorienting structure with cavernous underground vaults and ornate frescoed halls much like the dens of vice that abound in city-mysteries novels. Melville more than once called *Redburn* "trash," perhaps because he knew just how derivative of popular reform modes it was. Still, the novel must be recognized as Melville's plunge into the seamy world of dark reform (in contrast to the allegorical flights of *Mardi*) that exposed him to subversive forces of popular culture at a time he was trying to write for the masses.

Melville was less dismissive of *White-Jacket* than of *Redburn,* probably because his manipulation of dark reform at last seems to be leading him toward more original subversive generalizations. One element of Melville's originality in *White-Jacket* consists in his transference of dark city-mysteries imagery to nautical characters and settings, as well as his pressing beyond dark reform toward truly ambiguous pronouncements. In a passage in *White-Jacket* that directly recalls the half-buried, multitiered dens of sin in city-mysteries novels, Melville writes that the man-of-war "resembles a three-story house in a suspicious part of the town, with a basement of infinite depth, and ugly-looking fellows gazing out at the windows."[13] The city-mysteries comparison of modern cities to the biblical Sodom and Gomorrah is redirected by Melville, who writes: "The sins for which the cities of the plain were overthrown still linger in some of these wooden-walled Gomorrahs of the deep," and "The sea is the true Tophet and bottomless pit of many workers of iniquity." By fusing city-mysteries and post-Calvinist imagery with nautical scenes and characters, Melville is creating an absorption of the Subversive into the oceanic that anticipates the explosive symbolization of sea, ships, and whales in *Moby-Dick.*

In the process of transmuting popular imagery into the literary symbol, Melville continues his assimilation of reforms—here, temperance and naval reform. *White-Jacket* was favorably noticed by a temperance journal, the Honolulu *Friend,* while several other periodicals praised its exposure of injustices against sailors, showing that it was read in its own day as a straightforward reform novel. But, despite the undeniable earnestness of Melville's appeals for justice, reform here is principally exploited for its dark or subversive implications. Alcohol is again described in vivid post-Calvinist imagery, as the sailor who leaves the navy is predestined to return, "driven back to the spirit-tub and gun-deck by his old hereditary foe, the ever-devilish god of grog." Such protemperance touches, however, are fairly rare in the novel, which shows Melville moving toward a freer treatment of alcohol and its devotees. He paints notably sympathetic portraits of two heavy drinkers, the gruff, likable Mad Jack and a wry "old toper of a top-man" who, in answer to White-Jacket's appeal that he give up the bottle, replies he is too much "a good Christian" to give up drinking, because he loves his "enemy too much to drop his acquaintance." Melville is turning evangelical temperance against itself, as he does differently in *Moby-Dick* when he has Ishmael hop into bed with Queequeg with the pious rationalization: "Better sleep with a sober cannibal than a drunken Christian."[14] In short, Melville is now beginning to toy objectively with protemperance and antitemperance to create literary irony.

But it is not temperance but naval reform that occupies Melville's main attention in *White-Jacket*. Naval reform had been endorsed vigorously in several dark-reform works Melville is known to have read, most notably William McNally's brash exposé, *Evils and Abuses in the Naval and Merchant Service, Exposed* (1839). McNally's was very much a typical subversive reform work, since it combined vitriolic protest against maltreatment of sailors with some larger generalizations about the relativity of religions and moral codes. Several McNally passages seem to anticipate Melville: the portraits of extreme hardship at sea in *White-Jacket* are presaged by McNally's complaint that "a seaman may be flogged, starved, worked like a slave, imprisoned, beat, kicked and abused, at the mere whim of the master";[15] McNally portrays an amoral master-at-arms who not only behaves like the wicked Claggart in *Billy Budd* but even has the same nickname ("Jimmy Leggs") as Melville's master-at-arms; the famous description of the *Pequod* crew in *Moby-Dick* as an Anacharsis Cloots congregation of all races is anticipated by McNally's description of a crew, tyrannized over by a despotic captain, that "appeared like a general congress, to which every nation had sent a representative"; McNally describes one ship captain who strangely shifts from kindness to cruelty, rather like Melville's changeable Captain Riga in *Redburn*; McNally's contemplation of naval injustices occasionally leads him to cast quite cynical aspersions upon the United States government and mainstream Christianity, as Melville does in *White-Jacket*. As intriguing as such possible lines of influence are, they are actually less important than the fact that McNally's and Melville's works are both manifestations of the dark-reform style. The main difference is that McNally haphazardly strikes upon subversive themes and images that Melville treats with self-consciousness and intentionality.

McNally's reformist anger leads him to fabricate mythic metaphors—e.g., he once compares maltreated sailors to pursued "whales" wounded by "land-sharks" on shore and "thrashers" and "sword-fish" at sea—but he does not allow the imagination to revel in its own poetic subversiveness, to let symbols take on an independent life, as does Melville in his best moments.

To be sure, this symbolic process, which Melville had begun to explore in *Mardi,* would not be given full rein until he wrote *Moby-Dick.* But *Redburn* and *White-Jacket* were crucial transitional works. One reason that *Mardi,* for all its profundities, seems factitious and overliterary next to *Moby-Dick* is that its symbolic devices spring primarily from elite sources: from Plato, Spenser, Oriental scriptures, German romances, Coleridge, and so forth. In *Moby-Dick* Melville would again borrow heavily from classic literature but would breathe into classic models the distinct Subversive spirit of American popular culture, particularly the feisty spirit of dark reform that he had given vent to in *White-Jacket.*

The dark-reform mode, in fact, became Melville's primary means of moving from the rather postured, cerebral subversiveness of *Mardi* to the more energetic, salty artistry of *Moby-Dick.* In *White-Jacket* he intentionally dives into the mire of nineteenth-century social vice and tries to shed the somewhat cumbersome coat of classic literary influence. Thus, he includes in the novel a pointedly satirical portrait of a precious, intellectual clergy-man who studied philosophy and literature but "never, in the remotest manner, attacked the every-day vices of the nineteenth century" such as "drunkenness, fighting, flogging, and oppression."[16] Throughout the novel Melville makes it clear that he himself has cast aside his intellectual posture and is grappling with these grimy vices. Many American reformers before him had called themselves moral surgeons whose deep probings into festering vice were disagreeable but necessary. Melville uses an analogous rationalization in *White-Jacket* as he prepares us for a grisly account of a bloody flogging scene: "Some ignorant people will refrain from per-manently removing the cause of a deadly malaria, for fear of the temporary spread of its offensiveness. Let us not be of such. The more repugnant and repelling, the greater the evil. Leaving our women and children behind, let us freely enter this Golgotha."

Also, as in much dark-reform literature, the vividly described vice is so distant from American and Christian ideals that recording its horrors leads to larger subversive generalizations. While Melville may have undertaken *White-Jacket* with the righteous aim of exposing certain vices, he ended by aiming sharp barbs at revered political and religious conventions. His *vehicle* was naval reform but his *tenor* came to be the ironies discovered in the process of dark-reform writing. McNally had moved from the description of horrors at sea to brief subversive outcries such as "Oh man! oh savage mockery of his holy name!" or "[Religion] is a trade, which is followed from interest more than inclination, where tens of thousands preach to tens of thousands what they do not practice."[17] Melville takes this dark-reform tendency several steps further toward literary ambiguity. As mentioned, he wages his naval reform war in mythic city-mysteries images that create a broadening of symbol. At the same time, he goes beyond the fragmentary subversive generalizations in McNally and others to more consistently acerbic comments on the state, religion, and human nature. Sea horrors in *White-Jacket* reveal to Melville a chasm between noble American ideals and villainous American practice, between the gentle precepts of Christianity and the iniquities of many of its adherents. Calling flogging "utterly repugnant to the spirit of our democratic institutions," he stresses that for the sailor "our Revolution was in vain; to him our Declaration of Independence is a lie."[18] And the man-of-war itself symbolizes "much that is tyrannical and repelling in human nature," as everything connected with war is "utterly foolish, unchristian, barbarous, brutal." In such passages, Melville sounds like many dark reformers who were driven by social vices toward cynicism. Melville, however, is carried by such cynical reflection toward a recognition of dark outside forces that would assume titanic magnitude in *Moby-Dick.* For instance, he indicts war in ironic terms typical of many peace reformers, arguing that throughout history the most fiendish barbarities have been performed by persons claiming to be intensely religious. But he moves from this standard dark-reform view to a new revelation of moral relativism and implacable fate: "[A]ll events are mixed in a fusion indistinguishable. What we call Fate is even, heartless, and impartial . . . We may fret, fume, and fight; but the thing called Fate everlastingly sustains an armed neutrality." Likewise, he presses the mythic metaphors of popular reformers to new extremes, as contemplation of terrors aboard a man-of-war leads him often to large statements about "our man-of-war world" and even to an affirmation of ambiguity: "I love an indefinite, obscure background—a vast, heaving, rolling, mysterious rear!"

Although Melville in *White-Jacket* made original permutations of the dark-reform mode, these permutations were too subtle to be noticed by most contemporary reviewers, who accepted the novel as a seamy reform work quite typical of shocking exposés of the day. Simms was not alone in his stated opinion that Melville's role was that of the reformer. George Ripley wrote that Melville had "performed an excellent service in revealing . . . the indescribable abominations of naval life, reeking with the rankest corruption, cruelty, and blood."[19] The *Biblical Repository* admired Melville's "keen wit, pointed irony, sarcastic humor, biting invective, and fearless exposure of wrong." To be sure, a couple of reviewers charged Melville with wallowing in the mud he pretended to be cleaning up: a London paper complained of "disgusting details" and "horrible" wit in the novel, while a Boston one cast doubt upon "the soundness and knowledge of such a wholesale reformer." But even such criticism was itself quite typical in a day when dark-reform works were regularly called immoral. Moreover, most reviewers admired the aggressiveness with which Melville undertook to expose vice. Significantly, the most common metaphor surrounding dark reform—tearing away veils—was applied to the novel in a favorable review in *Saroni's Musical Times,* which declared that Melville has "lifted the veil which covers the . . . real 'life below stairs,' " as he remorselessly "tears the veil of romance which has been cast over the 'world in a man-of-war.' "

How seriously did Melville take the popular reforms he used so widely in his early novels? Just how deeply rooted was Melville's animus against flogging, against drinking, against missionaries, Roman Catholicism, slavery, war, class divisions, and so forth? His early novels prove that he was fascinated by the rhetoric and moral implications of popular reforms but viewed their ideological content with feelings that ranged from wry detachment to outright disgust. But this detachment, which made intriguing moral issues readily transferable to problematic fiction, was itself largely a product of the times. We have seen that by the 1840s American popular culture had freed several reforms of fixed referents and made them available for literary manipulation. This was particularly true in New York, where during the early 1840s reform lecturers absorbed the boisterous, rowdy spirit of the city's working classes and where popular publishers began to capitalize on the purely sensational possibilities of the dark-reform style. Morality and immorality became manufacturable, fluid, theatrical—and thus exploitable for professional authors like Whitman and Melville. It would be Melville's contribution to move from early manipulation of various reforms through a full symbolic projection of their energy and force (in *Moby-Dick*) to dramatizations, in *Pierre* and *The Confidence-Man,* of the moral fluidity and theatricality they implied.

The Stylization of Reform

Moby-Dick represents the coming of age of the dark-reform style. Poised between the intensely reformist *White-Jacket* and the ambiguous later novels, it shows the reform impulse being at last fully divested of didacticism and treated with self-referentiality. By experimenting with many different subversive reform voices in his early novels, Melville had finally reached a level of literariness whereby reform content was abandoned but reform images and subversive spirit were retained. When the reform impulse was unleashed in purely literary realms, an explosive symbolization resulted. The mythic images of reformers suddenly assumed universal proportions. The reformist instinct to tear veils off social evils became the titanic effort to rip "pasteboard masks" off perceived reality. Classic models like the Bible and Shakespeare became putty in the hands of the all-reforming literary artist. In the end, the dark-reform mode was consumed by its own paradoxes, and the furious quest for truth led to its own destruction.

It should be pointed out that the potential for a broadly imagistic work such as *Moby-Dick* had been intrinsic in America's reform culture since the early 1830s, when strident reformers began widespread experimentation with mythic metaphors—often pre-Melvillian ones pertaining to oceans, ships, whales, and so forth. For instance, in 1831 a contributor to Garrison's *Liberator,* alarmed by the rise of various social vices in America, wrote: "The whale which swallowed up the recreant prophet [Jonah] may be likened to the many monsters which swallow up the aberrant sinner of our own days," except that "the whales of this latter day are much more voracious than that of old; inasmuch as the whale which swallowed up the prophet Jonah cast him forth again after the third day. But in our days, when a hapless mortal once gets within the jaws of the monster, he is lost forever; he is not so fortunate as to be vomited forth on dry land."[20] In the dark-reform imagination, modern "whales" were far deadlier than the biblical one because they were ubiquitous and inescapable. And Melville's whale was deadliest of all because it was detached thoroughly from simple meaning—reformist, biblical, or otherwise. We have seen that dark-reform images had often verged upon assuming a life of their own, so that the tenor (reform of vice) was often threatened by the vehicle (mythic or post-Calvinist image). Melville was especially well positioned to allow this symbolizing process to reach literary fruition. Since in his early novels he had played with diverse reform attitudes, taking little heed of serious reform programs, he was prepared in *Moby-Dick* to explore the literary vehicle separate from the political tenor. He was ready to move beyond his interest in mere reforms to a larger concern with the operations of the dark-reform impulse unleashed by the creative spirit of the new American democracy. In *Moby-Dick* the mad pursuit of deadly "whales" and the ripping away of "veils" are elevated to gargantuan proportions, as standard reform images take on a multidimensional power of their own.

Since *Moby-Dick* can be viewed as the culmination of Melville's early permutations of the dark-reform mode, it is understandable that the novel has far more direct references to popular reform movements than even the most reform-minded of his previous novels. Ironically, however, *Moby-Dick* does not seem reformist at all. *This is because reform imagery has eventually become for Melville a colorful shell, largely devoid of political or didactic content, that can be arranged at will in the overall mosaic of a subversive novel.* Witness, for instance, his playful toying with subversive reform images in the following discussion of "fast fish" (things that are considered personal property merely because they happen to be in one's possession):

> What are the sinews and souls of Russian serfs and Republican slaves but Fast-Fish, whereof possession is the whole of law? What to the rapacious landlord is the widow's last mite but a Fast-Fish? What's yonder undetected villain's marble mansion with a door-plate for a waif; what is that but a Fast-Fish? What is the ruinous discount which Mordecai, the broker, gets from poor Woebegone, the bankrupt, on a loan to keep Woebegone's family from starvation; what is that ruinous discount but a Fast-Fish? What is the Archbishop of Save-soul's income of £100,000 seized from the scant bread and cheese of hundreds of thousands of broken-backed laborers (all sure of heaven without any of Savesoul's help) what is that globular 100,000 but a Fast-Fish?[21]

Here, in rapid succession, Melville brings together typical ironic imagery from antislavery agitation ("Republican slaves"), from property-law reform ("rapacious landlord"), and from socialist and city-mysteries writings ("undetected villain"; the banker cheating a starving family; a rich churchman living off the sweat of underpaid laborers). Melville leaves no doubt he sympathizes with the oppressed against their upper-class oppressors. At the same time, however, he is obviously just as concerned with literary effect as with reform statement. The popular reform images do make their ironic point against various forms of social oppression: but Melville is enjoying the sheer fun of coining new associations for the controlling metaphor of fast fish. In other words, dark-reform imagery retains its subversive impact but at the same time feeds into the purely literary.

This *stylization of reform devices* runs throughout the novel. It appears in Melville's expanded use of the oxymoronic character: he gives an updated sketch of the biblical rich man Dives, who, "a president of a temperance society, . . . only drinks the tepid tears of orphans";[22] he ironically portrays the Quaker captain Bildad as a penny-pinching philanthropist and a squabbling peace advocate; he has Jack Bunger, the captain of the *Samuel Enderby,* boast that he is "a strict total abstinence man" even though he gets drunk on the sly. In contrast to the rather haphazard arrangement of dark-reform images in his earlier novels, in *Moby-Dick* Melville carefully distributes images from city-mysteries fiction, antislavery reform, anti-Catholicism, and temperance literature to drive home the woeful wisdom of his novel. In all cases, Melville retains the ironic force behind dark reform but never allows moral message to gain supremacy over subversive metaphor.

Melville's stylized use of reform is most visible in his extensive reapplications of temperance images in *Moby-Dick*. Melville is now so sensitively attuned to all possible permutations of the dark-temperance mode that he can shift with ease between protemperance and antitemperance stances, giving full moral credence to no single viewpoint and always seeking the stylistic potentialities of whatever stance he assumes. He sounds protemperance in his portrait of the wretched Perth, the blacksmith who had been driven to sea after alcohol had shattered his family and who is now the lonely forger of harpoons for Ahab. In his review of Perth's life in Chapter 112, Melville sounds like a typical dark-temperance writer showing how alcohol can destroy the family circle and lead to suicide. But simply by exaggerating the dark images of temperance authors and leaving out their didacticism, Melville creates a moving picture of a truly wretched man whose dismal fate is metaphorically linked to that of Ahab and the entire *Pequod* crew. Melville tells how Perth had been a churchgoing artisan who lived happily with his young wife and three children until "a desperate burglar slid into his happy home, and robbed them all of everything. And darker yet to tell," Melville continues, "the blacksmith himself did ignorantly conduct this burglar into his family's heart. It was the Bottle Conjuror! Upon the opening of that fatal cork, forth flew the fiend, and shrivelled up his home." "Oh, woe on woe!" Melville laments as he describes the steady demise and death of the whole family as a result of Perth's drinking. The picture of the solitary Perth, "his every woe unreverenced," leads to the comment that death is "the only desireable sequel for a career like this," and death "is but the first salutation to the possibilities of the immense Remote, the Wild, the Watery, the Unshored"—and so Perth commits a kind of suicide by going to sea on the *Pequod.* Perth is left a stolid relic, a man "past scorching" who is well fitted to forge the harpoon that Ahab will baptize in the devil's name and hurl at the white whale. In the story of Perth, Melville is showing how an ostensibly moralistic mode (the temperance narrative) in fact carries the seeds of a cynical portrait of human despair. The Perth episode shows that the dark-reform mode can be used as an appropriate entrance to gloomy message and mythic imagery. Perth's movement from the shattered family circle to "the Wild, the Watery, the Unshored" parallels Melville's own movement from dark reform to oceanic symbolism, just as Perth's forging of Ahab's harpoon parallels Melville's use of the dark-reform stylistic "harpoons" to hurl at the truth that increasingly eludes him.

Just as the Perth incident demonstrates protemperance being converted into a dark episode, so an incident involving the harpooner Queequeg and the mate Stubb shows that the flexible Melville could readily adopt anti-temperance for humorous purposes. Just after he has emerged from his perilous descent into the whale in Chapter 72 ("The Monkey-Rope"), the exhausted Queequeg is handed a drink of ginger and water by Dough-Boy, the steward. The onlooking Stubb, a boisterous advocate of grog, furiously declares, "There is some sneaking Temperance Society movement about this business."[23] When Dough-Boy tells him that the social worker Aunt Charity has sent aboard ginger to enforce temperance among the harpoon-ers, Stubb throws the ginger to the waves and ensures that Queequeg benefits from the captain's command: "grog for the harpooner on a whale."

The fact is that Melville is now interested in temperance reform only as it can provide ironic or dark images for subversive fiction. In the novel, dark-temperance imagery becomes one locus of rebellion or ambiguity that stands opposed to the Conventional forces Melville is trying to subvert. In the course of the novel the temperate characters (Bulkington, Aunt Charity, Starbuck, Dough-Boy) prove powerless before the wickedly uproarious spirit-quaffing ones (the *Grampus* crew, Ahab, most of the *Pequod* crew). Melville neatly dramatizes this conflict and its outcome early in the novel, when Ishmael witnesses the *Grampus* crew, just home from a three years' voyage, rushing straight into the Spouter-Inn's bar (the entrance to which is a huge whale's jaw) and getting drunk on drinks poured by the bartender Jonah, while the temperate Bulkington watches aloof and then disappears. This symbolic scene shows Melville extensively using dark-temperance images as a means of moving toward subversive fiction. Just as popular reformers had described alcohol variously as an all-devouring "whale" or all-consuming "poison," so Melville describes the *Grampus* crew entering through "jaws of swift destruction" to be served "deliriums and death" by a prophetically named bartender. Just as the reformers had emphasized the illusoriness of alcohol's pleasures, so Melville writes: "Abominable are the tumblers into which he pours his poison. Though true cylinders without— within, the villainous green goggling glasses deceitfully tapered downwards to a cheating bottom." Just as dark-temperance literature had stressed the orgiastic extremes of inebriation rather than the remedies for it, so Melville suggests the relative impotence of Bulkington in the face of his shipmates' obstreperous carousing, which Bulkington witnesses with a "sober face" before he slips away unnoticed.

The disappearance of Bulkington here, presaging his later disappear-ance from the novel, epitomizes the victory of dark temperance, with its boisterous irrationalism and its mythic imagery, over the Conventional.

This imagistic victory is repeated throughout the novel, as when Ahab toasts his demonic crew and mates on the quarterdeck (Chapter 36) or when the harpooners and sailors hold a midnight orgy in the forecastle (Chapter 40). Indeed, Ishmael experiences a kind of conversion to the Subversive during the drunken orgy scene, as the formerly blithe narrator begins Chapter 41 by declaring that "my shouts had gone up with the rest; my oath had been welded with theirs. . . . Ahab's quenchless feud seemed mine." Given the number of dark-temperance images in the novel, it is possible to read the Spouter-Inn barroom scene as another preparatory literary exercise: just as the bartender pours poisonous drinks to rambunctious sailors who are inside symbolic whale's jaws, so in a sense the dark-temperance mode "pours" *Moby-Dick* by providing Melville with a variety of subversive images.

It would be easy enough to run through the entire novel and suggest specific reform influences for certain scenes. For instance, the city-mysteries mode enhances the gloom of Ishmael's opening entrance to New Bedford, as he stumbles over an ash box and asks, "Are these ashes from that destroyed city, Gomorrah?" Ishmael's ironic query "Who aint a slave?" would seem to owe much to the attitude of the fiery New York radical Mike Walsh, who in the 1840s famously universalized the notion of slavery by emphasizing that *both* Northern wage slaves and Southern chattel slaves were equally exploited. Sensational anti-Catholic imagery sometimes adds color or irreverence, as when Ishmael asks why an "unsophisticated Protestant of the Middle American States" is terrified by the mention of "a White Friar or a White Nun," or when the account of the mincer who wears the whale's cassock (i.e., penis skin) leads to the bawdy pun: "what a candidate for an archbishoprick, what a lad for a Pope were this mincer!"

Such individual sources, however, are less important than the overall dark-reform *écriture* that governs the novel. Scholars have long sought historical prototypes for several scenes and characters, but the results have often proved contradictory. Ahab, for instance, has been variously associated with the radical abolitionist William Lloyd Garrison, with Garrison's archopponent John C. Calhoun, and with the moderate politician Daniel Webster! Such historical source study can be delimiting, for the fact is that *Moby-Dick* moves beyond slavery or antislavery, protemperance or antitemperance—in short, beyond programmatic reform—to a literary realm in which subversive reform *energy* and *rhetoric,* rather than reform *message,* becomes the literary artist's central concern. In this context, a passage in Father Mapple's sermon can be taken as a gloss on Melville's attitude toward the dark-reform style. Toward the end of his sermon Father Mapple declares: "Woe to him who seeks to pour oil upon the waters when God has brewed them into a gale! Woe to him who seeks to please rather than to appal!" We have seen that from the 1830s onward, there had been a linguistic split between Conventional reformers (mainly Unitarians and rationalists), whose style was determinedly staid, and Subversive ones (particularly evangelicals and other so-called ultraists), who tried through stylistic violence to combat and overwhelm the irrationalism and ugliness of various social iniquities. Often Conventional reformers would directly lament the linguistic violence of their opponents, as when Lydia Maria Child wished to found a temperate antislavery paper as an antidote to "the wild spirit of ultraism" represented by Garrisonian abolitionists, whose rhetoric she found "irrational, unphilosophic, impracticable, mischievous." She was praised in her efforts toward Conventional antislavery by a friend who wrote: "You are just the editor we want. We need oil upon the waves" since "we have had too much of fighting."[24] In contrast, the Subversive reformers—from McDowall through Garrison to Mike Walsh and George Lippard—repeatedly denounced what they labeled "puny" or "effeminate" reformers whom they regarded as too timid to clench vice strongly and reproduce all its lurid horrors on the page. Father Mapple's real-life prototype, Father Taylor, was himself a roughneck reformer reportedly more at home jousting verbally with barroom drunkards than sermonizing to polite congregations. When Melville has Mapple lambaste those who would "pour oil upon the waters" he is aligning himself with the Subversive tradition.

The many explicit reform devices in *Moby-Dick,* therefore, are pushed toward literariness by Melville's devotion to the Subversive style, which formed a rhetorical sub-basis connecting *all* dark-reform writings. As a result, some of his central images seem titanic versions of dark-reform images. While it is misleading to equate Ahab either with the abolitionist Garrison or with the proslavery leader Calhoun, it is certainly possible to connect him with the suprapolitical, powerfully human volatility that linked Garrison, Calhoun, and many other clamorous reform orators as well. When Ahab is described paradoxically as an "ungodly, god-like man" or a "swearing good man," it may be useful to know that Daniel Webster had been famously satirized by one popular exposé novelist as "Gabriel Godlike," who seems noble but is in fact evil; but it is even more important to understand Ahab as the era's most fully developed oxymoronic character, attaining a kind of universality from the magnitude of the contrary impulses he embodies. This amplification of reform devices is perhaps best seen in Melville's use of mythic images. We saw that in popular reform literature, mythic imagery increasingly took on an independent life. The following metaphors from an 1847 New York exposé are typical:

The dark swelling tempest which rages over the wildest sea, is not more dissimilar from the tranquil ocean, when not a wave ripples, nor a breath fans the sails, than is the community of men, when surveyed at different times, and in varying aspects. All seems bright, and good, and glorious, to the superficial looker on, while to the experienced inquirer, and the laborious collector of facts, there is a dark understratum of guilt, and a wide expanse of material that is decayed, corrupt, offensive, and revolting . . . [as in the case of prostitutes, where] extremes meet in the same individual woman. Outward splendor covers internal sorrow. Flagrant vice walks forth in public places under the mantle and veil of virtue . . . [Apparently healthy womanhood] is but a mere vulgar compound of paint and silk and pasteboard, an image artificially made up.[25]

Like numerous dark-reform passages, this one verges on the literary because its supposed message (the lamentable rise of prostitution) is virtually smothered by images of the ocean, the swelling tempest, hidden corruption, cheating appearances, cosmetics, pasteboard coverings, and so forth. We should not be surprised that many of these images sound pre-Melvillian, for Melville in his early works had proved himself a uniquely flexible experimenter with dark-reform stances, preparing himself for the truly mythic subversiveness of *Moby-Dick*. The ungodly, godlike Ahab pursuing the demonic, divine white whale figuratively enacts the highly charged ironies of antebellum reform culture, in which pursuit of moral truth was often waged in a kind of divine madness, a righteous unrighteousness.

Ultimately, Melville in *Moby-Dick* is a gigantic dark reformer, towering above all reform programs but driven by the powerful reform impulse. If other reformers "lifted the veil" off social corruption or lamented the "pasteboard" artificiality of certain people, Melville has Ahab describe all visible objects as "pasteboard masks" and declare that man's highest goal is to "strike through the mask."[26] In this sense, the object of Ahab's quest is the ultimate dark-reform mythic image, which now has been granted a full independent life and an alluringly malevolent moral will of its own. The white whale brings together all the "whales" swimming in all the turbulent "oceans" described by the image-fashioning ultraists. If reformers had regularly seen surrounding society as a "whited sepulchre" hiding submerged evil, so the white whale is invested with the most apparently benign but most ultimately subversive qualities, suggesting to Ishmael that "all deified Nature absolutely paints like the harlot, whose allurements cover nothing but the charnel-house within." If the popular reformers liberally used post-Calvinist imagery, Melville secularly enacts the Calvinist God itself, as the whole novel culminates in the destruction of Ahab and his crew by the "predestinating head" of Moby-Dick, which is alive with "[r]etribution, swift vengeance, eternal malice." In the end, the liberated reform *vehicle,* released totally into mythic ambiguity, turns upon the equally liberated moral *tenor,* seeking desperately for connection with moral truth but lost hopelessly in its own paradoxes.

It is perhaps understandable that the subtitle of Melville's next novel was *The Ambiguities.* Melville's private comments on *Pierre; or, The Ambiguities* suggest that he believed the novel was broadly representative of American popular culture. Melville wrote his publisher, Richard Bentley, that the novel "was very much more calculated for popularity than anything you have yet published of mine."[27] At about the same time, his friend Sarah Morewood commented: "I think [Melville] cares very little as to what others may think of him or his books so long as they sell well."[28] It may seem odd that a novel designed for popularity would fail abysmally. *Pierre* had poor sales and received generally harsh reviews, including more than one charge that Melville had gone insane. How do we explain the negative reception given to a novel evidently written for the masses? The truth is that *Pierre* was *too* broadly representative of antebellum popular culture—with all its crippling moral paradoxes—to have wide appeal. In this paradigmatic novel are embodied the profound dualisms of American popular culture. The first half of the novel portrays the Conventional world of pastoralism, domesticity, the angelic exemplar, hopeful religion, military heroism, and innocence. The second half of the novel plunges us into the Subversive world of dark city mysteries, shattered homes, illicit love, social and philosophical radicalism, and bloody crime. Since both sections of the novel feature themes and characters that had proved extremely popular with American readers, we understand why Melville expected good sales. Perhaps he wanted to attract both those who loved Conventional novels like *The Wide, Wide World* (to Sophia Hawthorne he promised *Pierre* would be "a rural bowl of milk") and those who consumed Subversive exposés like *The Quaker City* (to Bentley he called the book "a regular romance, with a mysterious plot to it, and stirring passions at work").[29] Whatever his motivations, the fact is that by fusing the two realms he produced a highly explosive mixture that gave little pleasure to either class of readers. *Pierre* contained an unsettling truth about antebellum moral culture: the Conventional itself carried the seeds of the Subversive. In elaborating this theme, Melville dramatized a central paradox that had surrounded immoral reformers from McDowall through Foster: the strict insistence on moral rectitude ironically leads to immorality and violence.

From his contemporary popular culture Melville could learn firsthand that it is precisely when virtuous feelings become exaggerated and arouse reformist rage that they threaten to abolish the very premises of virtue and carry the writer into the Subversive realm. We should notice that most of the wrongdoing in *Pierre* results from two seemingly Conventional virtues: a love for sisters and a devotion to the ideal of chastity. Pierre, who early in the novel had declared: "It must be a glorious thing to engage in a mortal quarrel on a sweet sister's behalf!,"[30] has an almost brotherly affection for his mother and then sacrifices everything for his long-lost sister Isabel, whom he pities because she is the orphaned product of his father's illicit relationship with a French woman. In the end, devotion to a sister and to chastity breeds murder, as Lucy Tartan's brother leads the way in wreaking revenge on Pierre, his sister's ruiner. This ironic coupling of virtue and crime had governed much popular immoral-reform writing. Particularly relevant in this regard is Lippard's *The Quaker City*, which had woven a highly sensational plot around the thesis that sadistic murder was fully justifiable if done in the name of preserving a sister's chastity.

The central ambiguity in *Pierre* springs from an issue that had long preoccupied American reformers: how, precisely, is one to respond to illicit love? In a pivotal scene in the novel, Pierre, his mother, and the Rev. Falsgrave debate this issue as it applies in the case of Delly Ulver, the poor orphan girl with an illegitimate child by a seducer who has abandoned her. Mrs. Glendinning brands Delly as a fallen woman not to be pitied and her seducer as "worse than a murderer." She loathes both the man and the woman and never wants to see the child. Pierre is as appalled as his mother by Delly's situation but has a different reaction to it: he pities the wretched girl and wants to get directly involved to alleviate her misery. Pierre asks Falsgrave whether it is Christian to ostracize a fallen woman, but the oily minister temporizes by saying, "Millions of circumstances modify all moral questions."[31] He similarly equivocates when Pierre asks whether, given the Bible's injunction that we honor our father and mother, one should respect a parent known to have been a seducer—Falsgrave calls this matter "another question in morals absolutely incapable of a definite answer, which shall be universally applicable."

Melville is infusing new vigor and intentionality into reform ambiguities. Mrs. Glendinning's response to Delly Ulver (and to Pierre and Isabel when they go off together) is the typical Conventional reaction to immorality: a refusal to face harsh facts or even to think of them. Hers is the antiseptic world of domestic novels, in which ugly social realities are minimized and pure virtue is idealized. In contrast, Pierre takes the ultraist reformer's approach, i.e., that of trying to wash away sin by jumping into the mire and pondering its darkness. The distinction between the two attitudes reappears in the contrasting reaction to the revelation of the checkered past of Pierre's father. Pierre stares fully at his father's vice, which plagues him and drives him to take any action to rectify it. His mother refuses to even look at the portrait of her husband in his rakish youth, and she prudishly turns her back upon Delly, Pierre, and Isabel.

The irony is that both the mother's overprudish avoidance of vice and the son's masochistic wallowing in it are really two sides of the same coin. Both reflect America's neurotic obsession with puritanical virtue, an obsession which Melville shows as breeding human misery and moral relativism. Throughout the novel, pure love and virtuous motives always give rise to illicit love and conflict. Insistence upon chastity leads to immorality. Although Pierre is acting upon a pious motive that would have pleased most Americans—an instinct to protect his orphaned sister and her abandoned friend—he unwittingly sets off a string of gloomy events. Although his mother is devoted to the ideal of sexual purity, she rejects her own son and dies insane in its name. Even Lucy Tartan, the personification of the Conventional, gets sucked into an illicit live-in situation because of her devotion to a pure ideal: fidelity to her betrothed. When taken to an extreme, Melville suggests, the purity of the Conventional fuses with the viciousness of the Subversive, just as in the novel the idyllic village world of Saddle Meadows gives way before the grimy landscape of the big city. All the good American virtues, when exaggerated, nullify each other and strip virtue itself of all meaning. This dark lesson of antebellum culture is verbalized by Pierre, who concludes that "Virtue and Vice are trash!" and who cries in anguish: "If to follow Virtue to her uttermost vista, . . . if by that I take hold on hell, and the uttermost virtue, after all, prove but a betraying pander to the monstrousest vice,—then close in and crush me, ye stony walls, and into one gulf let all things tumble together!"[32] We have seen that Melville's America was full of earnest moralists going to immoral extremes, often in the name of Christianity, to locate, pursue, and extirpate sin. Melville was surrounded by people claiming to be angelic chronometricals but inevitably proving themselves all too horologically human. In *Pierre* Melville was writing the tragedy of his contemporary moral culture.

Pierre was Melville's summation of the immoral-reform paradox, the final sincere probing of his society's ambiguities. In much of the fiction he wrote between *Pierre* and *The Confidence-Man,* Melville seemed intent upon evading or untangling the moral knot he had fastened in *Pierre.* Among other things, this intermediary fiction shows Melville retreating to easily perceived social dualisms ("The Two Temples," "The Paradise of Bachelors. The Tartarus of Maids," "Poor Man's Pudding and Rich Man's Crumbs"); to rapid-fire adventure and "traditional" city-mysteries imagery *(Israel Potter);* and to before-and-after rising or falling sequences that reduced narrative complexity ("Jimmy Rose," "Cock-A-Doodle-Doo!,"

"The Apple-Tree Table," "The Happy Failure"). Instead of fusing the Conventional and the Subversive, as he had in *Pierre,* Melville in most of these works separates them or places them side by side. The result is fiction that shows Melville moving from the problematic realm of mythic symbol and moral ambiguity to the safer level of social irony. If reform issues had earlier led him into thematic quagmires, they now also provided a convenient escape route. He could now play the role of the Subversive reformer exposing the gap between callous aristocrats and wretched factory operatives (in "Paradise . . . Tartarus"), between frigid, wealthy churchgoers and brotherly, indigent theatergoers ("The Two Temples"), between the hypocritical rich and the wretchedly stoical poor ("Rich Man's Crumbs"). Or he could assume the part of the Conventional reformer singing praises to virtuous endurance of poverty with expectations of heavenly reward ("Cock-A-Doodle-Doo!" and "Jimmy Rose").

The two tales of the period that most clearly succeed, "Benito Cereno" and "Bartleby, the Scrivener," are precisely those in which Melville brings together the Subversive and the Conventional to produce enigmatic, imagistic fiction. In "Bartleby" a city-mysteries landscape of towering Wall Street buildings, milling Broadway crowds, and the Tombs provides a bleak symbolic backdrop to the central confrontation between the safe Conventional narrator and the puzzling, passively Subversive copyist. In "Benito Cereno" abolitionist and anti-Catholic imagery darkens the drama of the pious Amasa Delano confronted with the weird situation aboard the *San Dominick.* Although popular reform imagery abounds in these tales, however, it is not directed toward a clear political statement, as it is in dualistic sketches like "The Two Temples" or "Rich Man's Crumbs." Instead, it is pushed once more toward literariness and ambiguity, as potentially explosive social problems—the dehumanizing modern city in "Bartleby" and slave revolts in "Benito Cereno"—are viewed through the eyes of narrators whose shifting perceptions seem Melville's main objects of study.

The fact that Melville's two best stories of the period are dramas of distorted perception, passivity, and inertia makes it clear that the mad pursuit after truth launched in *Moby-Dick* and *Pierre* has now run into a dead end as dreary and blank as Bartleby's walls. The rather frenetic shifting between Subversive and Conventional voices in several stories of this period suggests a fragmentation of vision, a loss of the holistic symbolizing power that in *Moby-Dick* had given direction and force to subversive moral ponderings. The escape route had led to a surface that was as complex as—and even more chaotic than—the moral depths Melville had reached in mid-career. In *The Confidence-Man* Melville heroically forges art from this chaos of the surface. If Ahab was a grand oxymoronic character seeking moral truth, the confidence man is the fragmented modern self engaged in endless moral posturing. Melville's central character is no longer obsessed with tearing away veils or punching through pasteboard masks. Instead, he is himself an impenetrable veil, a constantly shifting mask. And several of the faces he wears are directly related to antebellum reform culture.

Given Melville's penchant for adopting images from popular culture, it is not surprising that in focusing upon a confidence man Melville was exploring a figure that was very much alive in the popular imagination. Scholars such as Johannes Dietrich Bergmann and John D. Seelye have performed the valuable service of unearthing several newspaper articles and popular pamphlets about confidence men that Melville may have used.[33] But there are even larger cultural sources of Melville's cosmic rendering of moral chicanery. Popular reports of confidence men were most often made in a dark-reform style that had transformed the common swindler into a more generalized Subversive force in American society. For instance, the reform-minded journalist George Houston, in an 1849 *New York Herald* article Melville may have read, denied that the imprisoned swindler William Thompson was America's principal confidence man:

> Let him rot, then, in "the Tombs," while the "Confidence Man on a large scale" fattens, in his palace, on the blood and sweat of the green ones of the land! . . . Let him rot in "the Tombs," we say again, while the genuine "Confidence Man" stands one of the Corinthian columns of society—heads the lists of benevolent institutions—sits in the grandest pews of the grandest temple—spreads new snares for new victims—and heaps up fresh fuel for the day of wrath, which will one day follow the mandate of the God of Justice and the poor man! Success, then, to the real "Confidence Man!"—the "Confidence Man" of Wall Street—the "Confidence Man" of the palace up town—the "Confidence Man" who battens and fattens on the plunder coming from the poor man and the man of moderate means! As for the "Confidence Man" of "the Tombs," he is a cheat, a humbug, a delusion, a sham, a mockery! Let him rot![34]

Already, in this dark-reform socialist indictment of the rich, we have a kind of mythic broadening of the definition of the confidence man (applying both to an incarcerated swindler and to a variety of aristocrats) that prepares for Melville's almost cosmic characterization of this popular figure. Melville was prepared to go beyond Houston or any other dark reformer toward a vision of truly universal chicanery. In every chapter of the novel some outwardly Conventional character uses such Christian

virtues as charity, morality, trust, benevolence, and above all confidence
for highly Subversive purposes. *Pierre* had showed how the Conventional
could turn into the Subversive. "Bartleby" and "Benito Cereno" had
begun to graft the two together, as the Subversive is viewed through the
eyes of the Conventional. In *The Confidence-Man* a complete fusion of the
two occurs, creating total fluidity in characterization and in moral statement. There is good reason that critics cannot decide whether the Confidence Man is Satan, Christ, or some middling figure. It is perhaps best not
to call him a *person* at all but rather a *text* or a *mode*. In the terms of this
study, he is the ultimate fictional embodiment of the benign-subversive
mode—a very slippery (and peculiarly American) mode which now has led
to a total dispersal of meaning.

As the final enactment of the benign-subversive style, *The Confidence-Man*
refers often to popular reform movements but never permits us, even
briefly, to rest securely in a single, clear attitude toward these movements.
It would appear that by the time he wrote the novel Melville had tried on
so many different Subversive and Conventional reform guises that the
mere shells of reform remained. Now reforms have been reduced to mo-
mentary postures as erasable as the different statements about charity
chalked on slate by the lamblike man in the opening scene of the novel.
The slavery issue is deflected into the pitiable theatricality of Black Guinea
and the unresolved debate over abolitionism between the mild herb doctor
and the fiery Pitch. Socialism and capitalism ironically conjoin in the man
in gray, who denounces businessmen as monstrous hypocrites and yet who
himself has the capitalistic dream of infusing reform work with "the Wall
street spirit" by levying "one grand benevolence tax upon all mankind."[35]
Anti-Catholic images undermine the apparent kindness of the herb doctor,
who is suspected of being "one of those Jesuit missionaries prowling all
over our country." Temperance and antitemperance again become a central locus of ambiguity. Paradoxically, Pitch (the moralistic total abstinence
man) is cantankerous and misanthropic, while the cosmopolitan (the supporter of tippling) seems moral and optimistic. As Frank Goodman, the
cosmopolitan decries temperance men as "[s]trange traducers, who see
good faith in nothing, however sacred," and concludes that "[t]hese dis-
trusters stab at the very soul of confidence." Frank startles his drinking
mate Charlie Noble by comparing temperance advocates to "gamblers and
all sorts of subtle tricksters" who avoid alcohol in order to keep a cool head
for business. Even though he sings praise to liquor and smoking, Frank
plies Charlie with wine but does not imbibe himself. When questioned by
the suspicious Charlie, Frank actually poses momentarily as a temperance
advocate himself, arguing that conviviality is good but sober congeniality
is better!

Melville is purposefully drawing upon the contradictions of reform to create a moral labyrinth in which the reader wanders helplessly among shifting reform signs. The novel enacts the bafflement expressed by a character in *Clarel* who asks, "Your word *reform* / What meaning's to that word assigned?" When at the end of *The Confidence-Man* the cosmopolitan announces himself as Philanthropos, the reader is confronted with a mythic embodiment of the antebellum immoral reformer, one who proclaims philanthropic love and trust but who almost certainly is one more instance of tainted benevolence.

This insoluble moral contradiction was, as we have seen, not new. It had been intrinsic in American reform culture since the 1830s and had fed into the complex themes of major American literature. In *The Confidence-Man* it had reached full artistic embodiment in a novel filled with reform emblems that are now thoroughly divested of determinate meaning. In *Moby-Dick* an extraordinary linguistic polarization had resulted when reform vehicles and tenors were violently torn asunder, when the oxymoronic character was magnified to titanic proportions, when Melville was exuberantly soaring on the powerful reform impulse in pursuit of elusive metaphysical truth. In *Pierre* this pursuit was turned inward, as the fluid interchange between virtue and vice became the premise for a more interior, psychological pursuit that led to a vision of moral ambiguity. In *The Confidence-Man* Melville surrendered metaphysical or psychological truth seeking and studied instead the empty shards of his reform culture. Having in the course of his career assumed virtually all possible reform postures, he then turned to the very process of moral posturing, to the sheer theatricality of reform stances. His society had led him toward literariness by offering him rich reform imagery and an energetic reform impulse that could be manipulated for artistic ends. In *The Confidence-Man* he created a new kind of literariness by exploring the activity of moral manipulation. If *Moby-Dick* had absorbed the immense energy released by the popular reform impulse, *The Confidence-Man* registered the fragmentation and dispersal of reform signifiers. In the final novel of Melville's major phase, the relativization implicit in the antebellum reform culture reached its ultimate stylistic projection.

Part Two

PUBLIC POISON:
Sensationalism and Sexuality

6

THE SENSATIONAL PRESS AND
THE RISE OF SUBVERSIVE
LITERATURE

Hawthorne's notion that the work of genius is the newspaper of its age applies even to some of the most apparently unconventional features of America's classic literature. Poe's portraits of psychopathic murderers; Melville's studies of incest and deceit; Hawthorne's probings into the psyche of social outcasts; Whitman's frank expression of sexual passion—these and other daring aspects of the major texts were artistic renderings of irrational or erotic themes predominant in a large body of overlooked sensational writings of the day.

The major writers were not, as is commonly believed, aliens in a literary culture of prudery or clear moral distinctions. Rather, they were responding to a heterogeneous culture which had strong elements of the criminal, the erotic, and the demonic. Although the hunger for sensationalism has been visible in all societies and periods, early-nineteenth-century America was unique, since for the first time this hunger could be fed easily on a mass scale. The right to freedom of the press made possible journalistic reportage of shocking stories that were censored in more repressive societies. Dramatic improvements in print technology and book distribution facilitated the publication of various kinds of racy literature that reflected the tastes of working-class and frontier readers. Popular newspapers made a dramatic shift toward the sensational, a shift whose effects are still felt today. Crime literature, ranging from trial reports to criminal biographies, enjoyed increasing popularity and had a demonstrable influence on several major works.

Along with such lively social texts there emerged a body of popular adventure fiction which, in its darkest manifestations, featured some of the most perverse scenes in literature. In much of this seamy fiction, popular writers forged a distinctly American irrational style whose linguistic wildness and dislocations were also visible in the grotesque American humor that arose during this period. Popular adventure fiction became increasingly subversive, both stylistically and thematically, as it became appropriated by a cluster of politically minded writers I call the radical democrats—authors whose hyperbolic reverence for America's republican ideals impelled them to go to unprecedented sensational extremes to expose what they saw as the betrayal of these ideals in contemporary American society. In time, all types of popular sensational literature fell into the hands of opportunistic publishers who took advantage of technological improvements, particularly the cylinder press (introduced in 1847), by manufacturing lurid pamphlet literature, most of it scabrous and some of it perversely pornographic. The various kinds of sensational literature, from the early penny papers through radical-democrat fiction and pornography, provide an intriguing cultural backdrop to both the political and the erotic themes of the major literature.

Another popular phenomenon that has not been adequately explored in terms of the major texts is pseudoscience: phrenology, animal magnetism, mesmerism, and spiritualism. No account of the antebellum scene is complete without consideration of these often bizarre but highly influential pseudosciences. They represented rich mixtures of the materialistic and the otherworldly that fed into the theory and practice of American literature, which characteristically occupied a dynamic middle ground between the realistic and the fantastic, the mimetic and the allegorical.

The sensational, the erotic, and the pseudoscientific were often linked in the antebellum imagination. Melville was tapping this odd combination in the second half of *Pierre* with his depiction of the subversive authors, sexual aberrants, and prophetic seers gathered together in the urban tenement, the Church of the Apostles. Hawthorne used the combination in his portrayals of Holgrave, the fiery reformer in *The House of the Seven Gables* who dabbles in mesmerism and writes popular sensational fiction, and Westervelt, the villain of *The Blithedale Romance* who is an amalgam of the deceptive crime hero and the exploitative pseudoscientist. A common character in popular fiction was the villainous pseudoscientist who used his magnetic powers to facilitate seductions and commit crimes.

As shall be seen in later chapters, the major writers had notably divided feelings about the explosively irrational forces within their literary culture. On the one hand, they associated these forces with a raw and vibrant Americanism they could exploit to combat staid, genteel aspects of foreign literatures. On the other hand, they were disturbed by the directionlessness and turbulence that characterized the more extreme sensational writings. They found in these writings a wild energy that reflected the brash spirit of the American republic but sometimes lapsed into formlessness and moral chaos. They therefore shaped indigenous sensational themes through reconstructive devices, such as narrative layering and symbol patterns, and achieved a new depth and universality through the use of stabilizing archetypes from history and myth.

Throughout the major literature we witness a dialectical engagement with bizarre or sensational aspects of American culture. We cannot appreciate the ubiquity of such popular imagery in the major works unless we study the emergence and literary absorption of significant popular phenomena to which I assign the umbrella term "sensational literature": seamy social texts such as penny papers, trial reports, and crime pamphlets; Romantic Adventure fiction (much of it quite dark) and the more politically radical genre of Subversive fiction; and erotic and pornographic writings.

The Press Ghoul

Poe once wrote that the rise of the sensational penny newspapers in the early 1830s had an influence upon American life and letters that was "probably beyond all calculation."[1] He was right: it is impossible to measure precisely the effects of a journalistic revolution that had a lasting impact upon all aspects of America's cultural life, including its major literature. The least that can be said is that the antebellum public was fed an increasingly spicy diet of horror, gore, and perversity in both the penny papers and in the closely allied genres of trial pamphlets and criminal biographies. The major writers were intimately aware of this shift toward the sensational. Emerson acknowledged in his journal that most of his countrymen spent their time "reading all day murders & railroad accidents" in newspapers.[2] Thoreau knew the popular press well enough to speak of "startling and monstrous events as fill the daily papers."[3] Whitman, weaned in the turbulent world of New York journalism, noted the special scurrility of American newspapers, and Poe famously borrowed crime stories from the penny press. Hawthorne was a lifelong addict of popular newspapers (he even had a friend send stacks of dailies to him when he moved to Liverpool in the 1850s), and he had what his son called a "pathetic craving" for trial reports and criminal biographies.[4] Melville also kept a close eye on the sensational press, which often featured bizarre or freakish images (e.g., destructive white whales, conniving confidence men, ship disasters) that may have sparked his imagination.

Sensational literature, of course, was not a uniquely American phenomenon. Such literature had precedents in foreign collections of criminal biography such as the *Newgate Calendar,* which had been popular since the early eighteenth century in Great Britain and which directly influenced a succession of British novelists, including Daniel Defoe, Edward Bulwer-Lytton, William Harrison Ainsworth, and Charles Dickens. Since there was still no international copyright, American publishers issued many cheap reprintings of such foreign sensational writings, which found a huge market in America.

Despite such foreign competition, however, American sensationalists quickly earned a worldwide reputation for special nastiness and grossness. Tocqueville associated the characteristic coarseness of American journalism with the universal agitation and thirst for novelty endemic to democratic societies. Whitman, as editor of the *Brooklyn Daily Eagle,* noted "the superiority of tone of the London and Paris press over our cheaper and more diffused press," emphasizing: "Scurrility—the truth may as well be told—is a sin of the American newspaper press."[5] The special scurrility Whitman recognized was not lost on foreign commentators. In 1842 the London *Foreign Quarterly Review* generalized: "[T]he more respectable the city in America, the more infamous, the more degrading and disgusting, we have found to be its Newspaper Press." Attributing the special dirtiness of the American press to the tyranny of the unrestrained mob, the essayist declared that an American newspaper is "popular in the proportion of its infamy and indecency."[6] In the same year, the visiting Charles Dickens, despite his own interest in criminality, was disgusted by the excessive sensationalism of the American penny papers, which he charged with "pimping and pandering for all degrees of vicious taste, and gorging with coined lies the most voracious maw; [and] imputing to every man in public life the coarsest and vilest motives." Although he found some "pure" papers in America, he wrote that "the influence of the good is powerless to counteract the moral poison of the bad."[7] So appalled was he that in *Martin Chuzzlewit* he drew a satirical portrait of American newsboys peddling scabrous papers with titles like the *New York Sewer* and the *New York Stabber.* The foreign animus against America's sensational press continued for decades. In the 1850s, a writer for the *Westminister Review* declared: "*Our* press is bad enough. . . . But its violence is meekness and even its atrocities are virtues, compared with that system of *brutal and ferocious outrage* which distinguishes the press of America."[8] Three decades later, the visiting British woman Emily Faithfull declared that "the American newspaper very often startles its more cultured readers with extraordinary sensational headings and the prominence it gives to horrors of all kinds—murders, elopements, divorces, and wickednesses in general."[9]

When did this shift toward sensational journalism begin in America?

Signs of this shift were visible as early as the first decade of the nineteenth century. In 1807 a Philadelphia humor magazine, *The Tickler,* printed a whimsical poem stating that all the world is a newspaper and all people merely readers. In America, according to the poem, a growing group of readers were *"Wonder-Hunters"* who looked always for stories of "dying speeches—hurricanes— . . . people drowned, or burned or suffocated."[10]

This demand for sensational news was rapidly answered by the appearance of several popular journals featuring the bizarre or perverse. Chief among these was a New York monthly edited by Donald Fraser, *The American Magazine of Wonders* (1809), which promised to print only what was "Miraculous! Queer! Marvelous! Whimsical! Absurd! Out of the Way! Unaccountable!"[11] The magazine more than lived up to its billing. It ran stories, ranging from the odd to the thoroughly disgusting, about juicy topics like cannibalism, live burial, destructive whales, krakens, witches, every variety of human and animal ghoul. Several stories introduced subjects or images that would reappear in the major literature. The treatment of cannibalism in Poe's *Arthur Gordon Pym* and Melville's *Typee* is relatively tame when compared with several articles on the topic in Fraser's magazine, such as the story of a frontier family whose main food for twenty-five years is their murdered victims, or that of ferocious religious fanatics who entered a gentleman's house, "bound him to a stake, violated, in his sight, the chastity of his wife and daughters; put him afterwards upon a spit, and having roasted him, compelled his lady and his children to eat his flesh and terminated the horrid scene by a general massacre of the whole family." Readers of Poe may be interested to know that the magazine also ran a story about "The Humanity of a Raven" and another about a "Wonderful Ape" who used scissors like a barber and ran wild all over town. Melville readers should be aware that at this early stage the American public was obviously fascinated by mythic sea monsters and by strange anecdotes like that of the Virginia man struck dead by lightning while smoking at his window who remained standing as though still alive—a story printed in Fraser's first issue and adopted later by Melville as a metaphor in "Bartleby, the Scrivener."

Although the major authors may have had no direct exposure to Fraser's magazine, they all had intimate knowledge of the increasing number of sensational papers that emerged during the 1820s and 1830s. By 1831 the New York *Genius of Temperance* could report that crimes "now form the 'Domestic News' of every journal. Once it was not so . . . That which was once too shocking for recital, now forms a part of the intellectual regalia which the public appetite demands with a gusto that will scarcely brook the disappointment, should the mails bring fewer murders than temperance meetings!"[12] The crucial transitional moment in American journalism was

1833, the year that the first penny newspapers, Horatio David Sheppard's New York *Morning Post* and Benjamin H. Day's New York *Sun,* appeared. Penny newspapers, aimed at the wallets and the tastes of America's increasingly rowdy working class, supplanted the respectable sixpennies of the past with a new brand of journalism that was brash, zestful, and above all sensational. Anything lively—a "Secret Tryst," a "Double Suicide," an "Awful Accident," a "Bloody Murder"—was fit news to print in the penny papers.

It was not long before every major American city had one or more penny papers. The Boston *Daily Times* and the Philadelphia *Public Ledger* were among the better-known penny papers, but none gained the notoriety and lasting influence of James Gordon Bennett's *New York Herald,* which appeared in 1835. In its first year the *Herald* was a pleasantly written, respectable paper, but Bennett quickly learned that American readers "were more ready to seek six columns of the details of a brutal murder, or the testimony of a divorce case, or the trial of a divine for improprieties of conduct, than the same amount of words poured forth by the genius of the noblest author of the times."[13] Realizing that the public would not look at him unless he "blacken his face," he began stirring up controversy and publishing highly sensational stories—all the while proclaiming himself, like many a Citizen Kane after him, a grand reformer who dealt frankly with vice only to expose and purge it. The reform pretense proved to be flimsy covering for opportunistic sensationalism. Bennett continued to print shocking stories with little or no moral comment, and he even courted insults to gain publicity. There was a standing joke that if you horsewhipped Bennett, he would "bend his back to the lash and thank you; for every blow is worth so many dollars." In the 1840s, a stock character in many American pulp novels was the amoral penny-press editor (in most cases patterned after Bennett) who libeled and praised everyone in turn according to the commercial needs of the moment and who kept the voracious public well stocked with murders, seductions, and rapes. Bennett drew fire from the young Walter Whitman, who as editor of the New York *Aurora* in 1842 blasted Bennett with these Gothic invectives:

> A reptile marking his path with slime wherever he goes, and breathing mildew at everything fresh and fragrant; a midnight ghoul, preying on rottenness and repulsive filth; a creature, hated by his nearest intimates, and bearing the consciousness thereof upon his distorted features, and upon his despicable soul; one whom good men avoid as a blot to his nature—whom all despise, and whom no one blesses—*all this* is James Gordon Bennett.[14]

Such tirades, predictably, only stimulated the public's curiosity and increased the circulation of the penny papers. By the 1850s, when the penny papers had long held undisputed dominance of the mass newspaper market, the public was so accustomed to sensational news that a feeling of glut had set in. As Lambert A. Wilmer wrote in a book on newspapers in 1859: "No narrative of human depravity or crime can shock or horrify an American reader."[15]

While the penny papers were chiefly responsible for this callous public attitude, we cannot overlook the importance of the allied genres of trial pamphlets and criminal biographies. The same technological innovations that sped the printing of sensational newspapers also made possible the rapid publication of pamphlets about current trials and about notorious American murderers, robbers, pirates, swindlers, and sex fiends. Popular crime pamphlets had a special fascination for Hawthorne, and Melville thought such pamphlets were significant enough to be featured in the opening scene of *The Confidence-Man,* in which he describes a man aboard a riverboat peddling "the lives of Meason, the bandit of Ohio, Murrel, the pirate of the Mississippi, and the brothers Harpe, the Thugs of the Green River country, in Kentucky."[16]

When we look at the popular crime literature of the day, we immediately see through the common myth that the major writers were distant from a popular culture that was easily optimistic or moralistic. Indeed, the unexampled depravity often described in such literature makes us wonder why the major texts, which frequently drew from such popular sources, weren't even darker than they are. Not surprisingly, trial pamphlets met heavy resistance in the early going. When a pamphlet about a scandalous incest case met a rapid sale in 1806, a Litchfield, Connecticut, paper editorialized angrily against its publication by declaring that such pamphlets "can be of no other use than to gratify a gross curiosity."[17] But such puritanical protests could not stop the trickle of popular crime narratives from swelling into a broad river by the 1830s and to a virtual flood by the 1840s. By then, almost every sensational trial, besides being played up in the penny papers, produced its own cheap pamphlet that was hawked in street bookstalls and railway depots. Given the ubiquity of the pamphlets, it is understandable that Hawthorne in "Earth's Holocaust" (1844) pictured them as an irresistible swarm: "[T]he last remnant of the literature was now descending upon the blazing heap, in the shape of a cloud of pamphlets from the press of the New World."[18]

While much of this ephemeral writing has disappeared, enough of it has survived to suggest just how dark a swarm these pamphlets were. At first, pamphlet publishers were careful to accentuate the pious, hortatory side of trials in a way that had characterized most American crime reportage since Puritan times. Such pious moralizing predominates in such early pamphlets as *Trial and Sentence of John Johnson* (1824), *Trial of the Three Thayers* (1825), and *Trial and Sentence of Moses Parker [and Six Others]* (1825). These pamphlets are filled with long warnings about God's anger against criminals and man's need to beg forgiveness in the face of divine wrath. Unusual among the early pamphlets was Henry Trumbull's *Life and Remarkable Adventures of Israel Potter* (1824), which so intrigued Melville that he used it as the basis for *Israel Potter* (1855). It is telling that Melville was drawn to Trumbull's pamphlet, which was a significant transitional work between the typically preachy early pamphlets and the more bleak, gory later ones. In fact, Trumbull emphasizes even more than Melville the tragic implications of the dispossessed Revolutionary War veteran forced to stay alive for four decades in London's rogue-ridden underworld. While Melville gives a highly foreshortened picture of Israel Potter's decline in London, Trumbull dwells on this decline, depicting an amoral, deterministic environment in which naturally good people are driven to poverty and crime by circumstances outside their control. The sympathetic treatment of criminals would become a central theme of much American crime literature and would feed directly into the resonant ambiguities of major works by Poe and Hawthorne.

The commercialization of crime pamphlets became a widespread phenomenon in the early 1830s, the period that also witnessed the rise of the penny newspapers. The crassly exploitative approach of the presses was summarized in one pamphlet: "If a publisher finds that his readers will feed upon poison, he is strongly tempted to procure or manufacture it for their use."[19] The nation was regaled by a succession of seamy trial pamphlets that withheld no detail in the description of perverse crimes. The grisly parade of trial pamphlets began in 1830 with the report of the famous murder of Captain Joseph White by hirelings of a person who wanted to destroy White's will. Nationally publicized in a trial pamphlet as "the Salem Murder," this case fascinated Hawthorne, who discussed it often in his letters and probably drew from it his story of Clifford Pyncheon's alleged murder of his uncle in *The House of the Seven Gables*. During the 1830s and 1840s, the public feasted on a whole succession of widely publicized cases: that of Ephraim K. Avery, a Methodist preacher who was tried in 1833 for seducing and then murdering a sluttish girl after a camp meeting; the scandal involving Richard P. Robinson, a New York dandy who was acquitted after a long trial for the murder of the New York prostitute Ellen Jewett in a house of ill fame; the 1841 trial and execution of Peter Robinson, a poor carpenter who had dragged his victim to the cellar, dug a grave before his eyes, and then buried the corpse under floor planks; that of Mary Rogers, the New York cigar girl whose mysterious disappearance and subsequent murder in 1841 was famously "solved" by Poe in "The Mystery of Marie Roget"; and that of John C. Colt (mentioned in Melville's "Bartleby, the Scrivener"), who was convicted for the Broadway office murder of Samuel Adams and then on the day scheduled for his hanging was married and committed suicide in prison. Not only were such cases publicized through individual trial pamphlets, but also multiple cases were gathered together in popular criminal anthologies, such as the massive *Record of Crimes in the United States* (1833), Joseph Martin's *Select Tales* (1833), and the very popular *Pirates' Own Book* (1837). The demand for crime stories was so great that the New York editor George Wilkes could make a good living from his weekly newspaper, *The National Police Gazette* (1845–1933), which ran narratives illustrating every variety of criminal activity. To increase his profit, Wilkes reprinted many *Police Gazette* cases in cheap pamphlets under the running title of *The Lives of the Felons* (1847 ff.), a series that included the crime pamphlets mentioned in Melville's *The Confidence-Man.*

Nowhere was unrepentant villainy so dramatically manifested as in the widely publicized case of the Harpe brothers. Melville had good reason to mention these figures at the beginning of *The Confidence-Man,* for in the antebellum imagination they were the very embodiments of cool-handed crime. In the first decade of the nineteenth century the Kentucky brothers John and James Harpe had formed a crime band that terrorized frontier communities, killing people indiscriminately not for money but for what was called "a savage thirst for blood—a deep-rooted malignancy against human nature."[20] When captured, John Harpe refused to repent, declaring to his captors: "I have not the least regret for the murders I have committed. I have taken pleasure in the sight of human blood shed by my own hands . . . I curse you and all mankind, for I hate you and the whole human race. *One of my own children* I have murdered . . . Think you then that I cared for the blood of strangers?"[21] The American public was obviously intrigued by the quintessentially amoral Harpes, whose lives were frequently retold in popular crime literature, most notably in a long pamphlet biography that appeared in 1847 as part of George Wilkes's series *The Lives of the Felons, or American Criminal Calendar.*

What relation did the penny papers and the crime writings have with the major literature? In the most direct sense, they generated popular images and stereotypes that were absorbed into the major literature. The adaptation of sensational images by specific authors (such as Hawthorne's use of the reverend rake and the dramatic scaffold scene, two favorite preoccupations of the sensationalists) will be discussed at length later. For now, it is important to recognize that the major literature, in its attempt to broadly represent American culture, took into account the dark themes and character types of sensational writings but earnestly tried to lend new suggestiveness to ironies that had lost resonance because of crass repetition in the popular press. In *The Scarlet Letter,* for example, Hawthorne makes a point of emphasizing the "awe" and "solemnity" of the Puritans' response to Hester's ignominy, a response that he says "had none of the heartlessness of another social state, which would find only a theme for jest in an exhibition like the present."[22] There was good reason for observant writers such as Hawthorne to wish to invest crime issues with literary depth, for one of the most disturbing features of the modern crime narratives was their frequent moral neutrality. Whereas previous American crime reports, from Puritan times through the mid-1820s, were careful to draw religious or moral lessons from criminals' experiences, the antebellum reports were, in the main, gloating records of unthinkable atrocities obviously designed to please a sensation-hungry public. To be sure, some religious imagery did remain in the modern narratives, but almost always it emphasized man's depravity without mentioning redemption. For instance, through the accounts of twenty-three criminals in *Record of Crimes in the United States* runs the theme of the basic sinfulness of mankind, as Americans of every profession and background are presented as capable of the most heinous acts. We hear that one murderer exemplifies "innate depravity" and that another reveals "the great wickedness of the human heart"—but nothing is said about God's saving grace.[23] In the post-Calvinist world of the crime narratives, depravity reigns while salvation is forgotten. In his notebook for 1836 Hawthorne drew a direct connection between human sinfulness and popular crime trials. "There is evil in every human heart," Hawthorne writes, "which may remain latent, through the whole of life; but circumstances may rouse it into activity." Jotting down imaginary sketches to illustrate this idea, Hawthorne pictured a woman who cheats on her husband out of mere whim and a young man who commits murder "out of mere thirst for blood." "This appetite," Hawthorne emphasizes, "may be traced in the popularity of criminal trials."[24]

The most popular and culturally influential stereotype that arose from the ascendant sensational press was the highly paradoxical one of the *likable criminal* or *justified pariah.* We are all familiar with American writers' fascination with cool villainy and smooth deceit, as evidenced by Hawthorne's frigid villains like Rappaccini and Roger Chillingworth, or Poe's crazy but oddly rational murderers, or Melville's gently satanic confidence man. It has not been recognized that such characters can be viewed as variations upon the emotionally detached, confident criminals that filled the sensational press of the day. The likable criminal gained grisly prominence during the 1840s in the Subversive fiction of the radical democrats but had arisen long before that in crime narratives. The most important early appearance of this smugly devilish stereotype was during the 1830 trial of Joseph and Frank Knapp for the murder of Captain Joseph White— the notorious "Salem Murder," which was destined to have a lasting impact on Hawthorne and Poe. "Here is a new face given to murder," declared the prosecuting attorney, Daniel Webster, "a new character given to the face of Moloch; no knitted brow, no bloodshot eye of passion disfigured the countenance of the assassin; but all was calm, smooth, and unruffled; . . . all was done in deliberation of purpose, and with consummate skill of execution."[25] Hawthorne, who kept a close eye on the trial proceedings, noted with surprise that while in jail awaiting execution Frank Knapp constantly joked and laughed with the jailer, showing a blithe indifference to his fate.[26] A similar attitude characterized most of the criminals described in the *Record of Crimes,* such as the convicted pirate and mass murderer Charles Gibbs, who in jail was so "mild and gentle" that "no one would have taken him to be a villain."[27] It was also visible in Major Mitchell, a Maine man whose trial for the castration of a young boy with a jagged piece of tin was one of the most sensational cases of 1834, provoking special interest because of the "freedom, indifference, and openness, with which he talks of a deed, the bare naming of which causes all else to shudder with horror."[28]

The most prominent example of the likable criminal in antebellum culture was John A. Murrell, the "Great Western Land Pirate." Once again, Melville manifested shrewd awareness of his popular culture by mentioning Murrell in *The Confidence-Man,* for few figures in American crime narratives were so surrounded with rich and conflicting legends as John Murrell. Born in 1804, Murrell from an early age misapplied his enviable mental and physical gifts, becoming the charismatic leader of a frontier crime band that terrorized the South through nefarious deeds such as robbery, counterfeiting, and slave stealing. After he was tracked down and captured by one Virgil A. Stewart, a spy who infiltrated his ranks by feigning friendship, Murrell became the subject of several popular biographies: Augustus Q. Walton's *A History of the Detection, Conviction, Life and Designs of John A. Murel, the Great Western Land Pirate* (1835), H. R. Howard's *The History of Virgil A. Stewart, and His Adventure in Capturing the Great "Western Land Pirate" and His Gang* (1836), and Howard's much expanded popular pamphlet *The Life and Adventures of John A. Murrell, the Great Western Land Pirate* (1847), which went through many subsequent reprintings. These successive biographies provide a capsule history of popular views of criminals, for they manifest an increasing sympathy with the "land pirate," Murrell, and a growing ambivalence about his captor, Stewart. In the moralistic early works, Murrell is drawn as a villain of the blackest dye, an example of the wages of misdirected genius, while Stewart is the unblemished hero. In the later version, the roles have almost been reversed: Murrell is portrayed as a heartless yet bold and shrewd warrior against a largely corrupt society; Stewart is the sneaking spy who uses cowardly means to entrap his victim. Melville's curiosity about the shape-shifting capacities of the confidence man is anticipated in Howard's portrait of Murrell, who dons various pious and impious personae with a skill that proves he was, in Howard's words, "the most capable man of his age in his profession" and "remarkably ingenious in the performance of every thing he undertook."[29]

The anomalous combination of virtuous and evil qualities inherent in the likable criminal was highly provocative for an attentive culture watcher like Melville, who in the opening scene of *The Confidence-Man* not only mentions pamphlets about Murrell and other popular criminals but also gives a mini-history of American crime narratives in preparation for his own depiction of the wily confidence man. Melville compares early American criminals to exterminated "wolves" who have left "comparatively few successors; which would seem a cause for unalloyed gratulation, and is such to all except those who think that in new countries, where wolves are killed off, the foxes increase."[30] Melville obviously knew that there was growing public fascination with the criminal who could manipulate others effectively, without recourse to brutish violence. In the crime pamphlets of the 1840s, it indeed seemed that as the "wolves" declined, the "foxes" increased. We have seen that in the Murrell pamphlets increasing attention was paid to the villain's uncanny power to use his sharp wits in duping others. By 1850 the New York journalist George Thompson could write: "To such a complete science has professional villainy of late years been reduced" that the successful criminal "is now generally looked upon somewhat in the light of a hero," as people frequently "look with admiration upon the genius of the criminal, and breathe something of sympathy with his fate."[31]

It was left to Melville to capture fully the strange combination of ingenuity and exploitativeness, innocence and deception inherent in the likable criminal—a combination so subtle and problematic that even today critics cannot decide whether Melville's confidence man is Christ or Satan. It would be left to Hawthorne in *The Marble Faun* to delve deeply into the psychological and metaphysical implications of the likable criminal, who in Hawthorne's novel becomes the center of a provocative debate over the value of admitting evil into the human consciousness. But long before Melville or Hawthorne studied the likable criminal, this character had been increasingly prominent in factual crime narratives and, as will be seen, in popular adventure fiction.

The likable criminal has been a popular figure in other cultures and enjoyed particular prominence in Romantic literature, as is seen in the alluring pariahs that fill the writings of Byron, Scott, Bulwer-Lytton, George Sand, and Eugène Sue, to name only the most obvious instances. But this mixed character was destined to have a special meaning in democratic America. In a sense, antebellum America as whole was a justified pariah—a nation that had recently waged holy war against a foreign oppressor and that still felt the paradoxical spirit of optimism and militancy, progressivism and pugnaciousness that would impel Melville to characterize America as "civilized in externals but a savage at heart, . . . the [John] Paul Jones of nations."[32] This fusion of cocksure confidence and scathing rebelliousness was manifested in many radical-democrat novelists of the day, such as George Lippard and George Thompson, who at once produced some of the most patriotic and the most radical, violent works of the period. And nowhere was this combination of warring impulses so evident as in the treatment of criminals. There was a growing fascination with the shrewd techniques of criminals and an even stronger democratic impulse to make heroes of those who lashed out angrily against what was viewed as deepening social corruption. At the very moment Melville was writing *Moby-Dick,* which contains the intriguing pariahs Ishmael and Ahab, his imagination was bristling with the polarities of his criminal culture. In a June 1851 letter to Hawthorne, Melville proclaimed himself one who feels a "ruthless democracy on all sides" and who "boldly declares that a thief in jail is as honorable a personage as Gen. George Washington."[33] In the next breath he confessed: "It seems an inconsistency to assert unconditional democracy in all things, and yet confess a dislike to all mankind—in the mass." The first of these statements shows the intensity of Melville's response to the American stereotype of the admirable criminal; the second shows him momentarily becoming absorbed into this stereotype, announcing himself the democratic misanthrope, the all-embracing rebel, much like the paradoxical heroes of popular crime literature.

The problematic stereotype of the likable criminal inevitably raised larger questions: can extreme evil and extreme good coexist in the same person? If such a mixture can occur, what happens to traditional moral codes and religious creeds? Sensational social texts such as penny papers and crime pamphlets raised these thorny issues but did not tussle with them creatively or project them stylistically. It was left to writers of popular fiction to rise above the stark, unembellished narration of the social texts and dramatize these issues in ways that directly prepared the way for the resonant ambiguities of the major literature.

Romantic Adventure and Subversive Fiction

The extraordinary popularity of adventure fiction about criminals and other dashing pariahs was noted by the respected Boston critic Edwin Percy Whipple, who in 1848 wrote that the rage of the hour was the "Romance of Rascality."[34] He was bemused over America's widespread interest in the likable criminal. The romancers of rascality, he wrote, assume that "the final cause of human society is the provision of a brilliant theatre for the exploits of its outcasts." Whipple believed that the effect of such fiction was to subvert all moral standards. "According to the philosophy obtaining among the romancers of rascality," he wrote, "the fact that an object creates physical disgust, is the reason why we should take it to our arms; the fact that a man excites moral reprobation, is his claim upon our sympathy." Whipple noted that not only were foreign sensational novelists immensely popular but that America had produced its own special rascalish literature whose effect was to "confuse our moral perceptions." The situation was particularly dangerous in America, he argued, because "this country is the only country where everybody reads," and American printing technology and book distribution were the most advanced in the world, making possible the rapid issuance and universal dissemination of cheap sensational novels. "Who will not commit suicide when the poison is cheap?" Whipple asked in despair.

These comments are not merely the paranoiac outcries of a stuffy Bostonian. They are an understandably concerned reaction to a school of highly wrought adventurous or satirical novels whose increasing popularity during the antebellum period is substantiated by other reviews and by publishing statistics. True, as many scholars have pointed out, there was a large market in antebellum America for pious domestic fiction, as is evidenced by best-sellers such as Susan Warner's *The Wide, Wide World* (1850) and Maria Cummins's *The Lamplighter* (1854). This domestic literature, which I classify as the Conventional, valorized the home, good works, stylistic clarity, and Christian virtues such as submission and endurance. To emphasize Conventional literature while excluding more sensational genres, however, is to distort dangerously the literary history of pre–Civil War America. Actually, the great Conventional best-sellers were rhetorical constructs in which the troubled social and philosophical climate of antebellum America was determinedly meliorated and an alternative world of village pastoralism and victorious moral exemplars were offered as mythic correctives for thorny realities such as crime, urbanization, tangled reform movements, and savage frontier life.

These more turbulent social realities were reflected in a largely forgotten body of seamy adventurous novels that enacted the fierce aggressions and political fantasies of the growing urban working class in a time of great social instability. Whipple was quite justified in identifying the Romance of Rascality as the rage of the day. The proportion of such fiction, when weighed against more decorous types of fiction, was always high in America and actually rose as time passed. Before 1831, American fiction was pretty evenly divided between adventurous fiction and the more genteel sentimental-domestic genre. Between 1831 and 1860, when printing improvements sped the publication of cheap sensational literature (particularly yellow-covered pamphlet novels), the proportion of adventurous or darkly humorous volumes rose to almost 60 percent, while the proportion of genteel volumes sank to about 20 percent.[35] The ambiguities of the major literary texts can be profitably studied as extensions of central conflicts within the ascendant sensational and satirical literature of the day.

In order to understand the major writers' use of sensational images, it is essential to review the categories I have devised to describe different kinds of antebellum adventure fiction: Romantic Adventure fiction (in its two predominant forms, Moral Adventure and Dark Adventure) and the more politically radical mode of Subversive fiction. Moral Adventure was an exploratory genre that probed the turbulence and linguistic violence of frontier or city life but tried to uphold firm ethical values through the portrayal of a central hero (Cooper's Natty Bumppo is the archetypal example) who sustains integrity and moral power. What I call Dark Adventure, typified by J. H. Ingraham's pirate novel *Lafitte* (1836) and hundreds of cheap adventure novels like it, presented a totally secular world of social outcasts whose often criminal adventures are described without explicit moralizing and with obvious fascination with the villainous or tabooed. This kind of fiction was written in a "flat," action-packed style with only occasional philosophical commentary, usually dark. Moral Adventure and Dark Adventure can be grouped together as different manifestations of the mode of Romantic Adventure, to be distinguished from the more politically oriented Subversive mode.

Subversive fiction, much of which has been overlooked by previous scholars, enacted fully the wild cultural forces that were evaded or glossed over in the other types of adventure fiction. In its most characteristic form, as in the novels of John Neal, George Lippard, and George Thompson, such literature was deliberately subversive in both the *stylistic* and the *political* sense: it forged a new irrational style aimed at reproducing the rebellious, savage forces of American culture; and its unmasking of the social elite was enforced through extreme violence, sexual scenes ranging from the suggestive to the disgustingly perverse, and new variations upon ironic stereotypes such as the reverend rake and the likable criminal. This kind of fiction often featured excessive gore and mass chicanery, conveyed in an intentionally disruptive, quirky style designed to outrage the genteel reader. Increasingly, Subversive literature was written by what I call *radical democrats*: writers so ardently devoted to the egalitarian ideals of the American democracy that their writings are filled with hyperbolic reverence for the Founding Fathers and, at the same time, with vitriolic bitterness against perceived inequities in nineteenth-century American society, which they regarded as a nightmarish realm of upper-class charlatans and political oppressors described in highly sensational images.

The writers we have come to regard as major had full knowledge of the various kinds of indigenous adventure literature but carefully resisted full identification with any one of them. What particularly distinguished the major authors was their bold capacity to absorb the disturbing stereotypes and ironies unleashed in Dark Adventure and Subversive literature but simultaneously to retain the reconstructive firmness of Moral Adventure and to introduce potent structuring devices of their own. In order to understand the cultural sources of the major writers' sensational images, we must look more closely at the main types of popular adventure fiction.

The most prominent writers in the first category, Moral Adventure, were James Fenimore Cooper, Catharine Sedgwick, Richard Henry Dana, and Francis Parkman. Often there were direct links between these writers and the major authors. Dana's *Two Years Before the Mast,* for instance, elicited a rich accolade from Melville, who declared he felt "a Siamese link of affectionate sympathy" with Dana.[36] Melville also had high praise for Parkman's *The Oregon Trail,* which he said had "the true wild-game flavor" and was full of "all manner of outlandish and interesting characters."[37] Both Melville and Hawthorne had high regard for their Berkshire neighbor Catharine Sedgwick, whom Hawthorne once called America's "most truthful novelist."[38] Cooper was generally admired by the major writers, particularly Whitman, who said Cooper's novels are "all racy of America."[39]

What attracted the major writers to the Moral Adventure novelists was their success in bringing intelligence and civility to the treatment of wild subjects. Indeed, many Moral Adventure novels are in some respects quite close to the major writings. In both groups of texts we witness a dialectical engagement with and disengagement from Subversive forces within American culture. The key distinction between the groups lies in the differing degrees of engagement and differing methods of disengagement. The major authors allowed the Subversive to flood their consciousness, to dissolve all religious and moral preconceptions, to energize their style. The depth of their engagement is mirrored in the creativeness of their strategies for reconstruction, their imaginative use of distancing or structuring elements such as the self, myth, history, science, even mathematics.

In contrast, the Moral Adventure novelists had only superficial engagement with the Subversive forces. Because they avoided complete immersion in these forces, their texts lack the linguistic experimentation and thematic complexity of the major writings. In Moral Adventure we see tentative, sometimes anguished perceptions of ambiguity that prompt a retreat to monistic meaning and to a rational style. For the modern reader, Moral Adventure is most intriguing for the very real cultural tensions it reflects—tensions which at moments become so prominent that they produce images or character types akin to those in the major literature.

The prototypical Moral Adventure novelist was James Fenimore Cooper. In 1821, at the beginning of his literary career, he wrote: "A good novel addresses itself very powerfully to our moral nature and conscience." The novelist, he insisted, should be careful as "he distributes virtues and vices" to ensure that retribution is apportioned in conformity to God's law and man's moral sense.[40] In his fiction Cooper never radically betrays this moral outlook. In fact, a major strength of his novels is their success in studying savage, potentially chaotic topics—Indian warfare and captivity, frontier living, sea battles, piracy, Arctic exploration—without sacrificing the firm authorial voice that enforces his moral vision. To be sure, some of the most intriguing moments in Cooper are those when this moral vision becomes temporarily blurred, when the rational surface begins to crack under the strain of perceived ambivalences or cultural pressures. We tend to be attracted to ambiguous characters who embody conflicting tendencies: Judge Temple in *The Pioneers,* who is torn between reason and passion, between the dictates of law and those of the heart; or several of Cooper's likable criminals, such as Harry Wilder in *The Red Rover,* Tom Tiller in *The Water-Witch,* or Captain Spike in *Jack Tier,* all of whom are disreputable or villainous but still admirable because of their heroism and their protection of the virtuous.

But in the end Cooper comes up on the side of restraint and moral clarity. His central likable pariah, Natty Bumppo, sometimes wars nobly against social corruption, but his rebelliousness is modified by a decorum and a natural decency that prevent him from being subversive. A walking embodiment of the Scottish Common Sense notion of man's innate ability to distinguish between right and wrong, Leatherstocking (particularly in his later appearances) leaves little room for ambiguity in Cooper's scheme. In *The Pathfinder* (1841) Cooper underscores this moral capacity when he emphasizes that "a disbeliever in the ability of man to distinguish between good and evil without the aid of human instruction, would have been staggered by the character of this extraordinary inhabitant of the frontier."[41] In the character of Leatherstocking, Cooper introduces the archetypal American *moral* pariah, an individualistic democrat who rebels against civilization's iniquities and yet retains salty good sense and intuitive morality. Leatherstocking is an appropriate ideological center in a fictional world where adventure is treated as a test of virtuous strength rather than as an illustration of human perversity. In *The Deerslayer* (1842) Cooper directly contrasts a "loud, clamorous, dogmatical" frontiersman, Hurry Harry, to the more sober Leatherstocking, who proved "by the moderation of his language, the fairness of his views, and the simplicity of his distinctions, that he possessed every disposition to hear reason, a strong, innate desire to do justice."[42] This grace and morality is mirrored in a style that avoids rhapsodic extremes or distortions of time and space. The stylistic stiffness and romanticism that Mark Twain saw in Cooper was to a large degree a rhetorical defense against explosive forces within American popular culture.

Cooper was particularly sensitive to these forces, which he regarded as the harbingers of moral chaos and linguistic confusion. His sense of shock upon returning in 1833 to America after his seven-year residence in Europe was registered in *Home as Found* (1838), whose returning protagonist discovers that "his country had undergone many changes since he last resided in it. . . . The spirit of misrule was abroad, and the lawless and unprincipled held bold language, when it suited their purpose to intimidate."[43] It is well known that Cooper had a compelling personal reason for concern: the public was trying to take over property that had long been in his family, and he had to file a libel suit against newspaper editors who opposed him in the case. The author who in Europe had been the great democratic spokesman for the rights of the masses ironically became the defender of the individual and of property. But there was a much larger reason for Cooper's new uneasiness about his nation. We should recall that it was precisely during the years Cooper was abroad, 1826–33, that America witnessed the dramatic rise of squabbling immoral reformers and sensational newspapers. Cooper's later writings betray his growing fear that ascendant mass culture might annihilate all fixed principles through the agencies of an amoral press, warring preachers, morally flabby politicians, and materialistic entrepreneurs. The press, he declares in *Home as Found,* had become "as much without restraint as without remorse," an argument he made again in "The American Democrat" (1838), in which he held the press mainly responsible for the fact that "the entire nation, in a moral sense, breathes an atmosphere of falsehoods."[44] Cooper was horrified not only by this moral fluidity but also by a linguistic indeterminacy which he also associated with popular culture. Complaining in "The American Democrat" about "popular abuses of significations" and "the effort to subvert things by names," Cooper found that the American language was flawed by "ambiguity of expression" and "many perversions of significations." He had a particular antipathy toward American slang, which in *The Crater* (1847) he called "the great and most powerful foe of justice."[45]

Cooper, therefore, was every bit as aware of volcanic disturbances within American mass culture as were writers like Melville and Hawthorne; but, unlike them, he did not permit these disturbances to infiltrate his consciousness, shake loose settled beliefs, and thus prepare the way for ambiguous literature. Instead, he created in his later works a huge stylistic shield against various forms of popular irrationalism—the sensational press, the loud revivalistic sects, the wild frontier spirit, acerbic slang—which he regarded as threats to moral stability and linguistic uniformity. His search for stability brought about a retreat to religious dogmatism, as manifested in the strongly pious themes of several of his late novels and his confirmation in the Protestant Episcopal Church shortly before his death in 1851. This need for moral anchorage was also reflected in the changing aspect of his principal character, Natty Bumppo. In the earlier Leatherstocking novels—*The Pioneers* (1823), *The Last of the Mohicans* (1826), and *The Prairie* (1827)—Natty had been a man of firm integrity, but he also occasionally betrayed cynical and sanguinary impulses that made him morally mixed. In the later novels, *The Pathfinder* (1841) and *The Deerslayer* (1842), he comes far closer to being the secular saint, with a pious respect for nature, a feeling of honor toward friend and foe alike, and a stoic calmness under pressure. He becomes everything that, in Cooper's eyes, American popular culture was not: forthright, genuine, cool, clear. Cooper, reacting against what he saw as a mass culture of moral chaos and linguistic distortion, had converted Leatherstocking into a mythic figure of honesty and calm virtue.

Two other leading writers of Moral Adventure, Richard Henry Dana, Jr., and Francis Parkman, were almost as successful as Cooper in fashioning stable alternatives to fluid popular culture. If neither of these writers succeeded in creating a legendary character like Natty Bumppo, they did manage to sustain moral firmness and stylistic clarity even when dealing with wild scenes and characters. Dana's *Two Years Before the Mast* (1840) brought a new realism to American sea fiction precisely because the novel's narrator remains a genteel, sensitive observer who, though sometimes depressed or angry, never allows his passions to blur his vision of surrounding reality. Like Melville's *Moby-Dick*, Dana's novel traces the passage of a young man from the relative security of shore life to a remote region where he encounters the primitive and uncivilized. Both heroes are cast into the turbulent realm of tyrannical ship's officers, drunken sailors, and strange barbarians, a realm filled with dark images lifted directly from the Subversive Adventure mode. The difference is that Melville's Ishmael undergoes a kind of conversion to the Subversive, joining in with the profane shouts of the "sharkish" crew and absorbing Ahab's mad vengeance, while Dana's narrator remains unchanged by his experiences. Melville's novel is a parable of initiation into the Subversive; Dana's is one of the victory of the Conventional. Dana's moral emphasis was glaringly evident at the end of the novel, which advocates the distribution of religious tracts among American sailors, and in Dana's own life—he became a confirmed Episcopalian and a secure member of the Boston Brahmin literary establishment.

In Parkman's *The Oregon Trail* (1847) we witness an intriguing intrusion of Subversive elements into the Moral Adventure mode. An autobiographical narrative about Parkman's life among Indians and frontiersmen in 1846, *The Oregon Trail* has the virtues of Dana's novel, including realistic reportage of primitive experiences, but adds the new dimensions of preimpressionistic effects and mixed characterization. At key moments in the narrative, Parkman strains to reproduce the distortions of vision and shifting appearances that occur in the vast expanses of the Western plain. He also explores man's capacity for moral doubleness when confronted with the harsh exigencies of frontier life. This strange mixture of qualities especially characterizes the guide Henry Chantillon, who is tough and explosive yet delicate and refined, and the fur trader Jim Beckwith, who would stab a man in his sleep but who has moments of magnificent daring. Throughout the book runs a deep fascination with physical peril, wild adventure, and elemental passions. On the other hand, Parkman never sacrifices his civilized priorities. A Harvard graduate and the son of an upper-class Unitarian clergyman, Parkman always assumes the role of the civilized Easterner observing inferior beings. Like Dana and Cooper, he refrains from excessive accounts of gore and perversity, and he remains fundamentally dedicated to what he calls the "powerful and ennobling influences" of Boston gentility.[46]

While Moral Adventure fiction gave final victory to tough virtue, the mode of Dark Adventure gave such primacy to violence and irrationalism that the forces of darkness shattered those of moral rectitude. I assign the term Dark Adventure to an evolving popular genre that before 1820 harked back to the Puritan captivity narrative and which in the 1820s and 1830s broadened notably to include violent frontier adventure novels, particularly those of the Southern novelists William Gilmore Simms and Robert Montgomery Bird, and dark novels of love intrigue, such as Laughton Osborn's *Confessions of a Poet* (1831). In the 1840s Dark Adventure fiction took the form of cheap pamphlet novels about pirates, corsairs, freebooters, swaggering ship's captains, mythic monsters, and so forth, novels distinguished by their emphasis upon fast-paced bloody adventure among outlaw heroes whose heretical exploits are often rendered without moral commentary. This later Dark Adventure fiction was churned out by mass publishing houses, such as Gleason's of Boston and T. B. Peterson's of Philadelphia, which answered growing popular demand for what Whitman called "blood and thunder romances with alliterative titles and plots of startling interest."[47] Typical titles (with the inevitable descriptive subtitles) included Harry Halyard's *Wharton the Whale-Killer! or, The Pride of the Pacific,* Frank Forrester's *Pierre, the Partisan; A Tale of the Mexican Rancheros,* Maturin Murray Ballou's *Fanny Campbell; or The Female Pirate Captain,* and Miss J. A. B.'s *Mary Bean, the Factory Girl; or, The Mysterious Murder.*

By the 1850s Whitman could write that such sensational fiction was "a power in the land, not without great significance in its way, and very deserving of more careful consideration than has hitherto been accorded it." Whitman's statement still holds true, for actually little has been written on the Dark Adventure mode, which constituted nearly 35 percent of all fiction volumes published in America between 1830 and 1860. Much of this fiction has disappeared from view because it appeared as cheap paper-covered pamphlets designed for immediate consumption and disposal. Many of the volumes that have survived seem comically unsophisticated to today's reader, but we should keep in mind that the major writers of the American Renaissance were intrigued by even the cruder examples of this mode. Whitman, in response to Emerson's query about the foreground of *Leaves of Grass,* identified "strong-flavored romances, widely circulated" and "low-priced flaring tales, adventures, biographies" as "prophetic" genres that contributed to the rise of America's great literature.[48] Melville, in his prefatory extracts to *Moby-Dick,* included passages from Harry Halyard's *Wharton the Whale-Killer!* and from *The Life of Samuel Comstock,* two of the numerous pulp novels that included scenes of huge whales smashing into ships. Emerson and Margaret Fuller were so excited by Paul Harro-Harring's *Dolores,* a whirlwind novel about love and murder in South America, that they exchanged enthusiastic letters about the novel, which impelled Emerson to exclaim: "If I could write the novels for the people!"[49] At another time, when Emerson told Thoreau he would love to produce a popular adventure novel, Thoreau at first demurred but then showed his agreement by coining adventure stories to enliven his lecture that night. Poe was particularly attentive of Laughton Osborn, William Gilmore Simms, Robert Montgomery Bird, and other writers of early Dark Adventure fiction, much of which (surprisingly enough, given the irrationalism of Poe's own fiction) struck him as repulsive and morally unsound.

While Dark Adventure literature of some sort has been a feature of many cultures, it gained new visibility in antebellum America because of the rise of the mass press. The frenzied pace at which sensational adventure tales were manufactured was humorously rendered in a poem read at an 1855 New York literary banquet:

> "The Sea of Blood!"
> A work of wondrous power,
> Of which we've sold ten thousand sets
> Within the last half hour!
> This is the new sensation book.
> A work of so much force,
> The first edition all blew up
> And smashed a cart and horse! . . .
> And here's a most astounding tale,
> A volume full of fire,
> The author's name is known to fame—
> Stupendous Stubbs, Esquire!
> And here "The Howling Ditch of Crime,"
> By a Sapphira Stress,
> Two hundred men fell dead last night
> A working at the press![50]

The immense popularity of Dark Adventure novels in America was attributed by William Ellery Channing to the "love of strong stimulants" on the part of a newly mobile American society. "To be stimulated, to be excited, is the universal want," Channing noted, explaining that the most popular books are those which can be "run through with a railroad rapidity, and which give a pleasure not unlike that produced by exhilarating draughts."[51] Tocqueville, likewise, explained that in their feverish, rapidly changing society, Americans looked to popular literature for the "unexpected and new. Accustomed to the monotonous struggle of practical life, what they want is vivid, lively emotions, sudden revelations, brilliant truths, or error able to rouse them up and plunge them, almost by violence, into the middle of a subject."[52] Such commentary sheds light on the antebellum public's voracious need for diverting novels filled with shocking events and unexpected plot twists. It also provided an intriguing backdrop to certain startling or sensational aspects of the major literature, such as Hawthorne's images of crime and vampirism, Emily Dickinson's often violent metaphors, and Melville's interest in outcasts and monsters.

While Dark Adventure literature had roots in British Gothic fiction and European Dark Romanticism, it took on distinctly American characteristics when reinterpreted by authors who wished to find literary correlatives for the horrific or turbulent aspects of perceived reality in the new republic. The American texts were distinguished by a special intensity of irrationalism and perversity. William Hazlitt captured this unique quality when he wrote that in America horror devices are "infinitely exaggerated, full (to disease) of imagination . . . forced, violent, shocking." Hazlitt had a socio-logical explanation for this phenomenon. In England, he argued, there was "an old and solid ground in previous manners and opinion for imagination to rest upon." In America, which lacked this solid ground, the imagination was never "natural," it had to be "excited by overstraining," it always ran to the savage and the monstrous.[53] Another explanation was offered by Tocqueville, who argued that American writers, faced with a huge vacancy between their narrowly individual concerns and "very general and vague conceptions," unduly inflate their imaginations "so that they achieve giganticism"; they abandon "truth and reality" and "create monsters."[54]

Hazlitt and Tocqueville were describing the literary imagination sud-denly liberated by American democracy, which provided few static forms on which to operate. The traditional trappings of horror—what Brockden Brown had called "puerile superstitions and exploded manners, Gothic castles and chimeras"—were quickly rejected as useless remnants of an artificial aristocracy. Republican ideology impelled the writer to look else-where for symbols or projections of horror. The two most intriguing settings for the American writer were the frontier, with its wild landscape and often savage inhabitants, and the city, with its dark slums, horrid plagues, and criminal classes.

When one reads the unfamiliar Dark Adventure writings of the day, one is struck by excesses that even today seem shocking. One of these excesses was overindulgence in the pornography of violence. We have seen that bloody violence of all sorts was a standard feature of sensational social texts such as the penny papers and crime pamphlets. The violence in much Dark Adventure fiction is different, however, because it is treated with a gleeful lyricism absent from the more objective social texts.

Blood drinking and cannibalism are common motifs of Dark Adventure fiction. In John Neal's *Logan* (1822) an Indian patriarch avenges years of injustice against his race by brutally killing and scalping whites, then throwing their reeking scalps into a receptacle that carries his newborn children, who lap up the blood. With a typical sanguinary flourish Neal describes the Indian as "the parent vulture, that perches above her young and flaps over them, while their clotted beaks are searching out their first banquet of blood and flesh."[55] Such images run through the frontier novels of William Gilmore Simms. Simms's *The Yemassee* (1835) is full of detailed accounts of Indians torturing their white captives and singing gruesome war songs like the following:

> See him tear Suwannee's [white man's] side,
> See him drink Suwannee's blood—
> With his paws upon his breast,

> Look, he pulls the heart away,
> And his nose is searching deep,
> Clammy, thick with bloody drink,
> In the hollow where it lay.[56]

In Simms's fiction, Indians don't have a corner on blood-drinking, for many of his outwardly civilized white characters have their vampire-like moments, such as a virtuous man in *Guy Rivers* (1834) who screams at his love rival, "I would have thy blood. I would drink it."[57] This theme reached a culmination in the late 1840s with the fiction of George Thompson, who has the dubious distinction of having written the most purely disgusting novels in pre–Civil War America. In Thompson's *Venus in Boston* (1849) a double-dealing butler, having murdered his lady's husband at her behest, chops up the corpse, puts it in a wine barrel, then a week later serves the wine to the lady and her paramour, vowing that "her ladyship and her lover shall banquet on human blood; the corruption of a putrefying corpse shall be mingled with the sparkling fluid that nourishes their unholy passions."[58] The lovers, pronouncing the wine very tasty, indulge in a long drinking bout that is spoiled when the butler confesses to them his ruse. Thompson outdoes himself in *Road to Ruin* (c. 1849), in which a starving man stays alive for days by devouring two rotting corpses and even eating flesh from his own arms. All these fictional representations of cannibalism were equaled by a real-life story in 1848 of man-eating among a stranded party of Sierra miners, a story that was reported in all the penny papers and sensationalized in a Dark Adventure pamphlet novel *Amelia Sherwood; or, Bloody Scenes at the California Gold Mines* (1849), which contains this passage:

> A woman sat by the side of the body of her husband, who had just died, cutting out his tongue—the heart she had already taken out, broiled, and ate! The daughter was seen eating the flesh of her father—the mother that of her children—children that of father and mother.[59]

Dark Adventure fiction also features riotous orgy scenes or devilish rituals which provide some of the most demonic, blasphemous moments in this literature. Such scenes are, of course, central in our major literary texts, as seen in the satanic ritual in "Young Goodman Brown" and the uproarious forecastle party in *Moby-Dick*. Hawthorne and Melville were making use of a popular convention, since in Dark Adventure texts drunken scenes inevitably embody attacks upon mainstream conventions. At key moments in Simms's novels, respectable and disreputable characters whip themselves to a drunken frenzy and make devilish toasts against religion or in praise of hedonism. When Hawthorne called *The Scarlet Letter* a "hell-fired" novel and when Melville said that *Moby-Dick* was baptized by the devil, they were placing themselves in an American literary tradition of consecration to the forces of darkness. Demonic rituals were particularly common in popular crime fiction, whose protagonists were often disillusioned rebels against society who denounce God and man in surrendering to a life of sin. For instance, in *The Female Land Pirate* the heroine, a hardened criminal being initiated into a crime band, is made to use the warm blood of a murdered victim to swear in writing that she will henceforth *"cling to every thing wicked, abjure every thing holy, deny God and the Bible."*[60]

Many Dark Adventure works express the same restless skepticism and ambiguities that have made Hawthorne, Poe, and Melville attractive to modern readers. Nothing is more misleading than the commonly accepted notion that the dark vision of the major authors was unusual for their day. In fact, the major writings—even the gloomiest of them—are in a sense more affirmative than several of the lesser ones because their ambiguities are crafted, they are projected into symbol or tight narrative, and thus controlled by the artist. As Henry James would later say, literary style itself offers the highest redemption for the modern writer. Many unfamiliar works come close to being cacophonic cries of nihilistic despair because their dark themes are not successfuly sculpted.

When did this tradition of shapelessly skeptical texts begin in America, and what were its successive manifestations? A spirit of doubt lies behind Charles Brockden Brown's major novels, particularly *Wieland* and *Edgar Huntly,* but Brown achieved sufficient artistic control over his dark themes so that he can be more properly analyzed in terms of the literary fusions to be discussed later. The main American texts in which we see artistry waging a losing battle to ambiguity and frenetic sensationalism are George Watterston's *The Lawyer* (1808), Samuel J. B. Judah's *The Buccaneers* (1827), Laughton Osborn's *The Confessions of a Poet* (1835), S. Austin's story "The Comet" (1839), Richard Burleigh Kimball's *St. Leger, or Threads of Life* (1849), and the anonymously published *Desultoria: The Recovered Mss. of an Eccentric* (1850). These novels are tormented records of a restless skepticism that underlies the entire Dark Adventure mode. In them we see the kinds of torrential passions and anguished speculations that were rechanneled and more firmly managed in the major writings. In this regard, it should be pointed out that some of these works were familiar to the major authors: Poe once called Osborn's *Confessions of a Poet* the best book of its kind written in American, and he used Austin's "Comet" as a source for his tale "Eiros and Charmion"; also, Melville and Hawthorne were almost certainly aware of Kimball's *St. Leger* (1849), a novel which created a great sensation.

All these works are more or less informed by a dark philosophy that can be summarized as follows. Humankind is vile, self-deceived, driven by greed and lust, and hopelessly selfish. God's existence is dubious, and even if God does exist it matters little, for He pays no attention to this world, which is a tiny speck in a universe whose immensity is hopelessly beyond the comprehension of insignificant man. All of life is a delusion. Virtue is inoperable in a sham-ridden world. Since philosophical investigation can never solve the riddle of life, the pursuit of knowledge is pointless. So is the pursuit of fame, because death nullifies everything. In the face of these dark truths, a person can easily go mad and die, but even that doesn't matter since no one cares, not even relatives and supposed friends.

Such gloomy musings appear mainly as digressions in wildly sensational narratives involving various kinds of criminals and adventurers. Watterston's *The Lawyer* is a Poe-like first-person narration by a venal lawyer, heartless seducer, and would-be murderer who frequently confesses his own depravity. Osborn's *Confessions of a Poet,* perhaps the darkest American novel written before Melville's *Pierre,* features two illicit live-in romances, a murder, a vividly described nightmare, and the horrid decapitation of a rotting corpse—all related by a crazed poet shortly before he shoots himself. Scattered liberally throughout the text, mainly in the form of expository footnotes, are extremely cynical comments, such as "How vile is human nature!" and "Thus it is with every thing,—delusion—delusion—delusion!"[61] This theme of the illusoriness of experience also runs through Judah's *The Buccaneers,* a gory historical novel about war and piracy that includes several bleak passages such as this: "Who will contend that life is not an evil gift—a foul image with a veil of loveliness— . . . an iceberg of death, glowing beneath the variegated hues of sky, beautiful as a palace of spirits to the sight, but destroying if approached." Just as Judah's images of life's tantalizing inexplicability point toward *Moby-Dick,* so his repeated emphasis on human knavery anticipates *The Confidence-Man.* "There is not a single occurrence," he writes, "that is not tainted with vileness and abandoned knavery; your very neighbour, nay, your dearest friend chuckles delighted, if for the value of a farthing he can cheat you . . . All is overreaching duplicity."[62] The universality of chicanery is also emphasized in *Desultoria,* whose suicidal, disillusioned narrator warns: "Never trust the face. . . . To deceive by the face is the study of the world."[63]

Thematically, then, many of these unfamiliar texts are not distant from the major writings of the period. What distinguishes the major authors was their ability to structure and dramatize skeptical themes that in the lesser works are thrown rather clumsily into meandering novels that seem always on the brink of total irrationalism. Despite the artistic inferiority of the unfamiliar works, it is important to recognize that bleak narratives of perversity and metaphysical angst were quite common during this period, contributing to the crude cultural material from which the major writers crafted lasting literature.

Besides establishing a precedent for the devilish, ambiguous themes of the major literature, Dark Adventure also generated wondrous or marvelous images analogous to those in the major texts. In particular, there was a notably pre-Melvillian preoccupation with mythic sea monsters in a substantial body of overlooked nautical adventure novels. In *The Raven and the Whale* Perry Miller suggests as a source for Melville's white whale the terrific antediluvian beast described in *Behemoth* (1839), a novel by Melville's New York literary associate Cornelius Mathews.[64] It is also common knowledge that Melville was familiar with Owen Chase's 1821 *Narrative* of the *Essex* wrecked by a whale and that he may have known of J. N. Reynolds's "Mocha Dick: or the White Whale of the Pacific," published in the *Knickerbocker Magazine* in 1839. In general, the American public had an extraordinary fascination with mythic sea monsters and such monsters were treated with particular liveliness in Dark Adventure works. Antebellum interest in huge sea monsters was stimulated initially by numerous reports of sightings of an enormous kraken (sea serpent) off the coast of Gloucester, Massachusetts, between 1817 and 1822. Eventually the Gloucester sightings were fantastically re-created in Eugene Batchelder's adventurous prose poem *A Romance of the Sea-Serpent,* published a year before Melville began writing *Moby-Dick.* In the intervening decades both krakens and whales had been frequently mentioned in adventure literature. Since *Moby-Dick* was itself a massive Dark Adventure novel, it is useful to consider key examples of mythic beasts in lesser-known writings of the period.

Fictional treatments of sea monsters appealed to the growing interest in marvels that was also being exploited by the master showman Phineas T. Barnum. The Boston *Uncle Sam,* one of the earliest story weeklies in which adventure fiction appeared, in October 1842 featured an adventure story, "Whaling in the Pacific. Encounter with a White Whale," in which a gigantic white whale crushes several whaleboats sent from a ship whose captain is named Coffin and whose mate is Starbuck (two names Melville would use in *Moby-Dick*). The mammoth story weeklies continued for more than a decade to run stories of destructive whales: *Gleason's Pictorial Drawing Room,* for instance, in July 1851 (just as Melville was in the final stage of writing *Moby-Dick*) ran an article, "Encounter with a Whale," about a South Pacific whale that swallowed whaleboats and rammed into a ship, which barely made it to shore for repairs. Spectacular whale chases, often punctuated with salty seaman's slang, were featured in many adventure novels. Harry Halyard, a pamphlet novelist quoted in the prefatory "Extracts" to *Moby-Dick,* published several novels in the late 1840s featuring dramatic whale chases. Halyard's *The Doom of the Dolphin* (1848) has a scene in which three boats pursue a tremendous sperm whale, described as "a regular old white-headed eighty barrel fellow," which upsets the boats with his tremendous flukes.[65] Halyard's *Wharton the Whale-Killer!* (also 1848) includes a sequence in which a ship's captain offers a reward to the first sailor who can raise a whale; his wager is met when a greenhorn sights a whale from a masthead, initiating a long whale chase sequence, made lively by a swearing mate who grins in the face of destruction, a sequence that culminates in the whale's being killed and drawn alongside the ship for cutting in. Since Melville uses a quote from *Wharton the Whale-Killer!* in his "Extracts," it is not overstepping the bounds of credulity to suggest that such images as Ahab's reward offer, the masthead scene, Stubb's humor in the midst of peril, and the cutting in of whales were designed, at least in part, for readers of popular nautical romances like Halyard's.

Also, Melville's emphasis on the unparalleled immensity and destructiveness of his white whale can be viewed as part of a growing fascination with mythic monsters of all varieties. There had arisen a wild one-upmanship among popular adventure writers competing against each other to see who could describe the most freakish, savage beast. For example, strange encounters between humans and sea monsters were regular fare in grotesque humor periodicals such as the Crockett almanacs. The 1838 Crockett almanac included a sketch, "Colonel Crockett and the Sea Sarpint," in which Davy Crockett battles a kraken said to be long enough to twist the hair of an angel who straddles the land and the sea. The 1849 Crockett almanac contained a story, "Crockett and the Great Prairie Serpent," about a monstrous snake, said to be larger than any kraken, which Crockett wrestles and lashes to death. In the Crockett almanac for 1850, Crockett's nautical friend Ben Harding tells a violent story about a time when he and a sailor friend harpooned a whale, climbed aboard the whale's back, and went for a dizzying ride until at last the whale vindictively rammed against their ship, which was saved from destruction only when the whale was killed by a lance.

Sea monsters were not merely exploited as terrific spectacles; in several Dark Adventure works they were also treated as emblems of larger truths about man or God. Melville was not alone in investing a sea monster with both human and divine characteristics. Melville's extensive connections between whales and fates or spirits, for instance, had been anticipated in the pamphlet novel *Romance of the Deep!* (1846), in which the sailor characters are said to feel that "their doom and every incident attending it was writ out at length previous to that eventful day—that it was revealed to them the moment they struck their whale—that its phantom voice urged them on, and that they had not the power to refuse to obey. . . . [W]hen you have sailed the blue seas for half a century you will believe that each of our destinies has a guiding star, and that sooner or later, and ere its accomplishment, our final fate is revealed to us through its spirit-agent."[66] While the phantom image in this passage anticipates the Spirit Spout in *Moby-Dick,* the references to fate presage Ishmael's reflection that his whaling voyage "formed part of the grand programme of Providence that was drawn up a long time ago." Modern readers who call attention to the allegorical elements of *Moby-Dick*—the dramatic references to fate and elusive quests—should be made aware that such connections between whaling and larger themes were not unusual in American adventure fiction of the day. It is significant that when Sophia Hawthorne tried to point out some "subtle significance" behind Melville's Spirit Spout images, Melville wrote her a letter saying that in writing *Moby-Dick* he had "some vague idea" that the novel was "susceptible of an allegoric construction" but that he had not intended specific images such as the Spirit Spout to have special allegorical meaning.[67] The fact is that linkages between whaling and larger philosophical speculations were not uncommon in popular nautical fiction, so that Melville had reason to believe he was doing nothing particularly unusual in fashioning suggestive images such as the Spirit Spout.

Perhaps the most important thing to recognize is that by the time Melville wrote *Moby-Dick,* mythic sea monsters had a firm grasp on the American popular imagination and had been treated regularly and creatively by various writers of Dark Adventure. The most imaginative fictional treatment of sea monsters in American fiction before *Moby-Dick* was Eugene Batchelder's *A Romance of the Sea-Serpent, or The Ichthyosaurus* (1849), a bizarre pamphlet novel about a sea serpent which terrorizes the coast of Massachusetts, destroys a huge ship in mid-ocean, repasts on human remains gruesomely with sharks and whales, attends a Harvard commencement (where he has been asked to speak), shocks partygoers by appearing at a Newport ball, and at last is hunted and killed by a fleet of Newport sailors. Although absurd, Batchelder's novel in certain ways anticipated the whaling novel Melville began the following year. Just as Melville would attempt to counterbalance his metaphysical themes with the expository "Cetology" section, so Batchelder includes extensive notes in which he records all known sightings and descriptions of the kraken in recent times. Just as Melville would try to lend religious and historical depth to his whale, so Batchelder quotes long biblical passages about "leviathan" and stresses that his monster "lived in the world before the flood" and roamed the sea "when Job and the Prophets roamed the earth."[68] The unearthly

majesty and awesome power of Batchelder's leviathan is repeatedly emphasized, as would be Melville's, and just as Ishmael alone survives Moby
Dick's assault on the *Pequod,* so in the ship wrecked by Batchelder's serpent
"all that were in it were lost, save one who held on to the keel." In light
of the popularization of sea monsters represented by books like Batchelder's, there may have been quite topical meaning in Melville's comment
to Hawthorne after he had finished *Moby-Dick*: "So, now, let us add Moby
Dick to our blessing, and step from that. Leviathan is not the biggest
fish;—I have heard of Krakens."[69]

When we turn from Dark Adventure to the final form of antebellum
adventure fiction, what I call the Subversive, we find many points of
similarity but also key differences that make the Subversive mode the most
intriguing of the adventure genres. Like Dark Adventure, Subversive
fiction featured racy, marvelous, often gory plots involving wild adventure
and social outcasts. Subversive literature can be distinguished from Dark
Adventure by two things: first, it was *a literature of protest* with an ardently
democratic *political* dimension, as it militantly took the side of oppressed
groups while exposing alleged corruption among respected pillars of society; second, it was more *experimental* both thematically and stylistically than
Dark Adventure. It was increasingly informed by a bitter radical-democrat
vision of nineteenth-century America, which was portrayed as a nightmarish society of class divisions and social inequities, a society that seemed to
have grossly violated the republican ideals enunciated by the Founding
Fathers and fought for in the American Revolution. Stylistically, it tried to
reproduce this perceived social nightmare in what I term the American
Subversive Style, a highly irrational style characterized by intentional disruptions of linear patterns and wholesale assaults on conventional literary
rules. Subversive literature in its earliest phase, as exemplified by the
sensational novels and literary manifestoes of John Neal in the 1820s, was
a pugnacious, partly political mode that tried to establish a defiant, quirky
Americanness whose excessive irrationalism was intended as a direct affront to what was regarded as the effete gentility of foreign literatures.
Subversive Adventure increasingly absorbed the fiery egalitarianism of
Jacksonian democracy and after the Panic of 1837 became a volcanic protest literature produced by *radical democrats* who could describe modern
America only in sarcastic, inverted terms, with bold social pariahs deemed
preferable to hypocritical social rulers.* Despite its serious political moti-

---

*Most of the writers I am calling radical democrats were at one time or another
associated with the liberal wing of the Democratic Party, but I use the lower-case
"d" in "radical democrat" as a means of deemphasizing party affiliations. Indeed,
the literary radical democracy of antebellum America grew from an increasing
disillusion with the established parties, which were seen as tainted by the general

vation, Subversive literature always verged upon the grotesquely sensational and by the late 1840s became wholly vulgarized by the mass publishers. One of the greatest accomplishments of writers like Melville, Hawthorne, and Whitman was their success in retaining the energetic Americanness and provocative paradoxes of Subversive literature while leaving behind its growing perversity and crassness.

Subversive literature in its crude popular state was a politicized, exaggerated product of the democratic impulse that impelled other adventure novelists to look for native settings and characters. The same democratic spirit that drove other writers to seek out native literary arenas prompted the Subversives' deep sympathy for various oppressed groups: Native Americans, maltreated throughout American history; the urban working class, increasingly poor and turbulent in a period of rapid industrialization; women, cut off from meaningful employment and political power; and criminals, often the product of unfavorable circumstances. The very patriotic ideals that made authors search out native materials, therefore, led some to the discovery that these materials contained disturbing inconsistencies and paradoxes. National ideology seemed to be mocked everywhere by perceived reality. In the 1790s Charles Brockden Brown became the first to probe several irrational features of American life, including the suffering caused by urban poverty and disease, with the direct aim of subverting rational perception, and occasionally with the goal of advancing radical political views.

Nevertheless, Brown's rather formal, Latinate prose suggests that his Gothicism was still under the influence of Godwin and other British novelists. It was not until the reform-minded John Neal in the 1820s wrote a series of novels and essays that a more peculiarly indigenous Subversive style came into being. Neal was the American writer who first publicly praised Poe, who developed experimental poetic theories anticipatory of Whitman's, and who had a marked effect on Hawthorne. Because Neal's crucial role in developing a native Subversive idiom has been unrecognized, his importance in the emergence of America's major literature is not adequately appreciated.

Neal was the most vocal participant in an intensifying debate between those who wished to retain what was regarded as the calmness and polish of British prose and those, on the other hand, who called for a distinctly American wildness, roughness, and savagery, even at the expense of all past literary rules. The conflict between the two schools became open warfare when Neal impugned leading American writers, including Wash-

---

social corruption, and from an eagerness to seek correctives or alternatives to the party system.

ington Irving and John Pierpont, as tame and imitative. The American author, he argued, should be a kind of swaggering giant always flexing his stylistic muscles and blustering loudly. To match the giganticness of his country, Neal wrote, the American author should be "a rude, coarse man" of "stout, original power."[70] Disgusted by tame, predictable writing, which he associated with a foreign gentility, he asked Americans to produce a "mischievous" literature that reflected what he saw as the tough rebelliousness of the American democracy. He not only tolerated but actually courted stylistic crudities, as long as they were genuinely American. "Let us have poison," he wrote, "for poison were more precious, than herbs of degenerate virtue." He put theory into practice in a series of remarkable novels, which are our earliest full examples of the American Subversive Style, characterized by emotions heightened to a fever pitch, extreme sensational action creating a dizzying effect, sudden shifts in perspective, and narrative discontinuities.

Subversive fiction, as introduced by Neal and developed by radical democrats like George Lippard and George Thompson, tried to be deliberately outrageous, inflammatory, disquieting. It spit in the face of conventional literature. It took the side of oppressed or minority groups while exposing what was seen as secret corruption among the pillars of society. In Subversive fiction rebels or outcasts become symbols of the democratic common man always reenacting the American protest against tyranny. But the emblems of tyranny had become part of American society itself—the statesmen, capitalists, lawyers, clergymen, and "idle" rich that the Subversives viewed as hypocritical. Subversive fiction thus represented a form of autocriticism within American society, a turning inward of the rebelliousness that had once been directed at foreign tyrants.

Underlying the violence and satanism of Subversive literature was a sympathy with the feisty rebel against the social establishment. The justified or likable criminal, who we saw was also featured in popular crime pamphlets, became a figure of almost mythic dimensions in Subversive fiction. The Indian hero of Neal's *Logan* (1822) is said to be justified for his sadistic warfare against whites because of America's record of gross injustice to Native Americans. In Neal's *Errata* (1823) a naturally good man is converted into a depraved criminal as a result of his shattering perception of universal corruption among the outwardly respectable. The hero of Laughton Osborn's *Jeremy Levis* (1831) becomes "roguish, sceptical, morose" after seeing that in a perverted world the wicked thrive while the good suffer.[71] An ironic theme running through William Gilmore Simms's darkest novels is that bold criminality is preferable to the sneaking, covert villainy that reigns in civilized life. In Simms's *Richard Hurdis* (1838) a frontier gang of murderers is ironically called "the most moral community under the sun," since mainstream society is full of rogues who cause grave injustices under the cloak of respectability.[72] The criminal hero of Simms's *Guy Rivers* (1834) is an intelligent and initially virtuous man who turns to crime only after perceiving damning hypocrisy among the socially established. The justified criminal became a particularly popular character in later radical-democrat fiction such as Ned Buntline's *The G'hals of New York* (1850), which contains a sympathetic portrait of a murderer who sarcastically declares that "there isn't no *real* witue and honesty nowhere 'cept among the perfessional *dis*honest."[73]

In some Subversive texts this ennoblement of the likable criminal gave rise to a complete inversion of values whereby even grotesquely evil figures were invested with admirable qualities. For instance, two characters that are among the most gleefully wicked figures in American fiction—Devil-Bug in George Lippard's *The Quaker City* (1845) and Asmodeus in George Thompson's *New-York Life* (1849)—are portrayed in such a way that we are forced to sympathize with them despite their unprecedented devilishness. The leering Devil-Bug supervises constant debauchery and crime among the upper-class Philadelphians who frequent his den of iniquity, Monk Hall. He is a monstrous pimp and murderer who loves, in Lippard's words, "not so much to kill, as to observe the blood of his victim fall drop by drop."[74] In the topsy-turvy world of Subversive fiction, however, even bloodthirsty sadism is deemed preferable to sham virtue: at one point Devil-Bug actually becomes a force for good, saving two imperiled women, whereas his well-heeled guests at Monk Hall prove irredeemably amoral. Thompson's Asmodeus, a grinning devil figure who has the magical ability to witness secretly corrupt activities among America's ruling class, is said to have "germs of goodness in his nature, yet he is so constituted that he pursues even his good designs with a spice of devilish malice."[75] Paradoxically enough, this amiable devil is shown to have more honesty and integrity than the two-faced aristocrats he witnesses everywhere in American society.

In paradigmatic Subversive writings, the central conflict is between various oxymoronic oppressors (the reverend rake, the Christian slaveholder, the churchgoing capitalist, and so forth) and some version of the likable pariah, who embodies the embittered vindictiveness of lower-class or disenfranchised groups. In several major works of the day we find a similar confrontation. Melville in *Moby-Dick* contrasts oxymoronic authority figures (the godly, ungodlike Ahab, the fighting Quakers Peleg and Bildad) with lowly likable pariahs (Ishmael, Queequeg, the whole genially wicked crew). Likewise, Hawthorne contrasts a secretly corrupt reverend rake, Arthur Dimmesdale, with the openly criminal Hester Prynne: as in the popular novels, honest sin proves superior to hypocritical virtue. The

chief difference is that major authors eventually fuse the opposing character groups: Ahab's purpose is absorbed by the crew, and Dimmesdale
finally becomes an *honest* sinner like Hester Prynne. This fusing of warring
viewpoints creates greater density and suggestiveness in the major texts
and at the same time avoids the cynical inversion of values that occurs in
several popular works in which the likable criminal assumes an ironic
ascendancy over social leaders whose outward virtue is found rotten to the
core.

While Subversive literature unleashed powerful social paradoxes that
contributed to the ambiguities of the major writings, it also prepared the
way for stylistic innovation in American literature. What may seem the
most glaring flaw of many Subversive novels—their formlessness, their
wildness—was an extremely important groundbreaker for the major writers. Mark Twain rightly noted that the most distinctly American genre, the
one that grew most completely from native soil, was the tall tale: the
structureless string of weird digressions that comically go nowhere. What
he did not mention is that the tall tale was just one of many kinds of
digressive writings which, taken together, form an indigenous *écriture* I call
the American Subversive Style.

The appropriateness of a defiantly disruptive style to democratic America was one of Tocqueville's main arguments in his discussion of this
country's literature. "By and large," Tocqueville wrote, "the literature of
democracy will never exhibit the order, regularity, skill and art characteristic of aristocratic literature; formal qualities will be neglected or actually
despised. The style will often be strange, incorrect, overburdened, and
loose, and almost always strong and bold." He noted that "Americans
often mix their styles in an odd way, sometimes putting words together
which, in their mother tongue, are carefully kept apart."[76] What Tocqueville described as the typical democratic style is precisely the irrational style
as developed by the writers I call Subversive. It was a style of intentional
narrative discontinuities, oddly juxtaposed imagery, confusions between
dream and reality, and feverish emotions creating distortions of perception.

It was, in short, a period when idiosyncratic rebelliousness against staid
literary norms became integrated into the theory and practice of American
literature. And nowhere did this rebelliousness have such extreme manifestations as among the unfamiliar Subversive novelists, who may be credited with experimenting adventurously with irrational images and devices
that were handled more artistically by the major authors. We might be
tempted to dismiss the frequent stylistic innovations in the unfamiliar texts
as signs of carelessness or mere chance. But, from the start, American
Subversives were quite direct and outspoken in their attempt to redefine

literary style in terms of a crude Americanness identified with the shocking, the impudent, the oneiric.

The intention to create a distinctly American irrational style was first expressed by the pioneering Subversive spokesman John Neal. With typical brashness, Neal announced that he wrote his turbulent war novel *Seventy-Six* (1823) "as an experiment" in an effort "to do what nobody else had done, or would have the impudence to attempt."[77] He declared that the American writer, in the effort to combat Anglophile tameness and match the roughness of his country, should exhibit "coarseness,—that other name for great vigor, wild power, and courageous peculiarity." While he admired Brockden Brown as an accomplished novelist of terror, he thought (with some justification) that Brown's rather formal style was too heavily influenced by foreign writers and showed few signs of distinctly American forms of linguistic irrationalism. In several of his novels Neal tried to introduce versions of what he termed "natural writing," or "how people talk when they are not talking for display."[78] Aiming to counteract Addisonian smoothness and Johnsonian stiffness, he developed a consciously disruptive style based on folk speech patterns and passionate excess. Among Neal's more inventive variations upon this "natural" style were the use of soldiers' vernacular in *Seventy-Six,* the crude colloquialisms of a cynical narrator in *Errata,* and the remarkable use of narrative ellipsis and directionless dialogue in the first half of *The Down-Easters.*

With his experimental outlook, it is understandable that Neal in various ways looked forward to several major authors. He began the American tradition of the cynical antipreface, or introductory comment intended to outrage or poke fun at the reader—a tradition that later would include the wry "Custom-House" section of *The Scarlet Letter* and the sarcastic remarks prefacing *Pierre, Israel Potter,* and *Huckleberry Finn.* "I hate Prefaces. I hate Dedications," Neal writes in *Logan*; he says he dedicates the novel to "any body; for I know nobody worth dedicating it to," least of all his countrymen, for "they are unworthy of me."[79] Initiating the sort of attack on literary sentimentalism that would run through Melville's writings and become fully dramatized in Mark Twain's portrait of the mawkish Emmeline Grangerford, Neal digressed in *Errata* to announce his disgust with "simpering, smooth, sweet" imitations of Addison by pious American poets like James G. Percival and John Pierpont.[80] Other of his stylistic experiments were prophetic too. When Hawthorne recalled that his "boyish brains" were "almost turned" by "that wild fellow John Neal,"[81] he may have been thinking of the frequent strident outbursts of Neal's characters, outbursts whose unprecedented intensity looked forward to the delirious shrieks of Robin Molineux, Ethan Brand, and Miriam Schaefer. Nearly two decades before Hawthorne made his famous distinction between the novel

and the romance, Neal in *Randolph* made the same distinction, asking
Americans to write not *novels* but *romances* based on "vivid and intense
. . . *exaggeration*" producing "trance-like agitation and excitement." In the
same work, Neal anticipated Whitman by asserting that America was on the
verge of a stylistic revolution whereby "the poetry of form, . . . of rhyme,
measure, and cadence" would be replaced by a new prose-poetry.[82] Also,
Neal was primarily responsible for bringing national attention to the struggling young Poe, whose early poems Neal praised in an 1829 magazine
article. Poe, who called these "the very first words of encouragement I ever
remember to have heard," stressed that his and Neal's sensibilities were
"always running in the same direction . . . and cannot help mingling."[83]
That aspect of Poe's style that the surrealist André Breton called *convulsive
beauty* (violent, shattering, explosive) owed much to the irrational style as
developed by Neal, who presaged Poe in detaching literature from morality and placing it in the realm of effect.

While Neal and several later Subversives introduced various forms of
literary irrationalism that were adopted by the major writers, they also
went in new directions, sometimes producing effects that anticipated not
Hawthorne or Poe but later writers instead. When in *Seventy-Six* Neal had
his ill-spoken narrator give "a fair chart of the rambling incoherent jour-
neying of my thought for hours," he was experimenting with a technique
that would later be called stream of consciousness.[84] When he described
the extreme distortions of perspective created by battle smoke and flame,
he was introducing a device that would be featured by Stephen Crane. Neal
often tries to undermine the genteel reader by deliberately violating predictable narrative patterns. "My style may offend you . . . I hope that it
will," announces the narrator of *Seventy-Six,* and offensive it often is, with
its rapid leaps between gory war scenes, weird visions, and feverish erotic
escapades.[85] Similarly, Neal warns us that the strange novel *Errata* is most
notable for "the want of arrangement; the incoherency; and the perpetual
shifting" of its narration.[86] When he called for a "natural writing" based
upon colloquial idioms, he was looking forward to Mark Twain and
Faulkner. When he registered the bizarre, rapidly shifting images flitting
through the minds of dreamers or madmen, he sometimes reproduced the
oneiric in a manner that presaged Lautréamont and the surrealists.

Such premodern elements of the irrational style became even more
pronounced in later Subversive texts, particularly the consciously outrageous novels of George Lippard. One of his contemporaries remarked
that "the Lippard style . . . requires the writer to be born with St. Vitus's
dance, to be inoculated with Delirium Tremens, take the nightmare in the
natural way, get badly frightened at a collection of snakes, and write under the combined influences of these manifold causes of inspiration."[87] As

bizarre as Lippard's style can seem—even by today's standards—it was thoroughly, indelibly American. That is, American in Tocqueville's sense of strange, bold, astonishing, and stylistically mixed. It was the democratic style taken to a new boisterous extreme. The quintessential radical democrat, Lippard was at once the most intensely patriotic and the most militantly radical novelist of the pre–Civil War period. His veneration for America's Founding Fathers verged upon the religious, as witnessed by his long, very popular collections of historical "legends" in which he mythologized the heroes of the past. At the same time, his perception of the distance between democratic ideals and the horrors of industrialized America impelled him to write lurid exposés of upper-class corruption in a style perhaps unparalleled in its irrationalism.

An espouser of radical causes like Neal, Lippard waged holy war against all kinds of social oppressors. His indictments of the rich and defenses of the poor were uncompromising. Although he stressed peaceful social change, he warned that if workers' demands were not met they would be forced "to go to War, in any and all forms—War with the Rifle, Sword and Knife."[88] Although he apparently never read the works of his German contemporary Karl Marx, he could sound much like a revolutionary Marxist in his calls for workers' unity and revolt. The famous passage in the *Communist Manifesto*—"The workers of the world have no country. . . . Workers of the world, unite!"—is similar in spirit to several of Lippard's declarations of international solidarity, such as this: "Call these nations as you will—call them French, English, German, Irish, Hungarian, or Roman—they are yet one people; they belong to one vast nation of the OPPRESSED" (*Quaker City* weekly, 1849). Such radical-democrat internationalism would also affect Melville, who made the *Pequod* the repository for representatives of many downtrodden nations, and Whitman, who frequently extended sympathy to foreign peoples. Lippard differed from these writers in the savagery of his rhetoric and the activist strategies he used to implement his goals. Despite their egalitarian sympathies, neither Melville nor Whitman had the militancy of a true radical activist like Lippard. "Arise, ye millions of the human race—Arise, ye races and tribes of the poor," Lippard wrote in *Paul Ardenheim* (1848), using words that strikingly prefigured the opening line of the revolutionary socialist battle hymn "The Internationale" (Paris, 1871): "Arise, ye prisoners of starvation! Arise, ye wretched of the earth." So dedicated was Lippard to the workers' cause that he founded a nationwide labor organization, the Brotherhood of the Union, designed to supplant the capitalist system with a network of workers' cooperatives patterned according to the republican principles of the Founding Fathers.

There was, however, a major complication in the radical-democrat imagination as embodied in Lippard and several other activist writers of the 1840s: its anticapitalist rhetoric lapsed all too quickly into the merely sensational and often into the downright disgusting. To be sure, sensational rhetoric is common enough among nineteenth-century radicals of other countries. In *Capital*, for instance, Marx states that capital comes into the world "dripping from head to foot, from every pore, with blood and dirt. . . . Capital is dead labor that, vampire-like, lives only by sucking living labor."[89] Still, Marx had an objective, scientific dimension completely lacking among the American radical democrats, for whom trenchant irony and verbal fireworks seemed the only effective means of communicating their ideas.

How do we explain the strange compound of serious social commentary and purely extraneous sensationalism that runs through Lippard's fiction? The fact is that he was both speaking *for* and speaking *from* American working-class culture. As an endorser of radical social change, he used violent imagery to unmask the social elite. As a product of the proletarian class he defended, he knew that this class took increasing pleasure in a gratuitous violence that embodied its fiercest aggressions. In the economically unstable decade following the Panic of 1837, the American working class took out its frustrations by forming gangs and clubs that engaged in frequent brawls. At the same time, popular newspapers and stage melodramas were tailored increasingly for the emerging urban classes whose rowdy jingoism Sean Wilentz aptly calls "the republicanism of the streets."[90] A committed radical democrat, Lippard exaggerated sensational rhetoric for the dual reason of exposing the rich and satisfying the poor. Fueled by political rage, he absorbed all the problematic features of Subversive popular culture—penny-press sensationalism, the justified criminal, the oxymoronic oppressor, the irrational style—and produced a novel, *The Quaker City*, that in a sense *was* this popular culture, with all its crudities and energies. He used words as weapons, much as a Philadelphia gang member would use clubs and daggers. A contemporary biographer of Lippard explained: "It was *his* business to attack social wrongs, to drag away purple garments, and expose to our shivering gaze the rottenness of vice—to take tyranny by the throat and strangle it to death."[91]

While Lippard's writings politically defend workers' interests, therefore, they also project the most violent fantasies of the working-class consciousness in a time of rapid urbanization. In *The Quaker City*, the archetypal radical-democrat novel, one quickly recognizes the self-subverting paradoxes of the popular Subversive imagination. The novel's hyperbolic sensationalism and voyeuristic eroticism compromise whatever political message it might contain. Dismayed by social injustice and economic inequities, Lippard exploits every device of popular sensational literature to expose the social elite; but time and again sensationalism becomes an end in itself. There is little social import to Lippard's long description of an old lady's brain splattered on the floor, or dismembered corpses in a dissecting room, or the images of gibbets and poisons that fill the novel. Although Lippard's motivation is to unmask the ruling class, the ironic images discovered in the unmasking process lead Lippard into the crassest forms of sensationalism. Blood, rotting corpses, gibbets, nightmare visions—such are the images that the radical-democrat imagination of the 1840s naturally coined.

The rebellion of the radical democrats was as much stylistic as it was social. Lippard was even more disgusted than Neal or Poe with staid, predictable sentimental literature, which he insisted was manufactured by a cadre of bourgeois magazinists upholding the economic and political status quo. He lamented that American fiction "of the present day, does not present extravagant views or life, or paint pictures that transcend probability; its delineations, on the contrary, are only extravagant in their tameness, and transcendent in their mathematical probability."[92] In his own novels he used a savage lyricism designed to challenge the Conventional literature that he associated with an effete aristocracy still clinging to foreign literary rules. Lippard brashly violated narrative linearity and chronological sequence, often shifting tone and perspective to create a kind of quicksand effect. He boasted that the plot of *Paul Ardenheim* was "utterly impossible" and "altogether improbable"; "the author . . . prides himself on having written *'the most improbable book in the world.'* " Similarly, he claimed that *The Nazarene* was "strange," at variance with the "rules of critics."[93]

The irrational style had a compelling attraction for the American public. Lippard's *The Quaker City* (1845) sold 60,000 copies in its first year and an average of 30,000 a year for the next five years, becoming the best-selling novel written by an American before *Uncle Tom's Cabin.* So popular did Lippard become that even *Godey's Lady's Book*—a magazine he detested— conceded in 1848: "He is unquestionably the most popular writer of the day, and his books are sold, edition after edition, thousand after thousand, while those of others accumulate, like useless lumber, on the shelves of the publishers."[94] The novel is the quintessential American Subversive text, as radical stylistically as it is politically. It absorbed many popular sensational characters and devices and exaggerated them to such a degree that it completely subverted rational expression and broke down unities of time and space. The novel is like Monk Hall itself, a labyrinthine structure riddled with trapdoors that are always opening beneath the reader's feet, tumbling him into another dimension. The texture of the novel is very much like life as it is described by one of the main characters: "Every thing increase of this public poison—a demoralizing literature, the real 'Pandora's box of evil passions'—the flood-gate, from beneath whose slimy jaws run a stream of pollution, sending forth its pestilential branches to one great ocean of immorality, let such a one take a trip with me through the length and breadth of our land."[101] The author noted that such racy fiction was peddled from bookstalls on street corners and in railway station depots all over the nation. In the United States, with its population of some twenty-four-million people, the writer noted, there was an "enormous circulation of over 2,500,000 volumes" exerting their poisonous influence "*directly* upon the minds of very nearly 9,500,000 of our population, and *indirectly* upon the GREAT MASS." In angry reaction against this fiction's inverted morality and its use of the likable criminal, the author declared: " 'Vice unmasked' say you; . . . but where is virtue portrayed? The murderer, robber, pirate, swindler, the grog-shop tippler, the lady of fashion, the accomplished rake and libertine, are meritorious characters, held up in a spirit of pride and levity, and surrounded by a 'halo of emulation.' " The volume contained as an appendix this statement by the Chicago Tract Society: "The popular press is teeming with works of vapid or unhallowed fiction, or grossly immoral books and prints" whose effect will be "to overturn all morality, to poison the springs of domestic happiness, to dissolve the ties of our social order, and to involve our country in ruin."

Nowhere was this vulgarization more evident than in fictional depictions of perverse sexuality, which had surfaced in early Subversive fiction but became grossly exaggerated by certain pamphlet novelists of the 1840s, most notably George Thompson. For the first time in American history, the erotic imagination was visibly unleashed by antebellum popular culture. That is a story worth telling on its own.

7

THE EROTIC IMAGINATION

I T has been well known, since Steven Marcus's *The Other Victorians*, that there was a subterranean genre of pornography in England, but the perception of a highly puritanical America still prevails.[1] I have found that antebellum America in fact produced a sizable body of hitherto overlooked erotic popular writings. The sexual images in the major literature may be profitably studied in the context of these writings.

The antebellum social and literary scene was deeply riddled with sexual tensions and perversions. Although reliable primary evidence of antebellum sexual habits is frustratingly scarce, enough evidence survives to explode the long-standing myth that there was an all-powerful cult of domesticity that governed daily behavior and kept America a prudish, highly moralistic culture. True, such a conservative outlook was promoted in popular ladies' magazines and etiquette books. But the cult of domesticity was itself, like Conventional fiction, an ideological response to reading habits that were far more inclined to the scabrous and illicit than is commonly supposed. Beginning in the early 1830s, sex scandals were often featured in penny papers, dark-reform literature, and trial pamphlets, and in time a frankly erotic popular literature emerged. Whitman mentions in his notebooks having read "erotic poetry and stories, dwelling on the lusty and copulative."[2] Such literature, much of it written by Americans, indeed enjoyed a great vogue, particularly during the 1840s. The unbridled sensualism and sadomasochistic violence of this popular pornography leads us to regard the relatively restrained erotic moments in the major literature

as another cultural corrective offered to counteract the mechanical prurience and crass titillation that characterized the popular erotic imagination.

Snowy Globes and Scarlet Prisons

The distinguishing feature of the American erotic writing of the 1840s
was its unique combination of prurient sexuality and grisly gore. Sadomasochism has, of course, been a common feature of all erotic literature.
But the same forces that produced unusual violence in America's sensational writings also contributed to excessive bloodiness in its erotic literature. By the 1840s, gross violence and explicit pornography were brought
together by various writers of popular pamphlet fiction, most notably the
New York radical democrat George Thompson. Long before that, there
had been tentative anticipations of this combination. John Neal, the father
of American Subversive fiction, experimented with the combined violence
and eroticism that would dominate later American pornography. In one
typical sequence in *Logan* a surgeon helping a bleeding soldier looks up
from his bloody task and stares with "rapturous delight" at the swelling
bosoms of a woman who offers help.[3] Neal also began the immoral-reform
tradition of pretending to denounce eroticism but showing undeniable
fascination with it. For example, when in *Errata* he criticizes American
women for wearing low-cut gowns, his apparent moralism is belied by his
irrepressible attraction to what these gowns reveal: "You go with your
bosoms naked, aye, your *bosoms,* whereon, if a man really loved you, he
would as soon another had placed his hand, or his mouth, as his eyes; aye,
your *bosoms*—the pillow, where a husband . . . will yet lay his aching
temples, with the thought of rapture—that he sleeps upon something
holy—unvisited, unprofaned."[4] In the same novel he suggests his actual
interests by describing a steamy scene in which a nubile woman enters a
man's room at night and faints, exposing her breasts; he loses control and
places his "passionate mouth to her bosom." The voyeur style, by which
the author dwells lasciviously on the private parts of his heroines, was
developed by Neal, who in a typical moment describes a woman wearing
a thin gown that reveals her "fine bosom; and, particularly, her right
breast, which was surprisingly beautiful and natural—unsustained by any
corset or stays, almost as if it had been naked." Neal was the first novelist
to portray sex at camp meetings, describing in *Errata* a religious revival
where nothing is seen but "tents full of legs and arms." In the same novel
he became the first American writer to recognize woman's strong sexual
drives. He has the narrator hide in a room where a bride-to-be slowly
disrobes while chatting with her bridesmaids—the girls are discussing sex.

He digresses to say that women of all kinds, even "the holy and conse-crate," privately express the most licentious fantasies.

In the 1830s it became evident that erotica had a large market in America. In 1833 the New York reformer John R. McDowall launched an investigation into the popularity of erotic books, prints, snuff boxes, and music boxes. He wrote that he was "completely astounded" to find that "our country was flooded with these obscene articles."[5] In 1834 he called together nearly three hundred clergymen in a New York chapel to display the many "obscene" items he had collected; the clerics were fascinated but became suspicious of McDowall's motives, and the meeting broke up with as many murmurings against him as against the displayed articles.

The reformers' discoveries were sensational enough to gain nationwide attention, both through their very popular publications and through the notoriety created by sallies against the reformers themselves. To many Americans, it must have seemed as though sexual deviation was the order of the day. One alarmed reformer warned in 1834 that masturbation was such a common indulgence that it threatened to "sweep in a wide-spread tide of desolation, over our land and the world."[6] Another found adultery and premarital sex to be so widespread that "virgin chastity, and conjugal fidelity, are imaginary virtues."[7] A favorite topic in reform literature was secret debauchery among outwardly respectable citizens and the degraded lives of urban prostitutes. Whorehouses were regularly described as the site of mass corruption, suicide, and infanticide. Prostitutes were portrayed as she-devils, driven to a life of sin by seducers' trickery and subsequent social ostracism. They were said to take poison regularly and kill their illegitimate offspring. In the words of McDowall: "Thousands of children are murdered. Dead infants are frequently found; sometimes in privies, wells, sewers, ponds, docks, streets, open fields, and in other places."[8] Stories of prostitutes and their customers rarely had happy endings: most ended as gloomily as "Young Goodman Brown" or Crane's *Maggie*. The story of Amelia Gray, featured in the April 1833 issue of *McDowall's Journal*, was typical. Amelia, a poor girl raised by a clergyman, is seduced and then abandoned by her protector's son. She goes insane, becomes a whore, is converted to religion, but then backslides into prostitution and dies miserably.

This seamy reform literature was only part of the overall shift toward the sensational and the darkly erotic in the American popular press. The 1830s, the decade that produced penny newspapers and crime pamphlets, was also marked by the rise of a new kind of dark literature featuring perverse sexuality. In terms of eroticism, Laughton Osborn's *Confessions of a Poet* (1831) was perhaps the most important American novel of the 1830s, because it combined a violent, gloomy plot with striking accounts of illicit love and woman's sexuality. The narrator has successive live-in relationships with two women: one is "never soft but when the stir of sexual passion was busy with her senses," while the other succeeds in carrying out a Hester Prynne–like plan to escape to Europe with her lover, to whom she cries, "I will fly with you! . . . Friend, lover, mistress, any thing,—make me what you please; I will be all to you,—every thing—or nothing—so that I be not from you!"[9]

Such willing women, however, are rare in the fiction of the 1830s, which was a decade of transition between the soft pornography of John Neal's novels and the more open sexuality of the 1840s. It was a decade of steady broadening, a time when the moralistic and the sensational began to overlap textually. On the popular level, this overlapping gave rise to the phenomenon I have described as immoral reform, epitomized by the sexually charged writings of antiprostitution, anti-Catholic, and temperance reformers, all of whom were forced to compete for the same readers who were being regaled by atrocities and sex scandals in the popular penny papers and crime pamphlets. This overlapping of genres was nowhere more clearly visible than in the fierce wars that raged between the reformers and the popular newspaper editors, who regularly charged each other with obscenity and crass sensationalism. Popular culture had suddenly become a miasma in which morality, sex, self-righteous indignation, and exploitative sensationalism on all sides became mingled in a swirling maelstrom of values. It was naturally a fruitful moment for ambiguous literature—in the 1830s Hawthorne produced some of his most successful tales of hidden corruption and Poe abstracted the essence of popular sensational and erotic writings in tales of sex and death such as "Ligeia" and "Morella."

It was in the 1840s that the burgeoning American erotic imagination at last came to full flower. After federal statutes banning the importation of erotic material were passed in 1842, American publishers redoubled their efforts to satisfy readers by publishing a far greater amount of native erotic literature than before. By 1845 a leading New York reformer expressed shock at "all the trashy and disgusting fictions with which our country is flooded," while another asked: "Will not the steam-presses create licentiousness faster than police regulations can drain it off? . . . While a thousand presses pander to the basest of human appetites, is it surprising that licentiousness abounds?"[10]

The sex drive was now generally recognized as powerful and irrepressible, largely because of the widely publicized discovery by the phrenologist Andrew Combe that the organ of "amativeness" was the largest in the brain. Voyeuristic shows of "model artists," also referred to as *tableaux vivants* or *poses plastiques,* became extremely popular during the 1840s. In these shows lightly draped women gave the illusion of nudity when they posed as classical deities or legendary women, ranging from "Eve in Eden" through "Venus in a Shell" to "Lady Godiva." The first of the shows was given at Palmero's Opera House in New York and was soon imitated in taverns nationwide at every price ranging from a sixpence to a dollar. Predictably, the model-artist shows created a scandal and were often raided by police. But they persisted through the decade and were warmly defended by Whitman, who in an article for the *New Orleans Crescent* declared that to denounce model artists was to brand as indecent "Nature's cunningest work—the human frame, form and face."[11] By the mid-1840s it became a fad among upper-class couples to copy the model-artist idea at home; often hostesses of dinner parties would dress in transparent gowns and give motionless portrayals of classical scenes. Such private theatricals fed into the erotic undertones of Hawthorne's *The Blithedale Romance,* in which the narrator more than once disrobes the beautiful Zenobia in his imagination and is even treated to actual *tableaux vivants* when she poses as legendary characters "holding a large piece of gauze, or some such ethereal stuff."[12]

This social voyeurism was reflected in an intensified use of the voyeur style in popular novels of the 1840s. In the racy pamphlet fiction that comprised almost two-thirds of American novels published in the decade, we find many languorous accounts of voluptuous women in total or partial dishabille. Many authors undertook their accounts of sensuous women in the spirit of Whitman, who would write in "Children of Adam": "[T]he female form . . . attracts with fierce undeniable attraction."[13] Whitman would famously give sensuous catalogues of physical beauty, from the "Head, neck, hair, ears" through "The womb, the teats, nipples" to "The beauty of the waist, and thence of the hips, and thence downward toward the knees." Such physical descriptions are relatively sanitized versions of a voyeur style that had produced more prurient, sometimes perverse effects in popular sensational fiction. In J. Henry Smith's *The Green Family; or, The Veil Removed* (1849) a scheming procuress entertains her male customers by drugging a lovely girl and putting her nude body on display. Struck by the special loveliness of the girl's vagina, one of the men struggles for the right metaphors to describe it (with rather unfortunate results): "What a splendid carnation adorns the main aperture, with its fascinating fringe of sea-moss. It more than rivals my conception of the beautiful line of Oliver Wendell Holmes: 'Like seaweed round a clam.' "[14] Sensational writers were adept at inventing situations in which women were either totally or partially nude. A dress "accidentally" unfastened during a scuffle; a black woman asked to stand naked on a slave block; a woman's corpse brought before a class of medical students; a sleeping woman with her nightrobe open—these and many other scenes were excuses for authors to linger over the female form, which was usually described minutely from the hair to the toes, with special emphasis on the "snowy globes" or "rose-tipped hillocks" that were always billowing into view.

The master of the voyeur style was George Lippard. In Lippard's hands, the voyeur style created an atmosphere of lust around even the most apparently virtuous heroine, so that whatever pious associations have gathered around the moral woman are negated by the lascivious "caress" of the aroused author. One bemused reviewer complained that Lippard carries "the demon of sensuality with him, even into the presence of earth's angels."[15] Lippard's descriptions, though rarely explicit, are always suggestive. Lippard instinctively grasped a concept that Hugh Hefner would later exploit: the American public is most excited not by explicit views of depraved women as by peekaboo glimpses of the girl next door. This typically American combination of purity and prurience grew directly from the antebellum Subversive imagination, whose most representative product on the popular level was Lippard's *The Quaker City.* This novel was widely damned as "the immoral work of the age," but Lippard insisted the book was "destitute of any idea of sensualism."[16] Lippard's moral pretense was, of course, standard immoral-reform apologia, just as his use of the voyeur style was polite pornography. His descriptions resemble the early *Playboy* centerfolds: glossy portraits of impossibly lovely women who are all the more tempting for not being fully revealed. Notice how a dreamy eroticism permeates even this comparatively tame account of the virtuous Mary Arlington—perhaps the *least* explicit picture of female charms Lippard ever penned:

> The maiden—pure and without a stain—lay sleeping on the small couch that occupied one corner of the closet. Her fair limbs were enshrouded in the light folds of a night-robe, and she lay in an attitude of perfect repose, one glowing cheek resting upon her uncovered arm, while over the other, waved the loosened curls of her glossy hair. The parting lips disclosed her teeth, white as ivory, while her youthful bosom, came heaving up from the folds of her night-robe, like a billow that trembles for a moment in the moonlight, and then is suddenly lost to view. She lay there in all the ripening beauty of maidenhood, the light falling over her young limbs, their outlines marked by the easy folds of her robe, resembling in their roundness and richness of proportion, the welling fullness of the rose-bud that needs but another beam of light, to open it into its perfect bloom.[17]

The sleeping heroine may be "pure and without stain," but the description of her is not. The style itself undercuts any pious message she may embody, as the erotic imagination exudes a succession of throbbing sentences filled with sexually charged metaphors betraying the author's undeniable sensualism.

Model artists and the voyeur style not only provided release for male fantasies but also reflected an increased interest in the sexuality of women. In a surprising number of novels of the 1840s, women are either willing partners or actually aggressors in the sex act. Among the many views of women circulating in antebellum America was that of John Humphrey Noyes's perfectionists, whose views were well known after their notorious "love feasts" of the 1830s and especially after Noyes's often reprinted "Battle Axe Letter" of 1837. The perfectionists regarded woman as an insatiable sexual vampire who demanded constant sexual stimulation but drained vital force from man every time he experienced orgasm. Celebrating "amative" sex while fearing the emasculating results of "propagative" sex, Noyes and his followers at the Oneida community (founded 1847) practiced a system of complex marriage whereby man was encouraged to have many sexual partners (therefore keeping lustful women satisfied) but always avoiding ejaculation (thereby saving himself from the dementia that was thought to accompany the release of semen). Although the perfectionists' view of woman as a sexual vampire may not have been openly accepted by most Americans, it clearly lies behind the portrayal of fictional heroines such as the animalistic Dora Livingstone in *The Quaker City.* It should be noted, moreover, that woman's sexuality was recognized by others than the perfectionists. The prominent reformer Mary Gove Nichols gave a widely publicized speech in 1846 announcing that masturbation was widespread in America, particularly among women. Three years later, Nichols's findings were confirmed by the New York writer George Thompson, who announced that masturbation was common even among "elegant young ladies, virtuous and modest," who seem "paragons of perfection" but who are dedicated to "the secret indulgence of passions which they would have people think they are too pure to possess."[18]

Several other popular novelists of the period were also intrigued by woman's sexual nature. Much of the crime fiction of the 1840s featured heroines who fearlessly indulge in the excesses of perverse passion. The devilish heroine of the lurid pamphlet novel *Narrative and Confessions of Lucretia Cannon* (1841) is raised as a teenaged prostitute and then marries a wealthy man whom she poisons (along with their child) because she is "very sensual in her pleasures" and tires of married life. In a career of crime that includes twelve murders and much sadomasochistic sex, she becomes "one of the most abandoned and notorious of women, giving loose to every species of licentiousness and extravagance."[19] Four other novels about woman criminals—*The Life and Sufferings of Cecilia Mayo* (1843), *Life and Confession of Mary Jane Gordon* (1847), *The Female Land Pirate* (1847), and A. J. H. Duganne's *Eustace Barcourt* (1848)—are even more explicit in their treatments of women's sexuality. Cecilia Mayo, seduced and abandoned at an early age, becomes an unregenerate whore who specializes in ruining innocent young men. Mary Jane Gordon resorts to "all licentiousness in the power of women" in order to entrap men and kill them; in the course of the novel she murders her husband, her father, her baby, two of her best friends, and several men she sleeps with.[20] Similarly, Amanda Bannoris, the "Female Land Pirate," takes revenge on her seducer, giving herself over to a career of unrestrained sex and amoral murder. Duganne's Eustace Barcourt likewise becomes wild with amorality, as she vows to a man that if he kills the criminal who raped her: "You shall possess my beautiful body, and make me your slave!"[21] He does so, and there develops between the two a vampirish partnership in crime. Certain elements of the novel directly anticipate *The Scarlet Letter*: for a while Eustace lives alone in a cottage near a village, where her illegitimate child is "nursed in solitude and apart from the world, feeding on the sadness and mystery of his mother's life"; and at the end Eustace and her lover escape on a pirate ship, the kind of flight planned but not realized by Hawthorne's lovers.

In other novels of the period the topic of women's sexuality becomes central. *Ellen Merton, The Belle of Lowell* (1844), traces the descent into prostitution of a sexually eager factory girl who "fell a victim to her own unbridled passions."[22] In J. Henry Smith's *The Green Family; or, The Veil Removed* (1849), a "warm and ardent" married woman takes several lovers, one of whom is carefully described as he gazes on her "rose-tipped hillocks" and parts "the folds of her dress" while his hand seeks "the soft, velvety orbs of her bosom."[23] Hawthorne may have made his letter scarlet for reasons other than just the obvious one of using a color often associated with sin; in Smith's novel (published the year Hawthorne was writing *The Scarlet Letter*) a girl who swallows an aphrodisiac is initiated into a secret sex club of which the final degree is "the *scarlet*, that fearful and most solemn of all degrees." Woman's love of sexuality is also featured in *Mary Ann Temple . . . [The] History of an Amorous and Lively Girl, of Exquisite Beauty, and Strong Natural Love of Pleasure!* (c. 1849). As a girl, Mary Temple has powerful sex fantasies from reading novels and anatomy books; she goes on to live out these fantasies in various amorous adventures, the first of which suggests the truth of the novel's subtitle: "He tore open my bosom, and putting his lips to the 'White Mountains,' caused me the most thrilling pleasures. I sank prostrate under him overpowered with delight, and sighing deeply, returned his passionate kisses." She stresses that she "was not a passive instrument in his hands. I hugged and kissed him with a voluptuous eagerness that, when I once began, was carried to the extreme by my uncontrollable passions."[24]

As daring as some of these novels were, none approached the explicitness of the fiction of George Thompson, the prolific New York writer of radical-democrat pamphlet novels in the late 1840s and 1850s. In works like *The House Breaker* (1848), *Venus in Boston* (1849), *The Countess; or, Memoirs of Women of Leisure* (1849), *City Crimes* (1849), *Adventures of a Pickpocket* (1849), *New-York Life* (1849), *The Ladies' Garter* (c. 1851), *The Gay Girls of New-York* (1853), and *Fanny Greeley; or, Confessions of a Free-love Sister* (c. 1853) Thompson portrayed or suggested every type of illicit sex. In all, Thompson is reported to have written nearly a hundred novels, which enjoyed a lively sale in their day.

Woman's powerful sexual drive is a constant theme of Thompson's fiction, which often features nymphomaniacs who demand constant variety. In *New-York Life* he depicts respectable New York women flocking to a doctor who finds it necessary in each case "to make an examination, *per vaginam.*" His "daily fingerings," when he applies an ointment to his patients' private parts, assures him a lively business from women who are "doctored for no other reason than a liking for the medicine."[25] In *Venus in Boston* women are directly said to be "even more ardent in their passions than those who have the happiness to be men." Hester Prynne's secretly rebellious feelings about marriage and sexuality are outdone by Thompson's heroines, several of whom are tied, like Hester, to frigid older men but are more successful than she in fulfilling their wildest fantasies of infidelity. One woman, enjoying a lover while her husband is away, declares: " 'Tis slavery, 'tis madness, to be chained for life to but one source of love, when a thousand streams would not satiate or overflow." Another woman with a cold husband asks: "How long must I remain here pining for the embraces of fifty men, and enduring the impotent caresses of but one?"[26] She doesn't wait long. The heroine of *City Crimes* refuses to sleep with her fiancé but has a torrid affair with her Negro servant. When her enraged fiancé discovers the affair, she tells him: "You cannot understand the fiery and insatiate cravings of my passions. I tell you that I consume with desire—not for enjoyment with such as *you,* but for delicious amours which are *recherché* and unique," such as this one with "my superb African."[27] In *The Countess* Thompson poses the curious theory that the great Roman nymphomaniac Messalina had founded a society of insatiable women that had gone underground in the Middle Ages and then resurfaced in a nineteenth-century New York group whose sexual frolics are the subject of the novel.

In addition to giving zest and variety to the topic of woman's sexuality, Thompson introduced more unusual themes as well. He was, as far as I know, the first American novelist to deal openly with homosexuality, lesbianism, transvestism, group sex, and child pornography. In his autobiography he reports having witnessed a lesbian relationship, which provokes the exclamation: "The idea of a woman falling in love with one of her own sex, is rather rich!"[28] In *Venus in Boston,* a girl being initiated into whoredom is kissed by a dozen half-naked prostitutes whose "libidinous natures derived gratification even in kissing one of their own sex."[29] In the same novel, an adulterous couple playfully exchange clothes during foreplay, the woman donning male attire and trying to rape her lover, who plays the part of a shy girl. *City Crimes* has an unusual sequence in which a Spanish man visiting New York approaches a young boy on the street for sexual gratification; Thompson tells us that in American cities "there are boys who *prostitute* themselves thus, from motive of gain." This novel also portrays poor people living in the squalid Five Points area of New York, where "the crime of *incest* is as common among them as dirt! I have known a mother and her son—a father and his daughter—a brother and sister—to be guilty of criminal intimacy."[30] He gives us a prolonged incestuous relationship in *The Ladies' Garter,* whose young heroine discovers that the old man she married was her grandfather. In *The House Breaker* private *tableaux vivants* at an upper-class party rapidly degenerate into an all-out sexual orgy where nude teenaged boys and girls serve wine; the next morning, it is clear that some of the teenagers have performed other services as well. In *The Mysteries of Bond Street* a man is sporting with a naked woman in bed when the pair is interrupted by an old man, who proceeds to fondle the woman's upper body while the other man hides by burying his head between the woman's legs with "his nose only a few inches from the portals of paradise."[31]

Antebellum erotic novels, most of which fall into the Dark Adventure or Subversive categories, commonly included scenes with necrophilic undertones. John Neal's *The Down-Easters* (1833) contains a striking sequence (which Hawthorne may have adapted and modified for "Rappaccini's Daughter") in which a woman who has arranged an assignation with her lover in a dark house takes a slow poison that will put her to death in the act of love; she leaves a note promising he will lavish his "caresses, [and] passionate love upon a dead body."[32] In Lippard's *The Ladye Annabel* (1842) the hero has a long vision of a dance of clattering skeletons, including that of his deceased lover, who gives him a grisly embrace. Lippard gives a psychological twist to the theme in *The Quaker City,* in which the greedy Dora Livingstone, lured by the prospect of wealth to her lover's country mansion, is followed all the way by a carriage holding her own coffin—she only learns of the horrid irony as she dies in her lover's arms after drinking the poisoned cocktail he gives her. In *New York: Its Upper Ten and Lower Million* Lippard describes a situation—one that has rightly been called "one of the most grotesque combinations of sex and death in literature"[33]—involving a woman who sweetly inveigles her paramour to her "bridal bed," where she has hidden the moldering corpse of her murdered husband as a horrid reminder of the paramour's sins. In George Thompson's *Venus in Boston* (1849) a man enters a dark room and takes delight in fondling the naked body of a woman until he comes to the horrified realization she had stabbed herself to avoid lowering herself to him.

Even when there is no direct suggestion of necrophilia, the sex/death combination is almost always featured in this fiction, which alternates between scenes of sexual rapture and scenes of unthinkable atrocity. A marked sadomasochistic streak runs through novels from *Mary Velnet* (1816), in which a nude woman is tortured on the rack, through Thompson's *Venus in Boston* (1849), in which a bestial Negro procuress strips and whips a young maiden, through *Revelations of a Slave Smuggler* (1860), in which we see two slave women dragged naked before jeering crowds, one with "both breasts cut smoothly off, stomach full of arrows" and the other with "breasts scewered by a knife."[34] The heroine of *Lucretia Cannon* (1841) is not only licentious but savage: in a typical scene she tears off the clothes of a crying child, beats it, and holds its face over a hot fire until it is scorched to death. Such amoral violence typifies these novels. In *Mary Jane Gordon* (1847) a woman decides to have fun by arbitrarily picking up a child on a city sidewalk, taking it to a back street, and suffocating it. The same woman says gleefully: "I must confess that I have many a time murdered young and old men when in their sleep in my bed at night."[35] Similarly, the criminal heroine of *The Female Land Pirate* (1847) learns to "look upon a murder as indifferently as a butcher would look upon the death of an animal."[36] We see the heroine of Duganne's *Eustace Barcourt* first violently raped and then turned into a maniacal sadist who, among other things, bathes her baby in the blood and brains of her murdered seducer.

It was a sign of the times that the two writers who produced the most daringly erotic fiction, George Lippard and George Thompson, also distinguished themselves by their special fascination with savage violence. Lippard is always shifting between voyeuristic sex and the grisly doings of perverse characters, ranging from the mad executioner in *The Ladye Annabel,* who rips out the eyes and heart of his victims, through the fiendish Devil-Bug in *The Quaker City,* who gleefully dashes out the brains of an old woman, to the strange battlefield ghouls of *Blanche of Brandywine,* who love to grope among the rotting remains of fallen soldiers. Thompson was simultaneously the most sexually explicit and the most purely disgusting novelist of the 1840s: he typically follows up a chapter of orgiastic sex with a chapter of equally orgiastic violence, often involving torture or cannibalism. A typical Thompson novel, *The Road to Ruin* contains a stomach-turning sequence in which a trapped man being tortured by starvation becomes a howling idiot after feasting for days on flesh from his own arms and on the corpses of his murdered victims, whose rotting remains he reluctantly devours; all the while, his torturer is upstairs engaged in "amorous and bacchanalian revelry" with a frolicsome woman.[37]

What bearing did popular erotic writings have on the major literature? A full answer to this question will emerge only when we look closely at sensational themes in the major texts. It should be initially emphasized that the 1840s, the decade immediately preceding the appearance of several major novels and poems, was the first time in American history that sexuality was publicly discussed on a mass level. Diverse theories of sexual antinomianism were not only circulating but also were acted upon: the polygamous Mormons established their Utah community in 1842; the pantagamous perfectionists gathered at Oneida in 1847; many of the prominent Fourierist communities sprang up during this decade; and in 1850 the first of the free-love communities was established. Also, the erotic imagination began to come out of the closet. Moving beyond the tortured sexual probings of the 1830s, America became a freer culture that permitted model artists, the voyeur style, an understanding of woman's libido, and the portrayal of all kinds of sex in popular fiction.

A freer culture, perhaps, but by no means a totally liberated one. There was no sexual revolution in the 1840s. In this decade the awakening recognition of sexual desire was waging a titanic struggle against the residual repressiveness of the Puritan conscience. As a result, public expressions of erotic impulses always had a perverse, bizarre aspect. Deep-seated guilt engendered a notably furtive quality in erotic expression, as seen in the cold posturings of the model artists, the prevalent use of euphemisms like "snowy globes," and the whole phenomenon of the voyeur style, which permitted indirect glimpses rather than warm exposure of human physicality. This furtive treatment of sexuality governs certain erotic tensions in our major literature. Hawthorne obviously has a voyeuristic fascination with his sensuous "dark" heroines: Hester, Zenobia, and Miriam. This typically antebellum two-sidedness is reflected in the way he stylistically "caresses" these richly voluptuous heroines but then withdraws from full enjoyment of their charms, punishing them and himself, as it were, by turning them into virtually sexless penitents (Hester, Miriam) or into a stiff corpse (Zenobia). Melville tentatively approaches the theme of incest in *Pierre* but gives us little explicit sex and certainly no happy eroticism. Even Whitman has a voyeuristic side. Although he once declared to Traubel that "sex is the root of it all," he often treated the erotic obliquely, as in the famous moment in "Song of Myself" when he has a voyeuristic woman fantasize from a distance about twenty-eight bathing men.

The popular fiction of the 1840s must be regarded as a preparatory lesson in guilty eroticism rather than an opening of the floodgates to free sexual expression. This sexual ambivalence actually fed into some of the more interesting effects of our major literary texts, in which we often see a dialectic of erotic enjoyment followed by recoil or deflection. While the major writers absorbed this cultural ambivalence, they also purposely avoided the freakish perversities that often accompanied this ambivalence on the popular level. This is not to say that such perversity is absent from the major literature: witness the way Hawthorne gloats over Zenobia's body both when she is alive and when she is dead. But there is nothing in the major literature to match the odd combination of furtive sexuality and unbridled violence that we find in the popular fiction. Primarily because the popular writers could not honestly express sexual yearnings, they instead projected these yearnings into voyeuristic sex and especially into horrible violence and gore.

When we survey the sensational literature of the day, particularly the novels I classify as Subversive, we recognize that sexuality in antebellum literature had little to do with natural passion or honest feeling. Increasingly, erotic themes became the special province of militant radical democrats who went to perverse extremes to expose what they viewed as the rottenness of America's ruling class. They believed that the most effective way of doing this was to depict outwardly respectable figures (businessmen, clergymen, lawyers, pious matrons, and so forth) engaged in secret sexual intrigues that exposed them as scheming and bestial. The portrayal of sexual aberration was an especially potent weapon against the upper classes, whose pretensions to virtue could most readily be exploded by recording their private sexual misdeeds. Hawthorne's Arthur Dimmesdale, the publicly respected but secretly adulterous preacher, and Jaffrey Pyncheon, the churchgoing judge who has a sex crime in his past, are quite characteristic figures in this regard. They suggest Hawthorne's awareness of his age's egalitarian sensibility, which was attracted to stories of sexual wrongdoing among the establishment.

As we shall see, however, Hawthorne and the other major writers departed from the popular sensationalists in significant ways. It should be emphasized that there was nothing clean or genuine about relations between the sexes for a Subversive radical democrat like Thompson, who described or suggested all varieties of sex: incest, sadomasochism, homosexuality, group sex, miscegenation, child sex, mass orgies. The accounts of such behavior were less explicit but more perverse than most of today's pornography. Since sex was being used as a weapon to unmask the social elite, it was treated as aberrant and furtive. In the twisted world of Subversive fiction, sex was unconnected with love. Instead, it was governed by violence, entrapment, manipulation.

This grotesque eroticism makes the frank sexuality of Whitman's poetry seem yet another corrective to popular treatments of sex. Whitman, despite his reputation to the contrary, always thought of his poetry as a pure, chaste alternative to a perverse brand of popular American literature that featured what he called "the love plot." As he wrote in his notebook: "In the plentiful feast of romance presented to us, all the novels, all the poems really dish up only one figure, various forms and preparations of only one plot, namely, a sickly, scrofulous, crude, amorousness."[38] Similarly, in his article "A Memorandum at a Venture," Whitman complained that "by far the largest" point of view toward sexuality in America was manifested in "erotic stories and talk," stories that repelled him with their "merely sensual voluptuousness" and that led him to declare that sexual passion was a proper literary theme only as long as it was "normal and unperverted."[39] In his own poetry Whitman tried to remove sex from the mire of perversity and place it on the higher level of hearty comradeship and natural desire.

This artistic transformation of sexuality was just one facet of a much larger process of studied assimilation of popular sensational themes by the major authors. By turning now to representative literary texts of the period, we see how the public poison of antebellum culture was carefully distilled into various forms of literary nectar.

8

POE AND POPULAR IRRATIONALISM

S ENSATIONAL literature is particularly worthy of study since the major authors generally associated Americanness with the kind of crude vigor and brash independence that characterized it. Thoreau expressed the common view when he wrote: "In literature it is only the wild that attracts us."[1] Melville wrote that American writers must "turn bullies" and defined American genius as "that explosive sort of stuff [that] will expand, though screwed up in a vice, and burst it, though it were triple steel."[2] This attraction to the savage and the sensational was variously manifested in the rampant irrationalism of Poe's fiction, in the weird imaginings and periodic eruptions of Hawthorne's characters, in Whitman's pose as "one of the roughs," and in Emily Dickinson's violent juxtapositions of strange images.

There is, however, an important distinction between sensational themes as they appear in popular literature and as they are transformed in America's central literary texts. The major writers fully absorbed the paradoxes of sensational literature but mightily resisted the prevailing tendency toward vulgarization and inhumanity in popular culture. Like the popular sensationalists, they often used disquieting images or character types which represented an American autocriticism, a turning inward of the rebelliousness once aimed at foreign rulers. And yet they were distressed by the unrestrained wildness and open defiance of extreme sensational writings, such as those I have designated as Subversive. In the literary text, the whirling paradoxes and ironies within the surrounding culture gather in upon themselves, creating both extraordinary proliferation and extraordinary compaction of image. Sensational themes were not repressed or wished away, as they were in Moral Adventure or Conventional literature. Because they were a crucial element of the American culture the major authors were trying to represent, they were boldly assimilated in a variety of ways. They were, however, purposely removed from the neutral and chaotic realm to which they were debased in many of their popular manifestations. In numerous literary works they gained a depth, an intensity, and, sometimes, even a beauty that was almost wholly lacking in popular sensationalism. While the major works were more dense and ambiguous than the lesser ones, they were at the same time more suggestive and controlled. It is this ability of literary texts to absorb the subversive images of its contemporary culture but at the same time to redirect these elements toward the suggestive and the genuinely human that accounts for their universality and enduring appeal.

Poe's Critique of the Sensational

Nowhere is the dual process of enthusiastic absorption and studied redirection of the sensational so visible as in Poe's writings. In the criticism on Poe, it has not been shown that his writings were, to a large degree, rhetorical responses to popular sensationalism. Intimately aware of every type of popular sensational literature, Poe repeatedly commented on such literature in his criticism and borrowed from it liberally in his tales and poems.

To some degree, Poe was clearly trying to tap the new market for sensational literature. When in 1835 his tale "Berenice" (about the grisly detoothing of a woman buried alive) stirred controversy after its appearance in the *Southern Literary Messenger,* he conceded to the editor that the subject was "far too horrible" and "on the very verge of bad-taste" but emphasized: "To be appreciated you must be *read,* and these things are invariably sought after with avidity."[3] The extreme popularity of sensational writings became the specific topic of his tale "The Psyche Zenobia" (1838), in which he said that any gory or thrilling subject—live burial, hanging, drowning, being bitten by a rabid dog—ensured a lively sale for a modern work, as long as the author paid "minute attention to the sensations."[4] Several years later he confessed to a friend that he wrote "The Raven" and "The Gold-Bug" "for the express purpose of running." He was proud to note that "The Gold-Bug" sold some 300,000 copies and was even prouder to report: "The bird beat the bug, though, all hollow."[5] He defended reprinting "Eiros and Charmion," his tale about the destruction of the world by a comet, by pointing up its attraction for many readers: "I believe that I am making a *sensation* which will tend to the benefit of the magazine."[6] Recognizing the salability of sensational literature, he once remarked that his tales were written "with an eye to the paltry compensations, or the more paltry commendations, of mankind."[7] He liked to brag that the circulations of the *Southern Literary Messenger* and *Graham's Magazine* increased dramatically under his editorship.

Poe frequently expressed a feeling of kinship with a popular culture he regarded as wild, racy, vigorous. In one of his pieces on Hawthorne he stressed: "It is, in fact, the excitable, undisciplined and child-like popular mind which most keenly feels the original," while the "cultivated old clergymen of the 'North American Review' . . . have a holy horror of being moved," asking only for repose.[8] In Poe's eyes, the masses demanded agitation and irrationalism in literature, while more cultivated readers looked for quietude and instruction. This view of the American public as sensation-hungry is visible in much of his literary criticism. For instance, he wrote that respectable quarterly reviews "have *never* been popular" because they are "too stilted. . . . In a word, their ponderosity is quite out of keeping with the *rush* of the age." He explained the rapid demise of Evert A. Duyckinck's short-lived literary journal *Arcturus* by saying it was "an *excessively tasteful*" periodical that could only attract "the literary quietists." In designing his own proposed magazine, *Stylus*, Poe consciously wished to supplant the old quarterlies with a livelier kind of magazine reflective of popular taste. Looking upon "the world at large as the sole proper audience for the author," he emphasized that in order to please this audience he would "eschew the stilted dulness of our own Quarterlies" and be "more vigorous, more pungent, more original, more individual, and more independent" than they.

While he decried genteel literature because of its distance from what he perceived as the tumultuous spirit of the age, he was not prepared to go as far as contemporary writers who dispensed with the rational altogether. He often expressed dismay at the wildness and repulsiveness of much American writing. For instance, his feelings about the father of American Subversive fiction, John Neal, were significantly mixed. On the one hand, he owed great spiritual and practical debts to Neal, who had been the first to publicly praise Poe's writings, who introduced several themes and devices Poe would exploit, and whose influence was acknowledged when Poe dedicated the 1829 edition of *Tamerlane* to him. And yet, though Poe once placed Neal "among our men of indisputable *genius*," he was repelled by Neal's volcanic, intentionally disruptive fiction.[9] Poe found that in Neal's work "there is no precision, no finish about anything he does,—always an excessive *force* but little of refined art." He stated that Neal wrote powerfully but "by fits, much at random" and noted elsewhere that his fiction was "excessively diffuse, extravagant, and indicative of an imperfect sentiment of Art." Neal himself, as we have seen, took delight in his reputation as a quirky stylist and even published mock reviews in which he branded his own fiction as impudent and poisonous. Poe, unwilling to share Neal's enthusiasm for the uncontrolled irrational style, called for unity, construction, climax.

The recoil away from unregulated manifestations of the Subversive imagination is a common thread running through much of Poe's literary criticism. Although he was attracted to the style of Thomas Holley Chivers, he complained that it was sometimes like "a wild dream—strange—incongruous, full of images of more than arabesque monstrosity."[10] In Poe's eyes, Maria Brooks's poems were striking but often bombastic and extravagant; Nathaniel P. Willis's sketches were bizarre; Charles Frederick Briggs was too vulgar; Christopher Pearse Cranch's poetry was full of odd, whimsical conceits; Longfellow's *Hyperion* was "without design, without shape"; Lambert Wilmer's *The Quacks of Helicon* was spoiled by "the gross obscenity, the filth, . . . [and] innate impurity" of the writer's mind. A British sensational novel, Harrison Ainsworth's *Guy Fawkes,* struck Poe as "monstrously improbable" and "inconsequential," like "some perplexing dream—one of those frequently recurring visions, half night-mare, half asphyxia."[11] George Lippard's *The Ladye Annabel,* a dizzying sensational novel involving medieval torture and necrophilic visions, struck Poe as "indicative of *genius* in its author" and yet chaotic.[12] Poe had strong reservations about popular serial fiction, which he found wanting in structure and design. For instance, a serialized sensational novel by Edward Bulwer-Lytton left him feeling "tantalized, wearied, and displeased" because of its "continual and vexatious shifting of scene."[13] His own insistence on artistic unity was related to his pained perception of the structurelessness of many popular texts. For instance, he found that the sensational play *Tortesa* by the American dramatist Nathaniel P. Willis suffered from "the great error [of] *inconsequence.* Underplot is piled upon underplot," as Willis gives us "vast designs that terminate in nothing." Cornelius Mathews's *Wakondah* (1842) he found "a mere jumble of incongruous nonsense" full of "unintelligible rant and cant" and having "neither beginning, middle, nor end." He saw "very little plot or connexion" in William Gilmore Simms's *The Partisan* (1836). Poe's famous definition of the plot as that from which nothing can be removed without detriment to the mass was, to a large degree, a direct reaction against the directionlessness of the popular irrational style.

Despite his own interest in violent crime and perversity, he could actually sound moralistic when lamenting the amorality and repulsiveness of popular sensational novels. He had little tolerance for the popular stereotype of the likable criminal or justified pariah. In his damning review of Morris Mattson's *Paul Ulric* (1836), which he called "despicable in every respect," he criticized the confusion between virtue and vice implicit in Mattson's portrait of a "metaphysical outlaw" who insists a common thief is no worse than a nation that seizes land from other nations.[14] He attacked J. H. Ingraham's best-seller *Lafitte, the Pirate of the Gulf* (1836) on moral grounds, complaining that Ingraham presented a horrid, swearing murderer as worthy of respect. Similarly, in an 1840 review of Frederick Chamier's novel *The Spitfire* he faulted the author for investing "the character of a pirate and a cutthroat with the attributes of a hero and a deserving man."[15] He lamented scenes of "slaughter and violence" in a war novel by Robert Montgomery Bird.[16] He found several novels by the prominent American sensationalist William Gilmore Simms in "villainously bad taste" because of the author's fondness for "the purely disgusting or repulsive," when the interest should be "merely the horrible."[17] He frequently objected to the gore and violent oaths that filled much adventure fiction of the day.

Poe's distaste for excesses of popular sensationalism was linked to an underlying dissatisfaction with what he perceived as the turbulence and fluidity of modern American life. In 1842 he wrote that "the onward and tumultuous spirit of the age" was threatening to cast literature into a pit of detestable "cant."[18] Clinging to rules of prosody and syntax with an almost neurotic devotion, he resisted what he termed "the new licentious 'schools' of poetry" which "in their rashness of spirit, much in accordance with the whole spirit of the age," would dispense with all poetic rules.[19] In "Mellonta Tauta" he expressed fear that American society was becoming an "insolent, rapacious, and filthy" mob that ignored the law of gradation governing the universe.[20] In "The Colloquy of Monos and Una" he lamented "wild attempts at an omni-prevalent Democracy" that created an urbanized environment destroying taste, which he saw as the last saving grace for modern man.

He was likewise disturbed by the cruelty and venality of the literary marketplace. His famous detachment of literature from morality was in part a reflection of the amoral publishing world in which he lived and breathed. He underscored the grim realities of popular publishing in several sketches: in "Secrets in a Magazine House," which shows American authors driven by lack of a copyright to do slave labor for popular periodicals; in "The Life of Thingum Bob," which satirizes sentimentalists elevated to spurious celebrity by paid puffers and critics; and in "The Psyche Zenobia," which parodies sensationalists who churn out horror tales for an amoral public. In his 1841 review of Lambert A. Wilmer's *The Quacks of*

Helicon he characterized the publishing scene as totally, almost irredeemably corrupt. There was, of course, some personal motivation behind such criticism. Poe regularly complained of being cheated out of a fair profit because of the copyright situation, and he had a frustrated dream of founding a magazine that would make him rich. Through much of his career he was a virtual slave to the popular magazines, whose different audiences he attempted to please in his notably variegated tales.

Though he always had his eye on the mass market for sensational literature, he never became as popular as he hoped or as one might expect, given the sensational tastes of the day. The main reason for his relative lack of popularity was his inclination to sculpt and depoliticize irrational themes that in popular texts had explosive social implications. Sensationalists like George Lippard and George Thompson enjoyed immense popularity because their fiction openly projected the common reader's most savage impulses and fantasies: violent antielitism, identification with monstrous outcasts and justified criminals, eroticism and gory violence, bizarre nightmares with revolutionary overtones. It was precisely these kinds of intensely democratic excesses that Poe constantly censured in his critical writings. In his fiction, he was like his own "natural aristocrat," using the tools of the rabble but not soiling his hands with them. His horror tales feature violence without repulsive gore, criminality without political import, women without sensuality, nightmares without revolutionary suggestions.

Poe's Artistic Sensationalism

Poe's best fiction is uniquely terrifying and yet somewhat removed because of its analytical rigor, its stylization, its distance from ordinary reality. It absorbs the agitation and perversity Poe perceived in American popular culture but leaves out politics and mob fantasy. It possesses the wildness that Tocqueville associated with the American literary imagination but has none of the social turbulence or moral confusions Poe reviled. It embodies an apolitical irrationalism, an artistic wildness. It was simultaneously a full enactment of the popular Subversive imagination and a careful containment of it. This doubleness is what gave pause to the surrealist devotee of automatic writing, André Breton, who admired Poe's irrational themes but was disturbed by his rational method. More favorably impressed by this quality was Dostoyevsky, who remarked that Poe always analyzed extravagant situations "with marvellous acumen and amazing realism," so that his "fantasticalness . . . seems strangely material."[21]

Poe brought control and intentionality to sensational themes that appeared more chaotically in many lesser texts. He believed that the popular mind was attracted to the wild, the exciting, the original. He also wanted to exploit the new market for sensational literature. But he detested the gore and repulsiveness of many novels, the hyperbolic, often inaccurate reportage of crime in popular newspapers, the strident calls for social change by modern reformers such as abolitionists and Fourierists (whom he denounced as noisy and even insane), the difficult plight of the American writer, and the overall turmoil of a democratic society. Doubtless Poe's infamous bouts with the bottle had something to do with his latent dissatisfaction with his surrounding culture. But his dissatisfaction had more positive results as well, for it fed into the energy and complexities of his fiction. Occasionally, his fictional attacks on American culture were fiercely explicit: witness tales like "Some Words with a Mummy" and "Mellonta Tauta," in which he characterizes republican democracy as a beastly, vile mob. More characteristically, he made this criticism implicitly in his fiction, often adopting popular themes with the aim of changing them and stripping them of specific qualities he detested. In this respect Poe was rather like the landscape gardener of "The Domain of Arnheim," who uses the artistic imagination to convert an untamed wilderness into a garden possessing both wildness and cultivation, both novelty and order.

The strategies Poe most commonly used for reshaping popular themes were what I call *exaggeration* and *analysis*. He described his method of exaggeration in an 1835 letter in which he says the terror writer's goal should be "the ludicrous heightened into the grotesque: the fearful colored into the horrible: the witty exaggerated into the burlesque: the singular wrought out into the strange and mystical."[22] In some tales, exaggeration brings about a fusion of the sensational with the arabesque, thereby creating a weird beauty; in other tales, it forces the sensational to deconstruct, to become an agency of its own subversion. The second method, analysis, shows Poe applying reason or science to sensational themes whose repulsiveness is therefore diminished. The ultimate example of analysis was the detective story, which Poe used as a means heralding the intellect's power over the sensational. Both exaggeration and analysis allowed Poe to capitalize on popular sensational themes but at the same time to gain firm control over them and to redirect their energy in taut, economical fiction.

Two of his best-known tales, "The Tell-Tale Heart" (1843) and "The Man of the Crowd" (1840), provide a good introduction to Poe's manipulation of popular stereotypes. "The Tell-Tale Heart" is based in part on the 1830 trial of Joseph and Francis Knapp for the murder of Captain Joseph White, the notorious "Salem Murder" that also intrigued Hawthorne. We have seen that a chief importance of the Knapp case was its popularization of the cool criminal, the detached and manipulative murderer whose type was mythologized in a number of popular crime heroes ranging from Simms's Guy Rivers through Lippard's Devil-Bug to John Murrell, the "Great Western Land Pirate." Another source of "The Tell-Tale Heart" would seem to be the nationally publicized case of Peter Robinson, a New Jersey man who in 1841 was hanged for the brutal murder of a rich banker, Abraham Suydam. Whereas the Knapp case had been the popular prototype of cool criminality, the Robinson case had been a primary instance of the American public's fascination with repulsive crime and with execution of criminals. The circumstances of the Robinson case make it seem like a real-life sensational tale: when the banker Suydam appeared at Robinson's house demanding payment of an old debt, Robinson knocked Suydam unconscious and dragged him to his basement, where he left him gagged for several days, then dug a grave before his eyes, bludgeoned him to death, and buried his body under planks in his cellar floor. The brutality of Robinson's crime was outdone only by the bloodthirstiness of the milling crowd who came to witness his hanging. At first disappointed when it was announced that Robinson had been hanged in an inner courtyard, the crowd burst through the prison gates to catch a glimpse of his body and eagerly seized the hanging rope, which was torn into pieces that were distributed as mementoes. As with most sensational cases of the day, the murder and the public hanging were vividly recounted in a lurid crime pamphlet, with a melodramatic cover engraving that shows Robinson hanging from a scaffold above a black coffin.[23]

In "The Tell-Tale Heart" Poe exploits the popular interest in sensational crime but at the same time avoids both the moral ambiguities surrounding the Knapp case and the grisly sensationalism surrounding the Robinson case. The rather amoral popular interest in terrible crime that had been catered to by crime pamphlets and by lyrically gory novels like Lippard's *The Ladye Annabel* (1842) is intentionally disregarded in this tale. True, Poe presents a story of murder, dismemberment, and burial under floor planks. But he avoids repulsive accounts of violence or blood, shifting his attention to the crazed mind of the obsessed narrator. By removing us from the realm of horrid gore to that of diseased psychology, he rises above the kind of tawdry sensationalism that had surrounded the Robinson case. At the same time, he purposely avoids the moral quagmire surrounding the figure of the likable criminal, as epitomized by Frank Knapp, who in jail was so cool and affable that even an intelligent observer like Hawthorne was inclined to admire him. In "The Tell-Tale Heart" Poe enters the consciousness of the cool murderer and watches this consciousness deconstruct due to terrors of its own creation. At the beginning of the tale, the murderer is boasting "with what caution—with what foresight" he executes the murder of the old man and the disposal of the body under floor planks.[24] His coolness carries over into his blithe explanations to the police, but then we see it quickly collapse as he becomes a shrieking mass of quivering remorse. Many popular crime narratives had confused the issue by portraying murderers sympathetically, concentrating not only on visions that haunt them but also their social motivations for crime and the many circuitous events that lead up to or stem from their crime. In Poe's tale there is no such excess and no such sympathy: there is simply a sharply focused dramatization of a "sane insane" criminal whose narration becomes the agency of its own subversion. The narrative voice itself undermines any sympathy we might have with this criminal. In the very first sentence Poe places us in the world of popular criminals—the world of the "sane insane"—but moral issues are quickly banished by the startling address to the reader: "True!—nervous—very, very dreadfully nervous I had been and am; but why *will* you say that I am mad? The disease had sharpened my senses—not destroyed—not dulled them. . . . Hearken! and observe how healthily—how calmly I can tell you the whole story." Poe avoids the moral problems surrounding the criminal simply by making the criminal's crazed narration itself a main object of our attention. We enjoy the sharp *effect* of the narration on our nerve endings and don't ask moral questions about a man whose sane madness is itself the point of the literary game. We are more engaged with this criminal on an emotional level but less enamored with him on a moral level than we are in much popular literature. We are given no motive or justification for his crime, other than the obviously insane one of his obsession with the old man's eye. We feel the intensity of this obsession, we are horrified by his crime, but we are not ever sympathetic with this psychopath. Poe has lifted us at once beyond sensationalism and beyond one of sensational literature's most problematic figures, the likable or justified criminal.

In "The Man of the Crowd" Poe takes a different look at the criminal. This time the moral dilemmas surrounding the criminal *are* directly confronted. But, again, we are lifted from the moral to the psychological and artistic realm. When the narrator, a man in a city coffeehouse "occupied in scrutinizing the mob" of passersby, sees the decrepit old criminal, he says "there arose confusedly and paradoxically" in his mind ideas of "vast mental power, of caution, of penuriousness, of avarice, of coolness, of malice, of blood-thirstiness, of triumph, of merriment, of excessive terror, of intense—of supreme despair."[25] We are here in the presence of a mixed criminal, one who embodies contrary qualities of intelligence and perversity, humor and malice, and so on. We are, in short, in the ambiguous realm of the popular crime narratives. But even though Poe will tell us this man is "the type and the genius of deep crime," he does not allow himself to be swept up in the bloody doings of the criminal, as would a popular crime writer. Indeed, he gives us no crime at all, nor does he tell us the old man is a criminal until the very end. Instead, he extracts the moral ambiguities of the stereotypical criminal—the sharply contrary values that puzzle the sensitive observer—and enacts these ambiguities in the narrative structure. The long opening section in which the narrator is "occupied in scrutinizing the mob" outside the coffeehouse is analogous to Poe himself scrutinizing the "mob" of his contemporary culture. The confusion and paradoxes that overwhelm the narrator when he focuses on the criminal are similar to Poe's recognition of the complexities within the popular criminal stereotype. The two-day journey through the gaslit streets, the slums, the saloon district is like the popular writer's plunge into the seamy urban underworld—except that Poe is interested not so much in dark city "mysteries" as in how these outer mysteries reflect the even darker soul of the criminal. We have seen that in his literary criticism Poe often criticized popular sensational literature as directionless, unregulated, amoral. Here the directionless wandering of an amoral man itself becomes the main action of the story. The author's critique of an uncontrolled popular genre is integrated into the structure of carefully controlled fiction. The character Poe isolates is indeed the "man of the crowd"; that is, the man who lives and moves only in the popular consciousness, the "crowd" of Poe's contemporary culture. The man is doomed to wander endlessly in the crowd that created him and that reflects him, just as the popular criminal stereotype is kept alive by the crowd of sensation lovers of Poe's day. Poe's response to the stereotype is one of simultaneous interest and puzzlement, fascination and disgust. It is fitting that, despite his intense observation of the criminal, the narrator ends where he began: in utter bafflement before the ambiguous criminal, about whom all that can be said, as about "a certain German book," is that " 'er lasst sich nicht lesen'—it does not permit itself to be read."

Another Poe tale that ponders the ambiguities surrounding the criminal is "William Wilson." In the opening paragraphs we learn that we are in the presence of an extraordinarily villainous man who nevertheless makes claims upon our sympathies. The narrator calls himself "outcast of all outcasts most abandoned," whose life has been one of "unspeakable misery, and unpardonable crime."[26] And yet he says he is telling his life story in order to inspire "the sympathy—I had nearly said the pity—of my fellow men," to show that he has been "the slave of circumstances beyond human control." In other words, he longs to establish his position as a likable pariah, a justified criminal. But Poe refuses to rest comfortably in this stereotype. To be sure, on one level the story is a prototypical popular tale that combines the dark-reform exemplum and the crime narrative. As in many popular stories, we follow a man's progressive descent into dissipation and crime as a result of constitutional flaws and parental maltreatment. We see Wilson confront a rather typical oxymoronic oppressor—the benign but cruel clergyman whose contrary qualities pose a "gigantic paradox, too utterly monstrous for solution"—and then rebelliously follow a downward path that leads to drunken orgies, illicit love, gambling, and finally murder. As if the typicality of Wilson's descent is not enough to establish him as a figure from popular culture, Poe constantly stresses Wilson's kinship with boisterous mobs. He is very much a "man of the crowd": in school he is the most popular boy in the class, and as an adult he is always among crowds of carousing cronies. This identification with wild mobs is enacted even in his moment of private revenge, for when he stabs his double he says, "I was frantic with every species of excitement, and felt in my single arm the energy and power of a multitude."

Figuratively, Wilson embodies the ferocity and chaos of popular sensationalism as it had been established in dark-reform literature and in crime narratives. His double, in contrast, is the solitary observer of this turbulent popular culture. Wilson, despite his popularity, recognizes the "true superiority" of the double and even says "his moral sense, at least, if not his general talents and worldly wisdom, was far keener than my own." While Wilson is the amoral, popular man who would flee into unbridled license, the double is the contemplative artistic conscience that would regulate and prevent such license. We should note that the three times the double reappears to confront Wilson are moments of unusual wildness: on the first occasion, Wilson is "[m]adly flushed with cards and intoxication" and giving "a toast of more than wonted profanity"; on the second, he has ruined a young wealthy nobleman by cheating at cards; on the third, he is excessively drunk and about to seduce the wife of an old man. In each case, the double quietly, almost wordlessly, restrains his folly, while Wilson is roused to an ever-crescendoing fury that culminates in the gory murder. The fact that the double may not exist outside Wilson's consciousness and that the murder is in fact self-murder underscores the devastating self-reflexivity of the tale. Poe is declaring his symbiotic kinship with and his simultaneous distaste for the popular Subversive imagination, which he allows here to turn violently against itself. The ultimate act of criminal aggression becomes the final act of suicidal despair. Instead of following the popular pattern of sympathizing with the justified criminal and his ugly doings, Poe watches how this criminal is tortured and finally destroyed by warring impulses in his own soul.

A similarly deconstructive use of popular sensational devices characterizes "The Fall of the House of Usher." In this tale Poe gives us three kinds of sensational texts: "The Haunted Palace" (Roderick Usher's song), which embodies the musical, poetic treatment of sensational themes; Launcelot Canning's "The Mad Trist," the action-packed, structureless story which whips Usher to a mad frenzy as he hears it read aloud; and the main narrative, which serves as a highly regulated battleground on which the other texts compete. "The Haunted Palace," the song about a mythical palace whose happy inhabitants are driven out by "evil things" and replaced by "vast forms" that move to "a discordant melody," possesses the ideality and the poetic structure that Poe regarded as the highest possible mode of dealing with the sensational.[27] "The Mad Trist," in contrast, possesses the prolixity, the flatness, and the merely adventurous action that Poe disliked—and that he often associated with popular sensational fiction. The narrator reads the story to Usher even though he knows "there is little in its uncouth and unimaginative prolixity which could have had interest for the lofty and spiritual ideality of my friend." But Usher's ideality collapses before the wildness of the story, which becomes fused in his mind with the raging storm and the horrid vision of his blood-covered sister rising from her coffin. In effect, poetic ideality is overthrown by gruesome, unartistic sensationalism. The clamorous noises described in "The Mad Trist" become fused with the sounds Usher hears, as the wildly sensational penetrates and destroys the realm of the poetically ideal. As a whole, the tale has built up to the forlorn musicality of "The Haunted Palace" and then has been deconstructed by the savage, directionless sensationalism embodied in "The Mad Trist." Figuratively, the fall of the house of Usher is a fearful projection of the fall of the house of Poe: that is, the fall of the artistic control and unity that Poe feared would accompany modern sensational writings, whose typical narrative patterns he knew to be as crooked as the zigzag fissure that splits apart Usher's mansion.

Whatever fears about his culture Poe may have been projecting, he created a memorable tale that has outlived lesser literature of his day precisely because it assumes thorough control over the sensational. The unexampled unity of the story is itself an assertion of faith—faith in ordered literary words as opposed to the chaotic words Poe saw all around him. The main narrative embodies what might be called the highest possible prose version of sensational themes. It is not a mere string of flat, adventurous events, as is "The Mad Trist" or the popular sensational writings of Poe's day. It has total unity; everything is interconnected. The house "is" Roderick Usher, who "is" his sister: none can exist without the other. Throughout the story, there is a complete interpenetration between the physical and the spiritual, between the psychological and the visionary. All the images mirror and amplify each other, from the dreary day to vacant, eyelike windows to the narrator's depressed spirits to Usher's pallid skin and growing agitation, to the storm and "The Mad Trist," through the shattering conclusion. Because of this interlocking structure, wild sensationalism does not overwhelm the narrative, as it does in many popular texts. Instead, it becomes just one element that is subsumed under a general artistic plan. "The Mad Trist" serves nicely to speed the terrifying denouement. The type of fragmented sensational text Poe despised becomes the final brick in the artistic house he has built. We watch with admiration as the careful placement of this brick brings the whole house tumbling down.

If "The Fall of the House of Usher" studies the destructive effects of the wildly sensational, "Ligeia" dramatizes the nurturing effects of the arabesque. It is understandable that Poe twice called "Ligeia" his best story, because it contains all the imagery that in Poe's eyes removed sensational themes from the crassly unartistic and placed them in the realm of the beautiful. The Lady Ligeia brings together everything Poe deemed worthy: supernal beauty, quietude, strangeness, musicality, immense learning in all the sciences, and poetic sensibility. Her poem about the "Conqueror Worm" that disperses the troupe of angel-mimes is, like "The Haunted Palace" in "Usher," an interpolated text that represents the graceful treatment of gory themes. The weird arabesque chamber in which Rowena dies and Ligeia comes back to life represents the nurturing power of Poe's art, the conversion of horror into fantastic beauty that both reflects and piques the creative visions of the narrator. Whether or not Ligeia's reappearance is merely the product of the narrator's drugged mind, the fact remains that, on a visionary level at least, she does come back to life and thus stands for the imaginative resurrection of all those values Poe respects. Moreover, as in many of Poe's better tales, here the first-person narrator serves as a firm device for controlling the sensational, since even the most bizarre moments in "Ligeia" can be attributed to the over-active fancy of the narrator. This use of the narrator as a controlling device was noted by a contemporary reviewer, who wrote of "Ligeia": "Mark the exquisite art, which keeps constantly before the reader the ruined and spectre-haunted mind of the narrator, and so suggests a *possible explanation* of the marvels of the story, without in the least weakening the vigor as an exposition of the mystical *thesis* which the tale is designed to illustrate and enforce."[28] Poe has managed to treat the strange and the gruesome without descending to the gory or the chaotic. Once again, the creation of unified effect becomes an affirmation of artistic power.

In "The Masque of the Red Death" Poe gives a symbolist, highly elliptical treatment of the tension between the wildly and the artistically sensational. Prince Prospero's ornately decorated castle with its colored rooms and gay revelers represents an arabesque retreat from the gory plague that has depopulated his kingdom. Figuratively, the castle is analogous to Poe's private kingdom of art and fancy established in direct opposition to the bloody, uncontrolled sensationalism in his surrounding literary culture. In this sense, it is like the chamber in "Ligeia." But whereas "Ligeia" affirmed the resurrection of beauty through arabesque terror, "The Masque of the Red Death" poses the possibility of the arabesque losing its battle against the merely repulsive. We should note that Prospero's castle contains the seeds of its own destruction. It has "much of the beautiful, much of the wanton, much of the *bizarre,* something of the terrible, and not a little of that which might have excited disgust."[29] Despite the six gaily colored chambers, there is the innermost, western chamber of horrid blackness and windows of "a deep blood color." And in this chamber, on the western wall, is the gigantic clock whose hourly gong freezes the masquers in the midst of their revels. The fearful western clock in the gloomy western chamber may embody the inevitable passage of time in the world's most "western" culture—Poe's own America, which during the 1830s and 1840s was witnessing the broadening popularity of the kind of wildly sensational literature Poe despised. And the shroud-covered, blood-bespattered death figure that enters the castle and plants itself in the western chamber may be precisely the gory literary gruesomeness Poe fears. When Prospero tries to stab the monster and the revelers attack him, they are giving in to the mere violence and murderousness of popular sensational literature. The last sentence of the story reflects Poe's deepest fears about the collapse of the artistic and the victory of the grossly sensational: "And Darkness and Decay and Death held illimitable dominion over all."

While in the above tales he allows sensational themes to self-destruct or to be converted into beauty, in other tales he uses reason to analyze them. In tales such as "A Descent into the Maelstrom" and "The Pit and the Pendulum" he records the terrified but scrupulously detailed responses of a narrator to unusual physical peril. In works such as *Arthur Gordon Pym* and "The Imp of the Perverse" he superimposes ideas from contemporary science or pseudoscience upon sensational situations. His virtual invention of the modern detective story stems directly from the latter procedure. These kinds of fiction show Poe consciously using a firm rationalism to regulate the kinds of themes and images he saw treated more loosely in popular culture.

In his tales of physical peril, he was adapting the most common and popular element in antebellum adventure literature: the detailed recording of sensations produced by dangerous or horrific situations. "MS. Found in a Bottle," "A Descent into the Maelstrom," and "The Pit and the Pendulum" are deservedly the most famous of his tales of peril. They were obviously designed for the readers of the kind of peril literature he discusses at length in "The Psyche Zenobia (How to Write a Blackwood

Article)." Through the dual title of this sketch, Poe is underscoring the universality of interest in peril literature: he derives the name "Zenobia" from an American adventure novel, William Ware's *Zenobia* (1836); and the subtitle refers to the famous *Blackwood's Edinburgh Magazine* (founded 1817), which for years had been publishing tales of peril and which in the mid-1820s had printed works by the pioneer of American irrational literature, John Neal. In "The Psyche Zenobia" Poe describes some of his own methods (derived from the popular sensationalists) by having a magazine editor instruct the Psyche Zenobia in the art of peril writing. Advising her to "get yourself into such a scrape as no one ever got before," the editor declares: "Sensations are the great thing after all. Should you ever be drowned or hung, be sure and make a note of your sensations—they will be worth to you ten guineas a sheet."[30] The more outlandish the situation, he emphasizes, the better, since already the public is surfeited with stories of people baked in ovens, buried alive, and so forth. He goes on to outline the various possible "tones" one can use for peril writing, and then Zenobia tries her hand at such writing by composing "A Predicament," a first-person tale in which she describes her sensations as her head is slowly sliced off by the descending hands of a gigantic church-tower clock.

In much of his own fiction Poe was clearly trying to exploit the market that had been created by the popular peril writers. His letters are peppered with excited boasts about how this or that tale has made a "sensation" or a "hit." Still, his negative feelings about popular peril writing run as a cynical undertone through "The Psyche Zenobia" and through much of his literary criticism. Paradoxically awful, "The Psyche Zenobia," despite its how-to subtitle, is an exemplum on how *not* to write a peril story. It is Poe's ironic rendering of perils as they are mishandled by popular writers. It shows Poe's keen awareness of—and dissatisfaction with—the popular irrational style, called here "the tone heterogeneous." Zenobia's tale, "A Predicament," is a zany caricature of the irrational style. Persistently digressive and virtually plotless, it reveals Poe's perception that sensationalism, when unchecked by firm authorial control, gives rise to stylistic chaos and thematic absurdity.

Behind the humor of "The Psyche Zenobia" lies Poe's very real concern about unregulated sensationalism, a concern he expresses more seriously throughout his literary criticism. The presurrealistic moments in Zenobia's story seem particularly parodic of Robert Montgomery Bird's *Sheppard Lee* (1836), a sensational novel of metempsychosis in which the hero's soul successively inhabits seven different bodies, having dialogues with these bodies even when he is detached from them. In his review of Bird's novel, Poe objected to the antinaturalism, the directionlessness, and the flatness of Bird's handling of this bizarre topic, which Poe insisted should be treated with tightness and high seriousness, "as if the author were firmly impressed with the truth, yet astonished at the immensity, of the wonders he relates."[31] Poe made sure that his own tales of metempsychosis— "Morella," "Ligeia," and "A Tale of the Ragged Mountains"—possessed these qualities: not only are they taut and full of awe but also they ground the apparently supernatural in fact (the visions of reanimation are connected to the narrators' distorted perception or, in the case of "Ragged Mountains," to mesmeric phenomena).

Poe's protest against the popular irrational style carried over into his principal tales of peril. For instance, his handling of the popular themes of the Flying Dutchman and the earth's hollowness in "MS. Found in a Bottle" shows him attempting to anchor the fantastic in the rational. At the start of the story, the narrator emphasizes that he is a highly educated man with "a strong relish for physical philosophy" and not given to "the raving of a crude imagination."[32] Accordingly, his report of the awesome spectral ship rushing toward the earth's axis is at once terrific and realistic. Similarly, "A Descent into the Maelstrom" replaces the diffuse, unrealistic treatment of a similar topic in Edward Wilson Landor's "The Maelstrom: A Fragment" with an economical, scientifically detailed account by a narrator who, while properly awestruck, has sufficient coolness to measure the relative velocities of objects as they whirl around the gigantic sides of the whirlpool. Likewise, the narrator of "The Pit and the Pendulum," though increasingly frenzied, takes care to measure the circumference of the black pit and to gauge the relative downward velocities of the descending pendulum. The unique intensity of Poe's peril tales results from his determination to magnify awe (thereby avoiding the flatness of many popular texts) and at the same time to magnify reason (thereby avoiding the merely fabulous and the unnatural).

To some degree, this fusion of the sensational and the rational had precedent in earlier American writing. In particular, Brockden Brown's fiction possessed what Hazlitt regarded as a characteristically American kind of horror that was at once monstrously exaggerated and scientifically mechanical: witness Brown's use of natural phenomena such as ventriloquism, spontaneous combustion, and somnambulism. While Poe may have noticed this fusion of opposite qualities in Brown, he definitely learned from a more updated kind of fusion in the penny newspapers of the early 1830s. We have seen that the early issues of the penny papers dealt with sensational themes in a fairly objective way; it was not until the mid-1830s that excessive violence and gore became the rule in the penny press. Poe looked to the very earliest issues of America's first penny paper, the New York *Sun* (founded 1833) for a lesson in rational manipulation of the sensational. In "The Literati of New York City" (1846) Poe commended Richard Adams Locke, an early editor of the *Sun,* for having "firmly established the 'penny system' throughout the country" and thus initiating what Poe called "one of the most important steps ever yet taken in the pathway of human progress."[33] Poe's combination of the marvelous and the realistic was directly influenced by Locke's notorious report of life on the moon as revealed through a powerful telescope, a report so detailed that it was widely accepted as true. From the perspective of thirteen years, Poe could still say that the "moon hoax" was "decidedly the greatest *hit* in the way of *sensation*—of merely popular sensation—ever made by any similar fiction either in America or Europe." The reasons Poe gave for the remarkable success of Locke's story were the novelty of the idea, the "fancy-exciting and reason-repressing character of the alleged discoveries," the "consummate tact with which the deception was brought forth," and the "exquisite *vraisemblance* of the narration."

In the formative stage of his literary career, therefore, Poe had learned from America's pioneering penny newspaper a lesson in conscious manipulation of sensational themes through a double-sided fiction that possessed both novelty and tact, excitement and control. The moon hoax exemplified the writer's ability to stir the popular mind through the creation of an effect, one of simultaneous wonder and belief. It is understandable that Poe wrote his own moon hoax, "Hans Phaall," and that throughout his career he enjoyed hoodwinking the public with scientific "reports" of fabulous events—most notably "Mesmeric Revelation," "The Balloon Hoax," and "The Facts in the Case of M. Valdemar." It is also understandable that in 1833 (the same year that produced the first penny papers) he published his first distinctive tale, "MS. Found in a Bottle," which featured marvelous events factually reported. Poe's preference of the short story to the novel was directly related to his interest in avoiding the directionless irrational style that he often complained of in his reviews of novels by Neal, Simms, Bird, Ingraham, and others. Concentrating on the terse pieces in penny papers and magazines, he stressed that "the whole tendency of the age" was toward "the curt, the condensed, the pointed, the readily diffused, in place of the verbose, the detailed, the voluminous, the inaccessible."[34] In making this statement he was being rhetorical. He knew all too well that many American fictionists, especially the novelists I have called Subversive, were purposely disjointed and extravagant, not at all concise. When he tried to think of models of the good American short story, he could only point to certain tales by Irving, Hawthorne, and Simms. And when he tried his hand at writing a long fiction, the result was an anxious struggle against excessive sensationalism and the irrational style. *The Narrative of Arthur Gordon Pym* shows Poe taking sensationalism to its natural end—presurrealistic imagery—but at the same time asserting the scientific with a desperate vigor unseen in his shorter fictions. Poe discovered that to move beyond "the curt, the condensed, the pointed" was to stray dangerously close to the kind of irrational excesses that he saw in many novels and that he satirized in "The Psyche Zenobia."

On one level, *Arthur Gordon Pym* was a popular performance aimed at the growing readership of sensational literature. Its long subtitle promised the public a variety of juicy horrors, including an *Atrocious Butchery* at sea, a *Shipwreck, and Subsequent Horrible Sufferings,* a *Massacre* of a ship's crew, then *Incredible Adventures and Discoveries still further South, to which that Distressing Calamity gave Rise.* Such gruesome topics were obviously meant to appeal to the many readers who during the 1830s were being regaled by seamy immoral-reform works like Maria Monk's racy *Awful Disclosures,* gory frontier novels like Simms's *Guy Rivers* and *Richard Hurdis,* the bloody war fiction of Robert Montgomery Bird, and popular crime narratives. Poe did not neglect the demands of these readers, for violence and gore dominate much of the novel in scenes of drunkenness, bloody fights, rotting corpses, and cannibalism—all of which were standard horrors in Dark Adventure and Subversive fiction. But in Poe's treatment, these horrors are filtered through a first-person narrator whose reports of remarkable events range from the frenzied to the objective. On the one hand, Pym is almost a caricature of the 1830s sensation lover, a man whose intense love for novelty and adventure enables him to be titillated even while he is appalled and who at one point allows himself to drop from a steep cliff just to enjoy the sensation of falling. On the other hand, he is a scrupulous observer who records factual information about exotic places and events with the exactitude of an objective scientist of the day. The novel as a whole can be seen as an attempted fusion of two modes—Dark Adventure fiction, featuring savagery and nightmare imagery, and the scientific social text, featuring mimetic reportage of intriguing facts. When taken to an extreme, the first mode culminates in presurrealistic distortion of perspective, the second in a valorization of mathematical signs and codes. It is this doubleness that explains the weirdly bifurcated conclusion of the novel: first, the appearance of the shrouded white figure looming miraculously in the mist as the ship approaches the South Pole; then, in the concluding editorial "Note," the explanation of Pym's earlier line scribblings as meaningful codes and word pictures. The novel ends in both ultrairrationalism and ultrarationalism, as Poe amplifies contradictory tendencies within his culture to move beyond literary mimesis into an alternate imaginary realm.

As significant as *Arthur Gordon Pym* is in the development of American sensational fiction, it must be said that Poe's attempted fusion of the irrational and the scientific is not altogether successful. The bifurcated ending is only the final example of an awkward split that runs through the whole novel: i.e., the split between the Subversive imagination and scientific reason. About three-quarters of the novel is devoted to Pym's compellingly terrified response to horrid occurrences; the rest takes the form of factual exotica that are only indirectly associated with the sensational sections. Poe here seems to be struggling to establish rational anchorage to popular sensational themes whose excesses he disliked; but he fails to produce literary fusion because the disciplines he uses in the factual sections (mainly geography and history) cannot be easily combined with the hyperbolic emotionalism of the main narrative. Several other Poe tales succeed because they use imagery from popular pseudosciences like phrenology, animal magnetism, and mesmerism, all of which themselves embodied a kind of "rational irrationalism" that was compatible with Poe's divided vision. It was in the strange "isms" of his day that Poe found scientific correlatives for the literary fusions he was attempting.

Pseudoscience was destined to have a marked effect not only on Poe but also on Hawthorne, Melville, and Whitman. These writers gave highly individualistic reinterpretations of various pseudoscientific images and principles. They were all profiting from the liberalized use of pseudoscience that accompanied its popularization in America. Although all the pseudosciences originated abroad, they gained in America unprecedented influence due to the efforts of business-minded, often showmanlike practitioners who gave lectures, exhibitions, and healing sessions throughout the 1830s and 1840s. Phrenology, the materialistic psychological school that linked emotions and attributes to distinct brain organs, was popularized by a number of American skull readers, most notably the New York brothers Orson and Lorenzo Fowler. Animal magnetism (the belief in a universal electrical fluid influencing physics and even human psychology) was combined with mesmerism (the control of a hypnotized person by a trance medium) by the likes of Andrew Jackson Davis, who gave many notorious diagnostic and healing sessions in the early 1840s. Spiritualism (direct communication with spirits of the deceased through trance visions or séances) became a mass movement after the famous "Rochester knockings" heard by Maggie and Katie Fox in 1848. In the open, fluid atmosphere of democratic America, these pseudosciences were handled with unprecedented flexibility and creativity. They were brought together in the form of hybrids like phrenomagnetism, and in time they merged with Transcendentalism and liberal Christianity to produce new faith-healing denominations like Christian Science. This distinctively American flexibility made possible the variegated adaptations of pseudoscience by the major authors.

For Poe, pseudoscience provided a means of anchoring the marvelous in the real and of gaining victory over darkly irrational forces which threatened to become chaotic. Animal magnetism and mesmerism seem to lie behind many of the subtler effects of Poe's early fiction, particularly the creative interpenetration of the spiritual and the material in tales like "Morella," "Ligeia," "The Fall of the House of Usher," and "The Masque of the Red Death." As Poe progressively tried to identify earthly causes for the supernatural, his use of these pseudosciences became more explicit, to the detriment of his literary art. In "Mesmeric Revelation" he portrays a man, placed in a hypnotic trance, answering questions about God and the afterlife. In the American spirit of creative reinterpretation of pseudoscience, Poe begins with a standard idea of animal magnetism—the existence of a universal electric fluid—and develops a notion of God as unparticled matter, a theme he would amplify in *Eureka.* More successful, because less preachy, is "The Facts in the Case of M. Valdemar," about a dying man placed in a magnetic sleep, from which he is awakened in seven months, upon which he immediately dissolves into a mass of loathsome putrefaction. Poe showed how profoundly indebted he was to America's flexible readaptations of pseudoscience in "A Tale of the Ragged Mountains," a tale of mesmeric reincarnation which contains the following statement: "It is only now, in the year 1845, when similar miracles are witnessed daily by thousands, that I dare venture to record this apparent impossibility as a matter of serious fact."[35] The fact that two of his mesmerism tales, "Mesmeric Revelation" and "Valdemar," were widely accepted as factual shows just how ready the public was to swallow even the embellished miracles of an inventive fictionist.

Animal magnetism and mesmerism were important elements in Poe's efforts to confront questions of spirituality and death. Phrenology, in contrast, was useful in his confrontations with psychological questions. In a rapturous review of Mrs. L. Miles's *Phrenology* (1836) he declared: "Phrenology is no longer to be laughed at. . . . It has assumed the majesty of a science; and, as a science, ranks among the most important which can engage the attention of thinking human beings."[36] The phrenological belief that mental attributes could be read through facial features permitted a new means of analyzing fictional characters. Poe's very careful descriptions of Roderick Usher, with his cadaverous skin and protruding brow, and Ligeia, with her lofty forehead and luminous eyes, typify his use of face-reading procedures to give a mystical depth to concrete physical description. Furthermore, phrenology directly influenced Poe's literary theory, which was based upon distinct portions of the mind devoted to different impulses. Just as phrenologists divided the brain up into apportioned functions, so Poe distinguished between pure intellect (concerned with truth), taste (concerned with beauty), and the moral sense (devoted to duty). Poetry, he argued, appealed only to the taste and therefore had nothing to do with truth or duty. His influential notion of art for art's sake was in part made possible by the compartmentalization of the mental faculties initiated by the popular psychologists of his day.

Poe was well aware of the vulgarization and commercialization of phrenology when it fell into the hands of businessmen like the Fowlers or histrionic lecturers like Robert H. Collyer. For instance, in an 1845 review he could decry the "marvels and inconsistencies of the FOWLERS *et id genus omne*" and felt compelled to write equivocally that "very many of the salient points of phrenological science are undisputable truths—whatever falsity may be detected in the principles kindly furnished to the science by hot-headed and asinine votaries."[37] Still, he profited greatly from the new flexibility and individualism of the American pseudoscientific scene. He took wry pleasure in the fact that even the practiced phrenomagnetic showman Robert Collyer was so excited by the apparent factuality of "The Facts in the Case of M. Valdemar" that Collyer wrote Poe an anxious letter requesting hard evidence of Poe's story so that he could publish it and thus salvage his flagging pseudoscientific career. Despite his criticism of the American commercialists, Poe shared their experimental outlook and extended it in his fiction.

His theory of the imp of the perverse and his creation of the detective story are the most memorable of his innovations directly attributable to the new experimental phrenology. Phrenologists generally agreed that there was a brain organ, combativeness, that made humans commit crime and take pleasure in the suffering of others. But American practitioners like the Fowlers and Collyer reinterpreted phrenological principles to advance the optimistic notion that this organ could be controlled and regulated. In "The Imp of the Perverse" Poe made the characteristically American gesture of applying phrenology individualistically; but the application he offered was a disquieting one that flew directly in the face of optimists. He gave his own startling psychological lesson by identifying a primal impulse for which "the phrenologists have failed to make room," one which he says must not be confused with "the *combativeness* of phrenology."[38] This impulse, which Poe calls perverseness, is the inclination to do wrong for wrong's sake, to perpetrate bad actions merely because we feel we should not. He goes on to use sensational fiction as a means of rhetorical argument, telling the story of a murderer whose crime goes undiscovered and who confesses his guilt precisely because he knows it will lead to his own death.

It might seem from "The Imp of the Perverse" that Poe was intent upon manipulating phrenology for solely negative, cynical ends, as a way of combating his age's optimism. But this was not so: his detective stories show he could use it to combat his age's sensationalism as well. It should be noted that even in "The Imp of the Perverse," phrenological terminology made possible a scientific, case-study approach to themes that in popular sensational literature too often gave rise to mere repulsiveness or unexplained violence. In the detective stories this use of phrenology to overcome sensational excesses was particularly pronounced. For Poe, phrenology represented an attractive means of studying the irrational without losing control of the subject. Poe's famous discovery of the detective tale was the direct outgrowth of his superimposition of phrenological principles upon the kind of bloody crime whose indulgent reportage by popular sensationalists he had repeatedly castigated. "The Murders in the Rue Morgue" (1841), the first popular detective story, does have vestiges of popular sensational literature. The premise of freakish actions by a humanoid orangutan had been introduced in America as early as 1807, with the story of a razor-wielding ape in the *American Magazine of Wonders,* and had been circulating later in works like Joseph Martin's *Select Tales* (1833), an adventure anthology that includes a story about an orangutan who kidnaps a child and suckles it for three months. The fact that the action begins when the narrator and his detective friend read a newspaper article with the headline "Extraordinary Murders" places the tale in the realm of popular crime reportage, as does the grisly violence of the murders. Still, I must take issue with Poe's modern editor, Thomas Olive Mabbott, who says the one fault of the tale is an excessively gory passage. Poe does include enough gore and violence to suggest to his contemporary readers that they are in the familiar world of sensational literature, but he in fact distinguishes himself by his *avoidance* of explicit violence, his innovative concentration on the observant intelligence of the detective, C. Auguste Dupin. And this detached, scientific feature of the story springs directly from phrenology. In the original magazine version of the tale, Poe begins with a long discussion of a specific organ in the brain devoted to analysis, a power linked with ideality that Poe insists is highly developed in imaginative people like Dupin. The detective, therefore, is constitutionally equipped to respond coolly to a horrible crime that has been sensationalized in the press and misinterpreted by more poorly endowed observers whose feeble guesses about the crime are as cacophonous as the fabled gruntings of the homicidal orangutan. Poe purposely avoids the flaws (repulsiveness, unreason, stylistic looseness) he had identified in the sensational fiction of Neal, Simms, Bird, and others. He virtually invents the detective story by taking a common popular premise—crime and its popular misinterpreters—and combining it with another powerful element from popular culture: the brain's analytical power, as defined by phrenology.

In his next detective story, "The Mystery of Marie Rogêt" (1842–43),

Poe is even more explicit in his effort to bring cerebral order to a horrid crime—this time a real crime involving a New York cigar girl, Mary Rogers, who disappeared on July 25, 1841, and whose body was found days later floating in the Hudson River. For the next several months the mysterious murder of the beautiful and well-known girl was sensationalized in notably conflicting newspaper reports; eventually, like most dramatic murders of the day, it was exploited in an opportunistic pamphlet novel, *La Bonita Cigarera: or The Beautiful Cigar Vender* (1844), by the same J. H. Ingraham whose earlier novel *Lafitte* Poe had attacked as immoral and violent. Throughout his story Poe makes it clear that he is writing with the specific aim of repudiating erratic, indulgent reportage of crime in the popular press. The masterful Dupin frequently quotes the contradictory press accounts of the girl's death and emphasizes that "it is the object of our newspapers rather to create a sensation—to make a point—than to further the cause of truth."[39] While the popular sensationalists quickly lose themselves in a maze of fervid responses and irrelevant guesses, the powerful brain of Dupin arrives at the "solution" by exercising imaginative faculties that are perfectly in tune with what Poe calls "the Calculus of Probabilities," a "purely mathematical" theory of chance and coincidence which presents "the anomaly of the most rigidly exact in science applied to the shadow and spirituality of the most intangible in speculation."

By the time he wrote "The Purloined Letter" (1844) he had moved so far away from the sensational that both crime and its detection operate on a purely intellectual level. Poe's statement that this was "perhaps the best of my tales of ratiocination" reflects his high regard for crime fiction totally removed from the mire of repulsiveness.[40] His previous two detective stories had affirmed the power of the analytical mind but still had devoted much time to popular reportage of gory events. In "The Purloined Letter" the emphasis is reversed: not only are there no gory events, but the crime is the bloodless one of letter stealing and the identity of the criminal is known from the start. Indeed, crime is absent from this story, which directs our attention to the mental principles behind crime. Poe now brings together many elements from his previous tales to forge his ultimate imaginary victory over the irrational. The amoral criminal who becomes the means of his own destruction (an idea he studied differently in "William Wilson," "The Tell-Tale Heart," and "The Imp of the Perverse") is represented here by the Minister D——, except that here the self-destruction is masterminded by the thoughtful detective who guesses D——'s mental operations. The abbreviated discussions of phrenological ideas in "Murders in the Rue Morgue" are replaced here by long, detailed monologues by Dupin on the science of the mind. Poe's rationalistic theory of poetry is echoed in Dupin's account of the faculty of analysis, which is said to bring together the mathematical and the poetical. Sensationalism is reduced to a disturbance in the street caused by a gunshot, which diverts D——'s attention and makes possible Dupin's switching of the letters. The fact that the disturbance is created by a man in Dupin's hire shows the large degree to which sensationalism is under the control of the intellect. As in "The Fall of the House of Usher," the sensational is put in place to create an effect. There is, of course, a key difference: in "Usher" the reading of "The Mad Trist" leads to the wild climax; in "The Purloined Letter" the gunshot leads to the intellectual victory of the detective. But the difference is more apparent than real, for in both cases the sensational is skillfully put in place by the literary artist with the effect of deconstructing the evil or bizarre images of the narrative: the House of Usher collapses, and D—— is outwitted. In the latter case, the victory of the analytical power is especially sweet, for Poe is imaginatively outwitting the heroic villain of popular crime narratives. In direct opposition to the popular stereotype of the sympathetic criminal, Poe establishes the detective as a force for both high intellect and high morality, one who can declare that he has "no sympathy—at least no pity" for D——, who is called "that *monstrum horrendum,* an unprincipled man of genius."[41] Poe has given us the ultimate example of a popular stereotype—the amoral, cool, brilliant criminal—and has defeated him through the creation of a character who is even more cool, more brilliant than he—and who upholds morality. In creating the brainy detective, Poe gained victory over the popular Subversive imagination.

9

HAWTHORNE'S CULTURAL DEMONS

W H E N Poe once mentioned Hawthorne's distance from the "excitable, undisciplined . . . popular mind" he was neglecting important ways in which Hawthorne was, like himself, engaged in using popular literary tools.[1] In one sense, Poe was right: Hawthorne's fiction does possess an allegorical element and a quietude that disqualified it for wide popularity among lovers of sensational literature. Melville made a similar point when he wrote in "Hawthorne and His Mosses" that Hawthorne "refrains from all the popularizing noise and show of broad farce, and blood-besmeared tragedy."[2] Still, Hawthorne was responding to noisy, blood-besmeared American popular culture just as much as Poe or Melville. Like them, he was a professional fictionist who was conscious of the growing market for sensational writings. Also like them, he was disturbed by unrestrained sensationalism and sought to assert artistic control over popular themes. The controlling devices he used—allegory, history, symbol, tight structure, tonal restraint—converted such stereotypes as the justified pariah and the oxymoronic oppressor into mythic figures that transcended the popular culture they grew from.

Hawthorne and Crime Literature

A voracious reader of what he called "all sorts of good and good-for-nothing books," Hawthorne had a special fascination for dark, sensational popular writings. In his youth he devoured Gothic novels by Horace Walpole, Ann Radcliffe, Monk Lewis, and Edward Maturin. He had a penchant for crime narratives that became a lifetime obsession. One of his favorite childhood books was an old crime anthology, translated from the Italian, entitled *God's Revenge Against the Crying and Execrable Sin of Murder!*, which had been passed down through Hawthorne's family for generations. Despite its religious title, it stressed the sensational so heavily that Hawthorne's son Julian in *Hawthorne's Reading* recalled it as "the forerunner of the yellow literature which is so much discussed and abused and is so signally popular nowadays," a "medieval Police Gazette" whose gory plots "would be a godsend to the criminal-fiction school of today." Julian noted that his father's "pathetic craving" for these murder tales was indicated by the worn condition of the volume, with its dog-eared and stained pages and its binding "completely wrecked" by Hawthorne's relentless thumbings-through.[3] This interest in crime narrative lasted until his death; one of Julian's last mental images was his aged father sedulously leafing through an enormous volume of trial reports.

A devotee of crime narratives in youth and old age, Hawthorne was especially attuned to popular criminal trials and famous scandals during his formative period as an author. The dark themes of his fiction were related to his apprehension of perversities and ironies in popular reports of criminal trials. In his notebook for 1836 he drew a direct connection between human sinfulness and popular trials. "There is evil in every human heart," he wrote, "which may remain latent, through the whole of life; but circumstances may rouse it into activity." Jotting down imaginary sketches to illustrate this idea, he pictured a woman who cheats on her husband out of arbitrary whim and a young man who commits murder "out of mere thirst for blood." Hawthorne emphasizes: "This appetite may be traced in the popularity of criminal trials."[4]

Throughout Hawthorne's private writings are scattered with his excited comments on popular trials of the day. His letters of 1830 show his special interest in the notorious "Salem Murder." The wealthy retired Salem merchant Captain Joseph White had been brutally murdered by a local criminal, Richard Crowninshield, who had been hired by two brothers of good family, John Francis and Joseph Knapp, who hoped to profit from White's will. Crowninshield, driven insane by remorse, committed suicide in jail while awaiting trial. The Knapp brothers remained cool through the sensational trial proceedings and even after they were both sentenced to death; Hawthorne noted that Frank Knapp actually "joked and laughed with the man who watched him, with as much apparent gaiety as if he had been acquitted, instead of condemned."[5] Knapp's equanimity made the Salem Murder an important episode in the development of the stereotype of the cool criminal—so important that twelve years later Poe would make it the basis for his famous deconstruction of cool criminality, "The Tell-Tale Heart." The case also had a lasting influence on Hawthorne, who used it as the probable basis for his portrait of the coldly malicious Roger Chillingworth in *The Scarlet Letter* and for a crime over a disputed will in *The House of the Seven Gables.*

Why did a simple murder case, of the sort we read about daily over our morning coffee, have such a profound impact on our literature? We should recall that the White murder occurred in 1830, just as the popular press was learning how to capitalize fully on the American public's thirst for sensational news. Crime was still naïvely treated as a relative novelty, as is evidenced by this passage in the Knapp trial pamphlet: "Never in our own quiet community, has an event occurred possessing such a deep dye of depravity as that characterising what is popularly denominated the Salem Murder. Guilt seems to have steeped the offence in its blackest hue, and humanity covers its face in horror at the recital of a deed so cruel and so causeless."[6] The Knapp trial and the sensational press reports it produced acted cumulatively as the American public's fall from innocence into grisly fascination with the details of crime. The oft-repeated theme in Hawthorne's fiction of damning effects of crime on the previously innocent was partly a reenactment of this momentous cultural event, about which the prosecuting attorney, Daniel Webster, declared: "So little had ever been known of a crime so deep in New England." Another favorite Hawthorne theme, the inward torment of the guilty individual, may have been partly inspired by Crowninshield's mad remorse, which became, in Webster's words, "a vulture, ever gnawing at his heart." Also, Hawthorne learned the feeling of combined horror and sympathy which criminals could provoke when their plight was sensationalized in the popular press. Hawthorne actually took a liking to the jocular Frank Knapp and stated in a letter he hoped he would escape. In his fascination with the case, he was sharing the paradoxical feelings of the American public as described by Webster:

A kind of morbid interest for the felon, was created within us, and following the course of the young and imaginative, the very horridness of the crime rendered it attractive. The monster presented to us, was rendered beautiful by its superlative ugliness. So strangely was the mind of man constructed, that pleasure could be gathered from the elements of pain, and beauty seen in the Gorgon head of horror.

The Knapp trial was a powerful lesson in various dark themes: cool villainy, the fall from innocence, sin among the respectable, the likable criminal, and the public's fascination with crime and sensationalism. All of these themes would appear repeatedly in Hawthorne's fiction.

Hawthorne was also pondering *other* prominent crimes and scandals in this developmental stage. In an 1830 letter to his Ohio friend J. S. Dike he dwelt upon grisly doings in New England, such as the case of a mad Cambridge man who killed himself and that of a dissipated Boston man who stabbed a fellow who had turned him out of a party. In 1831 he took note of a Salem minister's wife charged with slander by the editor of the *Salem Observer* for having publicly called him a blasphemer. Hawthorne wrote: "The trial of a minister's wife for slander would have caused nearly as great an excitement as the trial of the Knapps." His interest in corruption in high places was evidenced by his growing recognition of the moral turpitude of Daniel Webster, who, Hawthorne declared in an 1836 letter, is "altogether a disreputable character" who "drinks, and is notoriously immoral."[7]

If on the one hand his interest was provoked by crime cases reported in the press, at the same time it was stimulated by accounts of crime in popular works such as the massive anthology *The Record of Crimes in the United States* (1833), which was most likely his source of information for an 1838 notebook entry in which he proposed to write a "political or other satire" about "A show of wax-figures, consisting almost wholly of murderers and their victims."[8] He specifically mentions several of the most notorious American criminals: Charles Gibbs and Thomas J. Wansley, pirates who in the 1820s had captured nearly twenty vessels and had murdered over four hundred human beings; Ephraim K. Avery, the Methodist preacher who in 1833 was tried for seducing and murdering a sluttish convert in his charge; Jesse Strang, a doltish country boy taken as a paramour by Elsie D. Whipple, who in 1827 persuaded Strang to poison her husband; and Richard P. Robinson, the New York dandy accused of killing the prostitute Ellen Jewett but acquitted for lack of evidence.

Such criminal cases were a primary source of dark themes in Hawthorne's fiction. The volume in which he learned of many of these cases, *The Record of Crimes in the United States,* is so searing a record of human perversity and criminality, often punctuated by gloomy generalizations about human nature, that, given Hawthorne's interest in popular crime cases, it is surprising his fiction isn't even darker than it is. The introduction to the anthology explains that the organ of destructiveness in the brain gives everyone an intrinsic interest in witnessing executions and a latent capacity for committing crime. The anthology consists of twenty-three biographies of famous American criminals: wife stabbers, husband poisoners, child murderers, pirates, counterfeiters, and rapists. The careers of these criminals are portrayed in objective, neutral fashion, with little or no moral commentary. Most of the criminals are said to have committed a string of unthinkable atrocities for the sheer love of it. The narratives in *Record of Crimes* contain several themes or images that would appear in Hawthorne's fiction: the idea of the potential sinfulness of all human beings, as Americans of every profession and background are said to be capable of the most heinous crimes; dramatic scaffold confessions, any of which may have provided the basis for scaffold scenes in *The Scarlet Letter*; and an overall interest in persons outside the law, foes of mainstream civilization. Perhaps the most important stereotypes that emerge from the narratives in this volume are the secretly sinful churchgoer and the likable or justified criminal. A typical instance of the first type is George Swearingen, a respected, outwardly strict Methodist who is secretly involved with several "lewd and lascivious women," with one of whom he brutally murders his wife.[9] Pious women are portrayed as being just as capable of grisly murder as men: the case of Elsie Whipple is said to prove that "a woman makes more rapid strides in the path which leadeth to destruction, when she has once set her foot in it, than men." A chief example in *Record of Crimes* of the cool, likable criminal is the pirate Charles Gibbs, who in jail seems so "mild and gentle," so affably talkative that "no one would have taken him to be a villain." And a key instance of the justified criminal is Samuel Bellamy, a murderous pirate but also a democratic folk hero who insists that the rich "rob the poor under cover of the law, and we plunder them with no protection but our own courage." The final effect of the narratives is to describe such mixed characters so often that normal definitions of virtue and vice are directly threatened. Human nature is portrayed as notably ambiguous and fluid. In one narrative we have the following typical generalization: "Such is the strange and mysterious composition of our nature; so closely allied are our virtues and vices; so easily does the former degenerate into the latter, or the latter assimilate themselves, and assume the garb of the former, it is often difficult to determine where the one terminates, or the other commences."

Hawthorne's exposure to such popular crime literature in the early 1830s was largely responsible for the broadening awareness of universal sinfulness and moral fluidity, an awareness that had a significant effect on his fiction. The effect is best highlighted by a comparison of two tales with a similar theme: "My Kinsman, Major Molineux" and "Young Goodman Brown." "My Kinsman" was published in 1832 but had been written much earlier: Hawthorne had sent it to the editor Samuel G. Goodrich in 1829, reporting it had been "completed . . . a considerable time." It thus represents Hawthorne's earliest style, as compared with "Young Goodman Brown," which was written and published in the mid-1830s. Both of these tales involve a young man's initiation into evil resulting from a disillusioning perception about previously respected people. But there is an important difference: the later story universalizes the initiation parable that in the early tale is the discovery of individual infamy. In "My Kinsman" the fall from innocence is connected to the witnessing of the public punishment of a particular individual, Molineux, whose disgrace is given historical specificity by the introductory paragraph about popular insurrections against colonial governors. In "Young Goodman Brown" Hawthorne intensifies the irony and deepens the gloom by depicting the universality of sin and the grim aftermath of this perception. The following images used by the satanic preacher in the forest seem to show the influence of popular sensational literature, particularly the crime narratives Hawthorne was reading with special interest in the early 1830s:

> This night it shall be granted to you to know their secret deeds: how hoary-bearded elders of the church have whispered wanton words to the young maids of their households; how many a woman, eager for widow's weeds, has given her husband a drink at bedtime and let him sleep his last sleep in her bosom; how beardless youths have made haste to inherit their father's wealth; and how fair damsels—blush not, sweet ones!—have dug little graves in the garden, and bidden me, the sole guest to an infant's funeral.[10]

It is tempting to identify real-life analogues for the criminals mentioned here—to see the Rev. Ephraim K. Avery or George Swearingen behind the licentious church elders, Elsie Whipple behind the husband poisoners, the Knapp brothers behind the scheming inheritors of wealth, and John McDowall's child-killing prostitutes behind the baby buriers. The least that can be said is that by the mid-1830s Hawthorne had moved from a perception of individual sinfulness to a vision of universal gloom, a vision communicated in "Young Goodman Brown" through characters remarkably similar to those he was reading about in the popular crime narratives. We saw that the final effect of crime reports like *The Record of Crimes* was to break down the barriers between virtue and vice by showing that people of all backgrounds and dispositions are capable of evil. The moral relativism implicit in crime narratives is reproduced in Young Goodman Brown's progressive recognition of the hidden sinfulness of revered villagers and ancestors, a recognition that culminates in his outcry: "My Faith is gone! . . . There is no good on earth; and sin is but a name. Come, devil; for to thee the world is given."

An attentive observer of trials, Hawthorne was also a close reader of newspapers. His son Julian recalled that he read poetry and romances "for pleasure and relaxation . . . but if study were his object, he would resort to the newspapers and magazines."[11] He is known to have read the *Salem Observer* from the early 1820s on. He was a good friend of Caleb Foote, the editor of the *Salem Gazette,* who had published "The Hollow of Three Hills" (1830) and eighteen subsequent Hawthorne tales. Hawthorne also had high regard for James Kennedy Cook, publisher of the *Salem Commercial Advertiser* starting in 1832. An avid reader of the penny papers, Hawthorne and Longfellow made plans in 1840 to found what he called "a daily evening paper upon the cash principle, together with a weekly sheet—say the size of the [Boston Evening] Transcript."[12]

Since in the 1830s Hawthorne was competing against popular sensational newspaper writers, he knew that a reference to seamy or odd news was often useful in attracting attention. Notice, for example, how he begins his famous story "Wakefield" (1835): "In some old magazine or newspaper I recollect a story, told as truth, of a man—let us call him Wakefield—who absented himself for a long time from his wife," which was "as remarkable a freak as may be found in the whole list of human oddities."[13] Even Hawthorne's celebrated recovery of the darker aspects of Puritan history was in large part guided by this regard for modern sensation lovers. In "Old News" (1835) he assumes the persona of a man who comes upon a volume of old newspapers, which he calls the best reflection of an age: "Happy are the editors of newspapers! Their productions excel all others in immediate popularity, and are certain to acquire another sort of value with the escape of time." He goes on to write a sketch that reads like a penny newspaper report on Puritan culture. Bringing attention to diverting novelties about the Puritans, he writes: "There is no evidence that the moral standard was higher then than now. . . . There seem to have been quite as many frauds and robberies, in proportion to the number of honest deals; there were murders, in hot blood and malice; and bloody quarrels, over liquor."[14] Adultery was rife, he continues, and the whipping post, the gallows, and the prison all made the Puritan period a gloomy one indeed. Hawthorne is creating a kind of subversive national history by imposing the sensibility of the nineteenth-century sensation-monger upon the Puritan past. His age's interest in sensational news gives rise to gloomy reflections on American history. Hawthorne was hardly the first American fictionist to write about the Puritans: several novels of the 1820s, most notably Lydia Child's *Hobomok* and John Neal's *Rachel Dyer,* had anticipated him in this regard. But he was the first to use the persona of a newspaper reader in order to focus on tabooed or seamy Puritan images—adultery, child murderers, witches, robbers, and so on—that would have had natural appeal for many readers of his day. He does the same in the preface to *Mosses from an Old Manse* (1846), in which his persona rummages through old newspapers, almanacs, and other past ephemeral literature; he emphasizes that no old writings have "retained any sap, except what had been written for the passing day and year, without the remotest pretension or idea of permanence."[15] Presenting his tales as newspaper sketches of various aspects of the past, Hawthorne in effect joined the competition among journalists of his day. He became the news reporter of the Puritans.

The question arises: given his acknowledged interest in sensational writings like crime reports and penny newspapers, why did not he himself write contemporary journalism or crime narratives? If he used newspaper imagery in his fiction, why did he not deal more directly with nineteenth-century America?

While profoundly impressed by popular sensational writings, Hawthorne resisted their flatness and moral neutrality. He registered his dissatisfaction in his parody of newspaper writing, "The Sister Years" (1839), in which he assumes the persona of the *Salem Gazette* for 1838. Reality as reflected in newspaper reportage is full of chaotic political brawls, disappointed hopes, crime—the outgoing year says the new year should "expect no gratitude nor good will from this peevish, unreasonable, inconsiderate, ill-intending and worse-behaving world."[16] The dizzying speed and confusion of modern life is a common theme in Hawthorne's fiction. At the end of "Fire-Worship" (1843) he emphasizes that togetherness, the family, and moral values are giving way before fragmentation, debate, and atomism. In the preface to *Mosses from an Old Manse* he writes that the age has "gone distracted, through a morbid activity" that can be cured by repose, which is the only way of "restoring to us the simple perception of what is right, and the single-hearted desire to achieve it; both of which have long been lost, in consequence of this weary activity of brain, and torpor or passion of the heart, that now afflicts the universe. Stimulants, the only mode of treatment hitherto attempted, cannot quell the disease; they do but to heighten the delirium."[17] Here Hawthorne seems to be protesting against the feverish sensational literature that was being offered as a stimulant and diversion to the American public. He believed that such stimulation only worsened what he regarded as a prevailing hyperactivity and heartsickness in American society. The quietude that Poe and Melville noticed in his fiction was consciously cultivated in defense against terrifying cultural turbulences.

Hawthorne absorbed the negativity and ironic tone of popular sensational literature but above all tried to infuse new depth and meaning into it. He could retain the modern ironies but give them suggestiveness and intensity through the agency of Puritanism. In his eyes, modern sensationalism represented a fall from innocence into an arid wasteland of moral neutrality; Calvinism, in contrast, had taught that positive good can result from the honest exposure of sin. Hawthorne coupled the ironies of modern sensationalism with the resonance of Puritan Calvinism. "The Minister's Black Veil" (1836) is a paradigmatic combination of Puritanism and nineteenth-century ironies. The 1830s were full of examples of ministerial depravity, several of which Hawthorne noted in his journals. A common image in popular journalism was lifting the veil that covers hidden corruption. The prevailing feeling among reformers and sensationalists was that veils over hidden sin were virtually everywhere—among priests, ministers, politicians, and many other respectable pillars of society. Hawthorne evidently recognized that he could not present an unsullied minister in an age when ministers were quickly becoming laughingstocks in the popular press. But he did not want to follow the popular sensationalists into the amoral world of mere titillation by having his ministers cheat and seduce with gleeful disregard for all moral values. He thus decided to retain the modern stereotype of the tainted minister but imagine him as a Puritan Calvinist. Thus he removed sin from the realm of crass titillation and placed it in a moral context.

Given the savage Subversive ironies of the sensationalists, the best Hawthorne could do was to invest these ironies with depth, with a sense of awe, which was far preferable to the flat neutrality he saw in the popular writings. In his early tales, he accomplishes this by isolating a paradigmatic character (Robin Molineux, Goodman Brown, Edgar and Edith in "Merry Mount," the Rev. Hooper) and trace the fall from innocence into knowledge of sin. These characters have different responses to sin: Robin shrieks with laughter at his previously respected uncle; Brown is bitterly disillusioned by the revelation of hidden sin among revered townspeople; Edgar and Edith are deepened and chastened when they reject their former gaiety and join the dour Puritans; the Rev. Hooper becomes a better preacher, a counsel for troubled souls but also a wholly isolated and feared figure after he assumes the veil. In other words, sometimes the fall into sin is clearly fortunate, sometimes it is mixed, sometimes it is unfortunate because it breeds cynicism and mistrust. The common denominator is that in each case the fall has meaning within the context of the tale, which is structured and symbolic. Symbol, psychological depth, universality, allegorical suggestiveness themselves gather real value for a writer who cannot ignore modern ironies but who is repelled by their representations in popular sensational literature. In a self-critical moment, Hawthorne could declare he did not know what he meant in his "blasted allegories"—but meaning, in the simplistic sense, does not apply to the Hawthorne tale, which is typically suggestive but finally ambiguous. Suggestiveness itself became an assertion of value in the face of the often morally neutral social texts like the crime narratives and penny newspaper reports Hawthorne knew well.

Similarly, structure itself took on meaning in an age when many novels were consciously alinear and disorganized. When an editor asked him to produce a serial novel similar to those commonly published by the popular sensationalists, Hawthorne unequivocally rejected the proposal, insisting he could only write romances centered on "one prominent idea."[18] He stressed that his novels lacked "the variety of interest and character which seem to have made the success of other works, so published." His refusal to depart from his custom of developing "one prominent idea" in a romance showed his unwillingness to participate in the jerkiness and roller-coaster emotionalism of the serial novelists. Above all, he needed structure, unity, interconnectedness. It is significant that his feelings about the leading Subversive fictionist, John Neal, were, like Poe's, notably divided. On the one hand, Hawthorne had devoured Neal's fiction while a Bowdoin student. Clearly, some of Neal's dark images—nightmares, haunted minds, confusion between dream and reality, horrid shrieks by maddened characters, a feisty instinct to unmask authority figures—fed directly into Hawthorne's fiction, which is full of this sort of Subversive imagery. But, like Poe, Hawthorne had reservations about the stylistic irrationalism and abandon Neal championed. That is why he always associated Neal with madness, wildness, noise. In "P.'s Correspondence" (1845) he recalled: "There was that wild fellow John Neal, who almost turned my boyish brains with his romances."[19] His friend Jonathan Cilley, upon hearing Hawthorne was to become a professional writer, expressed an ardent wish that Hawthorne avoid producing fiction like "that damned ranting stuff of John Neal, which you, while at Brunswick [i.e., Bowdoin College], relished so highly."[20] Hawthorne had good reason to control the irrational style. He was certainly aware that Neal and others had associated Americanness with stylistic wildness and quirkiness. He did not want to omit this element altogether from his writings. But he feared the excesses of the Subversive imagination, a fear that emerged also in his recoil away from mesmerism, which drove him to warn his wife: "Keep thy imagination sane."[21]

He integrated elements of the irrational style into his fiction but subsumed them under a larger design. For instance, he doesn't simply follow the meandering thoughts of a dreaming person or a madman, as did Neal and the other Subversives. Rather, he makes madness and dream a carefully arranged element in a narrative structure that also contains realistic elements (grounding the tale in fact), allegorical elements (giving it larger suggestiveness), and often moral or religious context (giving an aura of didacticism, even when there is no single meaning). He therefore avoids both the flatness and moral neutrality of sensational social texts and the directionless emotionalism of sensational novels. He manipulates the Subversive imagination and gains control over it.

The Scarlet Letter and Popular Sensationalism

His literary reshaping of popular sensational themes is best exemplified by *The Scarlet Letter*. Hawthorne always thought of his novel as a popular performance. He would write to Horatio Bridge about his next novel, *The House of the Seven Gables*: "Being better (which I insist it is) than the Scarlet Letter, I have never expected it to be so popular."[22] He later wrote Bridge that *Seven Gables* was "more characteristic of my mind, and more proper for me to write, than the Scarlet Letter,—but, for that very reason, less likely to interest the public." And in reference to his plans for his third major novel, *The Blithedale Romance*, he promised Bridge he would "put an extra touch of the devil into it; for I doubt whether the public will stand two quiet books in succession, without my losing ground. As long as people will buy, I shall keep at my work; and I find that my facility of labor increases with the demand for it." The presumption here is that Hawthorne knew that the American public liked devilish books and that to sustain his popularity he must get out of the "quiet" mode of *Seven Gables* and resume the dark mode he had exploited in *The Scarlet Letter*. If Hawthorne regarded *The Scarlet Letter* as a popular effort, he also believed it was an exceptionally gloomy one—in his words, "positively a h-ll-fired story, into which I found it almost impossible to throw any cheering light." It was the product of a year in which he was under the combined influences of extreme financial pressure, grief over his mother's death, and bitterness over his dismissal from the custom house. He explained in a June 1849 letter to Longfellow that he wanted to retaliate against his political enemies by showing them what "the imaginative power . . . can do in the way of producing nettles, skunk-cabbage, deadly night-shade, wolf's bane, dogwood," when it leaves the realm of "beauty and beneficence" and becomes "a pervasive and penetrating mischief, that can reach them at their firesides and in their bedchambers, follow them to far countries, and make their very graves refuse to hide them." He was consciously trying to produce a novel that would be at once popular and poisonous, attractive to the public and subversive of his enemies.

Readers have long hunted among Puritan annals for sources of characters and scenes in *The Scarlet Letter* but have overlooked prototypes in antebellum sensational literature that were far more relevant to Hawthorne's stated goals. To be sure, he was probably aware of certain scandals in Puritan history, such as that involving a Maine minister's wife, Mary Bachelor, who was branded with the letter A for having adulterous relations with one George Rogers. But the existence of such Puritan sources does not explain Hawthorne's choice of such a topic at a time when he wished to produce a novel that would be both gloomy and popular. That choice was to a large degree guided by ironic stereotypes from his contemporary popular culture.

In particular, Hawthorne was exploiting interest in the popular stereotypes of the oxymoronic oppressor, representing hidden sin in high places, and the justified pariah or likable criminal. With growing frequency in popular sensational writings, the honest criminality of the justified pariah was viewed as preferable to the sham virtue of the oppressor. Hawthorne himself had experimented with this theme in some of his earlier fiction. In "The Procession of Life" (1843) he portrays "the brotherhood of crime," with a forger and a financier, a murderer and a reverend, whores and decorous maidens walking hand in hand. Like a typical defender of justified criminals, he writes: "Statesmen, rulers, generals . . . commit wrong, devastation, and murder, on so grand a scale, that it impresses them as speculative rather than actual," but they are in fact worse than "the meanest criminals."[23] This sympathy for outcasts and victims of oppression feeds into his portrait of Hester Prynne.

In opposition to the likable criminal, he places the oxymoronic oppressors, the moralistic but cruel Puritans that punish her. At the center of the novel he places a particular type of oxymoronic oppressor—the reverend rake—which had special appeal for his contemporaries. A common figure in sensational writings of the day, the reverend rake is the hypocritical minister, secretly involved with one of his parishioners, whose sinfulness is brought to light by the inquisitorial writer.

The antebellum public had a special fascination with sensational sex scandals involving clergymen. Stories of reverend rakes ensured a good sale for newspapers and crime pamphlets, while the more traditional virtuous preacher was considered too dull to sell copy. The New York doctor David Reese noted in *Humbugs of New-York* (1838) that "tales of lust, and blood, and murder" dominated the American press, tales particularly popular "when they are represented as transpiring under the cloak of religion, and the criminals occupying and disgracing the holy office of the ministry."[24] Among the most widely reported scandals were the aforementioned seduction and murder case of the Rev. Ephraim K. Avery, noted in Hawthorne's journal; the 1835 trial of a homosexual Massachusetts preacher, Charles L. Cook, who was removed from two pulpits for "perpetrating the vilest and most unnatural offences with persons of his own sex";[25] the so-called Great Divorce Case of 1839, in which a leading Episcopalian priest, Samuel F. Jarvis, was sued by his wife for ignoring her sexually while sleeping with their German governess; the ongoing drama of John N. Maffitt, the immensely successful itinerant who throughout the 1840s was regularly reported as having illicit sexual affairs; and, most shocking of all, the trial in 1845 of Benjamin T. Onderdonk, the Episcopalian bishop of New York, who was defrocked for seducing several of his female parishioners. In the late 1840s reports of ministerial depravity filled George Wilkes's weekly *National Police Gazette,* which played up such cases in long articles with lively headlines like "The Reverend Seducer," "More Religious Hypocrites," "Another Reverend Rascal," and "Incest by a Clergyman on Three Daughters." A typical tirade against popular preachers was this passage from an 1848 article in the *Police Gazette*:

> The reader now may see what some of these preachers are! Hypocrisy, cant, espionage, malice, lust, and all uncharitableness pour from their hearts as filth from a corrupted fountain, and while they raise their voices to rebuke the harmless derelictions of the common world, they stand chargeable with the most heinous crimes themselves and reeking with defilement to the very lips.[26]

Hawthorne's Arthur Dimmesdale, therefore, had numerous forerunners in the popular sensational press.

And his company was not confined to real-life religious hypocrites: he had even more friends in popular novels. In antebellum popular fiction, a good minister is hard to find. As scandals involving actual preachers and reformers began to fill sensational newspapers, popular American novelists virtually gave up trying to portray pure preachers, who they knew would bore a public that was getting used to seeing reverends portrayed as rakes. Novelists quickly gave new publicity to the reverend rake, who was typically portrayed as a harsh clergyman with an overactive sex drive. In one pamphlet novel, *The Confessions of a Magdalene* (1831), a popular revivalist drugs and ravishes a lovely parishioner, who goes on to become a whore. The widely reported Ephraim K. Avery case that intrigued Hawthorne was fictionalized in Catharine Read Williams's *Fall River* (1833), in which Avery appears as a lustful preacher notorious for his "frequent closeting in [his] study with females."[27] The popular anti-Catholic literature that arose during the 1830s gave the figure of the reverend rake unprecedented prominence. In particular, Maria Monk's best-selling *Awful Disclosures* (1836) portrayed the priests at a Canadian nunnery as inexhaustible lechers who had murdered so many illegitimate children they had to dispose of babies' corpses in a lime pit in the basement. Rosamund Culbertson's *Rosamund* (1836), a novel about Cuban priests who sanction the manufacture of sausages out of murdered Negro boys, contains such suggestive passages as "The adultery and fornication of the Clergy degenerated, in many instances, into incest and other abominations."[28]

In his own fiction of the 1830s, Hawthorne had a sharp enough sense of popular taste to steer clear of pure clergymen and emphasize instead ministerial wrongdoing. In "Young Goodman Brown" he revealed his kinship with popular writers by portraying preachers and their parishioners consorting at the devilish ritual with whores, criminals, and unbelievers of all stripes. He made sure to give the reverend rake a prominent place in the people cited in the devil's sermon, which begins by mentioning "hoary-bearded elders of the church [who] have whispered wanton words to the young maids of their households . . ." And he placed the church first in the list of sites of wrongdoing: "By the sympathy of your human hearts for sin ye shall scent out all the places—whether in church, bedchamber, street, field, or forest—where crime has been committed . . ."[29] In an equally famous story of the 1830s he made a veiled minister "a type and a symbol" of all human sin.[30]

By the 1840s the reverend rake had become so common a figure in popular fiction that Hawthorne could not overlook it in his search for a main male character for *The Scarlet Letter*. Almost every sensational novel of the decade contains at least one scene in which a seducer uses religion as an instrument of seduction. The popular pamphlet novelist George Thompson, who coined the phrase "reverend rake" to describe the modern preacher, generalized in *The Countess* (1849): "Within the pale of every church, hypocrisy, secret and damning hypocrisy, is a predominating quality." As a result, he concluded, "every church wants a purging, a complete cleaning out."[31] In particular, he wrote in *New-York Life* (1849), "the so-called reverend pastors of churches have been found to be on far too familiar terms with the young lambs of their flock."[32] Like most sensationalists, Thompson believed this cleaning out should begin by exposing the reverend rake in all his dimensions. He concocted a striking scene of reverend lechery in *Venus in Boston* (1849), in which a young girl is aroused to sexual frenzy when she peeps through a keyhole and sees her mother having sex with their clergyman, who later in the novel casts lustful glances at the girl herself. In all Thompson's novels clergymen and moral reformers are singled out as being especially libidinous. Thompson was outdone in this regard only by George Lippard, whose many portraits of reverend profligacy included the Rev. F. A. T. Pyne, in Lippard's best-selling novel *The Quaker City* (1845). Pyne is a combination of the Calvinist enthusiast, the nativist Catholic hater, and the unbridled debauchee, who nightly applies his ministerial earnings to the purchase of wine, women, and opium at Monk Hall.

Another feature of *The Scarlet Letter* that is directly connected to popular sensational writings is the dramatic scaffold scenes which provide the central organizing structure of the novel. It is not generally known that the antebellum public had an almost sadistic fascination with scaffold scenes, which were constantly featured in popular newspapers and crime pamphlets. As early as 1833 the *Morning Courier and New York Enquirer* noted: "If a graceless malefactor expires on the scaffold, whole columns of parado are displayed in the public journals, touching the circumstances of the execution. The very types are made to assume a blacker darkness, and the paper to seem blanched with agony."[33] The trial anthology Hawthorne is known to have read, *The Record of Crimes in the United States* (1833), had a long preface, "Curiosity of those who Go to Witness Public Executions," which argued that the organ of destructiveness in the human brain gave people an overpowering interest in scaffold scenes, particularly when criminals of high station or cultural prominence are involved. This anthology itself contains dramatic scaffold appearances by notorious American criminals like Jesse Strang, Charles Gibbs, Thomas J. Wansley, and Joseph Knapp—all of whom Hawthorne mentioned in his journal. Hawthorne was probably also aware of another trial anthology, Joseph Martin's *Select Tales* (1833), which included one scene of a woman in Puritan New England emerging from a prison and walking before a jeering crowd to a scaffold where she was subjected to long scrutiny. By 1853 a leading humor journal could characterize the American public as "the Scaffold Glutton" who constantly devoured juicy scaffold scenes served up in the popular press.[34]

Hawthorne may have had a timely reason for making *women* the special spectators of Hester Prynne's ignominy, for antebellum crime reports often underscored the irony of supposedly pure women taking delight in the criminal cases. The funeral of the murdered Philadelphia seducer Mahlon Heberton, for example, created a national excitement in 1843 because hordes of women showed "the most indecent and disgraceful inhumanity" by trampling over each other and fighting off police to catch a glimpse of the corpse of the celebrated rake.[35] Similarly, in what was labeled the "Savage Curiosity" on the part of people rushing over police barriers to see the death scene of a condemned New Hampshire man in 1846, "even females were offering to assist in pulling down the fences."[36]

It is understandable, therefore, that Hawthorne thought of *The Scarlet Letter* as a popular performance. Featuring a likable criminal, oxymoronic oppressors, a reverend rake, scaffold scenes, and sadistic women, the novel was a meeting ground for key stereotypes from the sensational press. *The Scarlet Letter* enjoyed a relatively good sale and made Hawthorne internationally famous largely because its central images sprang directly from popular culture.

Hawthorne draws off the sensational press not only in the use of popular stereotypes but also in the savagery and violence of many of his images. The "Custom-House" section was particularly popular among antebellum readers because it read very much like a blackly humorous sensational novel. We can understand the contemporary appeal of the "Custom-House" section, because it contains the kind of biting, sometimes gory images that sensation lovers feasted upon: the American eagle over the custom-house door is called an "unhappy fowl" who "is apt to fling off her nestlings, with a scratch of her claw, a dab of her beak, or a rankling wound from her barbed arrows";[37] the old Inspector is depicted as a beast who could "smack his lips over dinners, every guest at which, except himself, had long been food for the worms"; the garrulous officials trade adventure stories about exciting battles, and so forth. The discovery of the scarlet letter is itself very much a sensational experience; the narrator reports "a sensation . . . as of burning heat," as though the letter "were not of red cloth, but red-hot iron." "The Custom-House" ends with typically macabre newspaper imagery, as Hawthorne reports that after he had been "guillotined" by his opponents, "the press had taken up my affair, and kept me, for a week or two, careering through the public prints, in my decapitated state, like Irving's Headless Horseman; ghastly and grim, and longing to be buried . . ." *The Scarlet Letter* itself is full of images of burning, poison, nightmare visions, distorted perspective—all of which were naturally attractive to sensation lovers of the day.

Still, *The Scarlet Letter* is radically different from other antebellum sensational novels because of its psychological seriousness and its structural unity. Indeed, Hawthorne adopts popular sensational images with the conscious intention of rescuing them from the moral sterility and stylistic directionlessness that characterized their representation in the popular press. Both the "Custom-House" section and the novel itself operate simultaneously as modern sensational texts and as critiques of modern sensational texts. In both cases, sensational images are not exploited for purposes of crass diversion; rather, they are probed as fertile sources of moral ambiguity. The world of the Salem custom house—with its democratic flatness, its vulgarity, its shallow prolixity, its corrupt politics, its sensational newspapers—is a metonymy for the popular culture into which Hawthorne had plunged and from which he was now being resurrected. The world of the Puritan past—with its religious and political hierarchy, its earnestness, its genuine religiosity—possesses a depth Hawthorne sorely misses but also a rigidity that repels him. By fusing modern sensationalism with bygone Puritanism, Hawthorne creates a new world of ambiguous art, one which retains the paradoxical stereotypes and disturbing imagery of his day but invests them with a genuineness they lacked in the popular press.

Throughout *The Scarlet Letter* Hawthorne makes it clear that his treatment of sensational themes is designed to be distinguished from that of his popular contemporaries. Three times in the novel he pauses to indict the crassness of nineteenth-century sensationalism. At the beginning of Chapter 2 he underscores the soberness of public punishment in Puritan times by writing that "a penalty, which, in our days, would infer a degree of mocking infamy and ridicule, might then be invested with almost as stern a dignity as the punishment of death itself."[38] Later in the chapter he again indicts his callous contemporaries when he emphasizes that Hester's scaffold appearance "was not without a mixture of awe, such as must always invest the spectacle of guilt and shame in a fellow-creature, before society shall have grown corrupt enough to smile, instead of shuddering at it," as the Puritans "had none of the heartlessness of another social state, which would find only a theme for jest in an exhibition like the present." At the end of the novel, just before Dimmesdale's climactic procession to the scaffold, Hawthorne stresses that the Puritans valued "stability and dignity of character a great deal more" than nineteenth-century Americans, and they possessed "the quality of reverence, which, in their descendants, if it survive at all, exists in smaller proportion, and with a vastly diminished force . . ."

The protest against nineteenth-century America, more subtle yet even more significant than the simultaneous protest against the Puritans' rigidity, is enforced in almost every scene in the novel by Hawthorne's serious treatment of topics that in popular sensational literature had become matters of mechanical prurience and shallow irreverence. The difference between Hawthorne's use of sensational themes and that of popular novelists of his day is underscored by a comparison between *The Scarlet Letter* and George Lippard's sensational best-seller *The Quaker City* (1845). Superficially, there are many parallels between these novels—so many, indeed, that one is tempted to believe that Hawthorne, who after his removal from the custom house was intent on writing a novel that would be both popular and mischievous, was trying to tap the popular market created by *The Quaker City* and its many American imitations. Hawthorne's and Lippard's novels both involve a clergyman who has an affair with a young woman. In both works there is a dramatic recognition scene in which the cuckolded husband sees a shocking display of his wife's infidelity. The husbands in both novels postpone revenge in order to increase the agony of the unfaithful wife and her paramour. In both novels the lovers plan an escape across the ocean but the escape is foiled. Both Hawthorne and Lippard feature a villainous learned character who is connected with alchemy, homeopathy, and the pseudosciences, and both include a devil figure (Lippard's Devil-Bug and Hawthorne's Mistress Hibbins) who takes demonic glee in the crimes and flaws of the main characters. Irony and ambiguity reign in both novels, as the twisted relationships and demonic passions both authors dwell upon give rise to continual hypocrisy on the part of all the main characters.

Given these similarities, however, we can immediately discern ways in which Hawthorne has revised the Lippardian plot. For one thing, he fuses certain characters that in Lippard's novel remain separate, creating extraordinary compaction and complexity of character. The prying alchemist and the vindictive husband, which are separate characters in *The Quaker City*, are fused in Roger Chillingworth, just as the licentious clergyman and the marriage-breaking paramour (also separate figures in Lippard) are combined in Arthur Dimmesdale. As a result, *The Scarlet Letter* is a far more unified, more dense novel than *The Quaker City*, in which many interwoven plots and disparate characters disorient the reader.

But the most important difference between the two novels pertains to tone and style, particularly to contrasting uses of images derived from popular sensational literature. Lippard's novel is the quintessential example of popular sensationalism, because it permits all the most subversive aspects of American culture—excessive gore, immoral reform, urban violence, street slang, black humor, working-class politics, prurient eroticism—to enjoy unabashed expression. The novel shows what happens when sensationalism is not carefully checked: it becomes wildly gratuitous and fundamentally amoral. Throughout *The Quaker City* justified revenge quickly turns into sadistic fantasy, as all characters have gleeful visions of torturing their victims in the most grisly ways imaginable. The two lovers involved in Lippard's adultery plot epitomize the amorality of the novel as a whole: Algernon Fitz-Cowles is the cheerful confidence man totally devoid of feeling or virtue; Dora Livingstone is the brilliant but depraved social climber who uses sex to pursue her dream of a royal title. The cuckolded husband, Albert Livingstone, takes horrid pleasure in slowly torturing his wife after he has lured her to their country seat, where she is brought with her own coffin following in a carriage. The reverend rake, F. A. T. Pyne, is another monster without feelings or beliefs; the money he collects from his duped congregations he applies to the purchase of drugs and women at Monk Hall. Public knowledge of the main characters' crimes is highly distorted, for bribed penny papers like *The Daily Black Mail* heartlessly trump up false stories about the innocent while allowing the secretly guilty to remain corrupt behind their respectable disguises. It is, in short, a world where materialism and chicanery hold full sway. The supervising criminal in Lippard's novel, Devil-Bug, is a one-eyed beast who takes delight in seeing the blood of his victims fall drop by drop. Lippard, while ostensibly exposing the crimes of depraved aristocrats, becomes hypnotically fascinated by the crimes of every character and proves as ready to gloat over the splattered brains of a murdered old woman or decaying corpses in a dissecting room as he is to pause over the "snowy globes" of a voluptuous woman in heat.

In *The Scarlet Letter* we meet a similar cast of characters, often with similar motivations, and we have key moments of irony and black humor that place the novel in the American subversive tradition. But because Hawthorne allows modern sensational images to resonate within a Puritan culture that is described with sympathy and seriousness, these images never become gratuitous or perverse. Nineteenth-century paradoxes and ironies suddenly gain mythic resonance when coupled with Puritan social and religious views. Were Arthur Dimmesdale simply a reverend rake, he would be much like F. A. T. Pyne and the other coarse, lip-smacking reverend rakes in popular sensational writings of the day. On the other hand, were he solely a virtuous Puritan preacher, he would be a dreary anachronism unbelievable and unsympathetic to Hawthorne's contemporaries, who had little interest in virtuous clergymen characters. Because he is *both* a good Puritan and a reverend rake, he is at once sincerely tormented and explosively ironic. Since he is a believing clergyman, he is honestly tortured and humane in a way that the purely theatrical, wholly duplicitous F. A. T. Pyne cannot be. He declares to Hester Prynne: "Were I an atheist,—a man devoid of conscience,—a wretch with coarse and brutal instincts,—I might have found peace, long ere now."[39] He possesses both the profound convictions of a soul-searching Calvinist and the lawless passions of the reverend rake. Likewise, the novel's revenge figure, Roger Chillingworth, has a retributive function absent from Lippard's novel. Chillingworth's revenge is every bit as sadistic, perhaps, as that of Lippard's cuckold, but it is directed against a serious clergyman whose impulse to reveal his sin finally leads to a purgative public confession, whereas in Lippard's novel the paramour, Fitz-Cowles, remains unrepentant and unpunished, while the cuckold, Livingstone, takes pathological glee in torturing his wife. Hester, too, is a powerfully mixed character who is at once the modern likable criminal and the self-lacerating Puritan. Were she only the likable criminal, she would be on the same level as many gleefully wicked females in popular novels, such as Dora Livingstone. Because she brings Puritan soberness to her sin, she is tormented in a way that no popular likable criminal is. Little Pearl, the wild child of the likable criminal and the reverend rake, figuratively represents the aftermath of Puritan culture— the directionlessness, perversity, and irrationalism Hawthorne always associated with nineteenth-century America. She remains the wild embodiment of the antebellum Subversive imagination as long as her parents remain within the amoral value system of nineteenth-century sensationalism: that is, as long as Dimmesdale remains the reverend rake cloaking his sin and as long as Hester is the likable criminal brandishing her sin proudly but never truly confronting it. Pearl becomes a moral, respectable person only when her parents honestly expose their sin—when Hawthorne clearly leaves the realm of nineteenth-century sensationalism and recaptures the retributive world of Puritan Calvinism. Hawthorne allows all the ironies of

nineteenth-century America to gather in upon themselves, within the soul
of the tortured Dimmesdale and within the twisted relationships between
all of these mixed characters, and then watches them deconstruct as they
are reined in by the moral prerogatives of Puritan culture.

As important as the resonance gained from Puritanism is the control
gained through structure and symbol. Whereas Lippard bursts linear
narrative patterns with his fervid irrationalism, Hawthorne takes numerous popular sensational images and arranges them with almost mathematical care. The three gallows scenes, the seven-year time gap between
the opening and middle sections, the final festival scene, the studied alteration between public and private scenes, the tonal restraint and balanced phrasing: all these stylistic elements have almost moral meaning
for a writer who hated the disorganization of modern sensational texts.
The relationships between the characters are governed by a range of
feelings from neurotic symbiosis to sadistic vampirism. They have the
common denominator of profound interconnectedness. Within the
structure of the novel, none of the characters can exist without the others. Allegory and history also serve as important controlling devices. It
does not matter that there is no single allegorical meaning, within individual scenes and within the novel as a whole. We should not be
alarmed, for instance, that the letter A successively takes on different,
sometimes contradictory significations. The very capacity of the letter
and other allegorical elements to radiate meaning, the very *suggestiveness*
of these elements is an assertion of value when contrasted with the flat
sensationalism Hawthorne detested. The careful apportionment of Subversive imagery in a unified artistic structure is the author's highest
achievement.

Sensationalism in the Later Fiction

In Hawthorne's next novel, *The House of the Seven Gables,* we see resonance and structural unity being seriously threatened by turbulent forces
in American culture. In a key scene toward the end of the novel, Clifford
and Hepzibah Pyncheon, fleeing on a train, find themselves confronted
with a dizzying array of images from modern popular culture. The train
itself, the era's prime symbol of brute force and modern technology, seems
to make the outside world seem "unfixed from its age-long rest."[40] On the
train the fugitives see passengers reading "pamphlet novels" and "penny-
papers." Giddy with the excitement of the moment, Clifford engages in
conversation with a crusty old man, to whom he praises various aspects of
the modern scene: improved transportation, spiritualism, electricity, mesmerism—all of which, Clifford insists, are dissolving our ties to an oppres-

sive past and preparing the way for a more fluid, mobile existence. Several times his skeptical auditor grumbles "Humbug!" and so Clifford turns to another popular topic: the liberal treatment of criminals. Parroting the common view of the justified criminal, Clifford defends the "poor rogues, the bank-robbers . . . who, after all, are about as honest as nine people in ten, except that they disregard certain formalities, and prefer to transact business at midnight, rather than 'Change-hours." Murderers, he adds, "are often excusable in the motives of their deed, and ought to be ranked among public benefactors, if we consider only its result." When his auditor protests even more strongly, Clifford loses his excitement, falls silent, and is passively led by Hepzibah back toward home.

In this scene Hawthorne is repeating the process, seen in *The Scarlet Letter,* of dialectical engagement with and detachment from antebellum popular culture. Several of the images he isolates—pamphlet novels, penny papers, spiritualism, electricity, mesmerism, the justified criminal— are among those that constituted the most problematic issues of the modern scene. Such issues had begun to impinge upon Hawthorne's artistic consciousness and had notably disrupted it. Throughout the novel, he shows his profound awareness of antebellum sensational writing. When Phoebe reads aloud from "works of fiction, in pamphlet-form," Clifford, upset by the pamphlet novelists' callous treatment of tragic themes, demands that she stop. Hawthorne interjects: "And wisely too! Is not the world sad enough, in genuine earnest, without making a pastime of mock sorrows?"[41] In another scene, Holgrave, among whose many talents is writing magazine stories, reads Phoebe his sensational story of the haughty Alice Pyncheon, who was mesmerized and driven into groveling submission by the poor Matthew Maule. Phoebe is struck that the story has "a vast deal of trouble and calamity,—so, no doubt, the story will prove exceedingly attractive."

Hawthorne knew well that penny papers, pamphlet novels, and magazine stories filled with "trouble and calamity" had an immense readership in his day, and to some degree he tried to satisfy the demands of this readership. By organizing his plot around a crime resulting from a disputed will, he is returning to the paradigmatic antebellum crime case that had fascinated him in 1830: the murder of Captain Joseph White for his will. By making the alleged murderer, Clifford Pyncheon, a central character, he is probing the popular stereotype of the criminal who is both likable and justified. By having this criminal opposed by a churchgoing, corrupt wealthy man, Jaffrey Pyncheon, he is setting up the common opposition of the likable criminal versus the oxymoronic oppressor. By including in his novel images of animal magnetism, mesmerism, reform movements, and sensational literature, he is multiplying the popular imagery. He even borrows a device from popular pamphlet fiction: in the seven-gabled house hangs a magical mirror in which one can see departed Pyncheons "not as they had shown themselves to the world . . . but as doing over again some deed of sin, or in the crisis of life's bitterest sorrow"—an unmasking device that is similar to the "social kaleidoscope" through which the devilish hero of George Thompson's *New-York Life* (1849) views secret sin among the outwardly respectable.[42]

But Hawthorne admits this popular imagery with the conscious intention of revising it. He lends historical depth to modern themes by tracing the Maule/Pyncheon theme back to Puritan times. The use of the Gothic mansion inhabited by a comically old-fashioned spinster and her conventional niece adds a sense of fixity and moral centeredness lacking in popular sensational novels. These forces for history and tradition are presented as a direct counterweight to the images from modern popular culture. Holgrave is a full embodiment of the anarchic elements of the modern scene: he is a reform lecturer whose "wild and disorganizing" speeches are reported in the penny papers;[43] he is a writer of Dark Adventure fiction for the popular magazines; he is associated with every modern fad, from the daguerreotype to pseudoscience. But he finally marries Phoebe and turns conservative. Jaffrey Pyncheon is the archetypal oxymoronic oppressor, but Hawthorne does not dwell on Jaffrey's vicious (particularly licentious) activity, as would a popular sensationalist. A similar reticence governs his treatment of Clifford. We have seen that in the topsy-turvy moral world of sensational fiction, the likable criminal often became a kind of perverse hero whose dastardly exploits formed the center of the novel. In Hawthorne's handling, the likable criminal becomes totally passive, vacuous, dependent on others—and, in the end, he turns out to be no criminal at all (it is found that the man Clifford supposedly murdered died of natural causes). Indeed, Clifford is not so much a likable criminal as he is a parodic deconstruction of one, as his moral impotence embodies the metaphysical aporia implicit in this problematic popular stereotype. His exhausted return to the house of the seven gables after his brief excursion into popular culture—an excursion that had, significantly enough, ended with his failed defense of justified criminals—enacts Hawthorne's recoil away from the popular sensational issues that both intrigued him and baffled him.

In *The Blithedale Romance* no such recoil is possible, since Hawthorne chooses to concentrate on popular movements on the antebellum scene, with few counterbalancing devices such as history or gabled mansions. As a result, the dizzying sense of modern fluidity that Clifford feels briefly on the train becomes enacted in the dominant imagery of *The Blithedale Romance*. The entire novel is an exercise in distorted perception, as we view all the events through the consciousness of Miles Coverdale, a dilettante reformer and minor poet who comes to feel that "everything in nature and human existence was fluid, or fast becoming so; that the crust of the Earth, in many places, was broken, and its whole surface portentously upheaving; that it was a day of crisis, and that we ourselves were in the critical vortex."[44] The quicksand-like fluidity and incipient chaos that Hawthorne had often associated with modern American life becomes projected stylistically in the images of veils and illusions that govern the novel. Since Hawthorne is now concentrating on ambiguities within his contemporary culture, it is understandable that he would return again to the problem of criminals. In *The Scarlet Letter* he had portrayed a proud likable criminal, Hester Prynne, whose fearlessness is preferable to the cowardly secretiveness of her lover; in *The House of the Seven Gables* he had studied the crippling moral paradoxes embodied in the likable criminal figure; in *The Blithedale Romance* he places at the center of the novel a reformer who takes a kindly view of criminals but, ironically, becomes the greatest criminal of all. Like Clifford, Hollingsworth represents a deconstruction of justified criminality, but the irony has now deepened, since Hollingsworth actually becomes a criminal as a result of his monomaniacal devotion to the idea of criminal reform. When asked at the end by Coverdale how many criminals he has reformed, Hollingsworth can only stare sadly downward and murmur, "Not one! . . . Ever since we parted, I have been busy with a single murderer!" In his depiction of the erring criminal reformer Hawthorne showed how his age's liberal view of criminals could become the means of its own subversion.

He had left unresolved, however, important moral questions surrounding the popular stereotype of the likable criminal. How, exactly, were the paradoxes intrinsic in this popular figure to be interpreted? Didn't these paradoxes pose a profound problem in ethics and religion? If one accepted justified criminality, wasn't one edging toward moral relativism?

Obsessed by such questions, Hawthorne confronted them directly in his last major romance, *The Marble Faun*. The novel revolves around a grisly crime—the murder committed by the "faun," Donatello—and traces the effect of this crime on four people: Donatello himself, who moves from innocent happiness to dark wisdom and brooding remorse; the artist Miriam Schaefer, the majestic woman with a dark past who becomes a suffering but still proud penitent; the copyist Hilda, the pure moral exemplar for whom knowledge of the crime is a continual agony relieved only by confession to a Roman Catholic priest; and the sculptor Kenyon, who becomes entangled in the deepening gloom but remains a helpful observer of the other characters. Hawthorne achieves extreme tension by depicting two sympathetic criminals, Donatello and Miriam, whose crime not only seems justified (the murder victim, Miriam's model, is a despicable madman who gets what he deserves) but also is an almost accidental result of exterior circumstances (in an uncharacteristic moment of rage, Donatello, with an approving glance from Miriam, hurls the model over the cliff). Hawthorne makes us feel the tensions surrounding justified crime and likable criminals with an intensity unparalleled in antebellum fiction. In many popular sensational novels, ambiguity surrounds the criminal character. The popular authors often showed that crime resulted from exterior circumstances, and that the criminal often has good qualities, such as shrewdness and charisma, which in different conditions could have produced an admirable human being. Hawthorne deepens and probes the moral enigmas surrounding crime until they create human tragedy.

Specifically, he creates a painful dialogue between two contrasting views of the justified criminal. One view is aired by the pure Hilda, who rejects the sympathetic co-criminal, Miriam, since the moral mixture she represents threatens all standards and raises the specter of relativism. The other view is defended by Kenyon, who argues that it is ennobling and realistic to accept the mixture of good and evil in all humans, a mixture most dramatically visible in justified or likable criminals like Miriam and Donatello. Hilda embodies the Conventional outlook that it is best to adhere to preestablished moral rules rather than accept ambiguity or evil into the consciousness. Kenyon argues that sin and crime should be confronted and pondered. He tells Hilda that the murder of Miriam's model shows "what a mixture of good there may be in things evil; and how the greatest criminal, if you look at his conduct from his own point of view, or from any side-point, may not seem so unquestionably guilty, after all." Hilda's retort is unequivocal: "If there be any such dreadful mixture of good and evil as you affirm,—and which appears to me almost more shocking than pure evil,—then the good is turned to poison, not evil to wholesomeness."[45]

In the end, Hawthorne fails to resolve this thorny issue. In the last chapter, Kenyon repeats again his belief that crime has "educated Donatello, and elevated him," but Hilda again replies that his creed makes a mockery of "all religious sentiment" and "moral law." Perhaps reflecting Hawthorne's exhaustion with the issue of the likable criminal, Kenyon cries that "the mind wanders wild and wide" and begs Hilda to "guide me home."[46] This evasive conclusion is a forgivable flaw in a novel whose imposing magnitude and depth is itself a form of rhetorical victory, an assertion of creative power in the face of unresolvable paradoxes. We have seen that he had set much of his fiction in Puritan times because he wished to lend depth to contemporary ironies that were often treated with offhand indifference in shapeless modern texts. When he had tried to deal with ambiguity in the context of modern America, as in *The Blithedale Romance* and sections of *The House of the Seven Gables,* the result was a frightening perception of fluidity and chaos in modern life. In *The Marble Faun* he shifts the scene to Rome because he wishes to recover imaginatively the tradition, the permanence he found lacking in America, which he says has "no shadow, no antiquity, no mystery, no picturesque or gloomy wrong." The Roman setting provided a resonance that modern America lacked, just as Roman Catholicism provides an outlet for repressed sin. He believed that American Protestantism, allowing no confessional, had the effect of turning sin's "poison back among the inner vitalities of the character at the imminent risk of corrupting them all."[47] This self-poisoning process had consumed several of his American characters, from Arthur Dimmesdale through Clifford Pyncheon to Hollingsworth. *The Marble Faun* allows him the opportunity to enjoy vicariously the cleansing effect of Roman Catholicism. All the main characters (except the anti-Catholic Kenyon) enjoy the release or the sense of larger significance offered by Catholicism: Hilda, who is a kind of "Catholic Puritan" from the start, feels liberated when she confesses her dark secret to the priest, and Donatello and Miriam become long-suffering penitents surrounded by Catholic imagery. While the Roman setting and the Catholic imagery lend depth to modern ironies, reflective symbols give a constant suggestiveness. Most notably, the paintings and sculpture that fill the novel are always invested with thematic significance, so that virtually every scene has its own built-in imagistic reflector giving a constant sense of larger meaning.

Still, there are clear signs of a fragmentation of vision that is threatening Hawthorne's art. The structural unity and interconnectedness that had characterized *The Scarlet Letter* has collapsed. Despite the bond of sympathy between the main characters, they actually live isolated most of the time: Hilda in her high dovecote; Donatello in his lonely villa; Kenyon in his studio; Miriam in her nomadic wanderings. Because Hawthorne cannot satisfactorily resolve the moral issues he raises, he can no longer imagine characters who enjoy meaningful contact with other individuals or with the world at large. Arthur Dimmesdale had announced his sin to the whole community; Hilda blurts hers privately to a priest. Hester Prynne became a social worker helping others; Miriam becomes a solitary penitent who at the end seems to stand "on the other side of a fathomless abyss."[48] The defeated criminal Hollingsworth at least ended up with Priscilla; Donatello is buried in an Italian dungeon. Hawthorne tries to fill in the gaps between people with extensive references to Roman ruins, paintings, sculpture, religious icons—but all these reflective devices suggest a certain stiffening and reification, as though more genuine, human forms of connectedness can no longer be relied upon. It is significant that the novel ends by pondering the problem of the likable criminal. The gulf between Hilda's moral purism and Kenyon's chastened realism is not bridged by the rhetorical ploy of their marriage. By the end of *The Marble Faun* it appears that Hawthorne's mind, like Kenyon's, is wandering "wild and wide" in the effort to solve one of the central questions of his literary culture.

The lack of central fusing agents in *The Marble Faun* set the stage for the further fragmentation in the four novels he left uncompleted at the end of his life. In these narratives, Hawthorne seems to be floating among the surface shards of various popular genres, having left behind the attempted depth, reflective symbolism, and character fusion of his major novels. He often intrudes with frustrated confessions of artistic failure, as he can no longer locate a central narrative voice or consistent tone. *The American Claimant Manuscripts* are particularly revealing in this regard. In these three loosely connected narratives, Hawthorne retreats to popular sensational- ism of the crassest variety, as he spins a gory plot involving a Bloody Footstep left as a trail by a murderer in England and America, a plot filled with references to every sort of bloody crime imaginable. His earlier fears of moral neutrality and heartless sensationalism have been thrown to the winds. He still shows his heavy dependence on popular crime narratives for racy material: at one point he actually pauses in the narrative to write: "I wish I could get hold of the Newgate Calendar . . . or any other book of murders—The Causes Celebres, for instance."[49] As the narrative pro- ceeds, a restless despair creeps into his efforts to enliven the flagging plot. He becomes more and more grisly in his speculations as to how one of his characters is to accomplish a certain murder: "A peculiar kind of poison? An acquaintance with wizard-lore? Nothing of this. He is an eater of human flesh—a vampire—a ghoul. He finds it necessary to eat a young child, every year, in order to keep himself alive." Recognizing his plot has "Not a spark of passion yet," he writes long lists of criminals that he hopes will add life to his central character: in rapid succession, he imagines that his protago- nist is a gambler, a fiend, "a poison-breather, a Thug, a pirate, a pick- pocket," and later adds: "A cannibal? A ghoul? A vampire? A man who lives by sucking the blood of the young and beautiful? . . . What habit can he have? Perhaps that of having a young child, fricaseed, served up to him for breakfast every morning?" These passages read like a penny paper, the *National Police Gazette,* or Dark Adventure novels—they are unembellished lists of crimes and criminals written in a flat, nonmetaphorical style.

Having reached a philosophical stalemate with serious contemplation of the justified criminal in *The Marble Faun,* Hawthorne had decided to retreat to the realm of action-packed adventure and mere gory crime. Lacking unifying symbols and an authoritative voice, he tried to do what he had purposely avoided throughout his career: write straightforward sensa- tional fiction with little depth or resonance. In his major texts he had regulated and enriched the American Subversive imagination. In the end he surrendered to the directionless sensationalism he had feared all along.

10

MELVILLE'S RUTHLESS DEMOCRACY

L I K E Poe and Hawthorne, Melville frequently adapted images from popular sensational literature. He was even more willing than they to import into his fiction a large variety of popular stereotypes and to absorb the wild energy of the Subversive imagination. On the simplest level, his fiction registers a unique range of freaks or oddities, many of which had ample precedent in American popular culture. In a more subtle sense, it expands upon the skeptical philosophy that runs through much sensational literature. More fully than any other antebellum novelist, Melville explored the rich ironies and paradoxes inherent in America's sensational culture. His discovery of these ironies resulted directly from his professional engagement with popular culture. Early in his career he feverishly churned out escapist adventure novels that led to his adoption of certain popular stereotypes. These stereotypes in turn deepened his vision and impelled him to search for distinctly American themes and characters. Among such representative characters, he realized, were the oxymoronic oppressor and its opposite, the justified pariah or likable criminal. Like Hawthorne, he realized fully the disturbing ambiguities intrinsic in these characters. He was driven by an intensely democratic urge to absorb and fuse contradictory elements in American culture. His recognition of his culture's troubling paradoxes and his simultaneous desire to forge literary fusions gave rise to explosive works like *Moby-Dick* and *The Confidence-Man,* which are at once fully ironic but fully democratic realizations of popular themes and strategies.

It was shown earlier that the ambiguities of Melville's fiction grew in part from his wide-ranging use of popular reform (particularly dark reform) images. These ambiguities had an equally potent source in popular sensational writings. Melville knew such writings well: he was a devoted reader of James Gordon Bennett's *New York Herald*, the leading penny newspaper of the day; among the "Extracts" prefacing *Moby-Dick* are passages from adventurous pamphlet novels, including Harry Halyard's *Wharton the Whale-Killer* and Henry T. Cheever's *The Whale and Its Captors*; his novel *Israel Potter* borrows heavily from a pamphlet novel he found in a street bookstall; criminals or crime literature are mentioned at key moments in his fiction, such as the opening scene of *The Confidence-Man,* which describes riverboat passengers crowding around a crime poster and around a peddler of crime narratives.

In the excitement today over Melville's premodern themes, it is sometimes forgotten that he was a professional adventure novelist who tried hard to please American sensation lovers. He had reason to believe, as he told Hawthorne, that he would go down to posterity as the man who lived among the cannibals. Many of his fictional images are reflective of the tastes of antebellum sensation lovers. Cannibalism, South Sea adventure, destructive whales, the Ishmael figure, despotic captains, mutiny, devilish rituals—these are only a few of the sensational images that made Melville widely perceived in his own day as a diverting sensational novelist. *Moby-Dick* was usually placed in the popular adventure camp by both positive and negative nineteenth-century reviewers, from the *New York Evangelist,* which praised the "graphic and terrible hair-breadth 'scapes" in the novel, to the *Athenaeum,* which dismissed the book as "so much trash belonging to the worst school of bedlam literature."[1] In 1855 *Israel Potter* was considered sufficiently attractive to sensation lovers to be issued in London as a yellow-covered pamphlet novel and to prompt one reviewer to call it "not a bad shilling's worth for any railway reader."[2] Even *The Confidence-Man,* with its complexities and indirections, treated crime material familiar to such reviewers as the *Newark Daily Advertiser,* which said "a certain class of persons, those who read police reports, will relish this record of treachery and deceit."[3]

It was Melville's democratic openness to wild forces within his contemporary popular culture that distinguished him from his more snobbish literary colleagues. Like many American writers of the day, he wished to produce literature that was both national and universal: but for him nationality could be achieved only by immersion in the people's literature, even when it was crude and violent. This openness to sensational popular culture was not shared by his fellows in the Young America literary movement, which had been founded in the late 1830s by the New York novelist Cornelius Mathews and the editor Evert A. Duyckinck. Melville's literary friends became progressively more elitist in their literary aims, while Melville was virtually alone in his openness to irrational forces within American popular culture. The popular sensational literature that during the 1840s became infused with a spirit of working-class protest was distasteful to Duyckinck, who declared that the national literature should be "immune from democratic enthusiasms, and from the wildness of American life."[4] Similarly, Mathews asked for "nationality in its purest, highest, broadest sense," far above the rant of popular speakers and barroom brawlers, a nationality that was "majestic and assured as the action of [America's] institutions is calm and secure."[5] To avoid association with "ultraist" working-class protest, the Young America literary group broke its ties with the more fiery, radical Young America political movement. In this sense, Duyckinck and Mathews were part of the conservative backlash against popular turbulences on the part of many leading American writers. Orestes Brownson called for Americans to study German and French masterpieces, in which he said there is "nothing rash, nothing violent, destructive."[6] Longfellow demanded a literature "without spasms and convulsions," one that gains universality by being "the result of culture and refinement."[7] Lowell argued that literature is universal only when it escapes provincial boundaries.

While Melville shared with these writers a devotion to universality, he infused into classical images a distinctly American zest because of his special awareness of the indigenous themes and idioms that the other writers tended to snub. He had a personal connection with the political Young America movement, whose linguistic excesses dismayed the New York littérateurs: in the early 1840s his brother Gansevoort had been a fiery spokesman for the movement. He refused to follow his brother into political activism, perhaps because he recognized the destructive squabbles (such as the vitriolic attacks on Gansevoort by the rowdy politician Mike Walsh) that working-class radicalism could provoke. On the other hand, he resisted the littérateurs' flight into the airy realm of culture and refinement. An exuberant ex-sailor writing adventure novels for a sensation-loving public, he embraced the "democratic enthusiasms" and "wildness" that the more respectable Duyckinck decried. He read everything: not just the classics but also pamphlet novels and penny papers of the crassest variety. As for his fellow writers' idolatry of Shakespeare and other past greats, he wrote sarcastically: "You must believe in Shakespeare's unapproachability, or quit the country. But what sort of a belief is this for an American, a man who is bound to carry republican progressiveness into Literature, as well as into Life?"[8]

Melville created a new literary voice that possessed the linguistic fire of the Young America *political* movement but not its social commitments, the universality of the Young America *literary* group but not its sycophancy or stylistic conservatism. Driven by what he termed "republican progressiveness," he wished to forge a literature that captured the spirit but not the political content of working-class protest. He absorbed the searing ironies of the radical democrats but left behind their political programs. Popular adventure fiction was a particularly appropriate avenue for this apolitical literary explorer, because it provided a fund of intensely democratic stereotypes and unconventional themes.

Melville's Immersion in the Sensational

Several key questions about Melville's fiction have not yet been adequately answered. How did such provocative, universal symbols as the white whale, the *Pequod,* and the riverboat *Fidèle* emerge? How could an American in 1851 fabricate a mythic monster that seems to encompass everything good and everything wicked, pursued by a maddened captain who is both godlike and ungodly? That is, how did American oxymorons suddenly rise beyond narrow, localized meanings and produce literary symbols of gargantuan stature?

We can begin to answer such questions by considering Melville's declaration in a June 1851 letter to Hawthorne, written as he was in the final stages of *Moby-Dick.* Melville said that "when you see or hear of my ruthless democracy on all sides, you may possibly feel a touch of a shrink, or something of that sort. It is but nature to be shy of a mortal who boldly declares that a thief in jail is as honorable a personage as Gen. George Washington."[9]

Written at perhaps the most fertile moment in Melville's literary career, this statement suggests the profound debt he owed to contemporary sensational writings and particularly to the radical democrats of the 1840s. We have seen that during this decade the likable criminal or justified pariah had gained immense importance in the popular consciousness: novelists like Lippard, Buntline, and Ingraham had often featured such figures in best-selling novels designed both to entertain the masses and to criticize the social elite; George Wilkes's *Police Gazette* and the popular crime pamphlets associated with it brought a new objectivity to reportage of criminals, who were regularly portrayed as products of their environment or congenital disorders; and there arose an influential body of prison reformers who took a sympathetic view of criminals and their plight. Melville profited greatly from this general broadening of the popular consciousness. It was precisely because of this broadening that he could attain what he called a "ruthless democracy on all sides." This ruthless democracy permitted him to place a thief on the same level as George Washington; more important, it allowed him to create literary symbols that reflected the rich paradoxes of his contemporary popular culture.

The stereotypes of the likable criminal or the justified pariah are the single most commonly probed characters in Melville's fiction. Melville evidently believed that by studying these paradoxical figures he was getting to the core of America itself, a nation he described in *Israel Potter* as "civilized in the externals but a savage at heart."[10] At first, his approach was not distant from that of many popular writers: in *Typee* and *Omoo* he exploits pariahs mainly as entertainingly adventurous figures and, occasionally, as vehicles for attacking the social elite. In *Mardi,* where he makes the justified murderer Taji the central character, he begins to study the metaphysical ambiguities and the potential linguistic indeterminacy implied by the paradoxical stereotype. In *Redburn* he gives his first full portrait of the mixed criminal in the person of Henry Jackson, who combines elements of several different adventure characters and who is at once totally evil and yet pitiable, even admirable. *White-Jacket* constitutes a broadening of the likable criminal figure, as Melville describes a warship full of criminals and other outcasts who are villainous but still are sympathetically portrayed as victims of cruel captains and unfair naval laws.

In surveying these early novels, one clearly sees the emergence of Melville's "ruthless democracy on all sides," evidenced by his creative adoption and transformation of popular sensational stereotypes.

When Melville wrote that his first novel, *Typee,* was "calculated for popular reading, or for none at all," he betrayed his awareness of the native market for sensational adventure fiction.[11] He knew his experiences would have appeal for American readers who since the early nineteenth century had shown a growing interest in South Sea adventure and cannibalism. While trying to appeal to sensation lovers in his many accounts of exotic places and things, he also adopted certain paradoxical characters and ironic themes from the popular fiction of the 1840s. We have seen that by the 1840s Subversive fiction had become infused with working-class fantasies and socialist militancy. It stressed the crime, crushing poverty, and mob violence caused by callous aristocrats in a time of widespread unemployment. Absorbing this spirit of working-class protest, Melville sometimes pauses in *Typee* to indict the class divisions of white civilization. In addition to voicing such typical working-class attitudes, Melville experiments with the kind of mixed, paradoxical characters that had emerged in sensational fiction. The stereotype of the justified pariah rebelling against harsh authority is reenacted in the main characters, Tommo and Toby, who escape a tyrannical captain and who later become a vehicle of protest against oxymoronic oppressors, the white missionaries who are Christian but whose influence is corrupting. The most intriguing paradoxical characters are the Typees themselves, who are cannibals but are nevertheless described as more "humane, gentlemanly, and amiable" than the whites who intend to civilize them.[12] In his portrait of the Typees, Melville adds a wholly new dimension to popular stereotypes. Several popular novelists had pointed up the irony of wealthy, religious people giving money to convert South Sea Islanders while ignoring the poor at home. Melville makes the further point that South Sea Islanders themselves are worthier souls than white aristocrats. Melville is pushing beyond the bald sensationalism and negative social criticism of Subversive fiction to a positive reconstruction of value on the basis of a democratic awareness of an alien culture.

Melville's next novel, *Omoo,* is his closest approximation of the popular Dark Adventure mode. Like many yellow novels of the 1840s, it is a relatively unstructured, free-flowing record of wild events or outlaw figures, with occasional dark philosophical commentary. The first words of the Preface make it clear that he is aiming to please lovers of the untamed, the savage: "Nowhere, perhaps, are the proverbial characteristics of sailors shown under wilder aspects, than in the South Seas." The sperm whale fishery is called "a business, which is not only peculiarly fitted to attract the most reckless seamen of all nations, but in various ways, is calculated to foster in them a spirit of utmost license."[13] We learn that the crews of whaling vessels like the *Julia* are "for the most part villains of all nations and dyes." The early chapters of the novel are filled with scenes of drunken brawls and wild disorder aboard the *Julia,* and in one of its island stoppages the ship is met by one Lem Hardy, "a renegado from Christendom and humanity," a sailor "without ties, reckless, and impatient of the restraints of civilization," who had long ago deserted a trading brig and is now the tribal leader of a native island. Aboard the *Julia* is the eccentric doctor Long Ghost, who plays weird pranks on his mates, as well as many rambunctious sailors and mates, most of whom have a strong propensity for the bottle. The black cook Baltimore owns a book of the Dark Adventure variety, *A History of the Most Atrocious and Bloody Piracies,* which takes on special significance since blank pages at the end of the volume are filled in with the "Round Robin" list of sailors' grievances. A certain blending of the oxymoronic oppressor and the lowly criminal is achieved throughout the novel, as Melville shows several authority figures (a ship's captain, a priest, a consul) getting as uproariously drunk as the common sailors.

In *Mardi* we see Melville beginning to use popular wildness and sensationalism as a springboard to metaphysical adventurousness. The first part of the novel is not distant in spirit from that of *Omoo,* except that now we see a notable broadening in Melville's applications of sensational imagery.

For the first time he applies such imagery to sea creatures. We have seen that the antebellum public had a peculiar fascination with both mythic sea monsters and outlaws or criminals. In several early chapters that were warmly praised by many reviewers, Melville appealed to both tastes at once by using outlaw metaphors to describe sea creatures. He compares two tiger sharks to "a couple of highwaymen, biding their time till you come to the cross-roads"; he calls Algerine fish "Atrocious Turks!" deadly with "corsair propensities"; and in describing Indian swordfish, he says that "of all the bullies, and braggarts, and bravoes, and free-booters, and Hectors, and fish-at-arms, and knight-errants, and moss-troopers, and assassins, and foot-pads, and gallant soldiers, and immortal heroes that swim the seas, the Indian Sword fish is by far the most remarkable."[14] We should recall that the year Melville wrote the bulk of *Mardi*, 1848, was the year that the popular market was for the first time flooded with cheap yellow novels about exotic adventure figures like corsairs, pirates, highwaymen, soldiers, and so forth—novels whose rapid publication had been made possible by the introduction of the new cylinder press in 1847. This fiction had a special importance in America, where the overwhelming majority of the world's cylinder presses were in use. The long lists of adventure figures in *Mardi* show Melville joining the competition for the new market of sensation lovers created by the yellow novelists. Most notable about the lists are their fusion of contradictory elements. The swordfish is both noble (a knight, a soldier, a hero) and evil (a bully, an assassin, a footpad). He makes a similar fusion of opposite elements when he says of sharks: "[T]hat sharks are lovable, witness their domestic endearments. No Fury so ferocious, as not to have some amiable side." One effect of yellow fiction was to break down firm moral categories by valorizing both the heroic and the villainous, both the pious and the impious. Writing at precisely the moment that this morally complex pamphlet fiction was surging into the popular consciousness, Melville experiments with his own moral mixtures by applying typically mixed adventure imagery to sea animals. His creative redirection of sensational imagery is already leading him toward the creation of a highly paradoxical, thematically resonant sea creature. The white whale is already beginning to emerge from the turbulent ocean of American popular culture.

The deepening psychological and philosophical themes of *Mardi* emerge slowly in the course of the adventurous early sections, almost as though Melville's total immersion in sensational themes and devices impels him toward the innovative speculations of the allegorical later section. The opening escape from the ship (compared to a flight from Newgate Prison) prefigures the adventure into the unknown. Jarl's superstition that the vacated ship is haunted by ghosts introduces a menacing-spirit motif that is later developed more metaphysically. The story of Samoa's and Annatoo's dramatic escape from natives as well as Taji's murderous rescue of Yillah are both popular adventure scenes that prefigure later speculations on human violence and demonism. The perversity of Annatoo, who is "possessed by some scores of devils," anticipates the devil possession of Babbalanja and the threatening-woman role of Hautia. Taji's constant gruesome visions of his murdered victim, similar to terrifying visions in popular novels, creates a haunted-mind motif which prepares the way for the later voyage into a dreamlike landscape of the mind.

Several intriguing themes of *Mardi,* therefore, develop directly out of sensational images. Melville's vision, however, was not confined to the sensational. He perceived the deeply anomalous character of American popular literature in the late 1840s: on the one hand, there was the sudden explosion of sensational yellow novels that often featured gore and violence; on the other hand, there was a proliferation of Conventional literature featuring piety and sentimentality. He recognized that in the popular press both sensationalism and religiosity, both impiety and piety had become manufacturable items exploited by opportunistic authors and publishers. Given these anomalies, it is understandable that when Melville directly discusses popular literature in *Mardi,* he emphasizes its internal contradictions. When the voyagers visit the antiquary Oh-Oh, he shows them his large library, in which books are categorized according to several classifications. Under the heading of "popular literature" is a volume entitled "A most Sweet, Pleasant, and Unctuous Account of the Manner in which Five-and-Forty Robbers were torn asunder by Swiftly-Going Canoes."[15] The pious, pleasant first part of this title is subverted by the gory, sensational second section; the title metonymically suggests Melville's comprehension of curious tensions within contemporary popular literature. This perception of the paradoxes of popular culture is suggested by the wildly contradictory volumes in Oh-Oh's library, which includes both mawkishly sentimental titles ("Suffusions of a Lily in a Shower" and "The Gad-Fly, and Other Poems") and demonically sensational ones ("The Devil Adrift, by a Corsair," "Grunts and Groans, by a Mad Boar," and "Stings, by a Scorpion").

His new awareness of the provocative paradoxes of popular culture is made explicit in the portrayal of Yoomy, the Warbler. Of all the Mardian voyagers, Yoomy is most closely associated with popular literature: he is periodically asked to sing catchy verses that soothe, incite, or reflect the moods of the other travelers. It is significant that this popular bard, despite the apparent simplicity of most of his songs, is perhaps the most complex and ambiguous figure in the novel. "He was so capricious a mortal," Melville writes; "so swayed by contrary moods; so lofty, so humble, so sad, so merry; so made up of a thousand contradictions" that "no one in Mardi comprehended him."[16] His poems vary from the sentimental to the sensational: in one very bloody verse he sings praise to war clubs as follows:

> Skull breakers! Brain spatterers!
> Wielded right, and wielded left;
> Life quenchers! Death dealers!
> Causing live bodies to run headless!

This darkly sensational poem makes King Media declare to Yoomy that "thou and thy tribe have much to answer for; ye stir up all Mardi with your lays. Your war chants make men fight; your drinking songs, drunkards; your love ditties, fools. Yet thou sittest there, Yoomy, gentle as a dove." When Yoomy protests that minstrels "but sing out lays carelessly" and "few of us purpose harm," both Media and the philosopher Babbalanja insist that it is precisely the apparent harmlessness of such popular writings that makes them especially harmful to Mardi. In Yoomy, Melville represents the outwardly benign but internally contradictory, ambiguous American popular culture that by the late 1840s was manufacturing morality and sensationalism with blithe disregard for established moral standards. For the first time, Melville displays his profound awareness of the relativization of values implicit in his contemporary popular culture.

This awareness also makes possible his innovative exploration of the paradoxical figure of the likable criminal. Taji, a criminal who is at once justified and likable, is the first in a line of mixed criminal characters that would also include the confidence man and Billy Budd. We applaud when Taji kills the priest, we are terrified for his sake as he is constantly pursued by the priest's avenging followers, and we feel his despair when he loses and searches for his beloved Yillah. Still, we cannot forget that he is a murderer. Not only is he haunted by visions of his slain victim, but his crime prompts mixed reflections on ethics that show Melville probing a familiar popular paradox: does the justified criminal figure nullify moral standards? It was one thing to playfully combine opposite elements in sea creatures, as Melville does in the early chapters. It was a far more serious matter to combine contradictory tendencies within a thoughtful human being. Taji ponders whether his crime "was sprung of a virtuous motive, the rescuing of a captive from thrall; or whether beneath that pretense, I had engaged in this fatal affray for some other, and selfish purpose; the companionship of a beautiful maid."[17] Here the likable-criminal paradox leads to a recognition of the complexity of psychological motivations; later in the novel it gives rise to an even more subtle theme—the indeterminacy of language. We have seen that several antebellum reviewers had complained that the popular valorization of criminals or outlaws threatened to subvert the meanings of vice and virtue. Melville makes a similar point when he has the storyteller Mohi tell the history of the legendary Island of Rogues, a criminal colony in Mardi where pirates, thieves, and other malefactors are sent to live. Mohi says that only the superior, craftiest knaves were sent to the island, so that in time the island is inhabited by old graybeards who seem quintessentially respectable. The term "Island of Rogues," Mohi emphasizes, has come to mean nothing since the criminals seem as good as or better than average Mardians. The arbitrariness of definitions of roguery leads Mohi to make the declaration that "words are but algebraic signs, conveying no meaning except what you please." This sentiment is echoed later by the philosopher Babbalanja, who says that "truth is in things, and not in words: truth is voiceless." Probing the linguistic implications of his culture's paradoxes, Melville has begun to move toward a perception of the relativity of language.

The exploration of popular paradoxes in *Mardi* is somewhat removed and abstract; only in the process of writing *Redburn* and *White-Jacket,* adventure novels designed specifically for the mass audience, did Melville discover effective ways of dramatizing the sensational by drawing directly off of energetic popular stereotypes.

Throughout *Redburn* Melville refers by name to several paradigmatic popular sensational texts, which are mentioned rhetorically to contrast with the initial innocence of the young Redburn. Melville makes it clear that the central conflict in *Redburn* between innocence and evil, between religion and impiety, is part of a larger struggle between the two main kinds of popular texts representing two levels of consciousness: one the conventionally moral and the other the amoral, the wildly sensational. Weaned in a bourgeois American village, Redburn goes to sea expecting to find a tame world like that described in the conventionally pious periodicals like *The Sailor's Magazine* or tracts like *The Boatswain's Mate.* Instead, he finds a world of morally mixed characters, brash impiety, and unrestrained emotions—just like the world conjured up in popular crime narratives, yellow novels, and penny newspapers. When Redburn naïvely asks one crude sailor if he had "any good books in his chest," the sailor offers him *The Newgate Calendar* and *The Pirate's Own Book.*[18] Later, Redburn gets firsthand exposure to popular sensational literature when he reads two lurid volumes, one "an account of Shipwrecks and Disasters, and the other . . . a large black volume, with *Delirium Tremens* in great gilt letters on the back." Several of the swearing, drunken sailors in the novel are not so much characters as they are living sensational "texts." For instance, Redburn's shipmates embody the fluid, contradictory world of Dark Adventure: "Each man of them almost was a volume of Voyages and Travels round the World. And what most struck me was that like books of voyages they often contradicted each other, and would fall into long and violent disputes." Likewise, a ballad-singing sailor Redburn meets on the London streets "was full of marvelous adventures, and abounded in terrific stories of pirates and sea murders, and all sorts of nautical enormities. He was a monomaniac upon these subjects; he was a Newgate Calendar of the robberies and assassinations of the day." The salability of sensationalism is epitomized by this sailor, who makes money from writing ballads about local murders and selling printed copies on the street.

These references to sensational literature, along with the dark-reform and urban Gothic imagery discussed in my earlier analysis of *Redburn,* show that in this popular-oriented novel, which Melville said he wrote "to buy some tobacco with," he was plunging wholeheartedly into the mire of dark popular culture.[19] While his main goal was to make money, he seems also to have been consciously descending from the allegorical clouds of *Mardi* in search of energetic themes from his contemporary popular culture. He was reenacting the experience of Mardi's mythical poet Lombardo, who, according to Babbalanja, wrote his great poem "The Koztanza" only after he had been forced by hunger to write for the popular audience. Lombardo's creation of a literary masterpiece after absorption of popular themes teaches the lesson: "To scale great heights, we must come out of lowermost depths."[20]

Given his eagerness to incorporate sensational themes of every variety in *Redburn,* it is understandable that in this novel Melville fabricates his first fully American likable criminal, Henry Jackson. Writing as a popular adventure novelist in 1849, Melville participated in the general inversion of values that governed character depiction in radical-democrat fiction by Ned Buntline, George Thompson, J. H. Ingraham, and others, who in stereotypes like the lovably wicked Bowery "b'hoy" and the charismatic criminal were creating the sort of moral mixture that Melville intensifies in Jackson. Melville stresses that Jackson "dressed a good deal like a Bowery boy" and "had a good deal to say about *highbinders* and *rowdies.*"[21] In other words, he grows directly out of New York's feisty working-class culture of the 1840s. He also represents a fusion of other sensational characters: the dissipated criminal, the American pirate, the degraded slaver. He is the archetypal sensation lover who regales the other sailors with endless grisly stories. "His whole talk was of this kind," Melville writes; "full of piracies, plagues and poisonings." Representing the amorality and anarchy of sensational popular culture, Jackson (who has "yellow" skin, as though he were a personified yellow novel) is a kind of living Subversive text who undercuts faith and goodness with his savage stories, his black humor, his brash impudence. A "horrid desperado" who is "spontaneously an atheist and an infidel," he "would enter into arguments, to prove there was nothing to be believed, nothing to be loved, and nothing worth living for." He is a full embodiment of the likable criminal, since, despite his unparalleled villainy, he is pitiable and even admirable. Like several crime heroes of the 1840s, Jackson is at once despicable and lovable, and because of his mixed nature becomes a potent source for Melvillian ambiguity. Melville's notion of "the wisdom of woe," the enriching sadness he would famously praise in *Moby-Dick,* has roots in Jackson's character, as Redburn says that "there seemed even more woe than wickedness about the man; and his wickedness seemed to spring from his woe; and for all his hideousness, there was that in his eye at times, that was ineffably pitiable and touching." In the radical-democrat scheme of the novel, the honestly wicked Jackson is actually superior to more established characters such as the hypocritical Captain Riga, who is kind ashore but cruel at sea, or the effete, wealthy Harry Bolton, who under the pretense of friendship lures Redburn into a London gambling den and then abandons him. Redburn's sympathy toward Jackson extends to his villainous shipmates, whom Redburn first brands as "wicked hard-hearted rascals" but whom he eventually views with "more an eye of pity and compassion, as men of naturally gentle and kind dispositions, whom only hardships, and neglect, and ill-usage had made outcasts of good society." By creating a shipload of likable criminals, Melville is amplifying and extending a stereotype that in most popular narratives was confined to a single character. By having the initially innocent Redburn gain sympathy for these characters, he is signaling a conversion of the Conventional sensibility to the paradoxical truths this stereotype embodies.

In *White-Jacket* these popular-based paradoxes intensify as Melville describes the morally topsy-turvy world of an American naval ship. By focusing on a man-of-war, Melville is now bringing total attention to an arena of criminals and outcasts. "The Navy is the asylum for the perverse, the home of the unfortunate," he writes. "Here the sons of adversity meet the children of calamity, and here the children of calamity meet the offspring of sin."[22] The ship is called "a sort of sea-Newgate, from which [one] can not escape, either by the roof or burrowing under ground." Ironically enough, morality emerges from mass immorality: this crew of thieves and desperadoes all steal from each other, but they establish "a community of goods . . . and at last, as a whole, they become relatively honest, by nearly every man becoming the reverse." Moreover, the crew's bold depravity is found to be preferable to the institutionalized corruption embodied in tyrannical captains and the unfair naval laws they enforce. We have seen that in the late 1840s many popular novelists were driven by the dual instinct to entertain the masses through diverting sensationalism and to criticize the social elite through vitriolic reform rhetoric: as a result, their novels represented a fusion of bald sensationalism and working-class protest, a fusion that resulted in an ironic reversal of social roles and moral values within their novels. For instance, Buntline in *The G'hals of New York* portrayed a depraved criminal who boasted of being the most virtuous man in a corrupt society. A similar elevation of lowly criminals to ironic moral prominence occurs in several of the sensational exposés produced by Lippard and Thompson in the late 1840s. In *White-Jacket*, which like *Redburn* was consciously written for the mass audience, Melville probes seriously the subversive, intensely American paradox suggested by the popular working-class novelists.

Not only does he create a crew of likable criminals but he focuses on one particularly resonant character, the master-at-arms Bland, who epitomizes fully the deep ambiguities within this democratic stereotype. Bland is called the "neat and gentlemanly villain" for whom the narrator claims "a lofty and honorable niche in the Newgate Calendar of history."[23] Bland becomes Melville's newest version of the likable criminal whose presence shatters moral distinctions, since he is extremely wicked and yet irresistibly attractive, even admirable. Through Bland, Melville returns again to the common popular irony that bold villainy—even if it involves, as with Bland, cunning and duplicity—is preferable to institutionalized criminality masked by law and religion. The following comment by the narrator about Bland shows how fully Melville had absorbed his culture's sentiments about the likable criminal and his opponents, oxymoronic oppressors:

> I could not but abominate him when I thought of his conduct; but I pitied the continual gnawing which, under all his deftly-donned disguises, I saw lying at the bottom of his soul. I admired his heroism in sustaining himself so well under such reverses. And when I thought about how arbitrary the *Articles of War* are in defining a man-of-war villain; how much undetected guilt might be sheltered by the aristocratic awning of our quarter-deck; how many florid pursers, ornaments of the ward-room, had been legally protected in defrauding *the people*, I could not but say to myself, Well, after all, though this man is a most wicked one indeed, yet he is even more luckless than depraved.

In his admiration for a criminal of "deftly-donned disguises" whose clever villainy is preferable to established hypocrisy, Melville begins to manifest the sensibility that would take delight in portraying the shape-shifting confidence man. But before he could manipulate the likable criminal's disguises with literary ease, he first had to work out the deep ethical questions that this stereotype posed. Unlike popular sensationalists like Buntline or Foster, he could not simply ignore these questions or leave them unresolved. Unlike Lippard, he was not ready to move from a perception of upper-class corruption to radical activism: he was not prepared to found a nationwide working-class organization, such as Lippard's Brotherhood of the Union, designed to establish universal comradeship among oppressed or disenfranchised groups. In his first five novels Melville had experimented with a greater variety of dark-reform and sensational images than any other American novelist; he had accordingly immersed himself in the turbulent world of American popular culture. But he had shied away from working-class politics, and he never separated himself completely from the Young American *literary* group, which wished to establish a national literature on the basis of universal themes. By 1850 he was in a unique position in American letters: he had absorbed the energetic ironies and paradoxes of American working-class literature, and yet he also shared the New York littérateurs' devotion to universality. In short, he was in precisely the right frame of mind to produce a novel that fused American paradoxes with classical archetypes.

"Its Wood Could Only Be American!"

Melville had experimented so often with the paradoxical stereotype of the likable criminal that by the time he wrote *Moby-Dick* he could define Americanness and American literature in terms of the bristling polarities this stereotype implied. He himself had become a kind of likable criminal, a fully American metaphysical outlaw who could place a thief on the same level as George Washington. He could paradoxically proclaim himself the greatest democrat and the greatest misanthrope. As he expressed it in his June 1851 letter to Hawthorne: "It seems an inconsistency to assert unconditional democracy in all things, and yet confess a dislike to all mankind—in the mass. But not so."[24] Not so, we should add, because by 1851 to be a fully American democrat, one with a realistic vision of the world, was to be a justified pariah, a rebel against what seemed a corrupt society. The same radical democracy that drove Lippard to establish the Brotherhood of the Union, based on both intense disgust with America's foibles and patriotic devotion to her great promise, impelled Melville to assert simultaneously his democracy and his rebelliousness. Thus, in "Hawthorne and His Mosses" (1850) he could sound in one breath like a benign patriot, saying the American writer should "breathe that unshackled, democratic spirit of Christianity in all things," and in the next like a feisty militant, declaring that "we must turn bullies, else the day is lost."[25] He had arrived at the very core of the popular paradox that fused criminality and good-ness, iconoclasm and patriotism. He was prepared to write a novel that he would describe to Hawthorne paradoxically: "I have written a wicked book, and feel spotless as the lamb."

In *Moby-Dick* there are no longer schematic oppositions between the likable criminal and the oxymoronic oppressor, as there had been in *Redburn* and *White-Jacket.* True, we see residual signs of these familiar characters: the likable criminal appears in the interpolated "Town-Ho's Story," in which the wicked but admirable Canaller, Steelkilt, justifiably murders the oppressive mate Radney; and a typical oxymoronic oppressor appears in the person of Captain Bildad, the querulous Quaker and penny-pinching Christian. But in the main plot of *Moby-Dick* Melville creates great energy not by separating the oppressor and the criminal but by *fusing* them. Ahab is not only the oxymoronic oppressor, the "grand, ungodly, god-like" tyrant who lords over his crew; he is also the likable criminal, what Peleg calls "a swearing good man" who is on an insane yet justified quest for the whale that has wounded him.[26] The object of his quest is itself a magnificent fusion of opposite qualities: a glorious yet malicious, a beau-tiful yet all-destructive monster. And the *Pequod*'s crew is a gang of likable outcasts whose wild passions and demonic energy become absorbed into the captain's quest. No longer is a rebellious crew set against an oppressive master. Both are fused in one mad, grand purpose. And what fuses them is Melville's democratic vision of interlocking paradoxes, a vision resulting from his broad absorption of working-class themes. When explaining that he will ascribe "high qualities" to the "meanest mariners, and renegades and castaways," he explains he is impelled by the "just Spirit of Equality," the same "great democratic God" who had picked up Andrew Jackson from the pebbles, hurled him on a war horse, and thundered him higher than a throne. Indeed, *Moby-Dick* is the literary culmination of the radical egalitarianism that had its roots in Jacksonian democracy and that had taken on paradoxical, devilish intensity in the working-class fiction of the 1840s.

Moby-Dick is the grand proclamation of the democratic writer's power to fuse the opposing forces of the oxymoronic oppressor and the likable criminal. As Ahab says of the crew, "my one cogged circle fits into all their various wheels."[27] When the opposing paradoxes are fused, they simul-taneously turn inward and explode outward, so that both the inner and the outer world take on a paradoxical nature. Ahab is at once the towering self-asserter and the tortured self-consumer, one whose "special lunacy stormed his general sanity, and carried it, and turned all its concentred cannon upon its own mad mark." Other main characters similarly embody rich paradoxes. Queequeg is the humane cannibal. The mate Stubb, the figure closest to popular culture, actually speaks in contradictions: note the wild linguistic swing from the consoling to the fierce in his exhortations to his whaleboat crews: "Easy; easy; don't be in a hurry. . . . Why don't you snap your oars, you rascals?" and "[K]eep cool, keep cool—cucumbers is the word—easy, easy—only start her like grim death and grinning devils." The visible world is similarly imbued with resonant contradictions. The ocean has an outer "blue blandness" but an inner "devilish charm." The whiteness of the whale is at once "the visible absence of color, and at the same time the concrete of all colors"; it is the "colorless, all-color of atheism from which we shrink."

In this world of subversive fiction, anyone that does not participate in the overall spirit of contradiction or paradox is satirized or doomed to defeat. We saw that one reason Hawthorne used the figure of the reverend rake in *The Scarlet Letter* was that, in light of the universal attacks on preachers in sensational literature of the period, it was virtually impossible to generate interest or credibility in a conventionally virtuous preacher. A similar phenomenon governed Melville's description of authority figures. Given the precedent of popular paradoxical stereotypes, any mention of a *good* authority figure was almost automatically ironic. By having Peleg describe Bildad as "a pious, good man," Melville joins the ranks of the popular ironists, since Bildad (like many pretended religionists in popular novels) is a hypocrite. Similarly, when Starbuck is described as a "good man, and a pious," he is relegated to ultimate powerlessness.[28] The "demigod" Bulkington is mentioned early in the novel but then is left behind as an impossible ideal. Having entered the ironic world of popular sensationalism in his earlier novels, Melville can now deal convincingly only with swearing good men, justified pariahs, humane cannibals, and likable desperadoes—that is, only with paradoxical emblems of his newfound radical democracy. Through the character of Ishmael he announces his acceptance of these subversive paradoxes. Melville's earlier noble protagonists, such as Wellingborough Redburn or Jack Chase, had remained relatively detached, naïve spectators of Subversive people and events. Ishmael, in contrast, undergoes a kind of conversion to the Subversive. In Queequeg he finds a pagan with "no civilized hypocrisies and bland deceits," one who makes him resolve to "try a pagan friend, . . . since Christian kindness has proved but hollow courtesy." By befriending Queequeg, Ishmael takes radical democracy and radical Christianity to a new extreme: the protest against civilized hypocrisy is enacted in the embrace of a man who is both black and pagan. Later, Ishmael merges completely with the Subversive when he joins the swearing, carousing sailors in their demonic oaths against the white whale: "I, Ishmael, was one of that crew; my shouts had gone up with the rest; my oath had been welded with theirs; . . . Ahab's quenchless feud seemed mine." The disappearance of Ishmael as a visible presence in the novel is often regarded as a structural flaw, but in fact it points up the all-absorbing magnetism of the cultural paradoxes Melville is portraying.

Melville had absorbed all the energetic paradoxes of America's sensational popular culture but had found that the novel they produced was not widely appreciated or understood. Although *Moby-Dick* received predominantly favorable reviews, it did not sell very well and was not acknowledged for the distinctly American metaphysical masterpiece it became in later critical judgments. Before its publication Melville had predicted its poor reception when he had written to Hawthorne: "What's the use of elaborating what, in its very essence, is so short-lived as a modern book? Though I wrote the Gospels in this century, I should die in the gutter."[29] After its publication, his warm pride over Hawthorne's enthusiasm for the novel was diminished by the bitter realization that "not one man in five cycles, who is wise, will expect appreciative recognition from his fellows, or any one of them."

Melville was in an anomalous and painful situation. On the one hand, he had stated in "Hawthorne and His Mosses" that "great geniuses are parts of the times; they themselves are the times, and possess a correspondent coloring." In *Moby-Dick* he produced a novel that proved this argument, because it fully embodied its times and its culture. And yet, the culture it reflected did not fully appreciate it. Melville's difficulty was one that Whitman would experience with *Leaves of Grass*: the fusion of variegated American themes produced a new kind of literary text that could not be comprehended by the very culture that nurtured it.

Melville's strongest animus was against the Young America literary movement and, in a larger sense, against Conventional writers in general. The leaders of Young America, fearing the volcanic disturbance in working-class culture, had increasingly emphasized refinement and smoothness in American literature. In "Hawthorne and His Mosses" Melville had tried to stem the tide toward Anglophile tameness by indicting "these smooth pleasing writers that know their own powers" and by calling for an explosive national literature based upon native wildness, even crudeness. In essence, he was trying to usher into the Young America movement the savage energies and scathing paradoxes of the radical democrats and their Subversive literature. *Moby-Dick,* as we have seen, was the full literary realization of these native energies and paradoxes. While it possessed the kind of universality and the imagery from past classics that the Young America group prized, it breathed the harsh spirit of radical democracy through classic archetypes so that it was both universal and fully indigenous. To paraphrase Ahab's words, its wood could only have been American. When this radically American novel was not generally appreciated, Melville became understandably cynical and vindictive toward the Conventional culture that misunderstood him.

In his subsequent major works of the 1850s Melville utilized the sensational images of radical democracy in a far more vitriolic, rhetorical way than he had in his earlier fiction. He repeatedly used dark themes and experimental devices from popular sensational literature to attack the Conventional. In *Pierre* he directly satirized the conventionality of the Young America group, and he enforced the satire in a notably sensational plot involving incest, murder, and suicide. In "Bartleby, the Scrivener" and "Benito Cereno" he assaulted Conventional narrators with gloomy, terrifying sensational images. *Israel Potter* applies rapid-fire adventure toward the subtle redefinition of legendary American heroes from the ironic vantage point of radical democracy. *The Confidence-Man* showed that a wholesale inversion of moral values and of stylistic norms could result when a highly Subversive stereotype, taken from sensational popular culture, was invested with Conventional attitudes. Melville's bitter aim of attacking America's Conventional culture with weapons from popular sensationalism produced some of his most memorable fiction.

Pierre makes clear Melville's disillusionment with the Young America group, which had failed to comprehend his efforts to forge a powerful national literature out of raw, violent American materials. In the central chapter, entitled "Young America in Literature," Melville gets his revenge against the New York littérateurs by mocking their somewhat, effete literary goals. Producing sweet poems early in his writing career, Pierre at first identifies with the Young America group. He is praised for "the general symmetry of his style," "the highly judicious smoothness and genteelness" of his themes, his avoidance of "any thing coarse or new," his lack of "vulgarity and vigor."[30] But Pierre soon sickens of this Conventional literature and the swarms of publishers, magazinists, biographers, and so forth that try to exploit it. Young America, he learns, is a world of amorality, venality, and artificiality.

Throughout the rest of the novel Melville dramatizes the satire in a highly sensational plot that flies in the face of the kind of smoothness and gentility that the Young America group had increasingly prized. When Melville wrote his publisher that *Pierre* was "very much more calculated for popularity" than his previous novels, he must have had in mind the mass readership of sensational, gloomy novels. That *Pierre* did not sell well is perhaps owing to the fact that by 1852, the year it appeared, the American public had been surfeited for more than a decade with novels about fallen innocence, illicit love, revenge, murder, imprisonment, and suicide. Even the dark philosophizing in *Pierre* was familiar to American sensation lovers:

many Subversive novels contain pre-Melvillian passages about hypocrisy, shattered dreams, tabooed desires, death, time, and doubt. *Pierre* seems particularly reminiscent of the writings of the New York author George Thompson, whose sensational novels of the late 1840s and early 1850s represented a fusion of radical-democratic social militancy and hyperbolic sensationalism. In *The Ladies' Garter* (c. 1850) Thompson had anticipated the central recognition scene in *Pierre* by having his hero learn of the past sins of a respected older gentleman by noticing the slightly sensuous expression in a portrait of the gentleman in his younger days—exactly the way Pierre confirms his worst fears about his father's shadowy past. The incest motif of *Pierre* had been more pruriently treated in *The Ladies' Garter*, in which the heroine discovers she is her husband's granddaughter, and in *City Crimes* (1849), in which Thompson portrays a New York community where "the crime of *incest* is as common . . . as dirt," where it is the custom for "a mother and her son—a father and his daughter—a brother and sister—to be guilty of criminal intimacy."[31] In a larger sense, Thompson's novels show how the radical democrats' vision of secret corruption among American authority figures gave rise to pre-Melvillian reflections upon human chicanery and moral ambiguity. The hero of Thompson's *New-York Life* (1849), seeing in American society only "the counterfeit presentiments of paints and cosmetics," asks such cynical questions as "O, world of humanity! . . . art thou all a cheat?" and "What can be done for a world where the very good is evil?" He finds that the human race "has the elements of goodness so mixed up together, that the very good is evil."[32] The heroine of another Thompson novel is so shattered by hypocrisy among the outwardly respectable that she concludes that "the world is only a cheat and a continual lie."[33]

It is clear that Melville had the radical democrats and their ambiguities in mind when he wrote *Pierre*. At the beginning of the novel he tells the reader: "[Y]ou will pronounce Pierre a thorough-going Democrat in time; perhaps a little too Radical altogether for your fancy."[34] As it turns out, Pierre is indeed a radical democrat in his disenchantment with authority figures, his sympathy for the poor and oppressed (represented by Isabel and Delly Ulver), and his later association with radical reformers in the Church of the Apostles. The narrative pattern of *Pierre* is not distant from that of paradigmatic popular Subversive novels like Lippard's *The Quaker City* or Thompson's *City Crimes*: a patriotic, idealistic protagonist, shattered by the recognition of secret depravity of formerly respected authority figures, enters the lurid realm of crime and poverty in the American city. Melville changed the pattern by exaggerating both its piously Conventional introduction and its darkly Subversive aftermath, thereby intensifying the protagonist's crashing fall from innocence. Adventurous action, always predominant in the popular novels, is reduced in *Pierre* to a bare minimum, as is the sensationalists' prurient gloating over the sensuous details of illicit love. In contrast, the dark metaphysics and gloomy psychology of the sensationalists is given a prominence it had never known. Because of the intensity of Pierre's initial idealism—his pride over his grandfather's wartime heroism, his love of his mother and the angelic Lucy, his strong patriotism and piety—his later disillusion assumes gigantic proportions. Often Melville sounds like Thompson and other dark sensationalists in the phrases he chooses to communicate this disillusion. Just as many popular protagonists vow to tear away veils to reveal hidden corruption, so Pierre cries: "From all idols, I tear all veils; henceforth I will see the hidden things." Just as a Thompson character called the world "a cheat and a continual lie," so Pierre finds it "saturated and soaking with lies." Just as another Thompson character had found virtue and vice indistinguishable in a corrupt world, so Pierre declares that they are "two shadows cast from one nothing." The sensationalists' irrational style, with its narrative discontinuities and its dreamlike quality, lies behind the intentionally quirky style of *Pierre,* described aptly by Melville: "This history goes forward and goes backward, as occasion calls. Nimble center, circumference elastic you must have."

The main difference between Melville and the popular sensationalists is that he was driven by an especially fierce vindictiveness against the Conventional, so that his Subversive themes and devices are rhetorically taken to a new extreme and are treated with a new self-reflexivity. The second half of the novel is not only about the kind of dark city mysteries and philosophical ambiguities that typified popular sensationalism; it is simultaneously about the contemplation of such mysteries and ambiguities by the reflective American novelist. The same radical democracy that had impelled Pierre to abandon his Conventional village life and plunge into urban poverty makes him leave behind the Conventional themes and write a highly skeptical novel that flouts the staid norms of literary Young America. The Church of the Apostles offers no real alternative to Conventional society, because it consists of disparate "political propagandists of all manner of heterodoxical tenets" who are fragmented, penniless, and slavishly devoted to charismatic quacks like Plotinus Plinlimmon. While exploiting several radical-democrat themes to subvert Conventionalism, Melville cannot rest comfortably in the political activism of many radical democrats. He has entered a suprapolitical literary realm in which he uses popular sensational imagery to assault the staidly Conventional.

He continued this militant reapplication of sensational devices in his first magazine story, "Bartleby, the Scrivener. A Story of Wall-Street." Much of the imagery in "Bartleby" is directly related to popular sensational literature. In particular, a series of sensational exposés about New York life by George Foster, a popular novelist in Melville's circle, are especially pertinent to "Bartleby." In *New York in Slices* (1849) Foster had portrayed Wall Street as a totally dehumanizing environment producing puppetlike people and universal misery cloaked by gentility. "Wall-street!" Foster writes. "Who shall fathom the depth and rottenness of thy mysteries? Has Gorgon passed through thy winding labyrinth, turning with his smile every thing to stone—hearts as well as houses?"[35] In Wall Street, Foster continues, man has erected huge stone temples to "the one god—Mammon." Through the labyrinthine chambers of buildings rush throngs of people "as if they went whirling about in some gigantic puppet-show, while a concealed hand pulled convulsively at the wire." Every chamber has its "pale young man" who can lose his fortune in one quick business reversal, leaving him with "his position lost, and himself an outcast." Who can wonder, Foster asks, that this dispossessed pale young man in a "quiet and gentlemanly way" often "applies a razor to the jugular, and thus frees himself at once of earthly ills." Just after his section on Wall Street, Foster writes a depressing description of New York's famous prison, the Tombs, which he calls a "Grim mausoleum of hope! Foul lazar-house of polluted and festering Humanity!" Elsewhere in the volume Foster makes a harrowing contrast between Broadway alive with people at noon and totally deserted in the gray light of early morning. On Sunday afternoon, Foster says, Broadway is "a perfect Mississippi, with a double current up and down, of glossy broadcloth and unblemished De Laines"—but after hours it becomes "some Palmyra avenue, solemn and deserted." Later, pondering items in a New York pawnshop, Foster declares there is "no more melancholy thing" than to see all the possessions that once belonged to happy, prosperous people who are now dead or poor.

"Bartleby, the Scrivener" might be viewed as a literary version of several of Foster's central images. The confining, deadening Wall Street atmosphere Foster describes is symbolized by the blank walls that surround the office and that reflect Bartleby's total passivity as he loses himself in "dead-wall reveries."[36] The image of puppetlike workers is reproduced in the portrayal of Turkey and Nippers, whose nonhuman names and clocklike mood shifts underscore their drearily mechanical existence. The deadness of both the physical environment and the mechanical employees is reflected in the scrivener job itself; as the narrator says, copying law papers is "proverbially a dry, husky sort of business" and at times "a very dull, wearisome, and lethargic affair." When Foster writes that every building has its "pale young man" who quietly works and just as quietly sinks into ostracism and death, he seems to directly anticipate Melville's Bartleby, the "pallidly neat, pitiably respectable, incurably forlorn" man who drifts to his solitary end with horrifying decorum and gentlemanliness. Foster's contrast between the "perfect Mississippi" of busy Broadway and the street "solemn and deserted" is similar to Melville's contrast between the "bright silks and sparkling faces . . . swan-like sailing down the Mississippi of Broadway" and the pallid copyist in his office "as deserted as Petra." Both writers use the Tombs as the symbol of final despair, and Melville's concluding speculation about letters in the Dead Letter Office, whose intended recipients are perhaps now dead or poor, is similar in spirit to Foster's comments about the former owners of articles in pawnshops.

None of the elements in "Bartleby, the Scrivener," therefore, were new to American fiction—they were a direct inheritance from dark city-mysteries fiction of the late 1840s. What is new about Melville's story is its formal innovations: the skillful use of the flawed narrator; the symbolic setting; the psychological and metaphysical suggestions. In Bartleby, Melville creates Wall Street's ultimate "pale young man" who reflects the mechanical lifelessness that surrounds him and who represents the hollowness at the core of this Wall Street existence. Even his "rebellion" is an extension of his lifelessness, for it is performed in a totally passive, unemotional way. Both in his dogged work and his passionless refusal to work he combines qualities of his fellow workers and of his physical environment: he possesses the quiet respectability of his employer, the machinelike nature of Nippers and Turkey, and the deadness of the blank walls.

Furthermore, Bartleby embodies all the ambiguities of the likable criminal. A social outcast finally imprisoned in the Tombs, he falls in a long line of American criminals who could not be summarily dismissed as wicked but rather were regarded as an ambiguous mixture of good and evil, normal and abnormal qualities. In a story so broadly representative of sensational popular culture as "Bartleby," it is not surprising that we find mention of two of the most notorious criminal cases of the antebellum period: the 1841 Broadway office murder of John C. Colt by Samuel Adams, who on the day scheduled for his hanging committed suicide in the Tombs; and the famous "gentleman forger" Monroe Edwards, who furnished his cell in the Tombs elegantly, like a parlor. These cases had been publicized in all the sensational literature of the day, and a public fascination, even sympathy with the criminals had grown. Melville has the lawyer, meeting Bartleby alone in his office, recall "the tragedy of the unfortunate Adams and the still more unfortunate Colt," who in a moment of understandable rage committed "an act which certainly no man could possibly deplore more than the actor himself."[37] Later, the grub man in the Tombs compares Bartleby with Monroe Edwards, noting that "they are always pale and genteel-like, them forgers. I can't help pity 'em—can't help it, sir." By mentioning two of the period's most notorious crime cases and especially by underscoring the pitiable, likable aspects of the criminal, Melville shows he is drawing from ambiguous stereotypes in sensational popular culture.

As in *Pierre*, one of Melville's main reasons for using ambiguous sensational imagery is to undermine the Conventional. We view all the characters and events in "Bartleby" through the distorting lens of a lawyer who epitomizes bourgeois respectability. The narrator is genteel, pious, non-contemplative, mildly materialistic, passionless. He is another embodiment of the kind of decorous civility and bland conventionalism Melville had sharply satirized throughout *Pierre*. By his own admission, he is "an eminently *safe* man" doing business in "the cool tranquillity of a snug retreat" and priding himself on his "prudence" and "method." In the course of the story we witness the contortions of this Conventional sensibility as it is confronted with the inexplicable, the perverse. Melville's most disturbing message is that the normal and the perverse, the Conventional and Subversive are really two sides of the same coin. He had approached this realization at the end of *Moby-Dick,* in which Ahab, recognizing the underlying identity between the pious Starbuck and the blackly humorous Stubb, cries: "Ye two are the opposite poles of one thing; Starbuck is Stubb reversed, and Stubb is Starbuck; and ye two are all mankind[.]"[38] In *Pierre* he had again shown that the Conventional, when exaggerated, inevitably changes into its opposite. In "Bartleby," the Subversive ambiguities that exasperate and baffle the Conventional narrator are actually a reflection of the narrator's own characteristics. Bartleby's decorous passivity is merely an extension of the lawyer's own genteel lifelessness, just as one of the blank walls outside the office window is "rather tame than otherwise, deficient in what landscape painters call 'life.' "[39] The lawyer says he would have violently dismissed Bartleby "had there been any thing ordinarily human about him"—but there is nothing ordinarily human about the lawyer, who prides himself on the "perfect quietness" of his passive strategy for getting rid of Bartleby. Melville brings together Conventional images (piety, prudence, charity, method) and Subversive ones (the likable criminal, urban dehumanization, the grim Tombs) to show how they blend into each other and form a gray middle ground of valuelessness and moral neutrality.

In "Benito Cereno" Melville again focuses on the psychological contortions of a Conventional narrator who is confronted with images from Subversive adventure: this time, images of piracy, murder, and slave revolt. Once again, Melville creates a psychological suspense story by recording the shifting reactions of a Conventional narrator to a mysterious, threatening situation. Amaso Delano is "a man of such native simplicity as to be incapable of satire or irony." His nature is "not only benign, but familiarly and humorously so."[40] Throughout the story he misreads the situation aboard the *San Dominick* because of his inclination to pity sailors who are actually mutinous criminals. Melville once again returns to the paradox of the likable criminal, this time to gauge the distortions of perspective that result when the Conventional sensibility pities black criminals masquerading as obsequious slaves. Pity is misdirected right up to the crucial moment, for it is not until the piratical Babo leaps into his departing boat and tries to stab Benito Cereno that Delano discovers his mistake.

The conclusion presents a riddle that is as difficult to unravel as the Gordian knot the old sailor hands to Delano early in the story. Have Conventional values won the day, or have they been ironically exposed as blind and impotent? Delano insists that his good nature and charity suspended his distrust throughout his time on the *San Dominick,* therefore enabling Benito Cereno to leap on his departing boat at the end. But Cereno reminds Delano that his pity had been misdirected throughout and that his last act before the great revelation was to "clutch for a monster, not only an innocent man, but the most pitiable of all men. To such a degree may malign machinations and deceptions impose."[41] That is, until Babo showed his true identity, Delano had regarded Benito Cereno as a murderous pirate. Ironically, then, it is the wicked Babo, not Delano's beloved Providence, that brings about the climactic revelation. Even in the action that dooms him, the likable criminal governs the situation. In a sense, Melville does assign final victory to the Conventional (the mutineers are exposed and punished), but the victory is Pyrrhic, for the Conventional has been shown to be so naïve and so easily deceived that the reader is, like Benito Cereno at the end, contemplating the dark mysteries surrounding "The negro"—both his bloody rebellion and his clever deceptions.

Both "Bartleby" and "Benito Cereno" signal Melville's rise from the philosophical depths of *Moby-Dick* and *Pierre* toward the surface refractions and posturings of *The Confidence-Man.* In the earlier works Melville had invested his culture's paradoxes with metaphysical meaning and had heroically tried to confront and resolve this meaning. In the later works he turns from the problem of philosophical meaning toward the effects of stereotypical paradoxes on human psychology and behavior. "Bartleby" and "Benito Cereno" studied the angst of the Conventional mentality when confronted with Subversive mysteries surrounding pitiable criminals; *The Confidence-Man* would show that the Conventional mentality itself is a mere change of costume for the criminal. The confidence-man figure had emerged in the late 1840s in the sensational journalism and popular fiction of radical democrats. It was the ultimate Subversive stereotype of American working-class culture, for it grew from the bitter feeling that the knavery of hypocritical aristocrats could be outdone only by the wily manipulations of the justified criminal. Melville would take the confidence-man stereotype beyond working-class politics and convert it into a mythic embodiment of his culture's paradoxes. His perception of this stereotype as a broadly representative figure, however, was arrived at only after he had written a radical-democrat adventure novel, *Israel Potter.*

In a June 1854 letter to his New York publisher, George Putnam, Melville made clear the popular orientation of his new novel: "There will be very little reflective writing in it; nothing weighty. It is adventure."[42] Indeed, *Israel Potter,* based on Henry Trumbull's popular pamphlet novel of 1824, approximates the mode of Dark Adventure: a rapidly moving action narrative punctuated by very brief, usually dark, philosophizing. So close was it to popular sensational fiction that shortly after its publication in 1855 it was pirated by a London publisher and was issued as part of a "Cheap Series" of yellow-covered shilling novels. Its appeal to sensation lovers was enduring, for in 1865 a leading American publisher of sensational fiction, T. B. Peterson, reprinted a second pirated pamphlet edition, renaming the novel *The Refugee* and advertising it as a cheap, exciting tale. The novel is often overlooked today because it is a consciously popular performance that lacks the depth of *Moby-Dick* and the experimental style of *The Confidence-Man.* But it was precisely Melville's engagement with his popular sensational culture in this novel that made possible the experimentation of *The Confidence-Man. Israel Potter* is a reinterpretation of a key moment in American history—the Revolution and its aftermath—from the ironic viewpoint of Dark Adventure and radical democracy. The irony begins with the sarcastic dedication, "To *His Highness* the BUNKER-HILL MONUMENT," and lasts until the Revolutionary War veteran Israel Potter returns home after several decades abroad, only to be neglected by the country he had served in battle. In the novel, historical adventure becomes American autocriticism, as paradoxes of antebellum radical democracy gain a new universality when they are superimposed upon paradigmatic figures of the nation's past.

In *Israel Potter* Melville probes four central mixed characters, all of them preparatory to the confidence man. Benjamin Franklin, who in Trumbull's narrative had been presented as wise and benign, becomes a problematic figure who preaches humble penury but is himself a richly robed, worldly man described as "sly, sly, sly."[43] Also contradictory is Ethan Allen, who is at once the savage pirate and the justified outlaw, the bloody barbarian and the righteous patriot. Israel Potter is sucked into this world of contradictions with grim inevitability; even though (or rather, in the ironic terms of the novel, *because*) he practices all the Franklinian virtues he finds himself in a dizzying world of enclosure and escape, sea battles, imposture, urban poverty, and final isolation. Perhaps the most paradoxical character of all is Captain John Paul Jones. In nineteenth-century histories, opinion was divided between hostile and sympathetic views of this anomalous gentleman-warrior of the Revolution. Melville incorporates both positive and negative interpretations in portraying a man who is described paradoxically as one "combining in one breast the vengeful indignation and bitter ambition of an outraged hero, with the uncompunctious desperation of a renegade. In one view, the Coriolanus of the sea; in another, a cross between a gentleman and a wolf." In Jones, the outlaw and the poet, the criminal and the patriot are fused in an explosive center. He is the American legendary hero reconceived as the modern likable criminal. In depicting this paradoxical character, Melville reached a larger realization about America. The nation was itself, he realized, a kind of likable criminal constantly reenacting the brash violence of its initial rebellion but always sustaining itself with ideals of decorum and gentility. Melville could now see deep paradoxes in the nation as a whole: "[I]ntrepid, unprincipled, reckless, predatory, with boundless ambition, civilized in externals but a savage at heart, America is, or yet may be, the Paul Jones of nations."

Israel Potter had simultaneously intensified Melville's vision of cultural paradoxes and had removed him from the problematic realm of truth seeking. The Dark Adventure mode had ushered him to the relativist surface of a popular culture whose swirling paradoxes and contradictions were not probed deeply but instead were projected into narrative strategies of dramatization, rapid scene shifts, and sensationalism, punctuated by dark but undeveloped asides. Even the paradoxes surrounding Jones are avoided in the interest of adventure. "Much subtle casuistry," Melville writes, "has been expended upon the point, whether Paul Jones was a knave or a hero, or a union of both. But war and warriors, like politics and politicians, like religion and religionists, admit of no metaphysics." This statement seems strange coming from a writer who earlier had seen metaphysics in just about everything, including a whale's tail. But by the time he wrote *Israel Potter* he was willfully surrendering metaphysics. Dark Adventure provided an appropriate means of resurfacing. The metaphysical quest had led only to Pierre's ambiguities and Bartleby's inertia. Melville was now prepared to gauge the complex undulations of the surface. He could not, however, escape the woeful wisdom of his major novels or the pervasive paradoxes of *Israel Potter*. The best objective correlative for his current viewpoint was a Subversive stereotype that combined cynicism and playfulness, that had dark suggestiveness but could also be enjoyed as good theater. That figure was the confidence man.

Although it is well known that the confidence man had precedent in a variety of literary rogues and charlatans,[44] it has not been shown how deeply indebted Melville was to the pioneering innovations of various Subversive writers. John Neal, the father of the modern Subversive school,

had in the first half of his intriguing novel *The Down-Easters* (1831) penned
a highly experimental sequence of gamesmanship, violence, and sacrilege
aboard a riverboat. It was not, however, until the publication of George
Lippard's *The Quaker City* (1845) that literary charlatanism took on pre-
Melvillian energy and universality. Lippard wrote with the trenchant
radical-democratic aim of exposing America's ruling class as sham-ridden
and deceitful. As a result, he produced a novel in which virtually everyone
wears a false appearance and life itself is said to be a tissue of "deceits and
confidences."[45] Monk Hall, the central setting of the novel, is a place where
"the very devil is played under a cloak." America's aristocracy is dubbed
a "magnificent Pretension," "a specimen of paste-board statuary, giving
but a grotesque outline, of the reality which it is intended to represent."
The master charlatan in the novel is the eternally shape-shifting Algernon
Fitz-Cowles, the "prince of swindlers" who variously appears as a business-
man selling stock in a phony mining company, as a Southern plantation
owner, and in countless other disguises. Fitz-Cowles constantly dons different costumes and artificial limbs to dupe others—he becomes, as his
helper says, "so many tings, dat de debbil hisself could'nt [*sic*] count
them." Lippard likes to double and redouble impostures, as when the
arch-swindler Fitz-Cowles tries to con a Southern millionaire who is himself an imposter spying on Fitz-Cowles. Although Lippard defended the
poor, he believed that too often America's lower classes were the willing
dupes of wealthy oppressors and were taken with various popular humbugs. One character notes "the popular disposition to believe in—*moon-
shine*" and explains: "An unknown Pretender appears in the Quaker City,
and lo! Everybody hastens to entrust him with their own lives, and the lives
of those they love." Throughout the novel, both poor and rich are manipulated at will by the leeringly likable criminal Devil-Bug, who operates
according to the philosophy that "human natur' is very much like a piece
of putty in a baby's fingers." In *The Quaker City*, the quintessential radical-
democrat sensation novel, charlatanism is so widespread that the reader
sinks into a miasma of sham appearances.

Melville's famous novel of duplicity had precedent not only in *The
Quaker City* but also in other productions of the popular Subversive imagination. Although few of the working-class novels of the late 1840s have the
multilayered complexity of Lippard's, many of them share Lippard's bleak
vision of modern life. "In every branch of human interest," George Foster
typically generalized in *Celio* (1850), "Fraud and Falsehood rear their
heads, twin demons of the epoch." In another work Foster notices in urban
America "all the millions of deceits and degradations and hypocrisies and
miseries played off as in some ghostly farce."[46] In the numerous novels of
another radical democrat, George Thompson, the world is portrayed, to

use the words of one of Thompson's characters, as "a cheat and a continual lie."[47]

The confidence-man stereotype represented a fusion of the likable criminal with a cynical vision of universal duplicity. It was a proclamation of simultaneous disgust and affirmation: disgust with civilized hypocrisies and affirmation of expert gamesmanship in a world of knaves. Since all the world seemed an imposture, the craftiest impostor was regarded as the highest artist.

The first fictional use of a character actually called a "confidence man" was in Ned Buntline's intriguing pamphlet novel *The G'hals of New York* (1850). It is understandable that the confidence man would appear in a radical-democrat novel which portrays a world in which, as Buntline writes, one "must make up his mind whether he will cheat or be cheated, whether he will dupe or be duped, whether he will pluck or be plucked."[48] "The Confidence Man" Joseph Skinkle flits in and out of Buntline's novel, exploiting the word "confidence," always with the aim of extorting money from others and sometimes with psychological and linguistic gamesmanship. In one scene anticipatory of Melville, Skinkle, threatened by a person angry over an earlier duping, circumvents discovery by witty circumlocution and by optimistic argumentation. Skinkle insists that his victim's evil companionship "has given you a false opinion of human nature in general, and robbed you of all confidence in the honesty of truth of the great family of man!" Here Skinkle presages Melville's cosmopolitan by defending optimism and good cheer even while he is entrapping his newest victim. For the first time in American literature, we have in Buntline's confidence man a fully amoral but completely likable protagonist who blithely boasts that since he has "no shame, . . . no sensitiveness, no feelings," he can forever persevere in his villainous game "with all the coolness and confidence of one who has never known reverses or defeat!" Buntline emphasizes that Skinkle is "no worse than the rest of the world—for *who* lives not by *appearances*!" In the radical-democrat realm of knaves and dupes, the cleverest knave is the highest exemplar. The moral inversions that would produce Melville's most complex novel were already dominant in popular sensational literature by 1850.

We have seen that after the public's mixed response to *Moby-Dick* Melville used various weapons from sensational popular culture to subvert the Conventional. In the final novel of his major phase, he selected the ultimate weapon from this culture: the confidence man. Through this Subversive stereotype Melville could imaginatively beat the Conventional at its own game. He could expose the artificiality of Conventional virtues by showing how easily such virtues could be playacted. Optimism, charity, trust, moderation—these and many other mainstream liberal virtues, gathered in the central notion of confidence, become mere changes of costume for Melville's ingenious shapeshifter.

Ironically, Melville's confidence man is assaulted from all sides by pessimistic or violent images from Subversive popular culture, and he often confronts these assaults with a Conventional posture. In most scenes, he defends hope and cheer, while his foil is often a churlish misanthrope with a Subversive view of things. For instance, he retains his optimism even during his conversation with the dour, crippled ex-prisoner Thomas Fry, who as a poor man had been incarcerated in the Tombs for no reason and who had extreme difficulty getting released simply because he had no wealthy friends. A cynical pariah who embodies the familiar Subversive notion of the victimization of the poor by the rich, Fry is consoled by the confidence man, who takes the Conventional view that Fry will be strengthened by misfortune and who plays the kindly Christian by offering him free medicine. Just as here the confidence man resists the dark notion of the justified pariah, so in the Indian-hating sequence he decries the ambiguities surrounding the likable criminal. In this sequence Melville lifts a Subversive paradox straight from popular sensation literature, for the Indian-hating chapter is adapted from *Legends of the West* (1832), one of several bloody adventure narratives by Judge James Hall. Hall had presented the Indian-hater as one of a dozen backwoods types who were normally "simple, honest, and inoffensive" but who became murderous savages in battle.[49] Melville points up the ethical dilemma surrounding this sensational stereotype when he has a stranger paraphrase Hall's story of Colonel John Moredock, the civilized gentleman who is at the same time a horribly ferocious Indian-killer. Shocked by the moral paradox posed by this figure, the confidence man asks: "If the man of hate, how could John Moredock be also the man of love?"[50] Such puzzlement over the paradoxical likable-criminal stereotype also governs his interchanges with the misanthropic frontiersman Pitch, who is called "a sort of comprehensive Colonel Moredock." The "half-cynic, half wild-cat" Pitch is a likable misanthrope who distrusts both nature and man, particularly boys, whom he is tempted to shoot with his always ready gun. Appalled by Pitch's cynicism, the confidence man defends nature's benignity, man's perfectibility, and the value of Christian nurture in raising boys—all standard Conventional beliefs.

The underlying irony, of course, is that the confidence man, who is always resisting the paradoxes surrounding the likable criminal, is himself the ultimate likable criminal, the smooth deceiver for whom conventionalism is an easily donned cloak. In his adept portrayal of this all-deceiving figure, Melville is announcing the victory of popular Subversive paradoxes and gamesmanship over philosophizing and truth telling. In *Moby-Dick* he had earnestly sent representative American paradoxical characters on a grand philosophical quest. By the time he wrote *The Confidence-Man* he had virtually suspended the quest and turned his attention to the wily posturings of a paradoxical character. Through this character, Melville could register fully but implicitly the contradictions of the American experience and at the same time subvert the kind of earnest truth telling that had governed *Moby-Dick*. The supremacy of clever posturing over earnest philosophizing becomes particularly visible in the chapters on Emerson and Thoreau, who appear as Mark Winsome and his follower Egbert. In *Moby-Dick* Melville had utilized the Transcendentalist notions of self-reliance and symbolism. In *The Confidence-Man* he subverts the symbolic process and sharply satirizes America's leading Transcendentalist philosophers. Emerson had preached literary independence; Winsome slavishly quotes from Greek and Oriental writers. The Transcendentalists had taught firm self-reliance; Egbert is obsequious to his "master." The Transcendentalists had denounced materialism; Winsome looks like "a cross between a Yankee peddler and a Tartan priest," while the penny-pinching Egbert, who looks like "a thriving young merchant," quotes Winsome's essay on friendship to defend the unfriendly position that he cannot give loans, a position he illustrates through his tale of China Aster.[51] Both Winsome and Egbert are cold and selfish, impelling the confidence man to indict this "inhuman philosophy" of "a head kept cool by the under ice of the heart." Once again, the confidence man defends humanity and optimism in the face of coldness and mistrust.

The fact always remains, however, that the confidence man is a swindler and a weasel who never shows a true face. His Conventional attitudes are all a sham, and his benign poses cannot be trusted. He scolds the collegian for reading Tacitus, which he calls "poison, moral poison," and recommends "serene and cheery books, fitted to inspire love and trust." But the joke is on the reader, since, from a Conventional standpoint, *The Confidence-Man* itself is "moral poison." The satire on the Transcendentalists is part of *an overall rejection of philosophy, an admission that in this world of genial misanthropes and likable criminals clear thematic messages are impossible.* In *The Confidence-Man,* the interlocking paradoxes of the Subversive imagination become all-negating and undercut literary meaning itself.

Melville's last major work for more than three decades, *The Confidence-Man* was at once a culmination of Melville's paradoxical artistry and a bitter cry of exhaustion. The abortion of meaning in *The Confidence-Man* seems to have been accompanied by an abortion of creativity. The full projection of the paradoxes of sensational popular culture had led to their deconstruction and to the very negation of the representational process. When he did return to writing, in *Battle-Pieces* (1866), he left behind thematic paradoxes and stylistic circularities and adopted instead a more traditional literary form, poetry, directed toward the sympathetic representation of an actual event, the Civil War. In *Clarel* (1876) he used an especially regulated poetic form—rhymed couplets—and resumed the earnest philosophical quest he had begun in *Mardi* and *Moby-Dick*. This time he made sure to undertake the quest without use of those problematic paradoxical characters that had complicated his earlier quests and had led to the thematic stalemate of *The Confidence-Man*. Throughout *Clarel* runs a profound dissatisfaction with the fluid values of American culture that had permitted such ambiguous phenomena as likable criminals and the confidence man. Melville has a main character in *Clarel* complain that democratic America "gave me this vile liberty / To reverence naught, not even herself." He declares that people "Get tired at last of being free—/ Whether in states—in states or creeds."[52] Melville wanted to enjoy, at least on the imaginative level, the security of the Conventional values he had so devastatingly undermined in his earlier fiction.

In *Billy Budd*, the novel he wrote just before his death, he found such security. He did so by rewriting the story of the likable criminal. Billy Budd is the ultimate likable criminal: "lovable" is the appropriate term in his case. True, Melville's ironic imagination could not create a perfect fictional hero. Billy has flaws that contribute to his tragic end: his naïveté makes him blind to signs of Claggart's plot against him, and his vocal defect makes him unable to defend himself against the charge of mutiny. Flawed as he is, he does not pose the difficult moral paradoxes of Melville's earlier likable criminals. He is the likable criminal divested of any association of radical democracy. He was the product of a different time and culture than Melville's earlier mixed protagonists. In the late 1840s, when Melville had written *Redburn* and *White-Jacket* for the mass audience, he had absorbed the dark, ironic stereotypes of sensational literature of the time. Through likable criminals like Jackson and Bland, described according to the inverted value system of radical democracy, he had fully absorbed the paradoxes of American sensationalism. The pervasive ironies of the Subversive imagination, making it difficult to depict a truly *good* pious hero, had engendered such mixed characters as the "swearing good" Ahab and the playfully malicious confidence man.

Post–Civil War popular culture had introduced a new kind of hero—the muscular Christian—who was both mixed *and* virtuous. Paradigmatic popular novels of the 1870s and 1880s, such as Edward Eggleston's *The Circuit Rider* (1873) and Lew Wallace's *Ben Hur* (1880), gave mythic status to the male hero who combined opposite qualities—gentleness and pugnaciousness, piety and ferocity—and yet who was not at all ironic. In the American pulpit, prominent evangelical Protestants such as Henry Ward Beecher, T. De Witt Talmage, and Dwight Moody were promoting a tender but tough liberal religion. If the oxymoronic stereotypes of antebellum radical democracy had been devastatingly subversive, those of post–Civil War popular culture offered a means of reconstructing the Conventional without sacrificing complexity. They permitted Melville to fabricate his "fighting peacemaker," who, despite his flaws and his commission of a capital crime, can be seriously presented as Christ-like.[53]

In addition to creating a mixed but genuinely virtuous hero, Melville is now able to depict a complex but thoroughly bad villain. John Claggart is a smart, civilized man who cuts "no ill figure" and yet who maliciously plots against Billy. With this combination of qualities, he might appear to be another of Melville's ambiguous criminals. But, like Billy, he is the deconstruction of the likable criminal. Just as Billy is flawed but wholly virtuous, so Claggart seems civil but is totally evil. Unlike Melville's earlier villains, he is not presented from the morally ambivalent vantage point of radical democracy. His wickedness does not signal a justified rebellion against a corrupt social system. It is an innate, perverse wickedness that gets the punishment it deserves. Melville tells us that Claggart has "something defective or abnormal in the constitution and blood." As a villain totally removed from the justified criminality of radical democracy, Claggart has nothing to do with prisons or with common criminals. Popular reformers of prisons and foes of capital punishment had long argued that criminals were unfairly treated by an unjust society; popular crime pamphlets had valorized heroic villainy. Melville had adopted these popular viewpoints in *The Confidence-Man* through his portrayal of the unfairly imprisoned Thomas Fry and the cleverly villainous confidence man. Fully aware of the troublesome ambiguities surrounding the popular view of criminals, Melville says Claggart has "a depravity according to nature" and emphasizes: "Not many are the examples of this depravity which the gallows and jail supply." By the end of the novel, we see the jail and the gallows supply a thoroughly pure criminal, Billy Budd, whose crime is justified because it is directed not against society but against a satanic individual.

In his hero and his villain, therefore, Melville imaginatively unravels the metaphysical knot he had tied in his earlier dealings with likable criminals. Complexity and subtlety are retained, but moral clarity is introduced. A similar unraveling characterizes his treatment of the oxymoronic oppressor. On the surface, Captain Vere seems the last in a line of captain figures who combine opposite qualities. He is kindly disposed toward Billy and yet he orders that Billy be hanged. But, unlike Captain Riga of *Redburn* or the wartime officers of *White-Jacket*, he is not morally inconsistent; unlike the "swearing good" Captain Ahab or John Paul Jones, he does not embody internal contradictions; unlike Benito Cereno, he is not impotent. He is civilized but not corrupt, firm but not cruel. He is pulled toward natural justice, which makes him want to pardon Billy, but he remains loyal to the law of civilization. He is no radical democrat who, in the interest of defending justified criminality, is prepared to break society's rules. Both he and Billy are conjoined in their devotion to the King and to each other. Billy dies blessing Captain Vere, who dies murmuring Billy's name.

Melville's restoration of thematic suggestiveness in *Billy Budd* is accompanied by a restoration of stylistic directness. In his major works of the 1850s, his imaginative engagement with paradoxical sensational characters had been mirrored in disrupted narrative patterns and, ultimately, in a subversion of the signifying process. In *The Confidence-Man* he delightedly records the playacting of a likable criminal whose words can never be trusted. He subverts clear meaning by his willing adoption of a paradoxical criminal stereotype. By resolving the ambiguities of this stereotype in *Billy Budd,* he reactivates the signifying process. To be sure, irony and conflict abound: Billy's flaws contribute to his downfall, Captain Vere must punish the one he loves, the official report of Billy's crime wrongly paints him as a wicked criminal, and so forth. But because Melville is no longer writing as a radical democrat about explosive cultural oxymorons, such ironies can now coexist with narrative sequentiality and stylistic directness.

The unraveling of paradoxical stereotypes brings about a reassertion of literary mimesis. It is significant that Captain Vere, the novel's regulating voice, is an intellectual who inclines to "books treating of actual men and events" such as history and biography.[54] Vere's reading preferences are reflected in Melville's factual, descriptive style. From the first sentence of the preface—"In the time before steamships, or then more than now . . ."—we are in a narrative world of historical periods and verities, one in which all signs are presumed to be readable. We are light-years distant from the circumlocutions and disorienting ellipses of *The Confidence-Man,* which is an April Fools' joke on the Conventional reader. Toward the end of *Billy Budd* Vere says: "With mankind, forms, measured forms are everything." With Melville, measured forms became a means of reasserting linguistic power. The former rebel against stylistic authority became, in the end, as loyal to the signifying process as Captain Vere was to the King. He concluded his career with a novel that, despite its ironies, could take seriously the kinds of affirmative images that in *The Confidence-Man* had been violently torn from referents. When the hanged Billy is described ascending toward the rosy cloud that looks like "the fleece of the Lamb of God seen in mystical vision"; when it is reported that, miraculously, he did not quiver while dying; when the sailors are said to treasure chips of his spar as though they were pieces of the cross, we know we have entered a realm of rejuvenated meaning. Through a leap of literary faith, Melville transforms the likable criminal, which earlier had led him toward indeterminacy, into a redemptive figure of almost divine significance.

Melville had come full circle in his treatment of sensational themes. In *Typee* and *Omoo* he had entered the ambiguous realm of Dark Adventure and then in *Mardi, Redburn,* and *White-Jacket* had explored the complex themes and paradoxical stereotypes associated with radical democracy. Haunted by the cultural ironies and paradoxes he had discovered in these early novels, he launched in *Moby-Dick* a full-scale philosophical quest through characters and symbols that fully embodied these paradoxes. In the later works of his major phase, from *Pierre* through *The Confidence-Man,* he retained a profound sense of radical-democrat ironies, but instead of trying to resolve them through overt philosophizing he increasingly dramatized them and pondered them implicitly instead of explicitly. The complete dramatization of radical-democrat ironies in *The Confidence-Man* led to a virtual suspension of clear philosophical meaning. In *Billy Budd* he restored the signifying power of philosophical and religious images by pondering ambiguity through characters who, despite superficial affinities with his earlier paradoxical figures, nevertheless were conceived outside of the twisted moral framework of radical democracy, which had earlier led Melville into a metaphysical maze. Although there is no simple resolution of philosophical or moral questions in *Billy Budd,* there is a perceptible restoration of human intensity and narrative sequentiality. This restoration is made possible by the fact that problematic stereotypes, especially the likable criminal, have been wrenched from the inverted value system of radical democracy and reconceived by an author intent upon renewing stylistic referentiality and genuineness of tragic emotion.

11

WHITMAN'S TRANSFIGURED SENSATIONALISM

WHITMAN has long been considered highly unusual among nineteenth-century American writers in the frankness of his sexual themes, in his innovative use of free verse, and in the brash independence of his poetic voice. Whitman, however, saw his poem not as a rebellious gesture by an alienated genius but rather as an all-embracing record of nineteenth-century America by a democratic poet. He believed that the distinguishing feature of American writers was their deep affinity with the spirit and literary tastes of common people. In the 1855 preface to *Leaves of Grass* he stressed that the American poet fails if "he does not flood himself with the immediate age as with vast oceanic tides[,] . . . if he be not himself the age transfigured."[1] He understood that his poem was the natural successor to previous American writings. Since the ground was already "ploughed and manured," he wrote, he was free to produce a distinctly American poem that expanded upon the experimental themes and devices of previous native writers. Far from being a lonely rebel against his culture, he was a broad-ranging observer who made every effort to assimilate his culture's sensational themes and images and to reproduce them deliberately in sanitizing, transfiguring poetry.

Whitman the Radical Democrat

Whitman was keenly aware of sensational social texts such as penny newspapers and crime narratives, and he had a particular interest in the various kinds of adventure fiction. In his letter to Emerson on the foreground of *Leaves of Grass,* published as an appendix to the 1856 edition of the poem, he said he was powerfully influenced by "strong-flavored romances," by "low-priced flaring tales, adventures," and by popular newspapers of every variety.[2] Since youth he had been fascinated by reports of murders, shipwrecks, disasters, and other spicy topics in the popular press. He also had intimate knowledge of the highly wrought pamphlet novels of the day. In an 1846 editorial for the *Brooklyn Daily Eagle* he remarked upon the extraordinary popularity of the yellow-covered novels by Joseph Holt Ingraham and others, and in an 1858 article on "sensation tales" he emphasized that these "blood and thunder romances with alliterative titles and plots of startling interest" had "a power in the land, not without great significance."[3]

His attraction to sensational literature clearly influenced his own writing. Such early Whitman stories as "The Half-Breed" and "Richard Parker's Widow" (both 1845) are of the Dark Adventure variety, featuring bloody crime, insanity, and Indian warfare. He became the only antebellum poet to extensively incorporate sensational imagery in his major poems. Several commentators, including Emerson, compared *Leaves of Grass* to penny newspapers like the *New York Herald,* and for good reason: the poem is riddled with the kind of violent or shocking images that filled the penny press. The suicide sprawled "on the bloody floor of the bedroom"; the lunatic "carried at last to the asylum a confirmed case"; the amputated limb that "drops horribly into a pail"; the drowning of the beautiful swimmer; the sordid experiences of the opium eater and the prostitute; the constant references to diseased people and rotting corpses—these are typical images that made some regard *Leaves of Grass* as a kind of poetic penny paper reporting grimy aspects of American life.[4] The narrative adventure modes Whitman had experimented with in his early fiction also carried over into "Song of Myself." Sections 34–36 of the poem, describing a bloody battle in Texas and John Paul Jones's most famous naval skirmish, read like gory, action-packed Dark Adventure tales.

Whitman was not only attracted to the racy themes of the popular adventure writers; he was also a radical democrat who absorbed the combined jingoistic patriotism and stinging social criticism of the popular Subversives. As a liberal free-soil journalist during the 1840s, he spent most of his free time with artisans and activists. In an 1850 biographical sketch of Whitman, the editor James J. Brenton tersely identified him as follows: "Mr. Whitman is an ardent politician of the radical democratic school."[5] Whitman himself defined his poetic persona as a radical democrat. In one of his prose writings he said his poem was centered on "the relation between the (radical, democratic) Me" and the "Not Me, the whole of the material universe."[6] Radical democratic indeed: from the late 1840s onward, many of his views of American society bore striking similarities to those of popular radical democrats like Lippard and Thompson. Like them, he had a hyperbolic reverence for America's past heroes, whom he mythologized in several stories and poems. The sentimental patriotism that characterized popular works such as Lippard's *Legends of the American Revolution* and Joel Tyler Headley's *Washington and His Generals* was reflected in several early Whitman works. In his tale "The Last of the Sacred Army" (1842) Whitman pictures crowds of inspired spectators touching the garments of an old soldier who had fought with Washington. As editor of the *Brooklyn Daily Eagle* he wrote several anecdotes about the heroism and humanity of Washington that show him sharing the radical democrats' sentimental patriotism. His notebooks are scattered with ardent praise of America's Founding Fathers, the Declaration of Independence, and the Constitution. His major poems are also punctuated by the creative patriotism of the radical democrats. One thinks particularly of section 5 of "The Sleepers," in which he imagines the weeping Washington hugging and kissing his soldiers after the Battle of Brooklyn, and "Chants Democratic. 6," in which he demands that America's youth always remember the republican principles fought for by the heroes of the Revolution.

As was true with the other radical democrats, his patriotic reverence for national ideals was matched by a profound disappointment with the failure of these ideals in nineteenth-century America. Whitman echoed the subversive sentiments of the popular radical democrats when he wrote: "I can conceive of no better service in the United States, henceforth, by democrats of thorough and heart-felt faith, than boldly exposing the weaknesses, liabilities and infinite corruptions of democracy."[7] In several prose writings and throughout his journals he used the dark, scathing rhetoric of radical democracy to impugn the powerful and defend the oppressed. As he made clear in two of his major prose works, *The Eighteenth Presidency!* (1856) and *Democratic Vistas* (1871), he saw corruption everywhere in American public life. In this sense, he was every inch the radical democrat. America's rulers, he wrote in *The Eighteenth Presidency!* eat excrement and sit on cushions drenched with human blood; American public life is a wasteland of scheming politicians and callous materialists. In *Democratic Vistas* he argued that democracy had proved "an almost complete failure." American society, he generalized, is "cankered, crude, superstitious, and rotten."[8] Political life is "saturated in corruption, bribery, falsehood, maladministration." The cities reek with "robbery and scoundrelism," businessmen are no more than "speculators and vulgarians," and fashionable life is a parade of "flippancy, tepid amours, weak infidelism." He often uses unmasking imagery reminiscent of the popular radical democrats. Just as George Thompson in *New-York Life* has his hero peer at America through a "social kaleidoscope" and perceive massive chicanery and rottenness, so Whitman imagines in *Democratic Vistas* looking through a "moral microscope" in which American cities appear as "a sort of flat and dry Sahara . . . crowded with petty grotesques, malformations, phantoms, playing meaningless antics."

Whitman's militant poetic voice and shocking imagery stem largely from his belief that the social corruptions he perceived could be overcome only by passionate defiance. "Give us turbulence, give us excitement," he wrote, "give us the rage and disputes of hell, all this rather than this lethargy of death that spreads like a vapor of decaying corpses over our land."[9] Just as popular radical democrats used words as weapons to assault the social elite, so Whitman wrote in *Leaves of Grass*: "My call is the call of battle, I nourish active rebellion, / He going with me must be well arm'd."[10]

The radical-democrat concept of the justified criminal had special meaning for Whitman, who once called *Leaves of Grass* "a book for the criminal classes" because "the other people do not need a poet."[11] As a popular writer during the 1840s, he had learned about the Subversive stereotype of the justified criminal. His temperance novel *Franklin Evans* (1842) contains an ironic episode involving a poor man who is jailed simply for stealing bread, while the underhanded swindling of rich people is known to be protected by the law. Similarly, in his newspaper articles "A Dialogue" (1845) and "Hurrah for Hanging!" (1846) he stressed that by harshly punishing common criminals, society hypocritically overlooks the worse crimes of established citizens who cheat and defraud the poor. By the mid-1840s, so passionate had he become about the unfair treatment of criminals that he confessed in his notebook that he could not pass a respectable church without seeing "a ghastly gallows frame" and hearing the echo: "Strangle and kill in the name of God!"[12] His radical-democrat sympathy for criminals was a major element of his burgeoning poetic sensibility. In his earliest known jottings in free verse, in his notebook for 1847, he defined the American poet as one whose universal soul embraced not just heroes but murderers, thieves, and deformed people as well.[13] This identification with criminals explains his continual absorption into criminal personae throughout *Leaves of Grass*. When the "I" of the poem says he makes appointments with the wicked as much as with the righteous, when he calls himself the greatest traitor, when he temporarily becomes a handcuffed murderer awaiting execution or a fugitive slave shot down by pursuers, he is enacting poetically the radical democracy of antebellum popular culture.

His enthusiasm for the justified criminal led to the wholesale inversion of values represented by the militant poem "Respondez!" (1856), in which he imagines American society being ruled by all sorts of grotesques and outcasts, including the most notorious criminals. "Let judges and criminals be transposed!" he writes with radical-democrat glee; "let the prison-keepers be put in / prison! let those that were prisoners take the keys! (Say! why might / they not just as well be transposed?)"[14] So central was the justified criminal to his vision that when he cut "Respondez!" from sixty-eight lines to form the terse three-line poem "Transpositions" (1881), this line about criminals was one of the three retained. Another, significantly, was the line about "bawling" reformers discussed in Chapter 4. An acute observer of popular culture, he knew that immoral reform and justified criminality came from the same Subversive nexus in popular culture and that both served as excellent metonymies for the paradoxical values he championed.

Stylistically, Whitman projected this inversion of values in a brash prose-poetry that also owed much to the radical democrats and their literature. In part, his free-verse form was the outgrowth of the organic theory of poetry expounded by Emerson, who had famously declared in "The Poet" that "it is not metres, but a metre-making argument, that makes a poem."[15] Whitman also owed much to the British writer Martin Farquhar Tupper, whose free-verse poem *Proverbial Philosophy* (1838) sold nearly a million copies in the nineteenth century. But Whitman applied free verse in ways that neither the philosophical Emerson nor the decorous Tupper could have foreseen. The difference between Whitman and Tupper was evident even in reviews where the two were compared. One reviewer called Whitman "a wild Tupper of the West" and another said "as Tupper is to English Humdrum, so is Walt Whitman to the American Rowdy"—both were pointing up the unique savagery and working-class fervor that Whitman brought to free verse.[16]

Whereas Tupper restricted himself to genteel themes, Whitman adopted free verse in the spirit of an American Subversive trying to mock conventional literature through the introduction of explicit, rebellious images. The spirit of his poetry had been directly anticipated by the pioneering Subversive John Neal, who had announced in his novel *Randolph* (1825): "A great revolution is at hand.—*Prose will take precedence of poetry:* or rather *poetry* will disencumber itself of rhyme and measure; and talk in prose—with a sort of rhythm, I admit."[17] Neal stressed that it was the job of American writers, as part of a stylistic rebellion against foreign models, to do away with "the poetry of form, . . . of rhyme, measure, and cadence." The protest against poetic form became even more vehement in the 1840s, when radical-democrat novelists and journalists launched wholesale assaults on sentimental poets who purveyed what George Lippard called "Twaddle-dom" and "Lollypop-itude." The radical democrats had a special animus against rhymed verse, which they associated with the artificiality and constrictions of an effete literary establishment. At the same time, some Subversives achieved a kind of crude prose-poetry by introducing highly abbreviated prose paragraphs written in a passionate, throbbing rhythm aimed at giving vent to revolutionary passions. Notice, for instance, how the following paragraphs in Lippard's socialist novel *Adonai* (1851) have a pre-Whitmanesque flavor:

> And as they passed on along they beheld the faces of all nations. They saw the faces of all men that people the earth of God.
>
> Irishmen were there, raising their famine-wasted hands above their blasted foreheads.
>
> Frenchmen were there, kneeling on the earth, with their faces buried against the sand.
>
> Englishmen were there, carrying burdens on their backs, which bowed them to the dust.
>
> Russians were there in chains, with their eyes veiled even from the dim light.
>
> Hungarians were there, with their wasted faces covered with the blood of their murdered kindred.
>
> Romans were there, with the arms of every one tied behind his back to an Iron Cross which, sharp at the edges, cut the hands which it manacled.
>
> Negroes, Caffirs, Hindoos, Indians, the men of China, Japan, and the Islands of the sea—the men of Europe and the New World—these all were there, with their wives, their mothers, their sisters and their little ones.[18]

This poetic prose is not particularly artistic, but it bears comparison with Whitman's prose-poetry. Lippard's broadly international theme anticipates Whitman's "Salut au Monde!" and "Europe," poems which likewise extend sympathy to all oppressed peoples of the earth. Just as significantly, the stylistic features of Lippard's lines—the rhythmic repetitions, the catalogues, the panoramic sweep of vision, the emotional intensity—suggest that Whitman's poetry was part of a radical-democrat style.

Given the spirit of stylistic experimentation among the radical democrats, it is small wonder that Whitman's earliest known jottings in free verse were directly connected to his political writings in the radical-democrat vein. In the early 1840s, before he had taken up the free-soil cause in earnest, he had written many poems that were conventional both thematically and stylistically, possessing none of the stylistic rebelliousness that would become his trademark. It was only in the late 1840s, after his political passions about oppressed groups began to infiltrate his style, that he began to write in free verse. In his notebook for 1847 he scribbled several free-verse lines proclaiming himself the poet of slaves as well as masters, of women as well as men, of murderers and thieves as well as the virtuous, a poet that will "talk wildly" and act as "a Curse" on the world.[19] In typical Subversive fashion, Whitman here carries revolutionary politics to a flouting of stylistic conventions. His first published free-verse poems, which appeared in the *New York Tribune* and the *Evening Post* in 1850, corresponded with the general rage among liberals over the passage of the Fugitive Slave Law. These poems were filled with Gothicized rhetoric and scathing invective typical of the radical democrats: in "The Dough-Face Song" Whitman characterized his political foes as "Lice of Humanity" and "muck-worms"; in "Blood Money" he took the standard radical-democrat view of Jesus, who is said to be still sold by the Iscariots of the world; in "Resurgemus" he seems to borrow an image from the era's best-selling radical-democrat novel, Lippard's *The Quaker City,* when he imagines the ghosts of the oppressed rising up in revenge against the tyrants of the world—an image Lippard had used in describing Devil-Bug's apocalyptic dream of social revolution. Whitman thought so highly of "Resurgemus" that he later included it in *Leaves of Grass* (retitling it later: "Europe. The *72d and 73d Years of these States*"), where it remains as a testament to Whitman's deep debt to the revolutionary themes and stylistic flexibility of the radical democrats.

Not only were his free-verse experiments influenced by the popular Subversives; so were his rapid time-space shifts and his catalogues. We have seen that the stylistic strangeness that Tocqueville associated with democratic literature was particularly visible in the Subversives' irrational style, characterized by odd juxtapositions and radical disjunctions designed to shock the complacent reader. Whitman uses a version of this style throughout *Leaves of Grass.* He shifts time, place, and imagery with amazing rapidity. He outdoes even the most experimental popular novelists with his leaps into the past and the future, his jumping about between people, places, and things. The connection between this imagistic flexibility and the popular fictional style becomes clear when one looks at Whitman's early works and private writings. Whitman's earliest poems, like most poems of the period, were sequentially arranged verses developing a central theme. Only in his sensational fiction did he begin to experiment with the kind of time-space leaps that would characterize his major poetry. *Franklin Evans* (1842), his popular dark-temperance novel, is a free-flowing, episodic novel that moves in zigzag fashion between various disturbing scenes and images. Whitman's engagement with the irrational style of the sensational fictionists freed him from the constraints of narrative linearity and a uniform tone. It was the sensationalists' randomness and rapidity, tending toward what today is called automatic writing, that Whitman tried to capture in his notebook entry titled "Directions for Story Writing," in which he gave himself these instructions: *"Haste along* (Don't stop so long to think)—*write quick. Strongly lined and colored. . . . Dash off chapters at random,* and then fit them in afterward. *A strong beginning to arouse curiosity. . . .* Plenty of incident—Dialogues."[20] If we ignore the references to plot and dialogue, these instructions could be taken as a fair recipe for the imagistic experimentation of *Leaves of Grass*. Even the title of Whitman's poem has a connection with popular literature. Authors of American sensational novels were often called "feuilletonists" because many of them were adapting the *roman feuilleton*, or the episodic newspaper serial novel developed by French writers like George Sand and Eugène Sue. Whitman found this word suggestive. In an 1855 newspaper article he defined "Feulliton" [*sic*] as "little leaf."[21] His major poem, of course, would be a series of little "leaves." In the 1850s several writers in Whitman's circle, including Henry Clapp and Ada Clare, were producing what they called "literary feuilletons," and Whitman himself was placed squarely in the realm of the other authors when the *Brooklyn Standard* in 1860 noted that at Pfaff's beer hall "assemble the ablest Feuilletonists of the great city," including Walt Whitman.[22]

While Whitman profited from the irrational style, he was also influenced by a more realistic, reportorial style that emerged in some radical-democrat journalism and fiction of the late 1840s. Nightmarishly irrational passages appear side by side with more realistic ones in novels like Lippard's *New York: Its Upper Ten and Lower Million* or Henri Foster's *Ellen Grafton*. While the popular Subversives often rapidly shifted tone and perspective, within individual scenes they often strove to reproduce the grimy details of what Lippard called "the ACTUAL of the large city."[23] The later Subversive fiction occupied a dynamic middle ground between "Monk" Lewis and Sinclair Lewis, between bygone Gothicism and forthcoming realism. The Subversive novelist's style often swung like a pendulum between the wildly irrational and the descriptively naturalistic.

This new realistic style was especially visible in the best-selling exposés by George Foster, including *New York in Slices* (1849), *Fifteen Minutes Around New York* (1854), and *New York Naked* (1854). Foster rightly called himself "the philosophic explorer of the lowest phenomena of life and human nature," a writer devoted to "gathering up the fragments, the refuse, of every-day life."[24] As a radical democrat, he had a bleak view of modern society, which he declared was "in utter and apparently hopeless confusion" because of widening class divisions.[25] We have seen that, at moments, Foster's sketches of modern city life were so gloomy that they looked forward to Melville's *Pierre* and "Bartleby, the Scrivener." But Foster showed that there was also a bright side to the radical democrats' outlook: the world appeared to be falling apart at the seams, but the writer was now more free than ever to put aside restrictive conventions and to revel in the sights, sounds, and smells of the world around him. Foster's popular *New York in Slices* and many similar works about American cities manifested simultaneously a stylistic splintering (reflected in the fragmentations of the irrational style) and a democratization of vision, an instinct to embrace what Foster called "the actual consistency, color and dimensions" of perceived reality. When Foster described a city street as "one of the most absolutely democratic places in the world,"[26] when he wrote a chapter called "A General Dash at the Ferries" about rushing crowds and panoramic bay views, when he used catalogue rhetoric to describe burly workers, squalid prostitutes, dandyish theatergoers, he was lovingly recording the kinds of quotidian images that would have an undying fascination for Whitman.

In the decade before he wrote *Leaves of Grass* Whitman was part of the same bustling world of city journalism that produced Foster's realistic exposés and many like them. Foster's *New York in Slices,* which sold nearly 100,000 copies in pamphlet form, immediately spawned a host of imitations throughout the nation. In Foster's words, it was "adopted and imitated in all directions," and American publishers were suddenly issuing titles like *Hudson in Patches, Wisconsin in Chunks, Mississippi in Gobs,* "and all sorts of states, cities, and provinces, in all sorts of aliquot quantities."[27] Whitman seems to have taken special notice of one fragment collection, Sara Willis Parton's popular *Fern Leaves from Fanny's Port Folio* (1854), the title of which is thought to have struck a responsive chord in Whitman. Whether or not Whitman was directly influenced by Foster, Parton, or any other of the countless city realists, it can be safely said that a work called *Leaves of Grass* featuring fragmented, concrete catalogues of modern experience was hardly unusual in this publishing atmosphere, particularly since much of Whitman's own journalism was done in the spirit of the new realism. In several articles for the *Brooklyn Daily Eagle* Whitman had adopted this style. In "The Philosophy of Ferries" (1847) he took the typically bleak radical-democrat view of city life, describing frightening mobs rushing on and off a New York ferry, which Whitman says moves inexorably "like iron-willed destiny. Passionless and fixed . . ." Appalled by urban dehumanization, Whitman writes: "How it deadens one's sympathies, this living in a city!"[28] As with Foster and the others, this radical-democrat reportage had an affirmative side too, since Whitman's newspaper pieces often show him sensuously reveling in tangible aspects of perceived reality. Between 1855 and 1858, at precisely the moment he was issuing the early editions of *Leaves of Grass,* he published in popular periodicals like *Life Illustrated* several articles in the *New York in Slices* vein, filled with excited accounts of bustling sidewalks, gaslit theaters, gangs, shopgirls, and so on. Throughout these articles Whitman uses the realists' catalogue rhetoric, even when indulging in self-portraiture. The sidewalk frequenters he describes in "Street Yarn" (1856) include a "tall, large, rough-looking man" with a "coarse, sanguine expression" and a "careless, lounging gait. Walt Whitman, the sturdy, self-conscious microcosmic prose-poetical author of that incongruous hash of mud and gold—'Leaves of Grass.' "[29]

Leaves of Grass and the Cleansing of American Culture

Surveying the multitudinous influences on *Leaves of Grass,* we may well understand why Whitman emphasized that the literary ground was well "ploughed and manured" for him and that his poem could not be understood without a wide-ranging study of its cultural foreground. Despite his affinities with the adventure fictionists and the radical democrats, however, there is good reason why *Leaves of Grass* has survived while the other works have fallen from view. Whitman did not just *adopt* sensational themes and devices; he determinedly *transformed* them with the conscious aim of giving them a structure and a resonance that they lacked in their popular manifestations. Like Poe, he recoiled from the directionlessness of the uncontrolled irrational style. Like Hawthorne, he despised the moral neutrality of much sensational writing. In his poetry he strove to repair these deficiencies. He adopted the time-space shifts of the Subversives but gave them new structural unity through carefully regulated repetition and balanced rhythm. He adopted the realists' catalogues but ordered them in such a way that they communicated the dazzling variety of modern life but not the depressingly chaotic aspect it often assumed in the popular works.

Whitman knew well the stark realities perceived by the radical democrats. It was precisely his bleak vision of modern society that drove him to assert tyrannical artistic control over fragmented, fluid modern experience. As his notebooks and his political tracts make clear, he perceived a far deeper social malaise than the other radical democrats, one that called for a far more thoroughgoing literary solution than they were prepared to offer. Indeed, he believed that the popular sensational literature itself was a major part of America's problem. In *Democratic Vistas* he said that the American public was flooded with two kinds of popular literature, analogous to the opposing schools I have called Conventional and Subversive. On the one hand, there were the preciously sentimental genres, particularly popular poetry, that impelled Whitman to ask: "Do you call those genteel little creatures American poets?" On the other hand, there was the uncontrolled sensationalism of popular novels and newspapers, which Whitman said aimed only at satisfying "the sensational appetite for stimulus" with "seasoning hotter and more varied" than in any previous racy literature.[30] He stressed that America desperately needed a new kind of literature, one that would absorb the other kinds but introduce a genuineness, a moral depth, a firm artistry they lacked.

America would be rescued, Whitman believed, only by a race of "bards" who would register the multitudinous facets of modern life, link them together, and infuse into them a religiosity they had lost in the "dry and flat Sahara" of American society.[31] We have become so accustomed to regarding Whitman as a rebellious bohemian that we are apt to forget that he always thought of himself as a moral, religious poet trying to cleanse a dirty, immoral society. Many times he complained that America suffered from what he called "a hideous depletion, almost absence of [a] moral nature."[32] He believed the poet's role was to emphasize directness in response to universal hypocrisy, spirituality in response to arid materialism, interconnectedness in response to social fragmentation, and hearty individualism in response to the leveling effects of mass culture.

Prose-poetry seemed a particularly effective means of achieving these diverse goals. Whitman wished to record the dazzling diversity of American life but at the same time to proclaim an underlying unity. One of his principal means of accomplishing this task was the long catalogue (reflecting diversity) unified by repeated rhythm and sentence structure. Another was the imaginative leap into the past or the future, as in "Crossing Brooklyn Ferry." We should not be surprised that this affirmative poem is distant in spirit from his earlier journal piece, "The Philosophy of Ferries," in which the ferry was pictured as a passionless destiny and its passengers as heartless mobs. The fact is that, here as elsewhere in Whitman's poetry, intense negativity becomes the basis upon which Whitman constructs affirmative poetry. In "The Philosophy of Ferries" he had been the typical radical-democrat journalist gloomily recording the dehumanizing effects of modern city life. In "Crossing Brooklyn Ferry" he becomes the chastened but joyous poet willfully proclaiming humanity in the face of impersonality, nature in the face of technology, immortality in the face of annihilation. The poet's buoyancy is the reactive product of the journalist's cynicism. Without residual signs of negativity within the poem itself, "Crossing Brooklyn Ferry" would not be nearly as compelling as it is. Because Whitman manages to revel in nature's beauty while riding amidst urban crowds, because he can spite death by imagining future generations enjoying this beauty, because he confesses to wicked, murderous impulses along with loving ones, he establishes a rich medium between the simple pieties of the Conventional and the noxious ironies of the Subversive.

Much of Whitman's poetry can be viewed as the product of a creative mind forging affirmative alternatives to a society whose injustices loomed large in his radical-democrat imagination. At some moments, Whitman seems the stereotype of the radical democrat in his militant attacks on the social elite, his identification with criminals or other pariahs, his patriotic nostalgia for the Revolutionary past. Just as the popular radical democrats had divided the world into two classes, the oppressors and the oppressed, so Whitman could write in the original version of "The Sleepers":

> I have been wronged. . . . I am oppressed. . . .
> I hate him that oppresses me,
> I will either destroy him, or he shall release me.[33]

Just as the radical democrats ushered in a revolutionary rhetoric designed to unmask the ruling class, so he wrote: "Let others praise eminent men and hold up peace, I hold up agitation and conflict." Just as they used words as weapons, so he announced: "I know my words are weapons full of danger, full of death." Just as they used the justified-criminal stereotype to undermine aristocrats' pretensions to virtue, so his identification with criminals and outcasts sometimes led to an inversion of values, most notably in the poem "Respondez!," in which he says criminals and judges should exchange places, God should be proclaimed dead, only infidels should be countenanced, insanity should take charge of sanity, men and women should think only obscenely of each other, and so on for sixty-seven scathingly Subversive lines.

It might seem strange to find that in a poem like "Respondez!" everything that Whitman supposedly holds dear (morality, trust, genuineness, and so forth) is completely negated. But the intense negativity is in fact the substratum for intense affirmations. Whitman's ability to carry radical-democratic revolutionary rhetoric to new extremes is matched by his capacity to forge fresh poetic solutions. The universality of society's illness, as he sees it, leads him to seek universal remedies. His special insight was that popular literature was itself part of the problem. Unlike other radical democrats, he did not wish to revel in imaginings of secret corruption among the rich. He wanted to supplant the lurid social exposé with a new, sane poetry that absorbed all the rage of the radical democrats but also affirmed unity with nature, with death, with past and future generations. Subversive rhetoric was extremely valuable to him for clearing the air, for undercutting stale institutions. But he believed that, taken too far and pursued for its own ends, such rhetoric only worsened the fragmentation and amorality he perceived in American society. If corruption and commercialism had infected America's social elite, he argued, the sensationalists' efforts to expose this corruption led to a dangerous distancing from what he called the "primal sanities" of nature. The poet's job was one of cleansing and fusion; as he puts it in his poem "Song of the Exposition," it is "Not to repel or destroy so much as accept, fuse, rehabilitate."[34] In particular, Whitman wished to absorb all the images and themes of popular writers but reinterpret them in such a way that they were restored to the sane level of nature. In "Passage to India" he emphasizes that in the new American poetry "Nature and Man shall be disjoin'd and diffused no more, / The true son of God [i.e., the poet] shall absolutely fuse them."

In several of Whitman's best poems we see him incorporating radical-democrat negativity but willfully overcoming it by turning to universals such as nature, death, sleep, time, and so forth. His admission in "Crossing Brooklyn Ferry" that he has within himself elements of "the wolf, the snake, the hog" betrays an awareness of the inverted sensibility that in popular exposés gave rise to bestial characters like Devil-Bug and Asmodeus, just as his comment that social life is little more than role playing reveals his radical-democratic perception of human chicanery.[35] But, unlike the typical radical democrat, he refuses to revel gleefully in lurid examples of this perception. Through a dazzling leap of poetic faith, he turns instead to the lovely river and city scene, his deft description of which becomes his gift to the future generations he imagines enjoying the same scene. He similarly builds refreshing poetry upon radical-democratic negativity in "The Sleepers," in which he takes a typical Subversive viewpoint—the underlying similarity between criminals and supposedly respectable people—and, instead of dwelling on the cynical implications of this notion, stresses the beautifully equalizing effects of sleep. He lists disparate social types—the murderer, the judge, the onanist, the President—and says that in sleep "I swear they are averaged now—one is no better than the other."[36] His two best-known poems about the death of Abraham Lincoln, "O Captain! My Captain!" and "When Lilacs Last in the Dooryard Bloom'd," provide an intriguing contrast in sensational versus poetic responses to social tragedy. "O Captain! My Captain!" pictures Lincoln lying horribly dead on the deck of a ship he has safely conducted through storms; like a popular sensationalist, Whitman here emphasizes tragic irony through ghastly images of dripping blood and a cold corpse. In contrast, "When Lilacs Last in the Dooryard Bloom'd" shows Whitman seeking symbolic, universal anodynes to the pain caused by Lincoln's death, as Whitman rechannels his profound sorrow into the triad of nature symbols—the fallen western star, the caroling thrush, and the delicate sprig of lilac—that magnificently affirm the poet's rich, unifying aesthetic perception in the face of shattering grief.

Many poems in *Leaves of Grass* are regulated by this conscious strategy of taking disturbing, often shocking aspects of modern life and determinedly converting them into affirmations of the human spirit and the order of nature. This transfiguring strategy is visible even in the area for which Whitman has become notorious: his treatment of human sexuality. It is commonly thought that Whitman, America's great erotic poet, was daringly innovative among antebellum writers in his dealings with heterosexual and homosexual love. The fact is that, far from being alone in his treatment of sex, he was adopting and transforming sexual imagery from popular sensational writings. His treatment of sex had much in common with sensational popular culture. The voyeurism that prevailed in sensational novels governs many sexual images in *Leaves of Grass,* such as the woman who fantasizes about the twenty-eight nude bathers she sees frolicking in the nearby stream, or the image of a "man's body at auction" and a "woman's body at auction," or the exuberant catalogues of body parts.[37] Still, here as elsewhere Whitman adopts popular strategies only to transform them. Many sensational writers had used veil-lifting metaphors to justify their prurience: they often said they were boldly "lifting the veil" off social corruption, but in most cases this was a mere excuse to revel in the erotic results of this corruption, such as the exposure of a young woman's "snowy globes." In "Song of Myself" Whitman adopts the popular veil-lifting image, but notice how he changes its emphasis:

> Through me forbidden voices,
> Voices of sexes and lusts. . . . voices veiled and I remove
>   the veil,
> Voices indecent by me clarified and transfigured.[38]

"Clarified" and "transfigured" are the important words here: Whitman saw it as his task to clarify sexual themes that were repressed in conventional literature and trivialized in sensational literature; and he wished to transfigure these themes into something new by ridding them of both guilt and prurience. In an article entitled "A Memorandum at a Venture" he generalized that there were two popular ways of dealing with sexual impulses: "the first, the conventional one of good folks and good print everywhere, repressing any direct statement of them"; and, secondly, the "merely sensual voluptuousness" dwelt upon in sensational "erotic stories and talk." "The time seems to me to have arrived," he continued, "and

America to be the place, for a new departure—a third point of view." He went on to mention changes in science, in religion, in views of women that made nineteenth-century America particularly conducive to placing sexuality "in the demesne of poetry and sanity—as something not in itself gross or impure, but entirely consistent with the highest manhood and womanhood, and indispensable to both."[39]

If we look closely at Whitman's prose and poetry, we recognize that he was making every effort to cleanse sexual images that in American sensational fiction had been separated from genuine humanity and placed in the realm of prurience and perversity. Although he accepted the sensationalists' notion that American society was filled with corruption, he saw that the novelists' efforts to expose this corruption only exacerbated the problem. It is true, as we have seen, that by writing dark-reform and sensational works early in his career he had gained a moral expansiveness that allowed him to announce himself the poet of wickedness as well as of goodness. But he was not prepared to go to the amoral extreme of the sensationalists, who under the pretense of reform manufactured sex and violence to titillate the masses. In *Democratic Vistas* he stressed that it wasn't just the upper classes who were diseased: there was a prevailing lack of genuineness, morality, and true humanity on all levels of social life. And popular literature itself was a major cause of the nation's illness. Unlike the popular radical democrats, he did not move from disgust with society into a complete immersion in gore and pornography. Discussing the "current copious fields of print" that included romances and "the huge editions of the dailies and weeklies," he commented that literary success, particularly among novelists, was for writers who satisfy "the sensational appetite for stimulus." In popular fiction and plays he saw only "[t]he same endless thread of tangled and superlative love-story," more highly seasoned than any previous sensational literature.[40]

The love plot, Whitman believed, was at the very root of the problem of popular culture, for it was full of unhealthy distortions and perversions. We have seen that in Subversive fiction, which often exposed secret amours among the outwardly respectable, sex was treated as aberrant and furtive, characterized by treachery and manipulation instead of genuine feeling. To a large degree, Whitman's poetry was written in response to the perverse treatments of sex and criminality in popular sensational literature. His view of popular romances and newspapers as distressingly lurid and sensual runs through many of his private and public writings. He once wrote in his notebook: "In the plentiful feast of romance presented to us, all the novels, all the poems really dish up only one figure, various forms and preparations of only one plot, namely, a sickly, scrofulous, crude, amorousness." This plot pretends to describe love, he writes, "but this is not love" because it is not genuinely human.[41] Alarmed by the proliferating instances of the love plot in sensational fiction, he blasted such fiction in an 1857 newspaper article: "Who will underrate the influence of a loose popular literature in debauching the popular mind?"[42] He incorporated his protest against the love plot in *Leaves of Grass*, most directly in "Song of the Exposition," in which he writes:

> Away with old romance!
> Away with novels, plots and plays of foreign courts,
> Away with love-verses sugar'd in rhyme, the intrigues, amours of
>   idlers,
> Fitted for only banquets of the night where dancers to late music
>   slide,
> The unhealthy pleasures, extravagant dissipations of the few,
> With perfumes, heat and wine, beneath the dazzling chandeliers.[43]

In opposition to this sensational popular literature, he wanted to treat sex as natural and genuine, free of the hypocrisy and gamesmanship that filled sensational novels. He wrote in *Democratic Vistas* that the test of the great writer is "the absence in him of the idea of the covert, the lurid, the maleficent, the devil"—all of which Whitman saw in American sensational writings.[44] He thought America's illness was beyond political remedy; it was an illness, he wrote in his notebook, "in the blood," one that demanded a complete revolution in values and a return to the healthy *spirit* of democracy.[45] This spirit could be retrieved, he believed, only through a new generation of poets who absorbed their culture but at the same time purified it and transformed it into something better. Throughout *Leaves of Grass* he attempted to infuse meaning and earnestness into sensational images that he believed had contributed to the dissolution of America's moral fiber.

It is this purifying process that governs Whitman's treatment of sex. Alarmed by the bald prurience and inhuman deceitfulness of much popular writing, he made a conscious effort to restore sex to the level of naturalness, honesty, and genuine emotion. Given the ubiquity of sexual themes in popular sensational literature, he knew he could not avoid the topic altogether and still retain his stature as a fully representative poet who absorbed his culture. He therefore adopted sexual images and strategies of popular literature but tried to lift them out of the mire of crass sensationalism.

To counteract what he regarded as the perversity and inhumanity of the love plot, Whitman borrowed sanitizing images from modern sciences and from American religious and social movements that permitted redefinition of sexual mores on spiritual grounds. The most useful sciences for him were physiology and phrenology. The 1840s and 1850s produced several books on human physiology that brought a new objectivity to the exploration of human sexuality. Whitman had particularly high regard for two explicit but reasoned books on sex, Edward H. Dixon's *Woman and Her Diseases, from the Cradle to the Grave* and Lorenzo N. Fowler's *Marriage: Its Histories and Its Ceremonies.* As editor of the *Daily Eagle,* having previously indicted popular love novels as "unwholesome" trash filled with "vulgar coarseness," he pointed to books like Dixon's and Fowler's as illustrations of the proper method of approaching sex.[46] His comment on Dixon's volume showed that he viewed physiology as both liberating and properly restrained: "The verdant prudishness has passed way, which would be offended at any discussion—in the plain, comprehensive, and perfectly decorous style of this book—of the subject which it treats on."[47] Fowler's book, which contained extensive descriptions of the female anatomy, seemed equally valuable because of its factuality and naturalness: "Let any one bethink him a moment how rare is the sight of a well developed, healthy *naturally* beautiful woman: let him reflect how widely the customs of our artificial life, joined with ignorance of physiological facts, are increasing the rarity . . . and he will hardly dispute the necessity of such publications as this."

In *Leaves of Grass* Whitman tried to supplant the grotesque perversions of the love plot with the frank freedoms of physiology. In the 1855 preface to *Leaves of Grass* he decried literature "which distorts honest shapes or which creates unearthly beings" and wrote: "Exaggerations will be revenged in human physiology."[48] The first full passage on sex in "Song of Myself" shows him taking care to place his persona in the objective, clean realm of physiology, distant from the nasty arena of sensational sex:

> Welcome is every organ and attribute of me, and of any man
> hearty and clean,
> Not an inch nor a particle of an inch is vile, and none shall
> be less familiar than the rest.

Throughout his poetry, his explorations of sexual organs and passions are guided by his impulse to remove sex from the lurid indirections of the popular love plot. His sexual passages are more explicit and passionate but at the same time less scabrous than those in sensational literature. When in *Leaves of Grass* he writes: "Copulation is no more rank to me than death"; when he asserts: "Perfect and clean the genitals previously jetting, and perfect and clean the womb cohering"; when he lovingly records the private parts of men and women, he shows his interest in ushering sex from the coarsely sensational to the honestly physiological.[49] To make clear his scientific approach, in the 1867 edition of *Leaves of Grass* he added an introductory poem (retained in later editions) that contained the line: "Of physiology from top to toe I sing, / [. . .] the Form complete[.]" That his use of physiology was closely linked to his rejection of popular romances is made clear not only in the 1855 preface but also in the following passage from the 1860 poem "Says":

> I say the human shape or face is so great, it must never be made ridiculous; [. . .]
> And that exaggerations will be sternly revenged in your own physiology, and in other persons' physiology also;
> And that clean-shaped children can be jetted and conceived only where natural forms prevail in public, and the human face and form are never caricatured;
> And I say that genius need never more be turned to romances,
> (For facts properly told, how mean appear all romances.)

Here Whitman typically connects distortion and caricature with popular romances, while healthy sex and sane facts are celebrated in terms of physiology.

Of equal use to Whitman in combating the luridness of the love plot was phrenology. A friend and admirer of New York's leading phrenologists, Orson and Lorenzo Fowler, who made a reading of his skull in 1849, Whitman profited from the experimental recombinations of phrenology that American practitioners had introduced. So close was he in spirit to the Fowlers, whose many enterprises included a publishing business specializing in physiological and phrenological books, that they distributed the first edition of *Leaves of Grass* and published the second edition. For Whitman, phrenology provided another means of dealing with sex with combined candor and tact. In 1835 the leading phrenological theorist, George Combe, had underscored the naturalness of human sexuality when he had argued that two of the most powerful brain impulses were amativeness (sexual love between men and women) and adhesiveness (comradely affection between persons of the same sex). The Fowlers had advised that the amative and adhesive organs should be well exercised along with the rest of the body to maintain good health. Whitman recorded in his journal the Fowlers' advice, and he distributed phrenological terms throughout his writings. His preparatory jottings for "Song of Myself" showed him echoing the phrenologists' acceptance of sexuality to validate his poetic treatment of sex. He wrote confidently: "I know that amativeness is just as divine as spirituality—and this which I know I put freely in my poems."[50] Elsewhere he wrote that the underlying qualities of his poetry were "a powerful sense of physical perfection, size, health, strength and beauty, with great amativeness, adhesiveness . . ." In the 1855 preface to *Leaves of Grass* he included the phrenologist as one of "the lawgivers of poets" and tried to emphasize the scientific aspect of his poem by citing the phrenological concepts of amativeness, destructiveness, causality, and alimentativeness.[51] In his poetry, phrenological terms were a convenient means of deflecting criticism of potentially risqué passages. The addition of a phrenological term could lend scientific purity to bold passages. For instance, the manuscript draft of one line reads: "Not he whom I love, kissing me so long with his daily kiss . . ." To assure the reader he is talking about comradely rather than homosexual love, Whitman added a key word in the published version of this poem: "Not he, adhesive, kissing me so long with his daily kiss . . ."[52]

Whitman also profited from another antebellum phenomenon associated with sexuality: what I call sexual antinomianism, or the effort to redefine sexual norms according to religious or moral belief. This period was a particularly fertile one for sexual antinomians of various kinds: the Mormons, the Shakers, the Oneidan perfectionists, the Fourierists, the spiritualists, and the free-love advocates all introduced highly unconventional sexual codes based upon personal belief. These groups represented a broad range of sexual practices, from the Shakers' celibacy through the Mormons' polygamy and the Oneidans' pantagamy to the free-lovers' abolition of marriage. Varied as they were, the groups were linked by a conviction that sexual experimentation could go hand in hand with moral righteousness. All the groups wanted to repair perceived iniquities in the marriage relation and to establish sexual practices that were spiritual and rational. As iconoclastic as many of them were, they represented a massive cultural effort to restore morality and naturalness to relations between the sexes. They believed that in America these relations had become unequal or distorted and could be repaired only through creative, inspired sexual self-determination. In this sense, they were close in spirit to Whitman, who in *Democratic Vistas* complained of the "absence, or perhaps the singular abeyance, of moral conscientious fibre all through American society."[53] Relations between the sexes, he argued, were so twisted that real men and women could not be found. A prime function of poetry should be to instill "vigorous and clean manliness, religiousness" and to nurture "a strong and sweet Female Race, a race of perfect Mothers."

This brings up the much debated issue of Whitman's homosexuality. Despite some bold passages in the "Calamus" poems and despite his confessed affection for young men such as Peter Doyle and Harry Stafford, Whitman firmly denied that he was a homosexual. When the British author John Addington Symonds, after years of probing, asked point-blank about

Whitman's sexual status, Whitman replied that such questions "quite daze me," calling Symonds's remarks "morbid inferences which are disavowed by me and seem damnable."[54] Quite apart from whether or not Whitman was telling the truth, it should be noted that a primary reason heterosexual love does not have more prominence in *Leaves of Grass* is that Whitman above all wanted to avoid the deceit, the artificiality, the amorality that he associated with the heterosexual love plot of popular novels. The typical radical-democrat sensation novel portrayed upper-class hypocrites ensnaring and ruining women. Relations between the sexes had become a poisonous topic for the American writer, as Whitman recognized when he denounced "novels, plots" about "the intrigues, amours of idlers" and "extravagant dissipations of the few."[55] Since literary portrayals of male-female sexual relations were almost inevitably loaded with irony and double entendre, Whitman shifted emphasis away from courting and seduction to "adhesive" love between men and "amative" love between the sexes. This change of emphasis permitted him to include images of heterosexual love—procreation, parenting, the jetting of sperm into the womb—without straying into the false realm of the love plot, which he associated with hypocrisy and insincerity. Another means of avoiding the love plot was to emphasize adhesive love, or affection between men. Yet another was to use the spiritual language of the sexual antinomians to lend a sense of holiness and purity to sexual topics that in sensational literature were treated with pornographic prurience.

Without coming to a firm conclusion about Whitman's sexual preferences, we should keep in mind that in his poetry he was trying to avoid the pitfalls of the sensational love plot and accordingly deemphasized seduction scenes between men and women. As for the controversial "Calamus" poems, Whitman specified that these poems were meant to illustrate "adhesiveness, or manly love," which in the phrenological terms of the day was not associated with homosexuality.[56] Similarly, when he described in his journal his feelings toward Peter Doyle, he used the vocabulary of phrenology: "Depress the adhesive nature / It is in excess—making life a torment," and "Ah, this diseased, feverish disproportionate adhesiveness." These statements are a passionate expression of the need to control the brain's organ of adhesiveness by one who took phrenology quite seriously.

Throughout his poetry Whitman tries to overcome the iniquities of the love plot by mixing together images from physiology, phrenology, and sexual antinomianism. Sometimes he emphasized heterosexual love, sometimes comradely love—but above all he wished to present sex as a natural, unifying human impulse rather than the treacherous, divisive contest it became in the hands of the sensationalists. Witness the free fusion of images from various uplifting sexual schools in these characteristic lines in his poetry: "This is the female form, / A divine nimbus exhales from it from head to foot" ("I Sing the Body Electric"); "Perfect and / clean the genitals previously jetting, and perfect and / clean the womb cohering" ("The Sleepers"); "I announce adhesiveness, I say it shall be limitless, unloosen'd" ("So Long!"); "Prophetic joys of better, loftier love's ideals, the divine wife, the / sweet, eternal, perfect comrade" ("A Song of Joys"); "They shall report Nature, laws, physiology, and happiness, / . . . They shall be alimentive, amative, receptive" ("Mediums"); "I will make divine magnetic lands, / With the love of comrades, / With the life-long love of comrades" ("For You O Democracy").[57] In these Whitman poems, images from physiology (genitals cleanly jetting, female form) and phrenology (heterosexual amativeness, comradely adhesiveness) are fused by the kind of spiritualizing religious rhetoric that characterized sexual antinomianism ("divine nimbus," "prophetic joys," "the divine wife," "divine magnetic lands"). Whitman's creative fusion of various sexual schools ushers him into a broader poetic realm beyond any individual school. His oft-repeated declaration that the poet is the blender, the uniter, the arbiter of the diverse thus applies equally to the realm of sexuality as to other of his key themes.

Whitman's unifying imagination produced not only inventive combinations of popular sexual beliefs; it also engendered an unprecedented experimentation with fusions of sex and nature images. Since his overriding goal was to absorb his popular culture's shocking images but at the same time to purify them, he repeatedly used what might be termed *cleansing rhetoric*: that is, the yoking together of refreshing nature images and potentially scabrous sensational images in the effort to overcome prurient sexuality. Cleansing rhetoric dominates the famous opening sections of "Song of Myself." After the inviting opening section about the loafer's contemplation of a grass leaf, Whitman moves from a rejection of "Houses and rooms full of perfumes" through a cleansing line that fuses sex and nature images ("Echos, ripples, and buzzed whispers. . . . loveroot, / silkthread, crotch and vine") to a tentative sexual passage ("A few light kisses. . . . a few embraces. . . . a reaching / around of arms") to a completely cleansing picture of health in nature ("The feeling of health. . . . the full-noon trill. . . . the song / of me rising from bed and meeting the sun").[58] The rejection of perfumed houses and rooms seems to be part of Whitman's animus against lurid sensational fiction; he always associated such fiction with entrapment and artifice, as when in "Song of the Exposition" he denounced novels about "The unhealthy pleasures, extravagant dissipations of the few, / With perfumes, heat and wine, beneath the dazzling chandeliers."[59] In a sense, then, Whitman's famous embrace of nature was part of a dialectic involving a rejection of the love plot and an effort to place sexuality and other sensational themes on a purer level.

Cleansing rhetoric is so rife in *Leaves of Grass* that one is tempted to regard many erotic moments in the poem as intentional purifications of popular sexual images. Take, for example, the first long sex passage in "Song of Myself," describing the rich woman's erotic fantasy about the twenty-eight young men she sees bathing in a nearby stream. We have seen that women's sexual insatiability was a common theme among certain popular novelists, especially George Thompson. In the popular novels, however, nymphomania was always associated with perversity and duplicity, as is evidenced by such Thompson novels as *New-York Life*, in which rich women flock to a male doctor for "daily fingerings" of their vaginas, or *Venus in Boston*, in which society women fantasize about having hundreds of lovers, or *City Crimes*, in which a wealthy belle rejects the advances of her fiancé but has constant sexual intercourse with her Negro servant to satisfy her desire for "delicious amours which are *recherché* and unique."[60] To some degree, Whitman seems to be borrowing from the popular sensationalists in the woman's fantasy scene: like them, he stresses that the woman is wealthy, that her sexual thoughts about the men are secretive, and that she fantasizes not just about one but about many lovers. But here the similarities stop. Whitman adopts the voyeuristic eroticism of the popular sensationalists but revises it in ways that make it natural and redemptive rather than selfish or destructive. There is absolutely no seduction or manipulation involved in the scene of the woman viewing the bathers. Indeed, there is no sexual contact, since the bathers do not even see her staring at them. Voyeuristic fantasy is stripped of malice and is conveyed through refreshing, baptismal images of nature. The twenty-eight men, laughing and splashing in the water, are the picture of fun and health. Whitman suggests that the woman is masturbating as she observes them, but her rising orgasmic excitement is made beautiful and pure because it is adeptly fused with cleansing nature images:

> The young men float on their backs, their white bellies swell
>   to the sun. . . . they do not ask who seizes fast to them,
> They do not know who puffs and declines with pendant and
>   bending arch,
> They do not think whom they souse with spray.[61]

Not only does the carefree fun of the bathers preclude any sort of machination or intrigue, but the dazzling final image, in which the spray of the water is fused metaphorically with the spray of orgasm, weds the sexual act with innocent frolic in nature.

Another passage in "Song of Myself" in which Whitman typically fuses sexual and nature imagery is the one in which he temporarily imagines the earth as his lover:

> Press close barebosomed night! Press close magnetic
>   nourishing night!
> Night of the south winds! Night of the large few stars!
> Still nodding night! Mad naked summer night!
>
> Smile O voluptuous coolbreathed earth!
> Earth of the slumbering and liquid trees! [. . .]
> Smile, for your lover comes! [. . .]
>
> Thruster holding me tight and that I hold tight!
> We hurt each other as the bridegroom and the bride hurt
>   each other.

In this passage Whitman uses images that were common in his era's sensational writings, such as bare bosoms and voluptuousness, and converts them into lovely metaphors for his sensuous enjoyment of nature. He retains the erotic passion of the sensationalists but redirects this passion toward an affirmation of nature's ever-regenerative beauty. Instead of gloating lasciviously over a woman's "snowy globes," he hugs tight the "barebosomed night." Instead of smacking his lips over a voluptuous woman, he declares himself the lover of the "voluptuous coolbreathed earth." Instead of portraying sex as a violent game that thrives on sham marriages and broken homes, he makes sure to emphasize that his rapturous union with nature is a consecrated marriage in which the partners "hurt each other as the bridegroom and the bride hurt each other." As always in Whitman's poetry, sexual imagery is at once redirected toward the natural and carefully interspersed with cleansing rhetoric, here evidenced by phrases such as "magnetic nourishing night," "Still nodding night," and "Night of the large few stars."

This purifying fusion of sex and nature is equally evident in many other images in *Leaves of Grass,* such as the "Winds whose soft-tickling genitals rub against me" ("Song of Myself"), "the clasping and sweet-flesh'd day," "Bridegroom night of love" ("I Sing the Body Electric"), or "The mystic amorous night, [. . .] / The souse of my lover the sea, as I lie willing and naked" ("Spontaneous Me").[62] Kate Chopin would be so inspired by such lines that she quoted one of Whitman's cleansing passages in a short story and attempted her own inventive fusion of eroticism and nature in her novel *The Awakening.*

Whitman applies cleansing rhetoric not only to sexual themes but to many other sensational themes as well. Since he wanted to absorb all elements of his contemporary popular culture, even the most vile or grotesque, he regularly followed the strategy of introducing or following sensational images with affirmative, inspiriting ones. In section 3 of "Song of Myself" we are ready to accept the bold line "Welcome is every organ and attribute of me" because we have just read the spiritual assertion "Clear and sweet is my soul. . . . and clear and sweet is all / that is not my soul."[63] The disturbing line about the suicide sprawled on the bloody floor is preceded by a picture of a peacefully sleeping baby and romping children, and the mention of "Arrests of criminals, slights, adulterous offers made" is mollified by the lovely succeeding passages about a hay-filled barn, a sparkling clipper ship, and clam diggers gathered around a chowder kettle. The sheer rapidity of the shifts between variegated images itself has a cleansing effect, since the reader's attention is continually being diverted and pushed forward to a different sight, sound, or odor. It is therefore wrong to label Whitman an "erotic" or "radical" or "sensational" writer, just as it is wrong to label him a conventionally moral or religious one. His poetry is best understood as an arena for the confrontation of varied, sometimes contradictory cultural forces whose creative fusion is Whitman's poetic gift to a society he perceived as rotten and strife-ridden.

Sadly enough, the author who believed that America's only hope for salvation lay in its poets was hardly read by the mass readership of his day. Whitman had buoyantly concluded the 1855 preface by declaring: "The proof of a poet is that his country absorbs him as affectionately as he has absorbed his country."[64] The next year he exuberantly wrote Emerson that *Leaves of Grass* had brought together themes from all kinds of popular texts and soon would be selling more than twenty thousand copies a year. By the time he wrote his 1871 treatise, *Democratic Vistas,* the chastened Whitman conceded that his mass acceptance would come only with future generations. To the end of his life, he would be puzzled by his poem's lack of popularity. The common scholarly view that *Leaves of Grass* failed because it was too shocking for its day is almost a direct reversal of fact. The truth is that its sensational, explicit passages enabled it to have what little popularity it enjoyed. Whitman told his follower Traubel later in life that his poem sold well only on a few occasions when the law got after him and "stirred up a sort of indecent curiosity concerning my work."[65] The truth seems to be that by fusing disparate popular images Whitman alienated both readers of Conventional literature and sensation lovers who continued to demand the merely prurient and shocking. Whitman was in the painful position of Melville when he wrote *Moby-Dick*: he had produced a masterpiece of broad cultural representativeness that nevertheless was rejected by the culture that had produced it. Still, if Whitman sacrificed his contemporary readership, he ensured his enduring fame by cultivating new literary fruit on grounds that had been well ploughed and manured by others, particularly the sensationalists he knew so well.

Part Three

OTHER AMAZONS:
Women's Rights, Women's Wrongs, and the Literary Imagination

12

TYPES OF AMERICAN WOMANHOOD

Is there a gender-specific American literature?

This stimulating question has been raised by feminist criticism, which has provided provocative reconceptualizations of America's literary past. Feminist criticism of American literature is not a single enterprise but includes a variety of camps with differing goals and procedures. One camp has devoted itself to the rediscovery of forgotten women writers and the reinterpretation of popular literature by women. Another has focused closely on classic women's writing, especially the poetry of Emily Dickinson, with the aim of identifying a so-called *écriture féminine*, or inscription of gender difference in language. Yet another has concentrated on the treatment of women by male authors, particularly Hawthorne. Each approach has yielded valuable information and insights, but much remains to be done to recover the social and linguistic dimensions of nineteenth-century women's literature in the context of major and lesser authors of both sexes.

Discussion of American women's writing has suffered from a widespread miscomprehension of antebellum women's culture and popular literature. The standard view is that between 1800 and 1860 America was flooded with novels and poetry volumes, written mainly by women for women, that tended to be sentimental and socially conservative. This literature, so that argument goes, reinforced the so-called cult of domesticity (also purveyed in etiquette books and tracts), which taught American women the value of gentle virtues such as piety, purity, and passivity. It also sanctified woman's role as nurturing mother during a period of rapid industrialization when economic production shifted from the home to the male-dominated world of the factory and the office. By stressing woman's motherly role, popular literature validated a widening gap between distinct male and female spheres. Some critics claim that this literature degenerated into bathos and narcissism; they argue that it was a "feminized," mawkish literature that set the stage for the literary rebellions of such tough-minded authors as Margaret Fuller, Nathaniel Hawthorne, and Herman Melville.[1] Others argue that popular women's literature was a more positive force: even though it emphasized woman's domestic and religious roles, it illustrated her "sentimental power" and therefore was a document of ennoblement rather than degradation.[2] Most critics see Emily Dickinson as something of an anomaly among antebellum women writers. She is thought to have had several affinities with classic American iconoclasts such as Anne Bradstreet or Adrienne Rich but few with the popular women writers of her own day.

My research suggests that this standard view is misleading and simplistic. From a quantitative standpoint, it overestimates the popularity of women's literature. The claim that women's fiction began as a relatively sparse genre and then by midcentury assumed dominance of the popular scene has no basis. The reverse, in fact, was true: the only time that female-authored American volumes had anything close to a numerical parity with male-authored ones was during the earliest stage of American fiction, between 1784 and 1810, when 41 percent of all volumes were written by women and 44 percent by men (the remaining volumes were published anonymously). By the 1830–60 period the proportion of female-authored volumes had fallen to 23 percent, while the proportion of male volumes had risen to 57 percent. These statistics reveal a notable drop in the proportion of volumes written by women. It should also be noted that the sentimental-domestic fiction that is thought to have conquered the popular market actually ran a distant second to more sensational genres. For the whole 1774–1860 period, the proportion of highly wrought, adventurous volumes written by American authors was about 57 percent, while the proportion of sentimental or religious volumes was only 22 percent. Also, the idea that there was a single kind of fiction that can be absolutely designated as "women's fiction" is inaccurate. Several male authors, such as Timothy Shay Arthur and Charles J. Peterson, were among the most prolific authors of sentimental-domestic fiction, while certain women writers, such as E. D. E. N. Southworth and Mary A. Denison, produced lurid sensational literature. There was, in short, no single kind of literature written solely by either sex. Moreover, debates about women's issues were confined to neither kind of popular literature: they were as apt to occur in sensational literature as in domestic fiction.

If popular women's literature has been misjudged quantitatively, it has been undervalued from a literary standpoint. There has been neglect of the dazzling diversity of female character types in antebellum literature. Some of these types were indeed conservative, underscoring woman's domestic function, but passivity was rarely praised, and American writers were uniquely bold in fashioning alternative women characters representing a variety of protofeminist or feminist views, ranging from anger against exploitative males to revolutionary assertions of women's rights. Significant connections between popular literature and the ascendant women's rights movement have been overlooked. It was during the antebellum period that the world's first women's rights conventions were held—beginning with the famous convention at Seneca Falls, New York, in 1848—and, as will be seen, several demands of the suffragists grew directly from popular culture and fed back into it. Also, there was an important cross-fertilization between popular women writers and familiar authors like Fuller, Hawthorne, and Melville. As for Emily Dickinson, her tortured, elliptical poetry was far more than the anguished record of one trapped woman's private struggles. It can be profitably viewed as the highest product of a rich literary moment, roughly between 1855 and 1865, that I call the American Women's Renaissance.

In April 1873 a writer for the progressive New York newspaper *The Golden Age* pointed to America's women novelists and poets as evidence that "there are many ways of advocating a reform." Women's rights lecturers are perhaps "the noblest Romans of us all," the essayist noted, but the strength of America's female authors demonstrated that "there are other true Amazons, even if less Amazonian."[3] It is these other Amazons that are the focus of this section.

Literature and the Diversification of Women's Roles

A far more diverse range of female stereotypes was established in antebellum popular literature than has been recognized. Not totally adequate is one critic's generalization that popular literature centered on "the timid exploits of innumerable pale and pious heroines" or other critics' perception of powerful mother figures and female redeemers.[4] The term I assign to the affirmative, pious heroine of sentimental-domestic fiction is the moral exemplar. In some of her manifestations, the American moral exemplar was gentle, but more often she was notably spunky and active, especially when compared with her counterparts in British and Continental fiction. In some works she became so bold as to fight, explore, command, or shoot just like a man, creating an androgynous stereotype I call the adventure feminist. While the moral exemplar and the adventure feminist represented affirmations of woman's power, the figure of the woman victim (the brutalized drunkard's wife or the seduced and abandoned woman) embodied dark "women's wrongs" and manifested a variety of emotions, from torpid gloom to rebellious rage. Another character type, the working woman, was similarly a victim of male exploitation who was variously depicted as depressed, stoical, or revolutionary. When women's issues were taken up by radical-democrat novelists, two iconoclastic figures, what I term the feminist criminal and the sensual woman, appeared in a sizable body of pamphlet fiction. In time, the protofeminist assumptions behind several of these character types became fully politicized, as leading suffragists expanded upon issues that had been debated for years in popular culture. By the 1850s the women's rights movement was producing fiction of its own, adopting all previous character types and adding a new militant figure, the feminist exemplar, who openly demanded political rights for women.

The numerous character types, reflecting a broad range of aggressions and fantasies within American women, proliferated and diversified to such a degree that by the 1850s there was a great complexity in perceptions of women's roles. This complexity had important literary ramifications: it prepared the way for Hawthorne's complex women characters; it produced a new kind of women's literature, called by Samuel Bowles "the literature of misery," that was haunted and fragmented;[5] and it lay behind the universal themes and shifting personae of Emily Dickinson's poetry.

Surveying the remarkable variety of female character types in American literature, the prominent British feminist Emily Faithfull confessed in 1884: "I feel more and more bewildered as I try to think which should be taken as strictly typical." But, like many others, Faithfull did come up with a central type she called "the American woman," who she said was a rich compound of independence, sweetness, intelligence, generosity—quite different, Faithfull stressed, from the passive, retiring heroine that typified British and Continental fiction.[6] American feminists similarly viewed the typical foreign heroine as too weak. American novelists who imported British heroines into their texts were firmly chided. In an article entitled "The Typical Women of American Authors," published in the New York suffrage paper *The Revolution,* Emily E. Ford emphasized that Cooper's heroines were especially disappointing: "His ladies are not in the least American, but simply wooden portraits of what he supposes English gentlefolk." Ford was also disappointed by the heroines of Susan Warner, whose best-seller *The Wide, Wide World* Ford found full of sentimentality uncharacteristic of American womanhood. Ford cited Hilda of Hawthorne's *The Marble Faun,* Mary Scudder of Stowe's *The Minister's Wooing,* Rose Wentworth of Henry Ward Beecher's *Norwood,* and a few other bright

Ralph Waldo Emerson

Henry David Thoreau

Walt Whitman

Emily Dickinson

Herman Melville

Edgar Allan Poe

Nathaniel Hawthorne

THE MAJOR AUTHORS OF
THE AMERICAN RENAISSANCE

EDWARD THOMPSON ("FATHER") TAYLOR of Seaman's Bethel church in Boston. (Courtesy of American Antiquarian Society [hereafter called AAS])

JOHN BARTHOLOMEW GOUGH, the popular temperance orator, here pictured pointing in warning against receptacles filled with alcoholic beverages. (Courtesy of AAS)

THE DARK REFORM MODE, as
exemplified in this frontispiece to George
B. Cheever's popular temperance tale
Deacon Giles' Distillery (1835). Shown are
devils manufacturing alcohol that will
eventually doom its consumers.
(Courtesy of AAS)

WHALE CHASE SEQUENCES pictured in *The Doom of the Dolphin* (1848), ABOVE, and *Wharton the Whale-Killer!* (1848), BELOW, popular Romantic Adventure novels by Harry Halyard, who is mentioned in the prefatory "Extracts" to Melville's *Moby-Dick* (1851). (Courtesy of Harvard University Library)

GEORGE LIPPARD.
(Courtesy of the Historical
Society of Pennsylvania)

JOHN NEAL. (Courtesy of
the Maine Historical Society)

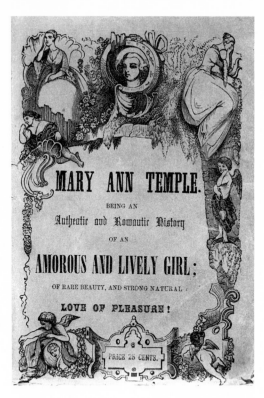

 EROTIC NOVEL,
Mary Ann Temple (c. 1849).
(Courtesy of AAS)

PAMPHLET CRIME
NOVEL, *The Female Land
Pirate* (1847). (Courtesy
of AAS)

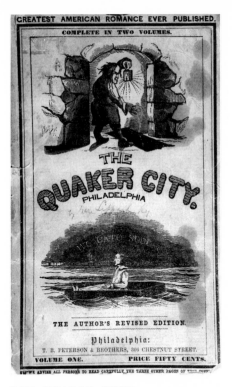

THE QUAKER CITY;
or, THE MONKS OF
MONK HALL (1845), the
sensational best-seller by
George Lippard. Pictured
on the cover page are
Devil-Bug in Monk Hall and
a vision from Devil-Bug's
dream of the cataclysmic
destruction of Philadelphia.
(Courtesy of AAS)

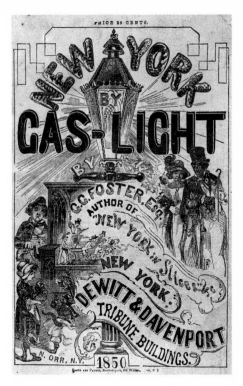

A POPULAR URBAN
EXPOSÉ, George G.
Foster's *New York by
Gas-Light* (1850).
(Courtesy of AAS)

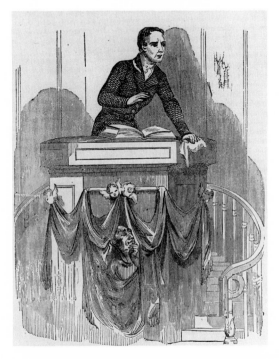

THE REVEREND RAKE,
as represented in George
Lippard's *The Memoirs of a
Preacher* (1849), in this
picture of a preacher
under whose pulpit lurks
a smirking devil figure.
(Courtesy of AAS)

THE ADVENTURE
FEMINIST, represented by
this portrait of an armed
woman soldier in the
pamphlet novel *The Female
Volunteer* (1851).
(Courtesy of AAS)

THE WORKING WOMAN,
exemplified by this woodcut
of a seamstress in George G.
Foster's *New York in Slices*
(1849). (Courtesy of AAS)

THE FEMINIST CRIMINAL, as represented in this frontispiece to
The Female Land Pirate (1847). (Courtesy of AAS)

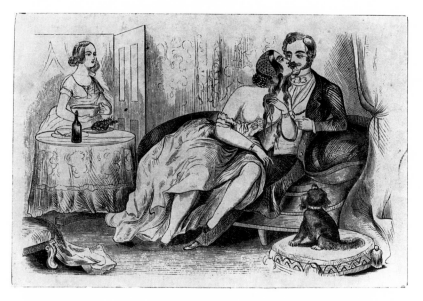

THE SENSUAL WOMAN. Shown in this frontispiece to George
Thompson's *Venus in Boston* (1849) is a bare-bosomed woman throwing
herself eagerly at her paramour while her maid and dog look on.
(Courtesy of Boston Public Library)

Alice Cary

Lillie Devereux Blake

Sara Willis Parton ("Fanny Fern")

Vol. 2.] "GO AHEAD!!" [No. 1.

THE CROCKETT ALMANAC
1839.

An Unexpected Ride on the Horns of an Elk. See Page 25.

Containing Adventures, Exploits, Sprees & Scrapes in the West, & Life and Manners in the Backwoods.

Nashville, Tennessee. Published by Ben Harding. See Page. 2

BESTIAL, GROTESQUE FRONTIER HUMOR, as represented by these illustrations from the popular Crockett almanacs. (Courtesy of AAS)

The Skeleton of Zebulon Kitchen.

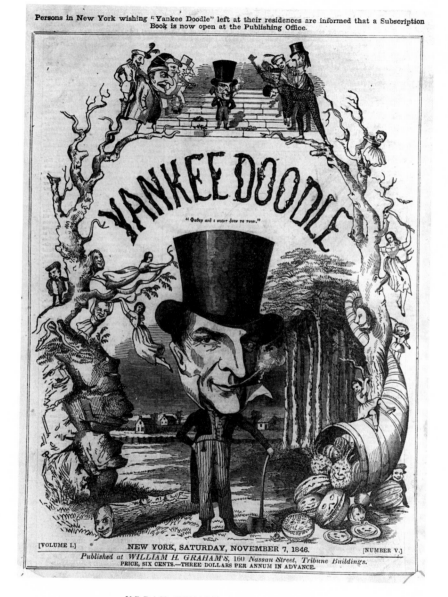

URBAN HUMOR PERIODICAL,
the *Yankee-Doodle.* (Courtesy of AAS)

"COMING EVENTS CAST THEIR SHADOWS BEFORE."

[President Pierce—" Another Insult to the American Flag!] Patience is no longer a Virtue. I must put a stop to this."

DARK HUMOR OF THE 1850S, stimulated by fear of the approaching Civil War. ABOVE: cartoon, from *The Lantern,* shows a glowering President Franklin Pierce about to shoot a black man who is blowing smoke on the American flag; BELOW: from *The New York Picayune,* depicting the many social evils flowing from the Pandora's box of slavery. (First picture courtesy of AAS; second courtesy of the New-York Historical Society)

SENATOR DOUGLAS OPENING PANDORA'S BOX.

heroines as examples of "New England girls" who "stand on their own feet, well planted, and maintain their poise, whatever wind may blow[.]"[7]

These comparisons are not altogether fair to foreign writers: one has only to think of the novels of Charlotte Brontë and George Sand to preclude any absolute generalization that American heroines had a corner on sturdiness. Still, twentieth-century scholarship confirms the thesis of Faithfull and Ford that American heroines had special strength. In a thoroughgoing study of popular novels and magazine fiction written in mid-nineteenth-century England, Margaret Dalzeil has found that the most common British heroine was the "lovely imbecile" inherited from eighteenth-century didactic fiction. This character was fragile, unathletic, vaguely religious, dependent on men. Dalzeil writes: *"Except by some American writers,* whose stories appear pretty frequently in certain periodicals at this date, it was taken for granted that women were inferior to men in all really important mental and moral qualities" [italics added]. The exception is important: Dalzeil finds that American heroines were tougher than their British counterparts in nearly all respects. This included a mind for business. The typical British heroine was incapable of business and fared badly when thrown on her own resources. If she worked, it was usually as a governess. Dalzeil notes that "when in penny periodicals we occasionally do find a heroine living by her own exertions and getting along tolerably well, the story is *almost invariably of American origin.* In England the heroine finds it almost impossible to achieve any sort of economic security" [italics added].[8]

Why was the American heroine more Amazonian than her foreign cousins? To begin with, the combined forces of Protestantism and democracy enabled American women to be more independent and morally self-controlling than those in more structured or aristocratic societies. Tocqueville wrote that in Europe women "almost think it a privilege to appear futile, weak, and timid. The women of America never lay claim to rights of that sort." The principal social and religious forces behind the American woman are summed up in Tocqueville's statement: "In the United States, Protestant teaching is combined with a very free constitution and a very democratic society, and in no other country is a girl left so soon or so completely to look after herself."[9] Tocqueville noted that the fluidity of economic fortunes in America and the exigencies of expansion into the Western frontier were other factors contributing to womanly strength. For Margaret Fuller, American women were naturally freer to develop themselves because of their democratic heritage and their lack of traditional restraints. "They have time to think," Fuller wrote, "and no traditions chain them, and few conventionalities compared with what must be met in other nations."[10] The superior sturdiness that several commentators have found in American heroines when compared with foreign ones was, therefore, at least partly a reflection of actual difference in women's roles within their respective cultures.

These cultural conditions gave rise to a popular kind of heroine, what I term the *moral exemplar*, who wielded great power within her fictional world. The moral exemplar enacted the spirit of Margaret Fuller's clarion pronouncement: "Women of my country. . . . If you have power, it is a moral power."[11] The power of the female exemplar grew in proportion to the decline of reliable male authority figures. One of the great effects of popular sensational literature, particularly the Subversive novels of the radical democrats, was to discredit formerly sacrosanct male figures such as clergymen, bankers, lawyers, and so forth. We have seen, for example, that by the 1840s it had become virtually impossible for an American novelist to portray a sympathetic clergyman figure because of the satirical stereotype of the reverend rake. The female moral exemplar became a chief means of reconstructing moral value in a world of devalued, amoral males. That is why many antebellum domestic novels, despite their religious intention, lack clergymen characters—the female moral exemplar takes the place of the male clergyman. This supplantation of male authority by the morally potent woman leads to straightforward declarations like this comment about a female exemplar in Warner's *The Wide, Wide World:* "I wish every minister was as good a one as you'd make."[12] Likewise, in Elizabeth Oakes Smith's popular story-poem "The Sinless Child" the heroine is called a "minister" who redeems a profane young man.[13]

In nineteenth-century American fiction there emerged two main types of moral exemplar: what may be called the angel (typified by gentle characters such as Eva St. Clare of *Uncle Tom's Cabin* and Beth March of *Little Women*) and the practical woman (such as the increasingly sturdy Gertrude Flint of Maria Cummins's *The Lamplighter*). While the angel and the practical woman both served as replacements for fallible male figures, each had a distinct function. The angel was rarely described in gender-specific fashion. Although she was a strong force for good, her strength did not have feminist implications. The angel's principal function was religious or philosophical. She first appeared as a rhetorical means of combating America's powerful tradition of scholastic Calvinism, particularly the absolutist theology of Jonathan Edwards and his followers. In the eyes of nineteenth-century liberal Protestants, Edwardsean Calvinism had cut off humanity from God by stressing God's terrifying inscrutability and man's utter worthlessness. The liberals wanted desperately to reestablish the link between the human and the otherworldly. One effective way to do so, they believed, was to depict an attractive heroine who either had many comforting celestial visions or who herself was referred to as an angel. The first important use of the angel was in Catharine Sedgwick's anti-Calvinist novel, *A New-England Tale* (1822), whose heroine, Jane Elton, is surrounded with angel imagery that provides a benign alternative to the harsh Calvinism of her protectress, Mrs. Wilson. Another dramatic example of the anti-Calvinist use of the angel occurs in Sylvester Judd's *Margaret* (1845), in which the heroine's many divine visions include a remarkable dream of Jesus and John, who embrace the loving Margaret while waving away several Calvinists who try to draw near. In effect, the angelic exemplar was introducing a sense of Roman Catholic ritualism to orthodox American Protestantism, which denied any mediation between the believer and God. This Roman Catholic function of the angel is visible in the scene in *Uncle Tom's Cabin* in which the dying Little Eva, who keeps a statue of Jesus on her bedroom shelf like a Catholic icon, hands out lockets of her hair as though they were the Word made flesh. The angelic exemplar was also useful in the struggle against skepticism and free thought. The nineteenth-century liberals saw free thought as a cheerless philosophy that denied the possibility of an afterlife. What better way to answer skepticism than through the angelic heroine who dies amidst a shower of celestial imagery? In *Uncle Tom's Cabin* Little Eva, with her beaming angel's face accented by the sculptured angel on her bed, is a rhetorical counterpoint to the arid cynicism of the freethinking Augustine St. Clare.

While the angelic exemplar was intended to present a benign version of God's relation with humanity, the practical exemplar was meant to show the efficacy of good works, particularly the good works of women. Phoebe Pyncheon of Hawthorne's *The House of the Seven Gables*—fresh, unconventional, active, orderly, efficient—typifies the practical exemplar. There were unique aspects of the American experience that gave the American practical exemplar a particular strength. If the angelic heroine embodied a gentle alternative to America's powerful orthodox religious tradition, the practical woman embodied a tougher alternative: her indomitable cheer flew in the face of Calvinistic gloom, and her persevering good works put the lie to Calvinistic predestination. The opposition between the hardworking, noble Hester Prynne and her dour Puritan persecutors was a version of a common contrast in American fiction between the practical exemplar and the Puritan Calvinist. In the three decades before the publication of *The Scarlet Letter,* this contrast had been made in various historical romances. Most of these works anticipate *The Scarlet Letter* by centering on the female exemplar, whose firmness and good works counteract the rigid intolerance of Puritan magistrates.

In several instances, the depiction of the practical exemplar in this Puritan fiction becomes gender-specific. There was, of course, the real-life example of Anne Hutchinson, the antinomian rebel mentioned in *The*

Scarlet Letter as a historical analogue to the independent Hester Prynne. Hawthorne was not alone in discovering protofeminist potential in Anne Hutchinson and in the fictional exemplar. Among the novelists who anticipated him in this regard was Harriet Vaughan Cheney, whose intriguing novel *A Peep at the Pilgrims* (1824) praised Hutchinson as "an uncommon woman; full of spirit and independence, with great strength of mind, and versatility of talents." Even more significantly, Cheney creates a heroine, Miriam Grey, whose exemplary fortitude gives rise to gender-specific comments such as this: "It is in circumstances of difficulty and distress . . . that the female character displays itself with particular loveliness; and man, with all his boasted firmness and superiority, will often sink beneath the weight of trials, which the unrepining constancy and unyielding patience of woman enables her to overcome."[14] A similar spirit informs another Puritan novel, Eliza Buckminster Lee's *Delusion; or, The Witch of New England* (1840), which Lee says is meant "to show how circumstances may unfold the inward strength of a timid woman, so that she may at last be willing to die rather than yield to the delusion that would have preserved her life."[15] Even more clearly gender-specific is Lee's depiction of Naomi Worthington in her later Puritan novel, *Naomi; or, Boston Two Hundred Years Ago* (1848). Naomi, an antinomian rebel who helps rescue a Quaker woman from Puritan persecution, "possessed a courageous, almost lion-hearted independence in the cause of humanity," proving that "women have often succeeded in enterprises so dangerous or delicate that men have shrunk from attempting them."[16] Hawthorne's contrast between the sturdy Hester Prynne and the cowering Arthur Dimmesdale thus drew directly off a common woman-man contrast in American fiction.

But Hawthorne need not have looked to previous Puritan fiction to learn the superior strength of the American practical exemplar. It was commonly agreed among antebellum Americans that woman was gifted with a peculiar capacity to endure misfortune. Even those who emphasized woman's domestic role pointed to the onerous burdens that the American homemaker bore with ease. In 1839 an essayist for the *Advocate of Moral Reform* wrote: "The truth is, the duties of women require as much promptitude in action, firmness of principle, and concentration of purpose, as those of men." Above all, the essayist emphasized, the homemaker must avoid "a morbid sentimentality, a vacillating weakness."[17] A relatively conservative magazine, the *Ladies' Repository,* actually sounded protofeminist when it asserted that the American woman was gifted with "a peculiar *power of endurance.* . . . She bears with meek composure what drives man to despair," and in the home she acquires a sovereignty more absolute than that of any monarch.[18]

Numerous domestic novelists, from Sarah Savage through Louisa Jane

Hall to Susan Warner and Maria Cummins, agreed that marriage was perhaps the culmination of a woman's life but that both before and during marriage the American woman must practice fortitude and moral power. In Louisa Hall's *Alfred* (1836) a woman's moral guidance of an erring brother is described as an Amazonian feat: "Other women have done great deeds,—they have fortified citadels, and led armies, and commanded empires. . . . Is it then more difficult, more daring, for one to attempt to mould a human heart?"[19] It was in the popular domestic novel that the practical exemplar came into her own. The two great domestic best-sellers of the 1850s, Warner's *The Wide, Wide World* and Cummins's *The Lamplighter,* are women's bildungsromans that trace the steady growth of heroines toward self-dependence. Cummins's Gertrude Flint is particularly exemplary in this regard. Even as a young girl, she faces life "with the simplicity of a child, but a woman's firmness; with the stature of a child, but a woman's capacity; the earnestness of a child, but a woman's perseverance." After the death of her foster father, she learns "more and more the power of governing herself" until she gains "complete self-control."[20]

In some novels, the moral exemplar is so sturdy that she confronts severe physical perils and survives them dauntlessly, often by temporarily assuming a male guise. The bold heroine who assumed male roles I call the *adventure feminist.* The adventure feminist is an especially tough, active version of the moral exemplar. In twentieth-century popular culture, such figures have become commonplace, as evidenced by Wonder Woman, the Bionic Woman, Police Woman, and other popular Amazons. These modern superwomen are the descendants of a number of adventurous heroines in novels written between 1790 and 1860. Again, Margaret Fuller epitomized the American spirit of adventure feminism in her memorable line about women: "Let them be sea-captains, if you will."[21] The first adventure feminist in American fiction was created by Charles Brockden Brown, a novelist whose heroines Fuller greatly admired. Martinette, the powerful warrior-woman of Brown's *Ormond* (1799), has slain men in two revolutions and holds distinctly progressive ideas about politics and sex roles.

A more distinctly American kind of adventure feminist appeared in nineteenth-century fiction about the frontier. Recently reprinted letters and diaries of nineteenth-century frontier women, along with the scholarship of Annette Kolodny and others, show that frontier life was a toughening experience known to American women alone. In the nineteenth century, a self-conscious awareness of this strengthening aspect of frontier life surfaced in popular newspapers and novels. One woman contributor to Garrison's *Liberator* wrote that American women "are just beginning to snuff the air of freedom, . . . and our thoughts and feelings have caught the spirit of the bounding deer and the dauntless prairie steed." In a jaunty reversal of sex roles, the essayist added: "Do not faint, dear reader, at the thought of woman shouldering the musket and starting for the frontier; for as men have taken the petticoats and crept into all the lighter employments, *we* must hold the plough and develop the physical, or the race will degenerate into monkeyism."[22]

The novelists who were most successful in registering this hardy frontier spirit among women were Catharine Maria Sedgwick, John Neal, James Fenimore Cooper, and William Gilmore Simms. In Sedgwick's *Hope Leslie* (1827) Magawisca, an Indian woman of shrewd intelligence and noble bearing, heroically saves the life of a white man about to be executed; she remains firm even though she loses an arm in the process. Equally bold is Hope Leslie herself, who intervenes to save an Indian woman from her white persecutors. Neal, a vocal supporter of the suffrage cause, depicted several strong heroines, such as one in *Logan* who, though bound to a tree by Indians and covered with the gore of battle, "neither fainted, nor flinched, nor wept!"[23] In the frontier novels of William Gilmore Simms, adventure feminism was the most common form of women's strength, combined occasionally with explicit advocacy of women's rights. Lucy Munroe, the daughter of a crime leader in Simms's *Guy Rivers,* is a tough, accomplished woman whose true grit is revealed when she confronts her murderous father with this protofeminist retort: "I am not the tame and cold creature that the world calls woman. . . . I can dare all, when my soul is in it, though the world sneer in scorn and contempt."[24] The wife of the trader Granger in Simms's *The Yemassee* has been so toughened by frontier life that she is called "a woman with a man's spirit."[25] Among her heroic feats is a remarkable sequence when she wields a hatchet in single-handed defense against a gang of Indians who invade her house.

Cooper's sensitive dramatizations of the frontier experience included several portraits of dauntless women. In his day and ours, Cooper has often been mocked for the passivity of his heroines, but this perception is only partly accurate. True, in his effort to accentuate the manliness of Natty Bumppo, Cooper does include many scenes enacting traditional sex roles, such as the famous sequence in *The Pioneers* in which Natty calmly shoots a panther just before it leaps upon two cringing women. The charge made by Lowell and others that Cooper's heroines are insipid perhaps applies to Cora and Alice Munroe in *The Last of the Mohicans* and the fair Spaniard Inez in *The Prairie*. But Cooper knew that the exigencies of frontier life elicited untapped powers in women. Mabel Dunham of *The Pathfinder,* for example, survives Indian ambuscades with nerves unshaken, remains fearless while caught on a lake during a storm, is ready to hold the blockhouse alone against an Indian siege, and shows a pioneer's aplomb when she embarks on a new life with a rough sailor. Ellen Wade of *The Prairie* is as independent and vigorous as Mabel, and even the weak-brained Hetty Hutter of *The Deerslayer* is "always intrepid in the cause of humanity," as seen in her bold rescue of Deerslayer as he is about to be tortured by the Indians.[26]

In the Dark Adventure pamphlet novels that emerged during the 1840s, the adventure feminist became a common figure. John K. Duer's *The Nautilus: A Collection of Select Nautical Tales and Sea Sketches* (1845) includes a scene in which a woman seizes a dagger and dies nobly after wounding a villain, whose injuries are called "lasting memorials to a woman's heroic spirit."[27] *The Life and Sufferings of Miss Emma Cole* (1844) is the first-person narrative of a woman who escapes a rich seducer, dons men's clothes, and embarks on a variety of sea adventures that include her heroic rescue of a drowning man. Another pamphlet novel, *The Remarkable Narrative of Cordelia Krats: or The Female Wanderer* (1846), features a woman disguised as a sailor who assures the captain she can take on the roughest jobs. Lorry Luff's *Antonita. The Female Contrabandista* (1848) depicts a bold woman chief of a pirate band who in the opening scene of the novel outdoes her male crew by scampering up her ship's rigging alone during a storm; through the rest of the novel she proves herself an intrepid warrior with firm control over her crew. Equally fearless are the heroines of three other pamphlet novels, Benjamin Barker's *The Female Spy* (1846), Maturin Murray Ballou's *Fanny Campbell, the Female Pirate Captain* (1845) and *The Outlaw; or, The Female Bandit* (c. 1850). Particularly intriguing is Ballou's Fanny Campbell, a pirate captain who helps the American cause during the Revolution by raiding British ships. Ballou underscores the adventure-feminist capabilities of his heroine by stressing that "Fanny could row a boat, shoot a panther, ride the wildest horse in the province, or do almost any brave and useful act."[28] The heroine of *The Female Volunteer* (1851) assumes soldier's clothing and fights in the Mexican War, surviving a series of calamities that would have spelled doom for more timid souls. A later pamphlet novel, *Dora, . . . The American Amazon* (1864), brings the adventure feminist into Civil War action, as the disguised heroine bravely rides through rebel lines and beats male soldiers in fights in a heroic effort to deliver military instructions to Union troops in the Deep South.

Having surveyed these different kinds of female exemplars, from the angel to the adventure feminist, it is useful to focus briefly on a single author—Catharine Sedgwick—whose exemplars are paradigmatic. Sedgwick's *Hope Leslie* (1827) and *The Linwoods* (1836) stand out as particularly sophisticated treatments of different kinds of exemplars. Sedgwick deserves more widespread appreciation than she has received. In her own day she drew warm accolades from Poe, who wrote: "All her stories are full of interest," especially *The Linwoods*.[29] She was the respected friend and neighbor of Melville when he was living in the Berkshires in the 1850s, and Hawthorne called her "our most truthful novelist."[30] She may well have been a literary role model for Emily Dickinson, because her novels gave Dickinson's father, in his words, "a conscious pride that women of our own country & our own state, too, are emulating not only the females but the men of England & France & Germany & Italy in works of literature."[31] Politically, Sedgwick was a moderate feminist in advance of her times. In 1839 she published an article, "The Rights of Women," in which she endorsed improved education and job opportunities for women, liberalized divorce laws, and equal property rights for husband and wife. All of these notions would later be adopted by the radical wing of the women's rights movement, led by Elizabeth Cady Stanton and Susan B. Anthony. But Sedgwick, who decried public agitation for women's rights, avoided outspoken feminist militancy and chose instead to advance progressive ideas indirectly through her fiction.

Sedgwick's *Hope Leslie* has, with some justification, been called the finest novel about Puritan times published before *The Scarlet Letter*.[32] Indeed, Sedgwick's novel is more skillfully crafted and more intriguing for the feminist critic than two other Puritan novels of the 1820s, Lydia Maria Child's *Hobomok* and Harriet Vaughan Cheney's *A Peep at the Pilgrims*. The difference between *The Scarlet Letter* and the earlier works was largely one of timing: writing his novel in 1849, Hawthorne could make use of several complex stereotypes—the reverend rake and other oxymoronic oppressors, the likable criminal, and several female character types—that had achieved cultural prominence only during the 1840s, two decades after Sedgwick and the others wrote their Puritan novels.

Given the relative sparseness of cultural materials available to her in the 1820s, Sedgwick produced a remarkable novel in *Hope Leslie*. Denounced in some circles as risqué and sacrilegious, the novel featured several unconventional characters and scenes: two feisty women, Hope Leslie and the Indian Magawisca, who brashly rebel against male authority; a miscegenation plot about a white woman's love affair with an Indian (a daring theme also treated in Child's *Hobomok*); and a rather perverse live-in relationship between a rake and a woman disguised as his manservant. These experimental themes are treated in a tightly woven narrative written with economy and elegance. Moreover, at key moments the language becomes gender-specific. Throughout the novel, the frontier experience of the early American settlers is used as a premise for demonstrating the strength and heroism of Hope Leslie and Magawisca, each of whom is at once a practical exemplar and an adventure feminist. The novel thus dramatizes one character's declaration that "our new country develops faculties that young ladies, in England, were unconscious of possessing."[33] At the same time, the timid, dependent Faith Leslie is satirized from the start. Female independence is prized above all, as in the following passage in which an old maid, Esther Downing, is used as a vehicle for Sedgwick's attack on the marriage institution: "She illustrated a truth, which, if more generally received by her own sex, might save a vast deal of misery: that marriage is not *essential* to the contentment, the dignity, or the happiness of woman." Here Sedgwick becomes the first American author in a line that would later include Margaret Fuller and Louisa May Alcott who used the old maid as a symbol of womanly self-reliance.

Sedgwick was also the first American novelist to treat conventional women with irony. She poked fun at old-fashioned women who accepted the domestic role with unthinking willingness. In *The Linwoods* she swiftly stabs one character, Mrs. Linwood, by calling her "a model of conjugal nonentity," one who believed "the husband rules by divine light."[34] Throughout *The Linwoods* she directs irony against the weak, sentimental Bessie Lee, who develops an unrequited crush on an aristocratic coxcomb and then drifts slowly into psychotic helplessness. While Bessie is a cautionary embodiment of the perils of dependent womanhood, Isabella Linwood is the chief of several female exemplars in the novel who demonstrate hardihood and heroism. Set in Revolutionary times, the novel gives a radical-democratic flavor to women's themes, for the colonists' rebellion nicely parallels the heroine's growing awareness of her powers as a woman. Both the nation and the heroine gain their independence. In the course of the novel we witness the interior growth of Isabella as she questions and then rejects the Tory sympathies of her father. By the end of the novel she and several other women have joined the colonial side. These women in fact control the war action, and their adventure feminism is rendered in gender-specific terms. When Isabella boldly argues with a British leader that he should release her jailed brother, "like many other great men, he yielded to a superior mind, albeit in the form of a woman." Even the release of Isabella's brother Herbert is governed by a woman: a black woman, Rose, boldly wrestles with a knife-wielding jailer and binds him up with his own garters. As she runs off with the freed prisoner, she sarcastically yells back that the jailer should always recall that he was "strung up there by a 'd—n *nigger*'—a nigger *woman*!" After this, four women, including Rose and Isabella, mastermind Herbert Linwood's final escape from the British by boat. Toughened by her war experiences, Isabella ends up in a marriage of equality with a man who loves her for "what most men like not at all—my love of freedom and independence of control." Having portrayed these spunky women, Sedgwick toward the end of the novel includes a digression calling for improved education for women so that they can contemplate serious topics like politics and business.

As Catharine Sedgwick's novels revealed, the female exemplar had definite protofeminist implications and needed only a highly sensitive, dedicated interpreter to be ushered into the realm of forthright political feminism. This interpreter arrived in the person of Margaret Fuller. To a large degree, Fuller's outlook can be summed up as moral exemplar feminism, influenced greatly by her reading in novels and popular etiquette books. Indeed, Fuller's pioneering volume, *Woman in the Nineteenth Century* (1844), contains several arguments that seem like explicitly feminist versions of Sedgwick's fictional themes. It is no surprise that in this work Fuller hails Sedgwick as "the clearest, wisest, kindliest who has yet used pen here on these subjects. . . . [Sedgwick] sets limits nowhere, and her objects and inducements are pure. . . . Her speech is moderate and sane, but never palsied by fear or skeptical caution."[35] Sedgwick's central point that a woman should seek equality in marriage and independence should she remain unmarried is fledged out by Fuller into an uncompromising demand for women's complete mental self-reliance. Just as Sedgwick had satirized women who idolize men, so Fuller wrote: "I wish woman to live *first* for God's sake. Then she will not make an imperfect man her god, and thus sink to idolatry." To underscore her argument for woman's self-dependence even in marriage, Fuller imaginatively differentiated between several kinds of marriages: the household partnership, with divided male and female roles; intellectual companionship, or mutual idolatry; and the highest form, "the religious, which may be expressed as pilgrimage toward a common shrine." Combining the philosophical individualism of her friend Emerson with moral exemplar feminism, Fuller asked women to devote themselves to truth, to the pondering of ultimate questions and the full development of inner capacities.

Despite the importance of *Woman in the Nineteenth Century* as an American feminist document, critics such as Perry Miller who have concentrated on Fuller to the exclusion of other women authors have missed a key element of antebellum woman's culture: the dark brooding and revolutionary rage that characterized many literary expressions of what was called "women's wrongs." The saneness and moderation that Margaret Fuller admired in Sedgwick's writings carried over into her own formal, sometimes stiff prose. Stylistically Fuller harks back to rational Enlightenment feminists and to certain women authors she praises, like Sedgwick and the Scotch didactic novelist Maria Edgeworth. Fuller endorses women's rights in non-sensational fashion, without using grotesque images or startling paradoxes. She is fully aware of woman's wrongs but shies away from detailing them. In a typical moment she brings up the topic of women victimized by dissolute men but skirts the issue by writing: "I would give instances that would startle the most vulgar and callous; but I will not. . . . If principles could be established, particulars would adjust themselves aright"[36] Throughout *Woman in the Nineteenth Century* she is so much more interested in principles than in startling particulars that topics which in other writers' hands would become the subjects of harrowing novels—the wretched working conditions of ill-paid seamstresses, the mistreatment of slave women, the social roots of prostitution, the bad lot of drunkards' wives— are mentioned by Fuller only in brief, passing sentences. Fuller's style reinforces her message: she views woman as "a harmonizer of the vehement elements," and so she avoids violence and quirkiness in her own prose.

The American Eve As Victim and Rebel

It was precisely the grim, workaday realities Fuller underplayed that became central in the *literature of women's wrongs*. Although Fuller was widely admired as a feminist theorist, she was roundly criticized in some quarters for her emphasis upon philosophy and self-culture, topics which seemed irrelevant to the thousands of working women who in the two decades after the Panic of 1837 were among the most cruelly exploited members of the American work force. The pioneering suffrage newspaper *The Una* ran a working-class serial novella, "Stray Leaves from a Seamstress's Journal," which said of Fuller: "[A] veil is between her and the rude, practical, every-day working world. She may write, and teach, and call herself a laborer, but this brings her only into distant relationship with us." Could Fuller look into seamstresses' comfortless homes and see them toiling fourteen to sixteen hours a day, the author continued, "she would then realize how difficult, how almost impossible is self-development, when there is only the means of keeping body and soul together."[37]

Moral exemplar feminism was not rejected wholesale by writers of women's wrongs literature. Rather, it was reinterpreted in light of a shattering perception of the American woman's economic and social degradation. The literature of women's wrongs emerged between 1832 and 1848 in dark writings connected with key reform movements—antiprostitution, antiseduction, temperance, antislavery—which frequently portrayed the miseries of American women, usually working-class women brutalized by dissolute men or exploited in the marketplace. Women's reform work and its accompanying literature produced a dialectical mixture of growing independence and perceived injustice, of women's consciousness of new power and also the perception of widespread suffering and exploitation. This dialectical combination of opposite sentiments, which burst forth in the mingled confidence and rage of the Seneca Falls convention, had been reflected in popular reform literature. This period witnessed the feminist coloration of two central stereotypical characters: the *working woman* (usually the starving seamstress but also other kinds of workers) and the *woman victim* (either the drunkard's wife, the slave woman, or the fallen woman). It was quickly seen that each of these characters could be featured either in gloomy narratives, illustrating women's wrongs, or in positive ones, demonstrating their strength and their assertiveness on behalf of rights for their sex. The gloomy narratives sometimes featured a wicked, violent character I call the *feminist criminal*, who enacted women's most savage fantasies by rampaging against mainstream society, especially the white males and conventional females who controlled that society. By the late 1840s, women's issues had infiltrated the sensational novels of the radical democrats, who created a militant inversion of sex roles and produced a complex character, the *sensual woman*, who spit in the face of Victorian propriety. By the time Hawthorne wrote *The Scarlet Letter*, the great variety of roles that would be recombined in his heroines had been firmly established in American literature.

The first of these characters in reform literature, the working woman, was a rich symbol of both the degradation and the stoical strength of American women in a time of great economic instability. Before 1855 the only jobs that were generally available to the mass of American women were the onerous, low-paying ones of sewing, factory work, teaching, and storekeeping. Women in the Eastern cities bore some of the heaviest burdens of industrialization. For example, in 1850 women constituted about a third of New York City's manufacturing work force, while the numbers in the apparel trades ranged from 43.5 percent to 62.7 percent.[38] By 1860 it was estimated that of the 48,900 operatives in American woolen factories, 41 percent were women; of the 118,920 workers in cotton factories, a staggering 62 percent were women.[39]

Behind these statistics lay many a tale of woe. Particularly wretched were seamstresses, who in the two decades after the Panic of 1837 often lived in squalid, crowded tenements and worked long hours for bare subsistence pay. During the 1830s and 1840s, the highest rate paid for a shirt was about fourteen cents, and few women could make more than ten shirts a week toiling twelve to fifteen hours a day. The situation was somewhat better for women factory workers, who at least were paid better than seamstresses, but the hours were long and the work was often monotonous and tiring. Melville had historical justification for using women factory operatives as symbols of deadening modern labor in "The Tartarus of Maids," in which the narrator is stunned by his first sight as he enters a New England paper factory: "At rows of blank-looking counters sat rows of blank-looking girls, with blank, white folders in their blank hands, all blankly folding blank paper."[40]

Melville wrote this in 1855; for more than two decades before this a body of American authors had depicted the trials and triumphs of American working women. "The Tartarus of Maids" was a literary culmination of a rich tradition of fiction about women factory workers. In the early going, this fiction was relatively benign. The heroine of Sarah Savage's *The Factory Girl* (1814) cheerfully does her job in a cotton factory in the happy knowledge that hard work is an ennobling activity for women. This emphasis upon the strengthening aspects of factory work would never be completely absent from popular literature—much of the poetry and fiction published in *The Lowell Offering, The Lady's Pearl,* and similar women's factory periodicals featured industrious women who persevered through loneliness and fatigue with the self-confidence of moral exemplars. This positive tone also characterizes certain stories in general magazines, such as Mrs. Joseph C. Neal's "The New England Factory Girl" (*Graham's Magazine,* 1848), which depicts a woman who pays for her brother's education by working for three years in a Lowell factory.

There is no doubt that such optimistic factory literature had some basis in truth. Factories were, after all, one of the easily available means for women to earn money and exercise the hardihood that was generally associated with active virtue. Still, one must be careful not to equate this cheerful literature with the realities of factory life. In the novel *Spiritual Vampirism* (1853) C. W. Webber emphasized that factory work damaged most women both physically and psychologically, leaving them with spinal diseases, bad lungs, twisted bodies, and crushed spirits. To fool the public, Webber has a character report, "[We] established a defensive literature, in the shape of dainty serials, announced as being edited by the factory girls themselves. These were filled with sentimental effusions, written principally to order, outside the factory, the general burden of which consisted in poetico-rural pictures of the joys brought home by the factory-girl, to some father or bedridden grand-papa."[41] This is a bit tendentious. *The Lowell Offering* and other factory periodicals at least represented a fervent effort among factory women to use their minds creatively and independently. Still, Webber seems to have been right in suggesting that these periodicals were less interesting as actual representations of factory women's lives than as willful meliorations of a generally dreary reality.

A more realistic literature of factory life appeared as early as 1834 with the publication of a pamphlet poem entitled *The Aristocrat and Trades Union Advocate, A Colloquial Poem . . . By a Working Woman of Boston.* This is not only America's first major antifactory poem but also one of the earliest pieces of trade-union imaginative literature published in America. It is also an early example of scathing radical-democrat rhetoric, as the author vents her rage against complacent aristocrats and stresses that American women are the special victims of the industrial age. Throughout the poem she complains that America's upper classes have become arrogant and corrupt, while the tide toward trade unions among working women and men is irresistible. "The simple ringing of a fact'ry bell," she writes, "To some men's ears is Freedom's funeral knell."[42] By the 1840s, when women and children constituted nearly two-thirds of the factory work force, such radical-democrat images had gained a new stridency. Ariel I. Cummings's novel *The Factory Girl* (1847), which depicts a young factory woman's struggles to retain strength and self-respect as she works to put her brother through college, contains several anticapitalist diatribes, such as:

> Horrid mockery of the equal rights of humanity! Vile lordlings! who would fain compromise the rights of fellow-beings to pamper pride! What think ye? Were ye born on other soil than that where *Freedom* was purchased at the point of the bayonet and the cannon's mouth, and the doctrine of *"equal rights,"* sealed with blood, ye need not blush so deeply with shame! But *here,* shame on the vile being who would fain raise an aristocracy to curse the land! The wrongs of *Factory Girls* shall not always sleep forgotten, and the instrument of high-handed monopoly go unchecked![43]

Walt Whitman, whose radical-democrat views were a principal basis for his egalitarian poetry, was so stirred by the report of a woman who had spent four decades as a factory worker that he wrote in the *Brooklyn Daily Eagle*: "Forty years of work in a cotton mill! in the close air, and deafened by the rumbling of machinery, and the freeness of the limbs all cramped by the restraint!"[44] The popular novelist George Lippard wrote a moving story, "The Sisterhood of the Green Veil" (1849), in which he described factory women as "that patient and gentle Sisterhood, whose order of worship has but one word for its litany, Toil, Toil, Toil; whose Convent is a Factory; whose way of life is darker and drearier than that of any Nun in the most severe of Catholic Convents."[45]

In antifactory literature the hardships of women workers were perhaps somewhat exaggerated, but in literature about seamstresses the reality was, if anything, worse than even the most lurid exposé fiction could make it. By all accounts, the plight of American seamstresses was miserable indeed. One of the reasons a talented novelist like Catharine Sedgwick missed true literary greatness was that she did not perceive the deep wrongs committed against her sex in the urban marketplace. In *Home* (1836) Sedgwick presents an idealized picture of a happy, hardworking seamstress earning good wages through diligence and cheer. Sedgwick even pauses to indict those who were agitating for higher pay for seamstresses. Such complacency can be attributed to Sedgwick's attempt, here as elsewhere, to underscore the sturdiness of her moral exemplar. But such idealization belied a reality that was darker than the upper-middle-class, rural-based Sedgwick could perceive. In the mid-1830s, at the time Sedgwick was denouncing those who called for higher wages, the typical city seamstress was earning a mere $2.00 a week, of which between $1.00 and $1.50 had to be paid for room and board, leaving very little money for clothing and emergencies. The situation actually worsened during the decade after the Panic of 1837, for seamstresses, deprived of the modest union support they had gained in the 1830s, were suddenly left to struggle alone in a wolfish environment of uncertain pay and fierce competition.

There emerged a seamstress literature that often became gender-specific in its language. On the one hand, this literature provided a new means of illustrating the special toughness and nobility of the moral exemplar when faced with seemingly insuperable misfortune. The typical seamstress novel featured a determined heroine who proudly eked out a meager living in the face of exploitation by heartless male employers and continual attempts at seduction by licentious roués. This was the premise of William B. English's *Gertrude Howard, the Maid of Humble Life* (1843), which tells of a poor but strongly virtuous seamstress who supports her family and resists tempting offers from wealthy men who offer money in return for sexual favors. In Charles Burdett's *The Elliott Family; or, The Trials of New-York Seamstresses* (1847), a similar plot leads to the protofeminist statement: "If there is a specimen of perfect sublimity on earth, it is the proud assertion of true female dignity, . . . [when] woman, amid the crush of hopes, the wreck of fortune, rises superior, yea amid the very ruins of happiness, to her misfortune, noble and dignified, erect, and stands in lonely majesty, bidding defiance to the crashing storm, before which *man,* self styled creation's Lord and King may droop—and fall—and die!"[46] The literary historian cannot help but muse that Hawthorne had good reason for making Hester Prynne (who herself stands in lonely majesty while her man droops and dies) a seamstress.

Whereas Hawthorne gave his heroine an aura of literary and social cohesiveness, several popular writers depicted the wrongs of seamstresses with unprecedented realism. There was a gloomy underside to seamstress literature. Despite the affirmative tone of the above quotation from Burdett's *The Elliott Family,* the novel is actually a harrowing work designed, as Burdett says in the preface, "to show the public the utter inadequacy of the compensation paid for female labor" and to expose "the most outrageous frauds and impositions practiced upon the seamstresses."[47] In the novel, although religious faith gives strength and hope to three indigent seamstresses, the widow Mrs. Elliott and her daughters Laura and Clara, there is no escape from the overwhelming forces of exploitation and poverty, and in the end all three family members die wretchedly. The fraudulent male characters include one employer who collects goods from seamstresses for almost nothing on the pretense that he's training them but fires them without pay and another who rents an upper floor, puts seamstresses to work there on the promise of a fair salary, and later flees with their produce without having paid them. A similarly bleak atmosphere governs *Edna Etheril, the Boston Seamstress* (1847) by the prolific popular novelist Mary Andrews Denison, who demands rhetorically: "Answer ye merchant tailors; ye traffickers in human life; are there not many more of our fair daughters, doomed daily to toil in want and wo over the six cent shirt?"[48] The indefatigable George Lippard registered the miseries of starving Philadelphia seamstresses in his radical-democrat story "Jesus and the Poor" (1848), and Walt Whitman, in an 1847 *Daily Eagle* article entitled "The Sewing Women of Brooklyn and New York," lamented "the miserably low rate of wages paid for women's work."[49]

When the tailoresses' cause was taken up by the women's rights movement in the 1850s, both the heroism and the gloom of seamstresses were brought together in fiction like the unfinished serial novella "Stray Leaves from a Seamstress's Journal" (1853–54), which ran in *The Una*, the monthly edited by the prominent suffragist Paulina Wright Davis. In this powerful novella, the narrator, Lucy Vernon, undertakes sewing to support two sisters and a sick mother, buoyed by a healthy resolve epitomized in her declaration: "It is only weakness that is incurable. Weakness is *the* only sin."[50] She manages to survive, but she not only endures unthinkable misery herself but also witnesses it in the lives of many other seamstresses, whose travails are described at length in interpolated tales. The rhetoric of this novella is gender-specific in a new revolutionary way. A tone of militant feminist anger has entered the seamstress genre, as the heroine cries:

> Are women to be born for this, to toil, shrivel, die and rot? Is there never to be an avenue opened for their powers? Is our country to grow old as Europe has with the same monotony, the same oppression for woman? My very soul is roused with indignation. The women of France once rose in rebellion. Their cry was "bread for our babes"; will the women of our country ever utter this cry as they gather in crowds from the attics, cellars, by lanes, and dark dens of filth and squalor? Alas! yes, if no change comes for the better, they too will thirst for the purple cup of revolution.

American women *did*, in effect, rise up in revolution, for in the 1850s, the same decade that this feisty feminist passage was written, tailoresses

and women factory workers were beginning to form unions and cooperatives that notably improved their lot. At the same time, more promising job
opportunities for women began to proliferate as a result of the unceasing
demands of women's rights leaders. Sexism and discrimination in the
workplace, of course, never disappeared, but slowly American women
gained entrance into previously sacrosanct male professions. The change
was reflected in some novels written by women's rights activists. In Laura
Curtis Bullard's remarkable (and hitherto overlooked) novel *Christine; or,
Woman's Trials and Triumphs* (1856) the heroine becomes first a famous
women's rights lecturer and then the founder of a women's employment
bureau that trains women for business, the law, medicine, and other
professions. In Lillie Devereux Blake's *Fettered for Life* (1874)—the most
comprehensive women's rights novel of the nineteenth century—the
wretchedness of seamstresses and factory operatives is contrasted with the
newfound confidence of the professional woman, represented in the novel
by the highly intelligent, uncompromisingly feminist doctor Cornelia
D'Arcy. Blake's novel reflects the fact that even though working-class
women still had a long way to go in redressing their economic wrongs,
improved education and job opportunities for women had already been
won by the American women's rights movement.

In addition to mirroring changes in the stereotype of the working
woman, Blake's emblematic novel also retained another long-standing
character type in popular reform literature—the *woman victim,* appearing
in the two forms of the drunkard's wife and the fallen woman. Blake's novel
contains a subplot about a working-class woman brutalized and finally
beaten to death by her drunken husband. In reference to such animalistic
male behavior, Dr. Cornelia D'Arcy, who has treated many women victims,
declares that "the record of what our sex has suffered from the other is a
long and bitter history that centuries of freedom and happiness can never
make us forget!"[51] Another subplot involves the abduction and attempted
seduction of the heroine by a licentious judge who joins a long line of
fictional Lovelaces borrowed initially from the Richardsonian seduction
novel but converted by American feminists into a political figure of male
chauvinism.

Both kinds of women victim, which are key stereotypes behind the
women's rights movement and behind certain major literary texts as well,
had first taken on gender-specific meaning in the reform literature of the
1830s and 1840s. Specifically, the drunkard's wife appeared in paradigmatic writings of the temperance movement, while the fallen woman
emerged in the literature of moral reform (by which was meant the fight
against prostitution and seduction). It should be noted how crucial these
reforms were to the emergence of the American women's rights move-

ment. From the 1830s onward, women were especially concerned with temperance since wives had no legal protection against drunken husbands. Too often true was the image in temperance literature of the husband who drank away his wages while his family went hungry at home. The two leading figures in the early suffrage movement, Susan B. Anthony and Elizabeth Cady Stanton, had begun primarily as temperance workers. So devoted was Anthony to the temperance cause that as late as 1851—three years after the Seneca Falls convention—she was still debating whether to devote herself to temperance or to women's rights. In the same year Stanton used temperance language when she called for relaxed divorce laws: "Let no woman remain in the relation of wife with a confirmed drunkard."[52]

The feminist applications for temperance reform discovered by the suffragists had in fact been implicit in the increasing sensational literature of temperance. We have seen that reform literature changed dramatically between 1820 and 1850, starting as a relatively hopeful genre emphasizing the remedies of vice but then becoming transformed into a more horrific genre featuring the grisly wages of vice. This change was reflected in the role of women characters in this literature. In early temperance stories like *Edmund and Margaret* and *The Lottery Ticket* (1822), the emphasis is on the successful efforts of the pious wife to save her erring husband. As increasing emphasis was placed on the unrelieved brutality of the husband, the wife's reformist efforts were rarely so easily successful. The wife character was often represented as the pitiable victim of male bestiality, a victim who became a particularly vivid emblem of women's wrongs and at the same time a kind of walking advertisement for the need for women's rights. As early as 1831 a feminist note had entered temperance literature, as evidenced by the pamphlet *Address to Females,* which demanded that laws should be changed to protect wives from drunken husbands; only then, writes the anonymous author, "shall woman attain her true rank, and no longer be the slave, but companion of man."[53] If one looks through a succession of popular temperance novels one sees a dreary catalogue of violence against women. In *The Catastrophe* (1833) a man in a drunken rage kills his wife with an ax. In Mary L. Fox's *The Ruined Deacon* (1834) a woman descends through skepticism and misanthropy to insanity as a result of her husband's habit—by the end, she has been reduced to a shrieking madwoman whose "rage was directed at her husband."[54] Another novel, *Letters from an Alms-House, on the Subject of Temperance* (1844), features a miserable woman reduced to beggary by a husband who constantly beat her and the children and finally fell to his death in a drunken stupor, leaving her hopeless and desperate. In *Autobiography of a Reformed Drunkard* (1845) the narrator has a horrid vision of drunkards' enormities against their wives:

"There was a man drawing his wife along by her hair. There was another with a club, driving a woman and children out of doors. There were a man and woman fighting with shovel and tongs. There was a man with an axe running after a woman, and another cutting his wife's throat with a carving knife."[55] John B. Gough, whose dramatic temperance lectures terrified thousands, including the young Walt Whitman, frequently acted out the domestic horrors created by drunkenness, such as a man laying his child on an open fire or clutching his wife's throat with a death grip.

These frightening tales of victimized drunkards' wives contributed to one of the most radical demands of the early women's rights movement: the call for laws that would facilitate divorce. When Elizabeth Cady Stanton declared that no woman should remain married to a drunkard, she shocked conservative women. In the late 1860s the American women's rights movement actually split apart because of the divorce question. The Boston wing of the movement, led by Lucy Stone, was alarmed at what it regarded as an attempt by Stanton's group in New York to subvert the marriage institution. The Bostonians formed an independent group devoted solely to gaining the vote for women, while the more radical New York group agitated not only for suffrage but for a whole range of social changes, including relaxed divorce laws. As progressive as Stanton seemed in her day, she was in fact taking to a natural conclusion the implicit message of dark-temperance fiction: the American woman needed some means of escaping the horrors of a degrading marriage.

Along with the drunkard's wife, there was concern for another type of woman victim—the slave woman—who was also destined to have significance for the women's rights movement. Lucretia Mott, Lucy Stone, and Angelina and Sarah Grimké were among the suffrage leaders whose roots were in the antislavery movement. In the famous feminist document *Letters on the Equality of the Sexes* (1837) Angelina Grimké focused on "the degradation of female slaves, and the licentiousness of the South."[56] She was referring to the practice of Southern slave owners to use their slave women as prostitutes, a practice made even more barbarous by the sadistic stripping and whipping of the women. This massive system of whoredom, Grimké pointed out, also affected the slave owners' wives, who had to live with men they knew were polluted by licentiousness. It became a commonplace in the North that women were the particular victims of the slave system. A marked feminist note had surfaced in abolitionist writings by the early 1840s, as evidenced by this passage in an article by Elizabeth Follen for *The Liberty Bell*: "Is it not natural that women should feel most for the sufferings and degradation of their own sex? And are not women the greatest sufferers from slavery?"[57] So closely associated did the extreme Garrisonian wing of the abolitionist movement become with the rising

women's rights cause that in 1840 a number of prominent reformers abandoned the antislavery cause because they thought it was straying toward
the "heresy" of women's rights. The escaped slave Frederick Douglass,
who became a leader in both abolitionism and women's rights, ardently
defended the Seneca Falls convention (at which he was vocally present)
and lampooned those who had left the antislavery cause in fear of "this
wicked idea" of women's rights.[58] One of the most memorable nineteenth-
century addresses on behalf of women's rights was delivered at an Akron,
Ohio, convention by the famous ex-slave Sojourner Truth. According to
one witness, Sojourner Truth's "almost Amazon form" towered majestically above the audience as she described her tough survival of slavery's
horrors, flexed her muscles defiantly, cracked jokes about white males, and
all the while repeated the rhetorical boast: "And a'n't I a woman?"[59] In
Sojourner Truth the ultimate woman victim became, through a sheer assertion of womanly pride, the ultimate adventure feminist.

The plight of the slave woman was vividly recounted in a small but
significant body of American fiction. The most powerful early fictionaliza-
tion of the slave woman's plight was Richard Hildreth's *The Slave: or Memoirs of Archy Moore* (1836), whose narrator is the son of a Virginia aristocrat
and his slave concubine. Though universally regarded as a man of piety
and honor, Archy's father was in fact a licentious tyrant who gave "a very
free indulgence to his amorous temperament among his numerous slaves,"
even to the extent of trying to seduce one of his own slave daughters.[60]
Throughout the novel the slave system is shown to be fatal to the marriage
institution, since at any moment a slave family could be disrupted by the
sale of one of its members. The character who embodies both the extreme
suffering and the noble sturdiness of the slave woman is Archy's wife,
Cassy, who endures whippings, near rapes, and forced separation from
loved ones with grim resolve.

When the slave woman character was adopted in women's rights fiction,
she displayed a new feminist fury. *L'eoline* (1855), a novella that ran serially
in Davis's periodical *Una,* featured a magnificent, strong aristocratic
woman courted by wealthy Southern men who discovers that her mother
had been a slave and her father a plantation owner. Although L'eoline at
first feels tainted by her Negro blood, she becomes proud of both her
blackness and her womanhood. She becomes fiercely vindictive against
Southern libertines who impregnate their slaves. Ironically, the people
who had always idolized the majestic L'eoline continue to do so, making
her burn inwardly with the knowledge that if they knew her true parentage
they would spurn her immediately. Continually approached by licentious
men, she develops a secret loathing for males that she sometimes expresses in gender-specific fashion. She therefore becomes a living protest

against the interlocking evils of slavery, racism, libertinism, and male oppression.

The broadening range of evils depicted in fiction about black women is also evidenced in Harriet Wilson's *Our Nig* (1859), which Henry Louis Gates has recently identified as the first novel published by a black person in America. As Gates points out, the uniqueness of this novel is that it protests against whites' racism in the North rather than slavery in the South. Wilson's heroine is not a slave woman but an indentured servant who, having been abandoned by her white mother after the death of her black father, was taken into a New England household where she is brutally maltreated. Gates, who claims that most antebellum novels were conventional affairs in which good triumphs and "everyone lives happily ever after," argues that *Our Nig* is special because of its rebellious themes and ambiguous ending.[61] Actually, though, the novel takes standard themes of popular Subversive fiction—deceitful authority figures, persecution of an oppressed character, the sufferings of a woman worker—and concentrates on a heroine who acts much like other nineteenth-century heroines, by turns weepy and resolute and in the end rebellious. Wilson's Frado is, like the typical heroine of women's wrongs fiction, at once horribly oppressed and stoically resolute. The originality of the novel lies in its occasional attacks on Northern racism, as seen in one character's rhetorical question: "Which would you rather have, a black heart in a white skin, or a white heart in a black one?"[62] Frado is a rich symbol of the woman victim, since she is exposed to exploitation in her successive jobs as a servant, a seamstress, a hatter, and at last a salesperson. By the end of the novel she has learned "to assert her rights when trampled on," as she is thrown on her own resources and left only with faith in herself.

The final woman victim character, the fallen woman, appeared mainly in the literature of moral reform. The issues surrounding the fallen woman were both economic and moral. The moral reformers claimed that prostitution was caused either by harsh economic conditions, which drove poor working women to the streets, or by the wiles of licentious men. In either case, a sympathetic view of the fallen woman emerged, since prostitution was said to be caused by outside forces and woman was viewed as the pitiable victim of an unjust society. In the 1830s there was great lobbying for tougher antiseduction laws, for the closing down of brothels, and for the establishment of halfway houses for reformed prostitutes. Moral reform newspapers were filled with early prototypes of Hester Prynne and Arthur Dimmesdale—that is, fallen women who were treated sympathetically while their secretly sinful male lovers were exposed to light. A major rationale behind reform efforts to aid "magdalens" was the view of prostitutes as pitiable victims of an unfair social system that tolerated male seducers but punished fallen women. In *New York by Gas-Light* (1850) George Foster summed up the general view when he wrote that prostitution "is invariably the result of man's individual villainy in seducing the pure being who trusts her destiny to his keeping—or of the monstrous crime of society which dooms its daughters to degradation, want, and misery, from which no virtuous effort of theirs can ever rescue them."[63] The prostitutes and female criminals that fill the sensational fiction of the 1840s are almost invariably portrayed as products of male duplicity or social injustice. One of George Thompson's fallen heroines typically says she would have taken on meaningful employment, "but society had built a wall I could not scale, and left no choice but sin or suicide."[64]

There was a special element of American moral reform that brought a feminist spirit to the exposure of male sinfulness. Like antislavery, the moral reform movement was a source of organizational power for women. In the early 1830s, when the great New York moral reformer John Mc-Dowall sank into infamy and then an early death after attacks from enemies, leadership in his New York Moral Reform Society and editorship of his reform newspaper were assumed by women. The women's accession to power was pronounced a sign of superior strength, as evidenced by this passage in the *Advocate of Moral Reform*: "*Man may* be overawed by persecution: but *woman never.* Ten thousand female hearts from Maine to Alabama, are pledged to each other in this work of reformation."[65] Among those active in moral reform were Susan B. Anthony, Lucretia Mott, and the Grimké sisters. Tocqueville captured the feminist quality of American moral reform when he noted that in Europe "our moral standards accord a strange immunity to man," while "the Americans know nothing of this unfair division of duties and rights. With them the seducer is as much dishonored as the victim."[66] The reason that militant suffragists emerged from moral reform ranks was that the effort to expose seducers had the effect of placing men and women on the same level. In this sense, the dramatic climax of *The Scarlet Letter,* in which Dimmesdale at last stands openly on the platform with his lover and child and confesses his complicity in sin, participates in the feminist equalization of the sexes that the moral reformers had initiated.

One outcome of the moral reformers' sympathy for fallen women was the featuring of seduced and abandoned heroines who retain their pride and dignity despite their sins. Hawthorne's sympathetic treatment of Hester Prynne actually had precedent in certain popular fiction about fallen women. Hawthorne, who kept a watchful eye on the popular press, may have seen a story entitled "The Magdalen," which appeared in 1833 in his hometown newspaper, the *Salem Gazette.* The story involves a seduced woman who, after a period as a prostitute, lives penitently in a solitary

"Magdalen Cottage" and finally dies a Christian. Like Hester Prynne, she is a pensive, noble woman who lives alone in a small cottage on the outskirts of a village and becomes venerated for her charitable work among the villagers.[67] An equally striking foreshadowing of *The Scarlet Letter* occurs in Sylvester Judd's popular novel *Margaret* (1845). One of the novel's subplots features a seduced and abandoned woman, Rose Elphiston, who has an illegitimate child and is punished for her sins by having "a significant red letter" sewn on her clothing.[68] Temperamentally Rose is not unlike Hester, for after her punishment she becomes a proud but skeptical woman. Just as the solitary Hester develops doubts about religion and social authority, so Rose becomes a wretched atheist for whom illicit love has been a passport to forbidden philosophical regions.

The moral reformers' sympathy with fallen women opened the way for the portrayal of two zestful characters—the *feminist criminal* and the *sensual woman*—who embodied the boldest, most rebellious fantasies of American women. The prominence of these two characters in sensational fiction of the 1840s puts the lie to the standard critical view that popular fiction featured only pure, gentle heroines. The fallen woman, we have seen, was in certain popular writings a cautionary figure intended to warn women against wily men and teach them noble endurance. But in many sensational novels the fallen woman became a fantasy figure of vindictive violence and unrestrained sexuality. It was taken for granted that woman, once seduced and released from the constrictions of female propriety, was capable of becoming more ferocious and more sexually aggressive than man. One crime pamphlet of the day contained the assertion that "a woman makes more rapid strides in the path which leadeth to destruction, when she has once set her foot in it, than a man";[69] another said similarly that "woman, by as much as in a virtuous state she is more pure and refined than man, when profligate sinks into a correspondent degree of depravity."[70] Poe's friend John Lofland summed up the feminist criminal when he wrote, in a story about a fallen woman, that "of all revenge, woman's is the most deadly, the most unrelenting when her affections have been trampled upon."[71]

The feminist criminal was the abandoned woman who avenges wrongs against her sex by waging war against society, especially against men and against proper women. The female rogue, of course, was not a new figure in literature. This character had been particularly prominent in the eighteenth-century British novel, as evidenced by well-known works such as *Moll Flanders, Roxanna, The Fortunate Transport,* and *Betty Ireland.* But in the radical-democrat fiction of the American 1840s the woman criminal took on a special ferocity and a gender-specific purpose she had not exhibited before. Like the figure of the likable criminal, the female rogue went through a sea change when reinterpreted by American writers who brought a new egalitarian sympathy for oppressed groups, in this case fallen women.

In sensational novels the seduced and abandoned woman was permitted to take militant revenge against what was perceived as the deceptiveness and tyranny of men. The period's most intriguing feminist criminals appeared in George Lippard's *The Quaker City* (1845) and Ned Buntline's *The G'hals of New York* (1850). It is understandable that these classic radical-democrat novels contained interesting heroines. The inverted value system of these novels, by which bold villainy is found preferable to sham virtue, gives rise to a reversal of female roles, as majestic but totally amoral women succeed in outsmarting men. Long-haired Bess of *The Quaker City* is a procuress who translates her hatred of a man who once abandoned her into a cool, manipulative rage against the male sex and against conventional females. Along with the gleefully wicked Devil-Bug, she supervises aristocrats' nightly seductions and debauchery in Monk Hall. A well-educated but unfortunate woman victimized by men's deceptions and society's discrimination against women, she inveigles innocent people into Monk Hall but, ironically, becomes a force for good when she helps Devil-Bug rescue two imperiled conventional women. In the topsy-turvy world of Subversive fiction, the fallen woman, sympathetically portrayed, is found to have more power and active virtue than the conventional moral exemplar. A similarly ironic reversal of women's roles occurs in Buntline's *The G'hals of New York*. Radical-democrat paradoxes so abound in this novel that a distinctly American ironic character, the confidence man, appears here for the first time in American fiction. As intriguing as is Buntline's genially malicious confidence man Joseph Skinkle, equally significant is the feminist criminal Constance Barton, who was taken as a mistress by a criminal on a promise of marriage and, after years of maltreatment, shrewdly plots his downfall. In Constance we see a keen woman triumph over an experienced libertine. A kind of confidence woman who uses intelligence and gamesmanship, she succeeds in outwitting her lover because, as Buntline explains, "hers was the clearer mind . . . trained and educated systematically, . . . she well knew how to take advantage of men's passions and weaknesses, and how to bend them to her purposes and will."[72] When she turns her lover in to the police, her words of denunciation have a feminist boldness: "You betrayed me, and knowing me a woman, absurdly imagined that I would tamely submit to the outrage and shame, and never dream of rising in my strength and avenging my lost honor and shame." As in the twisted world of *The Quaker City*, the fallen woman is rewarded with special power. Not only does Constance rescue two moral exemplars, whose conventional virtue is found less effective than her scheming vice, but in the end she is rewarded with wealth and a country seat on the Hudson, even though she has been living unmarried for years with an archcriminal.

The sensual woman was the other iconoclastic character that emerged from antebellum sympathy for the fallen woman. As discussed in Chapter 6, popular pamphlet fiction, especially sensational radical-democrat exposés of the 1840s and early 1850s, often featured sexually hungry heroines who put the lie to the standard image of nineteenth-century women as pure and passionless. In many sensational novels, depictions of fallen women became a pretext for exploring woman's strong sexual urges. In a number of novels of the 1840s, women are either willing partners or actual aggressors in the sex act. The secret sexual yearnings of apparently pure women was a favorite theme of the radical democrats, who wanted to reveal that the maligned fallen woman and the respected society woman were, after all, not at bottom terribly dissimilar. The hidden sexual yearnings of apparently virtuous women were a main preoccupation of George Lippard. In Lippard's *The Quaker City* the initially pure Mary Arlington falls victim not to her seducer's physical charms but rather to her gullible acceptance of his promise of their future domestic bliss together. Exposing the naïveté and blindness of the moral exemplar, Lippard writes of Mary: "She knew not that in her own organization, were hidden the sympathies of an animal as well as of an intellectual nature, that the blood in her veins only waited an opportunity to betray her, that in the very atmosphere of the holiest love of woman, crouched a sleeping fiend, who at the first whisperings of her wronger, would arise with hot breath and blood shot eyes, to wreak eternal ruin on her woman's honor."[73] As Mary listens to his idyllic fiction of a pious family life, she melts into an orgasmic ecstasy. Lippard is showing how excessive belief in the Conventional can be self-destructive, since the romantic Mary is led by her visions of a future "heaven on earth" to give herself to a man who in fact is arranging a sham wedding ceremony in order to possess her. If Mary Arlington embodies a pure woman's capacity to fall into sensuality, Dora Livingstone, the other main heroine of *The Quaker City*, embodies a sensual woman's ability to exploit sex for selfish ends. Perhaps America's most interesting fictional heroine before Hester Prynne, Dora is intellectual, tough, voluptuous, greedy, and deluded by visions of grandeur. She has married the old merchant Livingstone for his money and is now sleeping in Monk Hall with Algernon Fitz-Cowles, the confidence man who tells her he's an English lord who will bring her a title after they've killed her husband and fled to England. Dora is said to be "the perfect incarnation of the Sensual woman, who combines the beauty of the mere animal, with an intellect strong and resolute in its every purpose." To accomplish her nefarious goals, she not only sleeps with Fitz-Cowles but promises sexual favors to an old lover, Luke Harvey, and even to the monstrous Devil-Bug. As the embodiment of woman's sexual power, she is always described in the voyeur style. Applied indiscriminately to the virtuous Mary and the conniving Dora, the voyeur style serves to demolish simple moral categories and bring attention to woman's sexuality, which becomes alluring and all-powerful in the author's erotic imagination.

Woman's powerful sexual drive was a favorite theme of the popular pamphlet novelist George Thompson, whose fiction often features nymphomaniacs who demand constant variety. His variations upon this theme are revealed in a brief review of some of his typical heroines: in *City Crimes* (1848) a wealthy woman refuses to sleep with her fiancé but satisfies what she calls "the fiery and insatiate cravings of my passions" by having a torrid affair with her Negro servant; in *Venus in Boston* (1849) one adulterous woman pines "for the embraces of fifty men," a fantasy outdone by another heroine in the novel who declares it is madness to be chained to one man when "a thousand" would not satisfy her; *The Countess* (1849) portrays a club of ardent New York women who use sex to entrap and manipulate men, who are called "self-styled Emperors" here given a lesson in submission; in *New-York Life* (1849) we meet a gallery of society women who satisfy their insatiable longings in inventive ways, such as flocking to a New York gynecologist famous for his deft fingerings of his patients' vaginas.[74] Although Thompson was driven by the radical-democrat aim of exposing secret wrongdoing among upper-class women, he was actually less critical of these women than of the repressive society that did not permit open expression of their sexual yearnings, which Thompson frequently insists are even more powerful than those of men. In a characteristic moment, a heroine in *Venus in Boston* declares that women are especially unfortunate "because they *are* women; and because they are even more ardent in their passions than those who have the happiness to be men." Throughout Thompson's radical-democrat fiction runs a vehement protest against the double standard by which sexual excesses among men were pardoned while women were driven to passionless marriages, to perverse sexual intrigues, or, were they exposed, to disgrace and ostracism.

It should be noted that through the publication of *The Scarlet Letter* (1850), male authors were most successful in fashioning heroines that were complicated or iconoclastic (the main exception was Catharine Sedgwick, whose heroines are among the most interesting in pre-1850 fiction). While women reformers were largely responsible for generating such intriguing stereotypes as the fallen woman or the woman victim, it was the male novelists, especially the sensationalists of the 1840s, who most often translated these reform stereotypes into fictional characters. Hawthorne's stature as the period's earliest fabricator of truly complex heroines owes much to this phenomenon of male authors giving fictional life to cultural stereotypes that were provoking political action in women's reform circles. After studying the extraordinarily rich diversity of women's types in antebellum culture, it is useful now to show how these types were assimilated and transformed by Hawthorne, the era's most accomplished creator of fictional heroines.

13

HAWTHORNE'S HEROINES

A L T H O U G H Hawthorne is generally credited with having created the most intriguing heroines in pre–Civil War literature, little has been said about the relationship between these heroines and the women's culture of the day. The fact is that the rich variety of female character types in antebellum popular culture prepared the way for Hawthorne's complex heroines. Hawthorne's best fiction occupies an energetic middle space between the Conventional novel and the literature of women's wrongs. Skeptical of the Conventional and politically uncommitted, Hawthorne was in an ideal position to choose judiciously from the numerous female stereotypes and to assimilate them in literary texts. His career illustrates the success of an especially responsive author in gathering together disparate female types and recombining them artistically so that they became crucial elements of the rhetorical and artistic construct of his fiction.

Toward Hester Prynne

As a creator of heroines, Hawthorne began as an unusually flexible but rather haphazard experimenter with various native and foreign character types. His earliest fiction, published between 1828 and 1837, can be distinguished from that of other American authors by the heterogeneity of its heroines. None of his early tales contains a heroine that can be called complex, but, taken as a whole, the tales are a remarkable testament to

Hawthorne's ability to escape narrow, monolithic views of women. On the one hand, he proved himself capable of producing redemptive moral exemplars: in "Little Annie's Ramble" an angelic child revives and cheers an old man; "The Village Uncle" features a bright, sunshiny woman; in "The Vision of the Fountain" an angelic exemplar is the visionary creation of a narrator's fancy. On the other hand, he also gave graphic portrayals of female criminals, such as the wandering heroine who has cruelly abandoned her family in "The Hollow of Three Hills," and women victims, such as the persecuted Quaker woman in "The Gentle Boy" and the Puritan adulteress forced to wear a scarlet A in "Endicott and the Red Cross."

His most complex early use of women characters occurs in "Young Goodman Brown," in which the affirmative values embodied in the allegorically named exemplar, Faith, are shattered by the protagonist's recognition of universal sinfulness, represented by the gathering of saints and sinners in the forest. In previous chapters we have seen that "Young Goodman Brown" was in many senses a representative 1830s piece whose ambiguities owed much to dark popular writings of the decade. It also drew on the ironic perception of the underlying similarity of respectable and fallen women that was being discussed in reform writings. When Hawthorne describes "chaste dames and dewy virgins" consorting with "women of spotted fame" and when he mentions outwardly good women who kill their babies or husbands, he is tapping ironies that surrounded fallen women and women criminals in several popular works of the 1830s.[1] When he has the angelic Faith appear at this demonic gathering, he dramatically undercuts the power of the moral exemplar. For the first time in his fiction, real density of meaning surrounds his heroines because he boldly brings together under one fictional roof moral exemplars, fallen women, and women criminals, a combination that produces an explosion of ironic meaning. The explosion is all the more powerful because Hawthorne uses a Puritan setting, so that the contemporary ironies take on a universality and a resonance because they are treated with Calvinistic seriousness. It must be emphasized, however, that here Hawthorne creates a *combination* of character types but not a real *fusion,* as he would in more interesting later heroines. His portrayal of various kinds of women in a single tale is significant but is finally subordinated to his main purpose of studying the disillusionment of Young Goodman Brown himself.

In short, his early tales reveal his remarkable openness to various character types, his occasional success in bringing together different types in a single tale, but his minimization of gender-specific themes. It was only in the early 1840s that his fiction revealed his growing awareness of both women's wrongs and women's rights. It was during this period, we should recall, that he spent time at Brook Farm among progressive thinkers, including the period's leading feminist theorist, Margaret Fuller. His exposure to feminist ideas during a time of economic depression and widespread exploitation of working women had a strong impact upon his fiction. Unlike Catharine Sedgwick, he did not blithely dismiss the sufferings of American working women. He succinctly but powerfully registered the sufferings of seamstresses in "The Procession of Life" (1843), which contains the following alarmed description: "But what is this crowd of pale-cheeked, slender girls, who disturb the ear with the multiplicity of their short, dry coughs? They are seamstresses, who have plied the daily and nightly needle in the service of master-tailors and close-fisted contractors, until now it is almost time for each to hem the borders of her own shroud."[2] In "The Christmas Banquet" (1844), a dark tale about an imagined gathering of the most wretched people on earth, Hawthorne shows that his sympathy extends not only to seamstresses but to all women victimized by overwhelming wrongs against their sex. Among the guests at the sad Christmas banquet are two women: "one, a half-starved, consumptive seamstress, the representative of thousands just as wretched; the other, a woman of unemployed energy, who found herself in the world with nothing to achieve, nothing to enjoy, and nothing even to suffer. She had, therefore, driven herself to the verge of madness by dark broodings over the wrongs of her sex, and its exclusion from a proper field of action."[3]

While these tales reveal his new sensitivity to women's wrongs, other tales of the period demonstrate his simultaneous recognition of women's rights. Among the reformers who appear in "Earth's Holocaust" (1844) are a number of women who propose to fling into the bonfire their petticoats and gowns, "and assume the garb, together with the manners, duties, offices, and responsibilities of the opposite sex."[4] Although here Hawthorne gently satirizes public agitation for women's rights, in "The New Adam and Eve" (1843) he endorses a kind of moral exemplar feminism when, imagining the wholesome Eve sitting in an American legislative hall, he writes: "Man's intellect, moderated by Woman's tenderness and moral sense! Were such the legislation of the world, there would be no need of State Houses, Capitols, Halls of Parliament."[5] A new political consciousness, therefore, characterized his fictional treatment of women in the early 1840s.

By 1844 Hawthorne was in a unique position among American authors dealing with women's issues. No other American writer had approached him in producing so large a variety of fictional heroines, from his heterogeneous characters of the 1830s to his more topical, socially representative heroines of the early 1840s. He was now ready to produce a heroine who fused opposite qualities and thus assumed stature as a truly complex, memorable literary character. All his earlier tales had achieved *combinations* of different types of heroines but not *fusions* of different qualities in one person. In Beatrice, the poisonous angel of "Rappaccini's Daughter" (1844), he created such a complex heroine.

Beatrice Rappaccini is both the angelic moral exemplar and the feminist criminal, both the pitiable woman victim and the deadly avenger of women's wrongs. She even has the magnetic voluptuousness of the sensual woman. On the one hand, she is the ultimate disenfranchised woman, totally removed from meaningful employment despite her reputation as a learned woman capable of being a university professor. True, her scientist father has endowed her with fatal power that he believes will enable her to redress wrongs against her sex—in his words, to "be able to quell the mightiest with a breath" and to avoid "the condition of a weak woman, exposed to all evil and capable of none."[6] But the very thing that gives her power over the mightiest prevents her from having a normal human relationship. To her lover Giovanni she seems by turns a heavenly angel and a terrible monster. Torn between love and horror, worship and loathing, Giovanni suffers an emotional conflict summed up in Hawthorne's exclamatory comment: "Blessed are all the simple emotions, be they dark or bright! It is the lurid intermixture of the two that produces the illuminating blaze of the infernal regions." Giovanni's confusion seems to have mirrored a confusion in Hawthorne's own mind. According to his son Julian, when Hawthorne was writing "Rappaccini's Daughter" he read from the unfinished manuscript to his wife, who interrupted him with the question: "But how is it to end? . . . is Beatrice to be a demon or an angel?" Julian records his father's baffled confession: " 'I have no idea!' was Hawthorne's reply, spoken with some emotion."[7]

The tale itself provides no clear answer, for even though Beatrice is said to be headed toward heaven as she dies, she has proved poisonous to everything she touched. Given the inscrutability of his heroine, Hawthorne might, perhaps, be charged with equivocation or artistic confusion. But instead of criticizing "Rappaccini's Daughter," we should recognize it as a transitional tale in which contradictory female stereotypes are fused in a single heroine. And it must be noted that the process of creative fusion creates a character who, despite residual similarities to popular heroines, has a symbolic density that makes her altogether different from these heroines. She is like the plants in her father's garden—a strange hybrid of different strains forced together by the crafty experimenter. The "Eden of poisonous flowers" in which she lives is the beautiful but (from a conventional standpoint) deadly garden of Hawthorne's art. What makes this artistic garden so intriguing is the lurid intermixture of qualities that make

Beatrice Rappaccini at once the victim and the aggressor, the exemplar and the criminal.

Although interesting as an exercise in fused women stereotypes, Beatrice Rappaccini lacked the topicality and the Americanness of Hawthorne's next major heroine, Hester Prynne. The five years between the publication of "Rappaccini's Daughter" and the writing of *The Scarlet Letter* were, it should be recalled, important ones for literary treatments of American women. In popular sensational literature, the most important phenomenon was the devaluation of male authority figures and the intensification of iconoclastic female character types such as the sympathetic fallen woman, the feminist criminal, and the sensual woman. In popular Conventional literature, a defensive reaction against the sensationalists led to a valorization of the actively virtuous moral exemplar, leading toward the mythic exemplars in the famous domestic best-sellers of Maria Cummins and Susan Warner. Certain popular authors of the 1840s attempted crude but intriguing fusions of women character types. For instance, Lippard's *The Quaker City* traces the self-destruction of a moral exemplar, Mary Arlington, as a result of her deluded faith in the Conventional; it also includes the complicated Dora Livingstone, the intellectual, voluptuous, scheming confidence woman who sleeps around and even plots her husband's murder in order to get ahead. On the level of political activism, the late 1840s was the watershed moment when the Seneca Falls feminists initiated heated public agitation for women's rights.

Witnessing these swirling images of women in his contemporary culture, the observant Hawthorne brought them together in the figure of Hester Prynne. Given the cultural conditions and Hawthorne's personal experiences, it is understandable that he made a complex woman the center of his most famous novel. The widespread attacks on male authority figures in popular novels was paralleled in Hawthorne's experience at the Salem custom house, where his untimely firing by Whig merchants and officeholders gave him the bitter resolve to produce a poisonous novel that he said would act as "a pervasive and penetrating mischief" against his enemies.[8] At the same time, his suddenly tight financial straits made him wish to write a novel that would be popular and broadly representative. The novel he produced was indeed representative, since it featured both a secretly corrupt man and a strong, majestic woman. By 1849 the devalued male and the powerful female had become a commonly featured pair in both Subversive and Conventional novels, but in each case this pair had different significations. In the Subversive novel, devalued males such as the reverend rake or the churchgoing mogul were contrasted to a variety of women (the feminist criminal, the fallen woman, or the working woman) who were often strong and sympathetically portrayed but did not serve as moral replacements for the males. In the Conventional novel, the central figure of the female exemplar did function as potent alternative to weakened male authority.

In *The Scarlet Letter* Hawthorne retains the devalued male figure but takes the wholly original step of fashioning a heroine *who embodies all the dark female roles of the Subversive novel and who at the same time serves the redemptive function of the Conventional moral exemplar.* No character in antebellum fiction is so rich a compound of popular stereotypes as Hester Prynne. She is the sympathetically portrayed fallen woman whose honest sinfulness is found preferable to the furtive corruption of the reverend rake. She is the struggling working woman who plies her needle as a seamstress. She is the feminist criminal bound in an "iron link of mutual crime" with a man whose feebleness through most of the novel is contrasted with her indomitable firmness.[9] She is the sensual woman who has, in Hawthorne's words, "a rich, voluptuous, Oriental characteristic" and who is bold enough to whisper to her lover, "What we did had a consecration of its own." She is the feminist exemplar who privately broods over women's wrongs and dreams of a revolution in relations between the sexes. She is all of these iconoclastic things—but she is also a moral exemplar, in both the angelic and the practical sense. She elicits from the Puritans "the reverence due to an angel," and one of the meanings associated with her letter is "Angel." Along with her angelic quality goes a practical ability to help others as a charity worker and an adviser.

She is, in short, the quintessential American heroine, reflecting virtually every facet of the antebellum woman's experience. As was true with Beatrice Rappaccini, the innovative fusion of contrasting stereotypes creates a wholly new kind of heroine who bears little resemblance to any individual popular character. The fusion serves specific rhetorical functions for Hawthorne. The gathering together of different female types in Hester Prynne is an assertion of unity in the face of a fragmentation of women's roles that Hawthorne perceived in his contemporary culture. It was precisely this fragmentation of roles that would produce an indirect, elliptical style among some American women writers of the 1850s and 1860s. Through a majestic act of artistry, Hawthorne temporarily fends off the potential confusion inherent in shifting women's roles by creating a heroine who is magically able to act out several of these roles simultaneously.

What makes possible this complex heroine is Hawthorne's adept use of the Puritan past. Just as Puritanism added moral depth to sensational themes that had degenerated in popular literature into flat prurience, so it offered historical materials conducive to a serious, rounded treatment of women's issues that had become sensationalized in popular Subversive fiction and circumvented in Conventional fiction. In *The Scarlet Letter* Hawthorne not only adopts but also *transforms* popular female stereotypes, and the chief transforming agent is Puritanism. The sympathetic fallen woman, who in radical-democrat novels had led to a gleeful inversion of moral values, here is treated with high seriousness. We sympathize with Hester but, because of the enormity of her punishment (a punishment reflecting the moral severity of Puritan New England), we are impressed with the momentousness of her sin. That is to say, she is not the fallen woman of the antebellum sensational novel who becomes callously amoral or vindictively murderous. Similarly, she is not the typical working woman, one who either gives way to suicidal despair, or becomes a prostitute, or contemplates armed revolution. Hawthorne knew well the plight of American seamstresses, and in the novel he points out that needlework was "then, as now, almost the only one within a woman's grasp."[10] But instead of emphasizing the degradation accompanying woman's work, he transforms this work into a triumphant assertion of woman's artistic power, as evidenced by the intricate, superb patterns Hester produces. The sensual woman, who in pamphlet novels of the 1840s was an insatiable nymphomaniac demanding many sexual partners, is here changed into a passionate but restrained woman who worships the sexual act with just one partner and whose dream of escaping with her lover is carefully squelched by Hawthorne.

The feminist exemplar is another popular stereotype Hawthorne transforms. At key points in the novel we are told that Hester broods over women's wrongs and dreams of a total change in male-female relations. But she never agitates publicly for women's rights, and it is clear by the end of the novel that Hawthorne has in mind not a militant, angry feminism but rather a gradualist moral exemplar feminism with utopian overtones. As a counselor of troubled women, the aged Hester assures them that "at some brighter period, when the world shall have grown ripe for it, in Heaven's own time, a new truth would be revealed, in order to establish the whole relation between man and woman on a surer ground of mutual happiness." Not only is the feminist revolution delayed to a vague, ideal future, but also Hester discounts her own capacities as a feminist exemplar by stressing that "the angel and apostle of the coming revelation must be a woman indeed, but lofty, pure and beautiful" and wise "not through dusky grief, but the ethereal medium of joy."

Hawthorne, therefore, attempts in *The Scarlet Letter* to absorb his culture's darkest, most disturbing female stereotypes and to rescue them from prurience or noisy politics by reinterpreting them in terms of bygone Puritanism and by fusing them with the moral exemplar. Evidently, his attempted brightening of dark stereotypes through the character of Hester was not altogether successful for either Hawthorne or his wife. Hawthorne lamented what he described as the unrelieved gloom of *The Scarlet Letter*, which he hoped would be published in a volume that would also contain more cheerful tales. As for his wife, after reading the novel she reportedly went to bed with a throbbing headache. He had created a magnificent fusion of different character types in Hester but had in the process sacrificed clear meaning. If he and Sophia were puzzled whether Beatrice Rappaccini was an angel or a demon, they had reason to be even more puzzled over Hester. To this day, critics still argue over the degree to which Hawthorne sympathizes with his most famous heroine. Actually, as was true with Beatrice, no absolute meaning or distinct authorial attitude can be gleaned from the complicated Hester. He recognized the disparate female types in his contemporary culture and created in Hester Prynne a multifaceted heroine in whom these types were artistically fused.

Divided Heroines

Perhaps because he had strayed too close to the abyss of indeterminacy in creating the complex Hester, Hawthorne decided in his subsequent major novels to avoid so daring a fusion of various stereotypes. In each of his later complete novels there is a fairly straightforward division between a "light" heroine (usually a Conventional moral exemplar) and a "dark" one (embodying the paradoxes and fantasies intrinsic to women's wrongs, as seen in characters such as the fallen woman, the feminist criminal, the sensual woman, and so forth). It would seem that the main reason *The Scarlet Letter* gave his wife a headache and struck him as excessively gloomy was that in Hester he had essayed a highly unusual fusion of the moral exemplar and various dark stereotypes. There is reason to believe that in the eyes of Sophia and even Hawthorne himself such a fusion verged upon blasphemy.

Hawthorne had, therefore, compelling reasons for distinguishing his bright moral exemplars from his ambiguous dark women. He made an effort in his later novels to sustain at least the appearance of such a distinction. Having recognized the moral confusion inherent in his complex heroines, he tried in his later works to remain fully representative of current women's roles but at the same time to keep the moral exemplar sacred and inviolate.

The House of the Seven Gables is a good case in point. After Hawthorne had read the novel to his wife, she wrote in a letter: "There is an unspeakable grace and beauty in the conclusion, throwing back upon the sterner tragedy of the commencement an ethereal light, and a clear home-loveliness and satisfaction." She admired "the flowers of Paradise scattered over all the dark places, the sweet wall-flower scent of Phoebe's character, the wonderful pathos and charm of old Uncle Venner."[11] In other words, there were no headaches in store for Sophia, for Hawthorne was now cautious to avoid potentially disturbing fusions of light and dark female stereotypes.

Sophia had reason to be pleased with the novel's ending and with the character of Phoebe Pyncheon. As he was writing *The House of the Seven Gables* Hawthorne had written his publisher: "It darkens damnably towards the close, but I shall try hard to pour some setting sunshine over it."[12] Both at the conclusion and at other dark moments in the novel, the main dispenser of sunshine is the moral exemplar, Phoebe Pyncheon. Even though at some points Hawthorne gently satirizes Phoebe as shallow and narrow, he nevertheless allows her to win the day, get her man, Holgrave, and help restore the morbid Clifford and Hepzibah to some semblance of normality. Phoebe is the principal agent for adding the kind of cheer that Hawthorne thought was lacking in *The Scarlet Letter*. She is at once the angelic exemplar, compared by Uncle Venner to "one of God's angels," and the practical exemplar—active, efficient, cheerful.[13] She operates as a foil to the odd, cranky Hepzibah, who is a comic version of the oppressed working woman, a fallen aristocrat who sets up shop since she "must earn her own food, or starve!" Phoebe represents an ennoblement of the working woman, for she brings efficiency and practicality to the operation of Hepzibah's shop. She also functions much like the moral exemplar in Conventional novels: that is, she is a powerfully virtuous alternative to devalued males. What makes Hawthorne's novel far richer than the typical Conventional novel is that he places his moral exemplar alongside a variety of fallible males who were ordinarily mentioned only in Subversive fiction: the despicable oxymoronic oppressor (Jaffrey Pyncheon), the ambiguous likable criminal (Clifford), the chaotic reformer, mesmerist, and sensational writer (Holgrave). At the same time, the legendary curse on the Pyncheon family gives the novel a historical depth generally lacking in Conventional fiction. In effect, Hawthorne has repeated the innovative fusion of contrasting popular stereotypes that he had made in *The Scarlet Letter*. The key difference is that here the fusion does not take place *within* the central heroine, who is an actively redemptive moral exemplar rather than a problematic locus of disparate female roles.

In Hawthorne's next novel, *The Blithedale Romance,* there is an apparent division between light and dark heroines, with Priscilla as the moral exemplar and Zenobia as a combination of the feminist exemplar, the sensual woman, the fallen woman, and, eventually, the suicidal embodiment of dark women's wrongs. But the division is more apparent than real, for Hawthorne can no longer place faith in the moral exemplar. In Phoebe Pyncheon, Hawthorne had produced an actively virtuous exemplar who effectively redeems fallible characters. In Priscilla, he creates a heroine who has many attributes of the Conventional moral exemplar—a gentle but tough nature, optimism, likability—but in fact is the deconstruction of one. What makes her deconstruct is that Hawthorne, as though pulled inevitably toward complex heroines, once again fuses the moral exemplar with darker stereotypes: in this case, the oppressed working woman and the woman victim. Priscilla is the child of Old Moodie in his poverty-stricken period, when he was living in a squalid, crowded urban tenement amidst penniless wretches. His wife, significantly, was "a forlorn, meek-spirited, feeble young woman, a seamstress."[14] She dies, leaving him with their "pale and nervous child," Priscilla. Not only is Priscilla the offspring of a wretched seamstress, but she herself is a seamstress who is constantly at work sewing her silk purses. She is therefore anchored in the popular fictional stereotype of the seamstress, which, as we have seen, was the period's most common symbol for the degraded working woman. In *The Scarlet Letter* Hawthorne had converted the seamstress into a symbol of woman's artistic power. In *The Blithedale Romance* he returns to the disturbing image, common in dark popular literature and mentioned in his own tales of the early 1840s, of the seamstress as the deadened, passive victim of an unjust social system. From the start, Hawthorne presses home the connection between Priscilla and the popular seamstress stereotype. Priscilla is first described as a "depressed and sad" girl whose face has "a wan, almost sickly hue, betokening habitual seclusion from the sun and free atmosphere." Zenobia can sum her up as "neither more nor less than a seamstress from the city" whose paleness and fragility result from the fact that she has been "stifled with the heat of a salamander-stove, in a small, close room, and has drunk coffee, and fed upon dough-nuts, raisins, candy, and all such trash, till she is scarcely half-alive." As a working woman raised in an urban tenement, she has seen horrors that would cripple whatever hopes or good intentions she might otherwise possess.

But she is not only an indigent seamstress; she is also a woman victim of a special kind: the trance medium who becomes the tool of the manipulative pseudoscientific showman, Westervelt. As we know, Hawthorne had personal reasons for drawing a negative portrait of Priscilla's role as a mesmeric seer. In 1841, writing to his wife from Brook Farm, he upbraided her for consulting the Boston mesmerist Cornelia Park. He argued both against mesmerism, which he called a delusive confusion of physical and spiritual phenomena, and against the relation between the mesmerist and the trance medium, in which, he said, "the sacredness of the individual is violated."[15] In the novel, the manipulation of the clairvoyant Priscilla by Westervelt is portrayed as a violation of the seer's sanctity: in Coverdale's words, "the individual soul was virtually annihilated, and all that is sweet and pure, in our present life, debased" by the mesmeric connection.[16]

The main thing to recognize is that Priscilla's capacities as a redemptive moral exemplar are nullified by her simultaneous functions as a working woman and a woman victim. There seems to be a real intentionality behind Hawthorne's studied fusion of contrasting stereotypes, for his special target throughout the novel is moral exemplar feminism, as it was dramatized in popular Conventional novels and as it had been openly endorsed by Margaret Fuller. It is well known that, despite his respect for Fuller's intelligence, Hawthorne was repelled by what he saw as her derivativeness and her egotism. He once noted the irony of Fuller, the supposed champion of female independence, having fallen slavishly in love with an unintellectual Italian, Angelo Ossoli—as he expressed it, "this rude old potency bestirred itself, and undid all her labor in the twinkling of an eye," though actually Hawthorne liked her better for the inconsistency, since Fuller "proved herself a very woman after all, and fell as the weakest of her sisters might."[17]

It has long been guessed that Hawthorne satirizes Margaret Fuller in *The Blithedale Romance* but descriptions of his satiric materials and procedure have been imprecise. In his portrayals of both Priscilla and Zenobia he creates fused characters whose Fuller-like qualities fight a losing battle with contrasting qualities derived from other aspects of American women's culture. We have seen that Fuller, though widely respected, was attacked by some working-class feminists as an intellectual distanced from the realities of the average woman's experience. Hawthorne makes a similar satiric point in his depiction of Priscilla. The connection between Priscilla and Fuller is made by Coverdale, who, at the very moment that he opens a letter from Fuller, notices a striking physical resemblance between the two women. Indeed, in one respect Priscilla is the quintessential Fuller-like woman, as outlined in Fuller's *Woman in the Nineteenth Century.* "The especial genius of Woman," Fuller had written, "I believe to be electrical in movement, intuitive in function, spiritual in tendency."[18] It is this electrical, magnetic nature, Fuller argues, that makes women especially useful as mesmeric mediums. Priscilla is the intuitive, spiritual woman who is endowed with unique capabilities as a trance medium. But Hawthorne undermines this Fuller stereotype by showing how the magnetic medium can become the passive victim of a venal male pseudoscientist. He uses the grim realities of pseudoscientific histrionics and male manipulativeness to subvert Fuller's airy theorizing. At the same time, he dramatizes the working-class protest against Fuller by emphasizing Priscilla's background as a pale, poor seamstress. In this sense, he is not distant from the author of "Stray Leaves from a Seamstress' Journal," who aspersed Fuller's feminism as detached and idealistic.

His main vehicle for attacking Fuller, however, is Zenobia. The links between Zenobia and Fuller seem obvious enough: both began as outspoken defenders of women's rights and both (in Hawthorne's view) compromised their feminist principles when they fell desperately in love with unlikely men. If Hawthorne took wry delight in the fact that in loving her dull-witted man Fuller "fell as the weakest of her sisters might," so he probes the irony of the magnificent feminist Zenobia proving herself even weaker than the pale Priscilla in her willingness to relinquish her feminist views when she falls for the male chauvinist, Hollingsworth. The irony intensifies when we realize that Zenobia is probably named after a powerful moral exemplar featured in the popular novel *Zenobia* (1838), written by William Ware, a Unitarian novelist familiar to Hawthorne and Fuller. So important was the heroine's name to Hawthorne that he contemplated using the title *Zenobia* for his Blithedale novel, but, as he wrote to a friend, "Mr. Ware has anticipated me in that."[19] Ware's heroine, a sort of combination of the moral exemplar and the adventure feminist, had heroically defended her city, Palmyra, against invading Roman forces and had remained dignified even in defeat. Hawthorne's Zenobia is directly tied to Ware's character in several passages where she is called a "queen," as when Coverdale notes that she had "something imperial" about her and possesses "as much native pride as any queen would have known what to do with."[20]

But Hawthorne adopts these moral exemplar references only to deflate them. Just as the admixture of two dark stereotypes, the seamstress and the woman victim, had nullified the exemplary qualities of Priscilla, so other stereotypes—the sensual woman, the fallen woman, the brooder over women's wrongs—undercut the redemptive function of Zenobia. She seems "a woman to whom wedlock had thrown wide the gates of mystery"; as Coverdale says: "There is no folded petal, no latent dew-drop, in this perfectly developed rose!"[21] The persistence with which Hawthorne dwells on her physical charms, including Coverdale's voyeuristic imaginings of her nude body and her own theatrical *poses plastiques* before the Blithedale community, gives her the aura of the sensual woman. But her very sexuality contravenes her feminism, for her voluptuous womanhood is said to be more powerful than her tracts in defense of her sex. It turns out that indeed her sexual impulses win the day over her political views, for she sheepishly agrees with Hollingsworth even despite his sexist diatribe at Eliot's Pulpit. The formerly imperial heroine is reduced first to a cold actress and then to a suicidal emblem of women's wrongs. Just before she drowns herself she tells Coverdale there are two morals to her story: first, that in the battlefield of life the blow that would glance off a man's steel headpiece is sure to light on a woman's heart; second, that the world hates the woman who strays even slightly out of the beaten track. After her death, Coverdale adds a third moral: it is nonsense that, in a world that gives many avenues to men, a talented woman like Zenobia should have been forced to define her success or failure only in terms of romantic love.

Which of these morals are we supposed to accept? What exactly is Hawthorne saying about women's roles? As was true with *The Scarlet Letter,* no definite answer can be given to these questions. The novel's thematic complexities were noted in October 1852 by an essayist for the *Westminster Review* who complained: "So many morals—one a-piece for Coverdale and Hollingsworth, and two and a-half for Zenobia—are symptomatic of weak moral power, arising from feebleness of moral purpose."[22] The fact is that in *The Blithedale Romance* the proliferation of morals verges upon indeterminacy, and the proliferation of perceived women's roles signifies the annihilation of the efficacious exemplar. In *The Scarlet Letter* Hawthorne had managed to fashion a powerful complex heroine because his use of Puritanism gave depth and meaning to both dark and bright women stereotypes. In *The House of the Seven Gables* the fusion had been suspended, but real power was awarded to the Conventional moral exemplar. *The Blithedale Romance* dramatizes the inoperability of the moral exemplar in a morally fluid society of erring reformers, charlatans, degraded seamstresses, and voyeuristic bachelors. Since Priscilla represents the deconstruction of the moral exemplar, it is fitting that she gains a kind of pallid power over the other characters. Through much of the novel she behaves like a manic-depressive, varying between morbid inactivity and wild hyperactivity. Her mood shifts are of a piece with her divided role as a melancholy seamstress and cheerful moral exemplar. As the novel progresses, it becomes clear that the two sides of her nature cancel each other out, leaving a kind of black hole of moral nullity into which the other characters are inevitably sucked. She becomes the novel's central symbol of directionless passivity: she is once called "only a leaf, floating on the dark current of events," and she confesses that "I am blown about like a leaf, I never have any free-will."[23] In the end, the passive Priscilla has gained supremacy, while apparently tougher characters have either committed suicide (Zenobia), turned feeble (Hollingsworth), or become inert and passionless (Coverdale). It is fitting that "Priscilla!" is the last word in the novel, for the inertia and ambiguity she embodies can be viewed as Hawthorne's last word on the contemporary American culture whose fragmentations and contradictions he had so sensitively portrayed throughout the novel.

If *The Blithedale Romance* dramatized the collapse of the moral exemplar, *The Marble Faun* shows Hawthorne's rather desperate attempt to revive the moral exemplar, to restore its redemptive function. In *The Marble Faun* women's roles are divided more severely than ever; there is no precarious fusion of the moral exemplar with darker stereotypes. What makes *The*

Marble Faun powerful is that the collision between the moral exemplar and the dark heroine is a resounding one that gives off dazzling thematic sparks and is projected in suggestive, artistically managed images.

In order to reconstruct the redemptive moral exemplar, Hawthorne uses a variety of images derived from Italian culture and Roman Catholicism. *The Blithedale Romance* had been his swan song to the unaided Protestant American moral exemplar. Quite simply, Hawthorne's deep perception of contradictory elements in the American woman's experience—his awareness of seamstresses' suffering, of various kinds of women victims and women's wrongs in general—had made him incapable of using the Conventional moral exemplar in the traditional way. When he dealt with modern American women in a modern setting, as in *The Blithedale Romance*, his imagination could not help dwelling upon ironies and contradictions in American women's roles that invalidated the moral exemplar. In addition, he came to recognize how shallow were the popular novels that contained traditional moral exemplars. In a January 1855 letter to William Ticknor from Europe, he had made his now famous denunciation of the "d—d mob of scribbling women" whose "trash" was popular in America. He asked: "What is the mystery of these innumerable editions of the 'Lamplighter,' and other books neither better nor worse?—worse they could not be, and better they need not be, when they sell by the 100,000."[24] While he detested novels like *The Lamplighter* that featured Conventional moral exemplars, he was attracted to the new kind of women's wrongs literature of the 1850s—what others were calling the literature of misery—epitomized by Sara Parton's turbulent best-seller, *Ruth Hall.* "I must say I enjoyed it a good deal," he wrote of Parton's novel. "The woman writes as if the Devil was in her; and that is the only condition under which a woman ever writes anything worth reading."[25]

By the time he wrote *The Marble Faun* Hawthorne was in a highly delicate situation. The standard moral exemplar no longer had much attraction for him, and he was stirred by the devilish new literature of misery that enacted the dark women's wrongs he himself had long been contemplating. Also, his previous novel, *The Blithedale Romance*, had destroyed the moral exemplar and had ended on a bleak note of moral neutrality. His strategy in *The Marble Faun* was to reconstruct the moral exemplar through the figure of Hilda and, at the same time, to project all the most devilish women's stereotypes into the character of Miriam.

In refashioning the moral exemplar in Hilda, Hawthorne does not reject popular models but rather exaggerates certain qualities of previous exemplars to serve his own purposes. In several senses, Hilda is quite similar to the moral exemplars featured in the Conventional novels Hawthorne supposedly disliked. Like Gertrude Flint of *The Lamplighter* and many other popular heroines, she is an anomalous mixture of angelic gentleness and indomitable strength. Kenyon captures this paradoxical combination of qualities when he exclaims: "It is strange, with all her delicacy and fragility, the impression she makes of being utterly sufficient to herself!"[26] Miriam stresses that Hilda is living proof that women need not depend upon men for strength. Hawthorne exaggerates both her angelic and her practical side, since his exemplar must confront Subversive forces of criminality and perversity that few popular heroines were forced to face. He also exaggerates another feature of the popular exemplar: her Roman Catholic propensities. We have seen that, among other functions, the moral exemplar ushered a sense of Roman Catholic aestheticism and ritual into the American Protestant novel, as manifested in many popular heroines' love of beautiful religious symbols, in their habit of handing out homespun icons like locks of their hair, and in their overall function as lay priests. In his portrayal of Hilda, Hawthorne takes the exemplar's Roman Catholic tendencies to their natural conclusion. As a descendant of New England Puritans, Hilda of course denies that she is a Catholic, but she is associated with Catholicism in nearly every scene in which she appears. In her hermitagelike tower, she lives in nunlike solitude and keeps lit a lamp at the shrine of the Virgin that has been burning for centuries. In her period of torment, she makes a purgative confession to a Roman Catholic priest, and later she spends time in a Roman convent and finally becomes a "household saint" revered by Kenyon.

If Hilda is the exaggerated version of the moral exemplar, Miriam is the ultimate fusion of various dark female stereotypes. She is connected to the stereotype of the feminist criminal in several ways. Her sketch of Jael driving the nail through the temples of Sisera, in which Jael was converted into "a vulgar murderess," is only one of many works in which Miriam dwelt "on the idea of woman, acting the part of a revengeful mischief towards man."[27] To Hilda's dismay, she sympathizes with the woman criminal Beatrice Cenci (depicted in Hilda's copy of Guido) because, as she explains, "she was still a woman, Hilda, still a sister, be her sin or sorrow what they might." She becomes a kind of feminist criminal herself. She feels "a wild joy" when she sees her male pursuer thrown over the cliff, and after the murder she proves far stronger than her co-criminal, Donatello. When she sees the body of the murder victim laid out in the church of the Capuchins, Hawthorne writes, "it was wonderful to see how the crisis developed in Miriam its own proper strength." She tells the enfeebled Donatello that she will bear all the grief, "for I am a woman." As a woman criminal, she embodies women's fantasy of total freedom from conventional restrictions, for when rejected by Hilda, as she later recalls, "I had no longer any terms to keep with the reserves and decorums of my sex." Besides being a feminist criminal, she is a seamstress who frequently contemplates wrongs against her sex. She once cries: "A woman's days are so tedious that it is a boon to leave even one of them out of the account." Even though her crime nourishes her strength, it also increases her awareness of women's wrongs, for she tells Kenyon that she has "too much life and strength, without a purpose for one or the other. . . . Nothing is left for me, but to brood, brood, brood, all day, all night, in unprofitable longings and repinings!"

In his contrasting portrayal of Hilda and Miriam, Hawthorne is carefully unraveling the elements that had been fused in the character of Hester Prynne. He had learned from popular culture that devalued males could not be relied upon as moral centers in his novels. To feature solely the bright female exemplar would be to risk producing Conventional novels like those of the "scribbling women" Hawthorne disliked. To feature solely the dark heroine would be to present only a partial picture of a complex women's experience whose numerous facets he had long recognized. As *The Blithedale Romance* had shown, however, to attempt fusions of the two types in the context of modern America was to open the way for inertia and complete moral fluidity. What was left to Hawthorne was a firm division between the two main types, an exaggeration of the two until they became mutually repellent. Taken to an extreme, the moral exemplar becomes an absolutist who cannot admit a grain of sin into her consciousness and who is driven to torpid gloom by her friends' crime, a gloom expelled only when she confesses to a Catholic priest. Taken to an extreme, the dark woman thinks, acts, and creates like the feminist criminal, the voluptuous sensual woman, and the brooder over women's wrongs. Hawthorne, intent above all on avoiding problematic fusions of opposing stereotypes, creates a schematic world of divided heroines. He is left with the stark contrast between the severe, inviolate virtue of the moral exemplar and the full admittance of iconoclasm and rebellion by the dark heroine. He does establish a stylistic middle ground between the two in the symbolic use of women's art. But there is no central unifying symbol of women's creativity as there had been in *The Scarlet Letter.* Hilda's adroit but unoriginal copying is light-years distant from Miriam's turbulent, deeply personal paintings. The two cannot even agree over the interpretation of paintings: Guido's portrayal of the archangel defeating Satan, for instance, pleases Hilda as an emblem of the undisputed supremacy of good over evil but displeases Miriam, who thinks the angel should be depicted as stained with the gore of battle.

In order to forge any link between the two, Hawthorne must look outside woman's consciousness and outside American culture. He must resort to the deep traditions and long history of Rome and Roman Catholicism. What truly connects Hilda and Miriam is that both are types of American womanhood relocated and reconstructed on foreign soil. The moral exemplar, Hawthorne realizes, can neither be fused with the dark stereotypes nor relied upon for redemptive meaning. She must be exaggerated and, as it were, propped up with a variety of foreign images and icons that give her a new stability and depth. As for the dark woman, Hawthorne was not willing, as were several women authors of the literature of misery, to record the mercurially shifting faces of women. Hawthorne is perfectly aware of these shifting womanly roles, as is made clear by Miriam's lay figure that astonishes Donatello when he visits her studio. The lay figure, as Miriam explains, is "a lady of exceedingly pliable disposition; now a heroine of romance, and now a rustic maid; yet all for show," as "she pretends to assume the most varied duties and perform many parts in life, while really the poor puppet has nothing on earth to do." Her real self, as Donatello sees, is a dark-haired woman "who threw up her arms, with a wild gesture of tragic despair."[28] The lay figure embodies the shifting female personae, hiding a tormented inner self, that characterized the devilish literature of misery Hawthorne so admired. But, unlike Sara Parton or Emily Dickinson, Hawthorne was interested not in studying the intriguingly disparate pieces of the modern woman figure but rather in trying to make the pieces cohere. If Hilda is the moral exemplar as Catholic saint, Miriam is the dark heroine as Catholic penitent. In the final analysis, the profound moral differences between the two matter less than the depth, the traditions that eventually make them similar. On every page of the novel we see Hawthorne trying to deepen and enrich stereotypes that in *The Blithedale Romance* had led him to moral barrenness. Classic paintings and sculpture, the landscape and ruins of Rome, the long traditions of the Roman Church—all of these images give new resonance to flat stereotypes that could not be effectively treated in an America whose lack of shadow and mystery Hawthorne laments in his preface. Even though at the end Hilda and Miriam are said to be separated by "a fathomless abyss," it is precisely the "abyss"—that is, the dark depths of the novel's style and context—that connects them, despite their real differences. No longer capable of fusing opposite qualities in a single heroine, Hawthorne at least achieves an exterior fusion through a suggestive rendering of foreign symbols and settings.

This exterior fusion, however, proved a factitious alternative to the inward fusion he had achieved in Hester Prynne. By the late 1850s he had become uncomfortably aware of the multiplicity of his culture's female roles and poses. The late novel fragments he left uncompleted at his death show him groping about between alternative female roles in a futile effort to locate unified meaning and continuity. To the end he regarded the bright heroine as the main force of moral centeredness in a fictional world of devalued males. In a digression in *Etheredge* he expressed dismay at the gloomy aura of the story by writing: "I must moderate the horror of all this; or it will be absolutely intolerable."[29] What he most needed was a redemptive, cheerful moral exemplar along the lines of Phoebe Pyncheon. In outlining his plans for the character of Elsie, he wrote: "The girl must be cheerful, natural, reasonable, beautiful, spirited, to make up for the deficiencies of almost everybody else." Similarly, in Study 7 for *The Dolliver Romance* he gave himself these instructions: "All through the book, the prettiness, sauciness, cheerfulness of Alice, & her humor, expressions—as child, girl, woman, grandmother, must redeem the gloom, selfishness, morbidness, unnaturalness of the rest."[30] But this was easier said than done. Hawthorne had come too far to fashion an unironic moral exemplar. He had negated the power of the Conventional moral exemplar in *The Blithedale Romance* and had been forced to resort to massive stage props to buttress the exemplar of *The Marble Faun.* It was virtually impossible to call up the ghost of Phoebe Pyncheon now.

If he could no longer rely on the moral exemplar, neither could he draw a contrasting, more complex heroine representing women's wrongs or women's rights. Sybil Dacy, a melancholy, ethereal character in the *Elixir of Life Manuscripts,* is the closest he comes to producing a complicated figure of women's wrongs. An outgrowth of the same literature of misery that had also given rise to Miriam of *The Marble Faun,* Sybil wonders sadly why "woman gets so large a share of human misery laid on her weak shoulders" and whether there is "some deadly curse on woman" so that she has nothing to do "but only to be wronged by man and still to love him, and despise herself for it."[31] She insists that, given the world's gross maltreatment of women, the only solution is for all women to kill their female babies as soon as they are born. However, Sybil does not develop into a rounded dark heroine, because she is asked simultaneously to function as a bright counterpoint to the wicked Septimus Felton, who tells her, "I would reserve thee, good and pure, so that there may be to me the means of redemption; some stable hold, in the moral confusion that I will create around myself."

A similar dividedness of function spoils another potentially intriguing heroine, Alice of *The Ancestral Footstep.* The spunky, strong-minded Alice is intended to be both a progressive feminist exemplar and an old-fashioned Conventional moral exemplar. In describing her, Hawthorne reveals just how multifaceted the American heroine had become. Alice, he writes, is "free, wild, tender, proud, domestic, strange, natural, artistic; and has at bottom the characteristics of the American woman, with the principles of the strong-minded set."[32] The internal contradictions within this description constitute a major reason for the decline of Hawthorne's literary art. Alice is to be "free" but "domestic," "wild" and "proud" but "tender," "natural" but "artistic" and "strange." These qualities do embody, as Hawthorne notes, "the characteristics of the American woman" as she appeared to the observant novelist. But for Hawthorne, the fully characteristic American woman had become a self-subverting phenomenon, a troubling symbol of moral paradoxes and psychological ambiguity. For him, the American woman ends nowhere: his late heroines are figures of promise that never develop into fully realized characters. And with the absence of the unifying heroine, his art weakens. The author who had once crafted tightly structured literary texts around complex American heroines ended by surrendering structure and even meaning itself, largely because he had come to recognize just how complex these heroines were.

14

THE AMERICAN WOMEN'S
RENAISSANCE
AND EMILY DICKINSON

T URNING from Hawthorne to writings by American women published during the same period, we see that the very proliferation of stereotypes that in the end contributed to his confusion had a liberating effect on American women themselves. The 1850s was the decade when American women's culture came of age: what might be regarded as "the American Women's Renaissance." Most significantly, it was the period of the rapid maturation and the earliest literary productivity of Emily Dickinson. Dickinson, arguably the greatest female poet, has not yet been discussed in terms of the social and literary flowering that occurred in women's culture during the 1850s. Her development can be better understood when evaluated against this lively cultural background. On the political level, this was a decade of feminist agitation and organizing, which diminished just before and during the Civil War but then was resumed afterward. On the literary level, it was a decade of culturally influential and increasingly artistic women's literature, the most important of which I categorize as Conventional literature, women's rights fiction, and the literature of misery. Conventional literature generally avoided gender-specific issues and invested the redemptive moral exemplar with unprecedented power. Women's rights fiction was a political genre that dramatized the need for legal and social change on behalf of women. By the end of the 1850s, a profound disillusion with both the piously Conventional and the politically feminist began to be registered in the so-called literature of misery, an ironic, stylized genre which, as shall be seen, set the stage for Dickinson's elliptical poems.

The Enrichment of Women's Culture

What I am calling the Conventional novel, typified by Susan Warner's *The Wide, Wide World* and Maria Cummins's *The Lamplighter,* was culturally influential and yet lacked the gender-specific elements of other forms of women's literature of the day. The popular success of such fiction can be partly explained by the optimistic tone of these novels, each of which traced the development of a young woman from a troubled, somewhat unruly child into a self-reliant, upright woman. In these novels the moral exemplar was assigned a centrality that it never had before and has not had since. Because male authority figures had been devalued by Subversive literature of the 1840s, there was a desperate need to reconstruct moral value in the person of the female exemplar, who resisted all the troubling paradoxes of Subversive popular culture. In Warner's and Cummins's novels, the moral exemplar lived in an idealized fictional world unsullied by problematic social issues such as slavery, class divisions, factories, and so forth. The moral exemplar bravely confronted unparalleled personal misfortune, but by nature she was unequipped to ponder troublesome social realities or the ambiguities of sin. In *The Marble Faun* Hawthorne captured the moral exemplar's combined toughness and naïveté in Miriam's description of Hilda: "Of sorrow, slender as she seems, Hilda might bear a great burthen;—of sin, not a feather's weight."[1] Hawthorne knew the American moral exemplar well. Popular heroines like Warner's Ellen Montgomery and Cummins's Gertrude Flint face great calamities—loneliness, separation from loved ones, cruel treatment by tyrannical adults—but they never allow sin into their consciousness. Despite great sorrow and apparent moral wavering, they remain firm centers of virtue and moral clarity.

Harriet Beecher Stowe's *Uncle Tom's Cabin* can be distinguished from the other Conventional novels because of the turbulent social forces it confronts and the imposing variety of moral exemplars it uses to counteract these forces. Largely because the novel gave various moral exemplars uniquely redemptive power, it became the most popular literary work of the era, selling more than 300,000 copies in the United States and nearly a million in Great Britain. Like Hawthorne, Stowe gathered under one fictional roof both dark, iconoclastic women characters and brighter ones as well. There is a crucial difference, however, between these writers' treatment of women: because Stowe *mixes* but does not *fuse* character types, she retains a reassuringly simple division of functions absent from Hawthorne's complex texts. She portrays the suffering inflicted on both sexes by the slave system and gives the great optimistic message that anyone, no matter how terribly oppressed or constitutionally timid, has the capacity to be a moral exemplar. In a scene that has become an icon of American culture—the heroic crossing of the icy river by the slave girl Eliza—Stowe illustrates how the timid woman victim could be transformed into a magnificent adventure feminist. The novel's main exemplar, Eva St. Clare, neutralizes many of the evils that surround her through her cheerful activity and her angelic redemptiveness. As a sinless child redeeming a fallen world, Eva in life and death casts a halo of cheerful piety over the entire novel, suggesting that even the deepest injustices of the American social system can be imaginatively rectified by the moral exemplar.

While the Conventional best-sellers of the 1850s had immense cultural significance, they are of only secondary interest from a feminist standpoint because their language was rarely gender-specific. They advanced a popularized, Christian version of the moral exemplar feminism that had been introduced by Catharine Sedgwick and Margaret Fuller. The power that women characters wield in these novels is moral and religious rather than political. The authors of Conventional novels were, by and large, conservatives with a strong distaste for public agitation for women's rights. For them woman's great power was as a redeemer of devalued males and, in the case of *Uncle Tom's Cabin*, as a moral savior of a threatened social system.

It was rather in the women's rights novel that American authors called directly for political change. Surprisingly enough, America's rich tradition of women's rights fiction has been largely neglected by modern critics. It is commonly known that Charles Brockden Brown had advanced a rationalist Enlightenment feminism in his dialogue novel *Alcuin* (1798) and had dramatized his feminist views in *Ormond* (1799), which contains portraits of the self-reliant intellectual Constantia Dudley and the tough warrior-feminist Martinette de Beauvais. But most subsequent literary treatments of women's rights have been overlooked.

A number of American novels written between 1800 and 1850 endorsed what can be called utopian feminism. They depicted an imaginary society in which equal rights have been awarded to women. The deist novel *Equality; A History of Lithconia* (1802) portrays an idyllic island society where prostitution and female wretchedness have been eliminated as a result of a half-marriage system whereby husband and wife divide property equally and procure divorce easily. A later utopian piece, Mary Griffith's story "Three Hundred Years Hence" (1835), pictures America in the year 2135 as a liberated nation in which women have the same property rights, education, and job opportunities as men. The utopian Fourierist novel *Henry Russell: or, The Year of Our Lord, Two Thousand* (1846) similarly envisages a future model society in which, among other things, men and women work together in jobs of their own choosing. Likewise, Jane Sophia Apple-ton's "Vision of Bangor in the Twentieth Century" (1848) portrays a utopian nation whose feminist principles are summed up by a character who announces to nineteenth-century readers: *"Your* age *fondled* woman. Ours *honors* her. You gave her *compliments. We* give her *rights. "*[2] This projec-tion of feminist beliefs into a utopian future lies behind Hawthorne's statement on women's issues at the end of *The Scarlet Letter,* in which Hester Prynne comforts troubled Puritan women with the promise of "some brighter period" when "a new truth would be revealed, in order to estab-lish the whole relation between man and woman on a surer ground of mutual happiness."[3] Hawthorne here was drawing directly off a tradition of utopian feminism in American literature.

Although the utopian works were pioneering in their call for women's rights, they lacked the passionate vindictiveness against male tyranny and social injustice that would characterize later feminist fiction. Only one pre-1850 novel, Paul Harro-Harring's *Dolores* (1846), became strident in its defense of women's rights. This sensational, politically radical novel created such a stir upon its publication that Margaret Fuller and Ralph Waldo Emerson publicly came to its defense. Fuller's *New York Tribune* article defending the novel was so stirring that Edgar Allan Poe called it "one of the most eloquent and well-*put* articles I have ever yet seen in a newspaper."[4] Fuller had good reason to defend the novel, which contains some of the most forthright feminist passages in antebellum fiction. Throughout the novel Harro-Harring argues that society has reduced woman to a mere automaton and propagating machine; in the words of one character, "woman has been degraded, by disgraceful prejudice, to slavery, to legal bondage, under man."[5] Harro-Hanning points out that woman has the "same right to social independence" and "the same capacities and abilities for moral independence" as man. *Dolores* was original not so much for its argument, which had been made in several utopian novels, but in the militancy of its attacks on discrimination against women.

The rise of the American suffrage movement brought a new literature of women's rights, one that focused on current political issues and the activity of feminist lecturers. Sarah J. Hale's neglected novel *The Lecturess: or Woman's Sphere* (1839) stands as the earliest full-length treatment of a women's rights lecturer in literature. The heroine, Marion Gayland, is raised by a tough-minded woman who instills in her the values of industry and independence. At thirteen Marion has already become a committed feminist driven by a determination to combat male domination of women. When a conventional girlfriend warns her against lecturing, Marion re-plies: "I will spend my life, if necessary, in the endeavor to raise woman to that equality with man which is her right by the divine law of nature, and of which oppression alone deprives her."[6] She vows: "I will not be the slave of man," and she detests the common male view of woman as "the painted doll of the harem, or the mean drudge of domestic life." When she eventually is married, she accommodates somewhat to her husband's conservative views by giving up the lecture circuit, but she maintains that wifehood does not mean "a blind submission on my part to his opinions and will." She insists upon being treated as his intellectual equal, and she assumes the presidency of a woman's group. The novel ends with Marion declaring on her deathbed "how wrong were all my opinions," but this incongruously conventional ending seems designed to placate those readers who might have been shocked by the boldly feminist views aired earlier in the novel. Writing nearly a decade before the first organized women's rights convention, Hale knew that feminist opinions must be treated with caution and with attention to the still conservative attitudes of the American public.

It was only in the 1850s, when suffrage agitation was in full force, that American authors dared to be bold and uncompromising in their advocacy of women's rights. Hannah Gardner Creamer's novel *Delia's Doctors; A Glance Behind the Scenes* (1852) was the first novel that endorsed the vote for women. The novel features a sturdy, intellectual heroine who logically discourses on all the demands of the women's rights movement, including the demand for full political equality for women. A more passionate brand of women's rights fiction appeared in the suffrage newspaper *The Una* (1853–55). One *Una* story, Lizzie Linn's "Dependence" (1853), exposes the effects of unfair property laws by showing the impoverishment of a wife due to her husband's complete regulation of their wealth. Another Lizzie Linn story, "The Disappointed Wife" (1853), depicts a wealthy woman who marries a man who, with the sanction of law, takes over his wife's property and mismanages it until all their money is gone. Yet another ill result of woman's economic degradation is the topic of Linn's story "Marriage the Only Resource" (1854), in which the heroine wishes to support herself but finds that most job options are closed for women, so that she makes a marriage of convenience that leads to the dissipation of both spouses. *Lessons of Life* (1854), an anonymously published novel that ran serially in *The Una*, portrays a powerfully self-sufficient woman, Margaret Ramsay, who, despite severe misfortune, supports herself and her sister by teaching art. At one point in the novel, Margaret declares at a suffrage convention that woman should demand her rights "anywhere, and everywhere. . . . Why should she be the slave of a tyrant forever? . . . What right has man to control her?"[7] The *Una* fiction, while generally inferior from a literary standpoint, shows the growing breadth and passion of women's rights literature.

In the life and works of Laura Curtis Bullard this breadth and passion reached a kind of culmination. Of all the oversights of literary and social historians of America, few are more heinous than the almost complete neglect of Laura Curtis Bullard. Bullard's novel *Christine; or, Woman's Trials and Triumphs* (1856) was the first novel that not only endorsed every demand of the suffrage movement but also possessed the dramatic intensity and stylistic tautness of classic women's fiction. In the decade following the publication of the novel Bullard became active in the suffrage cause. She was selected to succeed Elizabeth Cady Stanton and Susan B. Anthony as the editor of the era's most radical feminist newspaper, *The Revolution.* Also, she was a pioneer in the women's club movement, which was intended to bring suffragists together with other women of all callings and professions. She was one of the founders of the first woman's club, Sorosis, and the leader of two employment organizations, the Women's Bureau and the Working Women's Association. What particularly distinguished Bullard was her breadth of vision. "The demand for suffrage," she wrote in an editorial for *The Revolution,* "is only one part of a greater demand which includes it. The woman question, as we understand it, is the comprehensive question of woman's rights—including her right to employment, wages, property, education, suffrage, marriage, and divorce. Our theme is *all* of these, not merely *one.*"[8] This breadth was manifested in her dedication to a uniquely varied range of women's activities, including the advocacy of women's rights abroad. A well-traveled woman who befriended several foreign progressives, including George Sand and Emily Faithfull, she attended the first British women's rights convention (in 1869), served as America's primary host for visiting feminists, and called for an international organization for women.

In addition, Bullard was one of the discriminating American women who had an unreserved appreciation for the poetry of Walt Whitman. In an 1876 letter to her fellow Brooklynite, asking for a complete edition of his poems, she announced herself as "one of the earliest readers of your Leaves of Grass, that unique book, which so startled the many and so delighted the few." Whitman was so pleased with Bullard's letter that years later, when Horace Traubel reread it to him, he exclaimed: "[D]on't think I don't appreciate such things—all such things: why, I live on them—they are all I have: cut them out and I am landed high and dry. . . . Yes: God bless her! God bless her!"[9] The link between Bullard and Whitman may have been even more significant than one of mutual appreciation: Whitman's broadly progressive attitude toward women—embracing the political, the passional, the economic, and the literary aspects of the woman question—greatly resembled Bullard's.

As intriguing as is the possible cross-influence between Bullard and Whitman, it is Bullard's hitherto neglected novel *Christine* that constitutes her real importance in American literary history. Bullard's first novel, *Now-A-Days!* (1854), had portrayed a young woman who develops independence as a schoolteacher in the backwoods of Maine. This novel was primarily important as a precursor of local-color realism, a woman writer's consciously restrained answer to the excesses of male sensational literature. Although a somewhat amateurish effort, *Now-A-Days!* lives up to Bullard's introductory boast that it is the first true portrait of "real life, New-England life," with salty Yankee dialect and realistic treatment of character.[10]

In her next novel, *Christine,* Bullard uses stylistic directness and subtle characterization to make a passionate case for women's rights. The heroine, Christine Elliott, is a women's rights lecturer and director of a women's employment bureau who in the end is married and abandons the lecture circuit but keeps up the women's bureau with the aid of her liberal husband. *Christine* is a tightly written, ardent novel filled with images of madness, imprisonment and escape, and open advocacy of political feminism. It might be called the *Jane Eyre* of women's rights fiction. Christine, a plain woman who as a child had suffered persecution and ostracism at a rigid boarding school, is inspired to become a suffrage lecturer by an older feminist, Helen Harper, who tells her: "Christine, it is yours to be the champion of your sex. The pioneer in the march of progress. You are to rouse the indifferent—to give voice to the suffering of your sex."[11] Indeed, on the lecture platform and in her private conversation Christine defends all the tenets of women's rights—the vote, equal job opportunities and equal pay, relaxed divorce and property laws—and even discovers in the Bible "texts in favor of women's rights."

In addition to advancing women's rights, the novel contains particularly powerful illustrations of women's wrongs. One of Christine's friends, Annie Howard, is a symbol of the unfairness of tight divorce laws, for she is tied to a husband whose cruelty and coldness finally impel her to escape into the squalid world of the city, where she becomes first a starving seamstress and finally a pathetic prostitute who gives her illegitimate child to Christine. Christine herself faces severe frustrations. Her efforts on behalf of women's rights are opposed at every turn. In a climactic sequence, her villainous aunt and conservative father, stunned by her radical views on women, lure her into an insane asylum, where she is wrongly imprisoned for years as a psychotic. She is repeatedly told she will be released as soon as she disavows her feminist views, but she stubbornly refuses to do so and escapes from the asylum only with the aid of a progressive friend. When she resumes the lecture circuit, she endures constant obloquy, even though, as Bullard emphasizes, at her lectures "all was decorous in the extreme." Bullard sensitively records the confrontation between feminism and marriage. Christine ends by giving up her lecturing after she is married, but she has a marriage of equality with her husband, who helps her run her employment bureau for women. What Bullard seems to be striving for is a rounded feminism, one that makes accommodations for both women's rights and heterosexual love, such as that advocated by her friend Elizabeth Cady Stanton.

The real success of *Christine,* however, lies not in its advocacy of women's rights or its portrayal of women's wrongs but in its power as a compelling, taut novel written by a progressive American woman who was extremely sensitive to the complexities of human relationships and the hidden tensions of the human psyche. It is not the political but rather the psychological images—the rage, the restlessness, the many hindrances repeatedly besetting Christine—that are most appealing to the modern reader. Here we come upon a central paradox of American women's fiction, indeed of women's literature in general: that is, it most often succeeds artistically when it leaves behind feminist politics. In this sense, it becomes women's *literature* when it refuses to be women's *propaganda* and asserts its power as an expression of universal themes.

The artistic superiority of literary as opposed to political treatments of women's issues becomes clear when we compare several women's rights novels of the 1855–75 period to more artistic forms of women's literature that emerged during this period. The women's rights novels are significant from a historical standpoint but are so lacking in complexity that few of them merit close reading. Henrietta Rose's *Nora Wilmot: A Tale of Temperance and Women's Rights* (1858), reflecting the link between the suffrage movement and temperance reform, is a long didactic novel arguing that women should be granted social and political power in order to provide an enduring moral corrective for corrupt men. Anna Argyle's *Money and Marriage* (1862) portrays several marriages that illustrate, as the author explains, "what has become habit and fixed usage—the complete pecuniary dependence of woman during her married life."[12] Caroline Fairfield Corbin's *Rebecca; or, A Woman's Secret* (1868) features an initially timid heroine who becomes increasingly enraged about male oppression and finally devotes herself to political activism on behalf of women. E. A. Berlin's *Earth's Angels* (1868) and Mrs. R. S. Hume's *Woman's Wrongs* (1872) return to the theme of woman's need to assume full political status in order to redeem an impure society, while Frances Dana Gage's *Steps Upward* (1870) reiterates the connection between women's rights and temperance. These women's rights novels, while interesting as courageous efforts to advance an unpopular cause, lack literariness.

The women's rights literature, although historically important, lacked the literary density of a new kind of literature of women's wrongs produced by women who felt disillusioned with public agitation and who believed that woman's angst lay on a deeper level than the political or economic. In this so-called literature of misery, all women's roles began to be perceived as easily changeable masks, beneath which was a hidden female self that was bitter, isolated but at the same time intelligent and proudly literary. A self-conscious artistry characterized the literature of misery, as certain American women—most dramatically Emily Dickinson—began to perceive that in a world from which they were still largely excluded their most effective weapon was the stabbing phrase and the ingenious, taunting ellipsis.

This literature of misery was described vividly by the newspaper editor Samuel Bowles, who today is most often remembered as Emily Dickinson's friend and, some have speculated, the possible intended recipient of the passionate love letters she wrote to the man she called "Master." Bowles's failure to appreciate fully Dickinson's genius was indicative of a worldly practicality that made him have reservations about the dark brand of women's writing he described in an 1860 editorial for the *Springfield Republican:*

> There is another kind of writing only too common, appealing to the sympathies of the reader without recommending itself to his judgment. It may be called *the literature of misery.* Its writers are chiefly women, gifted women may be, full of thought and feeling and fancy, but poor, lonely and unhappy. It may be a valuable discipline in the end, but for the time being it too often clouds, withers, distorts. It is so difficult to see objects distinctly through a mist of tears [italics added].[13]

More sympathetic responses to the literature of misery came from writers connected with the women's movement. In an 1855 article for *The Una* the prominent activist Caroline Dall had perceptively written: "Why is it that a low wail runs through all the literature that women have given to the world? It is because women feel a helplessness that they think without remedy."[14] Another *Una* writer, who called herself "Junia," described women writers as follows: "These are they, who have felt in all its bitterness their own impotence and powerlessness; felt that they had talents which they could not improve or abilities they could not exercise; have stood helplessly by, and seen the car of the social Juggernaut, roll over the throbbing hearts of sisters, mothers, daughters, till hope and life were crushed out, while legislators and divines and 'potent, grave and reverend seigniors,' have looked complacently on."

As these comments suggest, the literature of misery was produced mainly by women who felt to the depths of their being their painful power-lessness and their exclusion from a male-dominated society. This sense of exclusion from the male order, of course, was also the driving force behind public agitation for women's rights. But it was quickly discovered that public agitation had its drawbacks. Women's rights conventions were con-stantly assailed in the general press as unruly affairs conducted by squab-bling, mannish women. Squibs and burlesques caricaturing women's rights activists appeared regularly in penny papers and in popular magazines like *Putnam's* and *Harper's*. There even arose a genre of antifeminist novels, most notably Fred Folio's voluminous *Lucy Boston; or, Women's Rights and Spiritualism* (1855), which depicted chaos and confusion in an imaginary society run wholly by women. Battered by such criticism, suffragists risked becoming alienated from the society they wished to reform. Even worse, they risked cutting themselves off from average American women. By the mid-1850s, it was clear to perceptive leaders of the suffrage movement that efforts must be made to embrace the needs of women of all callings. A disillusion with women's rights conventions and an awareness of ordinary women began to surface in suffrage writings. In 1855 Caroline Dall empha-sized in *The Una* that "all noble souls must help us. . . . Every well-educated woman who leads an independent life, refusing to marry for bread, or managing her family interests as a widow, from wise and noble motives, helps us more than all speech-making. Speech-making is in fact the *lowest* duty in our temple of service,—a duty, yet the lowest."[15] Suffrage lecturers were so widely attacked that women activists recognized the need to broaden their appeal and to find more indirect, guarded ways to advance their views. This broadening definition of women's activity led in the 1860s to the rise of women's clubs, the product, as J. C. Croly explained, of "the stirring of an intense desire that women should come together . . . from all quarters."[16] It also led to the recognition of the literary text as one of the woman's chief means of self-assertion.

The recoil away from public activism and the diversification of perceived women's roles produced a new brand of women's writing that consciously asserted woman's power as image maker and role player while it retained the rage and sadness that had long characterized the literature of woman's wrongs. By becoming less openly political, women's writing in a sense became more "feminist," since it championed woman's ability to compete with man as a creator of universal art. The feminist critic Sandra M. Gilbert has recently argued that classic women's writing often is gender-specific in its quest to transcend gender.[17] As paradoxical as this theory sounds, it is in fact corroborated by the rise of a sophisticated American women's literature. By the 1850s there was a growing respect for nonpolitical means of advancing feminist or protofeminist principles. In 1854 Paulina Wright

Davis editorialized in *The Una* that women's rights are advanced not just by orators but by any independent working woman, by any woman novelist, by any woman editor. Reflecting the era's increased respect for woman as creator, Davis stressed: "The artist, in her studio, toiling patiently with her chisel, seeing in the marble forms of beauty, is the holiest reformer of them all, for she is creating."[18] The creative act itself, divorced from politics, became suddenly prized. This new emphasis on woman as creative artist fed into Hawthorne's portrait in *The Marble Faun* of two independent women artists, the adept copyist Hilda and the original painter Miriam. In key writings by American women, it was evidenced by a self-conscious promotion of complex, androgynous art. *Lessons of Life* (1854), a novel that ran serially in *The Una,* was representative in this regard. It described the harsh travails and final success of an artist, Margaret Ramsay, who at first protests publicly against male tyranny at a women's rights convention but then discovers that her art is her most potent means of self-expression. She concludes: "My life has been very free, and I have spoken in Art, yet I have at times felt the bitterness of a woman's lot. . . . My world is Art, and I know no sex there."[19] Margaret Ramsay was a heroine for her times, a maltreated woman, motivated by bitterness against males, who gains her triumph through the creation of art.

There were several real-life Margaret Ramsays—creative women on the fringes of the suffrage movement who occasionally wrote political tracts on behalf of women but whose best works represented an effort to move beyond politics into the free realm of art. Alice Cary, Lillie Devereux Blake, Sara Willis Parton, Louisa May Alcott, Rebecca Harding Davis, Harriet Prescott Spofford, and Elizabeth Stoddard were the principal figures whose finest works, written mainly between 1855 and 1865, may be placed behind Emily Dickinson's best poems (most of which were also written in these years) as the main texts of the American Women's Renaissance. To be sure, none of these lesser writers approached Emily Dickinson in terms of originality or artistic density. Still, their finest writings possess a complexity lacking in previous American women's literature, and as a group they can be said to have helped prepare the way for Emily Dickinson and, in a different sense, for Henry James and Edith Wharton.

These women writers were profoundly skeptical of the simple pieties of Conventional literature but they also shied away from public agitation for women's rights. Poised between the Conventional and the feminist, they took a fierce pride in their ability to manipulate and recombine the various women's roles offered by their contemporary culture. Their major texts are quirky but restrained, characterized by shifting imagery or broken narrative patterns and often by a terse, hard-boiled style. They often sought variety and changeability of tone for its own sake, as they began to test their literary powers by experimenting with changes of perspective, pungent wit, distortion, ellipsis. Samuel Bowles noticed such mercurial qualities in the literature of misery when he wrote that it often "clouds, withers, distorts."[20] Although the rather conventional Bowles was disturbed by this elliptical style, modern readers have good reason to be intrigued by it, for it shows the stormy passions of traditional women's wrongs literature being consciously sculpted and projected into experimental narrative structures and strange images.

Typical of this dark new women's literature was the best fiction and poetry of Alice Cary, the Ohio-born writer who moved to New York in 1850, when she was thirty, and produced several novels and poetry volumes. Cary believed in women's rights and became the first president of the first women's club, Sorosis. She was, however, a shy woman who once confessed: "I must work in my own way, and that is a very quiet one."[21] Shortly before her death in 1871, she published in the suffrage sheet *The Revolution* a women's rights novel, *The Born Thrall,* about which one reviewer declared: "What *Uncle Tom's Cabin* was to the anti-slavery movement, this work will be to the cause of women."[22] But *The Born Thrall* is another example of artistry being sacrificed to propaganda, for this women's rights novel has far less literary merit than her earlier, less obviously political works.

These early works had typified the literature of misery. Cary's poetry was sometimes criticized because it was filled with images of graves and death. One of her close friends noted that Cary's literary death laments were "the utterance of actual loss, not the morbid sentimentalism of poetic youth."[23] As a child she had lost her mother and two beloved sisters and had subsequently fallen in love with an older, cultured man who rejected her because she was poor, a story she retold in the novel *Hagar* (1852). Her first major poem, appropriately titled "The Child of Sorrow," was published in 1838, and soon she was receiving praise from established critics such as Edgar Allan Poe, Rufus Griswold, and Horace Greeley. Whatever pleasure she derived from this praise was diminished by the residual wounds from her early life, which she later recalled as a dreary round "of bereavement, of constant struggle, and of hope deferred." Her sister Phoebe said she never looked upon her face, even in sleep, without seeing "the sad characters of weariness and pain." While this pain had originally derived from her private troubles, in time it came to be associated in Cary's mind with the condition of all women. In her opening address to the Sorosis club, she generalized that women "are, in fact, weighed down with shame and humiliation, and impelled, while we are about it, to make full confession of all our wild and guilty fantasies." In short, Alice Cary was temperamentally and politically positioned to become a pioneering author of the literature of misery.

Although Cary was a skilled poet (her poem "The Pictures of Memory" was hailed by Poe as one of the most musically exquisite lyrics in the language), it is her forgotten novels *Hagar, A Story of To-day* (1852) and *Married, Not Mated* (1859) that most deserve reconsideration by modern readers. In these novels, the "wild and guilty fantasies" that Cary said were buried with all women explode to the surface. Because of their often offensive themes and experimental style, these novels were roundly damned by several antebellum reviewers. Even *The Una,* which was ordinarily tolerant of the darkest women's literature, complained that in *Hagar* Cary revealed "no aim or purpose but to give utterance to sickly, morbid fancies" and "had been down into one of Dante's hells to get her inspiration for her last chapter of horrors."[24] Evidently, even the progressive *Una* was not prepared to appreciate this novel about extramarital sex, crushing rejection and loneliness, and insanity, a novel filled with references to death and mutability. More than one reviewer compared *Hagar* to *The Scarlet Letter,* for it told the story of a woman who had an illegitimate child by a man who went on to become a widely respected minister and who eventually died in remorse, while his lover, like Hester Prynne, lived a life of penance in a solitary cottage near a village. Despite this similarity in plot, Hawthorne's and Cary's novels are quite different in tone, chiefly because Hester Prynne is a far brighter character than Hagar. In Hester, Hawthorne successfully brought together several key female stereotypes, some dark and some bright, and thus fashioned a broadly representative heroine who embodied at once the gloom of women's wrongs and the redemptiveness of moral exemplar feminism. Hagar, in contrast, embodies only women's wrongs, without any redemptiveness whatsoever. She endures abandonment and betrayal not with the haughty pride of Hester but with the grim stoicism of later American heroines, such as Crane's Maggie or Dreiser's Sister Carrie. The novel is darker than *The Scarlet Letter* in other ways too: whereas Hester's illegitimate child survives and becomes a respectable woman, Hagar's dies and leaves her mother miserable and her father haunted by guilt; whereas Arthur Dimmesdale purgatively confesses his sin in public, Cary's fallen clergyman becomes a skeptical misanthrope and at last is carted howling in a cage to an insane asylum; whereas Hester remains penitentially in her cottage, Hagar leaves her cottage with a dreary vow "to wander thirsty and alone in the desert."[25] It is no accident that Cary selected Hagar, who in the Bible is the tormented mother of the outcast Ishmael, as the archetype for her heroine. Just as Melville's Ishmael is the quintessential hero of dark male literature, so Cary's Hagar is the appropriate emblem of the American woman's literature of misery.

This new dark women's literature, lacking the redemptiveness of the Conventional or the political hopes of women's rights, was a transitional genre that looked forward to the fiction of the American naturalists. A prenaturalistic determinism governs Cary's *Married, Not Mated,* a novel, set in rural Ohio, that portrays a kind of moral wasteland where isolated, antagonistic people live in cynicism and complacent self-delusion. As in certain works by Crane and Wharton, characters in *Married, Not Mated* do not shape their own destinies so much as they passively flow according to the dictates of their temperament and their environment. The grim spirit of the novel is suggested by a brief review of the main characters: Annette Furniss, a "heartless, disappointed, and embittered" woman who has been jilted by a man of superior education and who frees herself from poverty only by marrying a man she despises;[26] her sister Nelly, who dies young and leaves Annette with a "settled and passionless sorrow"; their old grandmother, who lives in a messy attic with her deformed grandson, whom she savagely beats until he dies; the landowner Peter Throckmorton, who passes from robust healthy-mindedness to quivering nervousness as result of some imagined disease; his doting wife, Sally Ann, a virtual nonentity who eventually fades away and dies; Stafford Graham, the dashing but selfish doctor who coldly exploits his magnetic charm over women; and Orpha, the ugly, moody narrator of the second half of the novel, whose dark outlook contrasts with that of her cheerier but less interesting sister Rosalie. Just as remarkable as this array of strange characters is the senselessness of their interactions. They rarely communicate with each other; instead, they talk over each other and collide against each other. The prevailing noncommunication between the characters is epitomized in a long scene toward the end of the novel in which Throckmorton, suffering nervous collapse during his imaginary illness, has an insane conversation with his wife in which he frantically describes a nightmare and barrages her with absurd, contradictory commands. This nonsensical interchange is emblematic of Cary's strategy throughout the novel of distorting perspectives and playing off different points of view.

The intentional confusion is directly connected to women's issues, for in a central scene in the novel several characters attend a suffrage convention that begins decorously but rapidly deteriorates into a chaotic brawl between conservatives and radicals on the woman issue. The conservatives argue that woman's place is in the home, away from the corrupt political arena, while the radicals firmly defend women's right to equal employment and the vote. Although we know from Cary's life that her heart was with the radicals, this scene is most significant not for its feminist message but for its depiction of warring viewpoints, just as other scenes in the novel play popular fads like mesmerism, spiritualism, and phrenology against each other. *Married, Not Mated* succeeds precisely to the extent that it refuses to rest comfortably in a single political outlook. It transforms disparate voices of antebellum culture into an almost premodern text of conflict and disorientation.

Another example of the literature of misery is *Southwold* (1859), a novel by the largely forgotten author and suffragist Lillie Devereux Blake. A prolific writer who produced five novels and hundreds of shorter pieces, Blake also served as president of the New York Woman Suffrage Association and worked closely with Elizabeth Cady Stanton and Susan B. Anthony. As early as 1849, when she was sixteen, Blake had revealed strong feminist urges in a remarkable private document entitled "I Live to Redress the Wrongs of My Sex," in which she angrily wrote: "Women have been from time immemorial duped and deceived by men, their feelings trifled with and their hearts broken. . . . I give my heart and soul to making men miserable. . . . I will live but to redress these terrible wrongs!"[27] To a large degree, she lived up to this feminist vow. The fiction she produced in the 1850s and 1860s often featured scheming heroines who shrewdly subvert arrogant men. By the late 1860s, her instinctive feminism changed into political activism, for it was then that she concentrated on suffrage work. During this later political period she produced *Fettered for Life* (1874), the most comprehensive women's rights novel written in nineteenth-century America. This novel portrays a heroine who, distressed by the males' brutality and discrimination against women, accepts the progressive views of a woman doctor. Although *Fettered for Life* is a historically significant novel that should be read by those interested in the suffrage movement, it was, as a reviewer for *The Golden Age* rightly noted, "merely the vehicle for [Blake's] theories on the woman question" and lacked the artistry of some of her earlier fiction.[28] Among Blake's earlier works, none possessed more power or complexity than her first novel, *Southwold.* Produced at a fertile moment between Blake's protofeminist and politically active periods, *Southwold* possesses the fiery rage of her teenage document and signs of the political rebelliousness that would be stated more baldly in her suffrage writings.

Southwold is a gloomy novel about a woman, wounded by unrequited love, who vindictively manipulates men and eventually is driven to crime and suicide. The magnificent heroine, Medora Fielding, is a socialite with a turbulent inner life and a sharp, probing intellect. She becomes rapidly bored with her superficial life of parties and balls, and she falls desperately in love with a man who rejects her on behalf of another woman he marries for money. In revenge, Medora finds her own wealthy partner, Floyd Southwold, and inveigles him into a marriage proposal. The proposed match is vehemently resisted by Floyd's uncle. Medora successfully plots to murder the uncle, a crime that stuns the ingenuous Floyd and finally drives Medora to madness and suicide. Perhaps the most interesting aspect of the novel is the author's notably ambivalent attitude toward the heroine, who is a passionate, highly intelligent woman driven by outside forces into a labyrinth of evil. By far the most magnetic presence in the book, Medora is a free spirit trapped in the shell of a social butterfly. "Her mind," Blake emphasizes, "had a rare breadth and scope; indeed, it was almost masculine in its depth of thought and capability of analytical inquiry."[29] In the portrait of Medora, Blake implicitly criticizes a society in which women are not given an outlet for their intellect and their passions. Medora repeatedly outsmarts male characters in philosophical dialogues and dreams of a society in which women are granted full equality with men, but her own experience testifies to the tragic reality that, in a world of devalued males, women are driven to sexual manipulation and constant posing.

Given Blake's later commitment to the suffrage cause, these feminist undertones in the novel are doubtless intentional. Actually, however, the novel's feminist themes are not its most important feature. *Southwold* is a more powerful work than the later *Fettered for Life* because it possesses a density that the straightforward women's rights novel lacks. The surest sign of Blake's assertiveness is her success in creating a multifaceted heroine and placing her in a problematic fictional world in which the powers of darkness have full sway and forces for good are rendered inoperable. The novel is filled with penetrating questions about religious faith and with haunting images of death and mutability. The skeptical Medora becomes a vehicle for the author's doubts about Christianity. A disbeliever to the end, Medora refuses to pray even as she prepares to poison herself: "With fierce desperation she rebelled against her inexorable fate, and impiously dared to curse God and die!" Blake constantly broods over death and transience, as when she writes: "Oh! infatuated folly of humanity! . . . [W]hile we are constantly walking over graves and the whole world is one vast charnel-house, we still dance merrily and laugh carelessly, giving but a passing attention to that shadowy future whose momentous interest should absorb every thought of this brief existence." Several times in the novel Blake expresses the dark suspicion that belief in an afterlife is merely wishful self-delusion. The skeptical intellect of the restless, frustrated heroine is a projection of Blake's own attempt to venture ambitiously into the realm of dark philosophizing and complex artistry.

The complexity of American women's literature was also visible in another important novelist of the period, Sara Willis Parton (*pseud.* "Fanny Fern"). Parton has a special claim for critical attention, for she had direct connections with several major authors of the American Renaissance. Hawthorne was so pleased by her controversial best-seller *Ruth Hall* that he wrote his publisher asking for more information about "this Fanny Fern" and noting that when women "throw off the restraints of decency, and come before the public stark naked, as it were,—then their books are sure to possess character and value."[30] The devilish quality Hawthorne admired in Parton's style was apparently a source of titilation in the household of Emily Dickinson, as suggested by an extant description of Emily cheering up her father by reading to him "spicey passages from Fern leaves."[31] There were also links between Parton and Walt Whitman: the fern-leaf pattern he selected for the cover of *Leaves of Grass* was most likely derived from a pattern on her popular *Fern Leaves from Fanny's Port Folio*; his choice of "leaves" as a dominant metaphor in his poem may have been influenced by a desire to tap the market created by *Fern Leaves*; and Parton distinguished herself by becoming the first woman who publicly praised *Leaves of Grass*. In her 1856 review of the poem for the *New York Ledger* she commended the poem as "fresh, hardy, and grown for the masses" and perceptively noted that its open sexuality was far purer than the covert prurience of much popular American writing.[32]

The cross-influences between Parton and the major authors become particularly intriguing when we look at her main writings, which at their best possess a remarkable tonal flexibility and, on occasion, preliterary complexity. When Hawthorne commented that she wrote as if the Devil were in her, he probably had in mind the playful waspishness that characterized her style. She shifted between different female personae with chameleonlike ease. Her popular sketch collection *Fern Leaves* (1853), which sold more than 100,000 copies in its first year, was a patchwork portrayal of an extraordinary variety of female roles. In *Fern Leaves* the zestfully mercurial Parton is by turns cute, coy, vindictive, prissy, erotic, motherly, feminist—everything but shy and retiring. While few of the individual sketches have literary quality, taken as a whole *Fern Leaves* posed a significant challenge to monolithic gender roles. For the first time in American literature, a woman writer showed that conventional appearances could be donned and shed like changeable masks.

These shifts, predictably, gave rise to inconsistencies that bothered some reviewers. But inconsistencies were in fact a major element of Parton's shape-shifting strategy. In a sequence called "Fanny's Ideas about Babies" she boasts that "Fanny's sentiments on this subject are decidedly contradictory," a boast confirmed by the difference between a sketch that dismisses babies as disgusting "botherations" and another that hails them as adorable angels.[33] Conscious manipulation of attitudes and gender roles is sought by Parton for its own sake. At one point in *Fern Leaves* Parton makes clear that this manipulativeness springs from a desire to entrap men who have become wary of open lobbying for women's rights. Because by the mid-1850s the women's movement had prompted a backlash of harsh criticism, mainly from men, the rebellious woman writer was forced to disguise her feminism, to express it indirectly by fusing it with Conventional appearances. In a sketch about women's rights, Parton comments: "The instant the subject is mentioned, the lords of creation are up and dressed. Guns and bayonets the order of the day; *no surrender* on every flag that floats! The only way left is to pursue the 'Uriah Heep' policy; look *umble,* and be almighty cunning. Bait 'em with submission, and then throw the noose over the will . . . Make your reins of silk, *keep 'em out of sight, and drive where you like!*" Because open feminism had become too risky for the woman author who wished to reach the mass audience, a new style of indirection and disarming wit must be cultivated. As Parton saw it, the "lords of creation" were up in arms, and women must "bait" them with submission before throwing "the noose" over their will.

Her most deadly stylistic "noose" was her ability to shift tone and assume different guises rapidly. Parton was reportedly shifty and manipulative by nature. A friend recalled that in conversation she was "witty and pathetic by turns; now running over with fun, and now with tears."[34] She never kept a close friend for more than two years, she was married three times, she was disowned by her father because of her rebellious nature, and she had a strained relationship with her brother. It was her combined manipulativenes and her vindictiveness against family members that led to the writing of *Ruth Hall.* When it was published in 1854, *Ruth Hall* became an instant *succès de scandale,* for it was full of vicious caricatures of her family and friends. Parton was widely blasted in the press for what was called her filial disrespect and her religious irreverence, but perceptive reviewers saw the novel as an important moment in American women's writing. Hawthorne was not alone in his admiration for the devilish boldness of the novel. In an 1855 review of *Ruth Hall* in *The Una,* the suffrage leader Elizabeth Cady Stanton wrote: "In the name of womanhood, I thank Fanny Fern for this deeply interesting life experience. . . . When woman does at length divest herself of all false notions of justice and delicacy, and gives to the world a full revelation of her sufferings and miseries,—the histories of all other kinds of injustice and oppression will sink into utter insignificance, before the living pictures she shall hold up to the unwilling vision of domestic tyrants." In addition to revealing women's miseries, Stanton added, the novel teaches "the great lesson" that "God has given woman sufficient brain and muscle to work out her own destiny unaided and alone."[35]

As Stanton recognized, *Ruth Hall* is an innovative record of woman's suffering and of woman's triumph. Based loosely on Parton's troubled life, it dramatizes the almost unthinkable wretchedness of a young widow who, forever saddened by the premature death of her husband, is left unaided by her parents, her brother, and her in-laws, all of whom callously ignore her pleas for help, so that she is forced to raise her two children in a state of near starvation in a squalid urban tenement. Ruth takes on several lowly jobs in her struggle to escape poverty, until as a last resort she tries her hand at writing sketches for popular periodicals. Using the pseudonym "Floy," she succeeds as a popular author and finally settles down in a marriage of equality with an intelligent man. Despite the happy ending, the novel is dominated by images of gloom. Ruth is a harassed woman victim forced by ill luck and family indifference to become a working woman. Parton leaves little doubt that a gender-specific animosity fuels the novel. In a central chapter Ruth visits an insane asylum filled with women who have been abandoned, cheated, or brutalized by men. Ruth witnesses one screaming madwoman, Mary Leon, whipped to death in the hospital. The grim product of a society that discriminates against women, Mary had been abandoned by her husband, who carried off their child and who remained unpunished, because "the law, . . . as it generally is, was on the man's side."[36] The sexual discrimination that had driven Mary and the other hospital inmates mad confronts Ruth Hall herself at every turn. As a working woman Ruth is stunned by the paucity of meaningful jobs open to women. She continually encounters male chauvinism even when she becomes a successful author, as when one stuffy reviewer insists that "the *female* mind is incapable of producing anything which may be strictly called *literature.*" The pieces Ruth writes exemplify American women's literature of misery. They spring from her "bitter life experience" like "a wail from her inmost soul." Bereaved by the death of her husband, Harry, and maltreated at every turn, Ruth becomes the quintessential example of Parton's view that "no happy woman ever writes. From Harry's grave sprang 'Floy.' " In self-reflexive fashion, *Ruth Hall,* itself a prime text of the literature of misery, illustrates how this dark women's genre came into being.

But if the novel reveals the roots of the literature of misery, it also suggests how this literature could become the instrument of woman's triumph: the dual triumph of her self-support in a male-dominated world and of her canny manipulation of others. Ruth's sketches are so varied (they are aptly described as "a bundle of contradictions!") that they fascinate but confuse her readers, who vent a cacophony of outraged responses:

> All sorts of rumors became rife about "Floy," some maintaining her to be a man, because she had the courage to call things by their right names, and the independence to express herself boldly on subjects to which the timid and clique-serving, were tabooed. Some said she was a disappointed old maid; some said she was a designing widow; some said she was a moon-struck girl; and all said she was nondescript.

For Ruth Hall, as for Parton herself, literature is simultaneously a projection of woman's misery and a proclamation of her power. Literary creativity is fueled by the special anguish of woman's suffering, but at the same time it offers escape from the confining social conventions that surround her. The literary mask behind which Ruth hides is a tantalizingly variable one. It represents the woman writer's newly found ability to change kaleidoscopically, to free herself from male-defined categories that society imposes upon her. Readers of all kinds try to define the "real" Floy, but their definitions always come up short because they are founded upon bias and preconceptions. Floy is variously called a man, an old maid, a designing widow, a lovestruck girl. The truth is that, through the magic of the changeable literary persona, she is all of these at once. Woman's highest power, Parton suggests, is the ability to manipulate others while eluding definition, and the highest manipulative act is that of flexible writing.

Ruth Hall enacts structurally the changeability it heralds in its heroine's literary style. Just as the canny "Floy" frustrates her readers by producing contradictory sketches, so the mercurial "Fanny Fern" tantalizes her readers by playing games with narrative form. *Ruth Hall* was often attacked as formless. One reviewer remarked: "The story of *Ruth Hall* is nothing. There is no plot whatsoever; no thread of interest to hold one to its pages." Another complained: "Disjointed fragments of what should be a beautiful and complete edifice, are all that meets the eye."[37] These comments are accurate enough, but they overlook the intentionality behind Parton's formlessness. In her preface Parton says of her novel: "I am aware that it is entirely at variance with all set rules for novel-writing."[38] Throughout the novel (particularly in the first half) Parton experiments with the device of shifting point of view. Through much of the book we get little direct, firsthand description of Ruth Hall and her children; instead, we hear *reports* of the protagonists' experiences from other characters, reports that are almost invariably twisted or biased. Often there is no preparation for scenes and no sequential relation between chapters. The reader is continually shunted from perspective to perspective. This contravention of normal narrative pattern is a crude version of the carefully regulated formlessness of modern novelists. Although Parton's narrative shifts are sustained only through certain sections of the novel, they are intriguing disjunctions directly related to the willed evasiveness of the taunting woman writer. Significantly, the male-chauvinist reviewer in *Ruth Hall* who says literature cannot be produced by "the *female* mind" upbraids "Floy" for her lack of form: "[Y]ou violate all established rules of composition, and are as lawless and erratic as a comet." From Parton's vantage point, literary regularity and predictability are of a piece with the repressive male order that bans freedom for women. By the same token, irregularity and unpredictability—as manifested in the style of Floy and of Fanny Fern herself—are the sign of woman's liberating creativity.

The phenomenon of a popular woman writer's adept shifts in guises, engendering literary creativity, is also visible in the career of Louisa May Alcott. It is well known that Alcott began as a writer of lurid sensational fiction and then, at her publisher's demand, shifted her energies to moralistic children's literature, a genre which she once dismissed as "moral pap" but which gave her fame and financial independence. What has been overlooked is the crucial significance of popular culture in freeing Alcott's literary powers and especially in giving rise to *Behind a Mask* (1866), the complex novella that is beginning to be recognized as her most accomplished work and that is another example of the literature of misery.

The development of Alcott's literary sensibility is recorded in her largely autobiographical portrait of Jo March in *Little Women* (1868). After her family has been reduced to a state of near poverty, Jo decides to support it by writing popular fiction. At first she tries her hand at sensational stories that are "as full of desperation and despair as her limited acquaintance with those uncomfortable emotions enabled her to make it."[39] She ransacks all kinds of sensational social texts—police reports, the records of lunatic asylums, newspaper stories of accidents and crimes—for grisly material to weave into fervid serial novels with titles like *The Phantom Hand* and *The Curse of the Coventrys.* She is trying to tap the market for Romantic Adventure and Subversive literature, which, as we have seen in earlier chapters, were enjoying extraordinary popularity during this period. Like the writings by Parton's "Floy," Jo's fiction gets a notable mixture of responses. "Some make fun of it," she muses, "some overpraise, and nearly all insist that I had a deep theory to expound, when I only wrote it for the pleasure and the money." Although her sensational stories are profitable, they are dangerous to write, for in writing them Jo is "feeding heart and fancy on dangerous and unsubstantial food" and gaining "a premature acquaintance with the darker side of life." She therefore vows to write "no more sensational stories, deciding that the money did not pay for her share of the sensation, but going to the opposite extreme," she writes an "intensely moral" tale illustrating religion. But the feisty Jo "felt as ill at ease in this new style as she would have done masquerading in the stiff and cumbrous costume of the last century," and so she next attempts a children's tale but finds this equally awkward because of its didacticism. Jo finally reaches an impasse, declares, "I don't know anything," puts away her pen and ink, and whimsically decides to " 'sweep mud in the street,' if I can't do better; that's honest, at least." Instinctively inclined to write profitable sensational literature, therefore, Jo finds its dark realms precarious for her imagination, and so she recoils to an artificial commitment to the Conventional, only to find that the latter has become meaningless for her.

Jo March's pendulum swing from the Subversive to the Conventional, and her eventual recognition of the artificiality of both, signifies the moral relativism lurking behind the surface roles offered to the popular woman writer. Like Ruth Hall as "Floy," Jo March as popular author is shifty, detached from her work, misinterpreted by reviewers, and fundamentally cynical about the literary marketplace. Like Sara Parton, Louisa May Alcott knew the perils of the marketplace but at the same time profited artistically from the liberating variability it offered. The most significant reality that Alcott learned from her experience as a professional author is that in the fluid realm of American popular culture, moral values had become changeable objects of production rather than fixed entities with clear referents. Like her alter ego Jo March, Alcott was from an early age drawn instinctively to the writing of dark sensational literature. At fifteen she and her sister Anna co-authored thrilling melodramas with titles like *The Captive of Castille* and *Norna; or, The Witches' Curse.* In the 1850s and 1860s, using various pseudonyms, she produced for the story-papers numerous grisly sensational tales which provided psychological catharsis since they often involved wronged women wreaking violent vengeance on evil men. "I think my natural ambition is for the lurid style," she once confessed in conversation.[40] In an 1862 letter to a male friend she typically announced her intention "to illuminate the [New York] Ledger with a blood & thunder tale as they are easier to 'compoze' & are better paid than moral & elaborate works."[41] But by the late 1860s, she was willing to follow her publisher's suggestion to produce the didactic children's fiction that was to make her famous. The fact that she changed modes so easily and once derogated *Little Women* as "moral pap" need not shock us. For Alcott, as for Parton, the Conventional had become just another change of costume for the flexible popular writer who, like her heroine, always remained detached from the changing literary personae she donned in public.

As was true with Parton, this changeability paid literary dividends, for it made possible Alcott's intriguing novella *Behind a Mask; or, A Woman's Power.* As the title suggests, this work depicts a woman who gains power by remaining forever behind a social mask. The heroine, Jean Muir, is an amoral woman for whom Conventional values are mere cloaks worn to manipulate others. A wronged woman who has been severely wounded in love, she takes vengeance against men by attracting them with her sweet, docile appearance, scheming all the while to take advantage of them. She seems "meek, modest, faithful, and invariably sweet-tempered."[42] In short, she poses as the Conventional moral exemplar, and several men fall for the ruse, even though, ironically enough, she warns them to beware of her. Vowing at the start to take vengeance against men, she cries: "I will not fail again if there is power in a woman's wit and will!" In public she is a frail orphan forced by poverty to take on a lowly governess job. In the privacy of her room, with her false teeth out and her makeup off, she is revealed as "a haggard, worn, and moody woman of thirty at least" with a "weary, hard, bitter" expression caused by the "disappointment which had darkened all her life." In Jean Muir, the woman victim gains revenge by masquerading as the moral exemplar. By the end, her canny use of mock virtue has enabled her to become the wealthy Lady Coventry, victorious in the knowledge that her naïve old husband refuses to believe true reports about her murky past as an abandoned wife and a kept woman. As a marvelously two-faced heroine, Jean Muir is unusual among Alcott's characters since she is a fusion of opposite elements. She is a bitterly ironic version of the manipulativeness and changeability that had been expressed more positively in Parton's Ruth Hall.

Another novel that reveals the stylistic innovations of the literature of misery is Elizabeth Stoddard's *The Morgesons* (1862). Lawrence Buell and Sandra A. Zagarell, in their 1984 reprint of the novel, call Stoddard "next to Hawthorne and Melville, the most strikingly original voice in the mid-nineteenth-century American novel," notable particularly for an "astringent, elliptical style" attractive to the modern reader.[43] Actually, *The Morgesons* is a quite typical example of the dark genre of women's writings whose earlier texts included Cary's *Hagar* and *Married, Not Mated,* Blake's *Southwold,* Parton's *Ruth Hall,* and Harriet Prescott Spofford's haunting story "Circumstance." The novel's heroine, Cassandra, interesting as she is, in fact is less spunky and less forthrightly feminist than several other heroines of the 1850s and 1860s.

Contrary to critical myth, Stoddard's achievement was not to introduce a feminist rebelliousness to American fiction but rather to analyze strong rebellious impulses already there, to study the psychological traumas resulting from the thwarting of these impulses, and to project these repressed, frustrated feelings in a fictional style that anticipated the grimness and muted imagism of certain naturalistic authors. Like most works in the literature of misery, *The Morgesons* was sharply denounced for its unusual style. Henry James, for one, called it "a thoroughly bad novel . . . totally destitute of form," possessing "not even the slightest mechanical coherency," a nightmarish record of "disjointed, pointless repartee."[44] The novel's breaches of literary decorum were just as relevant to women's issues as were those in other women's writings of the day. The indirections and disconnections that outraged James were typical of the broken narrative patterns of the literature of misery. The heroine, Cassandra, is, in several senses, also typical: considered devilish and lawless as a child, she develops into a passionate, independent-minded woman whose frustrations in love and friendship eventually make her embittered and skeptical. Temperamentally akin to Cary's Hagar or Blake's Medora Fielding, she embodies the rich conflict between heterosexual love and womanly self-sufficiency. She greatly admires two independent women she meets, the intellectual Adelaide and the businesswoman Alice, but she is irresistibly attracted to a rakish man and is unsatisfied with intellectual or economic pursuits. In the portrait of Cassandra, Stoddard communicates the profound weariness and restless longing that lies beneath the shifting mask of the American heroine. Anticipating Edna Pontellier, the heroine of Kate Chopin's *The Awakening* (1899), Cassandra is driven by boredom and frustrated love to contemplate suicide. Like Edna, she studies the sea and feels "ever attracted by an awful materiality and its easy power to drown me."[45] Although she overcomes these suicidal impulses and is married, she remains until the end a largely unfulfilled woman haunted by the death of loved ones and made wretched by the economic decline of her family.

Like other central texts of the literature of misery, *The Morgesons* proclaims woman's power largely through stylistic innovations that show the author competing with male writers in the androgynous realm of literary art. Although narrative disjointedness and minimalist dialogue were not original with Stoddard—similar experimental devices had characterized American Subversive fiction since the days of John Neal—*The Morgesons* represents an effort to fuse such devices with the tone and themes of dark women's fiction. The result is a style that is purposely disorienting but at the same time carefully restrained. The style of male Subversive writers from Neal through Lippard was experimental in an eruptive, highly emotional way; that of women writers like Cary and Stoddard was experimental in a muted, withdrawn way. Just as the heroines of the literature of misery have powerful energies whose repression or submergence becomes a main concern of the author, so the author herself typically submerges powerful creative impulses that gather extraordinary force in a kind of violent implosion, evidenced in compactness of image. The real rewards of *The Morgesons* lie not in any overt feminist themes but rather in quietly potent, often wryly subversive images that attest to woman's artistic power. With economy and vividness Stoddard captures the benign boredom of Cassandra's bourgeois background when she has her heroine remember only "an eternal smell of cookery, a perpetual changing of beds, and the small talk of vacant minds."[46] Elsewhere, describing the bleak landscape of a town in winter, she makes a point that T. S. Eliot would differently express: "The desolation of winter sustains our frail hopes. Nature is kindest then; she does not taunt us with fruition." Cassandra's dour mood at the graveyard during her mother's funeral is succinctly communicated in this imagistic brushstroke: "[T]he whole round of gray sky was visible. It hung low over us. I wished it to drop and blot out the vague nothings under it." The real victory of the nineteenth-century American woman writer, as manifested in the work of Emily Dickinson and Kate Chopin, would be the ingenuity with which women's anger and women's power were projected in compelling images. Stoddard's *The Morgesons* is one of several works of the American Women's Renaissance in which we see this kind of victory beginning to be achieved.

A similar literary victory is gained in another paradigmatic women's text of the period, Rebecca Harding Davis's novel *Life in the Iron-Mills* (1861). As was true of previous complex women's writings, the success of Davis's novel lies in its objectification of women's anxieties and fantasies in moving images of universal appeal.

Life in the Iron-Mills has been revived as an exposé novel unique for its powerful accounts of working-class wretchedness. Tillie Olsen claims in the 1972 Feminist Press edition of the novel: "In the consciousness of literary America, there had been no dark satanic mills. . . . If working people existed—and nowhere were they material for serious attention, let alone the central subject—they were 'clean-haired Yankee mill girls,' and their mills were an industrial paradise."[47] This generalization, as we have seen, is inaccurate. The wretchedness of working people had since the 1830s been a common topic in American exposé literature, and the special misery of factory girls had been featured in a variety of novels and poems. *Life in the Iron-Mills* deserves study not for the originality of its topic but for its success in bringing to a familiar American theme—the plight of working men and women—a new stylistic density and a tonal grimness derived principally from the literature of misery. The novel involves a poor Virginia ironworker, Hugh Wolfe, whose wife, Deborah, picks the pocket of a visiting rich man and gives the money to Hugh, who reluctantly accepts it with the vague dream of buying escape from a life of drudgery. Arrested for the crime and sentenced to nineteen years' hard labor, he eventually kills himself in jail and leaves behind only an artistic legacy of working-class oppression: his rude but powerful iron sculpture of a miserable working woman. The sculpture embodies the new artistic self-consciousness of woman's wrongs literature. Witness the way the sculpture is described: "There was not one line of beauty or grace in it: a nude woman's form, muscular, grown coarse with labor, the powerful limbs instinct with some poignant longing. One idea: there it was in the tense, rigid muscles, the clutching hands, the wild, eager face, like that of a starving wolf's . . . A working woman,—the very type of her class." The whole movement of the literature of misery had been toward the artistic objectification of women's wrongs and women's potency in a compact image, and the sculpture (like

Miriam's lay figure of the wretched woman in *The Marble Faun*) is a result of that movement. Another result is the bleakly symbolic style of the entire novel. From the opening account of the "muddy, flat, immovable" sky looming over the mill town through the picture of Deborah Wolfe's "dead, vacant look" to the mention of Hugh Wolfe's "vile, slimy" life, we witness the real power of the woman writer—the discovery of metaphors that communicate the atmosphere of working-class life more effectively than speeches or political tracts.

The Strongest Amazon

Having surveyed key examples of the literature of misery, we can now turn to Emily Dickinson, who in a sense can be viewed as a composite of all the authors of the literature of misery. Although feminist criticism has produced valuable readings of certain Dickinson poems, her place in nineteenth-century women's culture has been largely misapprehended.

One of the most common errors of critics has been to focus closely on a handful of poems that seem to have gender-specific meaning. The fact is that Dickinson's poetry is most characteristic of her era's best women's writing in its extraordinary flexibility of tone, its refusal to rest comfortably in individual gender roles, its magnificent assertion of creativity through the fabrication of dense imagery, its gaps and indirections, and its gender-specific quest for a gender-free reality. We have seen that the height of the American Women's Renaissance came in the years 1858 through 1866, a time of temporary diminution in women's rights activity and of the search for more oblique means of expressing women's rage and fantasies. It was a time of extreme self-consciousness about the proliferation of varied women's roles in American culture. Mary Louise Hankins's *Women of New York* (1860) described no fewer than thirty-two kinds of American women—including, significantly, the confidence woman, who could playfully act out all the other women's roles with devilish ease. The variability Hankins perceived was enacted by women writers who took pride in literary acts of self-transformation and manipulation. In characterization, this pride was projected in characters like Medora Fielding and Jean Muir, canny heroines who avenge women's wrongs by feigning virtue. In plot, it produced broken narrative patterns. In atmosphere, it was reflected in tonal neutrality. In theme, it was evidenced by a preoccupation with doubt and negativity. In style it gave rise to minimalism, ellipsis, compaction. Intrinsic to this women's literature was a belief in the tormented but dauntless core self of the woman artist, lying below all gender roles and regulating them at will, asserting its power through waspish imagery and daring to tackle universal themes that lay beyond myth or gender. Given the extreme fertility of this historical moment in American woman's culture, it is perhaps understandable that of the 1,775 poems Emily Dickinson was to write in her lifetime a staggering 1,098 (62 percent of the total) were produced in the 1858–66 period. If we take into account both Dickinson's remarkable productivity during these years and the intriguing works written by less familiar women authors, this period might actually be regarded as the richest moment in the literary history of women.

Feminist criticism has discovered one of its best subjects in Emily Dickinson. Sandra M. Gilbert's and Susan Gubar's provocative analysis of Dickinson as madwoman and mythmaker; Wendy Martin's thoughtful comparison of her with Anne Bradstreet and Adrienne Rich; Margaret Homans's discussion of linguistic disruption as an element of her power as a woman writer; Vivian Pollak's notion of her "anxiety of gender"—these and other feminist-related approaches have reinvigorated the study of Emily Dickinson, who had long been the victim of misemphasis and even outright distortion by traditional critics dismissive of the importance of her womanhood to her art.[48]

There are, however, still areas of investigation open to those who wish to understand Emily Dickinson's role as a woman writer. In particular, it has not been shown that her gender-specific themes and devices were, in crucial ways, also *culture-specific and time-specific.* Precisely the opposite argument, in fact, has been offered by feminist critics, almost all of whom work from the assumption that she was distanced from a repressively conventional nineteenth-century American culture. This consensus is summed up by Suzanne Juhasz's introductory overview of the critics included in her recent volume, *Feminist Critics Read Emily Dickinson*: "All [the feminist critics] show Dickinson, of necessity, responding to repressions that surround her and threaten to control her, change her into something other than she is or might be."[49] Certain Dickinson critics—including George Frisbie Whicher, Richard Sewall, Ruth Miller, Barton Levi St. Armand, and Cynthia Griffin Wolff—have taken a somewhat more rounded view of her poetry, evaluating it in terms of familial and cultural context, but still have accepted the standard view that Dickinson was alienated from antebellum women's culture.[50]

Instead of focusing on "repressions that surround her," Dickinson critics would do well to turn their attention to the cultural forces that liberated her. By doing this, they will realize that she was not a solitary woman rebel but rather the highest product of a rebellious American sisterhood, a sisterhood of "other Amazons" whose best texts had constituted a real literary flowering between 1858 and 1866, the very years that were by far her most productive as a poet.

Emily Dickinson was the full embodiment of the proliferating stereotypes and literary strategies unleashed by antebellum America's women's culture. She had special affinities with the authors of the literature of misery, the genre named and described by Samuel Bowles, the energetic editor she knew well. If the women authors of the literature of misery sought to establish an artistic middle ground between the effetely Conventional and the openly feminist, so Emily Dickinson explicitly rejected both the "Dimity Convictions" of traditionalists and the public methods of women's rights activists, while she made the era's boldest quest for specifically artistic exhibitions of woman's power. If the other women writers typically hid behind shifting literary masks, she played so many roles, from the childlike "Daisy" to the regal "Empress," that it becomes difficult to identify her actual, biographical self. If they often shifted tone and perspective in successive sketches or chapters, she regularly did so in successive verses, lines, and even words. If their experimental style was attacked as crude and formless, so was hers, as is most famously evidenced by Thomas Wentworth Higginson's complaint about her "spasmodic" style. If their work grew principally from the severe inward pain that gave the literature of misery its name, some of her best poetry had a similar source, as is suggested by verses in which she describes grief or pain as exhilarating; one thinks especially of the poem "I can wade Grief— / Whole pools of it—"(#252). If along with this pain went a heady confidence in the creative act as the American woman's surest means of self-assertion, she too was nourished by this confidence, inherited partly from her father (an advocate of women's education and an outspoken admirer of the pioneering woman writer Catharine Sedgwick) and manifested continually by Dickinson's unparalleled poetic innovations. If they had redirected radical-democrat energies toward a search for a gender-free literary reality, she consummated this search in poetry which strains always toward the universal, poetry that reflects her great radical-democrat declaration: "My Country is Truth. . . . It is a very free Democracy."[51]

In addition to these overall affinities between Emily Dickinson and the other American women writers, there are more specific connections in the area of imagery and themes. Her repeated use of volcano imagery, for instance, is very much in the vein of the literature of misery. A basic assumption of this literature is that since women's energies were allowed no viable outlet, they gathered in upon themselves and lay burning inwardly, always threatening to erupt through a placid exterior. The heroines of the literature of misery often looked like sweet moral exemplars but raged inwardly with the ferocity of women victims bent on revenge. This fusion of docile and fiery qualities is summed up by a character in Parton's *Ruth Hall* who generalizes: "[W]henever—you—see—a—blue-eyed—soft-voiced—gentle—woman,—look—out—for a hurricane. I tell you that placid Ruth is a smouldering volcano."[52] In Blake's *Southwold,* the author describes Medora Fielding in a typical moment: "No one could have guessed that the calm indifference of her manner concealed a volcano of rage and scorn."[53] The heroine of the *Una* novel *L'eoline* declares: "A woman made reckless by wrongs, is without compassion," since beneath her gentle exterior lies "a spirit fearless and relentless as the untamed tigress."[54] Even the style of the literature of misery was a kind of dormant volcano, frequently muted and quietly imagistic but always with explosive implications. Emily Dickinson brought a full self-consciousness to the use of volcano imagery, recognizing that it applied both to women's lives and to women's literary style. Her sensitivity to these interrelated levels of meaning is powerfully captured in the first lines of the successive verses of poem #601:

> A still—Volcano—Life— [. . .]
> A quiet—Earthquake Style— [. . .]
> The Solemn—Torrid—Symbol—

These lines are a highly compressed, self-reflexive enactment of the thematic and stylistic polarities of American women's literature. Dickinson's irregular prosody, with its ubiquitous dashes and caesurae, shows rhythm and structure being shattered by the pressure of vehement emotion brought under severe restraint, a stylistic feature common in the literature of misery (witness, for example, the pre-Dickinsonian pauses in the above-quoted passage from *Ruth Hall* on "a—blue-eyed—soft-voiced—gentle—woman,—"). In Dickinson's case, there is evidence that confirms the connection between volcano imagery and women's issues. At a key moment in the longest of her three "Master" letters she communicates the extreme tensions created by her buried feelings as follows: "Vesuvius dont talk—Etna—dont—"[55] Although most generalizations about her character and personal life are tentative at best, the one that certainly holds true is that her extraordinary passional and intellectual powers were inevitably repressed and deflected, gaining full expression only in cryptic, loaded metaphors. It appears, therefore, that there is personal and gender-specific import in such famous Dickinson images as "Vesuvius at Home" (#1705), "the reticent volcano" (#1748), and "On my volcano grows the grass" (#1677). We might be tempted to look for specific biographical sources for Dickinson's volcano imagery (such as the much discussed issue of her possibly homoerotic attraction to her sister-in-law Susan Gilbert Dickinson), but more significant than such psychoanalytic guesswork is the realization that, whatever the personal motivations behind individual poems, Dickinson frequently discovered new poetic applications for the volcano, one of the most common images in American women's writing.

The literature of misery straddles the line between implicit explosiveness and actual frozenness, as though women's continual frustrations threaten always to negate their energies and destroy all feeling. In Sue P. K. Bowen's novella *Sylvia's World* (1859), a once idealistic woman becomes so disillusioned by the meaningless activities open to women that she becomes completely numb. She recalls a time when "I liked everybody, I believed in everybody. . . . Then, one day, came the reaction, and from the ashes of my buried hopes, from the wreck of all in which I believed, to which I clung, arose the woman that you see—cold, calm, scornful, cynical, wretched—no, not wretched—that belonged to my former state; for, if when I had a heart, it sometimes beat with deceitful happiness, it oftener paid for that short throb of bliss, with hours of crushing misery."[56] This passage is representative of a dark thematic substratum often visible in the literature of misery: the extinction of feeling that comes after great pain. Bowen's heroine typically confesses that she is "cold, calm, scornful, cynical"—but *not* "wretched," because wretchedness implies emotional expressiveness in a world where torpor is woman's most appropriate response to wrongs against her sex. Toward the end of Alice Cary's *Married, Not Mated,* the victimized Annette Furniss is pictured "pale and cold as marble, [sitting] quietly in moody and hopeless reveries."[57] The heroine of Cary's other major novel, *Hagar,* identifies wholly with a passage that she reads: "Despair, utter despair, is indeed passionless."[58] Similarly, a woman in a *Una* story, left with "a withered heart" after years of exploitation by males, says, "I no longer live to feel—but to know. Frigid indifference mantles all my sentiments."[59] In *The Marble Faun* Hawthorne, who was deeply attuned to the dark women's writings of his day, describes the cold impassivity (worse than passionate misery) that can result from woman's pains; the initially cheerful Hilda is so devastated by Miriam's crime that she experiences a period of stonelike indifference. There is an overall recognition in the literature of misery that women are subject to wounds unknown to men, wounds that may heal in time but that always leave a hard scar.

Given this emphasis on deadened feelings in American women's writings, it is perhaps understandable that Emily Dickinson wrote several poems that stand virtually alone in literature by having emotional numbness as their specific topic. Dickinson transforms one of her era's favorite subjects, the death of feeling after a crushing experience, into literary art by enlivening it with a metaphorical intensity and variety absent from the lesser literature. While some of her major poems were pain-inspired, they were distinguished among the literature of misery by their fresh metaphors and associations, which provide a kind of linguistic redemption from the very trauma they describe. Witness the artistic treatment of all-annihilating pain in these famous lines:

> After great pain, a formal feeling comes—
> The Nerves sit ceremonious, like Tombs—
> The stiff Heart questions was it He, that bore,
> And Yesterday, or Centuries before? [. . .]

> This is the Hour of Lead—
> Remembered, if outlived,
> As Freezing persons, recollect the Snow—
> First—Chill—then Stupor—then the letting go—

> (#341; c. 1862)

These lines capture precisely the chilly impassivity that characterized the American literature of misery. They were written at a moment when Dickinson confessed she was "afraid" and when, as her letters and her poems of 1862 suggest, she underwent some severe trauma. But they have endured while many similar mid-nineteenth-century accounts of emotional numbness have disappeared because of their poetic treatment of a common theme. In the lesser women's literature, the objects of the writer's attention are the wrongs that create woman's pain and her response to the pain. In Dickinson's poem, the attention is shifted away from the pain to the energetic invention of images to describe the pain. Even if, as her letters of the period would suggest, the pain is rooted in her experience as a woman, Dickinson purposely avoids gender issues in the poem and creates a string of surprising metaphors ("formal feeling," "Nerves . . . like Tombs," "stiff Heart," "Hour of Lead," and so on) that triumphantly proclaim artistic power. Though she may be treating a gender-specific theme for gender-specific reasons, she succeeds in escaping to the gender-free realm of imaginative artistry.

Emily Dickinson has frequently been placed in the company of two male authors, Hawthorne and Melville, as premodern authors who supposedly saw through the shallow optimism of their day and rebelliously studied dark philosophical truths. In my previous discussions of the largely male tradition of Subversive literature, I have shown that, in fact, the popular literature of the period was far bleaker than is ordinarily believed and that Hawthorne and Melville gave artistic renderings of many dark popular themes. Emily Dickinson can be said to have done the same for characteristic themes of the women's literature of misery. By the late 1850s skeptical intellectual probing in imaginative literature had become, to a large degree, the special province of women. By the time Melville wrote *The Confidence-Man* (1857) he had virtually suspended the philosophical quest begun in *Moby-Dick*, focusing instead on theatrics and style. When Hawthorne tackled dark philosophical issues in *The Marble Faun* (1859), it was mainly through the portrayal of the problematic *women* characters, Miriam and Hilda.

In the meantime, various women writers took up the philosophical quest in earnest. Religious authority and male authority were often viewed as twin demons in the literature of misery, whose authors wished to vent their growing doubts about both. Note the combined anguish and womanly independence in the following passage about the heroine of the anonymously published *The Female Skeptic*: "Alone she wandered in the wilderness of Doubt, taught, as a woman is ever taught to think, by the sorrow in her heart. . . . She felt a very Hagar in the desert. . . . Her brain was pregnant with Ishmael *thoughts*—wanderers and outcasts, but *free.*"[60] The Hagar reference reminds us that, just as Ishmael had been the archetype for the American male author's demonic philosophical quest, so Ishmael's wretched but free mother was an apt correlative for the independent woman seeker. If the heroine of Cary's *Hagar* vows to wander "alone in the desert," so, in effect, did several women authors of the 1850s.[61] Medora Fielding of Lillie Devereux Blake's *Southwold* shows her intellectual superiority to venal, mindless males by daring to apply her brilliance to a refutation of Christianity. Laura Curtis Bullard's tough heroine, Christine, "always restless and unhappy," chooses an independent course even though she knows it is painful. "Better to struggle always, if the goal is never reached," she cries inwardly, "than to pass on through life with calm indifference. Rather the hillside, bleak and cold though it may be, so that my course be upward, than the plain, bathed in sunshine, if I may never go beyond it."[62] So close was Emily Dickinson to this spirit of anguished independence that in her private writings she could sound much like the other women writers in her confessions of combined skepticism and resolution. Note the similarity between the above Bullard passage and this statement by Dickinson in a letter to her friend Abiah Root: "The shore is safer, Abiah, but I love to buffet the sea—I can count the bitter wrecks here in these pleasant waters, and hear the murmuring winds, but oh, I love the danger!"[63]

In women's literature of the 1850s, questions about God's existence and religion's validity recur with telling frequency. Constant exposure to wrongs against women lead Parton's Ruth Hall to murmur: "Is religion only a fable?"[64] Bullard's Christine is similarly impelled by discrimination against her sex to declare: "Sometimes, I don't know as there *is* a God."[65]

In Harriet Wilson's *Our Nig* it is the combined injustices of sexism and racism that lead the black heroine to ask many probing questions about Christianity. The heroine of *The Female Skeptic* whose religious doubts lead to a nightmarish vision of jeering demons who scream at her: "There is no God! There is no God!" vows in the end to trust neither in men nor in God but to rely wholly on herself.[66]

American women writers of the 1850s, therefore, revolted simultaneously against male authority and against religious authority and were left with a devotion to literary art. We have seen that, on occasion, women writers did fulfill their artistic goals. The writers whose main texts constitute what I have called the American Women's Renaissance—Blake, Cary, Bullard, Parton, Alcott, Spofford, Stoddard, Davis—sometimes achieved literary complexity by fusing contradictory female stereotypes, by disrupting normal literary structures, and by venturing into the dark but free territory of skeptical philosophy.

Only Emily Dickinson succeeded consistently in gaining the artistic sophistication and the philosophical originality many women writers were seeking. She did so because she observed her women's culture with unique attentiveness, tyrannically surveying the numerous roles it offered and bringing its artistic and philosophical aims to a poetic culmination. A primary reason for her success was her majestic refusal to accept monolithic gender roles. This refusal itself was largely conditioned by her culture, for the role fragmentations amply documented in antebellum women's literature created an atmosphere in which gender stereotypes could be amalgamated and recombined at will by the literary artist.

Her relationship to antebellum women's culture was not one of rebellion but rather of intense, unremitting pursuit of artistic ideals sought more tentatively by other women writers. When we survey the careers of the other women authors, we see that each approached a highly fertile moment of artistic autonomy but then withdrew from final, complete commitment to literary art. Blake, Cary, and Bullard each wrote intriguing novels in mid-career but then devoted themselves to the suffrage and women's club movements; Alcott reached a peak of literary complexity in the 1860s but then willfully turned to the writing of more conventional children's literature; Davis, after her triumphant portrait of class- and gender-related degradation in *Life in the Iron-Mills,* suffered a nervous collapse and then was forced by her family's poverty to write profitable domestic fiction for magazines. In Emily Dickinson's career, there was no such withdrawal from literary realization. There was instead a total commitment to literary art, a marriage to poetry, full loyalty to the country of truth.

In her artistic experimentation with newly defined women's roles and stylistic devices, she went beyond not only the other women writers but also two male authors, Hawthorne and Whitman, who were interested in women's themes. For Hawthorne, the proliferation of women's roles had made possible one fully realized American heroine, Hester Prynne, and several later heroines of varying complexity. For Whitman, it gave rise to the expansive treatment of women throughout *Leaves of Grass,* which incorporates the entire range of female stereotypes, from the moral exemplar through the adventure feminist to the sensual woman. On the surface, it might seem that Hawthorne's and Whitman's work is in fact more directly concerned with women's issues than Dickinson's. Nowhere in Dickinson's poetry do we find the direct, topical discussion of women's wrongs and women's rights that we find in works like *The Scarlet Letter, The Blithedale Romance, The Marble Faun.* No individual Dickinson poem contains so openly feminist assertions as Whitman's "Song of a Broad-Axe" or so broad a range of representative women stereotypes as "A Woman Waits for Me." Hawthorne and Whitman are thematically subtle but linguistically straightforward in their treatment of women. Dickinson is even more subtle than they and, at the same time, linguistically more shifty, metaphorical, oblique. Moreover, the large majority of her poems have no apparent gender-specific meaning whatsoever.

But it is precisely Dickinson's obliquity and elusiveness that make her far more representative of American women's culture than Hawthorne and Whitman. They address women's *issues*; she perfects women's *style.* They attempt literary fusions of women stereotypes in order to achieve a meaningful synthesis or contrast; she constantly impersonates shifting roles in full recognition that synthesis is what threatens to imprison women in male-defined categories. She was the final projection of all the energies of American radical-democrat feminism, that spirit of republican protest against male authority that had variously appeared in the Declaration of Sentiments at the Seneca Falls convention, in Fanny Fern's announcement of herself as "a little 'Bunker Hill'" who could outfight any man,[67] and in the ingenious role playing and philosophical speculations of the literature of misery. If the other women authors attempted to gain freedom by freely exploring dark philosophical realms, her poetic radical democracy led her to proclaim: "My Country is Truth. . . . It is a very free Democracy." If their efforts for freedom led to breaches of literary decorum, she could explain her "spasmodic" style to Higginson in radical-democratic terms: "I had no monarch in my life, and cannot rule myself, and when I try to organize—my little Force explodes—and leaves me bare and charred."[68] She had no monarch because she *chose* to have no monarch, and her little Force constantly exploded because she *allowed* it to. Emily Dickinson—not Fanny Fern—was the *real* "little 'Bunker Hill,' " the American woman who militantly asserted her creativity through ingenious metaphorical play and through brash imaginings of a gender-free literary reality.

Those who focus narrowly on a few Dickinson poems that seem directly feminist or on particular personality quirks that make Dickinson appear to be a nineteenth-century madwoman do not truly account for her stature as a paradigmatic American woman writer. Her real representativeness lies in her incomparable flexibility, her ability to be by turns coy, fierce, domestic, romantic, protofeminist, antifeminist, prudish, erotic. In this sense, of course, she was much like other authors of the American Women's Renaissance who evaded simple gender categories by freely combining the stereotypes generated by their culture, just as she shared their philosophical adventurousness and devotion to technique. But in Dickinson these common principles are so greatly exaggerated and intensified that they produce a wholly new kind of literature. The other women writers' manipulations of female stereotypes pale beside her endless adaptations and truly innovative fusions of these stereotypes. Their questions about religion and philosophy seem timid next to her leaps into an indefinite realm beyond all religion and philosophy. Their affirmations of women's creativity through stylistic experimentation are tentative when compared with her unremitting quest for the startling metaphor, the unusual rhyme, the odd caesura.

Even when she deals directly with gender issues, clear statement on these issues is abrogated on behalf of jaunty stylistic gamesmanship, signaled by tonal fusions and shocking images. Take the following poem:

> I'm "wife"—I've finished that—
> That other state—
> I'm Czar—I'm "Woman" now—
> It's safer so—
>
> How odd the Girl's life looks
> Behind this soft Eclipse—
> I think that Earth feels so
> To folks in Heaven—now—
>
> This being comfort—then
> That other kind—was pain—
> But why compare?
> I'm "Wife"! Stop there!

> (#199; c. 1860)

Some critics have interpreted this as a wry antimarriage poem extremely unusual in a day when marriage was extolled as the highest good. The fact is that American women's wrongs literature had long portrayed the suffering of wives; in particular, several works in the literature of misery, such as Cary's *Married, Not Mated* and Blake's *Southwold,* had underscored the impossibility of happy marriages. Indeed, the year before Dickinson wrote the above poem there had appeared a dark women's novel, *The Autobiography of a Married Woman,* whose heroine becomes so disillusioned with marriage that she exclaims: "O, mothers! Train your daughters to self-reliance, and not to feel that they are to marry simply because everybody does marry. . . . There are very few happy marriages; there can be but few, where interest and self-love form the tie."[69]

Dickinson's poem stands out not for any new statement about marriage it might contain but for its playful fusion of opposing views about the marriage relation that was circulating in American culture. One view, related to the Conventional ethos of domestic fiction, was that marriage was a state of heavenly bliss and of remarkable power for woman. In Dickinson's own life, this idealization of domesticity was reflected in her well-known enjoyment of housekeeping activities and in certain statements in her letters, such as her 1851 message to Susan Gilbert: "Home is a holy thing—nothing of doubt or distrust can enter it's blessed portals."[70] In the poem, this view is enforced by the images of the home as heaven and the wife as "Czar" and "Woman"—images that invest the marriage relation with both bliss and power for woman. The contrasting view, related to the more cynical outlook on marriage held by some suffragists and women's wrongs authors, saw marriage as an unequal state in which women suffered a range of ills, from economic deprivation to loss of independence. In Dickinson's life, this hostility to marriage was reflected in her indomitable spinsterhood and in direct cries of protest in letters, such as her exclamatory note to Abiah Root: "God keep me from what they call *households*" or her early comment to Susan Gilbert that their unmarried state must seem enviable to "the *wife,* . . . sometimes the *wife forgotten.* "[71] In the poem, the antimarriage view is crystallized in subtle images, such as "soft Eclipse" and "Stop there!," suggesting the termination of a woman's independence in marriage.

Dickinson was not the first American writer to incorporate both positive and negative views of marriage. Sara Parton, the author whose "spicey passages" Dickinson had read to her father, had done this in successive sketches in *Fern Leaves,* and many women writers of the 1850s had studied tensions between womanly independence and heterosexual love. Dickinson was the first, however, to *fuse contrasting views in a single text and individual metaphors.* The literary fusion enables her to achieve a far more rounded view of marriage than was advanced by either the promarriage or antimarriage groups. The message, if any can be gleaned, is that marriage is a heavenly state of power in which woman gains safety and comfort but at the same time loses the painful but exhilarating self-sufficiency of maidenhood. More important than the poem's message, however, is its stylistic power. How concisely Dickinson communicates the treatment of wife as the husband's objective possession through the quotation marks around "wife" and "Woman"! How subtle are the tonal shifts in the poem, as the persona wavers between enthusiasm and skepticism about marriage! How potently does the phrase "soft Eclipse" communicate that cushioned banality she envisages in marriage! As always in Dickinson's poetry, the highest triumphs here are stylistic.

Given Dickinson's literary aims, it is not surprising that she directly rejected women's rights and was notably inconsistent on women's issues. In the course of her close relationship with Thomas Wentworth Higginson she never showed interest in one of his favorite reforms, women's rights, and when the progressive popular novelist Elizabeth Stuart Phelps wrote her in 1872 asking for her aid in the women's cause, she burned Phelps's letter and mailed her a flat refusal. This indifference to political feminism was part and parcel of serious authorship during the American Women's Renaissance. It is no accident that Dickinson's most productive literary period was in the early 1860s, for this was the moment when all women's rights activity was suspended. As early as 1858, outside opposition and internal dissension had created a notable diminution of suffrage activity, and the Civil War brought a complete cessation of women's conventions between February 1861 and May 1866. Dickinson's earliest (and many of her best) poems were written between 1858 and 1866, precisely the years that produced some of the finest works of Blake, Stoddard, Davis, Alcott, Cary, and Spofford. Was Dickinson conscious that she was a member of this pioneering literary sisterhood? Little evidence survives to give us a sure answer, but her comments about one of these authors—Harriet Prescott Spofford—show that she was more moved by contemporary American women's writing than by any of her favorite classic authors, even Shakespeare. After she finished the last installment of Spofford's story "The Amber Gods" (in the February 1860 issue of the *Atlantic*) she begged her sister-in-law to send her everything Spofford wrote. "The Amber Gods," an imaginative tale involving mysterious amber beads and frustrated love, elicited this high compliment from Dickinson: "It is the only thing I ever read in my life that I didn't think I could have imagined myself!"[72] She was even more affected by Spofford's "Circumstance" (1860), a story about a woman alone in the Maine woods who fends off a half-human "Indian beast" by singing to him. Dickinson was so haunted by the story that she wrote Higginson in 1862: "I read Miss Prescott's 'Circumstance,' but it followed me, in the Dark—so I avoided her—"[73] Coming from a woman who believed that literature should be bewitching and devastating, this was high praise.

Whatever cross-influences between Dickinson and the other women writers may have existed, it is certain that she absorbed their overall goal of depoliticizing women's discourse and shifting creative energy away from monolithic expression toward flexible impersonation. Dickinson took to a new extreme the liberating manipulation of female stereotypes. In successive poems she assumed with ease an array of shifting personae: the abandoned woman ("Heart! We will forget him!" #47); the loving wife ("Forever at His side to walk—" #246); the fantasist of erotic ecstasy ("Wild Nights—Wild Nights!" #249); the acerbic satirist of Conventional women ("What Soft—Cherubic Creatures— / These Gentlewomen are—" #401); the expectant bride on the eve of her wedding ("A Wife—at Daybreak I shall be—" #461); the sullen rejecter of a lover ("I cannot live with You" #640). This is, of course, only a small sampling of her countless poses. We should not be concerned that these poses frequently contradict each other and that several of them seem far more conservative or obsequious to males than might be expected from the strongest woman poet in the English language. Instead, we should recognize her elusiveness as the major ingredient of her artistry and of her representativeness as a writer of the American Women's Renaissance. If Parton's "Floy" showed her power by sending impossibly mixed signals to baffled male reviewers, if Blake's Medora Fielding and Alcott's Jean Muir took vindictive pride in never showing a true face to men, if the "confidence woman" in Hankins's *Women of New York* proudly impersonated every female stereotype, Dickinson outdid them all by donning an unparalleled variety of masks behind which the core self lay as an ever-present but always invisible manipulator. Even in letters to confidants, Dickinson was quick to hide behind personae and to point up the totally fictive nature of her poetic poses. As she wrote Higginson in 1862: "When I state myself, as the Representative of the Verse—it does not mean—me—"[74] For Dickinson, all women's stereotypes become matters of literary theater and metaphorical play.

A result of this endless capacity for manipulation was her unusual fusion of female stereotypes with each other or with images from the physical or spiritual worlds. Take, for instance, her use of a very common stereotype, the drunkard's wife, in her poem "We—Bee and I—live by the quaffing—" (#230). In American popular culture and in suffrage ranks, brutalization of women by their drunken husbands was a very serious matter, one that arose in dark-temperance writings and that lay behind the political activism of many feminists. With characteristic playfulness, Dickinson strips the dark-temperance mode of terror and of feminist implications by using the drunkard's wife as a metaphor in an apolitical poem that celebrates a summer day. The second verse of the poem reads,

> Do we "get drunk"?
> Ask the jolly Clovers!
> Do we "beat" our "Wife"?
> *I*—never wed—
> Bee—pledges *his*—in minute flagons—
> Dainty—as the tress—on her deft Head—

It is fitting that Dickinson puts quotation marks around the phrases "get drunk," "beat," and "Wife," for, as in many other quoted passages in her poetry, these images are directly lifted from popular culture—in this case, from popular dark-temperance literature. But, here as elsewhere, Dickinson's strategy is one of quotation in the interest of transformation. Drunkenness, wife beating, and temperance pledges are adapted only to be transformed into something wholly new, because they are fused with nature imagery and directed toward the figurative expression of an ecstatic state, so distant from the dreary pictures of husbands' sadism and wives' suffering that abound in popular literature and suffrage speeches. Whereas many politically minded women writers had soberly portrayed drunkards' wives in order to effect legal change, Dickinson wittily changes this popular concept into a metaphor in order to gambol in the free realm of imagistic poetry.

Her powers of fusion and transformation of popular images are equally visible in "My Life had stood—a Loaded Gun—" (#754). Feminist critics have rescued this poem from obscurity and awarded it central status in the Dickinson canon but have missed its cultural dimensions. We have seen that a common stereotype in popular literature was the adventure feminist, the tough woman who could survive extreme physical peril and outbrave men in battle. We have seen that another image associated with women, the volcano, was commonly used in the literature of misery to represent the quiet but inwardly explosive woman who was denied a viable outlet for her energies. The first stereotype enacted fantasies of power; the second reflected the realities of repression and powerlessness. In her poem Dickinson takes the wholly original step of fusing these contrary images. On the one hand, the "I" of the poem is the ultimate adventure feminist, the omnipotent aggressor who does all the hunting and speaking for her man and always guards him from danger. On the other hand, she has a "Vesuvian face" that signals the total repression of her aggressions in deference to him. Whether or not the man here referred to as "Owner" and "Master" is the intended recipient of Dickinson's pained "Master" letters, the poem makes it clear that Dickinson is conjuring up an adventure-feminist fantasy and, simultaneously, suggesting the suspicion that this imagined power is an illusion. A loaded gun is not useful until it is fired, just as the "I" of the poem gains power only when carried off by her Master. The fantasies and frustrations the "I" embodies, however, are secondary to the potency of the poem itself. The ingenious fusion of contradictory female stereotypes sets off a string of lively metaphorical associations that themselves constitute the aggressiveness of the woman writer.

Her fusions of contradictory popular stereotypes are part of her overall effort to hide behind shifting masks while always asserting her creative powers. Time and again in her poems, popular images lose political meaning but gain literariness because they are recombined and treated metaphorically. This conscious stylistic manipulation of popular stereotypes is underscored by an accentuation of other experimental devices in women's literature—particularly ellipsis and shifts in perspective—that take on incredible energy when condensed into her abrupt, potent images. If the other writers of the American Women's Renaissance occasionally contravened the official language patterns of their culture, Emily Dickinson did so with a vengeance. No "Master" ever received such confusingly metaphorical, impossibly cryptic love letters as the three that she wrote. Few authors of any period made such quick shifts from the divine to the earthly, from the abstract to the particular, from the conventional to the subversive as she. Her experimental style represented an unremitting protest against the pretense that meaning could be summed up neatly or contained in an axiom. As she wrote:

> Experiment escorts us last—
> His pungent company
> Will not allow an Axiom
> An opportunity.
>
> (#1770; c. 1870)

The study of Dickinson in the context of American women's culture invites us to ponder the major stylistic question that has been posed by modern feminist criticism: is there an *écriture féminine*? Is sexual difference registered in literary language?

Dickinson's posture as a private woman poet with a highly experimental style would seem to place her in the ranks of the secretly subversive women authors that have been described by the French theorists of *l'écriture fémi-*

nine. Critics such as Hélène Cixous and Julia Kristeva have identified female discourse as a radically disruptive style that undermines the linguistic
and metaphysical conventions of the dominant culture. The woman writer,
they argue, allies herself with all that is muted or silenced in order to
subvert systems that repress sexual difference. In her essay "The Laugh
of the Medusa" Hélène Cixous writes: "When the repressed of their culture and their society return, it is an explosive, utterly destructive, staggering return, with a force never yet unleashed."[75] This statement could be
well applied to Emily Dickinson. Her poetry is a dialectical compound of
repression and explosiveness. In various characteristic poses, Dickinson is
the reticent volcano, the loaded gun, the little force constantly exploding
and leaving the inner self charred. To cite another of her emblematic
metaphors, she deals her pretty words like blades, each of which unbares
a nerve and wantons with a bone. On the metaphysical level, her poetry
challenges all fixed systems by constantly bringing attention to the inscrutability of truth. On the linguistic level, it purposely disrupts conventional
patterns at every turn.

The question remains, however: is hers a distinctly *feminine* subversive
style launched in protest against the linguistic structures of a *patriarchal*
culture? On this score, the French theory is of little help, for even though
it assumes that female discourse subverts male language systems, it is so
concerned with the personal, biological sources of *l'écriture féminine* that it
neglects socioliterary context, which alone can tell us whether or not
female discourse is indeed an act of rebellion against the dominant culture.
Those who have applied French theory to the study of Emily Dickinson,
such as Margaret Homans, have argued that Dickinson's disruptive style
was a gender-specific answer to patriarchal structures. The notion that her
linguistic disruptiveness is antipatriarchal or biologically induced, however, is demonstrably wrong. Dickinson's experimental style constituted
not a rebellion against fixed patriarchal systems but rather a transformation of progressive linguistic strategies, some derived from women's writings and others from men's writings, that were current in her culture.

Indeed, what distinguished Dickinson from other American women authors was her full attentiveness to linguistic experiments in male writings
as well as in female writings. During the 1835–55 period, as her poetic
sensibility was developing, linguistic disruptiveness was far more common
in male-authored than in female-authored American writings. The irrational style had arisen in Subversive novels by males and was brought to
an almost premodern level of linguistic experimentation by American
humorists, also male. An experimental female style did not emerge until
the mid-1850s, and its disruptiveness was restrained, ingrown, in contrast
to the zany exuberance that characterized the male irrational style. As we

have seen, Dickinson was influenced by the new female style—but she was just as strongly influenced by stylistic innovations in male-dominated writing. Indeed, she was the *only* woman writer of her day to incorporate fully the experimental devices introduced by males. Her linguistic disruptiveness does not represent a *rejection* of male language systems but rather a full *incorporation* of these systems. What some have called her *écriture féminine,* tied to biology and her personal experience as a woman, can be better described as an *écriture universelle,* engendered by her unique openness to innovations in both male and female discourse.

What, then, were the specific socioliterary forces that sped Dickinson's development and contributed to her poetry? We saw in Chapter 1 that the new religious style, introduced by imaginative preachers and popular writers, made possible her bold, jaunty reapplications of formerly sacrosanct imagery. At the same time that she was becoming increasingly attracted to the specifically stylistic dimensions of popular religious writing, she was constantly forced, under the pressure of repeated revivals in Amherst and South Hadley, to ponder ultimate questions about God, eternity, and the state of her soul. As her doubts about traditional Christianity mounted, culminating in her rejection of the conversion experience during the Great Revival of 1850, she experienced simultaneously a crisis of belief and an intensified interest in purely imaginative forms of religious expression. In her poetry she sustained the devotion to ultimate issues—time, death, God, the soul—but pondered them from a skeptical perspective in dense verses often full of highly innovative fusions of earthly and sacred images.

The new religious style was just one of several important cultural phenomena that Dickinson observed and poeticized. Critics who emphasize her religious background neglect the fact that she was intensely aware of much darker dimensions of America's popular psyche, associated with several of the subversive currents studied in this book. More clearly than any woman writer of her time, Dickinson saw that American popular culture was neither tame nor simplistic. Indeed, when Dickinson wrote poetry about this popular culture, her imagination was inevitably preoccupied with its violent, disorienting elements. Witness the following poem:

> The Popular Heart is a Cannon first—
> Subsequent a Drum—
> Bells for an Auxiliary
> And an Afterward of Rum—
>
> Not a Tomorrow to know it's name
> Nor a Past to stare—

Ditches for Realms and a Trip to Jail
For a Souvenir

(#1226; 1872)

In this poem Dickinson makes clear that the "Popular Heart" can best be described in violent images pertaining to war, weapons, drinking, ditches, prison. The popular culture she perceives is one that has been torn both from the future ("Not a Tomorrow to know it's name") and from historical memory ("Nor a Past to stare—"). It is fluid and ever-changing with the throes of the tumultuous present. It is associated with the muddy realm of ditches, and it thrives on a blithe acceptance of diverting crime ("a Trip to Jail / For a Souvenir").

When did Dickinson first become aware of these darker elements of popular culture and how did this awareness affect her literary development? From her letters we can see that the 1850–53 period—precisely the period in which she was rejecting formal Christianity and turning toward poeticized religion—was also the time that images of dark reform, sensationalism, and grotesque humor surfaced continually in her letters and disrupted their style. The open admission into her consciousness of several popular sensational elements prepared the way for the haunted themes and broken style of her poetry.

The sensational and blackly humorous images that abound in Dickinson's letters of the early 1850s stem from the male-dominated arena of popular newspapers and pamphlet literature. What is most striking about the appearance of such images is that they occur in the letters of a young woman. In the numerous volumes of private writings by antebellum American women I have read, I have found nothing even remotely comparable to the savagery (often the callous savagery) of these images in Emily Dickinson's letters. It is clear that, even as she was beginning to experiment with variations on the new religious style, she was also toying ambitiously with dark-reform and sensational imagery. In other words, she was boldly appropriating the discourse of various kinds of racy writing that previously had been the province of male writers.

In these letters we see a variety of sensational images whose sources can be readily traced to larger patterns in popular culture. For example, the increasing space given in American newspapers to crimes and tragedies was a great source of amused interest for Dickinson. In an autumn 1853 letter to Josiah G. Holland, who was connected with the *Springfield Republican,* she declared that the lurid contents of his paper had changed her into a quirky disturber of the peace. "One glimpse of *The Republican,*" she wrote, "makes me break things again—I read in it every night. / Who

writes those funny accidents, where railroads meet each other unexpect-
edly, and gentlemen in factories get their heads cut off quite informally?
The author, too, relates them in such a sprightly way, that they are quite
attractive."[76] Here Dickinson displays not only an excitement over her
era's sensational newspapers but also a shrewd awareness of the complex
mixture of grossness and offhand levity which which tragedies were reported in the popular press.

Similarly, in a June 15, 1851, letter to her brother Austin, who was
teaching in Boston at the time, she manifested interest in other modes of
sensational discourse, this time connected with crime reportage and dark
reform. Ever since the 1830s one of America's most powerful dark-reform
fantasies, related to the anti-Catholic or nativist movement, was that of
native American Protestants who remonstrated against the rising tide of
Roman Catholic immigrants, especially poor Irish, by publishing violent
literature in which Catholic characters were either portrayed as heartless
murderers or were retributively killed themselves. Dickinson, having heard
that Austin's students included many Irish boys, echoed this dark-reform
image by saying that she prayed for the "poor Irish boys souls. So far as
I am concerned I should like to have you kill some—there are so many
now, there is no room for Americans[.]" Elsewhere in the letter she betrayed her curiosity about popular crime cases. Fusing her dark-reform
fantasy of child murder with a notorious 1849 case involving a Harvard
professor, Dr. John W. Webster, Dickinson declares: ". . . we are quite
alarmed for the *boys,* hope you wont *kill,* or *pack away* any of 'em, so near
to Dr. Webster's bones t'ant strange you should have had temptations!"
Always hungry for sensational news from the big city, she reported that "I
gave the *manslaughter* extract to the infinite fun of Martha!" and requested
from Austin "anything else that's *startling* which you may chance to know—
I dont think deaths or murders can ever come amiss in a young woman's
journal."[77]

Dickinson's echoing of popular themes and images became especially
intriguing when she actually assumed sensational personae and registered
stylistically the fragmentations and time-space leaps that characterized
much sensational literature. In a January 1850 letter to her uncle Joel
Warren Norcross, whom she scolded for not writing her as he'd promised,
she humorously assumed the role of a likable criminal assailing another
likable criminal with exaggerated threats and epithets:

> You villain without a rival—unparraleled [*sic*] doer of crimes—
> scoundrel unheard of before—disturber of public peace—"creation's
> blot and blank"—state's prison filler—*magnum bonum* promise
> maker—harum scarum promise breaker—Oh what can I call you

more? Mrs Caudle would call you "a gentleman"—that is altogether
too good. Mrs Partington "a ver fine fellow"—neither does this
apply—I call upon all nature to lay hold of you—let fire burn—and
water drown—and light put out—and tempests tear—and hungry
wolves eat up—and lightning strike—and thunder stun—let friends
desert—and enemies draw nigh and gibbets *shake* but never *hang* the
house you walk about in![78]

This passage reflects the hyperbolic violence and disjointedness of popular sensational writings and makes direct reference to two strange characters of popular humor: Mrs. Caudle, a voluble scold created by Douglas
William Jerrold for *Punch;* and Mrs. Partington, a village malaprop created
in 1847 for a Boston newspaper by the humorist Benjamin P. Shillaber. In
the rest of the letter Dickinson amplifies her comic threats against her
uncle, vowing to kill him in a duel or shoot him, a fantasy that she expresses
in penny-press fashion: "It would do to go with a story I read—one man
pointed a loaded gun at a man—and it shot him so that he died—and the
people threw the owner of the gun into prison—and afterwards hung him
for *murder.* " For one who would later write "My Life had stood—a Loaded
Gun" this sensational story of the murder with a loaded gun had obviously
been provocative and suggestive.

The stylistic dislocations prompted by sensationalism and dark reform
are particularly visible in Dickinson's letter of January 23, 1850 (probably
to her friend George H. Gould), in which the stormy spirit of subversive
popular culture flares forth in her whimsical opening outburst: "Magnum
bonum, 'harum scarum,' zounds et zounds, et war alarum, man reformam,
life perfectum, mundum changum, all things flarum?"[79] The three opening phrases of this sentence seem merely like a girl's jumbled language
play; but the next four phrases, with their successive images of war, reform,
perfectibility, and social change give deep social meaning to the last half-
humorous, half-terrified phrase, "all things flarum?" The American culture that was dawning upon Emily Dickinson's imagination was one of
great vibrancy and activity but also one of confusion, moral fluidity, even
potential chaos. Significantly, later in this letter she vows that she and her
friend will become modern reformers whose activity can be expressed only
in the most jumbled, violent manner: "We'll build Alms-houses, and transcendental State prisons, and scaffolds—we will blow out the sun, and the
moon, and encourage invention. Alpha shall kiss Omega—we will ride up
the hill of glory—Hallelujah, all hail!" The persona she inhabits here is a
metonymy of American reform and criminal culture, with its curious contradictions: its endorsement of almshouses to prevent crime, its "transcendental" prisons to reform criminals, its love of scaffolds where criminals

were callously put on public display. The rapid image shifts and startling time-space leaps in Dickinson's prose are a kind of stylistic barometer of the cultural confusions she is describing.

It is fair to generalize from the letters of the early 1850s that Emily Dickinson was unique among women of her day in the breadth of her awareness of the most experimental—and most disturbing—tendencies in her contemporary American culture. Her attraction to the new religious style, her excitement over press reports of tragedies, her interest in popular crime and dark-reform rhetoric all reveal a sensibility that was voraciously absorbing various kinds of popular images. Precisely because she was far more responsive than other women to the energetic, contradictory images of popular culture, she recognized the need for an artistic form that would represent these often fragmented images but at the same time would serve to control and fuse these images. As the shifting, often jumbled passages from the above letters indicate, she was losing control over her culture's images and personae when she tried to use them in prose. She therefore took the wholly original step of appropriating the rhythm of English hymnody (which had been popularized in America by the hymns of Isaac Watts) as a controlling device to lend rhythm, structure, and even residual sacred resonance to themes that in prose threatened to fly toward the chaotic.

It was this treatment of highly experimental themes through dense images in rhythmic poetry that constituted her greatest departure from other women writers of the day. It will be noticed that my discussion of the American Women's Renaissance focused on the *prose* writings of American women. This is because the poetry that some of these writers produced was not nearly as complex as was their prose. Alice Cary, perhaps the most skilled poet of the group, did produce some intriguingly dark poems in which she assumed the persona of a woman stripped of religious faith and groping blindly for something to believe in. Although Cary's poetic lamentations have some thematic resemblances to Dickinson's contemplative poetry, it must be emphasized that Cary and the other unfamiliar writers most effectively registered their culture's disruptions in their prose works and that these prose works themselves often lacked central controlling devices. For Emily Dickinson, culturally representative prose was a virtual impossibility because it could lead only toward the formlessness and shiftiness that characterized her letters of the early 1850s and that was to become even more pronounced in her later correspondence (witness the fragmented "Master" letters). In poetry Dickinson could assimilate the subversive and at the same time regulate it. Poetry promised imaginative liberation from the increasing confusion she witnessed in her popular culture, that miasma of likable criminals, erring reformers, prisons,

ditches, weapons. Prose threatened her with suffocation and imprisonment—an idea she would develop in her poem "They shut me up in
Prose—" (#613). Poetry, in contrast, offered windows to a world of fresh
meaning and suggestions:

> I dwell in Possibility—
> A fairer House than Prose—
> More numerous of Windows—
> Superior—for Doors—
>
> (#657; c. 1862)

To recognize that Dickinson viewed poetry as an avenue of release and
possibility is not to say that she turned from the kind of sensational or
grotesque images she had discovered in the early 1850s. Quite the opposite, in fact, is closer to the truth: precisely because she appropriated a
rhythmic poetic structure, she was capable of fully admitting the sensational into her mature work and allowing its violence and weirdness to
create new disruptive poetic effects. Images of crime, weapons, pirates,
haunted minds, danger, and gore abound in her poetry. In her less complicated poems, such imagery is used with rather banal results. For example,
one early poem (#9) is a tiny poetic sensational narrative that describes
a wooded road by night haunted by banditti, a wolf, an owl, a serpent, and
so forth. In another early poem (#11) she assumes the persona of a hidden
onlooker watching the piratelike day burying its treasure in the surrounding hills. This rather simplistic use of the sensational is equally visible in
lines like these: "I never hear the word 'escape' / Without a quicker blood"
(#77); "My friend attacks my friend! / Oh Battle picturesque!" (#118);
"We like a Hairbreadth 'scape / It tingles in the Mind" (#1175). In these
poems Dickinson is not distant from the excited sensation-lover of the
early 1850s who ripped open newspapers to read about accidents and
begged her brother to send crime reports from the city.

Her most sophisticated poems are those in which she permits imagery
from radically different cultural arenas to come together in an explosive
metaphorical center. In some other women's writings of the 1850s, such
as Parton's *Ruth Hall* and Cary's *Married, Not Mated,* disparate cultural
images are *juxtaposed* in single texts, creating a certain density and stylistic
innovativeness. In Dickinson's poetry, such contrasting images are consistently *fused* in single stanzas, even in single words, so that they radiate with
fresh suggestions—and create intriguing puzzles for would-be interpret-
ers. Notice the poetic fusions in these famously cryptic verses:

> Mine—by the Right of the White Election!
> Mine—by the Royal Seal!

Mine—by the Sign in the Scarlet prison—
Bars—cannot conceal!

Mine—here—in Vision—and in Veto!
Mine—by the Grave's Repeal—
Titled—Confirmed—
Delirious Charter!
Mine—long as Ages steal!

(#528; c. 1862)

In this poem, negative images reminiscent of sensational or Subversive literature ("Scarlet prison," "Bars," "Veto," "Grave's Repeal") are fused with affirmative, ecstatic religious imagery ("White Election," "Vision," "Confirmed," "Delirious Charter!"). The lack of a clear referent for "Mine" points up the radical open-endedness of meaning that results from the creative fusion of opposing cultural elements. Dickinson had profited immensely from her earlier awareness of different progressive phenomena in popular culture: on the one hand, the sensational writings that had featured prisons, death, blood; on the other hand, relaxed religious discourse, which suddenly became available for creative recombination with secular imagery. Dickinson grafts together the two kinds of imagery and retains the ultimacy of vision that had long governed her ponderings of large issues. Dickinson's wholly original fusion of contrasting types of images in dense poetry truly distinguished her. If, as many critics believe, "Mine" refers to the poetic gift, it may be said that Dickinson is fully justified for the boasting, assertive tone of this poem. Through reconstructive fusion, she had managed to create a poem that salvages both the sensational and the religious by bringing them together and infusing them with new emotional intensity and metaphysical resonance.

A similar intensification through poetic fusion occurs in one of her most famous love poems:

Wild Nights—Wild Nights!
Were I with thee
Wild Nights should be
Our luxury!

Futile—the Winds—
To a Heart in port—
Done with the Compass—
Done with the Chart!

Rowing in Eden—
Ah, the Sea!

Might I but moor—Tonight—
In Thee!

(#249; c. 1861)

It is not known whether Dickinson had read any of the erotic literature of the day or if she knew of the stereotype of the sensual woman. Given her fascination with sensational journalism and with popular literature in general, it is hard to believe she would not have had at least some exposure to erotic literature. At any rate, her treatment of the daring theme of woman's sexual fantasy in this deservedly famous poem bears comparison with erotic themes as they appeared in popular sensational writings. The first stanza of the poem provides an uplifting or purification of sexual fantasy not distant from the effect of Whitman's cleansing rhetoric, which, as we have seen, was consciously designed to counteract the prurience of the popular "love plot." Dickinson's repeated phrase "Wild Nights" is a simple but dazzling metaphor that communicates wild passion—even lust—but simultaneously lifts sexual desire out of the scabrous by fusing it with the natural image of the night. The second verse introduces a second nature image, the turbulent sea and the contrasting quiet port, which at once universalizes the passion and purifies it further by distancing it through a more abstract metaphor. Also, the second verse makes clear that this is not a poem of sexual consummation but rather of pure fantasy and sexual impossibility. Unlike popular erotic literature, the poem portrays neither a consummated seduction nor the heartless deception that it involves. There is instead a pure, fervent fantasy whose frustration is figured forth in the contrasting images of the ocean (the longed-for-but-never-achieved consummation) and the port (the reality of the poet's isolation). The third verse begins with an image, "Rowing in Eden," that further uplifts sexual passion by yoking it with a religious archetype. Here as elsewhere, Dickinson capitalizes nicely on the new religious style, which made possible such fusions of the divine and the earthly. The persona's concluding wish to "moor" in the sea expresses the sustained intense sexual longing and the simultaneous frustration of that longing. In the course of the poem, Dickinson has communicated great erotic passion, and yet, by effectively projecting this passion through unusual nature and religious images, has rid it of even the tiniest residue of sensationalism.

If in "Wild Nights—Wild Nights!" Dickinson uses nature and religious imagery innovatively to reconstruct sensational themes, in other poems she uses psychological images as reconstructive devices. One of her major goals is to direct her reader's attention away from the senseless, flat sensationalism peddled in popular romances toward the interior drama of the soul. This objective is made clear in a poem such as the following:

No Romance sold unto
Could so enthrall a Man
As the perusal of
His Individual One—
'Tis Fiction's—to dilute to Plausibility
Our Novel—When 'tis small enough
To credit—'Tisn't true!

(#669; c. 1862)

The message of this poem—that the interior drama of the mind is far more exciting than any popular romance—is similar to that of "One need not be a Chamber—to be Haunted—" (#670), which argues that horror within is more terrifying than any fabulous fright. Such poems show Dickinson again redirecting horrific themes away from the neutral realm of exterior sensationalism toward the deeper abysses of the human mind. This psychological horror, enforced in both poems through a string of powerful metaphors, is far more intense than any outside horror, but its very depth and interiority provides relief from the kind of whirling, haphazard sensational images, derived from the popular press, that had created such great discontinuities and blackly humorous jesting in Dickinson's letters of the early 1850s. The potent metaphors and emotional depth of Dickinson's haunted poetry engendered a literary alternative to her previous toying with sensational images.

This studied redirection of dark themes controls another characteristic poem, "I felt a Funeral, in my Brain" (#280). This poem may be called a condensed, interiorized reconstruction of the American Subversive imagination, with its dour themes and its bizarre imagistic transpositions. As terrifying as it may seem, the poem actually offers literary solace from the merely sensational or grotesquely humorous imaginings of many popular writers. Like two other well-known Dickinson poems, "I heard a Fly buzz—when I died" (#465) and "Because I could not stop for Death—" (#712), this poem departs notably from popular sensational texts in several ways: it avoids sadistic physical violence or gore of the sort that filled sensational writings and that had appeared in Dickinson's early letters; it *looks back* upon the moment of death, therefore implicitly reassuring the reader that at least there *is* an afterlife (a possibility that several skeptical sensation writers denied); it subtly transfers the reader's attention from death itself to powerful metaphors and diverting physical images associated with death. That many of these metaphors (i.e., the treading mourners, the beating drum, the closing coffin) are intensely frightening actually serves a redemptive function, since intensity and suggestiveness are themselves a relief from the too often neutral sensational images in popular culture. Additional resonance stems from the dialectical interchange throughout the poem between disturbing concrete images ("Funeral," "Mourners," "Box," "Boots of Lead") and more abstract ones ("Sense," "My Mind," "my Soul," "Space," "Being," "Plank in Reason"). While Dickinson's doubts about religion prevent her from writing consolation poetry, she nevertheless fabricates a poem that fully incorporates the dark, twisted images of Subversive writers while investing such images with freshly abstract suggestiveness. The strange imagery of the last two verses, in which the Heavens become a bell and Being an ear while the persona hurtles through space hitting a world at every plunge, may be viewed as an inventive variation upon the presurrealistic American Subversive Style, mentioned previously in connection with popular sensational literature and to be discussed at greater length in the next chapter. Here as elsewhere, Dickinson adds emotional intensity and open-endedness of meaning, as the persona's plunge into space duplicates both psychological torment at the moment of death and release into the afterlife.

Dickinson's poetry, then, differed from other women's writings of the era primarily because of its openness to differing forms of popular discourse and its willed poetic reconstructions of this variegated discourse. Her incorporation of male strategies was gender-specific to the extent that it was performed in the indirect, quietly explosive style characteristic of the American Women's Renaissance, that moment when public feminist agitation was temporarily interrupted and women sought artistic outlets for their energies.

Although it is tempting to identify psychological reasons for Dickinson's experimental poetics (her apparent agoraphobia, say, or her homosocial bonding with strong women), it does a disservice to her complex makeup to place her in neat pigeonholes, such as nineteenth-century madwoman or secret man hater. Future psychological and feminist studies of Dickinson should be directed not toward the exploration of her tortured, isolated femininity but toward the discovery of reasons for her unique responsiveness to both male and female voices in her literary culture. Then we will better understand a poet who was by turns timidly obsequious and proudly imperious toward men, who juggled female stereotypes with dizzying bravura, who dared to combine the wild imagery of the male irrational style with the potent ellipses of the female literature of misery. Then we will truly know America's strongest other Amazon.

Part Four

THE GROTESQUE POSTURE:
Popular Humor and the American Subversive Style

15

THE CARNIVALIZATION OF AMERICAN LANGUAGE

W H E N in the first chapter of *The Confidence-Man* Melville has the barber of the riverboat *Fidèle* emerge from his shop and hang above his door a gaudy pasteboard sign that reads "NO TRUST," he seems to be underscoring not only a main theme of the novel, distrust or lost confidence, but also a primary stylistic strategy, distrust in the signifying process. At the very gateway of Melville's stylistic labyrinth the reader is presented with a sign that communicates an idea reinforced by every inconsequential chapter and circumlocutious sentence in the novel: in the world of American dark humor, trust between the author and the reader is violently undermined.

Nearly two decades before the publication of *The Confidence-Man*, *The Crockett Almanac* for 1839, an issue in a long-running series of popular frontier humor pamphlets, had featured an introduction that was just as appropriate, if far less subtle, than Melville's. After a paragraph promising "raal terrificashus" accounts of "wild scrapes" and "terrible fights," the author addresses us as follows: "And now, deer readers, I hope you will be satisfied with matters and things, and if you are not you may just top your boom, and make A General Clear Out." Printed just below this militant announcement is an engraving in which an angry old shrew (representing the author) is pictured driving a terrified general (the reader) out of her door with her broom. There is a sign above the shrew's cabin door that reads, in bold black letters, "NO TRUST."[1]

When we read the almanac itself, we recognize how meaningful this ominous engraving is in terms of the Crockett almanacs—and, indeed, in terms of many similar humor writings in antebellum America. In paradigmatic dark humor texts like the Crockett almanacs there is a suspension of trust, an unwillingness to permit the reader to repose in any single moral meaning, a conscious strategy of disorientation and assault on the reader's sensibilities. By comparison, even so experimental a novel as *The Confidence-Man* seems a studied effort to restore richness and literariness to a native humor that verged upon the nightmarish in its oddly juxtaposed images.

It is conceivable that Melville, who was a close reader of his culture's ephemeral literature and who mentions Davy Crockett more than once in his fiction, had read the *Crockett Almanac* for 1839, with its introductory "NO TRUST" sign warning genteel readers away from its savagely humorous domain. Whether or not there was a direct connection between the 1839 pamphlet and *The Confidence-Man,* there certainly was a broader cultural link between the two works. Both were different variations upon what I term the American Subversive Style, an indigenous style characterized by weird juxtapositions of incongruous images and by rapid shifts in time, place, or perspective. We have seen that the American Subversive Style had also appeared in the irrational style of sensational literature. In humorous texts such irrationalism is accompanied by a new detachment, an awareness of technique. In the humor writings wild irrationalism and perversity are tempered by stylistic manipulation, as is evidenced by a favorite humor character, the crafty democratic rascal-hero, and by an overall interest in unusual metaphors and experimental devices. The best popular humor was preliterary in a way that other popular texts were not, because it frankly confronted dark forces in human nature and in American society but sought to control them by rechanneling them into the arena of linguistic play.

American humor of the antebellum period is commonly divided into two camps. Constance Rourke has made a distinction between subtle, low-key Yankee humor and grotesque, macabre backwoods humor.[2] Similarly, Walter Blair and Hamlin Hill differentiate between what they call "reputable humor" and "subversive humor." Reputable humor, they show, was conservative and restrained, harking back to the smooth wit and polished periods of Goldsmith and Addison. It championed a moral and predictable universe and upheld decorum and a rigid social hierarchy. This patrician humor was written for mainly highbrow New England readers by authors such as George W. Arnold and Charles Augustus Davis of New York and Oliver Wendell Holmes, James Russell Lowell, and Asa Greene of New England. Subversive humor, in contrast, reveled in disorder, violence, amorality. It featured a dynamic rascal who flouted decency and the law and who embodied the dark view of man as a wily being who relies on cunning to survive in an unpredictable, inscrutable universe. Subversive humor, Blair and Hill point out, was particularly prevalent in the writings of Old Southwest humorists such as Thomas Bangs Thorpe and George Washington Harris.[3]

This useful distinction between reputable and subversive humor suggests that the contrast I made earlier in this book between Conventional and Subversive nonhumorous texts was paralleled by a similar difference in humorous writings. There are important areas of American humor that remain to be explored. This chapter points out that subversive humor was an evolving genre that began with certain key writings by Washington Irving and other early humorists and then became enriched with the appearance of the politically ironic humor of the radical democrats and the topical, all-encompassing humor of what may be called urban humorists. The stylistic innovations of American humorists, particularly those in the subversive camp, were characterized by linguistic dislocations that reflected larger forces in American culture and that were crucial in the shaping of the major literary texts. Subversive humor was largely responsible for the black jokes that abound in the major texts (even in optimistic ones by Emerson and Thoreau) as well as for the fertility of oddly juxtaposed images, the macabre outbursts of fictional characters, and the direct or implied assaults on trusting readers. Reputable humor was responsible for the lightly whimsical voice that characterizes many of our literary texts; it made possible a certain measure of stability and detachment from the subversive images or characters utilized. It is fair to say that without popular humor, particularly the subversive forms that are the focus of this chapter, America's major literature would have been far less zestful and vibrant than it is.

The Rise of Subversive Humor

The forces unleashed by America's young democratic culture had an impact on literary language that has not been adequately described. The profundity of this impact can be appreciated only by a close analysis of the developing style of American humor.

In his studies of Russian and French literature, Mikhail M. Bakhtin argues that in order for literature to appear there must be a preparatory stage in which language and value systems are relativized, or detached from single ideological meanings. In a period of relativization of literary-language consciousness, Bakhtin says, all "high positions and symbols . . . are transformed into masks in the presence of the rogue, into costumes for a masquerade, into buffoonery. A reformulation and loosening up of all these high symbols and positions, their radical re-accentuation, takes place in an atmosphere of gay deception."[4] Popular humorous genres such as *parodia sacra* and Menippean satire create a liberation from all logical links and a carnivalization of speech that prepares the way for dense literature. Satiric humor, in Bakhtin's view, is one example of carnival life, in which inequality or distance between people is suspended and a special carnival category goes into effect, whereby the sacred is united with the profane, the lofty with the lowly, the great with the insignificant.

As important as the carnival was in the European culture Bakhtin studies, it was perhaps even more so in democratic America, which was a kind of carnival culture, one that abolished the social distance between people and yoked together the high and the low in an atmosphere of jolly relativity. It is significant that carnivals or masques appear frequently in American literature, in Poe's "Masque of the Red Death" and "William Wilson," in Hawthorne's *The Blithedale Romance* and *The Marble Faun,* in the boisterous forecastle scene in *Moby-Dick,* and in popular exposé-novels like Lippard's *The Quaker City*—all of which show the American writer bringing the high and low together in carnival scenes with democratic implications.

Even more significant than such explicit carnival images was a widespread carnivalization of speech. A variety of foreign commentators noted that the disruptions of democratic society created linguistic strangeness in American writing. As early as 1809, a writer in the *Edinburgh Review* wrote that the "American bard frequently writes in a language utterly unknown to the prose or verse of this country," a language distinguished by the introduction of "a great multitude of words which are radically and entirely new" and by "the perversion of a still greater number of words from their proper use or signification."[5] At about the same time a British journal asserted that everything must be done to "stem that torrent of barbarous phraseology, with which American writers threaten to destroy the purity of the English language."[6] For Tocqueville, linguistic innovation was endemic to democratic culture. He noted that Americans "often mix their styles in an odd way," as "the continual restlessness of democracy leads to endless change of language." By often "giving double meanings to one word," Tocqueville argued, "democratic peoples often make both the old and the new significations ambiguous" so that "the phrase is left to wander free."[7] In other words, political and social freedom was reflected in a sudden linguistic freedom. Words were violently stripped from their normal associations and were left to float in ever-changing linguistic space.

It is this free-floating nature of democratic language that lies behind the linguistic theory proposed by nineteenth-century America's leading Protestant theologian, Horace Bushnell, in his famous "Dissertation on Language" (1849). Sounding at one point like a precursor of Jacques Derrida, Bushnell argued that words are only hints rather than embodiments of thoughts or ideas. Since words are merely "inexact representations of thought," Bushnell wrote, "it follows that language will be ever trying to mend its own deficiencies, by multiplying its forms of representation."[8] Bushnell declared that the only worthwhile authors and philosophers were those who refused to be tied to one symbol and who multiplied paradoxical, figurative expressions of a truth that remains forever indecipherable. When considered in light of Tocqueville's analysis of American language, Bushnell's theory was indelibly American, the product of a restless democratic culture in which multiple meanings proliferated and unambiguous language was automatically nullified.

The linguistic indeterminacy bred in the American cultural landscape could be accepted by Horace Bushnell with confidence because of his firm religious faith. For him, Christ was the most mysterious of all teachers and the Bible the most densely symbolic, paradoxical of all texts. A number of other early-nineteenth-century American writers shared Bushnell's perception of the insufficiency of language but did not enjoy his supportive faith in Christianity. They were aware of the linguistic dislocations created in the new democracy but sought other means than the religious to confront them. The genre most widely employed to confront them was humor.

The first American humorist whose writings reveal the linguistic changes created by democratic mass culture was Washington Irving, whose best works possess a density generally lacking in reputable humor because they register fully the excesses of American democracy instead of naïvely ignoring them. In *Salmagundi* (1807–8), which Irving co-authored with his brother William and with James Kirke Paulding, the American republic strikes several comic personae as turbulent and frenetic. For example, the Oriental visitor Mustapha Rub-A-Dub Keli Khan is appalled by "scenes of confusion, of licentious disorganization" in a presidential election, which he says gives rise to complete amorality in the popular press, with "individuals verbally massacred, families annihilated by whole sheets full, and slang-whangers coolly bathing their pens in ink, and rioting in the slaughter of their thousands."[9] Irving to some degree shared Mustapha's apprehension over such "orgies of liberty"; throughout *Salmagundi* he frequently brought attention to America's brawling politicians, noisy mobs, sensational papers, and other disruptive phenomena of popular culture.

Irving taught the great lesson of American humor: one could register democracy's disruptions but at the same time distance oneself from them and thus strip them of terror. In Irving's best works, the chief distancing device was comical commentary on the literary process itself. Self-referential humorous style provides a kind of artistic haven for the American writer. In the above passage, it is not Irving who expresses distress over the "orgies of liberty"; rather, it is the ridiculously named Mustapha Rub-A-Dub Keli Khan, a prejudiced Mohammedan visitor. Irving's contemporary readers would be especially tickled because they would know that in the Mustapha sketches Irving is parodying a literary genre—the Oriental spy narrative—that had been extraordinarily popular in America since the 1780s. Indeed, *Salmagundi* can be viewed as a pastiche of popular styles, as seen in the overblown neoclassical verses of Pindar Cockloft, the jerky Shandyisms of Pindar's son Jeremy, the smooth Addisonian articles of Anthony Evergreen, the pompous social commentary of Launcelot Langstaff, and the silly literary criticism of William Wizard. All these styles had rich histories in British and American popular culture. The *Salmagundi* authors shuttle between various comic personae and popular genres, thereby dissociating themselves from any single viewpoint. The flexibility and detachment gained through humor undermine the whole notion of a mimetic language system referring directly to perceived reality. Because of the proliferation of comic voices, "style" loses uniformity and abrogates referentiality. William Wizard's comments on style capture this studied slipperiness of meaning in the world of American humor: "This same word *style,* though but a diminutive word, assumes to itself more contradictions, and significations, and eccentricities, than any monosyllable in the language is legitimately entitled to. It is an arrant little humourist of a word, and full of whim-whams, which occasions me to like it hugely; but it puzzled me most wickedly on my first return from a long residence abroad."

If Irving's achievement in *Salmagundi* was to create humor out of the playful subversion of linguistic referentiality, his accomplishment in "Diedrich Knickerbocker's" *History of New York* (1809) was to demonstrate how the lack of referentiality could make a hilarious mess out of even the most apparently straightforward genre: history. The Knickerbocker *History* is prefaced by the comment: "The world—the world, is nothing without the historian!"; and yet a major point of this consciously rambling, discursive book is the unreliability of the would-be historian.[10] Knickerbocker immediately undercuts himself by announcing that his introduction is "nothing at all to the purpose" and may be skipped by most readers. He then gives a ridiculously foreshortened history of the world, of which he says there are a "thousand contradictory accounts." After many circuits, he finally does get to New York history, but even that has a discomfiting effect, because the historical record is often an unsettling one. We learn, for instance, that the maltreated Indians learned "to cheat, to lie, to swear, to gamble, to quarrel, to cut each other's throats, in short, to excel in all the accomplishments that had originally marked the superiority of their Christian visitors." In addition to making such ironic stabs at white civilization,

Irving constantly brings attention to the act of history writing, which for him is the act of comical mythmaking, of blending fact with fiction, and of debunking readers' expectations.

In his best-known works, "Rip Van Winkle" and "The Legend of Sleepy Hollow" (1820) Irving introduces to American literature a topic of native humor that would later intrigue writers like Hawthorne and Poe: the process of fiction making within the individual mind. The same distortions of perception that Irving's earlier works had dramatized with respect to literary genres and to history were now ushered into the private consciousness of a bemused, imaginative individual. In both tales an old-fashioned protagonist is confronted with terrifying, disruptive forces from modern American popular culture. Rip returns to his village after twenty years to find that "the very character of the people seemed changed. There was a busy, bustling disputatious tone about it, instead of the accustomed phlegm and drowsy tranquillity."[11] The "babylonish jargon" about elections and people's rights that bewilders Rip is similar to the "orgies of liberty" that had disgusted Mustapha in *Salmagundi*. But Irving is now prepared to study how democratic enthusiasms infiltrate and activate the creative consciousness. Rip is at first completely bewildered by this chaotic society but then becomes absorbed into it and turns into a venerable patriarch who endlessly spins his life story at the village inn. The story he tells, Irving writes, is known "at first to vary on some points, every time he told it," until it settles down to "the tale I have related." These imaginative variances in the retelling underscore the fictive nature of the tale the reader has just finished. A funny tale of supernaturalism—safely self-referential in its humor—has been spun out of disruptive democratic forces that are kept as distant and invisible as the far-off rumble of Hendrick Hudson's crew playing at ninepins.

In "The Legend of Sleepy Hollow" Irving again studies the collision between an old-fashioned quiet world and a more chaotic democracy but provides a more ambiguous denouement. Irving takes us to a village on the Hudson that is "one of the quietest places in the whole world," where all things "remain fixed, while the great torrent of migration and improvement, which is making such incessant changes in other parts of this restless country, sweeps by them unobserved."[12] Having established an almost dualistic contrast between the old, static village and restless, bustling nineteenth-century America, Irving presents two characters who embody the opposite sides of this dualism: the schoolteacher Ichabod Crane, whose mind is haunted by ghost tales reaching back to Puritan times; and the burly, roistering Brom Bones, who embodies the mischievous humor and comical trickery of modern America. If Rip Van Winkle had symbolized the power of the nostalgic fiction maker to re-create endlessly his lost predemocratic past, Ichabod Crane represents the powerlessness of the American past to withstand the onslaught of the ever-changing present. The rapidly riding Headless Horseman is an appropriate emblem of the mindless fury Irving associates with nineteenth-century society, driving away the timid, credulous world of bygone values embodied in Ichabod Crane. In the characterization of Brom Bones as the rampaging, destructive Headless Horseman, Irving seems to be apprehensively envisaging the coming victory of a new kind of American idiom: Old Southwest humor, which was just starting to achieve widespread popularity about the time Irving wrote this tale. The roistering Brom Bones is an early example of the nineteenth-century frontier "screamer" who would become a central figure in American humor.

Time proved Irving right: Brom Bones, in effect, did win the day. Although reputable humor was kept alive in the works of Holmes, Lowell, and others, it was subversive frontier humor that most captivated the reading public and that established a distinctly American voice that powerfully affected the major writers. In reputable humor democracy's disruptions would be rhetorically combated in the interest of preserving stability and clarity. In subversive humor they would be amplified and exaggerated until they became absurd.

If Irving had created humor from the collision of the quiet with the irrational, the frontier humorists created it by forgetting the quiet altogether and taking the irrational to a perverse, and therefore funny, extreme. Whereas Irving admitted into his creative consciousness just enough democratic disruptions to energize his imagination and to build fictive defenses against the real, the frontier humorists magnified the problematic features of the democratic experience until they became absurd. Irving had wittily distanced himself from the "orgies of liberty"; the subversive humorists exaggerated these orgies until they took on the aspect of a grotesque democratic carnival. They brought together all the dark aspects of nineteenth-century popular culture—gory violence, universal chicanery, the likable criminal, republican attacks on authority figures— and, by exaggerating them, made them ridiculous. In their humor, these phenomena became mechanistic and nonhuman. They were projected outward, away from ambiguity and introspection toward the surface. The irrational style, strange enough in nonhumorous Subversive writings, became in the humorous ones the zany and sometimes even premodern American Subversive Style.

These often raucous humorous writings held great interest for America's major writers. Emerson believed that stylistic vigor and originality came principally from the frontier. He referred to "the exploits of Boone and David Crockett, the journals of Western pioneers," and other frontier writings as "genuine growths" showing that America's eyes are "turned westward, and a new and stronger tone in our literature will be the result."[13] Thoreau claimed he had an inner needle that was constantly pulled South and West, areas, he wrote, that represented "a wildness whose glance no civilization can endure."[14] Melville, who famously denounced smooth Anglophile writers and called for an explosive American style, was aware of key heroes in frontier literature, as is shown by his description in *Mardi* of a swordfish's blade as "inflexible as Crockett's rifle tube; no doubt as deadly" and his reference in *Moby-Dick* to Hercules as "that antique Crockett and Kit Carson."[15] Whitman acutely noted that American humor, in contrast to British humor, was "very grim, loves exaggeration, & has a certain tartness & even fierceness."[16] Equally acute was Howells, who in the late nineteenth century recalled "those early humorists who antedated the romantic fictionists, who were often in their humor so rank, so wild, so savage, so cruel."[17] Mark Twain not only borrowed extensively from the early frontier humorists but once referred to the tall tale—the impossibly exaggerated, virtually structureless frontier narrative of improbable events—as the only literary form that was exclusively American. Although Mark Twain's generalization is perhaps too sweeping, it underscores the fact that wild hyperbole and structurelessness are instinctive products of the American psyche.

The analogies between the major writings and raw popular humor will be discussed at length in later chapters, but first we must explore this humor itself.

Nowhere is the wildness of American humor more apparent than in narratives about the most popular figure in early frontier humor, the "screamer" or "ring-tailed roarer," the loud backwoods braggart who spouted streams of strange metaphors. The most famous portrait of the ring-tailed roarer in American literature is that of the Child of Calamity in *Huckleberry Finn,* but Mark Twain's character is one of the last of a long line of popular figures that had long been featured in frontier humor. Starting in the 1820s, folk journalists and oral storytellers transformed the screamer into a kind of comic demigod whose superhuman antics centered on cruelty, violence, drunkenness, racism, eroticism. Americans were made acquainted with a succession of legendary screamers: Mike Fink was introduced in 1821, Davy Crockett and Nimrod Wildfire in 1830, Roaring Ralph Stackpole in 1837, and various other ring-tailed roarers in the following decades.

Although the screamer has often been discussed, the literary and cultural implications of this figure merit further exploration. The frontier screamer was a time-specific character who represented a stylization of the antebellum Subversive imagination, which became safely distanced because it was removed to the free world of absurdity. The screamer is the exaggerated version of the mixed figures that were appearing in popular sensational literature of the day. He was the ultimate likable criminal, the cosmic folk hero who used justified violence not just against social oppressors but against nature itself. He was also the ultimate immoral reformer, who, while supposedly a sympathetic figure, drinks and swears with gleeful disregard for moral values. His female counterpart, the screamer woman, was the ultimate adventure feminist, who could outfight, outdrink, outswear the toughest man. Exaggeration of popular themes in the figure of the screamer brought about a defusion of their threatening aspects. It also created an acceleration of sensational devices until they approached the presurrealistic. In the screamer we find the projection of the turbulence and linguistic anarchy that Tocqueville identified as distinctive features of American democracy.

In order to appreciate fully the significance of the screamer, it is useful to look closely at the Crockett almanacs, the popular series of humor pamphlets that gave wildly imaginative retellings of the exploits of Davy Crockett (1786–1836), the Tennessee frontiersman and politician who died heroically at the Alamo. Some fifty issues of Crockett almanacs (each of which enjoyed a widespread sale) were published in various American cities between 1835 and 1856, during which period Davy Crockett was the most visible and popular frontier roarer in American literature. The Crockett almanacs were paper pamphlets with brief humor passages, mainly first-person vernacular tall tales by the Crockett persona, interspersed with meteorological and astronomical information. Most were emblazoned with grotesque engravings of bestial-looking human beings or Crockett himself fighting alligators, riding streaks of lightning, and the like. Surprisingly, the stylistic aspects of Crockett almanacs have been largely neglected by literary historians, despite their vast popularity and despite the fact that several major writers (including Emerson, Melville, and Mark Twain) directly mention Crockett in their writings. The fierce protagonist of the antebellum Crockett almanacs bears little resemblance to the upright, clean-cut figure presented to American television viewers by Walt Disney in the 1950s. In fact, he has little in common with the real-life David Crockett, who was tough and colorful but restrained when compared with the almanac character, who is the self-reliant democratic man converted into a savage rascal god.

When Emerson declared that Americans should look to "the exploits of Boone and David Crockett" to discover "a new and stronger tone in our literature," he may have been referring to the thoroughly American experiments with theme and language that the Crockett almanacs represented. It might be hard to imagine Emerson enjoying gross frontier humor filled with eye gougings, nose chawings, panther skinnings, and so on, humor that invited readers to snicker continually at the pornography of violence. But let us not forget that Emerson himself sometimes used shocking images. If Crockett gouged out other people's eyes and carried them in his pocket, Emerson metaphorically transformed himself into a walking transparent eyeball. In a more general sense, the Crockett almanacs and Emerson's writings were different products of the American writer's instinct to exaggerate democratic individualism in both theme and language.

Throughout the Crockett almanacs standards of gentility are challenged at every level. The frontier children depicted in the almanacs are weaned on whiskey and taught from an early age how to scratch their parents and assault their grandparents. Courting between male and female screamers makes a mockery of normal courting practices. When Crockett's uncle is about to get married, he presents to his future wife two eyes he has gouged out; she dries out the eyes, hangs one in each ear, and wears them to church. Female and male roarers in the Crockett almanacs are engaged in a constant competition to prove their strength, their cruelty, and their tolerance for bad whiskey. A common figure of American adventure fiction, the adventure feminist, is converted in the almanacs into the savage screamer feminist, such as Sal Fink (who is tied to a stake by fifty Indians but manages to escape and tie them together by their heels), the six-foot Lolly Ritchers (who kills a bear with her hands and wears to church a necklace of eyes she has gouged out of other women), and Sal Fungus (who can "laugh the bark off a pine tree, swim straight up a cataract, gouge out alligators' eyes, dance a rock to pieces, sink a steamboat, blow out the moonlight . . .").[18] As for the male roarers, they are frolicking embodiments of ugliness and sadism—none more so than Davy Crockett himself. Davy boasts of being too ugly to get up in the morning, for fear of scaring the sun back to bed. Davy does all the things that a normal roarer does (he screams, claws, gouges, kills) but does them with a unique black delight in cruelty for its own sake. When he is cheated by a devious squatter, he forces the squatter at gunpoint to eat a pile of cow dung. A rampant racist, he takes special pleasure in gouging out the eyes of Negroes and Indians.

His open savagery, however, is found preferable to the underhanded corruption he sees everywhere in American society. As the ultimate likable pariah, he constantly impugns swindlers in government and double-dealers in business. "Whar's all the honor?" he demands in a typical congressional speech. "No whar! an thar it'll stick!"[19] He constantly reminds us that he lives in a world of untrustworthy appearances. "All natur is deceivin," he declares, "an in the course of this CHECK-ered life in sports an in pollytics, I've met a tarnal sight of deceivin things, statesmen, an pollytishuns in pertiklar."[20] Politicians are his chief but not his only gripe. He attends a camp meeting only to be shocked by the hypocrisy of preachers who sermonize on purity but secretly consort with women in their flock. With all his faults Crockett at least has the virtue of openness.

In the screamer character of the Crockett almanacs, the aggressive American individualist becomes the overreaching abrogator of nature's laws and the smirking warrior against normal language patterns. The Crockett almanacs were among the earliest examples of the socioliterary phenomenon noted by Tocqueville: political and social freedom in America was matched by a corresponding suspension of probability and linguistic uniformity in literature. It is important to note how persistently the laws of nature are violated in the strange world of the Crockett almanacs. In a typical story Crockett discovers while mountain climbing that the world's axis and the sun have become encrusted with ice and have frozen in place, posing severe danger to the human species. Crockett's solution for this problem is related in typically weird fashion. He seizes a tremendous bear and pounds it on the earth until warm blood oozes out. Then, as he tells it,

> I took an' held him over the airth's axes, an' squeezed him till I thaw'd 'em loose, poured about a ton of it over the sun's face, give the airth's cog-wheel one kick backward, till I got the sun loose—whistled "Push along, keep movin'!" and in about fifteen seconds the airth gin a grunt, and begun movin'—the sun walked up beautiful—saluten me with sich a wind o' gratitude, that it made me sneeze. I lit my pipe by the blaze o' his top-not, shouldered my bear, an' walked home, introducin' the people to fresh daylight with a piece of sunrise in my pocket, with which I cooked my bear steaks, an' enjoyed one o' the best breakfasts I had tasted for some time.[21]

This passage typifies the American Subversive Style. It is at once totally American and totally bizarre. Or, as Tocqueville might have put it, it is bizarre because it is totally American. Its Americanness lies in the brash self-confidence of the folksy persona, who squeezes bear's blood over the sun with the ease that one would squeeze dry a washcloth. This is democracy on a cosmic level. The earth's axis, the sun, the moon, the stars are within easy reach of the American screamer, who is the self-reliant American common man taken to an extreme. Nothing is impossible in this imaginary realm of hyperbolic democracy, for all aspects of perceived reality are dissolved and recombined at will by the imagination that reduces all things to the same level.

In the carnivalized world of the Crockett almanacs, the human and the bestial, the living and the inanimate exchange places with amazing ease. What modern scholars have identified as a distinguishing feature of surrealism—the juxtaposition of disparate realities—is commonplace in both the language and the illustrations of subversive American humor. The French surrealists took an interest in one antebellum writer, Edgar Allan Poe, and in the artist Thomas Quidor, whose grotesque paintings based on stories by Irving have a distorted, nightmarish quality. What they didn't recognize was that Poe and Quidor were at the tip of a huge cultural iceberg of a presurrealistic American style whose most bizarre manifestations appeared in the popular frontier humor Poe and Quidor are known to have enjoyed. Not only can Davy Crockett light his pipe with the sun and hop onto streaks of lightning, but his land is said to be so rich "that if you plant tenpenny nails at night, they will sprout crowbars by morning!"[22] And Davy is hardly alone. His neighbors "are half horse, half alligator, and a touch of the steam boat, besides being of the real meat-axe disposition, and always wolfish about the head."[23] All images in the Crockett almanacs are shifting and kaleidoscopic. Even many of the illustrative engravings in the almanacs have a distinctly premodern flavor—more so, actually, than the paintings of Quidor. *Crockett's Harrison Almanac, 1841,* for instance, features a weird picture of a huge fly, wearing a hat and fishing bag, that is standing with a fishing line in the water and a tiny human being swimming frantically at the end of his hook. Similarly, *Crockett's Comic Almanac* for 1840 has a picture of a prostrate man on a chopping block surrounded by an ax-wielding hog and two standing fish with smiling human heads. In another 1840 issue, the rough voice of a screamer is pictured as a jagged geometrical design extending as a cone from the screamer's mouth. This flagrant intermixture of disparate realities shows a presurrealistic style surging from the hot heart of democratic humor.

The shifting images that characterized the Crockett almanacs became, in more sophisticated examples of frontier humor, internalized in the psyche of the comic protagonist. The most notorious instance of this internalized shiftiness is the rascal-hero of Johnson Jones Hooper's *Adventures of Captain Simon Suggs* (1844). Hooper's volume illustrates just how popular comic rascality was in the 1840s, for it sold nearly ten thousand copies in its first year and went through eleven editions in the next decade. The kaleidoscopic shifts of the Crockett almanacs were thoroughly American in a volcanic and instinctive way. In the characterization of Simon Suggs they are American in a more intentional, self-conscious way. Suggs's concise motto—"It is good to be shifty in a new country"—shows how deeply attuned to democracy's fluid, potentially relativist environment subversive humor was becoming. Suggs differs from Crockett in that he takes pride in his own deceit and utter lack of principle. The deception

Crockett sees in high places now becomes a valued goal of the frontier hero himself. Exterior shifts in imagery are transformed into behavioral shifts in pose: Suggs is able to impersonate a member of the state legislature, a prosperous slave buyer, and a wealthy Kentucky drover with amoral ease. Suggs's deceptions are placed in competition with those he witnesses in civilized life. For instance, when he witnesses mass hypocrisy and sensuality at a camp-meeting revival, he sees "the whole affair as a grand deception—a sort of 'opposition line' running against his own, and looked on with a sort of professional jealousy."[24] Jealous he need not be, for, as always, he outdeceives the powers that be by feigning a conversion that eventually wins the hearts and the money of the pious. Suggs is the first figure in American literature who fully manipulates Conventional values—piety, discretion, honesty, entrepreneurial shrewdness—for purely selfish ends. The Conventional becomes fully relativized in the world of subversive humor.

It should be recognized that not all frontier humor was subversive: William Tappan Thompson's *Mayor Jones' Courtship* (1843), for instance, featured a hero who was neither a roarer nor a confidence man but rather a respectable, honest citizen. Still, it is the adventurous black humor and the rascalish protagonists of more typical frontier writings that have been most influential on major writers from Poe and Melville through Mark Twain and Faulkner. The humor of the Old Southwest repeatedly invites us to laugh at pranksters playing practical jokes at funerals and taking pleasure in the physical misery of their friends. In a characteristic sketch by Solomon Franklin Smith the narrator extends sympathy to the widow of a man who has just died accidentally; the widow callously shrugs off the death, saying her husband *"warn't of much account, no how!"*[25]

All the perverse tendencies of frontier humor culminate in two paradigmatic American comic heroes, Ovid Bolus, Esq., and Sut Lovingood. Ovid Bolus, the popular hero of Joseph Glover Baldwin's *The Flush Times of Alabama and Mississippi* (1853)—a book said to have been greatly enjoyed by Abraham Lincoln—is the democratic man as consummate liar. He does not deceive from self-interest, or necessity, or vanity. Instead, as Baldwin explains:

> What he did in that walk, was from the irresistible prompting of instinct, and a disinterested love of art. . . . Accordingly, he did not labor a lie: he lied with a relish: he lied with a coming appetite, growing with what it fed on: he lied from a delight of invention and the charm of fictitious narrative. . . . Bolus' lying came from his greatness of soul and his comprehensiveness of mind. The truth was too small for him. Fact was too dry and common-place for the fervor of his genius. . . . He had a great contempt for history and historians.

... He had long torn down the partition between his imagination and his memory.[26]

In Ovid Bolus, the American subversive imagination has become identical with perceived reality. There is no distinction between fact and fiction for the representative hero of American humor. We have seen that Tocqueville and other foreign commentators had argued that the linguistic effect of democratic society was to strip language from normal significations, and that the leading American theologian-linguist, Horace Bushnell, operated from the assumption that, given the absolute fictiveness of words, the enlightened writer infinitely multiplies forms of representation. In American humor, creative fiction-making becomes an act of play, as is evidenced by the endlessly accumulating fictions of Rip Van Winkle, the explosive strings of shifting images in the Crockett almanacs, the ever-changing roles of Simon Suggs. The instinctual, all-embracing lying of Ovid Bolus is merely an explicit version of the gleeful fiction-making of the other humor writings. Bolus is always giving sham representations of "the three cardinal virtues, Faith, Hope, and Charity; while, in the result, the chief of these was *Charity*!" Just as in the first scene of Melville's *The Confidence-Man* the erasable, shifting messages about charity on the lamb-like man's slate suggest the slippery meaning of sacred words, so in the character of Ovid Bolus Christian values are completely relativized when they become mere poses of an entrepreneurial comic showman.

In George Washington Harris's *Sut Lovingood Papers* (1854–58) we find a fusion of the anarchic violence of the frontier screamer and the artful malice of the rascal, along with a dimension generally absent from antebellum frontier humor: a carefully managed vernacular voice that enforces linguistically the subversiveness of the characters and events described. It has become a critical commonplace that beneath the sparkling surface of Harris's humor lurks a profound skepticism—some have even called it nihilism. This dark philosophical streak is most visible when Sut Lovingood denies he has a soul or gives examples of what he calls "universal, unregenerate human nature," such as every person's secret joy in the suffering of others (even of best friends) or the impulse to give a crying baby a vicious slap "to show it what's atwixt it and the grave."[27] It is equally apparent in the perversity and bestiality that reign in almost every scene. When Sut bridles and mounts his own father and rides him into the fields, when he ties a live rat in the pants of a sleeping friend, when he puts lizards up the trousers of the preaching Parson Bullen, causing him to strip naked and leap onto a fat listener who gallops off into the woods, we know that we are in a relativist realm where mainstream values—family love, religion, friendship—have little meaning.

Deep skepticism was hardly new to popular American literature; it had existed on many levels of American popular culture for decades. What made Harris unusual was not his underlying cynicism but rather the premodern imagistic effects that were produced when this cynicism was communicated in the strange idiom of Old Southwest humor. As in some previous frontier writings, grotesque imagery often takes on a weird life of its own, as humor creates a free linguistic space in which the human quickly changes place with the bestial or the inanimate. But Harris handles this odd juxtaposition of disparate images with a care unseen in previous frontier literature. Note the subtlety with which rapidly shifting metaphors, perspectives, and spatial relations are managed in Sut's macabre description of the sheriff's wife:

> She were bony and pale. A drunk Injun could a-read a Dutch almanac through her nose; and there were a new moon of indigo under her eyes. Away back into them, fifty foot or so, I seed her tear wells; their windlass were broke, the buckets in staves, and the waters all gone; and away still further back two lights shined, soft, like the stars above just afore their settin. . . . The hand itself were white, not like snow but like paint, and the forked blue veins made it look like a new map of the land of death.

On the one hand, this impressionistic passage tells us more about the woman than any abstract accounts of her qualities could communicate; her torpid sickliness, her quiet despair emerge more surely than they would in a more standard description. On the other hand, the passage is not so much about a sad woman as it is about the adventurous language experiments that a sad woman provokes in the imagination of the American humorist. Just notice Harris's dramatic leaps from strange image to strange image—from a drunk Indian reading a Dutch almanac to an indigo moon to tear wells fifty feet away to broken windlasses to setting stars, and so forth. If these disjunctive metaphors were painted as images on a canvas, the effect would be surrealistic indeed.

Throughout the *Sut Lovingood Papers* Harris communicates impressions or emotions but at the same time reveals the peculiar linguistic freedoms of American humor. The jittery stomach caused by a first infatuation is communicated both precisely and oddly when Sut declares that Sicily Burns makes him feel as if "I'd swallered a threshin-machine in full blast with a couple of bull-dogs, and they had set into fightin."[28] The rising frenzy of the young Skissum, as he discovers while sleeping that Sut had tied a rat in his pants, is wonderfully objectified in an account of his kaleidoscopic nightmare of a whip that turns into a huge boiling tea kettle that turns into "a steam engine a-drivin the wagon whip and a cotton gin with red-hot saws fifteen hundred licks a minute" while *"he were in the cotton hopper."* American subversive humor had always embodied a protest against predictable language patterns, but in Harris linguistic unpredictability becomes fully intentional and regulated. Note the contrasting use of words by Sut and a genteel friend: the friend "just rolls 'em out to the point like a feller a-layin bricks—every one fits," whereas, Sut boasts, "I ladles out my words at random like a calf kickin at yaller jackets." Elsewhere Sut explains that he can't help being a "durned fool" because his soul, instead of being forked between the ears and welded to the backbone, dangles loose and waves chaotically. He exclaims: "Oh, durn it. I thinks at random, just as I talks and does." The randomness, of course, is a purposeful authorial strategy and is entirely reflective of the democratic humorist's linguistic universe. The savage joy Sut feels as he bridles and rides his father seems an extension of the perverse glee Harris feels as he explores the wild metaphors and juxtapositions offered by carnivalized American language.

On the surface, it might seem that frontier humor was rather a specialized genre that had little direct influence on mainstream American culture. The opposite, however, is in fact closer to the truth. It is fair to say that no single indigenous literary phenomenon had so broad a cultural effect as this stylistically experimental humor. In the early stages, the spread of frontier humor owed much to the ascendancy of the new sermon style discussed in Chapter 1. The frontier circuit riders and urban revivalists that proliferated during and after the Second Great Awakening were often skilled humorists who ushered the backwoods idiom into the popular pulpit. Beginning in the 1820s, backwoods humorists themselves hit the lecture circuit; traveling humorists such as James H. Hackett and George Handel Hill made goodly sums from telling fantastically inconsequential tall tales to lecture audiences nationwide. Ring-tailed roarers were often featured in popular fiction and plays of the 1830s. Nimrod Wildfire, the roaring hero of James Kirke Paulding's farce *The Lion of the West* (1830), was one of the most popular of a group of literary screamers that also included Roaring Ralph Stackpole of Robert Montgomery Bird's *Nick of the Woods* (1837), Mark Forrester of William Gilmore Simms's *Guy Rivers* (1834), and the title character of John Pendleton Kennedy's *Horse-Shoe Robinson* (1835). In the meantime, frontier humor was popularized directly in cheap pamphlets like the Crockett almanacs and in popular newspapers, most notably William T. Porter's influential New York weekly *The Spirit of the Times* (1831–61), which brought Old Southwest humor to the heart of the urban Northeast. In short, the stage was set for the immense popularity enjoyed later by frontier humorists such as Artemus Ward, Bret Harte, and Mark Twain.

The infiltration of subversive humor into the Northern cities profoundly affected the style of various popular genres: sermons, newspapers, political speeches, poems, plays, novels. There was a sudden infusion of grotesqueness and sarcasm into these formerly staid genres. We should recall that the 1830s and 1840s were also a time of increasing sensationalism in popular reform writings and in working-class fiction, particularly that of the politically minded radical democrats. During the dark years after the Panic of 1837, the twisted idioms of frontier humor began to be fused with working-class sensationalism to produce what I term *radical-democrat humor.* Along with mythic immoral-reform rhetoric and gross sensationalism, subversive humor became a favorite weapon of the radical democrats in their effort to unmask what they regarded as the corruptions of America's ruling class. In *The Mysterious Stranger* Mark Twain would write: "Against the assault of laughter, nothing can stand."[29] It is in this militant spirit that humor was espoused by the radical democrats of the Northern cities.

The great popularizers of radical-democrat humor were the Bowery politician and editor Mike Walsh, the Philadelphia novelist-reformer George Lippard, and the sensational New York authors George Foster and George Thompson. While these were by far the most popular radical-democrat humorists, there was a young Brooklyn editor, Walter Whitman, who made quite a stir in the mid-1840s with his blackly humorous political articles, very much in the radical-democrat vein.

The flamboyant Mike Walsh was a pioneer of the new style. Walsh's infamous political newspaper, *The Subterranean* (1843–47), carried a heading—*"Independent in Everything, Neutral in Nothing"*—that was just as descriptive of its rhetoric as of its contents. Disparaging what he termed the "ultra dishwaterness" of Conventional magazine literature, Walsh made it clear that as the self-avowed champion of New York's working class he was going to bring both muscle and humor to American political prose. It is understandable that more than a dozen libel suits were filed against *The Subterranean* in its first four months of publication, for Walsh specialized in stabbing sarcasm, as when he dubbed Herman Melville's politician brother "Gansevoort or Gander-brained Melville" or when he branded an enemy as "one of the human stink weeds which are nurtured by the moral slime and putrefaction of that sink of iniquity, satirically denominated the 'Halls of Justice.' "[30] Typical of his black humor was a huge engraving, featured in the September 23, 1843, issue of the paper, entitled "Spirits of the Damned Exulting Over Our Anticipated Fall," which depicts Walsh and his friends boiling in a tremendous cauldron in hell while snickering demons (their political enemies) dance around the cauldron. Given his animus against maudlin literature and his devotion to working-class ideals, it is perhaps understandable that he had connections with another young firebrand, Walter Whitman. The first issue of Walsh's paper carried an early Whitman poem, "Lesson of the Two Symbols," that was an amateurish but intriguing effort from one who would rise from the radical-democrat depths to become the very embodiment of poetic unconventionalism. Whitman, for his part, in 1842 editorialized several times in his penny paper, the New York *Aurora,* on behalf of the Spartan Band, the gang of rowdy Tammany Democrats led by Mike Walsh.

In the fiction of George Thompson and George Lippard, radical-democrat humor was epitomized in the central figure of the sadistic devil-hero who used biting humor to unmask aristocrats. In Thompson's lurid novel *New-York Life* this figure appears as Asmodeus, described as "one of the most amiable of the fallen angels," who "pursues even his good designs with a spice of devilish malice." Exposing upper-class vice with "a malignant, sneering pleasure," Thompson's Asmodeus laughs continually as he uses his magic "social kaleidoscope" to reveal universal corruption beneath pious exteriors.[31] The Asmodeus figure was an important one in the humor of the radical democrats. This figure had derived originally from a character in an eighteenth-century French play who had the power to look through house roofs and see private goings-on. In the hands of the radical democrats Asmodeus became a political unmasking figure. In addition to Thompson's novel there appeared Harrison G. Buchanan's *Asmodeus; or, Legends of New York* (1848) and the anonymously published *Revelations of Asmodeus, or Mysteries of Upper Ten-Dom* (1849)—both of which use the smirking devil figure as an unmasker of social vice. Melville, who was living in New York at the peak of the Asmodeus craze, surely had this popular figure in mind when at the beginning of Chapter 18 of *The Confidence-Man* he featured a debate over the fairness of "unmask[ing] an operator," a debate in which one of the discussants asks whether it would be "the fair thing in Asmodeus" to walk into a stock exchange and reveal the true thoughts of those present.[32]

The period's most strikingly demonic unmasking character was Devil-Bug, the keeper of the Philadelphia den of vice in George Lippard's best-selling novel *The Quaker City.* Devil-Bug is the complete enactment of the savage fantasies of working-class readers, for he entraps, mocks, and tortures his upper-class guests at Monk Hall with almost unparalleled sadistic joy. He delights in watching the blood of his victims fall drop by drop, and every time one of them is endangered he lets go an uproarious laugh and mutters: "I wonders how that'll work!" He combines all the savagery of the frontier roarer with the political aims of the radical democrat. Like the fictional Davy Crockett, he is the mythically exaggerated likable criminal, the vindictive common man whose justified ferocity is found preferable to the sneaking vice that lurks everywhere in civilized life.

Devil-Bug is merely one instance of the black humor that rules in Lippard's quintessentially radical-democrat imagination. In the twenty popular volumes and countless essays Lippard wrote, there is scarcely a page that does not contain a black joke. Even his most sober work, the long initiation ritual, cryptically entitled "The B.G.C.," which he wrote in 1850 for his labor group, the Brotherhood of the Union, is loaded with humor of the most macabre variety. According to the ritual, the initiate is forced to watch a skit of three villainous capitalists shrieking with delight as they plot against the poor, waving an ax and drinking from a skull filled with red liquid that symbolizes the blood of American workers.[33] An orphaned and embittered product of Philadelphia's turbulent working class, Lippard saw style as nothing less than a political weapon that must be kept sharp with dark humor. Like his prototype Mike Walsh, he despised Conventional literature, which he called the poetry of "lollypop-itude" and "twaddle-dom."[34] His black humor had social import even when it was apparently gratuitous, for the ability to shock genteel readers through hilariously disgusting images seemed to him a source of power.

Since black humor was an intrinsic element of American popular culture, it is understandable that every scene of Lippard's culturally representative novel *The Quaker City* abounds with such humor. In one scene, a hangman and a mob of onlookers grin as they watch the black tongue and heaving body of a man dangling at the end of a rope. In another, a gang of medical students trade horrid jokes about rotting corpses they are dissecting. In another, a woman is followed home by a carriage carrying her own hearse, which is brought before her as she collapses from the poison her husband has given her. But it is pointless to isolate instances of Lippard's grotesque humor, for it permeates everything he wrote.

Literary scholars such as Leslie Fiedler have compared Lippard to two foreign popular novelists, Eugène Sue of France and G. M. W. Reynolds of England, who in the 1840s were also writing radical exposés of urban life. Although there is a rough similarity between Lippard's subject matter and theirs, in the area of style Lippard is wholly American, because his radical-democrat humor leads him into nightmarish extravagances that are absent from the more staid prose of his foreign counterparts. While Sue and Reynolds point toward the grim realism of the naturalists, Lippard points toward the unrestrained irrationalism and grotesqueness of other modern writers. It is understandable that Lippard has recently become a cult figure among American surrealists, because his fusion of the irrational and the blackly humorous gives rise to bizarre juxtapositions of the human and the nonhuman, the realistic and the abstract. Inanimate objects come to life and behave like human beings, as when through the eyes of a drunken character we see a watch box walking across the street and blacking the eyes of a lamppost. People, in turn, seem like strange pastiches of heterogeneous objects, such as a lawyer whose "small head overlooked his immense corporation, like a pea observing the circumference of a pumpkin," and a colonel whose face was "very much like a picture of a dissipated full-moon, with a large red pear stuck in the center for a nose, while two small black beads, placed in corresponding circles of crimson tape, supply the place of eyes."[35] As is true in some frontier writings, Lippard's imagistic juxtapositions are so strange that, were they rendered on a canvas, the effect would be surrealistic.

Also premodern are the zany dialogues, monologues, and puns that run through the novel. Notice the bizarre shifts created when a doctor sings praise to the statesman Henry Clay and a horse of the same name, all the while addressing a man with a heart ailment who wants to poison his wife: "Henry Clay—seen my blood horse, Henry Clay? Splendid creature, capital action, glorious gait. Paid eight hundred dollars for him. Make a good President; in favor of the Tariff, chivalrous fellow. . . . Ticklish disease *that*! One moment lively as a bird; the next, stiff as a poker! Have you seen Harry Clay lately? Grand speech that: his farewell to the Senate! Wait a moment and I'll go round to the stable and order the servant to trot him out. Would you like to see a manuscript of mine, on the Theory of Poisons?" André Breton couldn't ask for a more delectable bit of black humor than that! In the course of the doctor's speech the reader is thrown violently between different levels of reality—a blood horse, a statesman, heart attacks, poison—that intermesh to form a strange collage of disparate images. As weird as are some of the images in the major literature of the American Renaissance, Lippard's imagery is even more so, for it erupts unchecked from the volcanic imagination of the radical-democrat humorist. For example, if Poe creates an odd effect when he describes the eyelike windows of the House of Usher or if Melville seems bizarre when he describes the whale-jaw entrance to the bar in the Spouter-Inn, Lippard outdoes both of them in imagistic strangeness when he describes a hotel as "a monster-building, with some hundred windows varying its red-brick face, in the way of eyes, covered with green-blind shutters, looking very much like so many goggles intended to preserve the sight of the visual organs aforesaid; while the verandah, on the ground floor, affording an entrance to the bar-room, might be likened to the mouth of the grand-edifice, always wide open and ready to swallow a customer."

The extreme radical-democrat imagination, as embodied in Lippard, produced a new brand of humor that had the grotesqueness of subversive frontier humor but also something more: an impulse to assault larger themes from the zestfully republican perspective of the common American man. The radical democrats of the 1840s caused a notable broadening in

applications of unmasking humor. Dismayed by the contrast between
America's republican ideals and the unrepublican realities of growing class
divisions and sectional animosities, they began to sense that problems in
American life were more than merely political—they were part of the very
fabric of perceived reality. It was beginning to seem, as Lippard put it, "a
premium queer world."[36] Equality, religion, morality, didactic literature,
philanthropy—these valued American ideals and institutions seemed, in
the eyes of the radical democrats, to be savagely mocked by realities such
as poverty and slavery. For the radical democrats, unmasking humor became a chief means of underscoring the horrid ironies they perceived. The
abolitionist Frederick Douglass once remarked that, in light of the inequities in American life, the only proper style for the defender of the oppressed was stinging irony. In the central radical-democrat novel, *The
Quaker City*, we see irony fused with grotesqueness to create an intensified,
broadened dark humor.

A representative piece of radical-democrat humor is "Devil-Bug's
Dream," the nightmare sequence at the heart of *The Quaker City*. The
nightmare reveals the worst social fears of the radical democrats, for it
gives an imaginary rendering of Philadelphia in 1950, which has become
a horrible society in which poor blacks and whites—"the Slaves of Capital
and Trade"—are led in chains by grinning rulers of the social system.
Devil-Bug learns that this is the burial day of liberty, the funeral of America, which has been killed by "Priest-craft, and Slave-craft, and Traitor-
craft."[37] At the end of the dream we see the rulers being retributively
destroyed by the ghosts of the oppressed, who rise up and wipe out their
oppressors in a "massacre of judgment," while the words "WO UNTO
SODOM" blaze in the sky above. This sequence may not sound humorous,
but it is, for it is orchestrated throughout by the laughter of the onlooker
Devil-Bug, who explodes uproariously in cynical glee as he witnesses every
stage of the cataclysmic destruction of American society. Because Lippard
is here achieving a total fusion of radical-democrat social views and black
popular humor, it is understandable that the sequence seems more presurrealistic than any of its length in antebellum American fiction. In every
paragraph a new strange image appears, as the radical-democrat imagination becomes fully inscribed in a style that is as disorienting as the contents
are radical. At the beginning of the dream Devil-Bug is surrounded "by a
hazy atmosphere, with coffins floating slowly past, and the stars shining
through the eyes of skulls, and the sun pouring his livid light straight
downward into a wilderness of new-made graves which extended yawning
and dismal over the surface of a boundless plain." The images become
even wilder when he finds himself in twentieth-century Philadelphia, where
buildings rise and fall before him in broken perspective and where he is

shunted back and forth between impossible scenes. A typically bizarre moment comes when he envisages a tremendous battle between two huge coffin-fleets on the Schuylkill River; each coffin is driven by a putrid corpse that guides its boat into the furious fray. The nightmare culminates in a total disruption of physical laws, as the ground rolls like a massive ocean, people and buildings sink down, and a tremendous column of quivering earth shoots upward into the heavens, with three people on its peak caught in a grim death struggle. The delighted Devil-Bug shrieks with glee as he watches the cataclysm and the lurid words that signal the collapse of American civilization. The entire nightmare, its explosive social message enforced by its stylistic weirdness, represents the darkest, most experimental aspects of radical-democrat humor.

If vicious humor and disruptive style represented the darkest dimensions of the radical-democrat imagination, the popular figure of "the b'hoy" (street slang for "boy") embodied its most affirmative possibilities—affirmative, that is, before it was notably vulgarized in the popular literature of the late 1840s. The b'hoy figure has received inadequate attention from literary scholars. In their survey of American humor, Walter Blair and Hamlin Hill briefly point out that the b'hoy—the brash, swaggering lower-class urban youth—became such a popular character in American novels and plays that by 1848 he had replaced the frontier screamer as the premier character in antebellum humor.[38] The social roots of the b'hoy have been recently traced by Sean Wilentz, who shows that the real-life b'hoy grew out of New York fire gangs to become the main example of the boisterous "republicanism of the streets" that Wilentz says was the leading form of working-class protest in the 1840s.[39] In my view, the b'hoy represented the attempt of the radical-democrat imagination to reconstruct human value on the ruins of a civilization viewed as rotten to the core. The b'hoy was the red-blooded American worker who fully embodied the fervor of the republican patriot but also the feistiness and wickedness of the ring-tailed roarer. Because union activity declined during a decade of extreme economic instability, workers were forced to mythmaking and role playing, and the b'hoy persona embodied both deep hostilities and jingoistic nationalism. With his combined hyperbolic Americanism and jaunty defiance, he became the ideal mixed hero of radical-democrat humor. As a fully indigenous, complex character, he was destined to have a marked effect on American literature.

In the course of his transformation from real-life rowdy to a central character in popular literature, the b'hoy went through a remarkable broadening and deepening of his image. In the early going, he was little more than an unruly Bowery fireman. In the mid-1830s New York's fire companies, which once had been dominated by upper-class merchants, had turned into social clubs that provided comradeship and diversion for the city's lower-class citizens. Each club was also a fraternal organization with its own insignia and ritual, and a fierce competition between different clubs arose. Gang warfare began to emerge from fire companies. There developed a working-class culture that was boisterous, rough, sometimes brutal, full of intense masculine bravado. In time the chief representative of this culture was the Bowery b'hoy, the youthful working-class dandy who was distanced both from the marketplace and from trade unions but who was a rebel looking for fun and excitement, usually of an innocent nature. Gang leaders and firemen became party fixtures. Mike Walsh, the pugnacious leader of the New York Democrats in the early 1840s, was the prototypical b'hoy politician. George Lippard, Ned Buntline, J. H. Ingraham, and other pulp novelists were the favorite authors of this working-class culture and were themselves literary b'hoys fired by the animosities and the passions of this culture.

The b'hoy in time became absorbed as a character in popular literature. Novels such as Ned Buntline's *The B'hoys of Boston* (1850) and journalistic pamphlets like George Foster's *New York in Slices* (1849) featured the b'hoy, as did plays (more than twenty in all), newspapers, lithographs, humor periodicals, circuses, and, of all things, ballets. The b'hoy, often named "Mose" or "Sikesey," was the ringtail-roaring fireman who was always raring for a fight and spouting crude slang. He was as skilled in his proletarian activities, firefighting and target shooting, as the frontier screamer was in hunting and trapping. What made the b'hoy an especially rich figure was that he was not only feisty; he was also smart. Whereas the anti-intellectual screamer had firmly denounced "larnin'," the b'hoy was the punchy working-class man who behaved like a cultured dandy. He was reckless, wicked, pugnacious, but shrewd and altogether lovable. He struck out against aristocratic "upper ten-dom" but also aped its habits. Along with the b'hoy went the g'hal (usually named "Lize"), who was tough, active, athletic, good-hearted. As George Foster described a typical g'hal: "Her very walk had a swing of mischief and defiance in it, and the tones of her voice are loud, hearty and free."[40] She appeared as a main character in novels such as Ned Buntline's *Mysteries and Miseries of New-York* (1848) and *The G'hals of New York* (1850) and in George Thompson's *The G'hals of Boston* (1850).

By the late 1840s the b'hoy and the g'hal had become universal types of American youth, not just in the Eastern cities but even in distant frontier villages. The broadening of these figures was noted by George Foster, who wrote: "The b'hoy of the Bowery, the rowdy of Philadelphia, the Hoosier of the Mississippi, the trapper of the Rocky Mountains, and the gold-hunter of California are so much alike that an unpracticed hand could not distinguish one from the other; while the 'Lize' of the Chatham Theater and the belle of a Wisconsin ball-room are absolutely identical, and might change places without any body being the wiser."[41] On the eve of the central period of the American Renaissance, then, the b'hoy and the g'hal were firmly established cultural figures that awaited full exploration by sophisticated authors. Foster called them "the most original and interesting phase of human nature yet developed by American society," and demanded that American novelists and dramatists probe these characters more deeply. "To both these classes of writers," Foster wrote, "the b'hoy and the g'hal, and the great middle class of free life under a republic of which they are the types and representatives, afford an inexhaustible and almost untrodden field." He noticed, however, that by the late 1840s these figures were already being cheapened in pamphlet novels and stage melodramas that stressed their crudest, most savage qualities. He called upon serious American writers to stem this tendency to vulgarization and rescue these rich American figures from the merely sensational realm to which they were being debased.

As will be discussed later, two New York writers, Herman Melville and Walt Whitman, in effect answered Foster's request, for they presented the first full literary treatments of the b'hoy. Both writers were struggling to find a character who manifested the raw passions of red-blooded American people but also had intelligence and depth. They found this character in the b'hoy, who was the refreshingly unconventional and thoroughly shrewd working-class American. Melville's Ishmael, the democratic humor character who can both hobnob with renegades and spout philosophy, is a transformed version of the b'hoy, created by an author who had his eyes fixed on New York popular culture during the late 1840s, at precisely the moment when the b'hoy had his greatest cultural prominence. Even Melville's more isolated friend Hawthorne caught the spirit of the b'hoy, for when in 1854 he wrote his American publisher from England, he jauntily said that he didn't want to press their friendship, "but I really thought I was one of them—one of the b-hoys—and ought to have received the poems."[42] As for Whitman, he might be designated as "one of the b'hoys." He matured in the rowdy b'hoy culture of the 1840s and used the term "b'hoy" at least three times in his private writings. If the b'hoy, in Foster's words, was always striving to develop a sublime life of "independent loaferism," Whitman was loafing and inviting his soul.[43] Whitman's proclamation of himself as "one of the roughs"—a swaggerer, swearer, boaster, idler—is patterned almost exactly after the b'hoy.[44] The persona is very much in the b'hoy mold, since he is cultured enough to know Oriental mysticism but sufficiently lower-class to advertise himself continually as the average American. The flexibility of the b'hoy figure is suggested by his different literary manifestations: not only the salty worker-philosopher Ishmael or Whitman's rowdy mystic in *Leaves of Grass* but, eventually, Pete of Crane's *Maggie* and those preeminent scamp-heroes of American humor, Tom Sawyer and Huck Finn.

To mention these literary improvements upon the b'hoy figure, however, is to point up an underlying difference between them and the treatments of this figure by the popular writers. On the popular level, the b'hoy was usually associated with working-class politics; when assimilated by the major writers, he became a source of egalitarian sympathy but lost direct connections with political activism. The major writers treated the b'hoy, along with other elements of popular culture, with a new detachment that gave their texts a complexity and self-awareness that was generally lacking even in the most imaginative radical-democrat writings.

Urban Humor

This detachment was itself to a large degree culturally induced. Several major authors gained the ability to experiment ambitiously with radical-democrat imagery largely because they were under the influence of a sophisticated and self-consciously stylized brand of American humor— what I classify as *urban humor*—that was appearing in prominent humor periodicals of the 1840s and 1850s. The most representative of these periodicals were four influential New York humor sheets with a wide circulation: *The Yankee Doodle* (1846–47 and 1854–56), *The John-Donkey* (1848), *Diogenes, hys Lantern* (better known as *The Lantern*, 1852–53), and, most important of all, *The New York Picayune* (1847–60). Urban humor was also scattered liberally throughout other magazines, newspapers, almanacs, and books of the period.

What I am calling urban humor was produced mainly by popular Northeastern authors who were consciously trying to create a new kind of humor that possessed the subtlety of the British but also the brashness and strangeness of the American. Urban humor treated with wry detachment many of the problematic phenomena of popular culture: colloquial sermons, seamy reform literature, abolition and the slavery question, sensational literature, women's rights, spiritualism, mesmerism, radical-democrat politics. Taken together, these often puzzling phenomena were potentially a source of philosophical chaos in America's fluid, democratic culture. Through humor, these phenomena could be confronted directly but could be stripped of terror through comic exaggeration. When depoliticized and parodied through extreme caricature, they often seemed downright zany. The purely humorous use of strange pseudosciences like mesmerism and animal magnetism produced bold time-space distortions, while hyperbolic versions of sensational literature created an exponential acceleration of experimental linguistic devices. In general, urban humor was conservative politically, often making a mockery of sober national issues, but at the same time quite radical stylistically, reproducing linguistically the fragmentations and tensions within modern American culture. It therefore taught a dual lesson for the major writers: on the one hand, humor provided a haven from the stormy political movements and strange fads of modern times; on the other hand, it sped the carnivalization of American language, since the phenomena it parodied were intrinsically more disruptive than any that had yet appeared in American cultural history.

The interrelationship between popular urban humorists and the major writers was in several cases quite direct. At a key transitional moment in his career, during the summer of 1847, Melville published his series of popular humor articles, "Authentic Anecdotes of 'Old Zack,' " in the pioneering urban humor periodical *Yankee Doodle.* Several specific comic elements of his fiction, such as Fleece's absurd sermon to the sharks in *Moby-Dick* and the diddling of the barber in *The Confidence-Man,* can be directly traced to scenes in popular urban humor. Whitman, who once told Horace Traubel he would go down in literary history chiefly as a humorist, warmly praised two leading humor periodicals, *The Yankee Doodle* and *The John-Donkey,* and befriended several urban humorists, such as Benjamin Penhallow Shillaber. Hawthorne, though not often discussed today as a humorist, seemed sufficiently funny to a writer for the popular story weekly *Yankee Blade* who in 1849 cited Hawthorne's tales as main examples of the modern "Literature of Mirth." Emily Dickinson, as a student humorist at Amherst Academy, wrote a comic article in which she plagiarized from a series of burlesque sermons that had been appearing in New York newspapers since the early 1840s.

The relationship ran in both directions, for in the urban humor periodicals the major writers were mentioned with a frequency unprecedented in American literature. *The John-Donkey* had fun parodying Poe: in the June 3, 1848, issue it ran the absurdly sensational "Tale of a Grey Tadpole," announced as a tale by Poe; and in the next issue it featured a mock review by Poe that captured Poe's characteristic shifts between harsh criticism and unctuous praise. Another periodical, *The Lantern,* published in May 1852 an article, "Emersonia," that took Emerson's choppy logic and rhapsodic language to a wildly disorganized extreme. Hawthorne and Melville were well known to the popular parodists. They were often mentioned, for example, in *The Lantern,* which included in its June 1852 announcements of new books the following titles: *"The Pink Envelope*—By the author of *The*

Scarlet Letter," *"Hee Haw*—By the author of Omoo!,*"* and *"Excursions into the Middle of Next Week*—By the author of Mardi and a Voyage Thither." In other issues, Hawthorne's *Life of Franklin Pierce* and Melville's *Pierre* were similarly spoofed, and in April 1852, there appeared this wry paragraph:

> It is reported that when Herman Melville was wrecked on some outlandish shore, he saw a *gallows*; whereupon he fell upon his knees, and thanked "his stars" (and stripes) that he was thrown upon a *civilised* land. We doubt, however, had he known there was a new *code* attached to it, whether he would not have swam for his life once more, and trusted to *sea* rather than to *land sharks.*

The cross-influences and intermeshings between the major authors and the popular urban humorists, therefore, were in several instances very explicit. The major authors were not regarded as the towering, isolated giants they seem today but, instead, as amusing exhibits for the carnival of urban humor. The popular humorists, in turn, were hardly beneath the attention of the major authors, who recognized that native humor could be useful in the literary attempt to manipulate and recombine potentially disturbing aspects of contemporary popular culture. Humor proved to be a primary means of distancing subversive themes that in sober texts led to philosophical stalemate or stylistic failure. As Emerson expressed it, humor allows us to observe the world *"aloof,* as a man might look at a mouse," so that everything is "seen at a sufficient distance." In particular, Emerson wrote, humor provides "a protection from those perverse tendencies and gloomy insanities" that otherwise might lead to speechless depression.[45]

Permeating urban humor was the spirit of that greatest of all American carnivalists, Phineas T. Barnum. When Melville made Barnum the butt of several jokes in "Authentic Anecdotes of 'Old Zack,'" he captured metonymically Barnum's significance. In the course of the nine anecdotes, Melville has "Peter Tamerlane B——m" write excited requests to General Zachary Taylor for war memorabilia—an unexploded shell, the General's torn trousers, and finally the General himself—to be displayed in his famous museum along with other crowd-pleasing oddities. In his letter offering Taylor good money should he consent to be shown publicly in a cage like "all that is curious in nature and art," B——m promises he will "treat you no worse than he has the venerable nurse of our beloved Washington and the illustrious General Tom Thumb."[46] Melville here is concisely dramatizing the relativizing effect of the American humorous carnival as epitomized by Barnum. In this democratic carnival, intrinsic value is stripped from all objects or principles, so that a bomb shell, torn pants, an old black woman, Tom Thumb, and Zachary Taylor are placed on the same level by the entrepreneurial humorist. Distinctions of all kinds are eradicated, and the high and the low, the human and nonhuman meet on the flat level of humorous theater. When Melville has his B——m promise to treat Taylor "no worse than he has the venerable nurse of our beloved Washington," he is ironically underscoring Barnum's commercial exploitation of Joice Heth, the withered, hapless ex-slave, purporting to be 161 years old, who had been a huge sensation in the 1830s when Barnum had put her on display as the alleged nanny of George Washington. (Melville perhaps had this famous case of heartless racism in mind when in *The Confidence-Man* he drew his memorable portrait of the pathetic Negro poser, Black Guinea.) When Barnum opened his world-famous museum in New York, it was immediately apparent that even the most apparently serious aspects of American culture could be reduced to the theatrical when placed beside the merely bizarre. Crowds flocked to the museum to see a mermaid, the Bearded Woman of Geneva, the famous dwarf Tom Thumb, and a thousand other freaks—but at the museum they could also attend the "Moral Dramas" illustrating the Bible and temperance in excitingly updated fashion. Barnum unabashedly cast the profane and the sacred together into the arena of profit-making theater.

This purely histrionic conjoining of disparate value systems was actually just an explicit expression of democracy's ability to convert even sacrosanct things into objects for display. One of Barnum's contemporaries, Alexander Herzen, shrewdly wrote of him: "He understood the great secret of the age of rhetoric, the age of effects and phrases, exhibitions and advertisements; he comprehended that the most important thing for the contemporary nominalist is the poster!"[47] Indeed, Barnum was the natural product of a period that increasingly was, in Herzen's words, the age of rhetoric, effects, phrases, exhibitions, advertisements. We have seen throughout this book that in the relativist, entrepreneurial world of the young American republic a variety of serious phenomena—sermons, reform writings, phrenology, mesmerism, spiritualism—had, as early as the 1830s, been converted into diverting entertainment by many popular American showmen trying to satisfy a sensation-hungry public. Barnum was merely the master showman of the group, the one who capitalized fully on the carnival instincts of his democratic contemporaries. He had perhaps the most rubbery conscience of all antebellum showmen. He was the notorious "Prince of Humbug" who used often suspect means to make money, but he was also a temperance lecturer who faithfully went to church every Sunday. One of his many critics said his implicit motto for living was: "Lie and swindle as much as you please . . . but be sure you read your Bible and drink no brandy!" But his apparently massive hypocrisy was in fact merely a reflection of the intrinsic contradictions and paradoxes of a culture that produced showmanlike preachers, immoral reformers, and reverend rakes. In the relativizing environment of antebellum America, good morals and good religion could quickly change places with good theater and good humor.

It is this theatrical, stylized use of formerly sober things that constitutes the chief significance of the urban humor writers of the American 1840s and 1850s. Popular parody, of course, is common enough in all cultures and is known to have nurtured great literature: Bakhtin, for instance, shows how Menippean satire and *parodia sacra* contributed to the master-works of Rabelais and Dostoyevsky.[48] But parodic arrows are directed toward different targets in every culture, so that the literary manifestations of parody are inevitably time-specific and culture-specific. The urban humorists of antebellum America were trying to create a distinct brand of humor that fully embodied their time and place. The editor of *The New York Picayune,* arguing that each nation had its own humor, wrote: "Above all, we aim to be *Americans,* in the better and truer sense of the word."[49] It must be said that the urban humorists succeeded only partially in achieving this goal. It was not until Artemus Ward and Mark Twain fused the topicality of urban humor with the vernacular voice of frontier humor that a fully indigenous American humor appeared. Still, the urban humorists can be credited with paving the way for the more famous artisans of their craft. They brought a new literariness and genre-consciousness to American humor. More important, they removed all the problematic features of the contemporary scene to the realm of style. They were the Barnums of antebellum literature. By putting their own popular culture on display as a public joke, they prepared for the completely stylized use of this popular culture by the major writers.

Exploring the chief urban humor periodicals and books provides a comprehensive overview of all the elements of popular culture reviewed in this book. It also helps in understanding how the major writers recombined these elements with flexibility and artistry in literary texts. Let us see what happened to each distinct element as it was treated by the urban humorists.

The new religious style gave rise in urban humor to the burlesque sermon and jokes about what was described as the purely theatrical nature of American preaching. We have seen that popular preachers such as Father Taylor and Negro revivalists depended largely on homespun wit and racy anecdotes to make their points. It was no great leap from their pungent, often colloquial style to a parodic exaggeration of this style by the urban humorists. In "Dow's Patent Sermons," which began to appear in the *New York Sunday Mercury* in 1840, a salty revivalist persona gave comically jaunty accounts of the Bible, heaven, and other sacred topics. Emily Dickinson's early awareness of burlesque sermons in popular newspapers was a chief reason that she learned to deal with religious themes with a frolicsome drollery unprecedented in American literature. As a schoolgirl at Amherst Academy, where she wrote for a school magazine, she and another girl were, according to a classmate, "the wits of the school, and the humorists of the 'comic column.' . . . Emily's contributions were often in the style of a funny little sermon, . . . which went the rounds in the newspapers, . . . the art of which consisted in bringing the most incongruous things together[.]"[50] Modern scholars have identified Dickinson's specific source as William P. Brannan's farcical "The Harp of a Thousand Strings," a burlesque sermon reprinted in several popular newspapers; but what has been overlooked is the fact that Brannan's burlesque sermon and Dickinson's adaptations of it were part of a larger movement toward religious parody in the new urban humor of the 1840s and 1850s. The histrionic antics of pulpit showmen were commonly gibed in the urban humor periodicals, such as *The New York Picayune*, which in August 1856 featured an article introduced by this typical generalization: "Now-a-days a pastor must make sermons to draw big houses, and we have 'Star' sermonizers just as we have star actors, and star performing dogs at the museum."[51] The urban humorists discovered that in the carnivalized atmosphere of American culture, even God's highest servants were little different from performing dogs.

Popular parodies of the new religious style had a direct effect upon the most famous comic sermon in major nineteenth-century American literature—the absurd discourse to the sharks by the black cook Fleece in *Moby-Dick*, which I have found to have been adapted from a very popular series of burlesque sermons by William H. Levison that ran in many urban periodicals in the late 1840s. Levison's persona, Julius Caesar Hannibal, is a Negro preacher who in the course of his many sermons preaches in a Southern black dialect with laughable familiarity about every conceivable topic. Given the stylistic innovativeness of black American preachers, it is understandable that a Negro preacher would become the most famous burlesque sermonizer in urban humor. It is also understandable that Melville noticed the humor column of a New York writer, Levison, who was in his circle and whose strongest supporter was Melville's editor friend Lewis Gaylord Clark. The colloquial sermon of Melville's Fleece bears the obvious imprint of the Julius Caesar Hannibal series. Most important for understanding Fleece and, indeed, Melville's overall use of secularized religious discourse is the remarkable liberties that Julius Caesar Hannibal takes with sacred topics, as evidenced by his willingness to play daringly with biblical topics and expand upon them by inserting jokes and anecdotes. He sermonized imaginatively, for instance, about all kinds of monstrous animals, including the whale. Melville may have taken special interest in passages such as this one from a Hannibal sermon, *"De Whale"*:

> De whale am 'mong de fishes what de elemfint am 'mong beastesses; de biggest lofer ob dem all. A fisherman, named Jona, swaller'd one once; but it ober loded he stummuck to dat degree dat in tree days he leff 'em up agin. It war too much ob a muchness for him. . . .
>
> [Hannibal then digresses about whale chases, with a lively description of harpooned whales diving to the bottom, resurfacing, and then being killed, or "Sumtimes he hits de leetle bote, when all de men am in it, an' stabes it all to tunder, an' 'way flys de men up in de air, like man kites, an' kum down agin kerswat in de water."]
>
> De whale am de big fish—de codfish aristocracy ob de sees, de same as de big bugs an' de codfish aristocracy ob de lan' but de former hab got de 'wantage ob de latter, kase, notwidstandin' de whale dewoures a good eel, he produces sumfin, but de lan' codfish aristocracy dewours ebery-ting, an' produces nuffin'.[52]

What is most notable about this passage is the way it freely departs from the biblical text, which becomes thoroughly desacralized by being rendered in Negro dialect, and also the way it imaginatively interprets the whale from a working-class perspective, making it a symbol of the "codfish aristocracy" of the sea. (Recent scholars who have sought egalitarian, working-class themes in *Moby-Dick* might consider that in the popular humor Melville was reading the whale was being compared with America's hated ruling class.) Melville may have noticed many other burlesque sermons in the Hannibal series, such as "Quackery," which contains this assertion: "Dere am a great menny different kinds ob quackery runnin loose all ober de komunity. We hab de quack doctor, de quack preecher man, de quack lawyer, de quack boot-black, and de quack lecturer." This theme of universal deceit in American culture, a theme that Melville would famously treat in *The Confidence-Man,* was even more baldly put in another sermon, "Deceptions," in which Hannibal declares: "Neber Trust to 'Pearances. . . . My frens, dis am a wicked world—full ob deceit and nonsense, big pumkins and bigger lies, and all such warmints. It seems to be a wonderful disease on de part ob eberybody, to seem what dey are not, and derefore humbuggery am de order ob de day." In Hannibal's burlesque sermons we see the sacred and the cynical brought together in the demythologized realm of popular humor.

Just as parodies of the new religious style led to preliterary humor, so did parodies of a second major element of antebellum popular culture: immoral reform. The hypocrisy and increasingly sensational rhetoric of notable American reformers became a favorite topic among the urban humorists. John B. Gough, the great temperance speaker whose integrity was made suspect by repeated reports of his private backsliding, was a favorite target of the urban humorists. In a typical satirical poem published in *The Lantern*, the devil is described going to fish for temperance speakers, using a bottle of rum as bait: "Then, with a sly wink and dry cough, / A *temp'rance* air to himself did hum, / While he drew from the hook G—OFF."[53] Backsliding temperance lecturers were hardly the only reformers gibed. Abolitionists and philanthropists were frequently mocked for evidence of hypocrisy and rhetorical excess. In general, the urban humorists opposed slavery but were horrified by the hyperbolic, often seamy language of extreme abolitionists. *The Yankee Doodle* typically declared that it loved "the dream" of antislavery but hated the "foul and unseemly" language of many of its proponents.[54] When we ask why the major authors generally recoiled from direct involvement with the abolitionist movement, we should keep in mind the "foul and unseemly" tactics that also alienated the urban humorists.

As for philanthropy and charitable reform, it had become so corrupted in the popular mind that the humorists gleefully toyed with the total inversion of values that tainted reform suggested. In the preface to *Does-ticks' Letters* (1855), Mortimer Neal Thompson joked: "I shall not stand up for love and charity, for it might induce people to love the wrong persons, and to give their pennies to impostors."[55] The concept of morality was so twisted that moral institutions and Christian nurture became easy targets for satire. In an 1856 piece for *The New York Picayune*, entitled "Doesticks Founds a Great Moral Institution," Thompson makes light of subversive social messages by portraying a moral school where American reformers and statesmen are trained in their favorite activities: drinking, swearing, lying, confidence games.[56] The widespread inversion of values was capsulized in an 1853 *Lantern* article that stated: "Virtues having long since been twisted into fashionable vice, it was natural philanthropy should become hypocrisy."[57] So common did stories of false philanthropy become that by the mid-1850s such stories seemed hackneyed and beneath notice. Hence the apologetic tone of this introduction to an 1856 article, "The Woman with the Pious Mask, and Counterfeit Sunday Schools": "Those cases of grand larceny, in which the criminals have stolen the livery of heaven to serve the devil in, have become almost too common for special notice."[58] The writer goes on to describe an outwardly benevolent woman who inveigles people into giving money to a phony orphan asylum—rather like Melville's confidence man, who raises funds for fake charities. If *The*

Confidence-Man failed to sell well, it is in part because by 1857 stories of ersatz philanthropy had long since lost their power to amuse or titillate.

While hypocritical reform bred comedic toyings with inverted values, another popular phenomenon, sensational literature, bred new forms of black humor when parodied by the urban humorists. All types of popular sensational writings—crime pamphlets, penny newspapers, yellow novels—were regularly satirized in the humor periodicals. *The John-Donkey* in 1848 published many burlesques of sensational news reports that point up the American public's offhand familiarity with the bloody and the horrible. In one *John-Donkey* piece a man yawns comically as he reads a penny paper and comments: " *'Horrid Accident!'* Oh, I don't care about that. *'Wife Beaten by Her Husband!'* Poor fellow! Had to make his own coffee, I dare say. *'Suicide!'* Another victim to making his own coffee."[59] Another *John-Donkey* burlesque, called *"Stereotype Newspaper Reports,"* again parodies the penny press by describing an "Awful Explosion" (about a riverboat boiler that kills sixty-seven passengers), a "Charge of Seduction" (about a church board which, ironically, expels a female parishioner who has been seduced by the clergyman but exonerates him), and a "Mysterious Disappearance" (about the treasurer of a benevolent society who disappears with several thousand dollars).

As was seen earlier, such comic treatment of the sensational helps explain Emily Dickinson's jaunty use of oddly juxtaposed violent images. In the early 1850s, just prior to her earliest poetic phase, she manifested the spirit of the modern American humor in several letters, such as an autumn 1853 missive to the newspaper editor J. G. Holland, whose newspaper, the *Springfield Republican,* delighted her with its sensational news. She confessed she read the paper every night and took special pleasure in what she called "those funny accidents," such as railway collisions and factory disasters, that were related "in such a sprightly way, that they are quite attractive."[60] The distinctive combination in Dickinson's major poetry of savage and comical images was characteristic of an age when the sensational and the sprightly were increasingly conjoined in the popular press.

Crime pamphlets and pamphlet novels were other sensational genres parodied by the urban humorists. *The Lantern* in May 1853 gave mock praise to a Philadelphia publishing firm for printing such *"sound, healthy reading"* as the *Life and Adventures of Arthur Spring,* a crime pamphlet published "in the most approved fashion, being rolled up in a 'Daguerreotype Likeness of the Murderer Spring,' with a most correct view of the poor bodies of the poor [murdered] women as they were found weltering in their blood."[61] The crass popularization of crime was likewise mocked in a *Yankee Doodle* listing of "New Books," which promised forthcoming pamphlet novels with titles like *The Female Horse-Thief, Devils in Paradise,* and

The Triumphant Robber; or, Honesty Outwitted.[62] This kind of poisonous popular literature was targeted in another *Yankee Doodle* article, which described the devil visiting America and damning the nation's popular novels with the vow: "Let them read and be d—d, for I'll poison their books!"

Popular sensation novels provoked especially sharp barbs from a *John-Donkey* humorist who asserted that while sensational styles had appeared in all cultures, none had approached the unrestrained irrationalism of what it dubbed the "Horrible High-pressure Highfaluting Style" of the American sensationalists. Perceptively, the humorist identified George Lippard as the quintessential example of this new American style. After presenting a parodic version of a roller-coaster chapter from Lippard's sensational novel *The Ladye Annabel,* the writer gave a set of mock rules on how to write according to the Lippard formula: attend a popular melodrama to learn "gory, horrible, shrieking, bloody plots"; go home and tousle your hair, rip off your shirt, and upset the furniture; seize an iron pen and at least a gallon of black ink; and then write with total disregard of established literary rules about torture and similar grisly topics.[63] Similarly, Lippard was found typical of the American sensationalists by a humor writer for *Holden's Dollar Magazine* who wrote that Lippard and his ilk were using literary "brimstone, saltpetre, and kreosote" to "tickle the palate of our copper-throated public," producing fiction that was "a most delectable hash of horror, superstition and ribaldry, equalled in point of variety and cookery, by nothing but the witch-kettle of Macbeth."[64]

The *Macbeth* reference is significant, for it points up a joke commonly made by the urban humorists that even Shakespeare, the ever-popular master of blood and tragedy, had lost much of his entertainment value in an age that was surfeited with the sensational. In "Doesticks Writes a Play" (in the *Picayune* for October 11, 1856) Mortimer Thompson insisted that Shakespeare didn't "draw" any longer, since the American public was satisfied only with "unexpected and tremendous 'effects' in the scenery, and a most fiendish development and diabolical villainy in the characters." Comically enough, Doesticks concocts an impossibly sensational plot for a play only to find at the end that "in my anxiety to make a sensation, I had killed the hero at the end of each tableau—that my heroine had taken poison twice, and once had her head knocked off with a bombshell." In *Doesticks' Letters* Thompson again stresses that Shakespeare was considered too slow by the American public, since "usually nothing but the most slaughterous tragedies and melo-dramas of the most sanguinary stamp, give satisfaction."[65] It is understandable that Melville, despite his well-known admiration for Shakespeare, used Shakespearian devices extensively in only one novel, *Moby-Dick,* and even there modernized these devices by using bombastic rhetoric, black humor, and gory adventure derived largely from his own popular culture. The year before Melville wrote *Moby-Dick,* George Foster, a journalist in his New York circle, had written in *New York in Slices* (1849): "Shakespeare? yes, we think we have heard of him. Oh yes, now we remember—that is the name of the wooden effigy over the door. He is not to be seen *inside* of the house.—He doesn't *draw.*"[66] The hyperbolic, revised Shakespearian moments in *Moby-Dick,* such as Ahab's fervid soliloquies or the crew's violent party belowdecks, suggest that Melville, while drawn to the art of Shakespearian truth telling, recognized the need to add American embellishments to a writer who was widely regarded as too staid by the mass of Americans.

The urban humorists parodied not only sensational literature as a whole but also two paradigmatic characters in this literature: the reverend rake and the likable criminal. The notorious case of Benjamin T. Onderdonk, the New York Episcopalian bishop defrocked in 1845 for having seduced several parishioners, was exploited as humorous pornography in a Philadelphia humor pamphlet, *De Darkie's Comic All-Me-Nig* (1845), in which a black reverend rake, named "Under-Donk-En Dough Lips," is shown groping beneath a woman's dress while riding in a stagecoach. The current prevalence of reverend rakes in American society is underscored in the lewdly funny preface to this anecdote: "Ya, ya, ya! by smash, I blebe deer's no more human natur any more, when a bit o' women natur am about, for all our Deacons am gettin so fat dat de spiritual feelin am all smashed out of 'em like de yolk ob geese egg, and dar all flesh like ebery-oder body else."[67] The camp meeting, a common target in frontier humor, was satirized by urban humorists like Mortimer Thompson, who in "Doesticks Goes to a Camp Meeting" depicted lustful preachers drinking heavily and seducing their excited female converts. Thompson stresses that, here as elsewhere, "religion and rascality were so mixed up that it was hard to tell one from the other," as the preachers are adept in catering to "the spiritual wants of fast young men and even faster young women." Thompson wittily converts the popular metaphor of God's arrows into a sex pun: "There was a great deal of love-making going on in the bushes—smart young man got his sweetheart, who was 'pierced with the arrow of conviction,' behind a thorn bush."[68] In light of the mockery that such sexual humor made of religion, it is understandable that Hawthorne was careful to avoid the crassly prurient in his famous treatment of the reverend rake.

The other paradigmatic hero of antebellum sensational literature, the likable or justified criminal, yielded intriguing results when treated comically by the urban humorists, who brought to the surface several radically subversive themes that had remained implicit in the nonhumorous writings. We saw that in popular sensational writings the justified criminal became a common means of undercutting the false virtue of the American social elite and for singing praise to open villainy in a world of secretly corrupt respectability. The urban humorists took this inverted theme to a relativist extreme. An 1852 *Lantern* piece portrayed a man who tries desperately to succeed in several honest professions but then, finding that honesty is powerless in a world of knaves, decides to put out his shingle as a skilled robber and murderer. He justifies his open criminality as follows: "While I see around me many knaves succeed in every department, while thousands make large fortunes by *secret roguery,* I therefore propose to *openly profess* villainy, and pursue it as a legitimate calling to earn an *honest* penny."[69] Similarly, *The New York Picayune* ran a comic story of a lawyer who failed in virtuous endeavors and finally "emerged from the cocoon of honesty, a full fledged buttery rascal."[70] The humorists knew that the likable criminal was a stock character in sensational literature. In a literary parody published in *Young America,* a humor writer names several possible heroes for a proposed novel—including "a profligate clergyman," "a pious infidel," and "ladies in masculine attire"—and then decides that "a grand moral might be inculcated in the character of an amiable assassin" who "by means of murder, robbery and arson [will] rescue the good and immolate all the evil personages of the dramatis personae."[71] The ironic undercurrent of sensational novels, in which the boldly villainous was often more potent than the supposedly good, here surfaces in the flagrant moral inversions of urban humor.

Another phenomenon of the popular scene—women's wrongs and women's rights—also provoked many topical parodies. The urban humorists were deeply sensitive to the suffering of American seamstresses and female factory workers. The degraded condition of many working women was one of the few topics they did not make fun of. *The Lantern* typically drew impassioned portraits of what it called "soul-crushed, life-wasted" seamstresses and of female millworkers doomed to listless despair by "the *white slavery of New England.* "[72] Despite their sympathy for wronged women, however, the humorists had no tolerance for suffragists' efforts to improve woman's lot. They felt about American women as they did about slaves: although they perceived gross injustice against both groups, they were dismayed by the militant, potentially disruptive methods used to combat this injustice. They satirized women's rights conventions as unruly affairs governed by noisy, mannish women. In a typical antifeminist squib in *The Lantern* a suffragist rises at a convention and yells angrily: "I'll knock down the first fellow who has the impudence to be civil to me."[73] Constantly the humorists pictured the total confusion that they believed would result should the suffragists' goal of social and political equality between the sexes be achieved. In the humorists' eyes, woman's ascension to power would bring not equality but tyranny and eventual social collapse. They described querulous women wielding authoritarian sway in government and business, ushering in free love, and confining man to the home. The hopeful feminist utopia, which we have seen to have been a lively tradition in American literature since the 1790s, was answered by the humorists' cynical dystopia, which portrayed future societies in which sex-role reversal results in utter chaos and, in the end, a willing return to the male-dominated order of things. The *Penny Yankee Doodle* featured in its November 2, 1850, issue a poem, *"Vimmins Rights,"* depicting a confused society in which "daring Amazons" hold office and run businesses while the men serve as housekeepers. The Amazons come to recognize the folly of their ways and "soon with cause, / Wish things as they was." Similarly, in an 1852 *Lantern* piece a dreaming man sees an imaginary society in which sex roles have been reversed, with lustful women ogling shy young men and national peace being threatened by the gibbering of querulous women leaders. Another dystopic article in *The Lantern* moves from an alarmed account of a women-controlled society to the bleak generalization: "The world's topsy turvy—all things are so changed—/ And Nature, herself, seems going deranged. / . . . And the world is a Babel of tongues of acid."[74] In *Plu-Ri-Bus-Tah* (1856), Mortimer Thompson's dystopic parody of Longfellow's *Hiawatha*, America is portrayed as an increasingly fragmented country threatened by the combined forces of women's rights, free love, spiritualism, and abolitionism. In the poem, the hero marries a modern woman, Liberty, who is totally useless at home, who fights like a man, and who has affairs with numerous free-love partners. Her brawls and philandering ultimately speed the collapse of the American republic.[75]

The most notorious dystopia of the period was Fred Folio's long novel, *Lucy Boston; or, Women's Rights and Spiritualism: Illustrating the Follies and Delusions of the Nineteenth Century* (1855). The epigraph on the title page— "This is the age of oddities let loose"—anticipates the entire novel, which is motivated by the fear that anarchic fads, sects, and political movements are splintering the nation and leading toward its downfall. The plot involves the projected takeover in 1876 of the New York state government by women who are directed by spirit-women who at first communicate through mediums and then appear in real life. In the new feminist state, women assume leadership of government and public affairs, while men, wearing petticoats and dresses, take care of the home. Schools are established exclusively for women; a "Spiritual University" is founded whose professors are the spirits of great thinkers and writers from previous centuries; heroic women of the past like Dido and Catherine the Great are given seats in government; and, finally, marriage is abolished and free love reigns. After hundreds of pages devoted to exploring this role-reversed society, the author makes clear the wages of female control: all business and government comes to a standstill and the old patriarchal order must be reinstated. Feminists throughout the book are presented as pugnacious, querulous ultraists who claim not equality with, but superiority to, males. They are linked to spiritualists through the portrayal of guiding spirits who insist that heaven is controlled by women and thus the earth must be as well. Spiritualism is portrayed as a hoax palmed off as science by greedy mountebanks to sheepish fad lovers. Although women's rights and spiritualism are satirized, they are recognized as understandable products of an age of philosophical crisis. In a central scene of the novel, the spirits of Tom Paine, John Calvin, and St. Paul are shown having a long conversation in which they agree that the Bible is a jumble of absurdities and contradictions and that nineteenth-century Americans naturally turn to apparent panaceas like women's rights and spiritualism as the only sure beliefs in an uncertain world. Having been cast rudderless onto a terrifying ocean of doubt, Americans rush frantically to the nearest faddish port, using such "anchors" as spiritualism or women's rights. Although understandable, these fads strike the author as ultimately dangerous phenomena against which the best weapon is humor. By exaggerating the "oddities" around him, the author hopes to reduce them to absurdity. But behind the surface jocularity, there is irrepressible fear and gloom, as the author can believe in neither the pieties of the past nor the fads of the present. Occasionally, this gloom is expressed in images that are almost Melvillian. Notice the controlling image in this account of the final condition of the woman-controlled society: "The Ship of State, remodeled and new-rigged with such dispatch, launched so triumphantly, and without ballast, chart, compass, or practical helmsman, under the mighty press of her canvas, dashing through foam and spray, among rock, quicksands and whirlpools, on the sea of *Experiment,* had quickly foundered and gone to pieces amid darkness and tempest. From every quarter went up the cry for help."[76] The message of the book, as of so much urban humor, is that in the face of democracy's disruptions, the best one can do is to stylize these disruptions in odd, dystopic humor.

As is readily apparent, beneath the lighthearted satire of the urban humorists lurked a dark anticipation of impending social chaos. The retreat to humor represented a withdrawal from volcanic forces such as dark reform, women's rights, and pseudoscience. In this sense, the popular humorists were not unlike the major writers, all of whom saw in humor a useful means of distancing themselves from threatening social realities. But here a distinction must be made: the major authors conjoined humor with other literary devices, such as symbol and myth, while the popular humorists confronted social realities directly and permitted their style to mirror growing fragmentations in popular culture. As will be seen in later chapters, the major authors asserted firm artistic control over disruptive elements that created linguistic confusion among the lesser authors. Like several frontier humorists, characteristic urban humorists allowed democracy's disruptions to become enacted stylistically.

This stylized fragmentation seemed especially strange when it magnified already odd popular phenomena such as spiritualism, mesmerism, and the irrational style. When popular pseudosciences were caricatured they were taken beyond the strange to the downright zany, even to what we would call the presurrealistic. *The Yankee Doodle,* for instance, loved playing weird games with pseudoscience: in one issue it described a mesmerist who caused a child's nose to bend upward and blow on a handkerchief he had made to soar in the air above; in another, it ran a phony ad for a performing animal magnetist who could not only read without using his eyes but also eat without using his mouth or hands.[77] Similarly, in a *Picayune* story, a magnetically charged man sees someone falling from a high roof, "reaches out" mentally to arrest the fall, and several weeks later tells a fellow stage passenger he had left the man suspended in midair.[78] Spiritualism, always rather strange even when taken soberly, seemed even more so when treated humorously. A *Lantern* parody of spiritualism described a man who feels himself transported to a celestial sphere where he sees inanimate things like tables and chairs dancing freely about as if alive.[79] This piece was outdone by a *Picayune* spoof in which a spirit-rapping man sees his own kitchen furniture come alive and perform antics: the dining table does somersaults and a washstand does the polka while a bookcase beats time and umbrellas walk around the room.[80] In an even more adventurous *Picayune* spoof, a magnetized person holds regular conversations with his furniture. The animation of the lifeless is a common device in the humor of many cultures. But in nineteenth-century America, with the popularity of pseudoscientific performers who had large followings, this device took on a topicality and cultural representativeness it had never known before. In the spoofs of pseudoscience, perceived reality seemed totally fluid, and all inanimate objects were granted full power to behave like humans.

As strange as such burlesques of pseudoscience often were, they did not produce nearly as odd linguistic results as did parodies of another popular phenomenon: the irrational style. Comparatively literary and sophisticated, the urban humorists possessed a genre awareness generally lacking among the frontier humorists. They knew full well that popular sensational novels were typically alinear and centrifugal, with successive chapters often being so inconsequential that time-space unities were broken down. The humorists' genre awareness is revealed in the following mock advertisement for a forthcoming sensational novel in *The John-*

Donkey: "As each chapter of this work will not have the slightest connexion with the preceding number, nor with anything else, the lovers of the Disjointed Highfaluting Style may rely upon the invaluable pleasure of coming to the end of the work every week."[81] Elsewhere, *The John-Donkey* printed a "Lecture on Composition" which outlined qualities needed for a writer to achieve what it called "the Diabolic style" of popular novelists, qualities such as "Discontinuity" and "Incongruity" which consist in "the avoidance of too close a connection or relation between the different ideas and parts." According to the lecture, when you speak of religion you should "intersperse it as thickly as possible with slang phrases"; if you begin a sentence advancing morality, you should end it with a reference to an Ethiopian melody. Incongruity governs this popular style, as the remaining instructions reveal: "When you are writing of the heavenly bodies, allude to turnips. If you have occasion to speak of angels, make a reference to mouse-traps. In fine, let the ideas of your essay bear the same relation to each other, as subsists between the consecutive words of a dictionary."[82] The urban humorists knew well that carnivalization of language was endemic to the American popular imagination.

While some urban humorists joked about the irrational style, others inventively parodied it. Some urban humorists so exaggerated the irrational style that they produced new intensifications of what I have termed the American Subversive Style, characterized by extreme linguistic fragmentation and bizarre juxtapositions of disparate images. The most sophisticated urban humor periodical, *The New York Picayune*, ran parodies that produced linguistic dislocations that approached the premodern. Mortimer Thompson, the leading urban humorist of the 1850s, is particularly relevant in this regard. When Thompson was taken on in July 1856 as a regular contributor to the *Picayune*, his hiring was announced as follows: "He shall have full liberty to distort facts, pervert history, mystify the reader, contradict himself and others . . . He shall be false to the unities of time and space" and thumb his nose at "the rhetoricians of the schools."[83] Notably, Thompson's first piece for the *Picayune* was a long parody of a sensational novel by George Lippard. In the parody, Thompson exaggerates Lippard's distortions and alinear narrative patterns until they become nonsensical. Thompson knew just how iconoclastic were his comic exaggerations of the irrational style. In the preface to his narrative poem *Plu-Ri-Bus-Tah* he declared: "I have intended to compose a story without plot, plan, or regard for the rules of grammar. I have done it. . . . I intended to upset all commonly received ideas of chronology, and to transpose dates, periods, epochs, and eras, to suit my own convenience. I have done it."[84] For the American parodist of his country's irrational style, time, space, and linear chronology have no meaning. All are flouted by the democratic humorist who is trying above all to outdo in weirdness the oddities of his own popular culture.

The dislocations of sensational writings are registered linguistically with special effectiveness by Mortimer Thompson. Often in his humor perceived reality is transformed into a surrealistic pastiche of incongruous images. In a piece he wrote for the *Picayune,* a trip to the seashore becomes a strange phantasmagoria of transposed objects. The swimmer is tossed so violently by a wave that suddenly everything is mixed up: the porpoises had got into the bathing house, little shore trees were dancing furiously three miles out at sea, while a tugboat and a brig were having a scrub race over the sand dunes.[85] Distortions created by intense emotion or drunkenness, often a source of humor in American literature, are converted by Thompson into inventive linguistic transpositions that shatter normal associations. The surrealists would prize the capacity of dream to "tear up the real," in George Hugnet's words.[86] In Thompson, the tearing up of reality was achieved by parodic exaggeration of the American irrational style. In a typically jumbled moment, he describes a drunken man walking down the street and speculating whether it is "the custom, as a general thing, for the City Hall and Barnum's Museum to indulge in an animated contra-dance up and down Broadway in the middle of the night, accompanied in their fantastic movements, by the upper storey of Stewart's and the Bible Society's building?" In another Thompson sketch, a drunkard "called for a plate of beans, when the plate brought the waiter in his hand. I took it, hung up my beef and beans on a rail, ate my hat, paid the dollar a nigger, and sidled out on the step-walk, bought a glass of dog with a small beer and a neck on his tail," and soon the "station-house came along and said if I did not go straight he'd take me to the watchman—tried to oblige the station-house, very civil station-house, very—met a baby with an Irish woman and a wheelbarrow in it," and so on for several paragraphs.[87] In the urban humor of the *Picayune* and its chief writer, Mortimer Thompson, the American Subversive Style becomes completely liberated from politics and didacticism and is ushered into the realm of free language play.

As urban humor became increasingly adventurous in its dislocations and alinearity, so did the engravings used to illustrate it. Both the writers and the engravers for the popular humor periodicals seemed to work from the Barnumesque assumption that freakishness was the order of the day in America. An article, "The Characteristics of the Age," in *The John-Donkey* included a typical generalization: "Very extraordinary are the freaks of all sorts of humanity at the present remarkable epoch in the history of the world. Unless a man can walk on his hands, pick a friend's pocket with his toes, or stand on his head, there is no use of his staying in this world. . . . Hyperbole and exaggeration are the universal religion, from church to state, from the Capitol to the closet, and the Impossible is the only god of popular idolatry."[88] *The John-Donkey*, a relatively early urban humor periodical, did not translate this love of the impossible into premodern engravings, but the later humor periodicals did. The strangest aspects of *The Lantern*, for instance, are its pictures, which included grotesque, bestial people, odd word drawings (e.g., Senator Foote is pictured as a huge foot emerging from a fancy suit), and inanimate objects like scissors and thermometers portrayed as people. The strangest pictures appeared in *The New York Picayune*, which contained many bizarre engravings of beasts, insects, or fish dressed in human costume; extreme malproportions, such as a tremendous detached foot kicking a tiny man or a huge head perched on a minuscule body; more word pictures (e.g., a Judge Fish is portrayed as an ugly bass head emerging from a tuxedo); and some presurrealistic pictures, such as one of a man with a die for a head and scissors for a body.

As strange as were the verbal and pictorial transpositions of the urban humorists, they were actually just updated versions of the American Subversive Style, which had been noticed as early as 1809 by an *Edinburgh Review* essayist and which had appeared variously in successive schools of American humorists. All the schools produced humor that reflected democracy's disruptions, but these disruptions varied according to time and place. The relatively early humor of Irving reflected the passage of the colonial order and the upsurge of popular tumult during the early republic. Frontier humor reflected the savage conditions of backwoods life and the affront to literary propriety posed by crude frontier slang. Radical-democrat humor was politically motivated by perceived social injustices that impelled certain writers to go to nightmarish extremes to vent working-class aggressions and to shock genteel readers. Urban humor reflected the profound disturbances created by strange fads and equally strange popular writings of the 1840s and 1850s. At their best, these schools of humor yielded passages that possessed verve and preliterary complexity. On the other hand, most were marred by wildness and shallowness. As lively enactments of America's newly carnivalized culture, they lacked the subtlety and resonance of high literature. It was left to the major writers to orchestrate artistically the American carnival.

16

TRANSCENDENTAL WILD OATS

T HE literary careers of Emerson and Thoreau provide particularly striking illustrations of the effect of popular humor on the major literature. Despite differences in emphasis, these writers were quite similar in their adaptations of popular humor. They were intent on discovering a distinctly American literary voice, which they believed could be found not in parlors or universities but rather on the streets and on the frontier. The language of common life, of course, had long been a principal interest of the British Romantic poets, and it was not surprising that the American Romantics also made a conscious effort to explore what Emerson called "the near, the low, the common."[1] But the Americans believed that British writers had not gone far enough in incorporating popular idioms in literary texts. They argued that British literature was too often spoiled by a preciousness and fixity bred by a caste culture, and they decried certain American contemporaries they regarded as tamely Anglophile. In the energetic humor and slang of the American masses, they discovered a rich source of creative imagery that reflected what they saw as the zest, the toughness, and the fluidity of their own culture. For Emerson, the main influence was frontier humor, which he warmly praised and incorporated in his pungent, ever-shifting imagistic writings. For Thoreau, radical-democrat and urban humor provided a biting, blackly humorous voice and a means of toying freely with the often strange fads and movements of the American 1840s.

As strongly as they were affected by popular humor, however, the major writers saw in much of this humor an excessive savagery and a linguistic abandon that they associated with the worst aspects of democratic culture. On the one hand, it was precisely these features of humor that they hoped to exploit in their rebellion against what they regarded as stylistically staid foreign literatures. On the other hand, they were appalled by the growing materialism and shallowness of American life, and they hoped to rescue humorous idioms from the overall drift toward the frenetic and the theatrical. They sought to enrich the American Subversive Style by allowing it to resonate with larger themes, some derived from their native philosophical heritage and others from European and Oriental sources.

Emerson's Philosophical Humor

Emerson has a special claim on our attention, since he was the first to import the American humorous style into sophisticated philosophical writing. Emerson's witty, often racy metaphorical style contrasted sharply with the rarefied prose of Bronson Alcott, the rather stilted style of Margaret Fuller, the rational style of Orestes Brownson, the smoothness of Longfellow, and the workmanlike directness of Unitarian writers like William Ellery Channing and William Ware. The distinctly American shifts and paradoxes that enliven Emerson's best style derive from his peculiar sensitivity to lowly humorous idioms that the other writers tended to snub.

Perhaps the most convenient figure of comparison is Alcott, since he was close to Emerson personally and philosophically. As leading figures in the Transcendentalist movement, Emerson and Alcott held quite similar views—so similar, in fact, that Alcott noticed a "striking conformity of taste and opinion" between himself and his fellow Concordite.[2] Both writers knew, however, that stylistically there were deep differences between them, and that these differences sprang mainly from Emerson's sensitivity to popular idioms that the more idealistic Alcott resisted. The difference between them becomes apparent when we look at their early journals, written while both were still in their apprentice stage. As early as 1820 Emerson had announced in his journal: "My talents (according to the judgement of friends or to the whispered suggestions of vanity) are popular, are fitted to enable me to claim a place in the inclinations & sympathy of men."[3] He even had a secret desire for mass popularity, as was suggested in an 1827 journal entry in which he confessed: "I do not fully disclaim the vulgar hunger to be known, to have one's name hawked in the great capitals in the street." His instinctive openness to American popular culture proved to be a major reason for the development of his mature style. It led eventually to his definition of the genius as the *representative* man, the one who most successfully absorbed even the most vulgar or trivial interests of his countrymen.

Alcott, in contrast, was, by his own confession, distanced from the popular mind and committed to universal, metaphysical questions. "My thoughts do not easily flow out in popular terms," he wrote in his journal in 1835. "Intent on seeking the inner life, seeking to represent it to myself mainly; having little communication with the popular mind, whose associations and thoughts differ materially from my own, I come to the work of composition under great embarrassment."[4] He envied Emerson's common touch, which he attributed to the kind of popular grotesque-humorous images that he felt incapable of generating. Emerson, he commented, often wove into his discourse "pictures of vulgar life, . . . the under as well as the upper vulgar." He managed to use imagery of "beasts, vermin, the rabid mob, the courtesan" and then slid easily into the "refined, elegant." Along with Emerson's image leaps, Alcott wrote, went his extreme tonal flexibility: "The burlesque is, in a twinkling, transformed into the serious." Of his own writings, Alcott complained that they were "too general in their application, and too metaphysical in their character. . . . They are entirely destitute of wit and humor." Alcott had reason for self-criticism, for when we read through collections of his essays and addresses we encounter a mind well versed in classic literature and Romantic philosophy but totally removed from the idiosyncratic grotesque humor of his own culture.

In Emerson's best writings, on the other hand, we encounter a mind enlivened by this native humor. Among his contemporaries he was often regarded as a masterful American humorist. "Mr. Emerson is an inveterate humorist," wrote a reviewer for the *New Englander* in 1856. "He writes as if he were half quizzing and half in earnest. . . . He gathers up the widest analogies by the armful, and evokes at will the most striking illustrations from nature and history."[5] Another reviewer for the same journal remarked that one of his essay volumes was "enlivened by his well-known wit, running not infrequently into grotesque conceits, that are only saved from downright extravagance by the pithy sense and genial humor that relaxes the screwing lips of the critic into an irresistible smile, or a shouting peal of laughter." The qualities that these reviewers noted in Emerson's style—grotesqueness, extravagance, unusual analogies—were exactly those that distinguished the popular American humor Emerson admired.

It was in the crucial period of the mid-1830s, just before his major creative period, that Emerson had first recognized American popular humor writings as potent stylistic directives for American writers. We saw in Chapter 1 that Emerson's responsiveness to the new religious style, especially as it was manifested in the salty sermons of Edward Thompson Taylor, was largely responsible for his stylistic maturation. It should be added that it was because popular religious discourse had become deeply infiltrated by humor during this decade that Emerson learned so much from it. In Father Taylor's sermons, it was the shocking illustrations and humorous abandon that most intrigued Emerson. Emerson remarked on "the ridicule of all method, the bright chaos come again of his bewildering oratory," "the wonderful & laughing life of his illustrations," "the inexhaustible wit" that make his sermons "a perfect Punch & Judy affair."[6] Emerson was paying homage not so much to a particular style as to a free *mixture* of styles—in this case, the religious and the humorous—that liberated the American writer from the single-voiced genres of the past. It was in the 1830s, we must recall, that several seemingly contradictory genres began to merge: the illustrative sermon began to merge with the burlesque sermon, the moral-reform tract with the immoral reform exposé, the crime narrative with the sensational novel or newspaper. This period of extreme genre fluidity had its philosophical culmination in Emerson's polyvocal essays and addresses.

The infiltration of backwoods idioms into the urban Northeast was the particular instance of genre fluidity that had the most marked impact on Emerson as he searched for alternatives to a Unitarian style he considered tepid and a British style he viewed as earthbound. The 1830s marked the appearance of America's first purely comic almanacs (the first was published in 1831) and the sudden popularity of backwoods humor characters such as Jack Downing, Davy Crockett, Nimrod Wildfire, and a host of metaphor-spouting frontier screamers. For Emerson, raised in the rarefied realms of Boston and Cambridge but instinctively hungry for popular idioms, this invasion of the frontier signaled a welcome opportunity for stylistic change. The most important historical moment, he would later write, is when "the savage is just ceasing to be savage."[7] This statement has autobiographical import, for the moment of Emerson's literary maturation was also the moment when savage American humor was coming out of the backwoods and was appearing in the sermons, newspapers, and lyceum addresses of the Northeast. More acutely than any of his liberal colleagues, Emerson recognized the significance of the linguistic invasion from the frontier. Not only did he respond with unique rapture to the slang-filled sermons of Father Taylor, but he specifically called attention to the ingenious metaphors introduced in frontier humor. Like many religious liberals, he had long been attracted to secular illustrations and figures that were providing literary embellishments of sacred truths. But it was only in the mid-1830s that he distinguished himself from his liberal colleagues by identifying frontier idioms as a primary model for American writers. Shortly before he wrote *Nature,* his first major work, he delivered a lecture, in November 1835, that indicates the powerful impact that this ascendant frontier discourse was having on his imagination. Notice how his later theories on language are prefigured in this paean to the frontier style made in the 1835 lecture:

Good writing and brilliant discourse are perpetual allegories. The imagery in discourse which delights all men is that which is drawn from observation of natural processes. It is this which gives that piquancy to the conversation of a strong natured farmer or back-woodsman which all men relish. It is the salt of those semisavages, men of strong understanding, who bring out of the woods into the tameness of refined circles a native way of seeing things, and there speak in metaphors. "I showed him the back of my hand," says a backwoodsman, for *I broke friendship with him.* . . . The strong humor of Jack Downing's letters has not contributed so much to their pop-ularity as the just natural imagery in which all the thoughts are presented.[8]

Having underscored the suggestiveness of backwoods argot and humor, Emerson in the next breath defined the poet as the one who through the power of imagination "converts the solid globe, the land, the sea, the sun, the animals into symbols of thought."

The originality of this lecture lies less in its declarations about imagina-tion and the poetic process than in its linkage of this process with the imagery of frontier humor. What was new was Emerson's eagerness to reinterpret standard Romantic outlooks in terms of the linguistic strategies of the American backwoods. Like many writers in his circle, he had long been struggling to identify an indigenous literary voice for American writ-ers, but he was the first to dare to seek this voice in the crude realm of frontier humor. With the wisdom of hindsight, we can say that his interest in this humor was indeed justified. Few popular American literary genres possessed the raw imaginative energy of frontier humor, which featured vivid, often bizarre metaphors that created a dizzying world in which ob-jects floated, sometimes haphazardly, in free space. The special contribu-tion of the frontier "semisavages," Emerson stressed, was to "bring out of the woods into the tameness of refined circles a native way of seeing things, and there speak in metaphors." If, as he would later say, the important historical moment was when the savage became civilized, Emerson was fully conscious that he himself was living in such a moment. After a long search, he at last discovered a "native way of seeing things" in the image-filled frontier writings that began to flood the New England popular mar-ket in the 1830s.

His enthusiasm for the frontier humorists remained unabated through the period, roughly between 1836 and 1844, during which he produced his most memorable and characteristic writings. In an essay he wrote for *The Dial* in 1842, he outlined the future of American letters as follows:

Our eyes will be turned westward, and a new and stronger tone in our literature will be the result. The Kentucky stump-oratory, the exploits of Boone and David Crockett, the journals of the western pioneers, agriculturalists, and socialists, and the letters of Jack Downing, are genuine growths, which are sought with avidity in Europe, where our European-like books are of no value.[9]

In his 1835 lecture he had made an innovative connection between frontier metaphors and Romantic philosophy, and had used Seba Smith's Jack Downing series as an example of creative humor. Here he again mentions Smith's series and adds a number of other backwoods writings—the Davy Crockett and Daniel Boone narratives, Kentucky political speeches, pioneer journals—that he says will give rise to "a new and stronger tone in our literature." His perception of the fluidity of literary genres, which had been mainly stimulated by the incursion of frontier rhetoric into the Northeast, had now become explicit and complete. Almanacs, speeches, journals, and humor series all seemed interchangeable and equally provocative for the American philosopher who above all wished to establish the frontier as a schoolroom for American writers.

What was it about frontier humor that particularly attracted Emerson's attention? There was, of course, the egalitarian impulse of a Jacksonian American to counteract Anglophile literature by absorbing the language of American common folk, an impulse that had surfaced in this early journal entry: "We all lean on England. . . . I suppose the evil may be cured by this rank rabble party, the Jacksonism of the country, heedless of all English & of all literature . . . [that] may root out all the hollow dilettantism of our cultivation."[10] Repeatedly in the 1830s and 1840s, Emerson pointed in his private and public writings to a lowly American argot that he claimed had the kind of "nerve" and "dagger" necessary for energizing American literature.[11]

There were, however, deeper reasons for Emerson's fascination with frontier genres. In these genres he discovered a native metaphor-generating procedure that reflected the unique fluidity of the American democratic experience and that seemed the best available idiom for giving wholly indigenous expression to his philosophy. His improvements upon this idiom gave his major writings a distinctly American humorous voice. He frequently described American society as shifting and changeable, and he knew that the ever-changing metaphors of humor best reflected his culture's predominant qualities. What I have called the American Subversive Style reaches its earliest artistic transformation in Emerson's major essays. When Emerson's notions about the creative imagination and individualism were expressed in the disjointed, kaleidoscopic style of American humor, the result was a dazzling imagistic pastiche whose linguistic fertility enforced the philosophical freedoms it heralded. For a few of his contemporaries (particularly those devoted to English literary traditions) Emerson's typically American stylistic shifts compromised logic and consistency. The most famous denunciations of his style came from Lowell, who called it "a chaos full of shooting-stars," and Carlyle, who dubbed it a bag of duck shot held together by canvas.[12] Similar criticisms came from the *English Review,* which branded Emerson as "the American paradox-master" whose "grotesque extravagance becomes something more than a laughing matter," and from Henry Giles, who charged that in Emerson's essays things become "distorted, jostled, turned upside down in the giddy phantasmagoria of our borrowed vision, [and] are made to reel to and fro in a delirious or intoxicated dance."[13]

When compared with the wild, uncontrolled style of much popular humor, however, Emerson's style may be regarded as a notable enrichment and artistic improvement upon the American Subversive Style. It is actually in much frontier humor—not in Emerson's essays—that "grotesque extravagance" reigns and objects reel in a "giddy phantasmagoria." Emerson was well aware that the fluidity of democratic culture had profound perils. In a journal entry of 1847 he described America as "the ungirt, the diffuse, the profuse, the procumbent." In the same entry he declared: "America is formless, has no terrible & no beautiful condensation."[14] As much as he admired raw frontier humor, he recoiled instinctively from the emergent mass culture that was exploiting this humor and converting it, along with everything else, into crass theater. In 1837 he described America as a "tumultuous, insecure, unprincipled" society in which "what is gained in surface is lost in depth."[15] In his own writings, he used humorous images that were often grotesque and zany because he wished to mirror stylistically the predispositions of his own culture. At the same time, however, he was intent upon rescuing this culture from the incipient shallowness and materialism that threatened to convert the naturally wild into the merely freakish. It is no accident that Emerson's major essays appeared during the same decades (the 1830s and 1840s) that also produced the savagely humorous Crockett almanacs, the amoral heroes of Old Southwest humor, and the master showman of freaks, P. T. Barnum. Given his sensitivity to popular culture, Emerson may be said to have been himself confronted with a "giddy phantasmagoria" in a culture of "grotesque extravagance." His essays mirrored this phantasmagoria, absorbed many of its images, but tried to transform it into an inspirational affirmation of eternal verities.

When we look at specific images in his writings we recognize immediately how carefully planned was his literary rescue mission. Take this well-known passage in the first chapter of *Nature*: "Standing on the bare ground,—my head bathed by the blithe air, and uplifted into infinite space,—all mean egotism vanishes. I become a transparent eye-ball; I am nothing; I see all; the currents of the Universal Being circulate through me; I am part or particle of God."[16] This passage, one of the most famous in all of Emerson's writings, makes use of one of the most popular images in frontier humor—i.e., the taking out of eyes. In a lecture he had delivered the year before he published *Nature,* Emerson had abstractly described the influx of spiritual vibrations into his soul, and in the next breath had sung praise to the vivid metaphors of frontier humor. In the "transparent eye-ball" passage he achieves a *fusion* of Transcendentalist philosophy and popular image. The idealistic and the grotesquely humorous meet in an energetic metaphorical center. Emerson radically transforms two phenomena of his culture: on the one hand, he brings indigenous vigor and grotesqueness to New England Neoplatonism; on the other hand, he gives resonance and purity to a frontier image that in popular texts was inevitably linked with amoral violence. In a sense, the passage is shocking and humorous—so much so, indeed, that in Emerson's day it prompted funny caricatures, the most famous of which was Christopher Pearse Cranch's cartoon of a large eyeball perched on a sticklike body and wearing a hat and holding a cane. Still, its humor is elevated because it is infused with inspirational meaning. In frontier humor, the taking out of eyes was always a horribly antisocial act rendered in blackly humorous terms. In *Nature* it becomes a reassuring (if still humorous) metaphor of the gift of spiritual sight and receptivity.

This dual process of enlivening the Neoplatonic and uplifting the humorous runs throughout *Nature.* In discussing the first proposition of his theory of language—"Words are signs of natural facts"—Emerson cites as evidence the same frontier language that he praised in his 1835 lecture. Indeed, he repeats a sentence from the lecture: in describing the "immediate dependence of language upon nature" he writes: "It is this which gives that piquancy to the conversation of a strong-natured farmer or backwoodsman, which all men relish."[17] The difference between the lecture and *Nature* is that in the former he had followed this sentence with praise of metaphors in a specific popular humor text, Seba Smith's *Letters of Jack Downing,* while here he makes the more general assertion that as man becomes more civilized language loses its naturalness. "The corruption of man," he writes, "is followed by the corruption of language." Having attacked civilized language as fraudulent and artificial, Emerson invites us to take note of "the language created by the primary writers of the country, those, namely, who hold primarily on nature." It is only by learning from vivid popular metaphors, he stresses, that we can "pierce this rotten diction and fasten words again to visible things." Emerson has dropped the direct reference to popular humor texts and has abstracted from these texts what he saw as their central affirmative lesson—their fertility and naturalness of metaphor. He has stripped frontier humor of its anarchic savagery while retaining its bite and vividness.

As he soars continually higher in the philosophically ascending chapters of *Nature,* he never loses grasp of the kind of energetic imagery that he had discovered in the "primary writers of the country" like Seba Smith and other humorists. When he talks in *Nature* of travelers trying to roast eggs on the cinders of a volcano; when he describes the poet's ability to toss the creation like a bauble from hand to hand; when he discusses the imagination's power to visit the remotest points in time and space; when he describes man as broken and in heaps, he is lending fresh philosophical import to the kind of strange, often violent images that dominated grotesque humor. He is fully aware that on the popular level humor too often lapsed into the inconsequential and the absurd. In answer to nonsensical humorists he shows that the imaginative writer can toy with language and dissolve and recombine the physical world without compromising seriousness and ultimacy. As he writes in Chapter 6 of *Nature*: "The frivolous make themselves merry with the Ideal theory, as if its consequences were burlesque; as if it affected the stability of nature. It surely does not. God never jests with us, and will not compromise the end of nature, by permitting any inconsequence in its procession."[18] Since God never jests, Emerson suggests, man is free to retain a spirit of play without spoiling the underlying order of things. Several popular humorists had enacted linguistically the moral chaos of democratic culture; Emerson absorbs humorous language but invests it with a transcendence and referentiality totally lacking in the popular texts.

When we turn from *Nature* to another representative work, "The American Scholar," we see Emerson drawing more heavily upon popular humorous idioms while purposely transforming these idioms into meaningful receptacles of serious philosophical ideas. "The American Scholar" again underscores the significance of the language of common folk, culminating in the famous paean to common life: "I embrace the common, I explore and sit at the feet of the familiar, the low."[19] Emerson continued, however, to make pointed reapplications of grotesque images with the aim of demonstrating that humorous energy could be tapped without leading to relativism or stylistic disarray. Indeed, "The American Scholar" seems specifically designed to reproduce the grotesqueness and disjointedness of American humorous idioms and to uplift them by making them the vehicle of a philosophy that affirms underlying order and unity. "The American Scholar" is an attempted cultural rescue mission in a dual sense: thematically, it tries to counteract the fragmentation of modern man by positing wholeness and imaginative vitality; stylistically, it redirects grotesque native idioms toward higher social and spiritual meaning. Notice the string of strange metaphors that run through "The American Scholar," the kind of metaphors that made Emerson seem a humorist to some of his contemporaries:

> The state of society is one in which the members have suffered amputation from the trunk, and strut about so many walking monsters,— a good finger, a neck, a stomach, an elbow, but never a man.

> Let him not quit his belief that a popgun is a popgun, though the ancient and honorable of the earth affirm it to be the crack of doom.

> Men in history, men in the world of to-day are bugs, are spawn, are called "the mass" and "the herd."

> The poor and the low . . . are content to be brushed like flies from the path of a great person[.] . . . They sun themselves in the great man's light, and feel it to be their own element.

> [W]e are lined with eyes; we see with our feet . . .

As in many popular humorous writings, these weird, often violent images are radical juxtapositions which, if reproduced pictorially, would create a distinctly presurrealistic effect. The image of modern men as "walking monsters" and as body parts, bugs, spawn, and flies shows the kind of transposition of the human and nonhuman that abounded in popular humor. The image of people lined with eyes and seeing with their feet is an equally violent contravention of reality typical of subversive humor. But Emerson does not allow grotesqueness or violence to overwhelm his imagination; instead, he asserts control over grotesqueness and makes it a rhetorical vehicle for expressing higher truths. It should be noted that each of the above images has clear reference and meaning: the "walking monsters" image underscores the fragmented, ugly state of man in modern society; the "popgun" metaphor colorfully underscores the need for independent thinking; the picture of men as bugs and flies points up the leveling effects of mass societies upon individuals; "lined with eyes" suggests sickly introversion, and seeing with feet illustrates the downward, materialistic direction of people's vision. Although the weird string of images typifies the kind of monstrous humor that led some of Emerson's contemporaries to charge him with grotesque extravagance, Emerson's imagistic antics here are solidly grounded in the idea that modern society has reduced people to objects and destroyed their humanity. By right thinking and right acting, Emerson stresses throughout "The American Scholar," people may recover independence of thought and vitality of spiritual vision. Having used a variety of grotesque metaphors to underscore the broken condition of social man, Emerson moves at the end of the address to a ringing assertion of the dazzling unities perceived by the self-reliant thinker, for whom "the world lies no longer a dull miscellany and lumber-room, but has form and order; there is no trifle; there is no puzzle; but one design unites and animates the farthest pinnacle and the lowest trench."[20] In popular humor, bestiality and disorienting metaphors were the source of grotesque fun. In Emerson, grotesque metaphors prompt people to recover their full humanity and their spiritual sight.

The restoration of direction and reference to humorous images also occurs in other central Emerson texts. In the Divinity School Address, for instance, notice the rhetorical suggestiveness invested in the following comic or strange images: "Man under [the stars] seems a young child, and his huge globe a toy" delightfully enforces the majestic vastness of the perceived universe. "Once man was all; now he is an appendage, a nuisance" illustrates the reduced state of man in modern life. "That which shows God out of me, makes me a wart and a wen" uses a grotesque transposition to argue on behalf of the indwelling God within human beings.[21] The most daring reconstruction of grotesque imagery in the Divinity School Address occurs in this dazzling statement: "But the word Miracle, as pronounced by Christian churches, gives a false impression; it is Monster. It is not one with the blowing clover and the falling rain." The unexpected placement of the word "Monster" in the midst of this religious declaration is both arresting and dazzlingly rhetorical; it makes us laugh at Christian definitions of miracles, and it leads us to embrace warmly the loveliness of Emerson's redefined miracles, those associated with the irresistible images of blowing clover and falling rain. A similarly rhetorical adaptation of grotesque images helps enforce the central thesis of Emerson's essay "Self-Reliance," which contains the memorable declarations: "A foolish consistency is the hobgoblin of little minds, adored by little statesmen and philosophers and divines," and "Why drag about this corpse of your memory, lest you contradict somewhat you have stated in this or that public place?"[22] In the first statement, the grotesque becomes a potent vehicle of social criticism, as the word "hobgoblin" serves as a comic barb against staid, parochial people; in the second, it is a graphic promoter of fresh thinking, as memory becomes a "corpse" dragged about by the obsequious or unchanging person.

What has happened in Emerson's major writings is that American humor has been transmuted into a strategic rhetorical device by a philosopher who established firm control over the grotesque instead of allowing it to distort his imagination and ruin his style. For Emerson, humor was an effective means of gaining distance from the kind of perversities that so often overwhelmed sense and sanity in popular texts. In his 1839 lecture "The Comic" Emerson declared: "The perpetual game of humor is to look with considerate good nature at every object in existence, *aloof*, as a man might look at a mouse, comparing it with the eternal Whole; enjoying the figure which each self-satisfied particular creature cuts in the unrespecting All, and dismissing it with a benison." In the same lecture he stressed: "The perception of the Comic is a tie of sympathy with other men, a pledge of sanity, and a protection from those perverse tendencies and gloomy insanities in which fine intellects sometimes lose themselves."[23] For Emerson, then, humor served as protection against those "perverse tendencies and gloomy insanities" that threatened to engulf him. It allowed him to hold at a distance various aspects of the democratic experience, including frontier literature, that were leading some of his contemporaries toward stylistic and thematic chaos. Emerson redefined humor by allying it with Reason, that higher imaginative power that perpetually sought hidden analogies in nature.

When transformed by Emerson, humor aided in converting potentially annihilating forces in American life into affirmative qualities. His comments on nineteenth-century America in his journals and essays were generally quite negative. Modern American society, he often noted, is frenetic, maniacal, theatrical, and fundamentally desperate and sad. In his essay "Success" he charged "shallow Americanism" with creating a "life of show, puffery, advertisement and manufacture of public opinion."[24] Elsewhere he referred to his country as "a wild democracy; the riot of mediocrities and dishonesties and fudge."[25] Chaos and sadness, he knew, always lurked as the special nemeses of America. In an 1847 journal entry he called America "diffuse" and "formless."[26] Tocqueville's notion that a cloud always seemed to hang on an American's brow was seconded by Emerson, who generalized that "history gave no record of any society in which despondency came so readily to heart as we see it and feel it in ours."[27] The great twin consolers, Emerson believed, were the intellect (which he said "delights in detaching" and "converts the sufferer into a spectator") and humor (which regards the world aloof). The first American writer to place humor on the same level as intellect, Emerson offered a regenerative, philosophical humor to a society he believed was tending toward materialism and moral neutrality.

He knew that in order for his recuperative humor to have effect, he must create a heightened mirror image of American society, one in which his contemporaries could recognize themselves and yet see themselves changed. A constant theme of his major essays was the writer's need to reflect his own times and circumstances. An equally important theme was the necessity to use common images that all would recognize. "Small and mean things serve as well as great symbols," he wrote in "The Poet." "The meaner the type by which a law is expressed, the more pungent it is, and the more lasting in the memories of men."[28] The America he perceived was a uniquely fluid culture of constantly shifting values and appearances. He wished to mirror this culture but in the process to heal it by revising its preoccupations and images.

The cultural frenzy and distrust that popular humor merely *reflected* Emerson wished to *redirect* and *elevate*. If the Crockett almanac of 1839, for instance, had typified the subversive spirit of frontier humor with its picture of a "NO TRUST" sign over a door lintel, Emerson (who knew of the Crockett narratives) offered a hopeful version of this image in "Self-Reliance," in which he wrote: "I would write on the lintels of the door-post, *Whim.*"[29] If the rascal-heroes of popular humor often brandished their inconsistencies, Emerson wrote that a foolish consistency is the hobgoblin of little minds. If popular humorists regularly created premodern effects by dissolving normal linkages and bringing together grossly disparate images, Emerson converted this process into an assertion of idealism, as in the passage in "The Transcendentalist" in which he says if we ask a materialist a question or two beyond his daily questions suddenly his solid universe grows "dim and impalpable before his sense" and he "goes spinning away, . . . at a rate of thousands of miles the hour, he knows not whither,—a bit of bullet, now glimmering, now darkling through a small cubic space on the edge of an unimaginable pit of emptiness."[30] If popular humor increasingly valorized artful deception in an uncertain world of surfaces, Emerson insisted in "Experience": "We live amid surfaces, and the true art of life is to skate well on them."[31] For some of his readers, such statements were doubtless as bizarre or funny as any in the popular humor texts.

Indeed, he was, as one contemporary put it, "an inveterate humorist," and a distinctly American humorist at that. He had learned well from popular humorous writings that he himself credited with having introduced "a native way of seeing things." But he departed notably from the popular humorists in his ceaseless effort to lend philosophical depth to themes that in popular texts often pointed toward the superficial and the amoral. The humorists' changeability was answered by his notion of creative whim; their inconsistency by his proclamation of healthy nonconformity; their dizzying imagery by his poetic dissolvings of material reality in the name of idealism; their chaotic reflections of America's fluidity by his respect for the present hour. All the subversive cultural phenomena they reflected he willfully adopted only to transform them into affirmations of poetic vision and the human spirit. It is true, as his critics charged, that he sometimes ran toward the disjointed and the uncontrolled. As he himself confessed to Carlyle, he could write "with the most fragmentary result: paragraphs incompressible each sentence an infinitely repellent particle."[32] But given the prevalence of the American Subversive Style in the decades he produced his major essays, his disjointedness was itself directly reflective of a popular culture whose humor he thought pointed the direction American writers should take. His final success lay in his ability to suggest inspirational meanings even in the midst of his disjointedness. The linguistic-philosophical nexus that is called Emersonianism occupied a dynamic middle ground between the affirmations and the negations of the democratic experience. On the affirmative side was a heady self-reliance, a democratic faith in universal human perfectibility, a capacity for creative image making, and a suspicion of narrow ideologies and beliefs. On the negative side was a frightening perception of moral relativity and linguistic anarchy. While the popular humorists frequently tumbled headlong into the nightmarish underside of their culture, Emerson remained in his rich middle space because he regulated grotesque humor with a powerful intellect that never lost sight of the philosophical and the aesthetic.

Thoreau and "True Humor"

This instinct to rescue simultaneously a culture running toward materialism and a humorous language tending toward the absurd was shared by Thoreau. Like Emerson, Thoreau in his major phase was described as a humorist with a frequency that might surprise those who think of him only as a serious-minded philosopher. When *Walden* was published in 1854, it prompted several reviews that underscored its humor. The *Christian Register* commented that "playful humor and sparkling thought appear on almost every page."[33] The reviewer for *Graham's Magazine* was amused by its blackly humorous images, remarking: "Sometimes strikingly original, sometimes merely eccentric and odd, it is always racy and stimulating." "We might easily fill a page," the reviewer continued, "with short, sharp, quotable sentences, embodying some flash of wit or humor, some scrap of quaint or elevated wisdom, some odd or beautiful image."[34] The *Knickerbocker Magazine,* in a combined review of *Walden* and P. T. Barnum's autobiography, grouped the two works together as preeminent examples of what it called "Town and Rural Humbugs."[35]

It may be hard to imagine Thoreau, the apostle of simplicity and sincerity, being mentioned in the same breath as Barnum, the manipulative showman who epitomized the age's tendency toward humorous theatrical-

ity and freaks. In a larger sense, it is difficult to think of Thoreau, supposedly alienated from popular culture, being accepted in his time as a
diverting humorist. But Thoreau himself was the first to make the connection between *Walden* and popular humor. After he completed a draft of the
volume, he scribbled in his journal:

> My faults are:—
> Paradoxes,—saying just the opposite,—a style which might be
> imitated.
> Ingenious.
> Playing with words,—getting the laugh,—not always simple,
> strong, and broad.
> Using current phrases and maxims, when I should speak for
> myself.[36]

Indeed, what chiefly distinguishes *Walden* from Thoreau's other writings is the intentionality with which it devotes itself to "getting the laugh"
and "using current phrases and maxims." Although Thoreau criticizes
himself here for exploiting current humor, he had shaped *Walden* specifically with his contemporary readers in mind, and his guilt about adapting
popular idioms was doubtless alleviated by the generally positive reception
of *Walden*, which enjoyed a much livelier sale and was more favorably
reviewed than the unpopular *A Week on the Concord and Merrimack Rivers.*
Moreover, his adaptation of popular humor was an intrinsic element of his
self-appointed mission to absorb the language of common Americans and
make it the vehicle of uplifting notions about individualism and deliberate
living.

More frequently than any American writer of the period—more frequently, even, than Emerson—Thoreau underscored the necessity for
persons of genius to incorporate into their style the popular idioms of
their own time and culture. Witness some of his typical pronouncements
on the topic: "Anything living is easily and naturally expressed in popular language." "All true greatness . . . wears the homeliest dress and
speaks the homeliest language." "If a man is rich and strong anywhere,
it must be on his native soil." "Perhaps the value of any statement may
be measured by its susceptibility to be expressed in the popular language."[37] He had a special animus against the language of British literature, which he considered elitist and tame, and he wished his own writing
to reflect what he regarded as the wilder, more liberated language of
common Americans.

On the other hand, he was profoundly disturbed by the unregulated
black humor he discovered in much popular American writing. Theoreti-

cally committed to stylistic egalitarianism, he could not act fully upon his theory because he was appalled by the linguistic excesses that the democratic imagination produced when it was not carefully controlled. Recognizing that the most influential form of popular writing in America was the newspaper, he wrote: "If you do not read the newspaper, you may be impeached for treason. The newspapers are the ruling power."[38] But he knew that the popular penny papers were increasingly filled with gloating accounts of horrors and crime, often related in fiendishly funny terms. In *A Week* he firmly denounced the gratuitous dark humor of the popular press. He memorably described a time when he settled down at night by the fire to peruse pages of newspapers brought along by one of his fellow travelers. The newspapers' business columns and serious advertisements (not those, he stressed, "of the modern quack kind") pleased him because they were "useful, natural, and respectable."[39] The main news columns, however, showed "a singular disposition to wit and humor, but rarely the slightest real success; and the apparent success was a terrible satire on the attempt; the Evil Genius of man laughed loudest at his best jokes." The same instinct that impelled him to decry the "Evil Genius" of these newspapers made him elsewhere refer pejoratively to "startling and monstrous events as fill the daily papers."[40] He recoiled from the "Evil Genius" of popular humor because he saw that it lacked direction and purpose. "What a grovelling appetite for profitless jest and amusement our countrymen have!" he wrote in his journal. "Next to a good dinner, at least, they love a good joke[.]"[41] A nation's humor, he believed, was destined to be short-lived, while a nation's scriptures would be its only enduring documents.

Thoreau, then, was confronted with a problem which faced several other major American writers of the period: theoretically committed to incorporating popular idioms, he nevertheless recoiled from the directionlessness and devilishness that characterized these idioms as they usually appeared in the popular press. He was dismayed by what he called in *Walden* the "confused *tintinnabulum*" of his contemporaries, the endless noise that made him wish "not to live in this restless, nervous, bustling, trivial Nineteenth Century."[42] Popular humor and games, he saw, reflected the underlying despair of this frenetic society. What Americans called amusement he knew to be merely an evasion of deep sadness. In the famous paragraph in *Walden* on the "quiet desperation" of his countrymen, he wrote: "A stereotyped but unconscious despair is concealed even under what are called the games and amusements of mankind." He came to believe that unregulated humor was a sure sign of private ail. "A mere humorist," he wrote, "is an unhappy man; and his readers are unhappy also."[43] His aversion to popular humor was closely linked to his aversion to America's materialistic culture as a whole. The popular culture he surveyed was one in which capitalistic entrepreneurship was beginning to affect all aspects of life, including the popular press in which humor appeared. Just as he realized that the popularization of reform had brought about its desecration, so he recognized that the commercialization of humor had brought about its cheapening and sensationalizing. The "popular language" that he constantly insisted was the main ingredient of literary greatness had been spoiled by the nation's "Evil Genius," which leered from newspapers and sensational fiction. Thoreau saw that his mission was to salvage this language by adopting it and radically transforming it.

To many of his contemporaries, his adoption of American humorous language actually made him virtually indistinguishable from other humorists of the time. It was the bizarre, subversively humorous images in his writings that had the widest appeal in his own day. The success of "Economy," the trenchantly funny first chapter of *Walden,* is a case in point. When in November 1848 he first delivered "Economy" as a lecture, his listeners were not offended, as we might expect from its sarcastic gibes at American society, but instead were titillated and amused. The public's enthusiastic response was reported in the *Salem Observer,* which commented that the lecture "was done in an admirable manner, in a strain of exquisite humor, with a strong under current of delicate satire against the follies of the times. Then there were interspersed observations, speculations, and suggestions upon dress, fashions, food, dwellings, furniture, &c., &c., sufficiently queer to keep the audience in almost constant mirth. . . . The performance has created 'quite a sensation' amongst Lyceum goers."[44] The lecture and the audience's warm response are described in words— "exquisite humor," "satire against the follies of the times," "sufficiently queer," "constant mirth," " 'quite a sensation' "—that capture precisely the biting, oddly funny style that appealed to lyceum-goers in the late 1840s. Significantly, Thoreau's next lecture (which eventually became "Where I Lived, and What I Lived For," the second chapter of *Walden*) was less well received because it lacked the bizarre imagery of the first lecture. The *Observer* noted it was "less successful than the former one in pleasing all" because its style was considered "rather too allegorical for a popular audience."[45] Thoreau had learned a lesson about the popular appeal of sensational, darkly humorous imagery, a lesson reinforced by his later lecture experiences. Throughout the 1850s, lectures such as "The Wild" and the defense of John Brown—lectures filled with savage, grotesque imagery—were by far his most popular performances. He actually got a reputation as an entertaining, funny lecturer, as indicated by his wry journal entry:

Curators of lyceums write to me:—

DEAR SIR,—I hear that you have a lecture of some humor. Will you do us the favor to read it before the Bungtown Institute?[46]

By the same token, it was the freakish, wild passages in his major writings that were most frequently reprinted in the newspapers. Among the commonly reprinted passages was the strange one in *A Week* in which he fantasizes about standing neck-deep in a swamp "lulled by the minstrelsy of gnats and musquitoes." Also favorites for reprinting were his pungent expressions of wildness (e.g., "There is in my nature, methinks, a singular yearning toward all wildness," and "I grow savager and savager every day, as if fed on raw meat"), his memorable lines about the strange human psyche (e.g., "Nothing is ever so unfamiliar and startling to a man as his own thoughts"), and his accounts of gory action, such as the bloody moose-hunting incident in *The Maine Woods.* [47] These and other striking images were hardly out of place even in the penny newspapers of the day.

Thoreau's growing recognition of the popularity of sensationalism and humor helps explain several changes he made in *Walden* as he reworked various drafts between 1847 and 1854. In a word, he made *Walden* more acerbically humorous and more vividly grotesque in successive drafts. His description of the way his neighbors were doing penance (now the third paragraph of the "Economy" section) was lifeless in the original journal version, which dryly listed various self-inflicted tortures among Asians and Greeks.[48] For the final version, he provided shocking details with all the grisly humor of a penny-press humorist: he added images of tortured people suspended over four fires, being chained for life to a tree, looking at the sky with heads twisted until only liquid can pass down their distorted throats, and so on. Although in 1852 and 1853 he added inspiriting descriptions of the lovely pond, he also added several darker images, such as the battle of the ants, the haunting owl hoots in "Sounds," the thawing of the sandbanks in "Spring," and the details of the taunting loon and almshouse moron. His attacks on reformers, philanthropists, and popular authors also became more vitriolic in the later versions. His addition of grotesque, funny imagery helps explain the frequent references to his humor by reviewers. The revisions sometimes strayed too far toward the humorous and gave rise to serious misapprehensions. Some actually thought that all of *Walden,* even its factual and philosophical parts, was no more than a clever ruse. For instance, as Thoreau noted in his journal, a friend of Emerson viewed all of *Walden* "as a capital satire and joke, and even thought that the survey and map of the pond were not real, but a caricature of the Coast surveys."[49] For some, Thoreau's incorporation of humorous language placed him on the same level as the purveyors of freaks and fun that permeated popular culture.

The humor of *Walden* is indeed popular humor, but it is popular humor carefully transformed by a philosopher who wishes to salvage both his culture and his culture's favorite images. His strategies for transforming popular humor are much like Emerson's. Humor is itself a mode of detachment and manipulation, but Emerson and Thoreau distinguished themselves by manipulating even popular humor itself to serve their ultimately inspirational ends. They did so chiefly by discovering metaphorical use for humorous images that in popular writings were used literally. In effect, they disarmed grotesque images by converting them into figures of higher truths. They offered stylistic healing to savage humorous language even as they offered spiritual healing to human beings in restless modern society.

The main difference between the two is that Thoreau, who wrote his major works in the 1850s, nearly two decades after Emerson's major phase, took advantage of the rich variety of humorous techniques that had emerged in the interim. Like Emerson, he made use of images from frontier humor; but he took the further step of extensively incorporating the humor of radical democrats and urban humorists as well. Indeed, *Walden* as a whole may be viewed as a Transcendentalist refinement of central strategies in these later types of American humor. The popular radical democrats had often used humor to unmask the rich to defend the poor; Thoreau uses it to unmask riches and defend poverty. The popular urban humorists had converted many movements and literary genres of the day into objects of fun; he converted them into meaningful metaphors. The central theme of *Walden*—the necessity for thoughtful, deliberate living in an increasingly frenetic age—is reinforced by Thoreau's deliberate reapplication of popular humorous images. The most significant sociolinguistic feature of *Walden* is its rescuing of such images from the nonsensical and the pointless. Believing that his countrymen were given to "profitless jest," he showed that jest could be directed toward spiritual profit. Believing that the "mere humorist" was basically a "sad man," he showed that meaningful humor could instigate joy and self-confidence. In light of the pointlessly grotesque popular literature Thoreau was revising, even his most morbid images are in fact inspiring and health-engendering, since they have clear referents, whereas the popular humor often had no referents at all.

This infusion of popular humor with higher meaning is evident on virtually every page of *Walden*. Take, for example, the well-known line: "I do not propose to write an ode to dejection, but to brag as lustily as a chanticleer in the morning, standing on his roost, if only to wake my neighbors up."[50] One of the most common devices in popular frontier humor was the imaginative transformation of the screamer-hero into an animal, often a rooster. An example of such bestial humor is the portrayal of Roaring Ralph Stackpole in Robert Montgomery Bird's novel *Nick of the Woods* (1837). In a characteristic moment, the irrepressible Ralph performs many feats that are, as Bird puts it, "expressive of his hostile humor. He flapped his wings and crowed, until every chanticleer in the settlement replied to the note of battle; he snorted and neighed like a horse; he bellowed like a bull; he barked like a dog; he yelled like an Indian; he whined like a panther; he howled like a wolf; until one would have thought he was a living menagerie, comprising within his single body the spirit of every animal noted for its love of conflict."[51] When we compare this typical bit of popular humor with Thoreau's chanticleer line, we immediately notice key differences. Bird's passage begins and ends with references to hostility or conflict; Thoreau's is a ringing proclamation of joy and buoyancy. Bird's passage is a weird, shifting montage of bestial images, producing an almost presurrealistic conflation of the human and the nonhuman. Roaring Ralph is called a rooster and then in rapid succession is compared to a "living menagerie" of other animals, and there seems to be no object for these bizarre juxtapositions other than the "hostile humor" they convey. Thoreau's line revolves around a single, striking image that is grotesquely humorous but at the same time vividly illuminates the cheerful message Thoreau is sending to the world.

While the chanticleer passage exemplifies Thoreau's transformation of a frontier-humor image, most of the images in *Walden* seem to be reworkings of radical-democrat and urban humor. Nothing was more common in urban humor, for instance, than the exaggeration of sensationalism until it became absurd. Thoreau also takes the grotesque or the violent to a blackly humorous extreme, but with extremely different effect from what the urban humorists aimed at. Note *Walden*'s third paragraph, the description of self-inflicted tortures that was added in the more sensational later drafts of the book. The paragraph is a quintessential example of grotesque American humor, since it recounts in gleeful detail a rapid succession of tortures—humans burning over open flames, staring into the sun, chaining themselves for life to a tree, and so forth—in a way that recalls the wild string of horrors often featured in parodies of sensational literature by the urban humorists. Thoreau is reenacting the strategy of the urban humorists, with a key difference: the popular parodies are self-indulgently frenetic, pointless, while Thoreau's has a moral and social point that becomes clear when Thoreau writes that "even these forms of conscious penance are hardly more incredible and astonishing than the scenes which I daily witness."[52] The violent popular humor has no referent. His violent humor does: it points to his central argument that materialistic modern Americans torture themselves endlessly with mindless, earthly pursuits.

This revision of popular humor continues throughout *Walden*. Notice all the popular images he transforms. Urban humorists commonly spoofed sensational penny newspapers, with their reports of "A Horrible Accident," "A Lamentable Suicide," and so on. Thoreau makes the same kind of joke in his report of a crowd rushing aboard a train; when the smoke clears, he writes, "it will be perceived that a few are riding, but the rest are run over,—and it will be called, and will be, 'A melancholy accident.' "[53] Unlike the penny-press jokes that abound in urban humor, Thoreau's joke has a clear message: i.e., man's machines often turn against him and destroy him. Another typical strategy of popular humor was to present humans as beasts or inanimate objects. Thoreau often uses this strategy, but always with a definite aim. Note the transpositions in the following sentences: "The luxurious rich are not simply kept comfortably warm, but unnaturally hot; as I implied before, they are cooked, of course *à la mode.*" "We know but few men, a great many coats and breeches." "The head monkey at Paris puts on a traveller's cap, and all the monkeys in America do the same." These are a small sampling of typical Thoreau jokes of the kind that were thought "sufficiently queer" to keep his lecture audiences laughing. They have a radical-democrat flavor, for they impugn the rich from an egalitarian perspective. They also have a Barnumesque, urban flavor, since they invite us to laugh at the freakish or theatrical. They draw from the American Subversive Style, for they freely interchange the human and nonhuman, the high and the low. But they all use the weirdly sensational metaphorically and rhetorically rather than absurdly. They are Subversive images put into the service of unequivocal social commentary which prepares the reader for the affirmations that come later in *Walden.*

A few more examples of Thoreau's improvements upon popular humor suffice to suggest his overall reconstructive strategy. We have seen that as urban humor became progressively more self-consciously strange in the early 1850s, it had regularly used parts of the human body, such as a foot or an ear, to represent the whole human being. Thoreau makes use of this kind of grotesque metonymy when he writes that we tunnel under the Atlantic to hear foreign news, "but perchance the first news that will leak through into the broad, flapping American ear will be that the Princess Adelaide has the whooping cough."[54] Once again, he instills a social message—the American public's overeagerness for technological advance and for trivial news—into an image that was usually nonsensical on the popular level. Similarly, the urban humorists often spoofed spiritualism, but the result was inevitably an absurd exaggeration of the pseudoscience's bizarre visions. Thoreau mentions spiritualism only to reinforce his assault on materialism: "[T]hough you trade in messages from heaven, the whole curse of trade attaches to the business." Likewise, he parodies popular literature, just as the popular humorists often do, but always with a direct suggestion of alternative modes of thinking and living that he offers to counteract popular literature's degrading colorlessness. We laugh, for instance, when he writes that "we are a race of tit-men, and soar but little higher in our intellectual flights than the columns of the daily paper," and at the memorable passages on "Little Reading" in which he gives a lengthy parody of Romantic Adventure fiction. But our laughter has an edge to it. It reminds us constantly of the higher life we are missing when we give ourselves over to frivolous popular reading. Here as elsewhere, Thoreau adopts a humorous strategy from popular culture with the conscious goal of conducting readers out of that popular culture.

Thoreau wished to establish what he called "true humor," which, like popular humor, was grotesque but which had a fundamental seriousness and spiritual suggestiveness. In an early essay he writes: "Those who suspect a Mephistopheles, or sneering, satirical devil, under all, have not learned the secret of true humor, which sympathizes with the gods themselves, in view of their grotesque, half-finished creatures."[55] The true humor he defines here includes the grotesque but soars above it to the realm of the philosophical. In contrast to the flat, frequently hostile humor of his contemporaries, it had resonance and meaning. Popular humor was typically a series of grotesque vehicles without a tenor. His so-called true humor retained the grotesque vehicles but supplied an inspiring tenor. At several points in *Walden* he uses images that have the bizarre juxtapositions of the American Subversive Style but purposely convert these juxtapositions into dazzling affirmations. Take this line: "I would drink deeper; fish in the sky, whose bottom is pebbly with stars."[56] Like much popular American humor, this sentence strains the imagination by juxtaposing disparate realities. But the juxtaposed realities here are lovely nature images that form an impressionistic pastiche communicating Thoreau's yearning for philosophical living and oneness with nature's beauty.

This is not to pretend, of course, that Thoreau is always clear and unambiguous. To the contrary, he sometimes emphasizes his obscurities. But even when he does so, his attitude toward the reader remains fundamentally friendly. Witness this famous passage in *Walden:* "You will pardon some obscurities, for there are more secrets in my trade than in most men's, and yet not voluntarily kept, but inseparable from its very nature. I would gladly tell all that I know about it, and never paint 'No Admittance' on my gate." When we compare the latter all-welcoming sentence to the forbidding "NO TRUST" sign on the cover of the 1839 Crockett almanac, the difference between Thoreau and the popular humorists becomes clear. In the 1839 Crockett almanac we find ourselves in a disorienting world of gratuitous violence and odd metaphors, a hostile world whose most appropriate emblem is the "NO TRUST" sign engraved on its cover. In *Walden* we find ourselves in a sometimes mysterious, sometimes disquieting but always dazzling and finally reassuring world whose author is so kind as to ask us to pardon some obscurities. It is understandable that while disorienting popular texts like the 1839 Crockett almanac have been long forgotten, several generations of readers have gladly traveled through the open gate of *Walden*.

17

WHITMAN'S POETIC HUMOR

T H O R E A U ' S contemporary Walt Whitman also adopted and transformed popular humor. To his follower Horace Traubel, Whitman once declared: "Why, I pride myself on being a real humorist underneath everything else. There are some people who look upon Leaves of Grass as a funny book. . . . So I may go down into history, if I go at all, as a merrymaker wearing the cap and bells rather than as a prophet or what the Germans call a philosoph."[1] This prediction, of course, has proved inaccurate. Whitman has been variously studied as a mystic, a philosopher, an experimental stylist, a bohemian—but rarely as a humorist. Actually, though, he was all the former things largely because he was the latter. More precisely, he took certain ingredients of popular humor, most notably the character of the b'hoy and the American Subversive Style, and ushered them into a poetic realm where they gained new suggestiveness and control.

Whitman knew that American humor was a fertile but also potentially dangerous source of literary materials. A foreign friend, Rudolf Schmidt, once wrote him a letter requesting samples of American humor because, as Schmidt explained, he wished to write an article on " 'American fancy' contrasting the grotesque humor that is scattered with no pretension in your newspapers with the humor of Luther and Shakespeare." Whitman sent along a few popular humor volumes and emphasized in his reply: "The subject of American humor is difficult to treat fully & satisfactorily, even for a native. . . . American humor is still in its nebulous state—

unformed—*struggling to be born.* Some traits already appear—it is very grim, loves exaggeration, & has a certain tartness & even fierceness."[2] Few brief descriptions of nineteenth-century American humor are so shrewd and accurate as this interchange between Schmidt and Whitman. Schmidt stresses that American humor is characteristically grotesque, and Whitman replies that is it nebulous, unformed, tart, grim, fierce, full of exaggeration. While Whitman was diffident about this subversive American humor, he was clearly excited about its literary possibilities. It was a humor, in his italicized words, that was *"struggling to be born."* In *Leaves of Grass* the American humor Whitman called grim and unformed *was* born—that is, it was refashioned by a poet who retained its innovativeness but divested it of its inhumanity and directionlessness.

Walt Whitman, One of the B'Hoys

Nowhere was Whitman's reconstructive poetic power so visible as in his transformation of that central popular humor figure, the b'hoy. A real distinction between Whitman and his New England contemporaries Emerson and Thoreau was, as they claimed and as he himself stressed, that during his formative period he had been a member of the "rowdy" or "loafer" class of New York youths—the firemen, cab drivers, dockworkers, and other middle-class urban workers that made up the b'hoy population. He had been one of the b'hoys, and he transformed the b'hoy persona into the genially wicked, brashly wise persona of *Leaves of Grass.* For him, the b'hoy figure was a device he needed desperately in order to affirm heartiness and vibrancy in a society he feared was straying toward materialism and hopelessness. Whitman needed a more earthy, humanistic reconstructive device than he could find in Emerson's philosophy. He found such a device in the figure of the b'hoy, who was at once a real-life phenomenon and a famous character in American humor, at once an earthbound reality and a compelling public myth. Whitman recognized, however, that the b'hoy must be salvaged from the increasingly trivial and vulgar manifestations that it was assuming in popular culture.

Whitman mentioned the b'hoy several times in his early writings and even assumed the b'hoy persona in his own journalistic writings. As early as 1840, he showed deep sympathy for one of the b'hoy's favorite pastimes, loafing, in an article for the *Long Island Democrat,* in which he wrote: "How do I love a loafer!" Noting that all the great philosophers were loafers, he fantasized about a future "nation of loafers, . . . an entire loafer kingdom."[3] At this early date, he seems not yet to have discovered a fully American prototype for the philosophical loafer; as time passed he discovered one in the figure of the b'hoy. He developed an ardent interest in the emerging b'hoy class, as is suggested by his 1842 editorials in the New York *Aurora*, in which he risked his reputation by defending nativist riots instigated by rowdy b'hoy gangs such as the Spartans, led by Mike Walsh and the prizefighter Yankee Sullivan. Whitman's overt recognition of the b'hoy figure came in his unfinished temperance story, "The Madman" (1843), whose hero is said to be representative of an emerging class of indolent street people:

> Any one who has been familiar with life and people in a great city cannot fail to have noticed a certain class, mostly composed of young men, who occupy a kind of medium between gentility and poverty. By soul, intelligence, manners, and a vague good taste, they assimilate to the former method. By irresolution of mind, evil acquaintances, a kind of romance which pervades their character, an incapacity for the harder and more profitable purposes of life, they attach to the latter.[4]

Even in this ambivalent early passage it is evident that the b'hoy figure already held promise for Whitman. On the one hand, the b'hoy is intelligent and inclined to copy the taste and manners of gentility. On the other hand, he is a loafer, a street-wise person who has dropped out of the social mainstream. It would not be long before Whitman would assume a notably broad persona in *Leaves of Grass,* one intelligent enough to cite Oriental scriptures but lowly enough to pronounce himself one of the roughs, one who could loaf and invite his soul but also plunge wholeheartedly into the activities of city life.

Before arriving at this rich poetic persona, he had observed the popular b'hoy figure with growing interest. In an 1848 newspaper article he described a crude but witty barroom customer as follows: "This is one of the 'b'hoys' of the Bowery."[5] Whitman gave a fascinated description of the b'hoy, who, he pointed out affectionately, is proud of his crimson necktie, praises the classical performances by the Shakespearian actor James Hudson Kirby, damns the sentimental writer N. P. Willis, and sings praise to the boisterous Tammany politician Mike Walsh. The reference to Walsh, the chief spokesperson for New York City's b'hoys, is significant, especially since Whitman had contributed a radical-democrat poem to the first issue of Walsh's lively working-class paper, *The Subterranean.* In an 1848 article for the *New Orleans Crescent* Whitman again mentioned the b'hoy in a report of a dance where he rose as best he could "amidst the yelling of a crowd of b'hoys trying to sing 'Old Dan Tucker.' "[6] In the *Daily Eagle* he ardently defended b'hoys in an article on New York's firemen, arguing that they had earthy geniality and intelligence along with animal spirits.[7]

He not only defended b'hoys against their detractors but went so far as to assume the b'hoy persona in some of his journalism. The most popular sobriquet for the b'hoy—"Mose"—became his pseudonym in his notebooks and in several of his egalitarian newspaper pieces. In 1855, the year in which he greeted the world as "Walt Whitman, one of the roughs" in the first edition of *Leaves of Grass,* he also published an article in the popular *Life Illustrated* under the name "Mose Velsor, of Brooklyn." The article, entitled "The Opera," is very much in the New York-by-gaslight genre popularized by George Foster and others, a genre produced by and for New York's b'hoy population. Like Foster and his ilk, Whitman as "Mose" describes a fashionable opera crowd with a mixture of awe and irreverence, describing this gathering of "the aristocracy—the upper ten" as an example of "polished, high-bred, deliberate, heartless, bland, superb, chilling, smiling, repelling fashion!"[8] He continued to exploit this popular gaslight genre in several other *Life Illustrated* articles: in "Broadway" (1856), a jaunty, detailed account of a bustling city street scene; in "Advice to Strangers" (1856), a warning against the "traps" of city life, such as gambling and licentiousness; and in "Street Yarn" (1856), a description of several people on a New York sidewalk, including a "Tall, large, rough-looking man, in a journeyman carpenter's uniform. Coarse, sanguine complexion; strong, bristly, grizzled beard; . . . careless, lounging gait. Walt Whitman, the sturdy, self-conscious microcosmic, prose-poetical author of that incongruous hash of mud and gold—'Leaves of Grass.' " As this amusing self-portrait suggests, even as *Leaves of Grass* was passing through its majestic early editions Whitman wished to ground himself fully in the consciousness of the crude but smart American b'hoy.

From popular accounts of the b'hoy written by Whitman's contemporaries, we can understand why this figure had great appeal for him. The b'hoy detested the affectation of aristocrats and yet was intelligent enough to absorb upper-class culture. He was fundamentally virtuous but had a full awareness of the darker aspects of American life. He wore his shirt open at his chest and his straight-brimmed hat tilted jauntily over his forehead. His companion, the g'hal, walked with a swing of mischief and defiance. Her voice was hearty and free, and she wore her dress high in rebellion against French fashion. As a New York journalist with his eye on popular culture, Whitman observed the emergence of these popular figures and doubtless knew the popular literature in which they were described. It is likely, for example, that he was aware of the comment in *New York by Gas-Light* (1850), by fellow journalist George Foster, that "the b'hoy and the g'hal, and the great middle class of free life under a republic of which they are the types and representatives, afford an inexhaustible and almost untrodden field [for American writers], with a rich and certain harvest."[9] Whitman was the first major writer, in a line that would also include

Stephen Crane and Mark Twain, who reaped that harvest by discovering literary applications for the b'hoy figure.

Before this figure yielded literary fruit, however, it had to be rescued from the increasingly frivolous uses to which it was put in American popular culture. It is significant that the b'hoy, who had originally been a serious figure of working-class needs and fantasies, had by the late 1840s become a frolicsome character in American humor. Whatever redemptive value the b'hoy offered was increasingly compromised by portraits in pamphlet novels and melodramas of "Mose" or "Sikesey" as merely a punchy gangster or an uproarious funnyman. Extremely popular plays like Benjamin A. Baker's *A Glance at New York in 1848,* in which Frank S. Chanfrau played the swaggering b'hoy "Mose," spread the image of the b'hoy as wild and anarchic. In 1896, nearly half a century after the heyday of the b'hoy plays, William Dean Howells would still remember the immense cultural impact these plays had:

> It was interesting to note that the first successful attempt to represent the life of our streets was in dramatic form. Some actor saw and heard things spoken with the peculiar swagger and whopper-jaw utterance of the b'hoy of those dreadful old days, when the blood-tubs and the plug-uglies reigned over us, and Tammany was still almost purely American, and he put them on stage and spread the poison of them all over the land, so that there was hardly anywhere a little blackguard boy who did not wish to act and talk like Mose.[10]

What Howells calls "those dreadful old days" when the b'hoy plays "spread the poison" of comic violence over the land were precisely the years when Whitman watched b'hoy plays along with many of his b'hoy companions. Whitman recalled the momentous period in the 1840s when in New York's Bowery district "cheap prices and vulgar programmes came in. . . . [T]he young shipbuilders, cartmen, butchers, firemen (the old-time 'soap-lock' or exaggerated 'Mose' or 'Sikesey,' of Chanfrau's plays,) they, too, were always to be seen in these audiences, racy of the East River and the Dry Dock. Slang, wit, occasional shirt sleeves, and a picturesque freedom of looks and manners, with a rude good-nature and restless movement, were generally noticeable."[11] As attracted as he was to the b'hoy figure, he was distressed by the increasingly negative associations this figure had. By the late 1840s the b'hoy figure had become infected by the grotesqueness and violence that had long characterized frontier humor and that was by then permeating the urban literary markets. Howells had some justification for describing the b'hoy plays as "poison," for they presented the b'hoy as little more than a gangster whose amoral brutality was a source of crude fun for rambunctious audiences. George Foster, noting that the plays presented only the "faults, vices, and barbarisms" of the b'hoy, regretted the fact that "the getters-up of these execrable representations should have gained a temporary popularity by bringing out only the coarser and more vulgar traits, and thus enlisting the brutal sympathies and passions of their audiences."[12] A similar exploitation of the b'hoy's brutal side is visible in popular pamphlet novels of the late 1840s, such as George Lippard's *The Killers* and Ned Buntline's *The B'hoys of Boston*, in which the alleged viciousness of b'hoy gangsters is portrayed with smirking black humor.

Whitman feared that popular depictions of the b'hoy had tainted the image of America's middle-class workers. In the January 9, 1847, issue of the *Daily Eagle* he ardently defended New York's firemen as follows: "It is too common among supercilious people to look on the Firemen as turbulent noisy folk, 'b'hoys' for a row and 'muss,' only: this does the great body of them a prodigious injustice." As this sentence makes clear, Whitman knew that the b'hoy had come to be viewed as a "turbulent noisy" figure distant from the democratic common man whose freshness and heartiness he wished to restore in his own writings. One of his main efforts in his major poetry would be to preserve the best qualities of the b'hoy figure but leave behind the nonsensical violence and farcical humor with which it had become associated. Just as Thoreau had supplanted the "profitless jest" of his countrymen with meaningful humor, so Whitman wished to restore depth and sensibility to a figure that had been cheapened by popular literature.

He successfully accomplished this deepening process by transforming the *b'hoy* of popular culture into the *boy* of his mature writings, most notably the "I" of "Song of Myself." Like the b'hoy, Whitman's boy was swaggering, cocksure, indolent, wicked, acute, generous, and altogether lovable. Unlike the b'hoy, he was never amoral or needlessly violent. Whitman's boy was the b'hoy taken seriously, reinterpreted by a thoughtful poet with a profound devotion to the aesthetic and the moral. Without the preparatory appearance of the b'hoy in American culture, Whitman's poetic persona would have lacked its extreme flexibility, its all-absorptive power. The main attraction of the b'hoy for Whitman was that he seemed a walking solution to twin paradoxes in American culture: he was fiercely individualistic but at the same time democratically loving; he was unconventionally wicked but fundamentally moral and honest. The New York streets, he once wrote, provide "the solution of that paradox, the eligibility of the free and fully developed individual with the paramount aggregate."[13] Since the b'hoy was a notably *mixed* figure, he could accommodate the most paradoxical aspects of American society and the most disturbing elements of human nature. By definition, the b'hoy was in part a devilish figure whose defiant wickedness represented a healthy alternative to effete or artificial social conventions. Whitman's realistic, mixed view of common people resulted largely from his awareness of the popular b'hoy figure, who was intrinsically both wicked and moral at the same time.

Whitman knew well that *Leaves of Grass* grew directly from the boisterous working-class consciousness as represented by the b'hoy. In his early notebooks he declared that he had "deliberately and insultingly ignored all the other, the cultivated classes as they are called, and set himself to write 'America's first distinctive Poem,' on the platform of these same New York roughs, firemen, the ouvrier class, masons and carpenters, stagedrivers, the Dry Dock boys, and so forth."[14] He was inspired by the paradoxical union of contrary qualities within the boys of this class. He filled his notebooks with glowing descriptions of the mixed natures of these boys, such as the 1854 account of a "Peter" as a "Man of strong-will, powerful coarse feelings and appetites. . . . I like his refreshing *wickedness,* as it would be called by the orthodox. He seemed to feel a perfect independence, dashed with a little resentment, toward the world in general." The crucial significance of the b'hoy—or rather, in Whitman's revised version, the boy—was captured in his late confession to Traubel:

> What did I get? Well—I got the boys, for one thing: the boys: thousands of them: they were, they are, they will be mine. I gave myself for them: myself: and I got the boys: then I got Leaves of Grass: but for this I never would have had Leaves of Grass—the consummated book (the last confirming word): I got that: the boys, the Leaves: I got them.[15]

Some might call this passage the confessions of a doddering pederast, but there is much more in it than retrospective homosexual ardor. Whitman, indeed, had "got the boys" and, as he put it, "then I got Leaves of Grass." If he had merely got the *b'hoys* he would have remained on the level of many popular writers of the 1840s who were exploiting the b'hoy figure in violent, seamy humor. But Whitman got the *boys*—the deletion of the "h" marks his willful intensification and poetic broadening of this popular character, whom he rescued from the mire of popular humor. Whitman's fellow radical democrats had vitriolically attacked the ruling class in blackly humorous terms but had failed to capitalize fully on their most powerful alternative to aristocrats' corruptions, the b'hoy. In popular melodramas and pamphlet novels, the b'hoy was, in effect, fused with two subversive characters from American popular culture—the screamer of frontier humor and the likable criminal of sensational literature—so that he was transformed into an entertaining figure of wild fun, devoid of seriously redemptive qualities. Although several commentators (such as George Thompson) lamented this trivialization of the b'hoy and called for literary reconstructions of this figure, only Whitman and a tiny handful of other writers, including Melville and Mark Twain, succeeded in rescuing this rich figure by transforming it in literary texts.

As he appears in *Leaves of Grass,* the b'hoy has elided into the Whitmanesque boy, who possesses the b'hoy's contradictory qualities but who nevertheless emerges as a renovated, inspiring democratic figure. Witness these lines in the 1855 edition:

> The boy I love, the same becomes a man not through derived
>   power but in his own right,
> Wicked, rather than virtuous out of conformity or fear,
> Fond of his sweetheart, relishing well his steak,
> Unrequited love or a slight cutting him worse than a wound
>   cuts,
> First-rate to ride, to fight, to hit the bull's eye, to sail a skiff,
>   to sing a song or play on the banjo,
> Preferring scars and faces pitted with small pox over all
>   latherers and those that keep out of the sun.[16]

This is an inspiring, mythical representation of a figure who had been cheapened by popular culture. In nearly all respects, Whitman's boy is the popular b'hoy: he is self-reliant, wicked rather than conventionally virtuous, hearty, animalistic, proud, active, a good sportsman, a hater of the cloistered rich. He is not, however, senselessly violent or merely clownish, as were the "Mose" and "Sikesey" of melodramas and pamphlet novels. He is not, in fact, the b'hoy as American culture had come to know him by the 1850s. He was instead a thoroughly reconstructed b'hoy, one who fully embodied all the b'hoy's rich paradoxes but who was treated seriously by a poet who wished to restore the pristine virtues (*wicked* virtues, of course) of this thoroughly American character.

It is clear that the "I" of *Leaves of Grass* is also a revised version of the b'hoy. In fashioning his poetic persona, Whitman wished to establish a fully democratic first-person voice, one that could fuse the contradictory phenomena in American culture, who could be individualistic yet democratic, unconventional yet acceptable to all, radically egalitarian yet cultured. In order to fuse the disparate thematic and stylistic strategies of his culture, he needed a persona who was tonally and morally flexible. He found this persona in the b'hoy, who becomes in his revision the cocky, rowdyish, but basically sound and redemptive boy. "Arrogant, masculine, naive, rowdyish," the persona says of himself in the 1856 version of "Song of the Broad-Axe." "Reminder of animals, meeter of savage and gentleman on equal terms, / . . . A Manhattanese bred, fond of Brooklyn, fond of Broadway, fond of the life on the wharves and the great ferries." In the same poem he says: "Already a nonchalant breed, silently emerging appears on the streets."[17] This persona, then, springs from the same Manhattan streets that had bred the b'hoy, his popular twin. But in Whitman's reconstruction, this figure is the great intermediary between the civilized and the savage, the one who emulates the intelligence of the former but possesses the vibrancy of the latter. Like the popular b'hoy, he is a loafer, but he loafs and invites his *soul,* instead of inviting trouble, as the b'hoy was wont to do. He can absorb into his consciousness the best and worst features of democratic culture: as Whitman writes in the 1860 edition: "Me, so puzzling and contradictory—Me, a Manhattanese, the most loving and arrogant of men[.]"[18] This persona has far more complexity than the b'hoy figure, since he incorporates a far greater range of cultural and philosophical tendencies than any b'hoy was called to do. Along with this increased complexity, the persona is distanced from the chaotic realm of relativism and flatness that the b'hoy, in his meretricious humorous forms, often inhabited. He is a heightened version of the b'hoy's "worst" qualities (indolence, rebelliousness, conceit, pugnaciousness) and his "best" qualities (loyalty, heartiness, generosity, endurance, devotion). Because Whitman invested the b'hoy figure with philosophical resonance derived from various sources, including Oriental religions and Transcendentalism, he was able to lift the b'hoy out of the mire of popular culture. Notice how the b'hoy is rescued from mere tawdriness in the following famous poetic proclamation:

> Walt Whitman, an American, one of the roughs, a kosmos,
> Disorderly fleshy and sensual. . . . eating drinking and
>   breeding,
> No sentimentalist. . . . no stander above men and women or
>   apart from them. . . . no more modest than immodest.[19]

The mixture of qualities that made one contemporary reviewer call Whitman "a compound of the New England Transcendentalist and New York rowdy"[20] is evident here in his rhetorical placement of an uplifting philosophical word, a "kosmos," in a string of descriptive words ("one of the roughs," "Disorderly," "No sentimentalist," "no stander above men and women") which, unleavened by this word, would place the persona on the common level of the b'hoy.

This transformation of the b'hoy figure shows Whitman engaged in the same kind of artistic process as Emerson and Thoreau: like them, he creates a cultural mirror in which contemporary readers might recognize themselves but at the same time see themselves subtly changed. Having emerged out of New York working-class culture, Whitman mirrored a popular culture that was more turbulent, sensual, and politically radical than theirs. His literary mirror, therefore, was in several senses different from theirs; but many of his reconstructive strategies were essentially the same. All three writers were incorporating popular images with the aim of giving them suggestiveness and direction, whereas in their crude state they often remained savage and uncontrolled.

Reshaping the Subversive Style

Whitman's statement that he was a humorist beneath everything else holds true when we recognize the affinities between his poetic style and the American Subversive Style as it had been developed by the popular humorists. Whitman disliked smooth American poets who ignored the crude energy of American popular idioms. He commented, for example, that Longfellow "brings nothing offensive or new, does not deal hard blows."[21] *Leaves of Grass,* he declared pointedly, was "sharp, full of danger, full of contradictions and offence."[22] He knew that democratic culture had a harsh, destructive side whose grimness and disorderliness were reflected stylistically in the slang and humor of the American masses. He was not, however, prepared to go so far in the direction of stylistic abandon as those typical American humorists he described to Rudolf Schmidt as "fierce," "grim," "nebulous." His choice of free verse as his preferred genre was guided largely by his instinct to strike a middle note between the controlled but often saccharine tones of Conventional poetry and the lively but wild howlings of Subversive prose. Because his verse was free, it could incorporate some of the weird effects of popular prose stylists. Because it was rhythmic and creatively metaphorical, it exploited the regularity and control offered by the genre of poetry.

Notice what happens to a common element of American humor—radical leaps in time or space—when it is transformed by Whitman. We have seen that centrifugal forces in democratic culture gave rise to the American Subversive Style of dark humor, characterized by discontinuous images and time-space leaps. In frontier humor, the screamer had such democratic force that the sun and stars were as easily handled as a cup of coffee. In radical-democrat humor, the perception of an unjust American society as nightmarish and grotesque gave rise to dizzying, kaleidoscopic visions such as Devil-Bug's dream in Lippard's *The Quaker City.* In urban humor, time-space leaps were especially common in parodies of strange fads like mesmerism and spiritualism. In several popular parodies an entranced person moved freely into the past or future or to distant places, often conversing with the dead on humorously familiar terms.

Throughout *Leaves of Grass,* particularly in the early editions, Whitman toys with time, space, and distance as adventurously as any popular humorist. The following lines typify his playful dislocations and image shifts:

> Voyaging to every port to dicker and adventure,
> Hurrying with the modern crowd as eager and fickle as any,
> Hot toward one I hate, ready in my madness to knife him,
> Solitary at midnight in my back yard, my thoughts gone from me
>   a long while,
> Walking the old hills of Judea with the beautiful gentle God by
>   my side,
> Speeding through space, speeding through heaven and the
>   stars[.]²³

These lines suggest that Whitman knows perfectly well that time-space shifts are customary for modern Americans: he is, as he says, "Hurrying with the modern crowd as eager and fickle as any[.]" Like other American writers of the "modern crowd," he playfully reproduces the fluidity of the American experience by allowing his persona to shift rapidly between moods, from murderous hatred through dreamlike piety, and between physical scenes, from his back yard through a biblical landscape to outer space. As characteristically American as these shifts and leaps are, however, they are unlike anything that can be found in popular literature because they are carefully *regulated.* Like a master of the American Subversive Style, Whitman strings together radically incongruous images but departs from popular writers by conjoining them through poetic syntax and sentence structure. His introductory participles ("Voyaging," "Hurrying," "Walking," "Speeding") and adjectives ("Hot," "Solitary") establish a rhythm that has a powerful unifying effect, so that the reader feels exhilarated rather than confused by the abrupt image shifts. And all the modifiers refer back to the "I" who is the agent of these disparate activities. The "I" is not the passive witness of a kaleidoscopic panorama but rather is the controlling element of the entire scene. Moreover, his one anarchic, negative impulse (his instinct to knife his enemy) is rhetorically surrounded by refreshing images of voyaging, meeting the amiable Jesus, and soaring through space. The passage therefore includes the subversive, by shifting wildly and by noting human perversity, but it purposely overcomes the subversive through its rhythm, its authoritative first-person voice, its careful placement of negative and positive images. As odd as Whitman's juxtaposed images are, they have far more order and meaning than those of subversive American humor.

Similar controlling devices lend symmetry to the image shifts in what is perhaps Whitman's most stylistically experimental poem, "The Sleepers." This poem is often singled out as particularly adventurous in its changes of perspective and scene. The editors of the *Comprehensive Reader's Edition* of *Leaves of Grass,* for instance, call this "perhaps the only surrealist American poem of the nineteenth century, remarkable in its anticipation of later experiment."[24] "The Sleepers" might indeed be described as presurrealistic, but, far from being unusual for its day, it actually is a regulated, humanized version of the kind of bizarre oneiric images that were common devices of the American Subversive Style. It is true that this is one of the few *poems* that fully utilize this style, and the genre switch is all-important. The rhythms and structures of poetry enable Whitman to lend order to image shifts that in popular prose were usually formless. When "The Sleepers" is compared with a typical dream sequence in popular prose, a blackly humorous chapter in George Lippard's *The Midnight Queen* (1853) describing a madman's nightmare, the literary control of Whitman's poem becomes immediately apparent. In the Lippard sequence, an insane narrator describes a "grotesque and nightmare panorama" in which his soul flies to a barren planet and then back to earth to take on the successive shapes of a putrescent corpse, a howling animal, the bloodthirsty Napoleon in battle, and an old hag strung up on a noose but never dying. "[D]ream succeeded dream," the narrator says, "not like the visions of a fever, but most strangely and horribly palpable."[25] This surrender to a free-floating dream world, typical of popular subversive texts, has no direction and no point other than grisly diversion for the reader. It is arbitrary and merely grotesque.

Whitman's dream-reverie is equally wild in its time-space leaps and occasionally as grotesque as Lippard's, but it consciously incorporates such Subversive devices and images only to transform them into carefully arranged elements of a poem that is often disorienting but ultimately affirmative. Notice the structure of the two opening verses of "The Sleepers":

> I wander all night in my vision,
> Stepping with light feet, swiftly and noiselessly stepping and
>   stopping,
> Bending with open eyes over the shut eyes of sleepers,
> Wandering and confused, lost to myself, ill-assorted, contradic-
>   tory
> Pausing, gazing, bending, and stopping.

> How solemn they look there, stretch'd and still;
> How quiet they breathe, the little children in their cradles.[26]

With characteristic care, Whitman places the most negative, potentially subversive image (the line describing the persona as lost, confused) in the midst of uplifting images that assure the reader that, no matter how strange the dream sequence may get, it will be ultimately meaningful and inspiring. The passage is firmly governed by the "I" whose tenderness and compassion is obvious from the start. The persona may announce himself as "lost to myself" and "ill-assorted" but is nevertheless sensitive enough to step lightly amidst the sleepers and to take delight in the quiet breathing of children in their cradles.

This dialectical process of engagement with the negative or the weird followed by incessant iteration of the hopeful or the richly human governs the entire poem. Aware of the grimness and amorphousness of many popular texts, Whitman knows that in order to produce a fully American poem he must simulate the grotesqueness and shifts of the American Subversive Style. He does so by having his persona view a succession of horrid images: pale corpses, livid drunkards, sick-gray onanists, gashed bodies on battlefields, insane people, murderers, a drowning swimmer, a shipwreck, the defeat of Washington's army at Brooklyn. As disturbing as some of these images are, there is a central redeeming quality about them when they are compared with grotesque popular humor: they all involve the suffering of human beings, whereas such image strings in popular humor inevitably mingle the human and nonhuman with the effect of desecrating the human. Whitman restores full humanity to the American grotesque. Moreover, for every horrible sufferer mentioned in the poem, there is a counterbalancing reference to affirmative images, including sleeping children, spouses lovingly entwined, the beauty of the soul and of nature. In the few moments when the persona is temporarily absorbed into the nonhuman, the effect is not dehumanizing but rather life-affirming, as in the exuberant lines "I am a dance—play up there! the fit is whirling me fast!" and "I am the ever-laughing—it is new moon and twilight[.]"[27] This affirmative effect is produced even by the frightening lines in which he becomes momentarily absorbed into a death shroud:

> A shroud I see and I am the shroud, I wrap a body and lie in the
>   coffin,
> It is dark here underground, it is not evil or pain here, it is blank
>   here, for reasons.

(It seems to me that everything in the light and air ought to be
    happy,
Whoever is not in his coffin and the dark grave, let him know he
    has enough.)

Here Whitman takes absorption into the nonhuman to a precarious limit,
verging on a chilling contemplation of annihilation after death, but then
moves from the shroud image to an existentialist assertion of life. The
reader is assured that if it is blank after death, it is blank "for reasons" and
that, at any rate, death represents an escape from "evil or pain" as well as
a reason for living with joyful intensity.

Whitman has incorporated the dark images and time-space shifts of the
American Subversive Style only to make them sane, orderly, human. As
"The Sleepers" follows its dialectical course of negative images followed
by positive ones, it becomes clear that the poem's controlling metaphor,
sleep, was chosen because of the all-equalizing forgetfulness it embodies
and the all-restoring promise it holds. "The antipodes," Whitman writes
toward the end of the poem, "and every one between this and them in the
dark, / I swear they are averaged now—one is no better than the other, /
The night and sleep have liken'd them and restored them. / I swear they
are all beautiful, / [. . .] The wildest and bloodiest is over, and all is peace."
Whatever terrors the darker aspects of American culture may suggest are
erased by the poet's intensely human and refreshingly aesthetic re-creation
of the night and sleep. Although the poem brings together violently disparate images, the disparateness never suggests a fragmentation of experience, a shattering of perceived reality. "The soul is always beautiful,"
Whitman writes, "The universe is duly in order, every thing is in its place."

All things are in place, Whitman knows, because the poet puts them
there. The poet discovers controlling metaphors, such as grass leaves or
lilacs or the ocean or sleep, that symbolize the ultimate restorative function
of nature. The poet regulates image patterns and rhythms carefully with
the aim of reproducing stylistically this organic vision of decay and resurrection. It is significant that the concluding verses of "The Sleepers"
imagine the restoration to health of many of the sufferers mentioned
earlier in the poem: the insane become sane, the pain of the diseased is
relieved, the felon steps from prison, and so forth. In the jubilant closing
lines, the night is addressed as the fertile "Mother" to whom the persona
will always return, always to be reborn. This affirmation of renewal in the
face of annihilation, this vision of universal rebirth shows that the poem
itself has had a restorative function: it has absorbed the kind of nightmarish images and dislocations that characterized Subversive popular writing and has converted them into nourishing images of well-crafted poetry.

To underscore the restorative function of Whitman's poetry is not to pretend that it is *always* restorative. A poem like "Respondez!" (1856; later changed to the short poem "Transpositions") shows Whitman as a rather typical vitriolic American humorist. "Let churches accommodate serpents, vermin, and the corpses of those who have died of the most filthy diseases!" he writes here. "Let marriage slip down among fools, and be for none but fools! / Let men among themselves talk and think forever obscenely of women! and let women among themselves talk and think obscenely of men!"[28] "Respondez!" and the handful of other Whitman poems which gleefully subvert all mainstream conventions represent American black humor of the raw, crude variety, unsculpted by the creative imagination that Whitman used in his best poems to salvage and transform his culture.

When the rather excessive "Respondez!" is contrasted with a truly effective poem such as "Crossing Brooklyn Ferry," the primacy of poetic reshaping becomes immediately evident. "Crossing Brooklyn Ferry" stems from the same Subversive cultural nexus that produced "Respondez!" Throughout the poem Whitman daringly contravenes time-space restrictions and mentions the kind of perverse human impulses featured in American subversive humor. But, as in "The Sleepers," the human and the aesthetic are willfully asserted as counterweights to the blackly humorous, whose odd effects suddenly take on universal meaning. Witness these lines in "Crossing Brooklyn Ferry":

> Nor is it you alone who know what it is to be evil,
> I am he who knew what it was to be evil,
> I am he who knitted the old knot of contrariety,
> Blabb'd, blush'd, resented, lied, stole, grudg'd,
> Had guile, anger, lust, hot wishes I dared not speak,
> Was wayward, vain, greedy, shallow, sly, cowardly, malignant,
> The wolf, the snake, the hog, not wanting in me[.][29]

The last line seems to draw from the American tradition of bestial humor, a tradition that impelled Whitman to identify fierceness and grimness as peculiar traits of American humor. But in popular humor and in unartistic Whitman poems like "Respondez!" animal images are reveled in merely for their diverting grotesqueness. In these lines, such images are deepened by the preceding six lines, in which the poet confesses to evil impulses that make him fully human. This persona is not just another horrid "living menagerie" like Bird's Roaring Ralph Stackpole, Lippard's Devil-Bug, or other bestial characters of American humor. He is a wolf, a snake, a hog *because* he has lied, had hot wishes, held grudges, and so forth.

The bestial metaphors are not arbitrary but rather have psychological referents that invest this passage with a humanity and universality absent from subversive humor. The remainder of "Crossing Brooklyn Ferry" likewise redirects the Subversive style toward an affirmation of the universal. Whitman's imaginative visitation of future generations of ferry passengers would seem to place the poem in the realm of time-leaping popular writings, especially in explicit lines such as "It avails not, time nor place—distance avails not, / I am with you, you men and women of a generation, or ever / so many generations hence." But even these experimental lines reveal the humanistic revision of time-space travel Whitman is making. The "I" is with future generations because he is constantly resurrected as those generations read the poem. The poem's majestically described ferry crossing and the rounded, fully human persona become Whitman's gifts to future generations of readers. The grotesque and the discontinuous are absorbed into the poem only to be transmuted into the beautiful and the permanent. We are moved to accept the declaration that all humans are part of a "simple, compact, well-join'd scheme" and that all things furnish their parts toward eternity and the soul.

If Whitman was, as he claimed to be, a humorist beneath all else, his humor was a radically *transformed* American humor, one in which the experimental devices of popular humor were changed for the better. In "Song of Myself" Whitman stresses that his real self is untouched by the harsher aspects of modern life and "Stands amused, complacent, compassionating, idle, unitary, / Both in and out of the game and watching and wondering at it."[30] Significantly, the first adjective he uses to describe himself is "amused," a word that underscores the humorous side of his vision. Equally significant is Emerson's praise of *Leaves of Grass* as "the most extraordinary piece of wit and wisdom America has yet produced."[31] Here again the primacy of humor is emphasized, as "wit" is the first term Emerson associates with Whitman's masterpiece. It is the witty Whitman who reigns over this poetic universe, because humor permits him to be simultaneously in and out of the game, regulating and reorganizing cultural images from his amused vantage point. In poems like "Resurgemus" and "Respondez!" black American humor seems to overwhelm aesthetic sensibility, and Whitman descends to rant. Occasionally, this black humor is adeptly fused with sharp insights to produce pungent one-liners such as "And as to you Corpse I think you are good manure" or "And a mouse is miracle enough to stagger sextillions of infidels."[32] More characteristically, however, Whitman's humor is not black at all, especially when compared with the popular humor he accurately called formless and grim. If frontier humor had portrayed people as strange beasts, Whitman portrayed them as hearty animals with compassionate souls. If radical-democrat humor had sneered devilishly at the rottenness of civilization, Whitman affirmed the permanence and fruition of nature. If urban humor trivialized even reconstructive devices of popular culture such as the b'hoy, Whitman restored the power of such devices by investing them with new philosophical and psychological depth. If Whitman has not come down to posterity as "a merrymaker wearing the cap and bells," as he said he might, it is not because he ignored the rich humor of his culture. To the contrary, it is because he took his culture's humor seriously and made every effort to immortalize its best features in poetry of enduring value.

18

STYLIZED LAUGHTER IN POE, HAWTHORNE, AND MELVILLE

S U B V E R S I V E American humor had a particularly strong impact on the so-called dark writers: Poe, Hawthorne, and Melville. These authors were more open than Emerson or Thoreau to the iconoclastic psychological and metaphysical themes of this humor. One of them, Melville, made memorable improvements upon the American Subversive Style, which reached a kind of artistic apotheosis in *The Confidence-Man*. Nevertheless, it must be recognized that all these writers were just as eager as the Transcendentalists and Whitman to bring resonance and control to humorous idioms they believed tended toward the chaotic. They used a variety of literary devices—most notably the fusion of American humor with other popular phenomena and with classic literary archetypes—that converted the anarchic laughter of popular culture into a carefully controlled, stylized laughter.

Poe's Regulated Humor

The artistic regulation of popular humor is visible in the tales of Edgar Allan Poe. Poe took a great pride in his humorous works; as the novelist Charles F. Briggs noted in a letter to Lowell, "[Poe] has an inconceivably extravagant idea of his capacities as a humorist."[1] Poe's comic theory and practice was, to a large degree, a direct rhetorical response to a popular American humor he found simultaneously fascinating and disturbing. Poe grew out of the early phase of American subversive humor, the phase of Washington Irving and John Neal as well as the blackly humorous penny press, the interspersed humor in adventure novels by Robert Montgomery Bird and John Pendleton Kennedy, and the early frontier humor of Seba Smith and Augustus Baldwin Longstreet. He was clearly attracted to and influenced by this emerging tradition of subversive humor. He placed Irving's darkly humorous *Tales of a Traveller* (1826) among a select group of American tales of high merit, and he frequently referred to the force and energy of Neal's fiction. He laughed heartily over Longstreet's *Georgia Scenes* (1835), a frontier humor volume that he said "forms an era in our reading,"[2] and Seba Smith's Jack Downing was the one fictional character he included in his lengthy list of celebrated Americans whose signatures he includes in "Autography." His definition of the comic as the combination of elements that do not belong together derives from the American subversive tradition, as does his remark that the most widely read periodical fiction was that in which the ludicrous is heightened into the grotesque and the witty into the burlesque.

Still, Poe was profoundly dissatisfied with the directionlessness of much popular humor. In most of the pieces of Irving's *Tales of a Traveller,* he argued, "the interest is subdivided and frittered away, and their conclusions are insufficiently *climactic.*"[3] Neal's stories, he wrote, "ramble too much, and invariably break down just before coming to an end."[4] As much as he liked Longstreet's *Georgia Scenes,* he was repelled by some "horrible and disgusting details" in it. The humorous accidents in Robert M. Bird's *Sheppard Lee,* he remarked, were tonally inconsistent and in need of a unifying narrator and greater authorial seriousness in order to gain coherence. A common denominator of his criticism of popular humor texts was that they were admirably energetic but often lapsed into the formless and merely repulsive.

Poe was ambivalent, then, about American humor, as can be seen in his complaints about Irving's lack of structure, about Neal's directionlessness, about the gratuitous violence of Longstreet and Bird. He artistically transcribed this criticism of his fellow humorists in his own comic tales, many of which can be read as dialogic responses to the subversive themes and devices of his contemporaries. In Chapter 8 I identified two strategies, which I termed exaggeration and analysis, that were his principal means of transforming excessively sensational images into self-subverting artifacts in his tales of terror. In his comic tales he used similar strategies to transform popular humor.

In several of his comic tales he deliberately exaggerates the zany elements of popular humor until they become ridiculous in their contraventions of perceived reality. When he wrote of the witty heightened into the burlesque, he was pointing up his strategy of exaggerating popular humorous devices until they burlesqued themselves and became the agents of their own subversion. His tales of comic exaggeration outdo the bizarre mixtures of human and nonhuman images produced in those types of popular humor that reveled in the sensational and grotesque. In one sense, the effects Poe produces are more weird, more truly premodern, than even the most daring experiments on the popular level. On the other hand, because these effects are so ridiculous, they provoke laughter without provoking the hypnotic engagement with anarchic violence or moral evil that the popular texts often do.

An example of this distanced, stylized laughter is "The Psyche Zenobia (How to Write a Blackwood Article)," which exaggerates popular black humor until it becomes absurd. Poe makes it clear from the start that he is parodying the directionless sensationalism of his day, for he devotes the first half of the tale to the portrait of a Philadelphia woman who gets information from a magazine editor on how to write *"bizarreries,"* or popular tales filled with pointless rant and sensationalism. The second part of the tale is Zenobia's interpolated story, "A Predicament," in which she tries out the editor's instructions. Her tale is a caricature of the popular Subversive Style. Persistently digressive and virtually plotless, it reveals Poe's perception that humorous violence, when unchecked by firm authorial control, gives rise to stylistic chaos and thematic absurdity. We have seen that popular humor often created startling juxtapositions and violations of physical law that produced almost presurrealistic images. It is precisely such images that Poe exaggerates in Zenobia's tale, "A Predicament." To make his parodic point, Poe incorporates one of the favorite images of violent American humor: the dropping out of eyes. Toward the end of the story, Zenobia becomes so excited about a church clock's descending minute hand that one of her eyes pops out, rolls to the ground, and winks continually at the terrified Zenobia, who is temporarily relieved when the other eye drops out and joins its fellow. But then her head is chopped off by the minute hand and she is faced with another quandary: is she her head or her body? Getting contrary arguments from her body and her head, she is about to make a decision when she sees that her black servant has run away terrified and her dog has been devoured by a rat, leaving her alone to cry, "Dogless! niggerless, headless, what *now* remains for the unhappy Signora Psyche Zenobia? Alas—*nothing*! I have done."[5] Poe here is pushing black humor out of the realm of the savage into the stylized realm of the absurd. In popular frontier humor, the taking out of eyes, as well as other kinds of dismemberment, was always a bestial act performed by a wild character whose amoral violence was meant to seem funny. In Zenobia's tale, the removal of body parts is merely a silly, impossible occurrence in a tale that deliberately parodies a popular genre. The bodily deconstruction of the heroine enacts Poe's implied criticism of popular black humor. In a typical work of comic exaggeration, Poe has shown that even the most violent kinds of popular images are, like the heroine at the end, *"nothing."*

Another Poe tale that deconstructs popular humor by exaggerating its weirdness is "The Man That Was Used Up" (1839). Although this tale was so highly regarded by Poe that he gave it a place of honor, second only to "The Murders in the Rue Morgue," in his tale arrangement in both *Prose Romances* and the projected *Phantasy-Pieces,* scholars have long been mystified by this apparently frivolous comic tale about a fine-looking soldier who turns out to be no more than a talking bundle who had lost his arms and legs in battle and now has artificial limbs. In view of the dark humor Poe was reacting against, the significance of this tale becomes evident. Just as "The Murders in the Rue Morgue" had represented Poe's effort to assert rational control over popular sensationalism, so "The Man That Was Used Up" showed him trying to exaggerate subversive humor until it becomes merely inane. Violent humor texts like the Crockett almanacs and some of John Neal's stories had invited the reader to snicker at bloody war action, often involving battles against Indians. Davy Crockett, for example, regularly gouges out Indians' eyes, scalps them with his teeth, disembowels them, salts them, and eats them for dinner. Poe pointedly overturns this kind of dismemberment humor in "The Man That Was Used Up." The narrator of the tale meets the fine-looking General A. B. C. Smith and then hears confusing reports about Smith from various people who mention that Smith had been badly hurt in a campaign against the Indians. To learn the truth about the mystifying General, the narrator goes to Smith's home and on entering kicks aside a bundle that, shockingly enough, yells aloud and commands a servant to give him his arms, legs, and so forth, until the bundle materializes as the General himself. After he is completely put together, the General heartily damns the Indian "vagabonds" who had dismembered him, and the narrator declares that the mystery of this strange man has been cleared up. The apparent triviality of this tale has puzzled scholars; but it is its very triviality that constitutes its main meaning and explains its importance for Poe. As in Zenobia's absurd tale, comic violence here is exaggerated to such a degree that it becomes distanced and therefore harmless. Poe does not ask us to laugh at gory pictures of whites massacring Indians, as do several frontier humorists and novelists, but purifies the comedy by asking us to snicker at a ridiculous situation in which dismemberment is safely removed to the realm of the impossible.

He uses a similar strategy of exaggeration in two other humorous tales,

"Never Bet the Devil Your Head" (1841) and "The Angel of the Odd" (1844), tales which parody, respectively, immoral reform and sensational newspapers. It is understandable that "Never Bet the Devil Your Head" appeared in the early 1840s, the same period in which Poe also wrote "The Black Cat," for this was the time when the moral and the immoral were becoming so jumbled in popular reform circles that reform imagery could be used for either horrific or comic purposes by an observant writer like Poe. If in "The Black Cat" intemperance rouses the narrator to a murderous frenzy, in "Never Bet the Devil Your Head" it is an oath about gambling that makes the protagonist comically lose his head to the devil. In both tales Poe is converting the paradox of immoral reform into a self-subverting artifact, for in the terror tale the gin-driven narrator ends by defeating himself while in the comic tale the errors of the swearing Toby Dammit (who in youth had also rejected the temperance pledge and had been amorous with young girls) lead to his decapitation, so that he dies, Poe writes, "a lesson to all riotous livers."[6] This concluding moral is actually a humorous nonmoral that brings attention to the awkward, hypocritical mixture of morality and sensationalism that Poe saw in popular writings of his day. Exaggerated humor again becomes a weapon against a popular cultural mode, as Toby Dammit first loses his head, then sickens, and finally dies after homeopathy fails to cure him. Through abrogation of natural laws Poe once more extends popular humor into the realm of the outlandish.

In "The Angel of the Odd" sensational press reportage meets with similar comic exaggeration. At the beginning of the story the narrator looks through several dull books and then turns to livelier reading in the daily paper, only to be outraged by a typically sensational story about a man who died in an odd accident. The narrator angrily denounces what he calls the wretched concoctors of accidents who, "knowing the extravagant gullibility of the age, set their wits to work in the imagination of improbable possibilities—of odd accidents."[7] Just after he knowingly refuses to believe in any such reports, he is shocked to see a strange monster with two kegs as legs and two long bottles as arms. This is the Angel of the Odd, "whose business it was to bring about the *odd accidents* which are continually astonishing the skeptic." In the course of the story, the narrator is subjected to a variety of strange mishaps that make him finally confess in the possibility of the odd. Poe creates a surrealistic dreamscape that grows from the popular sensational press. The kinds of weird accidents that every day regaled American newspaper readers are mixed with impossible occurrences, such as the Angel's pouring oceans of liquid from his bottle arms, until they become merely ridiculous. Once again, Poe exaggerates a strategy from popular humor—the parody of sensational literature—until it effectively deconstructs the object of parody by converting it into an absurdity.

Analysis, Poe's other favorite strategy for gaining imaginative victory over disturbing elements of popular culture, is the controlling device in such tales as "The System of Doctor Tarr and Professor Fether" (1845), "Raising the Wind (Diddling)" (1843), and "The Gold-Bug" (1843). These tales make rational use, respectively, of bestiality, confidence games, and romantic adventure, themes that in popular humor texts frequently were treated in uncontrolled, even amoral fashion. Transposition of the human and nonhuman (a device that creates bizarre, savage effects in wild popular humor) becomes rationally sculpted in "Tarr and Fether." In various humor texts that Poe knew, the human and the bestial are transposed so freely that verisimilitude and artistic control are sacrificed altogether. Throughout Bird's *Nick of the Woods,* for example, Roaring Ralph Stackpole is said to be a whole menagerie of strange beasts, and at the end he is reported to have changed into a swamp alligator. Even more strange are the transpositions described in Bird's *Sheppard Lee,* in which the entranced hero describes vividly his experiences as he changes into many different things. In his 1836 review of *Sheppard Lee* Poe noted: "As Mr. Arthur Megrim, he passes through a variety of adventures, and fancies himself a coffee-pot, a puppy, a chicken, a loaded cannon, a clock, a hamper of crockery ware, a joint stock, a Greek Demi-God and the Emperor of France."[8] Poe complained that this "confused and jarring system of transmigration" was presented in a way that was neither wholly fanciful nor convincingly realistic. It was this muddy middle ground between the imagined and the scientifically demonstrable that Poe tried to avoid in his own fictional transpositions. When he exaggerated such transpositions, as in the portrait of the talking bundle in "The Man That Was Used Up," they became safely absurd. When he chose to analyze them, as in "Tarr and Fether," they became safely clinical because they were shown to be produced by diseased minds. In the tale, the narrator visits a French insane asylum headed by a Monsieur Maillard, who describes various past patients: one man who fancied himself a teapot, another a donkey, another a frog, another a pinch of snuff, and a woman who thought she was a rooster and thus often flapped her wings and crowed. We soon learn that Maillard himself is a disturbed man who led a patient revolt in which the actual asylum chiefs were tarred and feathered and a "lunatic government" was established. The climax of the story comes when the asylum suddenly explodes with the bestial cacophony of the patients, who are acting out their various animal roles, so that the narrator flees in fright. This comic tale transfers the bestial transpositions of popular humor into the rational realm of human neurosis. The use of the asylum setting and the case-history framework automatically makes clinical a topic that in popular humor was anarchic and violent.

"Raising the Wind (Diddling)" analyzes another leading preoccupation of popular humorists, confidence games, that also had been treated haphazardly by lesser writers of the day. Significantly, in the opening paragraph of the tale Poe parodically refers to John Neal, mentioning Neal's admiration for the utilitarian philosopher Jeremy Bentham. This reference is ironic, for Poe's scientific treatment of diddling appears to be a direct challenge to the bizarre, irrational treatment of the subject by Neal and his ilk. The original title of Poe's tale, "Diddling Considered as One of the Exact Sciences," underscores Poe's rationalistic emphasis, as does the listing of specific qualities and case histories that throughout the tale are said to exemplify diddling. One of the examples Poe cites, swindling on a steamboat, seems a tame version of the riverboat confidence games that are recounted in highly distorted, grotesque fashion in the zany first section of Neal's novel *The Down-Easters*. Another, swindling at camp meetings, seems a controlled version of the sacrilegious, sexually charged camp-meeting scenes in wild frontier humor, in which a roguish hero was often described as feigning religion to win a variety of illicit prizes, from cash to sexual favors from aroused female converts. The amoral, pornographic portrayals of diddling in American popular culture reached a culmination in Lippard's portrait in *The Quaker City* of the great shapeshifter Algernon Fitz-Cowles, who constantly changes faces and costumes in his unending search for sexual enjoyment, financial power, and sadistic pleasure in regulating others. Poe's "Raising the Wind" is a humorously scientific rendering of the confidence-man theme. Beginning with the assertion that diddling has been widely distorted and misrepresented, it rationally lists the diddler's traits: "minuteness, interest, perseverance, ingenuity, audacity, *nonchalance*, originality, impertinence, and *grin.*"[9] After elaborating on these traits, Poe gives several illustrative examples, all of which involve diddling for mere money rather than for sexual or psychological power, as it frequently was in the popular texts. In Poe's analytical interpretation, diddling is a coolly managed business, an exact science rather than a wildly subversive confidence game. By carefully analyzing a topic that often was fiendishly distorted in popular writings, Poe once more achieved comic control over a perverse preoccupation of his literary contemporaries.

The most dramatic instance of Poe's analytical permutation of popular themes is his famous tale "The Gold-Bug." In the eyes of Poe and his contemporaries, "The Gold-Bug" was a determinedly popular performance. One of his literary acquaintances, Thomas Dunn English, said Poe's intent "was evidently to write a popular tale," and Poe himself boasted that more than 300,000 copies of the tale had been circulated within a year, making it even more popular than his widely read poem "The Raven."[10] One explanation of the tale's success was its use of themes and images that had proved popular in previous American writings. Modern scholars have shown that a main source for the tale was a humorous story in Washington Irving's *Tales of a Traveller*, "Wolfert Webber," about a New York Dutchman who becomes obsessed by the notion that a treasure is buried in his cabbage farm and enlists the aid of a German doctor-astrologer (the prototype of Poe's Legrand) and an old black fisherman (the model for Poe's Jupiter). Another probable source, it has been suggested, was Bird's *Sheppard Lee*, in which a man, hearing a tale of buried treasure from his old Negro Jim Jumble, sets out one night in search of the treasure, sees demons dancing around graves, and digs under a tree but fails to find the treasure. Poe was also exploiting the story of the well-known pirate William Kidd. Moreover, there was a widespread fascination in America with pirate narratives, from factual volumes like *The History of the Pirates* (1825) to novels such as *The Memoirs of Lafitte* (1826), Samuel Judah's *The Buccaneers* (1827), and J. H. Ingraham's best-selling *Lafitte, the Pirate of the Gulf* (1836), which Poe had reviewed for the *Southern Literary Messenger*.

To point out such prototypes for "The Gold-Bug," however, is to notice immediately that in adopting popular images Poe notably changes them. Indeed, it seems that he specifically selected popular modes that intrigued him but that he believed were in dire need of revision through artistic analysis. All the popular sources of "The Gold-Bug" tended toward the digressive, the superstitious, the blackly humorous; Poe purposely added rigorous structure and intellectuality to modes he believed lapsed into formlessness or grotesqueness. Both Irving's "Wolfert Webber" and Bird's *Sheppard Lee* connect gold seeking with horrid distortions created by the diseased imagination. The obsession of Irving's gold seekers reaches almost psychotic proportions, as they have a horrific vision of William Kidd glaring down at them while they dig fruitlessly for their imagined treasure. The similarly delusive buried-treasure obsession of Bird's gold seekers leads to a vision of dancing demons and then to a mishap when the digging gold seeker wounds himself and falls into a trancelike state which sets off a string of odd transmigratory adventures. If Irving and Bird err in the direction of the deluded and the supernatural, American pirate volumes, typified by Ingraham's popular *Lafitte*, inevitably erred in the direction of the repulsive and the amoral. Poe's main criticism of *Lafitte* was that it gleefully dwelt upon bloody atrocities committed by a pirate who was presented as a hero worthy of respect. A common denominator of all these tales was their narrative shapelessness. When Poe complained that the stories in *Tales of a Traveller* lacked structure, when he noted that *Sheppard Lee* was confused and jarring, when he wrote that *Lafitte* was crowded with "unnecessary detail," he was bringing attention to a rampant digressiveness in popular narratives that he wished to repair in his own fiction.[11]

"The Gold-Bug" was his analytic revision of popular literary modes. The tale restores connection, meaning, and reason to a premise that in its popular prototypes gave rise to irrationalism and narrative discontinuity. The comic servant Jupiter embodies the kind of wild imaginativeness and supernatural fears that governed the popular texts. His master, William Legrand, with his directed imagination and his all-solving intellect, represents the connectedness introduced by Poe's ratiocinative technique. Poe reverses the emphasis of the popular writers. In Irving's story, the hero's weird imaginings of buried treasure infect two others, who aid him on his hopeless quest; in Bird's, a Negro's delusions infect the hero's mind and set him on his mistaken search. In Poe's tale, the hero refuses to be affected by the strange imaginings of his servant and asserts complete mental control over the situation as he unravels the twisted knot of evidence that leads eventually to the discovery of the treasure. Legrand's translation of the mysterious cipher and his other masterful detective efforts lend credence to his comment that the human mind cannot "construct an enigma of the kind which human ingenuity, may not, by proper application, resolve."[12] Irving's and Bird's tales are comic studies of mental aberration and distortion engendering delusive quests; Poe's tale is a study of mental rigor making possible the successful figuring out of a problem. This does not mean that Poe overlooks the irrational or the adventurous. To the contrary, Legrand gets feverishly excited when he discovers the mysterious parchment, and the whole topic of pirates and buried treasure would naturally raise the pulse rate of an American readership taken with pirate fiction. But even here Poe makes important revisions. Legrand's excitement is that of an imaginative thinker faced with a challenging enigma, and the main drama of the tale lies in the mental process by which Legrand traces mysterious clues to a solution. Similarly, Poe shifts the popular images of piracy away from the sensational toward the intellectual. Although we learn that Kidd has murdered followers to cover up the location of the treasure, there is none of the gratuitous violence that filled novels like *Lafitte*. Rather, the pirate is a smart strategist whose clever cipher is decoded by the even smarter Legrand. As in "The Purloined Letter," black humor and sensationalism are pushed aside as Poe fashions a war between interesting minds. Stylistically, "The Gold-Bug" was Poe's rhetorical answer to popular modes he had criticized for their inconsequentiality and unnecessary detail. It survives as an archetypal example of his definition of the plot as that from which nothing can be taken without detriment to the whole, for none of the mental steps that Legrand follows to his exciting discovery can be omitted in the context of the tale's crescendoing drama. The narrative unity and singleness of effect that Poe deemed essential to fiction became, here as in his other major tales, a rhetorical assertion of structure in an era of popular structurelessness.

Hawthorne, Melville, and Popular Humor

Hawthorne, too, used fictional structure as a means of controlling the more savage forces of his culture, among them subversive humor. Like Poe, Hawthorne was aware that native humor tended toward the grotesque and wild, and a major part of his artistic mission was his fashioning of well-sculpted tales in which this humor was ordered and redirected. The anarchic laughter of frontier humor is transcribed into key images in Hawthorne's fiction: in the hysterical shriek of Robin Molineux, in the demonic scream of Goodman Brown, in the resounding laugh of Ethan Brand, in the devilish imaginings of Arthur Dimmesdale on the scaffold at night. There is good reason to believe that these and several other blackly humorous images in Hawthorne's fiction are directly related to his knowledge of popular American humor. Still, Hawthorne was more intent than Poe on apportioning such images carefully in such a way that they did not disrupt his style. Unlike Poe, he had no inclination to exaggerate the American Subversive Style in order to create absurd effects. Nor did he have such faith in the rational mind that he used Poe's analytical devices. Instead, he structured much of his fiction in such a way that it vented the wildest impulses of popular humor but at the same time asserted control over these impulses by regulating them through various controlling devices, including a genial narrative voice, reference to historical factuality, allegorical suggestiveness, and images of the religious and the genuinely human.

Hawthorne provided a shrewd and accurate description of his artistic manipulation of humor in the late, unfinished novella *Etheredge*, in which, after listing many gloomy criminal types that he might use for his dark plot, he suddenly gives himself the following instructions: "Now, if this great blackness and horror is to be underneath the story, there must be a frolic and dance of bacchanals all over the surface; else the effect would be utterly miserable. There may be a steam of horror escaping through the safety-valves, but generally the tone must be joyous."[13] This moment of self-instruction is quite revealing of the two principal features of Hawthorne's humor, as it had been integrated in his fiction since his early tales. On the one hand, the "surface" of Hawthorne's fiction—its narrative voice, its tone—is often frolicsome and genial. On the other hand, there is often a "blackness and horror" underneath that periodically escapes through what Hawthorne calls "safety-valves." Hawthorne did not overlook the grim, grotesque laughter of American humor. Rather, he counterbalanced this laughter with a narrative voice that was witty and controlled, and he positioned this laughter rhetorically in his fiction in such a way that it escaped periodically without threatening the firm structure of his narratives. Also, he imbued this laughter with a resonance, a historical meaning, and a human depth that were absent from popular humor writings.

The urbane, subtly ironic narrative voice of Hawthorne's fiction sprang from the humorous tradition that Walter Blair and Hamlin Hill designate as "reputable"—a tradition that derived from eighteenth-century British humorists such as Goldsmith and Addison and that was adopted in America by Northeastern (generally Bostonian) writers such as Oliver Wendell Holmes, James Russell Lowell, Henry Wadsworth Longfellow, and Washington Irving in his gentler moments. Those who focus only on the gloomy aspects of Hawthorne's fiction neglect the humor that is integrated in the narrative voice of even his darkest fiction. As Henry James noted: "Hawthorne's observation has a smile in it oftener than may first appear." Viewed from the perspective of antebellum popular culture, with its often anarchic and shapeless humor, Hawthorne could actually appear to be a cheerful, happy writer. It is significant, for instance, that one of the most popular weekly newspapers, *The Yankee Blade,* featured in a September 1849 issue an article entitled "The Literature of Mirth," in which he was placed in a tiny group of bright American writers who carried on the eighteenth-century British tradition of humor. According to this article, Hawthorne was "deserving a place second to none in that band of humorists, whose beautiful depth of cheerful feeling is the very poetry of mirth. In ease, grace, delicate sharpness of satire, in a felicity of touch which often surpasses the felicity of Addison, in a subtlety of insight which often reaches farther than the subtlety of Steele—the humor of Hawthorne presents traits so fine as to be almost too excellent for popularity, as, to every one who has attempted their criticism, they are too refined for statement."[14] Similarly, a reviewer for *The Literary World* wrote in an 1851 essay: "Life, whatever view he paints it, always comes forth an harmonious picture from Hawthorne's pen."[15]

Ease, grace, delicacy, depth, subtlety, refinement, harmony—these are the characteristics of Hawthorne's narrative voice that made many of his contemporaries view him, as Melville noted, as a pleasant writer with a pleasant style, a writer with sunlight beaming on the hither side of his soul. From a purely structural standpoint, Hawthorne's fiction has much in common with reputable humor but little in common with subversive humor. Hawthorne purposely avoided the narrative breaks, the weirdly transposed imagery, the bestiality and tonal irrationalism of subversive humor. "No rollicking rudeness," Melville wrote of Hawthorne's humor in "Hawthorne and His Mosses," "no gross fun fed on fat dinners, and bred in the lees of wine,—but a humor so spiritually gentle, so high, so deep, and yet so richly relishable, that it were hardly inappropriate in an angel. It is the very religion of mirth; for nothing so human but it may be advanced to that."[16] This refined, gentle humor in Hawthorne, however, is not an end in itself, not a means of easy consolation or moral reassurance as it often is in Longfellow or Holmes. Instead, it is a carefully regulated structural element used rhetorically to provide what M. M. Bakhtin would call a loophole: a linguistic device of adding open-endedness of meaning.[17] For Hawthorne, the open-endedness provided by a controlled humorous voice was a crucial element of his literary function, as he understood it. When he wrote that the effect of *Etheredge* would be "utterly miserable" without "a frolic and dance of bacchanals all over the surface," when he wrote elsewhere of the same work: "It must be a humorous work, or nothing else,"[18] he was openly expressing his long-standing view that genial humor was an essential means of regulating the wilder elements of his imagination and his culture.

Hawthorne had emerged against the background of early subversive humor. His earliest works were written in the late 1820s, the decade when the frontier screamer had first surfaced in popular literature, when bizarre texts such as Irving's *Tales of a Traveller* and John Neal's blackly humorous fiction were published. The structure of Hawthorne tales in which he uses anarchic laughter, such as "My Kinsman, Major Molineux" and "Young Goodman Brown," was not unlike that of fiction by other American authors who emerged during this period, most notably Robert Montgomery Bird and William Gilmore Simms. In works like Simms's *Guy Rivers* and Bird's *Nick of the Woods,* the generally staid prose of the main narrative is periodically interrupted by the explosive laughter and animalistic invectives of the frontier screamer, who enters and leaves the narrative with arbitrary unpredictability. These appearances of the frontier screamer in otherwise stylistically calm novels signal the release of trapped subversive forces that escape as if through an open steam valve. Hawthorne, instinctively attracted to this escape-valve device, used it in key moments of his own fiction. It should be noticed that his blackly humorous, screeching characters are all linked to the frontier: Robin Molineux, we are constantly reminded, is from the backwoods; Goodman Brown is in the heart of the forest when he screams; Ethan Brand's laugh roars through a backwoods landscape of wild mountains and lonely lime kilns; Arthur Dimmesdale's interior laughter about his perverse wish to subvert the ideals of various townspeople occurs after his forest meeting with Hester Prynne. The screeches of these characters were in the tradition of the backwoods-screamer humor that Hawthorne, a close reader of popular newspapers and pamphlets, surely knew.

The key difference between Hawthorne and other novelists who incorporated the screamer character is that his characters' laughter, though often blackly humorous, is never accompanied by the unrestrained bestiality and anarchic expletives that were trademarks of the popular screamer. The screaming laughter in Hawthorne has all the wildness and grotesqueness of the popular laughter, but it also possesses a context, a meaning, and a structural purpose that are absent in the popular texts. This context and purpose derive principally from the fact that Hawthorne never portrayed the screamer character in a nineteenth-century setting but rather surrounded it with settings and images that imbued it with a resonance it lacked in its crude popular surroundings. In "My Kinsman, Major Molineux" the hero's screeching laughter at his degraded uncle is horribly perverse, but it is the natural culmination of a unified tale which begins with a historical review of popular revolts against colonial governors and which builds through gathering images of sarcastic laughter to the climactic screeching scene. This calibrated, artistic use of the scream is light-years distant from that in a novel like Bird's *Nick of the Woods,* in which Roaring Ralph Stackpole periodically appears to flap his wings, bark, growl, and yell at nobody and nothing in particular. Hawthorne again regulates the frontier scream in "Young Goodman Brown," in which the growing cynicism of the protagonist is explosively released in his long laugh as he seizes the devil's staff and runs furiously to the witch meeting in the woods. Religious imagery is the main controlling device in this tale, for the linkage of the frontier screamer with the howling devil automatically lends religious resonance to a figure that in popular humor was totally secular and desacralized. Hawthorne again used the religious to lend depth to the savage screamer in "Ethan Brand," in which the hero's unearthly shriek provides explosive release of his horrifying knowledge that he carries the Unpardonable Sin within his own breast. As gloomy and perverse as these moments of anarchic laughter in Hawthorne's fiction are, they at least have context and significance in the tales wherein they appear, and they are always positioned strategically by a literary craftsman. Hawthorne's artistic regulation of an anarchic popular phenomenon becomes itself a kind of affirmation.

Hawthorne's restoration of depth and significance to popular humor is nowhere more visible than in *The Scarlet Letter.* It has long been noticed that the "Custom-House" preface is full of humor, often black humor, and that even *The Scarlet Letter,* somber as it is in many places, has distinctly humorous images as well. The humor of the novel, however, has not been adequately studied in terms of the popular brands of humor that had emerged in the American 1840s. Once again, Hawthorne incorporates popular humor only to revise it. Toward the beginning of the "Custom-House" preface he introduces a darkly humorous image that mocks a revered national emblem: the American eagle over the custom-house door is described as a vixenly creature who is "apt to fling off her nestlings, with a scratch of her claw, a dab of her beak, or a rankling wound from her barbed arrows."[19] Such ironic undercutting of national emblems was common in the dark humor of radical democrats, who believed that America's republican ideals were mocked by grave injustices in modern America. The abolitionist Frederick Douglass, for instance, insisted that national holidays like the Fourth of July could be viewed only with ironic disdain; similarly, Devil-Bug's nightmare of social apocalypse in Lippard's *The Quaker City* is filled with images of fallen national icons, such as the shredded American flag and the collapsed Philadelphia State House.

Hawthorne, then, was very much in the spirit of the radical-democrat humorists when he began his novel with a sarcastic debunking of a national icon. Indeed, one reason the "Custom-House" preface as a whole was among his most popular performances was that it sustained the black humor that had been introduced in this bloody-eagle image. Many of his contemporary readers were doubtless entertained by the long string of subversive images in the preface. We may imagine them chuckling, for example, at his transposition of the human and the bestial in the description of the Inspector, who has barely enough spirituality to prevent him "from walking on all-fours" and whose voice and laugh "came strutting out of his lungs like the crow of a cock, or the blast of a clarion."[20] They would naturally enjoy reading that the Inspector smacked his lips over dinners "every guest at which, except himself, had long been food for the worms." The entire sequence in which Hawthorne describes his loss of his surveyorship in images of decapitation, suicide, and murder was undoubtedly attractive to those familiar with the black humor of the radical democrats. In his brief preface to the second edition of *The Scarlet Letter,* Hawthorne describes the "unprecedented excitement" created by the "atrocities" of his political satire and then insists the satire consisted only of "frank and genuine good-humor."[21] In light of the subversive humorous devices he was exploiting, we may agree that the trenchant, often grotesque "Custom-House" section was "good-humor" of a genuine American variety.

Hawthorne adopted humorous idioms, however, with the direct aim of *escaping* the miry political and social conditions that had created these idioms. He did not, like popular radical democrats, allow himself to become entangled in the thorny social issues addressed by the dark political humor of his era. Instead, he ambitiously sought artistic receptacles for images and themes that in their crude popular state inevitably ran toward the scabrous and the sensational. "The Custom-House" is a dialectical construct in which he re-creates the custom-house world (figuratively, nineteenth-century America, with its political backbiting, its materialism and flatness, its directionless humor) and at the same time discovers a rich alternative to this modern wasteland in the depths of the past, both his own ancestral past and the nation's past. Hawthorne shows that he can use subversive political humor as effectively as any radical democrat but that finally such humor belongs to the flat, neutral world of the nineteenth century. He wished to retain the ironies and biting images provided by contemporaneous humor but at the same time to imbue them with the resonance provided by the Puritan past, as he understood it. Without this deepening process, modern humor, he suggests, would remain as meaningless as his associates' endless conversations about bygone dinners. The barrenness of the modern scene, as Hawthorne sees it, is epitomized in the Inspector, who seems to have "no soul, no heart, no mind; nothing . . . but instincts."[22] Salem itself has a "flat, unvaried surface" and looks like "a disarranged checkerboard," making one "weary of the old wooden houses, the mud and dust, the dead level of site and sentiment, the chill east wind, and the chillest of all social atmospheres." In this atmosphere, Hawthorne declares, his literary faculties had become "pointless and inefficacious"— they had no direction, no referent, because they had been overwhelmed by the aimless anecdotes and stale humor of his custom-house cronies. Throughout "The Custom-House" he writes political black humor with the aim of leaving behind the world to which that humor belongs. Contemplation of what he calls the "dusky grandeur" and the "moral quality" of the Puritan past regenerates his literary powers by investing them with depth and structure.

Having rhetorically dismissed contemporary humorous idioms in "The Custom-House," he redirects and reconstructs these idioms in The Scarlet Letter. Many of the humorous moments in the novel can be linked in some way with the imagery or themes of nineteenth-century humor. The unmasking humor of the radical democrats, with its devilishly gleeful exposure of hidden sin beneath respectable exteriors, is visible in virtually every chapter of the novel. The explosive humor of the American frontier, with its anarchic laughter, surely contributed to the conception of the second scaffold scene, in which Arthur Dimmesdale, overcome by "a grisly sense of the humorous," lets go a shouting peal of laughter that echoes through the town and the surrounding forest.[23] Even the Barnumesque urban humor of the 1840s was not neglected by Hawthorne. Henry James declared that the appearance of the great A in the heavens, the reference to the scorching quality of Hester's badge, and other strange images in the novel verged upon "physical comedy" because of their outlandishness;[24] but we should recall that in the 1840s, this public parading of the marvelous was an important popular phenomenon prompted by Barnum and the urban humorists. Two years before the publication of *The Scarlet Letter, The John-Donkey* had declared: "Hyperbole and exaggeration are the universal religion, from church to state, from the Capitol to the closet, and the Impossible is the only god of popular idolatry."[25] What might be called the "physical comedy" of *The Scarlet Letter*—the references to supernatural marvels, the theatrical posturings and gloating spectatorship of the scaffold scenes, the constant display of Hester's shame, the electrical, magnetic relationship between main characters—clearly draws from the theatrical manipulation of oddities by Barnum and his ilk.

But the crucial point to recognize is that in Hawthorne's novel all such images of popular humor gain a depth and intensity they lacked in their native state, because they are rechanneled into a religious and historical context that imbues them with connectedness and meaning. In popular humor texts, such images are inevitably exploited for the black humor or freakishness they prompt. In *The Scarlet Letter* they are probed for the psychological torment they cause, the metaphysical speculations they suggest, the deep ironies they engender. As an American novelist addressing a public that had a proven attraction to subversive themes, he had inherited humorous images and idioms he could exploit in his effort to let off the trapped steam of his darkest impulses. But because he allows modern black humor to resonate within a Puritan culture that is described with sympathy and seriousness, this humor never becomes gratuitous or sensational. The thoughtful use of the Puritan context makes possible a serious reconstruction of topics that were often reduced to the trivial in Hawthorne's contemporary popular culture. All the dark humor in the novel is ultimately retributive. It has reference and direction, even while it has extraordinary irony and complexity. Indeed, the whole premise of adultery and revenge is treated much the way Hester's appearance on the scaffold is treated in the opening scene. In the nineteenth century, Hawthorne writes, this scene would be merely "a theme for jest" among heartless spectators enamored of the sensational.[26] In Puritan times, it was a matter of sobriety and magnitude. *The Scarlet Letter* is ample proof that Hawthorne had successfully escaped the neutrally humorous world of the custom house by imaginatively reconstructing a meaningfully humorous fictional world in the Puritan past.

Hawthorne's fusion of nineteenth-century humor devices with historical and literary archetypes was an artistic strategy shared by the writer who most ardently praised Hawthorne's humor, Herman Melville. The predominant narrative voice of Melville's early fiction derived, like that of Hawthorne, from the tradition of reputable humor. When Melville's friend Evert A. Duyckinck wrote in 1847 that Melville "models his writing evidently a great deal on Washington Irving," he was most likely referring to the blitheness and gentle irony that linked Melville's early narrative voice to that of Irving in his most benign moments.[27] The most common adjectives used by reviewers to describe Melville's early novels were "agreeable," "pleasant," "lively," and the like. A typical review, in the *Daily Wisconsin* in 1847, remarked that "Mr. Melville has a peculiarly *popular* style, . . . and therefore whatever he writes is *agreeable,* and will take with the people."[28] As Melville's narrative voice was infiltrated by more subversive elements, reviewers' responses became more ambivalent, as is evidenced by William Harrison Ainsworth's outburst against *Moby-Dick*: "The style is maniacal—mad as a March hare—mowing, gibbering, screaming, like an incurable Bedlamite, reckless of keeper or strait-waistcoat."[29] One of the principal reasons for the increasing complexity of Melville's narrative voice was his openness to humorous idioms that exploded onto the literary scene in the late 1840s. Although certain other writers in Evert Duyckinck's sophisticated literary circle incorporated one or two of these idioms, Melville alone absorbed and artistically reconstructed *all* of them. His unique responsiveness to the tone and images of popular humor accounts for the special zest and pungency of the humorous moments in *Moby-Dick*.

Melville's humor must be evaluated in light of a hitherto unnoticed type of popular American humor, what I term nautical humor, which was a kind of fusion of frontier humor and Barnumesque urban humor, featuring wild comic violence and often an emphasis upon bizarre monsters of the deep. Nautical humor surfaced in certain of the Crockett almanacs of the 1830s, infiltrated the popular pamphlet fiction of the 1840s, and produced at least one long work, Eugene Batchelder's narrative poem *A Romance of the Sea-Serpent* (1849). A main source of fun in nautical humor was the strange pranks that tars played on each other and the wild scrapes they fell into. The pamphlet novel *Life in a Whale Ship* (1841) contains a typical prankish incident in which the narrator is engaged in fisticuffs but is swept up by a running hog (which has been made crazy by raucous boys) and is carried off while a mob of spectators, including his own girlfriend, scream in wild derision. The same novel includes an episode in which a sailor who tumbles into the ocean has a long, terrifying ride on the back of a porpoise. Melville exploited this sort of nautical prankishness in his early novels, particularly in *Omoo,* in which the harpooner Mowree is taken for a wild ride on a whale's back and the eccentric ship's doctor, Long Ghost, plays practical jokes, such as hoisting shipmates aloft by their feet or shoulders while they are asleep. Melville explains the tricks of this "decided wag" as follows: "Every one knows what lovers of fun sailors are ashore—afloat, they are absolutely mad after it. So his pranks were duly appreciated."[30] The jovial, sometimes savage fun of nautical humor was never distant from Melville's imagination in his formative stage.

While popular nautical humor had prepared the way for Melville's use of the prankish, it helps to explain only a small part of the humor in *Moby-Dick.* The special Americanness of Melville's masterpiece lies in the breadth of native humorous idioms it incorporates. It was Melville's responsiveness to other forms of popular humor—particularly radical-democrat humor and urban humor—that most distinguished him from other nautical romancers of the period. Radical-democrat humor lies behind the bitingly subversive tone of *Moby-Dick* and behind the strongly egalitarian characterization of Queequeg, Ishmael, and Stubb. Urban humor directly influenced specific scenes, such as the cook Fleece's comic sermon to the sharks, and generated a fund of inventive reapplications of popular fads and movements throughout the novel. The humor of *Moby-Dick* has been called Shakespearian in its use, for instance, of the madman-fool relationship between Ahab and Pip, obviously reminiscent of *King Lear.* But the Shakespearian elements of *Moby-Dick* are, by and large, reconstructive devices used to enrich native humorous idioms that Melville was seeking to rescue from the savage or the merely perverse.

The importance of radical-democrat humor for Melville's literary development is capsulized in his portrayal of a central character in *Moby-Dick,* Queequeg. The Negro characters in Melville's earlier novels, such as Baltimore of *Omoo* or Mr. Thompson of *Redburn,* had been caricatured stereotypes who lacked Queequeg's unique combination of savagery and humaneness, principally because they had not been treated from a radical-democrat perspective. Melville arrived at the rich character of Queequeg after observing closely one of the most progressive tendencies of popular literature of the late 1840s. The broadening of his sensibility had resulted from his growing sensitivity to the combined grotesque humor and extreme egalitarianism of popular radical-democrat literature, which had depicted even the most fierce oppressed peoples and minority groups as more noble than secretly corrupt social leaders. In his characterization of Queequeg, Melville seems to have been particularly indebted to George Lippard, the most popular radical-democrat novelist of the day. Lippard's best-selling volumes *Blanche of Brandywine* (1846) and *Washington and His Generals* (1847) both had included memorable episodes involving a massive Negro soldier of the American Revolution, Black Sampson, who slashed through British lines with his tremendous scythe waving and his dog "Debbil" by his side. The Black Sampson episode suggests both the positive and the negative sides of the radical-democrat imagination in its crude popular state. Throughout his historical fiction Lippard underscores the special heroism of common people—farmers, blacksmiths, and so forth—who during the Revolution showed their combined patriotism and working-class fervor by seizing instruments of their trade, such as hammers and axes, as they rushed into battle. This radical-democrat egalitarianism had special import in the portrayal of Black Sampson, who is not only poor but also a Negro savage haunted by memories of his former noble stature as the son of the king of an African tribe. Lippard makes an innovative contribution to American literature when he stresses that Sampson, a pagan Negro, was one of the proudest and best soldiers in General Washington's army. This extremely sympathetic treatment of a Negro character was a testament to Lippard's sympathy for oppressed groups. But, in typical fashion, Lippard allows the Black Sampson episode to degenerate into grotesque black humor. Sampson seizes his gigantic scythe and rushes into battle, decapitating and dismembering British soldiers with utter brutality and with obvious love of gore. He screams to his dog, "We am gwin' mowin' today," and indeed mows down every soldier in sight; Lippard's potentially refreshing humanistic message about the innate nobleness of Negroes is lost in his gleeful fascination with perverse violence.[31] This blackly humorous interest in sheer brutality is epitomized in a long digression in *Blanche of Brandywine* that includes the following grisly words: "Dark and mysterious are the instincts of man. . . . [M]ost horrible of all, is the instinct of Carnage! Yes, that Instinct which makes a man thirst for blood, which makes him mad with joy, when he steeps his arms to the elbows in his foeman's gore, which makes him shout and halloo, and laugh, as he goes murdering on over piles of dead!"[32]

In portraying Queequeg, Melville reverses the pattern of the Black Sampson episode. He begins with blackly humorous images but moves to a fully humane treatment of the noble black man. Lippard had concluded his episode with a fiendish picture of his Negro savage mowing down humans with his tremendous scythe. Melville begins with the image of the deadly scythe and then progresses through various blackly humorous scenes toward a consoling portrait of Queequeg's redemptive humaneness. When in Chapter 3 Ishmael enters the Spouter-Inn, he sees hanging on the wall several "heathenish" weapons, the most terrifying of which is "sickle-shaped, with a vast handle sweeping round like the segment made in the new-mown grass by a long-armed mower," making Ishmael wonder "what monstrous cannibal and savage could have ever gone a death-harvesting with such a hacking, horrifying implement."[33] Having initiated the Spouter-Inn sequence with this Lippardian image, Melville remains, through this and the following chapter, in the realm of popular black humor: Ishmael learns that Queequeg is having trouble selling his head because "the market's overstocked"; we hear that the previous Sunday Queequeg had left the inn to sell a string of heads that looked like onions; when Queequeg leaps into bed next to Ishmael he screams, "Who-e debel you?" and Ishmael in turn yells for the landlord, Peter Coffin. To this point, the tone of Melville's episode is not distant from the end of Lippard's. The huge deadly sickle, the images of mowing and death harvesting, the references to decapitation and dismemberment, the word "debel"—all of these images place Melville's episode in the familiar arena of popular dark humor.

Melville, however, prevents the sequence from descending to the merely perverse. Rather than allow his savage character to become a grisly emblem of gleeful carnage, as does Lippard, Melville makes him an emblem of universal love. He is able to do so primarily because he is more open than Lippard to the *reconstructive* possibilities of the radical-democrat vision. He is able to lift Queequeg out of the mire of black humor primarily because he has him embraced by a narrator who has all the markings of that flexible American character, the b'hoy. In "Hawthorne and His Mosses" Melville had stressed the need for the American writer to "carry republican progressiveness into Literature" by seeking indigenous themes and characters.[34] He found such a character in the b'hoy, a character that Melville's fellow New Yorker George Thompson had identified in 1850 as the most distinctly American of all cultural figures. The b'hoy had gained prominence in New York popular literature between 1848 and 1850, at precisely the moment when Melville was a struggling New York novelist churning out the popular-oriented *Redburn* and *White-Jacket,* novels with strong radical-democrat themes. Having inundated himself in the popular radical-democrat consciousness, he emerged in *Moby-Dick* with a narrative voice that was different from that of his earlier novels, one that profited greatly from the complex b'hoy figure. In the opening pages of the novel Ishmael is established as the indigent, loafing, acute, brash, genially wicked New Yorker who plays pranks, hates respectable jobs, and aches for adventure. Melville's contemporary readers surely saw the signs of the b'hoy in an unconventional narrator who boasts that he travels not with commodores and who abominates "all honorable respectable toils, trials, and tribulations of every kind whatsoever."[35] Ishmael's declaration "Who aint a slave? Tell me that" would have had a familiar ring to those aware of the great b'hoy leader Mike Walsh, who by 1850 had become nationally famous for his argument that both Northern wage earners and Southern chattels were equally slaves of the capitalist system. The capacity of the b'hoy to be simultaneously virtuous and wicked is echoed in Ishmael's flexible spirit, as typified by his comment: "Not ignoring what is good, I am quick to perceive a horror, and could . . . be social with it[.]"

But in the process of adopting the b'hoy Melville reconstructs him. Ishmael was not the first b'hoy narrator in American fiction, but he was the first who was pressed as far as possible in the direction of the humane and the broadly tolerant. He is the b'hoy reconceived by a writer who recognized the universal, fully human potentialities of his own culture's popular images. The early chapters of *Moby-Dick* make clear that Melville was thoroughly familiar with the blackly humorous, cynical underside of radical-democrat humor; but they also show that he was more willing than any other novelist of his day to capitalize upon the affirmative, richly emotive possibilities as well. Ishmael is not merely the "Mose" or "Sikesey" of popular fiction and plays, the punchy b'hoy who mocks aristocrats and elicits snickers with his latest prank. He is also the flexible, loving youth who stirs our deepest democratic sympathies when he embraces a man he had previously feared as a bloodthirsty cannibal. Queequeg, for his part, is not another Black Sampson, the patriotic soldier who dissolves into a sanguinary demon of battle. At first he does seem a sanguinary demon, but he proves himself a fully realized embodiment of Black Sampson's best qualities. Whereas Black Sampson goes to perverse extremes as a member of George Washington's army, Queequeg is, as Ishmael declares, "George Washington cannibalistically developed," a pagan savage who becomes admirable because of his tenderness and generosity.[36] The "marriage" between Ishmael and Queequeg has been interpreted by Leslie Fiedler and others as Melville's projected homoerotic fantasy. There may indeed be sexual overtones in the scene in which Ishmael awakes to find himself half buried in Queequeg's affectionate embrace. More to Melville's point than sexual fantasy, however, is the fully human version of his culture's stereotypes he achieves. He rescues both the brash b'hoy and the savage warrior from the barren arena of black humor by burrowing beneath the cheapened radical democracy of popular culture to a genuine radical democracy signaled by deep affection between two good-hearted human beings of different races.

The bond between Ishmael and Queequeg is not the only example in the novel of Melville's ennoblement of radical-democrat humor. Other key instances appear in his treatments of the mate Stubb and the crew of the *Pequod.* Stubb is described as "one of those odd sort of humorists, whose jollity is sometimes so curiously ambiguous."[37] This comically churlish, grinning mate is highly derivative of radical-democrat humor in its darkest form. We have seen that the irony of radical democrats often went beyond social criticism to dark generalizations about a world that suddenly seemed profoundly awry. The word "queer" had a special significance in the radical-democrat lexicon, for it summoned up the skewed reality that these dark humorists perceived. George Lippard again stands out as the main popularizer of this word, for his writings are filled with sarcastic comments about the "queer" arrangement of things. "Queer world this!" exclaims a character in a typical moment in Lippard's *The Quaker City.* "Don't know much about other worlds, but it strikes me that if a prize were offered somewhere by somebody, for the queerest world a-going, this world of ours might be rigged up nice, and sent in like a bit of show beef, as the premium queer world."[38] So significant was this term to Lippard that in 1849 his weekly reform newspaper, *The Quaker City,* featured a regular column entitled "It Is a Queer World," which reported grotesque social injustices. Melville, who in 1849 probed social wrongs in his reformist novel *White-Jacket,* also came to view this wry word as especially descriptive of perceived reality. As he was in the final stage of writing *Moby-Dick* he wrote Hawthorne a letter in which he imagined the two of them sitting cross-legged in heaven, drinking champagne, and singing what he called "humorous, comic songs, 'Oh, when I lived in that queer little hole called the world[.]' "[39]

In *Moby-Dick,* this radical-democrat sarcasm is embodied in Stubb, whose favorite word is "queer." When Ahab strikes him and sends him below, Stubb mutters, "It's very queer. . . . It's queer; very queer; and he's queer too; aye, take him fore and aft, he's about the queerest old man Stubb ever sailed with. . . . Damn me, but all things are queer, come to think of 'em."[40] In his midnight soliloquy on the forecastle he declares that "a laugh's the wisest, easiest answer to all that's queer," and his response to the doubloon is a dismissive "Humph! in my poor, insignificant opinion, I regard this as queer." The ship's carpenter sums Stubb up well when he comments that "Stubb always says he's queer; says nothing but that one sufficient little word queer; he's queer—queer, queer; and keeps dinning it into Mr. Starbuck all the time—queer, sir—queer, queer, very queer." In addition to parroting the radical democrats' favorite cynical word, Stubb is closely linked to the bizarre, nightmarish imagery of the popular subversive imagination. We have seen that much popular humor became so experimental in its kaleidoscopic imagery that it verged upon the presur-realistic. Two of the strangest moments in *Moby-Dick* pertain to Stubb's overactive, disordered imagination. In Chapter 31 he reports his "queer dream" in which he tries to kick Ahab, who, shockingly enough, turns into a pyramid, which Stubb pummels with his leg until he is approached by a humpbacked merman, who turns threateningly to show Stubb a back studded with marlinespikes and then, after advising Stubb not to kick the pyramid anymore, seems "in some queer fashion, to swim off into the air." The second bizarre moment is when Stubb tries to comment on the doubloon: his remarks are a strange tangle of shifting, circular astrological readings.

In his portrayal of Stubb, Melville captures with marvelous concision the leering sarcasm and nightmarish imagery of popular humorists, particularly extreme radical democrats. Stubb represents the centrifugal forces of popular dark humor, the forces that fly quickly into the cynical and the chaotic as a result of a disillusion with perceived reality. These centrifugal forces are also embodied in the *Pequod*'s crew, particularly in the picture in Chapter 40 of the crew's boisterous revel in the forecastle. The black humor of the radical democrats was often punctuated by scenes of orgies meant to reflect the wildness and savagery lurking below the civilized surfaces of life. In Lippard's *The Quaker City* there is the freakish scene in which drunken characters whip themselves into a frenzy reflected in incoherent exclamations, erotic oaths, and complete noncommunication. It is this kind of disorganized blasphemy that Melville re-creates in the forecastle revel. Like much American Subversive humor, it firmly dismisses the Conventional (the first Nantucket sailor exclaims, "Oh, boys, don't be sentimental; it's bad for the digestion!"[41]) and proceeds into an inconsequential succession of oaths and jests that include a Lippardian mixture of sexual and dark images, such as warm bosoms, dancing on graves, lithe limbs, and the brevity of life. Like so many scenes in popular Subversive texts, this one culminates in sadistic threats between bloodthirsty characters who engage in a terrible brawl.

In addition to adopting savage radical-democrat humor, Melville incorporates in *Moby-Dick* techniques and images of urban humor. Melville had immersed himself in the new urban humor in his comic series "Authentic Anecdotes of 'Old Zack,'" which he had written in 1847 for Cornelius Mathews's pioneering urban humor periodical *Yankee Doodle*. Perhaps the chief strategy Melville had learned from the "Old Zack" series was that many phenomena of the contemporary cultural scene could be used with the zestful theatricality of the master-showman Phineas T. Barnum. He mentioned Barnum constantly throughout the "Old Zack" series, and surely the spirit of this great peddler of freaks and oddities lies behind many of the wondrous images in *Moby-Dick*, including the bizarre sights Ishmael encounters in New Bedford, the grotesque decorations that adorn the *Pequod*, and the overall interest in the monstrous and the outlandish. Melville seems to have been most directly indebted to Barnum in his conception of the crew of the *Pequod*. In 1849, the year before Melville began to write *Moby-Dick*, Barnum had publicized his lifelong plan for convening a "congress of All Nations," an assemblage of representatives of all the nations that could be reached by land or sea. He later recalled: "I meant to secure a man and a woman, as perfect as could be procured, from every accessible people, civilized or barbarous, on the face of the globe."[42] What Barnum failed to do in reality, Melville came close to accomplishing in fiction, for representatives of numerous nations are gathered on the *Pequod,* whose crew, Melville stresses, is an "Anacharsis Clootz deputation from all the isles of the sea, and all the ends of the earth."[43]

An even more direct influence of urban humor upon *Moby-Dick* is visible in the portrayal of the black cook Fleece and the crazed cabin boy Pip. Both are variations upon the Negro preacher featured in William H. Levison's burlesque sermon series published in *The New York Picayune* from 1847 onward and later collected in two popular volumes, *Julius Caesar Hannibal* and *Black Diamonds.* Fleece's comic sermon to the sharks in Chapter 64 is an adaptation of the style and content of burlesque sermons by Levison's Julius Caesar Hannibal, the pedantic, ill-spoken black preacher who regaled antebellum humor readers with his darkly humorous discourses (called "black diamonds") on countless topics. Just as Levison's Hannibal inevitably began his sermons with blessings such as "Blubed Sinners" or "Helpluss Brutheren," so Melville's Fleece addresses his congregation as "Belubed fellow-critters." Melville's contemporary readers would have found a familiar amusement in the fact that Fleece uses sharks as his text, because Levison's Hannibal had preached funny sermons about many strange animals: the crocodile, the lobster, the monkey, the elephant, the hog, and the whale. Nor would they have been surprised by Fleece's ultimately cynical message—the horrifying voraciousness of the sharks, symbolizing the universal cannibalism of humankind and nature—for Hannibal frequently emphasized human savagery. In a typical sermon on "Future Punishment" Hannibal stressed that the concept of an afterlife, though dubious, was necessary for preventing humans from becoming totally amoral; without some hope of heaven or fear of hell, Hannibal said, "man wouldn't stop to oney murder he feller man, but he'd sell de bones to de button factory and de flesh to de sassenger makers de same as dey do dogs in dese days," and "de kanal botes would float in de blood ob mankind, and all creation would stan palsied wid a fright."[44] This pronouncement is similar in spirit to that of Fleece, who talks about the afterlife to the bloodthirsty sharks, while Hannibal's image of all creation being "palsied wid a fright" is close to Ishmael's conclusion that "the palsied universe lies before us a leper."[45] It is not surprising that even some of Melville's most devilish reflections in *Moby-Dick* were thus anticipated in popular culture, for Levison was writing in the vein of subversive American humor. Fleece's conclusion that it was "no use a-preachin' to such dam g'uttons" would seem a natural piece of dark humor to readers of Levison's burlesque sermons.

Melville's adaptation of Levison's Hannibal not only produced Fleece;

it also influenced the portrayal of Pip, the black cabin boy who goes crazy after falling into the ocean and whose commentary on the main characters is a kind of insanely inspired chorus running through the late chapters of the novel. Levison had popularized "black diamonds"—that is, the darkly humorous sayings of Julius Caesar Hannibal. Melville took the further step of creating an actual black diamond: a character who emerges from the depths inspired with a dark wisdom that can be expressed only in mad laughter. The connection between Melville's and Levison's characters would have been immediately apparent to nineteenth-century readers, for when Pip is introduced he is compared at length to a diamond. Emphasizing that "this little black was brilliant, for even blackness has its brilliancy," Melville describes the increased brilliancy created by Pip's dreary nautical environment by noting: "[W]hen the cunning jeweler would show you the diamond in its most impressive lustre, he lays it against a gloomy ground, and then lights it up, not by the sun, but by some unnatural gases. Then come out those fiery effulgences, infernally superb; then the evil-blazing diamond, once the divinest symbol of the crystal skies, looks like some crown-jewel stolen from the King of Hell."[46] In time, Pip becomes a kind of living embodiment of the "black diamonds" Hannibal delivers in his lectures, for the darkest of Hannibal's reflections, pertaining to relativism of all human viewpoints, are acted out by the insane cabin boy. A bleak undercurrent of the burlesque sermons of Levison's Hannibal is the suspicion that warring interpretations of God and the world invalidate absolute truth. In a typically cynical moment Hannibal declares that religious denominations "all tell you dat if you don't belibe jis as dey do, and come into de 'stablished church, you am lost obberboard in de big gulf ob sin; *all* de churches am 'tablished churches, and dey all tink de rode dey hab picked out trough de miserable thickets ob trouble, wexations, and odder grevences ob dis life, am de rite one, and de odders am all rong."[47] While Hannibal's perception of relativism is punctuated by the image of falling "obberboard in de big gulf ob sin," Pip's similar perception comes after he literally falls overboard and plunges to the ocean's depths, where he has a shattering vision of primal truths. The madness that overtakes him is most memorably expressed at the end of the scene in which he overhears the main characters' radically heterogeneous views of the doubloon. The kind of bemused bafflement that Hannibal expresses when he contemplates warring faiths is concisely communicated in Pip's relativist outburst: "I look, you look, he looks; we look, ye look, they look."[48] Melville has converted the "black diamonds" of one of his age's leading urban humorists, Levison, into a memorable fictional character whose insane wisdom shines luridly over the conclusion of his wicked novel.

Much of the demonic energy and subversive reflectiveness of *Moby-Dick*, then, derives from Melville's openness to the dark radical-democrat and urban humor of his day. While these, along with nautical humor, were the predominant humorous influences on the novel, Melville did not neglect wild frontier humor of the Crockett-almanac variety. In the course of *Moby-Dick* he mentions three frontier heroes—Davy Crockett, Daniel Boone, Kit Carson—and in his characterization of Peleg and Stubb he captures the hyperbolic oaths and comic violence of frontier humor. Peleg's vow that he will "swallow a live goat with all his hair and horns on" and Stubb's boast that he will pull off the devil's tail and sell it as an ox whip are typical of frontier humor, as is the tinder-box pugnaciousness of these characters.[49]

Surveying the comic elements of *Moby-Dick,* we can safely say that this is the *only* American literary work of the antebellum period that incorporates *all* popular humorous idioms of the day. Ahab's symbolic outcry— "Its wood could only be American"—is particularly descriptive of the dark humor that Melville absorbed from popular American literature. In "Hawthorne and His Mosses" Melville defined the "American genius" as "that explosive sort of stuff [which] will expand though screwed up in a vice, and burst it, though it were triple steel."[50] This explosive force of American genius was felt particularly in the wild, often black humor that had surged into the urban literary market in the 1840s and that was fully represented in *Moby-Dick.* The American Subversive Style, which had been most visible in the shifts and quirks of dark popular humor, helps account for the stylistic richness of Melville's masterpiece. The centrifugal forces of subversive humor give rise not only to many bizarre images, such as Stubb's dream or Pip's disjointed outbursts, but also to the overall stylistic flexibility and variety of Melville's masterpiece. This stylistic fluidity is captured in Ishmael's comment: "Out of the trunk, the branches grow; out of them, the twigs. So, in productive subjects, grow the chapters."[51] A novel so inclusive of centrifugal humorous modes as *Moby-Dick* naturally becomes stylistically experimental.

Here, however, a crucial distinction must be made between subversive humor as it appears in popular texts and as it is transformed by Melville. At least since he had written *Mardi,* Melville had been aware that to incorporate demonic humor was to risk sacrificing unity and depth. "Authentic Anecdotes of 'Old Zack,' " the one wholly humorous work he had produced, had been characteristic of popular humor in its disjointedness and tonal inconsistency. Stubb, the one wholly humorous character in *Moby-Dick,* is a living emblem of such tonal inconsistency, as is evidenced even in his most apparently spontaneous utterances, his exhortations to his boat crew during whale chases. Note the wild shifts from the softly consoling to the devilishly urgent in this Stubb command: "Easy, easy; don't be in a hurry—don't be in a hurry. Why don't you snap your oars, you rascals? Bite something, you dogs! So, so, then;—softly, softly! . . . The devil fetch ye, ye ragamuffin rapscallions; ye are all asleep."[52] Stubb's schizoid commands are among the phenomena that lead Ishmael to describe him as "one of those odd sort of humorists" whose jollity is "curiously ambiguous." Stubb epitomizes a tendency toward the stylistically chaotic that Melville recognized was the final literary expression of the subversive energies of America's democratic culture. In *Mardi* he had described Mardi's great national epic, Lombardo's "Kostanza," as a dense but structureless poem which, in the words of the philosopher Babbalanja, "lacks cohesion; it is wild, unconnected."[53] In writing his own national epic, *Moby-Dick,* Melville knew that it was precisely such wildness and structurelessness that spoiled much popular humor and threatened to destroy the fully absorptive literary text. As a counterbalance to the centrifugal forces of popular humor, he introduced humanizing and structuring devices that rechanneled these forces toward the deeply philosophical and the fully human.

Throughout *Moby-Dick* every potentially anarchic image or character related to American black humor is fused with some counterbalancing image or character that prevents it from tumbling into the netherworld of thematic chaos. In the hands of a typical radical-democrat humorist, Queequeg would have quickly degenerated into an uncontrolled savage like Lippard's Black Sampson, just as Ishmael would have become just another punchy Mose or Sikesey. Because he avoids such cheapening and discovers the *truly* democratic possibilities of the radical-democrat vision, he forges their "marriage," which humanizes them and mollifies their potential savagery. Such images of human interconnectedness or union can be seen almost everywhere in the novel: in the crew's adoption of Ahab's monomaniacal purpose; in Ishmael's joining the wild shouts of the crew after its forecastle revel; in the reference to the motley crew as "federated along one keel"; in the passage praising the "great democratic God" that unites all human hearts; in the image of the monkey-rope, showing the symbiotic relationships among all human beings; in the loving squeeze of hands in the sperm vat.[54] Blackly humorous images are never allowed a long life of their own, as they often are in the less structured popular texts. Instead, they are always reined in by contrasting images or levels of rhetoric. Thus, the bizarre Chapter 31, describing Stubb's queer dream, is immediately followed by the rational, expository "Cetology" chapter. The sharkish crew is counterbalanced by the practical Starbuck, the rambunctious Stubb and insane Pip by the tyrannical Ahab, and all the sailors are driven by the common incentive of winning the doubloon and the common goal of destroying the white whale.

Besides introducing these fusing devices, Melville generates depth and meaning by coupling nineteenth-century images with archetypes from classic literature and philosophy. Perhaps the best example of this strategy is the characterization of Ahab. In fashioning Ahab, Melville was confronted with a delicate problem. Driven by an instinct to carry what he called "republican progressiveness into Literature,"[55] he must forge a thoroughly American character who could reflect or absorb the energetic, often disturbing images of democratic culture. At the same time, he wished to make use of literary archetypes that would aid in giving control and depth to these images. The character he created is a fully American figure who nevertheless transcends American culture. Ahab's Americanness lies in his stature as an imaginative synthesis of many of the most visible stereotypes in American popular culture. Ahab is simultaneously the towering immoral reformer striking through the mask, the ungodly, godlike oxymoronic oppressor, the justified criminal taking revenge against a being that has injured him, and the attractively devilish sea captain of Dark Adventure fiction. He is not, however, *only* quintessentially American. He is also a literary figure of mythic stature: he is the evil Ahab described in I Kings; he is the doomed overreacher of Renaissance drama; he is Faust, Lear, Prometheus. Permeated with archetypal resonances, he represents the contemplative Melville who sets out adventurously on a philosophical quest for truth. The quest is ultimately self-destructive and truth remains tantalizingly elusive; but this ambiguity does not place *Moby-Dick* at odds with American culture, as is commonly believed. What distinguishes this novel from its many popular prototypes is that it absorbs numerous American images and treats them not frivolously or haphazardly, as did popular texts, but instead takes them seriously, salvages them from the anarchically directionless, and gives them new humanity and mythic reference. Melville's philosophical quest may be dangerous, but it is also exhilarating and finally joyful. Its joy lies in its unparalleled intensity. Upon completing the novel Melville could express his paradoxical feeling of danger and peace by writing to Hawthorne: "I have written a wicked book, and feel spotless as the lamb. Ineffable socialities are in me."[56] Having written a novel that fully absorbed the subversive forces of his own culture, Melville could nonetheless feel warmly calm and loving because he had produced a lasting testament to the creative spirit of humankind.

Just as *Moby-Dick* salvaged several types of popular humor that had reached their height of popularity during the American 1840s, *The Confidence-Man* (1857) transformed the even stranger humor that flowered during the 1850s. It was in the 1850s, we should recall, that frontier humor reached a sophisticated level of stylization in the writings of George Washington Harris, while urban humor reached an experimental extreme in periodicals such as *Diogenes, hys Lantern* and *The New York Picayune,* as well as in the writings of Mortimer Neal Thompson. It was in this later humor that the disruptive American Subversive Style was consciously sought as a goal in itself, while many popular phenomena, from women's rights to sensational literature, were manipulated and toyed with from a purely comic perspective. In the intensifying debate over the slavery issue, the air was electric with cries of "Disunion!" and the social tensions that later would explode in the Civil War were enacted in a humorous style that was more disorienting than any that had yet appeared. Harris's Sut Lovingood characteristically boasted: "I ladles out my words at random like a calf kickin at yaller-jackets."[57] Mortimer Neal Thompson, recording his fears of national disunion in his blackly humorous narrative poem *Plu-Ri-Bus-Tah* (1856), described in the poem's preface his intention to "distort facts, to mutilate the records, to belie history, to outrage common sense" in a work "without plot, plan, or regard for the rules of grammar."[58] This militantly fragmented humor of the 1850s was a half-funny, half-cynical reflection of a social reality that struck the humorists as coming apart at the seams. By exaggerating the disunifying effects of sectional controversies and modern fads, the humorists inscribed the rising cultural complexities that intrigued and appalled them.

The Confidence-Man was simultaneously an enactment of and a commentary upon the themes and devices of this new popular humor. The first chapter of the novel shows immediately that Melville had reached the same conclusion about American society that many humorists of the 1850s had: in the Barnumesque carnival of popular culture, all is reduced to theater and entrepreneurial manipulation. Biblical verities have no real voice, no potent means of expression in this culture: they are chalked on a sign for public display and are carried by a jaded deaf-mute who fails to divert the crowds that are gathered eagerly around a sensational criminal poster and buying lurid crime pamphlets. The crowds push aside the deaf-mute, with his sign about charity, but they feel perfectly comfortable with the churlish barber whose pasteboard sign "NO TRUST" epitomizes the prevailing subversive spirit of the scene.

Indeed, subversiveness defines the stylistic texture of the entire novel, which is in many senses a quintessential example of the late American Subversive Style as developed by the humorists of the 1850s. Just as George Washington Harris had featured a comic hero who ladled out his words at random, so Melville cultivated the illusion of randomness in many of the dialogues and chapter sequences in the novel. Just as Mortimer Neal Thompson bragged of producing a narrative without plot or plan, so Melville produced a radically experimental novel that thrives on discontinuity and disorientation. Just as P. T. Barnum in his 1855 autobiography blithely gave his recipes for humbugging the gullible American public, so Melville made smooth chicanery the premise of his novel. Just as the urban humor periodicals increasingly mocked modern fads and movements, so Melville left barely a popular movement unmentioned in *The Confidence-Man,* which contains comic references to women's rights, spirit rapping, quack doctors, philanthropy, temperance, abolitionism, and other cultural phenomena commonly featured by the urban humorists.

In addition to these overall affinities to late subversive humor, *The Confidence-Man* utilizes several images that link it to specific humorous texts. Chicanery aboard riverboats was hardly a new topic in American humor: it had been treated skillfully in the first half of John Neal's *The Down-Easters* (1833) and in a brief episode of Poe's "Diddling" (1843) and had been updated in Barnum's popular autobiography, published just two years before Melville's novel. Barnum, declaring that he had a special attraction for tricking boat passengers, confessed he had played "numerous" hoaxes on boats, including several that involved barbers.[59] When Melville made double-dealing related to a boat barber central in *The Confidence-Man,* he may have had in mind the famous incident, retold in the Barnum autobiography, involving Barnum's trickery of a credulous barber aboard a Louisville steamboat on the Mississippi. When Barnum caused a quarter to disappear beneath a card, the barber swore Barnum was in league with the devil. Barnum, conceding he had been in league with the devil for several years, terrified the barber by using apparent black magic to transfer the barber's money from a safe to a drawer and by threatening to change him into a black cat. The devil imagery surrounding Melville's confidence man and the hoax involving the *Fidèle*'s barber and his money was, therefore, part of a tradition of Barnumesque humor.

Other major sources of the novel's topical humor include the two leading urban humor periodicals of the 1850s, *The Lantern* and *The New York Picayune.* Melville had special reason to take note of *The Lantern,* for in 1852 and 1853 this feisty biweekly ran spoofs of several of his novels, including *Typee, Omoo, Mardi,* and *Pierre.* In its October 16, 1852, review of *Pierre* it had declared: "We hereby commend our friend, Herman, either to resign his pen altogether or to choose different subjects." In *The Confidence-Man* Melville did choose different subjects, some of them directly connected to topics that were the source of comedy or satire in *The Lantern.* For one thing, he seems to be satirically answering the magazine's attacks on him in the heated conversation between the Cosmopolitan and Pitch about Diogenes. Now, the full name of *The Lantern* was *Diogenes, hys Lantern,* and it featured several darkly comic articles and poems with titles such as "The Didactics of Diogenes" or "The Philosophy of Diogenes." When at the end of Chapter 24 of *The Confidence-Man* Pitch declares that the Cosmopolitan is Diogenes in disguise, the Cosmopolitan angrily retorts: "I, Diogenes? I, he who, going a step beyond misanthropy, was less a man-hater than a man-hooter?"[60] In addition to linking his central character with the cynical Greek philosopher Diogenes, Melville here seems to be throwing a barb at *Diogenes, hys Lantern,* the humor magazine that had proved itself an unfriendly "man-hooter" in its attacks on his fiction.

But Melville was interested less in personal reprisal than in the studied assimilation and transformation of subjects and devices popularized in the urban humor periodicals. Melville's debt to the contemporary urban literary marketplace is underscored in the digression on fiction writing in Chapter 44, which contains the generalization: "In nearly all the original characters, loosely accounted such in works of invention, there is discernible something prevailingly local, or of the age[.]" In particular, the novelist looks to the urban scene for rich character types. "Where does any novelist pick up any character?" Melville asks. "For the most part, in town, to be sure. Every town is a kind of man-show, where the novelist goes for his stock, just as the agriculturalist goes to the cattle-show for his."[61] To a large degree Melville here was describing his own strategy in *The Confidence-Man* of adopting many of his culture's favorite stereotypes. His themes and characters were indeed "prevailingly local" and were discovered mainly "in town"—that is, in the urban literature of his day. We have traced in previous chapters how he revised popular stereotypes such as the immoral reformer, the confidence man, and the likable criminal. If he raided reform and sensational literature for these types, he scoured urban humor writings for equally rich material.

Indeed, the novel he calls "our comedy"[62] seems almost a pastiche of comic images from the urban humor of the 1850s. Witness the satirical use of the notion of charity that runs throughout *The Confidence-Man,* particularly in the early chapters. In exposing charity as a mechanical ruse and a heartless business, Melville was reiterating a common satiric theme of urban humor. *The Lantern,* for example, had in February 1853 run a cynically humorous piece indicting modern forms of charity as follows:

At present day Charity is fashionable, but fashion in fathering charity has corrupted it as it corrupts everything which is brought within the reach of its artificial touchstone. The history of the world is one great game of *leap-frog,* in which the savage has leapt over the brute, the man over the savage and oh, enlightened age! the philanthropist over the man. Virtues having long since been twisted into fashionable vice, it was natural that philanthropy should become hypocrisy.[63]

This passage on the corruption of charity could be used as a gloss of a good part of *The Confidence-Man.* From the first scene, in which charity is reduced to easily erased inscriptions on the deaf-mute's placard, through the false charity shown toward Black Guinea and the later references to commercialized philanthropy to the final transformation of the wily confidence man into Philanthropos, Melville constantly dramatizes the concept of twisted charity that was a standard joke among the urban humorists. He even adopts specific ruses from popular exposés of false charity. The man in gray's appeal for donations to his phony Seminole Widow and Orphan Asylum recalls a humorous piece in the February 9, 1856, issue of *The New York Picayune* about a pious woman who inveigles people to give "in support of an Orphan Asylum that had no existence, except in the imagination of the directress." In studying with bitter humor various poseurs of charity, Melville was very much in the spirit of the popular urban humorists.

Ersatz charity was not the only subject that Melville shared with the urban humorists. The theatricality of contemporary preachers was another. When in Chapter 6 of *The Confidence-Man* the man in gray points to the Methodist clergyman, asking, "Does all the world act? . . . Is my reverend friend here, too, a performer?" he is playing with the sort of irony that had governed an 1852 piece in the *Picayune* which characterized the typical American minister as "the head performer," one of "the fashionable actors of the present day."[64] Melville's interpolated story of Thomas Fry, the honest cooper unfairly turned into an imprisoned criminal and cynical drifter, is not distant from a June 1856 *Picayune* article, "Cell 39; or The Convict's Story," about a hardworking, honest man whose virtue goes unrewarded and who soon "emerged from the cocoon of honesty, a full fledged buttery rascal."[65] Melville's satire on Emerson and Thoreau, who appear as Mark Winsome and his follower Egbert, is also in the satirical spirit of the urban humorists. "Emersonia," a typical anti-Transcendentalist piece in *The Lantern* on May 1, 1852, had taken Emerson's choppy logic, rhapsodic language, and recondite allusions to a ridiculous extreme in a long parody that is full of obscurities and circular reasoning. Similarly, Melville parodies the Transcendentalists' inconsistencies and learned double-talk in his portrayal of Winsome and Egbert. The interpolated tale of Goneril, the mannish woman who successfully uses the services of a women's rights lawyer to regain custody of the child she had maltreated, driving her wretched husband into lonely world wanderings, is Melville's version of antifeminist satire, one of the most common forms of urban humor in the 1850s. In general, the humorous use of popular fads and movements throughout the novel shows Melville manipulating contemporary cultural phenomena with the bitter irony of the urban humorists.

Despite its many affinities with urban humor, however, *The Confidence-Man* achieves unique literary status because it fuses disparate popular images and imbues them with new resonance and structure. In Chapter 33, containing a digression on the art of fiction writing, Melville writes that he sympathizes with readers who seek in novels not merely "novelty" but "nature, too; . . . nature unfettered, exhilarated, in effect transformed."[66] This transforming power of the good novelist leads to the creation of an artifact that is linked closely to its own culture but at the same time transcends this culture. As Melville puts it: "It is with fiction as with religion: it should present another world, and yet one to which we feel the tie." This passage is descriptive of *The Confidence-Man* itself, which presented a world to which nineteenth-century readers would feel a tie and yet which was another world, or rather their world transformed and exhilarated.

The Confidence-Man is not another piece of 1850s humor whose fragmentations and zany images reflected extreme cultural tensions in a society on the brink of a bloody civil war. Beneath the distortions of popular humor ran a deep fear of national tragedy posed by proliferating reform movements and intensifying sectional controversies. Melville's novel too is filled with culturally induced distortions, but they are carefully sculpted by a literary artist intent upon salvaging them from the chaotic. Melville's achievement can be appreciated when we compare *The Confidence-Man* with paradigmatic comic American volumes of the 1850s, such as C. W. Webber's *Spiritual Vampirism: The History of Etherial Softdown* (1853), Fred Folio's *Lucy Boston; or Woman's Rights and Spiritualism* (1855), and Mortimer Neal Thompson's *Plu-Ri-Bus-Tah* (1856). Typical of much 1850s humor, these volumes anticipate *The Confidence-Man* by dramatizing the chicanery associated with a variety of modern fads and movements. Also typically—but *unlike* Melville's novel—they descend rapidly into the nonsensical and inhuman, as the social fragmentations they reflect tear apart narrative continuity and give rise to cheerless reflections on the modern scene. In Webber's bizarre, paranoiac novel *Spiritual Vampirism,* virtually all contemporary movements—Transcendentalism, women's rights, free love, socialism, temperance, the pseudosciences—are grouped together as branches of a secret Council of Disorganization whose main agent is Etherial Softdown, a "feminine Proteus" who uses many disguises to draw unwitting men and sentimental women into the chaos-breeding Council.[67] Fred Folio's *Lucy Boston* features an epigraph on its title page—"This is the age of oddities let loose"—which speaks for the entire novel. Folio pictures the utter confusion resulting from an imagined takeover of the New York state government by a group of angry feminists directed through spirit mediums by an odd array of spirits, including Tom Paine, John Calvin, and St. Paul. The combined forces of feminism and spiritualism lead to a "universal smash up" and the book ends with the declaration that the Ship of State, dashing "among rocks, quicksands and whirlpools, on the sea of *Experiment,* had quickly foundered and gone to pieces amid darkness and tempest."[68] Equally gloomy is Thompson's *Plu-Ri-Bus-Tah,* a dystopic version of Long-fellow's *Hiawatha* that sold some 13,000 copies within its first five days of publication. In his preface Thompson ironically vows "to slaughter the American Eagle, cut the throat of the Goddess of Liberty, annihilate the Yankee nation, and break things generally," and his deepest fears for his nation's demise are allegorized in the narrative's portrait of America's collapse as a result of the destructive forces of slavery, false charity, women's rights, and rampant materialism.[69]

The humor of these writers was black in a way no previous American humor had been, for it grew from a vision of impending national doom. In a typical piece of bleak comedy written in November 1856 for *The New York Picayune,* Thompson, upset by the results of the recent presidential election, wrote that he wished to gather armies and lead them into Washington, shouting the ironic words: "Division, Disunion, *Blood!,* BLOOD!!, BLOOD!!""[70] The inevitability of civil war gave rise to a humor that dwelt on the mockery of national ideals and the gory death of national symbols. Bitterness and nervous anticipation run through many passages in this humor, such as this one by Thompson in the *Picayune*:

> The end approaches. The Sun of Freedom is quenched in human blood—the music of the Union ceases with a grand final discord—the Ship of State is wrecked and gone to everlasting smash—the Constitution is scattered to the four winds—the Declaration of Independence is fizzled out. The Star Spangled Banner is ripped, ragged, and forgotten. The American Eagle has lost his tail feathers, and the Goddess of Liberty has barked her shins on the rocks of disunion, and distractedly calls for a whiskey sour.

Stylistically, this dystopic humor was manifested in the intensification of centrifugal forces of the American Subversive Style. When Thompson designed *Plu-Ri-Bus-Tah* as a narrative without plot or design, when the *Picayune* editors equated American humor with intentional disorientation of the reader, when George Washington Harris had Sut Lovingood ladle out his words at random, they showed that American humor was reflecting the disunities of a society approaching its greatest national calamity.

The Confidence-Man is an ennobled, artistic reconstruction of the bitter humor of the American 1850s. Like much progressive humor of the day, it studies human chicanery and a wide array of cultural phenomena in a purposely disorienting style. But the riverboat *Fidèle* is not merely the site

of senseless confidence games, nor is the vision of American society ultimately as dismal as that of the popular humorists. Toward the beginning
of the novel Melville lists the confusing array of contradictory types aboard
the *Fidèle*: Quakers and soldiers, Mormons and Catholics, teetotalers and
convivialists, the rich and the poor, deacons and blacklegs, slaves, Span-
iards, French Jews. In the course of the novel, the *Fidèle* becomes the
repository of virtually every form of popular stereotype, real or imagined,
produced by American popular culture. We meet intemperate temperance
men, justified criminals, an angry feminist, hypocritical philanthropists,
materialistic Transcendentalists—all observed and manipulated by the
most curious figure of all, the confidence man. Melville was more aware
than any popular humorist of the eradication of sure meaning implied by
these problematic stereotypes. But he was also more willing than the
others to rebuild artistically on the ruins of secure meaning or unified
national ideals. After listing the contradictory American types in Chapter
2, he writes: "Here reigned the dashing and all-fusing spirit of the West,
whose type is the Mississippi itself, which, uniting the streams of the most
distant and opposite zones, pours them along, helter-skelter, in one cosmopolitan and confident tide."[71] It is this "dashing and all-fusing spirit of
the West" that Melville offers as a remedy for the bleak suspension of
meaning represented by late popular humor. Having given up the earnest
philosophical quest of *Moby-Dick,* he turned now to the spirited play of
poses and dialogues that American culture revealed when viewed by a
sophisticated ironist in the late 1850s.

Melville's confidence man is the artistic flowering of previous fictional
confidence men, such as Lippard's Algernon Fitz-Cowles, Hooper's Simon
Suggs, and Baldwin's Ovid Bolus. If these characters lie from a delight in
artistic invention, Melville's character constantly re-creates and redefines
himself according to the fictional necessity of the moment. Although he
never shows a true face, his playacting more often than not uplifts others.
If his fellow passengers often pay for being duped, just as often they get
renewed confidence and hope, as though they had taken a psychological
placebo. Through much of the novel, the confidence man is in the ironic
position of trying to defend human goodness in the face of the gruff,
morose skeptics he meets. The novel is less a social satire or a metaphysical
treatise than it is a study of the creation of fictions, of the supremacy of
style over content. Melville's confidence man is the most skillful—the most
confident—fictionist in a sham-ridden world. All the other characters are
somehow stiff and narrow, locked in their stereotypical attitudes or their
profound prejudices. The novel is at once a renunciation of truth seeking
and a majestic assertion of stylistic creativity and flexibility. In the sheer
variety of his poses and the adeptness with which he carries off his ruses,

the confidence man becomes a creative hero in a culture whose internal contradictions preclude definitive interpretation.

The Confidence-Man can be viewed as the final stylized representation of the dominant popular modes—the Conventional, Romantic Adventure, Subversive—I have reviewed in this book. In the first chapter Melville makes clear that, like other humorists of the 1850s, he recognizes that each of these modes had been reduced to theater and show. If popular humorists frequently underscored the theatricality of the Conventional, Melville shows that biblical verities have been reduced to shifting phrases on a deaf-mute's chalkboard. If the humorists frequently noted that the American public was foolishly taken with sensational Romantic Adventure works, Melville likewise shows the *Fidèle* crowd mobbed around a criminal poster and buying crime pamphlets from money-hungry hawkers. If the humorists recognized the supremacy of the Subversive vision and suspension of authorial trust, Melville pictures a crusty barber whose pasteboard sign "NO TRUST" is a kind of malediction hanging over the gateway of the novel. If the humorists studied the disunifying effects of all the paradoxical stereotypes growing from these modes, Melville, too, includes virtually every conceivable popular stereotype in his novel.

But Melville was not prepared to follow Fred Folio, Mortimer Thompson, and the *Picayune* editors into a kind of torpid despair over complex literary stereotypes and collapsed national ideals. He showed that the theatricality of all popular modes in America's Barnumesque culture offered new rewards to the creative artist. The main reward was a renewal of the art of dialogue. The novel's first dialogue, the haphazard remarks at the start of Chapter 2 about Black Guinea by a crowd of spectators, could have been written by a black humorist like George Lippard or Mortimer Thompson. In rapid succession, unidentified speakers utter a series of nonsequential epithets, such as "Odd fish," "Poor fellow," "Green prophet from Utah," "Humbug," "Spirit-rapper," "Moon-calf," "Piteous," "Escaped convict, worn out with dodging."[72] The topical references to spiritualism, Mormonism, pitiable criminals, and humbug make it clear that we are in the realm of directionless popular humor. But Melville plunges us into the world of popular culture only to restore a sense of order and reference. His main reconstructive agent, the confidence man, is himself the most problematic product of this culture. Paradoxically, Melville uses this ultimate embodiment of cultural indeterminacy to refine the Subversive imagination. He fashions a confidence man who, even while he is duping people, becomes deeply engaged with them and in most cases manages to uplift their sense of self-worth. The confidence man is himself the "dashing and all-fusing spirit of the West" praised at the start of the novel. His creative posturing becomes a form of affirmation because it embodies the fertility of the fiction maker in a Barnumesque culture. Of course, this is a highly ambiguous affirmation, one that has no message in a conventional sense. But, when compared with the listless fragmentations of late subversive humor, it is the highest sort of affirmation Melville can offer without losing his cultural representativeness.

If he can no longer place faith in any single popular mode, he can nevertheless enjoy the creative sparks that fly when these modes interact and engage in rich dialogues. The Conventional mode appears in the numerous references to piety, optimism, good works, and temperance in the novel. Romantic Adventure surfaces in the images of the crafty diddling, justified criminals, and popular crime pamphlets. The Subversive mode penetrates the other two modes, showing how the paradoxical stereotypes produced by their commercialization undermine any potential meaning they may have originally contained. The American Subversive Style is the governing *écriture* of the novel.

But in *The Confidence-Man* the American Subversive Style is taken seriously and ushered to literariness. Melville does not merely exploit it cynically for the bizarre effects it could produce, as did, say, many popular parodists of mesmerism or spiritualism. Nor does he descend to the level of the grotesque or the sensational. Instead, he enriches it with archetypal allusions and humanizes it through witty interchanges between cleverly sparring conversers. *The Confidence-Man* was the first full example of the American Subversive Style made intelligent and humane. The string of incongruous epithets hurled in Chapter 2 at Black Guinea are steadily replaced by alternate, more compelling forms of dialogues and fictions as the book progresses. Although these dialogues may have no ultimate referent, they have the resonance and cool creativity provided by the reconceived, intelligent confidence man. Melville *did* present a world that had many ties to its own time and culture, but it was a world transformed and exhilarated by the all-fusing spirit of an American master of literary art.

Epilogue

RECONSTRUCTIVE CRITICISM: LITERARY THEORY AND LITERARY HISTORY

This book has used a critical methodology one might call reconstructive criticism, a term that applies both to the process of literary criticism and to the internal workings of literary texts. As a description of the critic's task, this approach calls upon the historical critic to reconstruct as completely as possible the socioliterary milieu of literary works through the exploration of a broad array of forgotten social and imaginative texts, paving the way for responsible reinterpretations of canonized works and making possible the rediscovery of lost literature. Ideally, the reconstructive critic would read *all* extant published writings of a given period with the aim of gaining a comprehensive, scientific overview. Given the exigencies of time and professional responsibilities, such comprehensiveness is virtually impossible, unless one limits oneself to an extremely brief historical period. If comprehensiveness is an improbable goal, however, representativeness is not. One should not make historical generalizations about literary works until one has sampled a large number of representative social and imaginative texts produced in different regions and by different social groups.

Applied to the internal workings of literary texts, reconstructive criticism views the literary work as simultaneously self-sufficient *and* historically shaped by environmental factors in society and personal life. In the case of the literary masterpieces of the American Renaissance, textual self-sufficiency does not constitute a rejection or evasion of socioliterary forces but rather a full assimilation and willed transformation of these forces. This process of assimilation and transformation—which might be called artistic or aesthetic—is another important aspect of reconstruction. The literary text reconstructs disparate socioliterary elements from its contemporary culture. In effect, it tries to save the society by giving certain popular elements new emotional resonance and artistic meaning. By "meaning" I do not suggest theme or message. Instead, I point to the intensification and ordering of cultural material that in its native state is often formless, contradictory, chaotic, indeterminate. Even when a literary text subverts itself (as it sometimes does), its self-subversion is carefully arranged and therefore is epistemologically meaningful. The literary work provides resonance where there is only flatness, it supplies moral suggestiveness where there is only moral naïveté or neutrality, it lends human intensity to images that in lesser hands give rise to inhumanity and emotional sterility.

The reconstructive approach might be said to provide a means of integrating various disciplines that in the past have been fragmented. Like several forms of formalist criticism, it recognizes literariness and forbids simplistic generalizations about the correspondence between the exterior world and the text. On the other hand, it does not sacrifice meaning to the gray arena of linguistic relativism or shifting reader response. It assumes that although a text lacks a transcendental signified, its uniqueness lies in the potency of its effort to find replacements for a transcendental signified, to restore suggestiveness by filling desiccated cultural chronotopes with the refreshing waters of human feeling and artistic order. Even modernist works that have been esteemed because of their self-conscious *dis*order possess an intentionality and an intense nihilism that distinguish them from the merely haphazard amoralism of many lesser-known works. Overemphasis of the subversive among many critical schools is based upon an inadequate understanding of a text's socioliterary environment. Like past extrinsic approaches, the reconstructive approach uses factors outside the text—personal life, historical facticity, popular literature—to evaluate literature. Like psychoanalytic or biological-feminist criticism, it seeks to establish links between private, sometimes gender-specific neurosis and the literary artifact, but it does not see literature as the mere transcription of repressed fantasy or gender difference. Projected private fantasy, however powerful, becomes literary only when it participates fully in the shared value and language systems of a specific time and culture. This does not mean that literature is a simple compound of historical facts or images. Rather, socioliterary environment supplies a mode of public discourse. Private life and sometimes gender difference are a text's catalyst and motivation, while the transcendental signified is its never attained but always suggested destination. Interpretation of a text varies over time, but appreciation of a text's density and universality does not. The "meaning" of a text lies in the richness of its texture, the emotions it stirs, the metaphysical speculations it instigates.

The literary text can be distinguished from other types of texts both by its openness to the most subversive forces in its immediate socioliterary environment and by its simultaneous endeavor to lend depth and artistry to these forces. Both the radical openness and the instinct to restructure must be present, or the literary text will not appear. The literary text fully confronts the subversive—plunges wholly into it, as it were—but at the same time removes itself through an assertion of the humanizing artistic imagination. During the American Renaissance, literary texts can be thus distinguished from the main types of unfamiliar literature: what I have called the Conventional, Romantic Adventure, and the Subversive. Conventional writings are characterized by an evasion of the subversive and by an excess of reconstructive devices, which form a tight shield against disturbing cultural forces. Romantic Adventure is another form of subliterary evasion. Particularly in the crude form of popular pamphlet novels, Romantic Adventure represented a total escape into episodic plot, with little attention to thematic resonance or moral suggestiveness. What I have termed Subversive literature (the most irrational examples of dark reform, sensational literature, and grotesque humor) openly admits dark cultural forces but runs toward the blackly humorous and the antihuman and thus misses literary status.

Each of the major texts is a case history in creative reconstruction. For Hawthorne, the principal reconstructive elements are Puritan culture and secularized allegory; for Melville, radical democracy, the Old Testament, and Renaissance drama; for Whitman, the b'hoy, Oriental philosophy, Emersonian self-reliance, and the Quaker inner light. The result of artistic fusion is extraordinary density of image and complexity of character. When different cultural images are fused with each other and with reconstructive devices they often lose their original connotations and take on entirely new dimensions of suggestiveness. The art of literary fusion rechannels the metaphorical energy of naïve or vulgarized popular images and releases a flood of fresh associations. In the literary text, there is a vast range of fused images, some relatively simple and still close to their popular meaning and others extraordinarily dense because they are receptacles of an unusually large variety of popular strategies and reconstructive devices. In *Moby-Dick,* the opening barroom scene in the Spouter-Inn and the sad life story of the blacksmith Perth are relatively simple images, quite close to the dark-temperance stories popular in Melville's day. A far more complex fusion of images occurs in the figure of Ahab, who is an amalgam of popular stereotypes (the grand sermonizer in the new religious style, the towering immoral reformer piercing through veils, the likable criminal, the oxymoronic oppressor) and reconstructive archetypes (Prometheus, Lear, Faust, and the biblical Ahab). Even more complex is the white whale, which is simultaneously the white sepulchre through which the mad reformer wishes to plunge, the marvelous Barnumesque freak, the great white god and great white devil objectified by the antebellum religious imagination, and numerous other things popular and archetypal. The white whale is indicative of a central feature of literary texts of the American Renaissance: many of these texts are so broadly representative of contemporary popular images that they contain central symbols or characters that are multidimensional repositories for most or all of the other images, both popular and reconstructive, in the work. Thus, Hawthorne's scarlet letter operates at once as the unmasking immoral reformer, the sign of the fallen woman in her shame, the extension of women's work, the symbol of the moral exemplar's abilities as an able social worker and a redemptive angel, the magnetic radiator of intense sensations, and so forth. Arthur Dimmesdale is a combination of the hypocritical reverend rake and the serious Puritan minister; Hester Prynne is an unprecedented fusion of at least five popular female stereotypes; and all the characters are deep Puritan versions of cheapened nineteenth-century characters such as the immoral reformer and the likable criminal. In *Leaves of Grass* Whitman amply fulfilled his goal of transfiguring the age, for his poem in fact surpasses even *Moby-Dick* and *The Scarlet Letter* in the breadth of its cultural representativeness and the variety of reconstructive devices it uses to salvage the cheapened images of its time.

It is possible to arrive at an integrative historical "close reading" of each of the major works by superimposing upon each the separate analyses I've made of these works in the foregoing chapters. Such final integrative close readings, however, might lead us toward a complacent neglect of the radical open-endedness of the critical endeavor and of socially representative literary texts. We have seen that each thematic strand in the major texts can be traced backward into a tremendous body of submerged works that have previously been hidden from view. I leave it to future critics to take up where I have left off in what is only a partially completed enterprise. I am also hopeful that sociocritical scholars in other fields will succeed in their current endeavors of reconstructing the literatures of other cultures. In a more general sense, I trust that we are leaving the period of hermetic close readings, based on the myth of textual autonomy, and are entering the era of reconstructive close readings, based on the reality of socioliterary dialogism.

It should be expected that the reconstructive enterprise will lead to the discovery of lost literary texts and to the cessation of the pointless fetishizing of a few so-called literary giants. Throughout this book I have of necessity focused on already acknowledged major works, with the aim of bringing to light unperceived influences and unexplored dimensions of familiar works. On the other hand, I have tried along the way to communicate my conviction that there are a good number of unfamiliar writings that merit attention on their own. To search for lost literature is to share the democratic spirit of the familiar authors themselves. Whitman, for example, used a vivid astronomical metaphor to express to Traubel his belief in the existence of forgotten classics. Denouncing the idolatry of Shakespeare and a few other "greats," he exclaimed:

> It is wrong! wrong! wrong! It is as if we should fix our eyes on one of the stars there: should say: Let that be the only star: let that alone stand out in glory, purpose, sacredness: let all the rest be wiped out: let that alone be declared legitimate: let that alone be our guide. Yet there are millions of other stars in the heavens: millions: some as great, some greater: perhaps some we do not see surpassing the best we see: so there are writers—countless writers: some swept away, lost forever: some neglected: some yet to be recognized for what they are.[1]

As much as Whitman desired greater recognition in his own lifetime, he would doubtless decry critics in our time who have tended to isolate him and a handful of other literary stars from the rich galaxy of their surrounding culture.

Although we should look diligently for lost luminaries, it is a mistake to simply dismiss the existing canon or pretend that it is an arbitrary grouping of works selected by biased critics. It is true that for decades there has been an overconcern with canonized texts to the exclusion of unfamiliar writings. On the other hand, I would argue that it does make sense to speak of "major" authors, as long as we recognize that additional major authors may be identified in the future. The problem of canon formation brings up the fundamental question: why do some texts emerge as classics while others fall from view? Margaret Fuller had an intriguing image for the selection over time of certain works as classics. "Time," she wrote, "holds a strainer like that used in the diamond mines; have but patience and the water and gravel will all pass through and only the precious stones will be left."[2] Henry James, discussing Hawthorne's ascendancy to classic status, used an equally endearing image: "The grand sign of being a classic is that when you have 'passed,' as they say at examinations, you have passed; you have become one once for all; you have taken your degree and may be left to the light and the ages."[3]

The problem of revising the canon can be best resolved if we respect the decision of time by preserving the already recognized classics but leave ourselves open for the possible rediscovery of other classics. To mix the above metaphors, we should earnestly seek lost stars in the literary galaxy without ignoring the diamonds that are already caught in Time's strainer or the classics that have passed the examination of the ages. There are viable reasons that Emerson's essays, *Walden, Moby-Dick, The Scarlet Letter,* and *Leaves of Grass* have emerged as the classic texts of the antebellum period. These reasons have little to do with linguistic indeterminacy or aporias of thought. To be sure, the inability of words to convey exact meaning is assumed in these classic texts, as it was in many unfamiliar writings of their day. But the pleasure of these texts lies in their bold assimilation of the most subversive forces in their socioliterary culture (including the slipperiness of language) and their simultaneous rechanneling of these forces in ways that are both intellectually challenging and emotionally moving. As is shown repeatedly in this book, the classic American texts were affirmations of suggestiveness in a period of increasing imagistic flatness, of psychological earnestness and artistic order in a time of commercialized feelings and centrifugal styles.

To call a text's density and intensity a form of humanistic affirmation, in spite of deep ironies that compromise clear meaning, is to recall one of Henry James's most subtle points about Hawthorne. James was fully aware of Hawthorne's ambiguities—so much so that he called *The Scarlet Letter* the most consistently gloomy novel of the first order in the English language. Nevertheless, he was outraged by critics who characterized Hawthorne as a bleak *romancier pessimiste.* Denying that Hawthorne had an intrinsic "relish of gloomy subjects," James wrote: "What pleased him in such subjects was their picturesqueness, their rich duskiness of colour, their chiaroscuro; but they were not the expression of a hopeless, even of a predominantly melancholy feeling about the human soul. . . . [T]here has rarely been an observer more serene, less agitated by what he sees and less disposed to call things deeply into question."[4] Indeed, the very reason Hawthorne had become a classic writer, James argued, is that his assertion of inwardness and artistry was a much needed relief from what James called the "monster" of nineteenth-century America—that is, the dizzying, shallow forces of popular culture, which James summed up as "the journalistic—so pervasive, so ubiquitous, so unprecedentedly prosperous, so wonderful for outward agility, but so unfavourable, even so fatal, to development from within."

James sensed that Hawthorne was nurtured by his contemporary culture. In discussing Hawthorne's sources he stressed that "the flower of art blooms only where the soil is deep" and that "it needs a complex social machinery to set the writer in motion." Hawthorne and the other authors discussed in this book fully assimilated their popular culture only to transcend it through the affirmation of the suggestive and the subtly human. They struggled mightily with what James called the journalistic monster—the sprawling mass of nineteenth-century subliterature, much of it in newspaper or pamphlet form—and they learned much from the struggle. In particular, their deep engagement with the popular subversive themes and idioms supplied them with literary material. But they refused to sacrifice their artistic powers in the fight. Instead, they victoriously created literary works in which the monster of popular culture suddenly took on human aspect and lasting appeal. In different ways, they memorably reconstructed the popular subversive imagination.

NOTES

ABBREVIATIONS FOR FREQUENTLY CITED PRIMARY SOURCES

CWE   *The Complete Works of Ralph Waldo Emerson.* Centenary Edition. New York: AMS Press, 1968 (first published 1904).

EAP   *Collected Works of Edgar Allan Poe,* ed. Thomas Olive Mabbott. 3 vols. Cambridge, Mass.: Harvard University Press, 1978.

EDL   *The Letters of Emily Dickinson,* ed. Thomas H. Johnson. 3 vols. Cambridge, Mass.: Harvard University Press, 1958.

EJ   *Emerson in His Journals,* ed. Joel Porte. Cambridge, Mass.: Harvard University Press, 1982.

EL   Ralph Waldo Emerson, *Essays and Lectures.* New York: Library of America, 1983.

"HawMoss"   Herman Melville, "Hawthorne and His Mosses" (1850). Reprinted in "Reviews and Letters by Melville," afterword to H. Melville, *Moby-Dick,* ed. Harrison Hayford and Hershel Parker. New York: Norton, 1967.

HDT   *The Writings of Henry David Thoreau.* Riverside Edition. Boston: Houghton Mifflin, 1906. Reprint: New York: AMS Press, 1982. Vol. I: *A Week on the Concord and Merrimack Rivers.* Vol. II: *Walden.* Vol. III: *The Maine Woods.* Vol. IV: *Cape Cod.* Vol. V: *Excursions and Poems.* Vol. VI: *Familiar Letters. Anti-Slavery and Reform Papers.*

HP   Harrison Hayford and Hershel Parker, eds., afterword to H. Melville, *Moby-Dick.* New York: W. W. Norton, 1967. The afterword includes *"Moby-Dick,"* "Reviews and Letters by Melville," "Analogues and Sources," "Criticism."

ISit   Walt Whitman, *I Sit and Look Out: Editorials from the Brooklyn Daily Times,* ed. Emory Holloway and Vernolian Schwarz. New York: AMS Press, 1966.

JE   *The Journals and Miscellaneous Notebooks of Ralph Waldo Emerson,*
            ed. William H. Gilman et al. Cambridge, Mass.: Harvard Uni-
            versity Press, 1960–82.

JHDT   *The Journal of Henry David Thoreau,* ed. Bradford Torrey and
            Francis H. Allen. New York: Dover, 1962.

LE   *The Letters of Ralph Waldo Emerson,* ed. Ralph L. Rusk. 6 vols.
            New York: Columbia University Press, 1939.

LEAP   *The Letters of Edgar Allan Poe,* ed. John Ward Ostrom. 2 vols.
            Cambridge, Mass.: Harvard University Press, 1948.

LecE   *The Early Lectures of Ralph Waldo Emerson,* ed. Stephen E.
            Whicher and Robert E. Spiller. Cambridge, Mass.: Harvard
            University Press. Vol. I: 1833–1836 (1959). Vol. II: 1836–1838
            (1964). Vol. III: 1838–1842 (1972).

LGC   Walt Whitman, *Leaves of Grass, Comprehensive Reader's Edition,* ed.
            Harold Blodgett and Sculley Bradley. New York: New York
            University Press, 1965.

LGV   Walt Whitman, *Leaves of Grass. A Textual Variorum of the Printed
            Poems,* ed. Sculley Bradley, Harold W. Blodgett, Arthur
            Golden, William White. New York: New York University Press,
            1980. Vol. I: Poems, 1855–1856. Vol. II: 1860–1867. Vol. III,
            1870–1891.

MD   Herman Melville, *Moby-Dick; or, The Whale* (1851), ed. Harrison
            Hayford and Hershel Parker. New York: W. W. Norton, 1967.

ML   Jay Leyda, *The Melville Log: A Documentary Life of Herman Melville,
            1819–1891.* New York: Harcourt, Brace, 1951.

Mosses   Nathaniel Hawthorne, *Mosses from an Old Manse* (1846). Centen-
            ary Edition. Ohio State University Press, 1974.

NF   Walt Whitman, *Notes and Fragments,* ed. Richard Maurice Bucke.
            Ontario: A. Tallbot & Co., n.d.

NHL   Nathaniel Hawthorne, *The Letters,* ed. Thomas Woodson,
            L. Neal Smith, Norman Holmes Pearson. 2 vols. Centenary
            Edition. Ohio State University Press. Vol. XV: 1813–1843
            (1984). Vol. XVI: 1843–1853 (1985).

NUPM   Walt Whitman, *Notebooks and Unpublished Prose Manuscripts,* ed.
            Edward F. Grier. Chicago: University of Chicago Press, 1955.

NYD   Walt Whitman, *New York Dissected,* ed. Emory Holloway and
            Ralph Adimari. New York: Rufus Rockwell Wilson, 1936.

PER   Edgar Allan Poe, *Essays and Reviews.* New York: Library of
            America, 1984.

PIPCUB   Herman Melville, *Pierre, Israel Potter, The Piazza Tales, The Confi-
            dence-Man, Uncollected Prose, Billy Budd.* New York: Library of
            America, 1984.

PW   Walt Whitman, *Prose Works, 1892,* ed. Floyd Stovall. 2 vols. New
            York: New York University Press. Vol. I: *Specimen Days* (1963).
            Vol. II: *Collect and Other Prose* (1964).

QC   George Lippard, *The Quaker City: or, The Monks of Monk Hall. A
            Romance of Philadelphia Life, Mystery and Crime* (1845). Reprint:
            The Monks of Monk Hall, ed. Leslie A. Fiedler. New York: Odys-
            sey, 1970.

SL   Nathaniel Hawthorne, *The Scarlet Letter* (1850). Centenary Edi-
            tion. Ohio State University Press, 1962.

TEM   Henry David Thoreau, *Early Essays and Miscellanies,* ed. Joseph
            J. Moldenhauer and Edwin Moser. Princeton: Princeton Uni-
            versity Press, 1975.

TTT Nathaniel Hawthorne, *Twice-Told Tales* (1837). Centenary Edition. Ohio State University Press, 1974.
WC Walt Whitman, *The Correspondence,* ed. Edwin Haviland Miller. 2 vols. New York: New York University Press. Vol. I: 1842–1867 (1961). Vol. II: 1868–1875 (1964).
WCP Walt Whitman, *Complete Poetry and Collected Prose.* New York: Library of America, 1982.
WEP Walt Whitman, *The Early Poems and the Fiction,* ed. Thomas L. Brasher. New York: New York University Press, 1963.
WUP *The Uncollected Poetry and Prose of Walt Whitman,* ed. Emory Holloway. 2 vols. Gloucester, Mass.: Peter Smith, 1972.
WWC Horace Traubel, *With Walt Whitman in Camden.* New York: Mitchell Kennedy, 1915.
WWW *Walt Whitman's Workshop: A Collection of Unpublished Prose Manuscripts,* ed. Clifton Joseph Furness. New York: Russell & Russell, 1964.
YH Jay Leyda, *The Years and Hours of Emily Dickinson.* 2 vols. New Haven: Yale University Press, 1960.

INTRODUCTION

1 *EJ,* p. 344.
2 "HawMoss," p. 543.
3 *Pierre; or, The Ambiguities,* in *PIPCUB,* p. 330.
4 *White-Jacket, or The World in a Man-of-War* (1850; rpt., Evanston: Northwestern University Press, 1970), p. 169.
5 Quoted in Julian Hawthorne, *Hawthorne Reading* (Cleveland: The Rowfant Club, 1902), p. 64.
6 *Mosses,* pp. 20–21.
7 *NF,* p. 130.
8 F. O. Matthiessen, *American Renaissance: Art and Expression in the Age of Emerson and Whitman* (New York: Oxford University Press, 1941).
9 Harold Bloom, *The Anxiety of Influence: A Theory of Poetry* (New York: Oxford University Press, 1973).
10 *EL,* p. 627.
11 *EL,* p. 711.
12 L. Trilling, *The Liberal Imagination* (New York: Doubleday, 1950), and R. Chase, *The American Novel and Its Tradition* (Garden City, N.Y.: Doubleday, 1957).
13 A useful overview of recent historical studies of American literature may be found in Russell J. Reising, *The Unusable Past: Theory and the Study of American Literature* (New York: Methuen, 1986), especially Ch. 5. In addition to the books and articles mentioned by Reising, see the historically oriented discussion of pre–Civil War literature in the following studies: Carolyn Porter, *Seeing and Being: The Plight of the Participant Observer in Emerson, James, Adams, and Faulkner* (Middletown, Conn.: Wesleyan University Press, 1981); Larzer Ziff, *Literary Democracy: The Cultural Declaration of Independence in America* (New York: Viking, 1981); Alfred Kazin, *An American Procession: The Major American Writers from 1830 to 1930, the Crucial Century* (New York: Alfred A. Knopf, 1984); Michael T. Gilmore, *American Romanticism and the Marketplace* (Chicago: University of Chicago Press, 1985); *The American Renaissance Reconsidered,* ed. Walter Benn Michaels and Donald E. Pease (Baltimore: Johns Hopkins University Press, 1985); Philip Fisher, *Hard Facts: Setting and Form in the American*

Novel (New York: Oxford University Press, 1985); Irving Howe, *The American Newness: Culture and Politics in the Age of Emerson* (Cambridge, Mass.: Harvard University Press, 1985); *Reconstructing American Literary History*, ed. Sacvan Bercovitch (Cambridge, Mass.: Harvard University Press, 1986); *Ideology and Classic American Literature*, ed. Sacvan Bercovitch and Myra Jehlen (New York: Cambridge University Press, 1986); Lawrence Buell, *New England Literary Culture: From Revolution Through Renaissance* (New York: Cambridge University Press, 1986); and Donald E. Pease, *Visionary Compacts: American Renaissance Writings* (Madison: University of Wisconsin Press, 1987).

    While the present book shares with these studies a concern with the social dimensions of literary texts, it presents new readings and conclusions based upon discussion of the major literature in the context of numerous hitherto neglected writings.

14 H. Melville, "HawMoss," p. 543, and W. Whitman, *PW*, II, 454.

15 I have arrived at these and other statistics relating to early American fiction after a comprehensive review of the volumes listed in Lyle Henry Wright, *American Fiction, 1774–1850: A Contribution Toward a Bibliography* (San Marino, Cal.: Huntington Library, 1957).

16 *MD*, p. 468.

CHAPTER 1

1 "The Present Age" (1841), in *The Works of William E. Channing, D.D.* (Boston: American Unitarian Association, 1875), p. 164.

2 *Sinners in the Hands of an Angry God* (1741), in *The Norton Anthology of American Literature*, ed. Ronald Gottesman et al. (New York: W. W. Norton, 1979), I, 253, 252.

3 *A Divine and Supernatural Light* (1834), in *Jonathan Edwards, Representative Selections*, ed. Clarence H. Faust and Thomas H. Johnson (New York: Hill and Wang, 1962), p. 105, and *A Treatise Concerning the Religious Affections*, in *American Thought and Writing*, ed. Russel B. Nye and Norman S. Grabo (Boston: Houghton Mifflin, 1965), I, 406, 417.

4 For a full discussion of changing sermon style, with examples from nineteenth-century sermons, see David S. Reynolds, "From Doctrine to Narrative: The Rise of Pulpit Storytelling in America," *American Quarterly*, XXXII (Winter 1980), 479–98.

5 *Uncle Tom's Cabin; or, Life Among the Lowly* (1852; rpt., New York: Collier, 1967), p. 83.

6 Quoted in William H. Pipes, *Say Amen, Brother! Old-Time Negro Preaching: A Study in American Frustration* (New York: William-Frederick Press, 1951), p. 65.

7 See G. Campbell, *The Philosophy of Rhetoric* (1776; rpt., Carbondale, Ill.: Southern Illinois University Press, 1963), p. 111, and H. Blair, *Lectures on Rhetoric and Belles Lettres* (1783; rpt., Philadelphia: S. C. Hayes, 1860), p. 314.

8 "Historic Notes of Life and Letters in New England," in *CWE*, X, 333. For a discussion of Edward Everett and two other popular orators, William Ellery Channing and Daniel Webster, in the context of Transcendentalist oratory, see L. Buell, *New England Literary Culture*, Ch. 6. See also Taylor Stoehr, *Nay-Saying in Concord* (Hamden, Conn.: Archon, 1979) and Gay Wilson Allen, *Waldo Emerson. A Biography* (New York: Viking, 1981), esp. Chs. 25 and 26.

9 *EJ*, pp. 38 and 43.

10 *EJ*, p. 46.

11 R. W. Emerson, "The Christian Minister: Part I," in *Young Emerson Speaks*, ed. Arthur C. McGiffert (Boston: Houghton Mifflin, 1938), p. 28.

12 R. W. Emerson, letter to Henry Ware, Jr., December 30, 1828, in *LE*, I, 257.

13 W. Whitman, *PW*, II, 549.
14 The quotations in this and the above paragraph are from Robert Collyer, *Father Taylor* (Boston: American Unitarian Association, 1906), pp. 27, 4, 49, 55, 52.
15 *JE*, VII, 360.
16 R. Collyer, *Father Taylor*, p. 51, and Emerson, "Self-Reliance," in *EL*, pp. 260, 261.
17 Letter to William Emerson, January 7, 1835, in *LE*, I, 431, and *JE*, V, 255.
18 *JE*, V, 287.
19 *JE*, IX, 236.
20 *Nature*, in *EL*, pp. 34–35.
21 *LecE*, III, 362.
22 "The Poet," in *EL*, p. 463.
23 "The Poet," in *EL*, p. 463.
24 The quotations in this and the following paragraph are from the Divinity School Address, in *EL*, pp. 84, 85, 75, 91, 80, 91.
25 *WWC*, I, 10, and *PW*, II, 551, 549.
26 Quoted in J. T. Trowbridge, *My Own Story: With Recollections of Noted Persons* (Boston: Houghton Mifflin, 1903), p. 367.
27 *WUP*, II, 255, 293.
28 *PW*, II, 551, 549.
29 *LGC*, p. 83.
30 *LGC*, p. 75.
31 *LGC*, pp. 58, 59.
32 *WCP*, p. 51. The next indented quotation is on p. 85.
33 *MD*, pp. 43–44.
34 David H. Battenfeld, "The Source for the Hymn in *Moby-Dick*," *American Literature*, XXVII (November 1955), 393–96.
35 R. Collyer, *Father Taylor*, p. 40.
36 *The Sailor's Magazine and Naval Journal* (New York, 1839–40).
37 *MD*, p. 45. The subsequent quotations in this paragraph are on pp. 46, 51, 50.
38 H. Melville, letters to N. Hawthorne, June 29, 1851, and November 17, 1851, in *HP*, pp. 561, 566.
39 *YH*, I, 53, and *EDL*, II, 251–52. In this chapter and elsewhere in the book, all texts of Emily Dickinson's poems, as well as numbers and dates for the poems, are from *The Poems of Emily Dickinson*, ed. Thomas H. Johnson (Cambridge, Mass.: Harvard University Press, 1955), 3 vols.
40 *EDL*, II, 475.
41 *Kavanagh* (1849), reprinted in *Hyperion and Kavanagh* (Boston: Houghton Mifflin, 1886), pp. 325–26.
42 *YH*, I, 287.
43 Quoted in *YH*, I, 296.
44 *"A New Lion," Springfield Republican*, October 22, 1850, reprinted from the *New York Evening Post*.
45 *YH*, II, 112 ("Mark Twain contributes to the *Golden Era*, 'Reflections in the Sabbath' ").
46 *EDL*, III, 901 and 703.
47 This statement from T. W. Higginson's 1852 installation sermon as minister of the Free Church in Worcester, Mass., is quoted in Tilden G. Edelstein, *Strange Enthusiasms: A Life of Thomas Wentworth Higginson* (New Haven: Yale University Press, 1968), p. 131.
48 "Letter to a Young Contributor," reprinted in T. W. Higginson, *Atlantic Essays* (Boston, 1871), pp. 90, 91.
49 *Fern Leaves from Fanny's Port Folio* (Auburn: Derby and Miller, 1853), p. 228.

50 Quoted in *The Life and Beauties of Fanny Fern* (New York: H. Long and Brother, 1855), pp. 184, 181.
51 *Reveries of a Bachelor* (1850; rpt., New York: Charles Scribner's Sons, 1907), p. vii. The subsequent Mitchell quotations in this paragraph and the following one are on pp. 219, 221, 254.
52 *EDL*, I, 144.
53 *EDL*, I, 195.
54 *EDL*, I, 120.
55 *EDL*, I, 272.
56 Review of *Twice-Told Tales* and *Mosses from an Old Manse* in *Godey's Lady's Book* (November 1847), reprinted in *PER*, p. 587.
57 *TTT*, p. 472.
58 Letter to James T. Fields, quoted in J. Donald Crowley, "Historical Commentary," *Mosses*, p. 522.
59 *Southern Quarterly Review*, II (January 1852), 262.
60 "HawMoss," p. 539.
61 "Education," in *The Complete Writings of Ralph Waldo Emerson*, II (New York: W. H. Wise, 1929), 984.
62 *LGC*, p. 412.
63 For extensive examples of religion in Oriental and visionary fiction, see David S. Reynolds, *Faith in Fiction: The Emergence of Religious Literature in America* (Cambridge, Mass.: Harvard University Press, 1981), Chs. 1 and 2.
64 *The Algerine Captive; or, The Life and Adventures of Doctor Updike Underhill . . .* (Walpole, N.H.: David Carlisle, Jr., 1797), II, 146.
65 *Letters of Shahcoolen* (1802; rpt., Gainesville, Fla.: Scholars' Facsimiles and Reprints, 1962), p. 89.
66 W. Irving, *History, Tales and Sketches* (New York: Library of America, 1983), p. 144.
67 Quoted in *The Unknown Poe*, ed. Raymond Foye (San Francisco: City Lights, 1980), p. 96.
68 Quoted in *The Unknown Poe*, p. 3.
69 "The Poetic Principle," in *PER*, pp. 75, 80, 82.
70 "The Poetic Principle," in *PER*, pp. 77, 78.
71 "Ligeia," *EAP*, II, 313.
72 John H. Amory, *Old Ironside, The Story of a Shipwreck* (Boston: James B. Dow, 1840), pp. 39–40.
73 Nathaniel Ames, *Nautical Reminiscences* (Providence: William Marshall, 1832), p. 58.
74 Charles W. Denison, *Stories of the Sea . . . Including a Residence among Cannibals on Wallace Islands* (Boston: John Putnam, 1844), p. 76.
75 Nathaniel Ames, *An Old Sailor's Yarns* (New York: George Dearborn, 1835), p. x.
76 Letter to John Murray, January 29, 1847, in *ML*, I, 233.
77 H. Melville, *Typee. A Peep at Polynesian Life* (1846; rpt., Evanston: Northwestern University Press, 1968), p. 179.
78 *Mardi and a Voyage Thither* (1849; rpt., Evanston: Northwestern University Press, 1970), pp. 633, 577.
79 *MD*, p. 61. The subsequent quotations in this paragraph are on pp. 82, 52.
80 *MD*, p. 54. The subsequent quotations in this paragraph are on pp. 83, 108.
81 *MD*, p. 349. The subsequent quotations in this paragraph are on pp. 347, 130, 409, 468.
82 *PIPCUB*, p. 1225.

CHAPTER 2

1 *Critics of Culture: Literature and Society in the Early Twentieth Century,* ed. Alan Trachtenberg (New York: John Wiley & Son, 1976), pp. 18, 23.

2 L. Trilling, *The Liberal Imagination;* R. Chase, *The American Novel and Its Tradition;* H. N. Smith, *Democracy and the Novel* (New York: Oxford University Press, 1978).

3 Paul Zweig, *Walt Whitman: The Making of the Poet* (New York: Basic Books, 1984), p. 12.

4 Michael Paul Rogin, *Subversive Genealogy: The Politics and Art of Herman Melville* (New York: Alfred A. Knopf, 1983), p. 190.

5 *The Dialogic Imagination: Four Essays by M. M. Bakhtin,* trans. Caryl Emerson and Michael Holquist (Austin: University of Texas Press, 1981), p. 418.

6 See Bruce Laurie, *Working People of Philadelphia, 1800–1850* (Philadelphia: Temple University Press, 1980), and Sean Wilentz, *Chants Democratic: New York City and the Rise of the American Working-Class, 1788–1850* (New York: Oxford University Press, 1984).

7 See Rush Welter, *The Mind of America, 1820–1860* (New York: Columbia University Press, 1975); Sacvan Bercovitch, *The American Jeremiad* (Madison: University of Wisconsin Press, 1978), pp. 156 ff.; Ann Douglas, *The Feminization of American Culture* (New York: Alfred A. Knopf, 1977).

8 R. Barthes, *Image—Music—Text* (New York: Hill and Wang, 1977), p. 200.

9 Quoted in Lewis Leary, *The Book-Peddling Parson: An Account of the Life and Works of Mason Locke Weems* (Chapel Hill: Algonquin Books, 1984), p. 12. The quotations in the next paragraph are on pp. 14, 101.

10 Mason Locke Weems, *Three Discourses* (New York: Random House, 1929), p. 93.

11 Quoted in L. Leary, *The Book-Peddling Parson,* pp. 145–46. The W. G. Simms statement, from his volume *Views and Reviews* (1845), is also quoted in Leary, p. 154.

12 R. W. Emerson, "Historic Notes of Life and Letters in New England" (c. 1867), in *CWE,* X, 337.

13 F. Wright's 1830 address is reprinted in *Religion, Reform, and Revolution: Labor Panaceas in the Nineteenth Century,* ed. Leon Stein and Philip Taft (New York: Arno, 1969), p. 11.

14 J. Tuckerman, "An Essay on the Wages Paid to Females" (1830), in *Religion, Reform, and Revolution,* pp. 30, 32.

15 *Morning Courier and New York Enquirer,* October 5, 1833.

16 *New York Commercial Advertiser,* August 8, 1836.

17 "Extra" edition of *McDowall's Journal* (New York), October 1, 1833.

18 *Memoir and Select Remains of the Late Rev. John R. M'Dowall, the Martyr of the Seventh Commandment in the Nineteenth Century* (New York: Leavitt, Lord, & Co., 1838), p. 213.

19 *History of the Preliminary Proceedings of the Third Presbytery, in the Case of J. R. McDowall, New York Observer,* May 1836 (pamphlet reprint).

20 See *Letters of Gallowrake: Being a Series of Communications Originally Published in the Ohio Star* (Ravenna: Ohio Star, 1834). This sensational pamphlet enjoyed a wide sale in the mid-1830s.

21 *WWC,* I, 147.

22 *"Horrid Case of Intemperance,"* in *Salem Gazette,* January 3, 1834; E. Everett's address to the Young Men's Temperance Association is reprinted in *Salem Gazette,* June 18, 1833.

23 *Poems of M'Donald Clark* (New York: J. W. Bell, 1836), p. 124.

24 This 1846 declaration appears in Theodore Parker, *Social Classes in a Republic,* ed. Samuel A. Eliot (Boston: American Unitarian Association, n.d.), p. 122.

25 *Autobiography and Personal Recollections of John B. Gough* (Toronto: A. H. Hovey, 1870), pp. 199–200.

26 Quoted in Albert Parry, *Garrets and Pretenders: A History of Bohemianism in America* (1933; rpt., New York: Dover, 1960), p. 48.

27 *Easy Nat; or Boston Bars and Boston Boys* (Boston: Redding and Co., 1844), p. i.

28 *PER,* p. 948.

29 "The Black Cat," *EAP,* III, 851. The subsequent quotations in this paragraph are on pp. 851, 858.

30 "The Cask of Amontillado," *EAP,* III, 1257. The subsequent quotations in this paragraph are on pp. 1259, 1260, 1262.

31 Introductory note to "The Cask of Amontillado," *EAP,* III, 1252.

32 *A Hasty Defence of the Farmers and Distillers of York County, Against the Aspersions of Temperance Societies, &c.* (York: W. C. Smyth, 1833), p. 3.

33 *TTT,* p. 148.

34 David Meredith Reese, M.D., *Humbugs of New-York: Being a Remonstrance against Popular Delusion, Whether in Science, Philosophy, or Religion* (New York: John S. Taylor, 1838), p. 217.

35 "The Present Age" (1841), in *Works of . . . Channing,* p. 167.

36 B. R. Hall, *Something for Every Body: Gleaned in the Old Purchase, from Fields Often Reaped* (New York: D. Appleton & Co., 1846), pp. 126, 134.

37 *Social Classes in a Republic,* p. 29.

38 *Social Classes in a Republic,* p. 29.

39 *The Liberator* (Boston), January 29, 1831; February 26, 1831; November 5, 1831.

40 *American Spectator* (Washington), July 14, 1831.

41 For accounts of Garrison's quarrel with the *National Intelligencer,* see *The Liberator,* October 8, 1831, and October 15, 1831.

42 Lydia Maria Child, *Selected Letters, 1817–1880,* ed. Milton Meltzer and Patricia G. Holland (Amherst: University of Massachusetts Press, 1982), pp. 207, 197.

43 *The Slave: or Memoirs of Archy Moore* (Boston: John H. Eastburn, 1836), I, 158. The remaining quotations from *The Slave* are in I, 46, 82.

44 Frederick Douglass, *The Narrative and Selected Writings,* ed. Michael Meyer (New York: Modern Library, 1984), p. xiv. The remaining quotations from this volume are on pp. 65, 85, 81, 112, 367, 365, 257.

45 *Uncle Tom's Cabin,* Introduction to the 1881 edition, p. 14.

46 The sentimental aspects of the novel are stressed, for example, in A. Douglas, *The Feminization of American Culture;* the novel's cultural influence is emphasized in Jane P. Tompkins, *Sensational Designs: The Cultural Work of American Fiction, 1790–1860* (New York: Oxford University Press, 1985), Ch. 5; the radical aspects of Stowe's sentimentalism are discussed in P. Fisher, *Hard Facts,* Ch. 2.

47 *Uncle Tom's Cabin,* p. 170. The subsequent quotations in this paragraph are on pp. 418, 450, 206, 284, 360.

48 H. B. Stowe, *Dred: A Tale of the Great Dismal Swamp* (1856; rpt., New York: AMS Press, 1967), II, 212.

49 Quoted in Thomas F. Gossett, *Uncle Tom's Cabin and American Culture* (Dallas: Southern Methodist University Press, 1985), p. 341.

50 Quoted in T. F. Gossett, *Uncle Tom's Cabin and American Culture,* p. 190. The subsequent *Picayune* quotation is in Gossett, p. 191.

51 Quoted in *The Liberator,* March 4, 1853. The subsequent quotation is from Henry C. Wright, " 'Uncle Tom's Cabin'—Questionable Characteristics," in *The Liberator,* July 9, 1852.

52 *Uncle Tom's Cabin,* p. 22.
53 *The Subterranean* (New York), September 9, 1843. The following attack on Gansevoort Melville appeared in the January 24, 1846, edition of the paper.
54 G. Lippard, preface to 1849 edition of *The Quaker City,* in *QC,* pp. 1, 2.
55 *QC,* p. 71. The subsequent quotations in this paragraph are on pp. 366, 23.
56 N. Hawthorne, *The Blithedale Romance* (1852; rpt., New York: W. W. Norton, 1978), p. 131.
57 A. J. H. Duganne, *The Knights of the Seal; or, The Mysteries of the Three Cities* (Philadelphia: Colon and Adriance, 1845), p. 112.
58 G. Foster, *New York Naked* (New York: De Witt and Davenport, 1850), p. 26.
59 J. Boughton, *Solon Grind: or, The Thunderstruck Hypocrite* (New York: Burgess, Stringer, & Co., 1845), p. 29.
60 *Orthodox Bubbles, or a Review of the "First Annual Report of the Executive Committee of the New York Magdalen Society"* (Boston, 1831), p. 3.
61 G. Thompson, *The Countess; or Memoirs of Women of Leisure* (Boston: Berry and Wright, 1849), p. 48.
62 E. Bennett, *Oliver Goldfinch; or, The Hypocrite* (Cincinnati: Stratton and Barnard, 1850), p. 40.
63 *QC,* p. 170.
64 C. W. Webber, *Spiritual Vampirism: The History of Etherial Softdown, and the Friends of the "New Light"* (Philadelphia: Lippincott, Grambo, & Co., 1853), p. 28.
65 H. Clapp, "Modern Christianity," in *The Liberty Bell* (Boston, 1844), p. 177.
66 Quoted in *Memoirs . . . of the Late Rev. John R. M'Dowall,* p. 267.
67 *The Solitary Vice Considered* (New York: John N. Bolles, 1834), p. 4.
68 *McDowall's Journal,* June 1833.
69 *Easy Nat,* p. [i].
70 The most vivid example of such modernized damnation imagery is Devil-Bug's dream of the last day of Philadelphia (signaled by a lurid "WO UNTO SODOM" in the sky) in G. Lippard's *The Quaker City.* See *QC,* pp. 369–93.
71 *QC,* pp. 1, 2.

CHAPTER 3

1 *EL,* p. 135.
2 *EL,* pp. 158, 159.
3 *CWE,* VII, 95.
4 Journal entry for October 1837, *EJ,* p. 169.
5 *EL,* p. 262.
6 "Nature" (in *Essays: Second Series*), *EL,* p. 549.
7 Journal entry for May 1839, *EJ,* p. 218.
8 "Reforms" (lecture of January 15, 1840), in *LecE,* III, 259.
9 "Reforms," in *LecE,* III, 257.
10 "New England Reformers" (lecture of March 3, 1844), *EL,* p. 592.
11 *LE,* II, 222.
12 "Lecture on the Times," *EL,* p. 162.
13 *EL,* p. 162.
14 *EL,* p. 127.
15 *EL,* p. 175.
16 *Nature* (1836), in *EL,* pp. 11, 46, 18.
17 *EL,* pp. 262, 263.
18 *EL,* p. 146.
19 *Thoreau* (1862), in *CWE,* X, 456.

20 *CWE*, X, 457.
21 *JHDT*, VII, 7.
22 F. O. Matthiessen, *American Renaissance*, p. 98.
23 Quoted in Walter Harding, *The Days of Henry Thoreau* (New York: Alfred A. Knopf, 1968), p. 337.
24 *TEM*, p. 92.
25 *HDT*, I, 136.
26 *HDT*, VI, 96, 97.
27 *HDT*, VI, 102.
28 *JHDT*, I, 240.
29 *HDT*, VI, 163.
30 *HDT*, I, 130.
31 *JHDT*, V, 264.
32 *The Writings of Henry David Thoreau. Reform Papers*, ed. Wendell Glick (Princeton: Princeton University Press, 1973), VI, 184. The subsequent quotations in this paragraph are on p. 191.
33 *HDT*, II, 82. The subsequent quotations from *Walden* in this and the following paragraphs are on pp. 2, 240, 100, 164.
34 *HDT*, VI, 295, 296.
35 *PW*, II, 473.
36 *PW*, II, 668.
37 *WWC*, V, 509.
38 *WWW*, p. 62.
39 This comment, which appears in Burroughs's notebooks, is quoted in *WWW*, p. 223.
40 *PW*, II, 724.
41 *WEP*, p. 125.
42 *WWC*, I, 93.
43 *WEP*, p. 124.
44 "The Eighteenth Presidency!" (1856), in *NUPM*, p. 2135.
45 "Origins of Attempted Secession," *PW*, I, 427.
46 *ISit*, pp. 118, 119.
47 *Brooklyn Daily Eagle*, December 22, 1846.
48 *WWC*, I, 223.
49 *WUP*, II, 69, 71.
50 *LGC*, p. 11.
51 *LGC*, p. 50.
52 *LGC*, p. 386. The subsequent quotations in this paragraph are on p. 385.
53 *LGC*, p. 588. The next indented quotation is on p. 585.
54 *LGC*, pp. 591, 593, 594. The next quotation in this paragraph is on p. 592.
55 *ISit*, pp. 44, 83.
56 *LGC*, p. 593.
57 *LGC*, p. 390.
58 *WWW*, p. 62.
59 *WWC*, V, 490.

CHAPTER 4

1 H. James, *Hawthorne* (1879; rpt., Ithaca: Cornell University Press, 1956), p. 145.
2 Julian Hawthorne, *Hawthorne Reading*, p. 107.
3 "A Select Party," *Mosses*, p. 68.
4 N. Hawthorne, *The American Notebooks* (Centenary Edition, Ohio State University Press, 1932), p. 12.

5 *Hawthorne's Lost Notebook* (University Park: Pennsylvania State University Press, 1978), p. 17. The subsequent quotations in this paragraph are on pp. 26, 58.

6 "A Rill from the Town Pump," in *TTT*, p. 148.

7 *Letters of Gallowrake*, p. 40.

8 *McDowall's Journal*, May 1833.

9 *Literary Comment in American Renaissance Newspapers: Fresh Discoveries Concerning Emerson, Thoreau, Alcott and Transcendentalism*, ed. Kenneth Walter Cameron (Hartford: Transcendental Books, 1977), p. 87.

10 "Young Goodman Brown," *Mosses*, p. 83.

11 *Mosses*, p. 180. The subsequent quotations in this paragraph are on pp. 218, 399, 402.

12 *SL*, p. 8. The subsequent quotation in the paragraph is on p. 43.

13 This newspaper interchange about Hawthorne's firing from the Salem custom house is reprinted in *Literary Comment in American Renaissance Newspapers*, ed. K. W. Cameron, pp. 16–17.

14 *NHL*, XVI, 269–70.

15 *SL*, p. 43.

16 E. Whipple, *Graham's Magazine* (September 1852), cited in Bertha Faust, *Hawthorne's Contemporaneous Reputation* (New York: Octagon, 1968), p. 100; A. C. Coxe, *The Church Review* (January 1851), included in Kenneth Walter Cameron, *Hawthorne Among His Contemporaries* (Hartford: Transcendental Books, 1968), p. 17.

17 H. James, *Hawthorne*, p. 87.

18 E. A. Duyckinck quoted in B. Faust, *Hawthorne's Contemporaneous Reputation*, p. 70; A. D. Mayo's review in the *Universalist Quarterly and General Review* quoted in Faust, p. 93.

19 "HawMoss," p. 549.

20 *TTT*, p. 309.

21 *TTT*, p. 432.

22 *Mosses*, p. 127.

23 "HawMoss," p. 539.

24 *SL*, p. 217. The subsequent quotations in this paragraph are on pp. 220, 195, 260.

25 *Margaret: A Tale of the Real and Ideal, Blight and Bloom* (Boston: Jordan and Wiley, 1845), p. 253.

26 A. C. Coxe's review included in K. W. Cameron, *Hawthorne Among His Contemporaries*, p. 18.

27 *SL*, p. 54. The subsequent quotations in this paragraph are on pp. 67, 86.

28 *SL*, p. 63.

29 *NHL*, XVI, 312 and 461.

30 *The House of the Seven Gables* (Centenary Edition, Ohio State University Press, 1965), p. 84. The subsequent quotations in this paragraph are on pp. 84, 177, 214, 307.

31 Journal entry for April 8, 1843, included in "Backgrounds and Sources," afterword to *The Blithedale Romance*, ed. Seymour Gross and Rosalie Murphy (New York: W. W. Norton, 1978), p. 239.

32 July 14, 1852, letter to George W. Curtis, included in afterword to the Norton edition of *The Blithedale Romance*, p. 241.

33 *The Blithedale Romance*, p. 12. The subsequent quotations in this paragraph are on pp. 13, 37, 21.

34 *The Blithedale Romance*, pp. 65, 66. The subsequent quotations in this paragraph are on pp. 73, 123.

35 *The Blithedale Romance*, p. 226. The subsequent quotations in this paragraph are on pp. 131, 132, 130.

36 *The Blithedale Romance,* p. 41. The subsequent quotations in this paragraph are on pp. 155, 158.

37 *The Marble Faun; or, The Romance of Monte Beni* (Centenary Edition, Ohio State University Press, 1968), p. 3.

38 *The French and Italian Notebooks* (Centenary Edition, Ohio State University Press, 1980), p. 60.

39 *Our Old Home: A Series of English Sketches* (Centenary Edition, Ohio State University Press, 1970), p. 242.

40 *The American Claimant Manuscripts* (Centenary Edition, Ohio State University Press, 1977), p. 220.

41 *The Elixir of Life Manuscripts* (Centenary Edition, Ohio State University Press, 1977), p. 529.

CHAPTER 5

1 Hawthorne's review appeared in the *Salem Advertiser,* March 26, 1847.

2 *White-Jacket,* p. 283.

3 c. June 1, 1851, letter to Hawthorne, included in *HP,* p. 557.

4 M. P. Rogin, *Subversive Genealogy,* p. 190.

5 W. G. Simms's review appeared in the *Southern Quarterly Review* (July 1850).

6 *Typee,* pp. 6–7. The subsequent quotations from *Typee* in this paragraph and the following two paragraphs are on pp. 15, 258, 126, 125, 189, 132, 157, 192.

7 *Omoo,* p. xiv. The subsequent quotations from *Omoo* in this paragraph and the following one are on pp. 142, 11.

8 *English Review* (March 1848). The subsequent reviews cited in this paragraph are G. W. Peck, *American Review* (July 1847), and J. Auld, *New York Evening Mirror,* July 21, 1847. All the reviews are discussed at length in Hugh W. Hetherington, *Melville's Reviewers: British and American, 1846–1891* (New York: Russell and Russell, 1961), pp. 75, 86, 88.

9 *Mardi,* p. 261. The subsequent quotations from *Mardi* in this paragraph and the following three paragraphs are on pp. 224, 259, 489, 577, 533, 534, 532.

10 "HawMoss," p. 540.

11 This comment in a letter to his father-in-law, Lemuel Shaw, is included in *ML,* p. 316.

12 *Redburn, His First Voyage. Being the Sailor-boy Confessions and Reminiscences of the Son-of-a-Gentleman, in the Merchant Service* (1849; rpt., Evanston: Northwestern University Press, 1969), p. 42. The subsequent quotations from *Redburn* in the next three paragraphs are on pp. 31, 42, 44, 245, 184, 186, 191, 201, 184.

13 *White-Jacket,* p. 75. The subsequent quotations from *White-Jacket* in this paragraph and the following one are on pp. 375–76, 377, 390, 54.

14 *MD,* p. 31.

15 William McNally, *Evils and Abuses in the Naval and Merchant Service, Exposed: With Proposals for their Remedy and Redress* (Boston: Cassady and March, 1839), p. 81. The subsequent quotations in this paragraph are on pp. 90, 79, 21.

16 *White-Jacket,* p. 15. The subsequent quotation in this paragraph is on p. 369.

17 W. McNally, *Evils and Abuses . . . Exposed,* p. 80.

18 *White-Jacket,* pp. 146, 144. The subsequent quotations in this paragraph are on pp. 208, 315, 320, 396.

19 *New York Tribune,* April 4, 1850. The subsequent reviews cited in this paragraph are in the *Biblical Repository and Classical Review,* included in H. W. Hetherington, *Melville's Reviewers,* p. 180; the *London Morning Post,* January 12, 1850; the Boston *Post,* cited in Willard Thorp's "Historical Note" to the

Northwestern University Press edition of *White-Jacket*, p. 435; and *Saroni's Musical Times*, March 30, 1850.

20 *The Liberator*, January 22, 1831.

21 *MD*, p. 333.

22 *MD*, p. 19. The subsequent quotations in this paragraph and the following one are on pp. 367, 401, 402.

23 *MD*, p. 272. The subsequent quotations in this paragraph and the following one are on pp. 273, 21, 23, 155, 18, 15, 167, 351, 50.

24 This exchange between Child and her friend Abby Kelley is in L. M. Child, *Selected Letters, 1817–1880*, ed. M. Meltzer and P. G. Holland, pp. 207, 193.

25 *National Police Gazette* (New York), October 23, 1847.

26 *MD*, p. 144. The subsequent quotations in this paragraph are on pp. 170, 468.

27 Quoted in *ML*, p. 450.

28 *ML*, p. 441.

29 *ML*, pp. 444, 450.

30 *Pierre*, in *PIPCUB*, p. 12.

31 *PIPCUB*, p. 124. The subsequent quotation in this paragraph is on p. 125.

32 *PIPCUB*, pp. 319, 318.

33 See J. D. Bergmann, "The Original Confidence Man: The Development of the American Confidence Man in the Sources and Backgrounds of Herman Melville's Novel," Diss. University of Connecticut, 1969, and Bergmann, "The Original Confidence Man," *American Quarterly*, XXI (Fall 1969), 560–77; and J. B. Seelye, *Melville: The Ironic Diagram* (Evanston: Northwestern University Press, 1970).

34 *New York Herald*, July 11, 1849.

35 *The Confidence-Man: His Masquerade*, in *PIPCUB*, pp. 883, 881. The subsequent quotations in this paragraph are on pp. 938, 1013, 1017.

CHAPTER 6

1 "The Literati of New York City" (1846), in *PER*, p. 1214.

2 Journal entry for May 1852, in *EJ*, p. 433.

3 *JHDT*, IV, 267.

4 Julian Hawthorne, *Hawthorne Reading*, p. 467.

5 *Brooklyn Daily Eagle*, February 8, 1847, and February 26, 1847.

6 *Foreign Quarterly Review* (London), October 1842.

7 C. Dickens, *American Notes and Pictures from Italy* (London: MacDonald and Sons, n.d.), I, 114, 321.

8 Quoted in Lambert A. Wilmer, *Our Press Gang; or, A Complete Exposition of the Corruptions and Crimes of American Newspapers* (Philadelphia: J. T. Lloyd, 1859), p. 261.

9 E. Faithfull, *Three Visits to America* (Edinburgh: David Douglas, 1884), p. 336.

10 *The Tickler*, March 1, 1807.

11 *The American Magazine of Wonders, and Marvellous Chronicle* (January 1809), p. 1. The subsequent quotation in this paragraph is on p. 170.

12 *Genius of Temperance* (New York), November 2, 1831.

13 Isaac Clark Pray, *Memoirs of James Gordon Bennett and His Times* (New York: Stringer and Townsend, 1855), p. 255.

14 *Walt Whitman of the New York Aurora: Editor at Twenty-Two*, ed. Joseph J. Rubin and Charles J. Brown (Westport, Conn.: Greenwood Press, 1950), p. 115.

15 L. A. Wilmer, *Our Press Gang*, p. 312. The next quotation in this paragraph is on p. 173.

16 H. Melville, *The Confidence-Man,* in *PIPCUB,* p. 841.

17 *The Witness* (Litchfield, Conn.), January 29, 1806.

18 *Mosses,* p. 398.

19 *The Trial of Singleton Mercer, for the Murder of M. Hutchinson Heberton* (New York: Herald Office, 1843), p. 6.

20 *The Record of Crimes in the United States* (Buffalo: Charles Faxon, 1833), p. 335.

21 *The Lives of the Felons, or American Criminal Calendar. John and James Harpe* (New York: Burgess & Stringer, 1849), pp. 104–5.

22 *SL,* p. 56.

23 *Record of Crimes,* pp. 232, 257.

24 N. Hawthorne, *American Notebooks,* p. 29.

25 *Trial of George Crowninshield, J. J. Knapp, Jun. and John Francis Knapp, for the Murder of Capt. Joseph White . . .* (Boston: Beals and Homer, 1830), p. 92.

26 For Hawthorne's response to the Knapp trial, see *NHL,* XV, 207–8.

27 *Record of Crimes,* p. 36.

28 *Report of the Trial of Major Mitchell, for the Felonious Assault and Maiming, on the Person of David F. Crawford* (Portland: Colman and Chisholm, 1834), p. 4.

29 H. R. Howard, *The Life and Adventures of John A. Murrell, the Great Western Land Pirate, with Twenty-One Spirited Illustrative Engravings* (New York: H. Long and Brother, 1847), pp. 13, 25.

30 *PIPCUB,* p. 842.

31 G. Thompson, *Life and Exploits of Bristol Bill, the Notorious Burglar* (Boston: Willis Little & Co., 1850), p. 5.

32 H. Melville, *Israel Potter. His Fifty Years of Exile* (1855; rpt., Evanston: Northwestern University Press, 1982), p. 120.

33 *HP,* p. 557.

34 E. Whipple, "The Romance of Rascality" (1848), in *One Hundred Years Ago: American Writing of 1848,* ed. James Playstead Wood (New York: Funk and Wagnalls, 1948). The quotations for this paragraph are in Wood, pp. 478, 479, 483, 484, 479.

35 I have arrived at these statistics after a review of the volumes listed in Lyle Wright, *American Fiction, 1774–1850: A Contribution to a Bibliography.*

36 *ML,* p. 374.

37 H. Melville, "Mr Parkman's Tour," in *PIPCUB,* pp. 1149, 1148.

38 N. Hawthorne, *A Wonder Book and Tanglewood Tales* (1851, 1853; rpt., Centenary Edition, Ohio State University Press, 1972), p. 169.

39 *WWC,* III, 550.

40 Quoted in James Beard's introduction to J. F. Cooper, *The Pioneers, or The Sources of the Susquehanna* (1823; rpt., New York: State University of New York Press, 1980), pp. xxii, xxiii.

41 J. F. Cooper, *The Leatherstocking Saga,* ed. Allan Nevins (New York: Pantheon, 1954), p. 530.

42 *The Leatherstocking Saga,* p. 64.

43 J. F. Cooper, *Home as Found* (1838; rpt., New York: Capricorn, 1961), p. 207.

44 *Home as Found,* p. 238, and "The American Democrat," in *James Fenimore Cooper, Representative Selections,* ed. Robert E. Spiller (New York: American Book Co., 1936), p. 213. The subsequent quotations in this paragraph are on pp. 206, 208, 205.

45 *The Crater; or, Vulcan's Peak* (1847; rpt., New York: G. P. Putnam's Sons, n.d.), p. 473.

46 Francis Parkman, Jr., *The Oregon Trail,* ed. David Levin (1847; rpt., New York: Penguin, 1982), p. 135.

47 Whitman, *Brooklyn Daily Times,* in *WUP,* II, 21. The first quotation in the following paragraph is also on p. 21.

48 Whitman, *LGC*, p. 733.
49 *The Letters of . . . Emerson,* ed. R. L. Rusk, III, 387.
50 *New York Times,* September 28, 1855.
51 *Works of . . . Channing,* p. 105.
52 Alexis de Tocqueville, *Democracy in America,* ed. J. P. Mayer (1835; rpt., Garden City, N.Y.: Anchor, 1969), p. 474.
53 *Edinburgh Review,* L (October 1829), 126, 127.
54 *Democracy in America,* p. 488.
55 J. Neal, *Logan* (Philadelphia: Carey and Lea, 1822), I, 8.
56 W. G. Simms, *The Yemassee, a Romance of South Carolina* (1835; rpt., New York: A. C. Armstrong, 1882), p. 189.
57 W. G. Simms, *Guy Rivers, a Tale of Georgia* (1834; rpt., New York: A. C, Armstrong, 1882), p. 266.
58 G. Thompson, *Venus in Boston: A Romance of City Life* (New York: n.p., 1849), p. 37.
59 *Amelia Sherwood; or, Bloody Scenes at the California Gold Mines* (New York: C. W. and G. E. Kenworthy, 1849), p. 31.
60 *The Female Land Pirate: or Awful, Mysterious and Horrible Disclosures of Amanda Bannoris* (Cincinnati: E. E. Barclay, 1847), p. 18.
61 L. Osborn, *Confessions of a Poet* (Philadelphia: Carey, Lea, and Blanchard, 1835), II, 126, 171.
62 S. Judah, *The Buccaneers; A Romance of Our Country, In Its Ancient Day* (New York, 1827), I, vi.
63 *Desultoria: The Recovered Mss. of an Eccentric* (New York: Baker and Scribner, 1850), p. 54.
64 P. Miller, *The Raven and the Whale: The War of Wits and Words in the Era of Poe and Melville* (New York: Harcourt, Brace, 1956), p. 86.
65 *The Doom of the Dolphin; or, The Sorceress of the Sea* (Boston: F. Gleason, 1848), p. 83.
66 *Romance of the Deep! or The Cruise of the Aeronaut, . . . During a Three Years' Voyage in an American Whale Ship* (Boston: Redding and Co., 1846), p. 25.
67 *HP,* p. 568.
68 *A Romance of the Sea-Serpent, or The Ichthyosaurus* (Cambridge, Mass.: John Bartlett, 1849), p. 57. The next quotation in this paragraph is on p. 31.
69 *HP,* p. 567.
70 John Neal, *American Writers: A Series of Papers Contributed to Blackwood's Magazine (1824–1825),* ed. Fred Lewis Pattee (Durham: Duke University Press, 1937), pp. 202, 201. The subsequent quotations in this paragraph are on p. 201.
71 L. Osborn, *Sixty Years in the Life of Jeremy Levis* (New York: G. & C. & H. Carvill, 1831), I, 121.
72 W. G. Simms, *Richard Hurdis: A Tale of Alabama* (1838; rpt., New York: Belford, Clarke, & Co., 1888), p. 239.
73 N. Buntline, *The G'hals of New York* (New York: Robert M. De Witt, 1850), p. 76.
74 *QC,* p. 106.
75 G. Thompson, *New-York Life: The Mysteries of Upper-Tendom Revealed* (New York: Charles S. Atwood, 1849), p. 5.
76 *Democracy in America,* pp. 474, 478.
77 J. Neal, *Seventy-Six* (Baltimore: Joseph Robinson, 1823), I, v.
78 J. Neal, *Errata; or, The Works of Will Adams* (New York, 1823), I, 59.
79 *Logan,* I, i.
80 *Errata,* I, 58.
81 "P's Correspondence," in *Mosses,* p. 378.
82 J. Neal, *Randolph, A Novel* (1823), II, 183, 184.

83 *The Unknown Poe*, p. 3.

84 *Seventy-Six*, I, 214.

85 *Seventy-Six*, I, 17.

86 *Errata*, I, v.

87 This comment by Jane Grey Swisshelm was quoted by G. Lippard in the *Quaker City* weekly, August 18, 1849.

88 *Quaker City* weekly, September 9, 1849; for this and the subsequent Lippard citations in this paragraph, see *George Lippard, Prophet of Protest: Writings of an American Radical, 1822–1854*, ed. David S. Reynolds (New York: Peter Lang, 1986).

89 For a discussion of this and other Lippardian passages in Karl Marx's writings, see D. S. Reynolds's introduction to *George Lippard, Prophet of Protest* and Franklin Rosemont, "George Lippard and the Worker's Movement," *Free Spirits*, no. 2 (1983).

90 Sean Wilentz, *Chants Democratic*, p. 263.

91 [John Bell Bouton], *The Life and Choice Writings of George Lippard* (New York: H. H. Randall, 1855), p. 96.

92 G. Lippard, *Paul Ardenheim; The Monk of the Wissahikon. A Romance of the American Revolution* (1848; rpt., Philadelphia: T. B. Peterson, 1876), p. 533. The next quotation in this paragraph is on p. 534.

93 G. Lippard, *The Nazarene; or, The Last of the Washingtons* (Philadelphia: G. Lippard & Co., 1846), p. vii.

94 Quoted in the *Quaker City* weekly, May 12, 1849.

95 *QC*, p. 23.

96 E. Whipple, *Lectures on Subjects Connected with Literature and Life* (Boston: Ticknor, Reed, and Fields, 1849), p. 20. The next quotation in this paragraph is on p. 8.

97 N. Hawthorne, "Earth's Holocaust," in *Mosses*, p. 398; J. H. Ingraham, *The Adventures of Will Wizard!* (Boston: H. L. Williams, 1845), p. 4.

98 *The Literary World*, February 9, 1850.

99 J. B. Jones, *Freaks of Fortune; or, The History and Adventures of Ned Lorn* (Philadelphia: T. B. Peterson, 1854), p. 199.

100 *New York Times*, September 18, 1855.

101 *Confessions and Experience of a Novel Reader* (Chicago: William Stacy, 1855), p. 27. The subsequent quotations in this paragraph are on pp. 39, 48, 73, 77.

CHAPTER 7

1 For example, Walter Kendrick generalizes that in the first half of the nineteenth century pornography was virtually "a non-issue in the United States" (*The Secret Museum: Pornography in Modern Culture* [New York: Viking, 1987], p. 129).

2 *WWW*, p. 233.

3 J. Neal, *Logan*, I, 41.

4 J. Neal, *Errata*, I, 136. The subsequent quotations in this paragraph are in I, 286, 217, 274, 129.

5 *Memoir . . . of the Late Rev. John R. M'Dowall*, p. 222.

6 *The Solitary Vice Considered*, p. 12.

7 *Letters of Gallowrake*, p. 11.

8 *McDowall's Journal*, May 1833.

9 L. Osborn, *Confessions of a Poet*, I, 205, 158.

10 *Advocate of Moral Reform* (New York), March 1, 1845, and May 15, 1845.

11 *WUP*, p. 191.
12 *The Blithedale Romance*, p. 99.
13 *LGC*, p. 96. The next quotation in this paragraph is on p. 101.
14 J. H. Smith, *The Green Family; or, The Veil Removed* (Springfield: Smith and Jones, 1849), p. 68.
15 *Holden's Dollar Magazine* (New York), I (July 1848), 423.
16 G. Lippard, *QC*, pp. 1, 2.
17 *QC*, pp. 83–84.
18 G. Thompson, *New-York Life*, p. 78.
19 *Narrative and Confessions of Lucretia P. Cannon . . . Containing an Account of Some of the Most Horrible and Shocking Murders and Daring Robberies Ever Committed by the Female Sex* (New York: n.p., 1841), p. 11.
20 *Life and Confessions of Mary Jane Gordon* (Augusta: n.p., 1847), p. 9.
21 A. J. H. Duganne, *Eustace Barcourt: or The Illegitimate* (Philadelphia: G. B. Zieber & Co., 1848), p. 32. The next quotation in this paragraph is on p. 65.
22 *Ellen Merton, The Belle of Lowell: or, Confessions of the "G.F.K" Club* (Boston: Brainard & Co., 1844), p. 11.
23 *The Green Family*, p. 64. The next quotation in this paragraph is on p. 70.
24 *Mary Ann Temple. Being an Authentic and Romantic History of an Amorous and Lively Girl, of Exquisite Beauty, and Strong Natural Love of Pleasure!* (New York: Henry S. G. Smith & Co., c. 1849), pp. 76, 77.
25 G. Thompson, *New-York Life*, p. 78.
26 *Venus in Boston*, pp. 65, 40, 25.
27 *City Crimes; or, Life in New York and Boston* (New York: William Berry & Co., 1849), p. 49.
28 *My Life: or The Adventures of George Thompson. Being the Auto-Biography of an Author* (Boston: Federehen & Co., 1854), p. 57.
29 *Venus in Boston*, p. 98.
30 *City Crimes*, pp. 138, 131.
31 G. Thompson, *The Mysteries of Bond Street; or, The Seraglios of Upper Tendom* (New York, 1859), p. 78.
32 J. Neal, *The Down-Easters* (New York: Harper & Brothers, 1833), II, 92.
33 David Brion Davis, *Homicide in American Fiction, 1798–1860: A Study in Social Values* (Ithaca: Cornell University Press, 1957), p. 206.
34 *Revelations of a Slave Smuggler: Being the Autobiography of Capt. Richard Drake, An African Trader for Fifty Years* (New York: Robert M. De Witt, 1860), p. 95.
35 *Life and Confessions of Mary Jane Gordon*, p. 11.
36 *The Female Land Pirate*, p. 20.
37 *The Road to Ruin: or, A Felon's Doom* (New York: Frederic A. Brady, c. 1851), p. 49.
38 *NF*, p. 146.
39 *WCP*, p. 1032.

CHAPTER 8

1 "The Wild" (1851), *HDT*, V, 231.
2 "HawMoss," p. 545.
3 *LEAP*, I, 58.
4 *EAP*, II, 340.
5 *LEAP*, I, 287, 253.
6 *LEAP*, I, 227.
7 From Poe's preface to *The Raven and Other Poems*, quoted in T. O. Mabbott's introduction to *EAP*, II, xv.

8 *PER*, p. 579. The subsequent quotations in this paragraph are on pp. 1414–15, 1161, 1035, 1034.

9 *PER*, p. 1448. The subsequent quotations in this paragraph are on pp. 1151 (two quotations), 573.

10 Quoted in A. H. Quinn, *Edgar Allan Poe*, p. 367.

11 *PER*, pp. 670 (on Longfellow), 1005 (on Wilmer), 102, 101 (on Ainsworth).

12 *LEAP*, I, 242–43.

13 *PER*, pp. 152, 153. The subsequent quotations in this paragraph are on pp. 367, 833, 893.

14 *PER*, pp. 860, 855.

15 *Burton's Magazine*, February 1840.

16 *Complete Works of . . . Poe*, ed. J. A. Harrison, VIII, 32.

17 *PER*, p. 903.

18 *Complete Works of . . . Poe*, ed. J. A. Harrison, XI, 3.

19 *PER*, p. 445.

20 *EAP*, III, 1300. The subsequent quotation in this paragraph is on II, 610.

21 *The Edgar Allan Poe Scrapbook*, ed. Peter Haining (New York: Schocken, 1978), p. 81.

22 *LEAP*, I, 58.

23 The pamphlet was entitled *Trial, Confession, and Execution of Peter Robinson for the Murder of Abraham Suydam, Esq., of New Brunswick, N.J.* (New Brunswick, 1841).

24 "The Tell-Tale Heart," *EAP*, III, 792. The subsequent quotation in this paragraph is on p. 792.

25 "The Man of the Crowd," *EAP*, II, 511. The subsequent quotations in this paragraph are both on p. 514.

26 "William Wilson," *EAP*, II, 426. The subsequent quotations in this paragraph and the following one are on pp. 427, 429, 447, 432, 438.

27 "The Fall of the House of Usher," *EAP*, II, 407. The subsequent quotation in this paragraph is on p. 413.

28 This review, which appeared in the *New World* in February 1845, is quoted in *The Poe Log: A Documentary Life of Edgar Allan Poe, 1809–1849*, ed. Dwight Thomas and David K. Jackson (Boston: G. K. Hall, 1987), p. 503.

29 "The Masque of the Red Death," *EAP*, II, 673. The subsequent quotations in this paragraph are on pp. 672, 677.

30 "The Psyche Zenobia," *EAP*, II, 340. The quotation in the following paragraph is on p. 342.

31 *PER*, p. 402.

32 "MS. Found in a Bottle," *EAP*, II, 135.

33 *PER*, p. 1221. The subsequent quotations in this paragraph are on p. 1220.

34 *PER*, pp. 1414–15.

35 "A Tale of the Ragged Mountains," *EAP*, III, 941–42.

36 *PER*, p. 329.

37 *PER*, p. 760.

38 "The Imp of the Perverse," *EAP*, III, 1221.

39 "The Mystery of Marie Rogêt," *EAP*, III, 738. The subsequent quotation in this paragraph is on p. 724.

40 *LEAP*, I, 258.

41 "The Purloined Letter," *EAP*, III, 993.

CHAPTER 9

1 *PER*, p. 579.
2 H. Melville, "HawMoss," p. 542.
3 Julian Hawthorne, *Hawthorne Reading*, p. 39.
4 *The American Notebooks*, p. 29.
5 *NHL*, XV, 207.
6 *Trial of George Crowninshield, J. J. Knapp, and John Francis Knapp . . .* , p. 4. The subsequent quotations in this paragraph are on pp. 92, 93.
7 *NHL*, XV, 217, 230.
8 *The American Notebooks*, pp. 178, 176.
9 *Record of Crimes in the United States*, p. 44. The subsequent quotations in this paragraph are on pp. 205, 36, 86, 301.
10 "Young Goodman Brown" (1835), *Mosses*, p. 87. The quotation in the following paragraph is on p. 83.
11 J. Hawthorne, *Hawthorne Reading*, p. 107.
12 *NHL*, XV, 489.
13 "Wakefield," *TTT*, p. 130.
14 N. Hawthorne, "Old News," *The Snow-Image and Uncollected Tales* (1851; rpt., Centenary Edition, Ohio State University Press, 1974), II, 132, 135.
15 *Mosses*, p. 20.
16 "The Sister Years," *TTT*, p. 340.
17 *Mosses*, p. 30.
18 *NHL*, XVI, 518.
19 "P's Correspondence," *Mosses*, p. 378.
20 Quoted in Julian Hawthorne, *Hawthorne and His Wife: A Biography* (1885; rpt., Boston: Houghton Mifflin, 1892), I, 145.
21 *NHL*, XV, 590.
22 *NHL*, XVI, 435. The subsequent quotations in this paragraph are on pp. 462, 312, 270.
23 "The Procession of Life," in *Mosses*, p. 215.
24 D. M. Reese, *Humbugs of New-York*, p. 217.
25 *Trial (Before the Municipal Court) of Charles L. Cook, Late Preacher of the Gospel of the Orthodox and Restorationist Denominations . . .* (Boston: S. N. Dickinson, 1835), pp. 2–3.
26 *National Police Gazette*, December 9, 1848.
27 C. R. Williams, *Fall River. An Authentic Narrative* (Boston: Lilly, Wait and Co., 1833), p. 144.
28 R. Culbertson, *Rosamund; or, A Narrative of the Captivity and Sufferings of an American Female under the Popish Priests in the Island of Cuba* (1836; rpt., Pittsburgh: John Sharp, 1848), p. 63.
29 "Young Goodman Brown," *Mosses*, p. 87.
30 "The Minister's Black Veil," *TTT*, p. 46.
31 G. Thompson, *The Countess*, p. 19.
32 G. Thompson, *New-York Life*, p. 53.
33 *Morning Courier and New York Enquirer*, October 31, 1833.
34 "The Banquet of the Gallows," *Diogenes, hys Lantern* (New York), February 12, 1853.
35 *Advocate of Moral Reform* (New York), March 1, 1843.
36 *Uncle Sam* (Boston), July 3, 1846.
37 *SL*, p. 5. The subsequent quotations in this paragraph are on pp. 19, 31, 41, 43.
38 *SL*, p. 50. The subsequent quotations in this paragraph are on pp. 56, 237.

39 *SL*, p. 189.
40 *The House of the Seven Gables*, p. 256. The subsequent quotations in this paragraph are on pp. 257, 265.
41 *The House of the Seven Gables*, pp. 145, 146. The next quotation in this paragraph is on p. 212.
42 *The House of the Seven Gables*, p. 21, and G. Thompson, *New-York Life*, p. 88.
43 *The House of the Seven Gables*, p. 84.
44 *The Blithedale Romance*, p. 130. The next quotation in this paragraph is on p. 224.
45 *The Marble Faun*, p. 384.
46 *The Marble Faun*, pp. 460, 461. The next quotation in this paragraph is on p. 3.
47 *Our Old Home*, p. 242.
48 *The Marble Faun*, p. 461.
49 *The American Claimant Manuscripts*, p. 82. The subsequent quotations in this paragraph are on pp. 198, 265, 267.

CHAPTER 10

1 *New York Evangelist*, November 20, 1851, and *Athenaeum*, October 25, 1851, included in *Moby-Dick as Doubloon: Essays and Extracts (1851–1970)*, ed. Hershel Parker and Harrison Hayford (New York: W. W. Norton, 1970), pp. 41, 8.
2 *Athenaeum*, June 2, 1855.
3 Quoted in "Editorial Appendix," *The Confidence-Man: His Masquerade*, ed. Hershel Parker et al. (Evanston: Northwestern University Press, 1983), p. 298.
4 Quoted in M. P. Rogin, *Subversive Genealogy*, p. 73.
5 *The Native Muse: Theories of American Literature*, ed. Richard Ruland (New York: E. P. Dutton, 1972), I, 302.
6 *The Native Muse*, p. 275.
7 *The Native Muse*, p. 305.
8 "HawMoss," p. 543.
9 *HP*, pp. 556–57.
10 *Israel Potter*, p. 120.
11 June 15, 1846, letter to John Murray, quoted in Merrell R. Davis, *Melville's Mardi: A Chartless Voyage* (1952; rpt., New Haven: Archon, 1967), p. 24.
12 *Typee*, p. 126.
13 *Omoo*, pp. xiii. The subsequent quotations in this paragraph are on pp. 14, 28.
14 *Mardi*, pp. 41, 42, 103. The subsequent quotation in this paragraph is on p. 40.
15 *Mardi*, p. 383.
16 *Mardi*, p. 197. The subsequent quotations in this paragraph are on pp. 436, 437.
17 *Mardi*, p. 135. The subsequent quotations in this paragraph are on pp. 269, 283.
18 *Redburn*, p. 48. The subsequent quotations in this paragraph are on pp. 86, 46, 190.
19 *ML*, p. 327.
20 *Mardi*, p. 595.
21 *Redburn*, p. 57. The subsequent quotations in this paragraph are on pp. 58, 104, 105, 48.
22 *White-Jacket*, p. 74. The subsequent quotations in this paragraph are on pp. 176, 39.

23 *White-Jacket*, p. 187. The indented quotation at the end of this paragraph is on p. 188.

24 *HP*, p. 557.

25 "HawMoss," p. 546. The next quotation in this paragraph, from Melville's November 17, 1851, letter to Hawthorne, is on p. 566.

26 *MD*, pp. 76, 77. The subsequent quotations in this paragraph are on pp. 104, 105.

27 *MD*, p. 147. The subsequent quotations in this paragraph are on pp. 161, 185, 235, 169.

28 *MD*, pp. 76 and 93. The subsequent quotations in this paragraph are on pp. 53, 155.

29 *HP*, p. 558. The subsequent quotation in this paragraph, from Melville's November 17, 1851, letter to Hawthorne, is on p. 566. The quotations in the next two paragraphs are in "HawMoss," pp. 543, 545.

30 *Pierre, PIPCUB*, p. 287.

31 *City Crimes*, p. 31.

32 *New-York Life*, pp. 92, 96.

33 G. Thompson, *The Mysteries of Bond Street*, p. 58.

34 *PIPCUB*, p. 18. The subsequent quotations from *Pierre* in this paragraph are in *PIPCUB*, pp. 80, 244, 319, 67. The quotation in the following paragraph is on p. 313.

35 George G. Foster, *New York in Slices* (New York: William H. Graham, 1849), p. 16. The subsequent quotations in this paragraph are on pp. 18, 19, 20, 11, 30.

36 "Bartleby, the Scrivener," *PIPCUB*, p. 653. The subsequent quotations in this paragraph are on pp. 642, 652, 651.

37 "Bartleby," *PIPCUB*, p. 661. The next quotation in this paragraph is on p. 670. The first quotations in the following paragraph are on p. 635.

38 *MD*, p. 452.

39 "Bartleby," *PIPCUB*, p. 636. The subsequent quotation in this paragraph is on p. 643.

40 "Benito Cereno," *PIPCUB*, p. 692. The next quotation in this paragraph is on p. 716.

41 "Benito Cereno," *PIPCUB*, p. 754.

42 June 7, 1854, letter to George P. Putnam, in *ML*, 489.

43 *Israel Potter*, p. 54. The subsequent quotations in this paragraph are on pp. 95, 120. The quotation in the next paragraph is on p. 96.

44 See especially the fine discussions of the topic in Gary Lindberg, *The Confidence Man in American Literature* (New York: Oxford University Press, 1982), and William E. Lenz, *Fast Talk and Flush Times: The Confidence Man as a Literary Convention* (Columbia: University of Missouri Press, 1985).

45 *QC*, p. 23. The subsequent quotations in this paragraph are on pp. 23, 182, 37, 155, 436.

46 G. Foster, *Celio: or, New York Above-Ground and Under-Ground* (New York: De Witt and Davenport, 1850), p. 68.

47 *The Mysteries of Bond Street*, p. 31.

48 N. Buntline, *The G'hals of New York* (New York: Robert M. De Witt, 1850), p. 25. The subsequent quotations in this paragraph are on pp. 134, 197.

49 James Hall, *Legends of the West* (Philadelphia: Harrison Hall, 1832), p. 3.

50 *The Confidence-Man, PIPCUB*, p. 1008. The subsequent quotations in this paragraph are on pp. 1007, 954.

51 *PIPCUB*, pp. 1043, 1054. The subsequent quotation in this paragraph is on p. 1081. The quotations in the following paragraph are on pp. 866, 868.

52 H. Melville, *Clarel: A Poem and Pilgrimage in the Holy Land*, ed. Walter E. Bezanson (1876; rpt., New York: Hendricks House, 1960), pp. 234, 233.

53 *Billy Budd, PIPCUB,* p. 1357. The subsequent quotations in this paragraph are on pp. 1372, 1373, 1384, 1383.

54 *Billy Budd, PIPCUB,* p. 1371. The subsequent quotations in this paragraph are on pp. 1430, 1427.

CHAPTER 11

1 *WCP,* p. 23.

2 *WCP,* p. 1329.

3 *Brooklyn Daily Times,* December 13, 1858, in *WUP,* II, 20, 21.

4 *Leaves of Grass* (1855), in *WCP,* pp. 33, 39. For a discussion of the journalistic aspects of Whitman's poetry, see Shelley Fisher Fishkin, *From Fact to Fiction: Journalism and Imaginative Writing in America* (Baltimore: John Hopkins University Press, 1985), Ch. 1. See also Justin Kaplan, *Walt Whitman, A Life* (New York; Simon & Schuster, 1980), Chs. 5–7, and Gay Wilson Allen, *The Solitary Singer: A Critical Biography of Walt Whitman* (New York: New York University Press, 1955), Chs. 2 and 3.

5 *Voices from the Press,* ed. James J. Brenton (New York, 1850), p. 88.

6 *PW,* I, 258.

7 *PW,* II, 529.

8 *Democratic Vistas,* in *WCP,* p. 938. The subsequent quotations from *Democratic Vistas* in this paragraph are on p. 937, with the exception of the final quotation, which is on p. 939. The quotation from George Thompson is in *New-York Life,* p. 88.

9 *WWW,* p. 81.

10 *LGV,* I, 237.

11 *WWC,* I, 375.

12 *WUP,* I, 103.

13 *WUP,* II, 71.

14 *LGC,* p. 593.

15 *EL,* p. 450.

16 The first reviewer is quoted in P. Zweig, *Walt Whitman: The Making of the Poet,* p. 153; the second, from the *Westminister Review,* is in *NYD,* p. 175.

17 J. Neal, *Randolph,* II, 190. The Neal quotation in the next sentence is on II, 84.

18 Included in *George Lippard, Prophet of Protest,* ed. D. S. Reynolds, p. 224.

19 *WUP,* II, 71.

20 *NUPM,* I, 407.

21 *NYD,* p. 64.

22 A. Parry, *Garrets and Pretenders,* p. 31; and *NYD,* p. 175.

23 G. Lippard, *The Empire City: or, New York by Night and Day* (New York: Stringer and Townsend, 1850), p. 205.

24 G. Foster, *New York Naked,* p. 12.

25 G. Foster, *Celio,* p. 68.

26 G. Foster, *Fifteen Minutes Around New York* (New York: De Witt and Davenport, 1854), p. 53.

27 *New York Naked,* p. 10.

28 *Brooklyn Daily Eagle,* August 13, 1847.

29 *NYD,* p. 130.

30 *Democratic Vistas,* in *WCP,* pp. 955, 974, 975.

31 *WCP,* p. 939.

32 *PW,* II, 638–39.

33 *LGV,* I, 116. The subsequent quotation in this paragraph is on II, 549.

34 *LGV*, III, 612. The subsequent quotation in this paragraph is on p. 568.
35 *LGV*, I, 219.
36 *LGV*, I, 118.
37 *LGV*, I, 129.
38 *WCP*, p. 50.
39 *WCP*, pp. 1031, 1032.
40 *Democratic Vistas*, in *WC*, pp. 974, 975.
41 *NF*, p. 146.
42 *ISit*, p. 113.
43 *LGC*, p. 202.
44 *WCP*, p. 982.
45 *WUP*, VI, 2136.
46 *Brooklyn Daily Eagle*, July 11, 1846, in *NF*, p. 103.
47 *Brooklyn Daily Eagle*, March 4, 1847; the subsequent quotation in this paragraph is in the *Brooklyn Daily Eagle*, April 2, 1847. The quotations are included in W. Whitman, *The Gathering of Forces*, ed. C. Rodgers and J. Black, II, 305, and II, 304.
48 *WCP*, p. 19. The next quotation in this paragraph is on p. 29.
49 *LGV*, I, 32, 119. The subsequent quotations in this paragraph are in *LGC*, pp. 1, 594.
50 *NF*, p. 40. The next quotation in this paragraph is on p. 66.
51 *WCP*, p. 15.
52 *Whitman's Manuscripts: Leaves of Grass (1860), A Parallel Text* (Chicago: University of Chicago Press, 1955), pp. 18–19.
53 *WCP*, p. 939. The subsequent quotation in this paragraph is on p. 941.
54 Quoted in Edward Carpenter, *Days with Walt Whitman* (London, 1906), pp. 142–45.
55 "Song of the Exposition," in *LGV*, III, 619.
56 *NUPM*, I, 413. The subsequent quotations in this paragraph are on I, 889, 890.
57 *LGC*, pp. 96, 432, 504, 182, 480, 117.
58 *WCP*, p. 27.
59 *LGC*, p. 202.
60 G. Thompson, *New-York Life*, p. 78, and *City Crimes*, p. 49.
61 *WCP*, p. 36. The quotation in the next paragraph is on p. 47.
62 *LGC*, pp. 53, 96, 105.
63 *WCP*, p. 29. The subsequent quotation in this paragraph is on p. 34.
64 *WCP*, p. 26.
65 *WWC*, II, 525.

CHAPTER 12

1 See Ann Douglas, *The Feminization of American Culture*, as well as George B. Forgie, *Patricide in the House Divided: A Psychological Interpretation of Lincoln and His Age* (New York: W. W. Norton, 1979), and Mary Kelly, *Private Woman, Public Stage: Literary Domesticity in Nineteenth-Century America* (New York: Oxford University Press, 1984).
2 See J. P. Tompkins, *Sensational Designs*, Chs. 5 and 6, and Nina Baym, *Women's Fiction: A Guide to Novels by and about Women in America, 1820–1870* (New York: Cornell University Press, 1978). See also P. Fisher, *Hard Facts*.
3 *The Golden Age* (New York), April 19, 1873.
4 A. Douglas, *The Feminization of American Culture*, p. 1.
5 *Springfield Republican*, July 7, 1860.

6 Emily Faithfull, *Three Visits to America,* pp. 317, 318.

7 *The Revolution* (New York), August 4, 1870.

8 M. Dalzeil, *Popular Fiction 100 Years Ago: An Unexplored Tract of Literary History* (London: Cohen & West, 1957), pp. 87, 90.

9 Tocqueville, *Democracy in America,* p. 602.

10 "Woman in the Nineteenth Century," in *The Writings of Margaret Fuller,* ed. Mason Wade (New York: Viking, 1941), p. 172.

11 *Writings of Margaret Fuller,* p. 210.

12 Susan Warner, *The Wide, Wide World* (1850; rpt., Philadelphia: J. B. Lippincott & Co., 1869), p. 263.

13 E. O. Smith, *The Sinless Child and Other Poems* (New York: Wiley and Putnam, 1843), p. 132.

14 *A Peep at the Pilgrims in Sixteen Hundred Thirty-Six* (Boston: Wills and Lilly, 1824), II, 64, 32.

15 E. B. Lee, *Delusion; or, The Witch of New England* (Boston: Hilliard, Gray and Co., 1840), p. iii.

16 E. B. Lee, *Naomi; or, Boston Two Hundred Years Ago* (Boston: Crosby and Nichols, 1848), p. 233.

17 *Advocate of Moral Reform,* May 15, 1839.

18 *The Ladies' Repository* (Cincinnati), February 1841.

19 Louisa Hall, *Alfred* (Boston: Munroe, 1836), p. 13.

20 M. Cummins, *The Lamplighter* (Leipzig: B. Tauchnitz, 1854), pp. 97, 151.

21 *Writings of Margaret Fuller,* p. 215.

22 *The Liberator,* April 11, 1851.

23 J. Neal, *Logan,* I, 80.

24 W. G. Simms, *Guy Rivers,* p. 390.

25 W. G. Simms, *The Yemassee,* p. 392.

26 J. F. Cooper, *The Leatherstocking Saga,* ed. A. Nevins, p. 251.

27 J. K. Duer, *The Nautilus: A Collection of Select Nautical Tales and Sea Sketches, With an Authentic Narrative of the Mutiny of the Somers, in the New World,* ed. Park Benjamin (New York, 1845), p. 29.

28 M. M. Ballou, *Fanny Campbell: or The Female Pirate Captain. A Tale of the Revolution* (New York: Samuel French, 1845), p. 12.

29 *PER,* p. 1201.

30 N. Hawthorne, *A Wonder Book and Tanglewood Tales,* p. 169.

31 This passage from a letter by Edward Dickinson is quoted in Richard B. Sewall, *The Life of Emily Dickinson* (New York: Farrar, Straus and Giroux, 1974), p. 49.

32 Edward Halsey Foster, foreword to Catharine Maria Sedgwick, *Hope Leslie; or, Early Times in . . . Massachusetts* (1827; rpt., New York: Garrett Press, 1969), p. iv.

33 *HopeLeslie,* I, 164. The subsequent quotation in this paragraph is on II, 292.

34 *The Linwoods; or, "Sixty Years Since" in America* (New York: Harper & Brothers, 1835), I, 34, 229. The subsequent quotations in this paragraph are on II, 97, 238, 223.

35 *Writings of Margaret Fuller,* pp. 207–8. The subsequent quotations in this paragraph are on pp. 215, 153.

36 *Writings of Margaret Fuller,* p. 122. The subsequent quotation in this paragraph is on p. 176.

37 *The Una* (Providence, R.I.), October 1853.

38 S. Wilentz, *Chants Democratic,* p. 118.

39 *A Moral Response to Industrialism: The Lectures of Reverend Cook in Lynn, Massachusetts,* ed. John Taylor Cumbler (Albany: State University of New York Press, 1982), p. 34.

40 H. Melville, "The Tartarus of Maids," *PIPCUB*, p. 1270.

41 C. W. Webber, *Spiritual Vampirism*, p. 241.

42 *The Aristocrat and Trades Union Advocate, A Colloquial Poem* (Boston: Leonard K. Kimball, 1834), p. 30.

43 A. I. Cummings, *The Factory Girl; or Gardez La Coeur* (Lowell: J. E. Short, 1847), p. 135.

44 *Brooklyn Daily Eagle*, June 17, 1846, in W. Whitman, *The Gathering of Forces*, p. 158.

45 G. Lippard, "The Sisterhood of the Green Veil," *The Nineteenth Century. A Quarterly Miscellany* (Philadelphia), II (1849), 746.

46 *The Elliott Family; or, The Trials of New-York Seamstresses* (1845; rpt., New York: Baker and Scribner, 1850), p. 26.

47 *The Elliott Family*, p. vii.

48 M. A. Denison, *Edna Etheril, the Boston Seamstress* (New York: Burgess, Stringer, & Co., 1847), p. 40.

49 *Brooklyn Daily Eagle*, January 29, 1847, in W. Whitman, *The Gathering of Forces*, p. 148.

50 *The Una*, March 1854. The subsequent quotation in this paragraph is in *The Una*, September 1853.

51 L. D. Blake, *Fettered for Life; or, Lord and Master* (New York: Sheldon & Co., 1874), p. 257.

52 Quoted in Miriam Gurko, *The Ladies of Seneca Falls: The Birth of the Women's Rights Movement* (New York: Macmillan, 1974), p. 157.

53 *Address to Females* (New York: George S. Sickels, 1831), p. 11.

54 M. L. Fox, *The Ruined Deacon. A True Story* (1834; rpt., Boston: D. H. Ela & Co., 1846), p. 33.

55 *Autobiography of a Reformed Drunkard* (Philadelphia: Griffith and Simon, 1845), p. 38.

56 Grimké's *Letters on the Equality of the Sexes*, reprinted in *The Feminist Papers: From Adams to Beauvoir*, ed. Alice S. Rossi (New York: Bantam, 1974), p. 314.

57 *The Liberty Bell* (Boston, 1842), p. 7.

58 F. Douglass, *The Narrative and Selected Writings*, p. 278.

59 *The Feminist Papers*, ed. A. Rossi, pp. 427, 428.

60 R. Hildreth, *The Slave*, I, 7.

61 H. L. Gates quoted in Leslie Bennetts, "An 1859 Black Literary Landmark Is Uncovered," *New York Times*, November 8, 1982.

62 Harriet E. Wilson, *Our Nig; or, Sketches from the Life of a Free Black, in a Two-Storey White House, North* (Boston: George C. Rand & Avery, 1859), p. 12. The subsequent quotation in this paragraph is on p. 108.

63 *New York by Gas-Light* (New York: De Witt & Davenport, 1850), p. 36.

64 G. Thompson, *The Mysteries of Bond Street*, p. 35.

65 *McDowall's Journal*, May 1833.

66 *Democracy in America*, p. 602.

67 *Salem Gazette*, January 29, 1833.

68 S. Judd, *Margaret*, p. 253.

69 *Record of Crimes in the United States*, p. 205.

70 *A Report of the Trial of the Rev. Ephraim K. Avery . . . for the Murder of Sarah Maria Cornell* (Boston: Russell, Odione and Co., 1833), p. 132.

71 William W. Smithers, *The Life of John Lofland, "The Milford Bard," the Earliest and Most Distinguished Poet of Delaware* (Philadelphia: Wallace M. Leonard, 1894), p. 221.

72 N. Buntline, *The G'hals of New York*, p. 191. The subsequent quotation in this paragraph is on p. 231.

73 *QC*, p. 85. The subsequent quotation in this paragraph is on p. 137.

74 G. Thompson, *City Crimes*, p. 49; *Venus in Boston*, pp. 93, 40; *New-York Life*, p. 78. The subsequent quotation in this paragraph is in *Venus in Boston*, p. 65.

CHAPTER 13

1 "Young Goodman Brown," *Mosses*, p. 85.
2 "The Procession of Life," *Mosses*, pp. 209–10.
3 "The Christmas Banquet," *Mosses*, p. 303.
4 "Earth's Holocaust," *Mosses*, p. 389.
5 "The New Adam and Eve," *Mosses*, p. 253.
6 "Rappaccini's Daughter," *Mosses*, p. 127. The next quotation in this paragraph is on p. 105.
7 Julian Hawthorne, *Hawthorne and His Wife*, I, 360.
8 June 1849 letter to H. W. Longfellow, *NHL*, XVI, 270.
9 *SL*, p. 160. The subsequent quotations in this paragraph are on pp. 83, 195, 32.
10 *SL*, p. 81. The quotations in the next paragraph are on p. 263.
11 J. Hawthorne, *Hawthorne and His Wife*, I, 383.
12 *NHL*, XVI, 376.
13 *The House of the Seven Gables*, p. 82. The subsequent quotation in this paragraph is on p. 38.
14 *The Blithedale Romance*, p. 170. The subsequent quotations in this paragraph are on pp. 26, 31.
15 *NHL*, XV, 589.
16 *The Blithedale Romance*, p. 183.
17 Quoted in J. Hawthorne, *Hawthorne and His Wife*, I, 261, 262.
18 *Writings of Margaret Fuller*, p. 176.
19 *NHL*, XVI, 536.
20 *The Blithedale Romance*, p. 13.
21 *The Blithedale Romance*, p. 44.
22 *Westminster Review* (October 1852); review reprinted in afterword to the Norton Critical Edition of *The Blithedale Romance*, p. 273.
23 *The Blithedale Romance*, pp. 155, 158.
24 Letter to William Davis Ticknor, quoted in Caroline Ticknor, *Hawthorne and His Publisher* (Boston: Houghton Mifflin, 1913), pp. 141–42.
25 Letter to W. D. Ticknor, quoted in C. Ticknor, *Hawthorne and His Publisher*, pp. 142–43.
26 *The Marble Faun*, p. 121.
27 *The Marble Faun*, pp. 43, 44. The subsequent quotations in this paragraph are on pp. 68, 172, 191, 198, 286, 15–16, 280.
28 *The Marble Faun*, p. 41. The subsequent quotation in this paragraph is on p. 461.
29 *American Claimant Manuscripts*, p. 292. The next quotation in this paragraph is on p. 333.
30 N. Hawthorne, *Elixir of Life Manuscripts*, p. 542.
31 *Elixir of Life Manuscripts*, p. 171. The subsequent quotation in this paragraph is on p. 174.
32 *American Claimant Manuscripts*, p. 87.

CHAPTER 14

1 *The Marble Faun,* p. 128.
2 J. S. Appleton, *Voices from Kenduskeag* (Bangor: David Bugbee, 1848), p. 251.
3 *SL,* pp. 263.
4 *PER,* p. 1172.
5 Paul Harro-Hanning, *Dolores: A Novel of South America* (New York: Marrenna, Lockwood & Co., 1846), p. 135. The subsequent quotations in this paragraph are also on p. 135.
6 Sarah J. Hale, *The Lecturess: or Woman's Sphere* (Boston: Whipple and Damrell, 1839), p. 25. The subsequent quotations in this paragraph are on pp. 38, 39, 65, 120.
7 *Lessons of Life,* in *The Una,* October 1854.
8 *The Revolution,* June 23, 1870.
9 Bullard's letter and Whitman's response to it are included in *WWC,* III, 555–56.
10 L. C. Bullard, *Now-A-Days!* (New York: T. L. Magagnos, 1854), p. vi.
11 L. C. Bullard, *Christine; or, Woman's Trials and Triumphs* (New York: De Witt and Davenport, 1856), p. 169. The subsequent quotations in this paragraph are on pp. 185, 286.
12 A. Argyle, *Money and Marriage. A Modern Story* (New York: S. & A. Hoyt, 1862), p. iii.
13 *Springfield Republican,* July 7, 1860.
14 *The Una,* October 1855. The subsequent quotation in this paragraph is in *The Una,* July 1, 1853.
15 *The Una,* October 1855.
16 *New York Times,* August 13, 1869.
17 Gerald Graff, "Feminist Criticism in the University: An Interview with Sandra Gilbert," in *Criticism in the University,* ed. Gerald Graff and Reginald Gibbons (Evanston: Northwestern University Press, 1985), p. 117.
18 *The Una,* December 1854.
19 *The Una,* October 1854.
20 *Springfield Republican,* July 7, 1860.
21 Quoted in Mary Clemmer Ames, *A Memorial of Alice and Phoebe Cary, with Some of Their Later Poems* (New York: Hurd and Houghton, 1873), p. 75.
22 Untitled newspaper review, *Susan B. Anthony Scrapbooks, 1848–1900.* Berg Collection, New York Public Library.
23 M. C. Ames, *Alice and Phoebe Cary,* p. 22. The subsequent quotations in this paragraph are on pp. 99, 145, 80.
24 *The Una,* May 2, 1853.
25 A. Cary, *Hagar, A Story of To-day* (Redfield: Clinton Hall, 1852), p. 300.
26 A. Cary, *Married, Not Mated; or, How They Lived at Woodside and Throckmorton Hall* (New York: Derby and Jackson, 1859), p. 59. The subsequent quotation in this paragraph is on p. 140.
27 Quoted in Katherine Devereux Blake and Margaret Louise Wallace, *Champion of Women: The Life of Lillie Devereux Blake* (New York: Fleming H. Revell, 1943), p. 25.
28 *The Golden Age,* May 16, 1874.
29 L. D. Blake, *Southwold: A Novel* (New York: Rudd & Carleton, 1859), p. 18. The quotations in the next paragraph are on pp. 235, 140.
30 Letter to W. D. Ticknor, quoted in C. Ticknor, *Hawthorne and His Publisher,* pp. 142–43.
31 Millicent Todd Bingham, *Emily Dickinson's Home: Letters of Edward Dickinson and His Family* (Toronto: Masson, 1955), pp. 312–13.

32 *New York Ledger,* July 23, 1855.
33 *Life and Beauties of Fanny Fern,* pp. 72, 76. The subsequent quotation in this paragraph is on p. 276.
34 *Life and Beauties of Fanny Fern,* p. 32.
35 *The Una,* February 1855.
36 Sara Payson (Willis) Parton, *Ruth Hall: A Domestic Tale of the Present Time* (New York: Mason Brothers, 1855), p. 212. The subsequent quotations in this paragraph are on pp. 317, 268, 33. The indented quotation in the following paragraph is on p. 255.
37 *Life and Beauties of Fanny Fern,* pp. 67, 181.
38 *Ruth Hall,* p. iii. The subsequent quotation in this paragraph is on p. 316.
39 L. M. Alcott, *Little Women; or, Meg, Jo, Beth and Amy* (1869; rpt., London: Collier Macmillan, 1962), p. 301. The subsequent quotations in this paragraph are on pp. 305, 387, 394, 395.
40 Quoted in LaSalle C. Pickett, *Across My Path: Memories of People I Have Known* (1916; rpt., Freeport, N.Y.: Books for Libraries Press, 1970), p. 107.
41 L. M. Alcott to A. Whitman, Concord, June 22, 1862. Houghton Library, Harvard University.
42 *Behind a Mask: The Unknown Thrillers of Louisa May Alcott,* ed. Madeleine Stern (New York: William Morrow & Co., 1975), p. 25. The subsequent quotations in this paragraph are on p. 12.
43 Elizabeth Stoddard, *The Morgesons and Other Writings, Published and Unpublished,* ed. L. Buell and S. A. Zagarell (Philadelphia: University of Pennsylvania Press, 1984), p. xi.
44 Henry James, *Literary Criticism* (New York: Library of America, 1984), p. 614.
45 *The Morgesons,* p. 143.
46 *The Morgesons,* p. 23. The subsequent quotations in this paragraph are on pp. 155, 212.
47 R. H. Davis, *Life in the Iron-Mills; or, The Korl Woman,* ed. Tillie Olsen (1861; rpt., Old Westbury, N.Y.: Feminist Press, 1972), p. 88. The subsequent quotations in this paragraph are on pp. 32, 11, 22, 25.
48 Sandra M. Gilbert and Susan Gubar, *The Madwoman in the Attic: The Woman Writer and the Nineteenth-Century Literary Imagination* (New Haven: Yale University Press, 1979); Wendy Martin, *An American Triptych: Anne Bradstreet, Emily Dickinson, Adrienne Rich* (Chapel Hill: University of North Carolina Press, 1984); Margaret Homans, *Women Writers and Poetic Identity: Dorothy Wordsworth, Emily Brontë, and Emily Dickinson* (Princeton: Princeton University Press, 1980); Vivian R. Pollak, *Dickinson: The Anxiety of Gender* (Ithaca: Cornell University Press, 1984). See also Cristanne Miller, *Emily Dickinson: A Poet's Grammar* (Cambridge, Mass.: Harvard University Press, 1987).
49 *Feminist Critics Read Emily Dickinson,* ed. Suzanne Juhasz (Bloomington: Indiana University Press, 1983), p. 17.
50 George Frisbie Whicher, *This Was a Poet: A Critical Biography of Emily Dickinson* (New York: Charles Scribner's Sons, 1938); Richard B. Sewall, *The Life of Emily Dickinson* (New York: Farrar, Straus & Giroux, 1974); Ruth Miller, *The Poetry of Emily Dickinson* (Middletown: Wesleyan University Press, 1968); Barton Levi St. Armand, *Emily Dickinson and Her Culture: The Soul's Society* (London: Cambridge University Press, 1984); Cynthia Griffin Wolff, *Emily Dickinson* (New York: Alfred A. Knopf, 1986).
51 Quoted in Richard B. Sewall, *The Lyman Letters: New Light on Emily Dickinson and Her Family* (Amherst: University of Massachusetts Press, 1965), p. 71. In the present chapter, as in Ch. 1, all texts of Emily Dickinson's poems are from *The Poems of Emily Dickinson,* ed. Thomas H. Johnson.
52 S. P. Parton, *Ruth Hall,* p. 133.

53 L. D. Blake, *Southwold,* p. 47.

54 *The Una,* June 1855.

55 *EDL,* II, 374.

56 Sue P. K. Bowen, *Sylvia's World. Crimes Which the Law Does Not Reach* (New York: Derby and Jackson, 1859)), p. 11.

57 A. Cary, *Married, Not Mated,* p. 414.

58 A. Cary, *Hagar,* p. 170.

59 *The Una,* March 1854.

60 *The Female Skeptic; or, Faith Triumphant* (New York: Robert M. De Witt, 1859), p. 176.

61 A. Cary, *Hagar,* p. 300.

62 L. C. Bullard, *Christine,* p. 23.

63 *EDL,* I, 104.

64 Parton, *Ruth Hall,* p. 229.

65 L. C. Bullard, *Christine,* p. 18.

66 *The Female Skeptic,* p. 286.

67 *Life and Beauties of Fanny Fern,* p. 270.

68 *EDL,* II, 414.

69 *The Autobiography of a Married Woman. No Girlhood* (New York: S. A. Rollo & Co., 1859), p. 155.

70 *EDL,* I, 150.

71 *EDL,* I, 99, 210.

72 *YH,* II, 6.

73 *EDL,* II, 404.

74 *EDL,* II, 412.

75 Hélène Cixous, "The Laugh of the Medusa," trans. Keith Cohen and Paula Cohen, in *New French Feminisms,* ed. Elaine Marks and Isabelle de Courtivron (Amherst: University of Massachusetts Press, 1980), p. 256.

76 *EDL,* I, 264.

77 *EDL,* I, 113, 114.

78 *EDL,* I, 78. The quotation from this letter in the next paragraph is on p. 79.

79 *EDL,* I, 91. The subsequent quotation in this paragraph is on p. 92.

CHAPTER 15

1 *The Crockett Almanac 1839. Containing Adventures, Exploits, Sprees, and Scrapes in the West and Life and Manners in the Backwoods* (Nashville: Ben Harding, 1839), p. 2.

2 Constance Rourke, *American Humor: A Study of the National Character* (New York: Harcourt, Brace, 1931), Chs. 1 and 2.

3 Walter Blair and Hamlin Hill, *America's Humor: From Poor Richard to Doonesbury* (New York: Oxford University Press, 1978). See especially pp. 35–41, 173–83, 196–220.

4 M. M. Bakhtin, *The Dialogic Imagination,* ed. M. Holquist, p. 408.

5 Francis Jeffrey, quoted in *The Native Muse,* ed. R. Ruland, p. 74.

6 *The Annual Review,* quoted in *The Native Muse,* p. 79.

7 Tocqueville, *Democracy in America,* pp. 478, 479.

8 Horace Bushnell, *God in Christ. Three Discourses, Delivered at New Haven, Cambridge, and Andover, with a Preliminary Dissertation on Language* (Hartford: Brown and Parsons, 1849), p. 55.

9 Washington Irving, *Salmagundi,* in *History, Tales and Sketches* (New York: Library of America, 1983), pp. 202. The quotation in the next paragraph is on p. 162.

10 W. Irving, *History, Tales and Sketches*, p. 380. The subsequent quotations in this paragraph are on pp. 383, 391, 418.

11 W. Irving, *History, Tales and Sketches*, p. 779. The subsequent quotations in this paragraph are on pp. 783, 784.

12 W. Irving, *History, Tales and Sketches*, pp. 1058, 1060.

13 *EL*, p. 1250.

14 *JHDT*, II, 171.

15 *Mardi*, p. 105, and *MD*, p. 306.

16 *WC*, II, 176.

17 William Dean Howells and Henry Mills Alden, *Southern Lights and Shadows* (New York: Harper & Brothers, 1907), p. vi.

18 *Crockett's Almanac, 1848* (Boston: James Fisher, 1848).

19 *Davy Crockett's 1844 Almanac* (Boston: James Fisher, 1844). For a useful discussion of the nineteenth-century Crockett phenomenon, see *Davy Crockett: The Man, the Legend, the Legacy, 1786–1986*, ed. Michael A. Lofaro (Knoxville: University of Tennessee Press, 1985).

20 *Davy Crockett's Almanac for 1845* (Boston: James Fisher, 1845).

21 *Crockett Almanac for 1856* (New York: Philip J. Cozans, 1856).

22 *Davy Crockett's 1837 Almanack of Wild Sports in the West, Life in the Backwoods, and Sketches of Texas* (Nashville, 1837).

23 *Crockett's Yaller Flower Almanac for '36* (New York: Elton, 1836).

24 Johnson Jones Hooper, *Adventures of Captain Simon Suggs, Late of the Tallapoosa Volunteers* (1844; rpt., Chapel Hill: University of North Carolina Press, 1969), p. 1.

25 *Humor of the Old Southwest*, ed. Hennig Cohen and William B. Dillingham (Boston: Houghton Mifflin, 1964), p. 74.

26 *Humor of the Old Southwest*, p. 253. The quotation in the next paragraph is on p. 254.

27 G. W. Harris, *Sut Lovingood*, ed. Brom Weber (New York: Grove Press, 1954), p. 138. The indented quotation at the end of the next paragraph is on p. 149.

28 *Sut Lovingood*, p. 41. The subsequent quotations in this paragraph are on pp. 21, 172, 171, 200.

29 *The Complete Short Stories of Mark Twain*, ed. Charles Neider (New York: Bantam, 1958), p. 674.

30 *The Subterranean*, January 24, 1846, and September 9, 1843.

31 G. Thompson, *New-York Life*, pp. 5, 88.

32 H. Melville, *The Confidence-Man*, in *PIPCUB*, p. 935.

33 A representative segment of the ritual is reprinted in *George Lippard, Prophet of Protest*, ed. D. S. Reynolds, pp. 80–84.

34 Quoted in *George Lippard, Prophet of Protest*, ed. D. S. Reynolds, p. 250.

35 *QC*, pp. 165, 7. The quotations in the next paragraph are on pp. 210, 211, 151.

36 *QC*, p. 34. The reference later in this paragraph to Frederick Douglass's irony is in F. Douglass, *The Narrative and Selected Writings*, ed. M. Meyer, p. xiv.

37 G. Lippard, *QC*, pp. 389, 388. The subsequent quotation in this paragraph ("by a hazy atmosphere . . .") is on p. 370.

38 W. Blair and H. Hill, *America's Humor*, p. 150.

39 S. Wilentz, *Chants Democratic*, p. 263.

40 G. Foster, *New York by Gas-Light*, p. 107.

41 *New York by Gas-Light*, p. 101. The subsequent quotations in this paragraph are on pp. 108, 109.

42 Quoted in C. Ticknor, *Hawthorne and His Publisher*, p. 138.

43 G. Foster, *Fifteen Minutes Around New York*, p. 34.

44 *WCP*, p. 50.

45 R. W. Emerson, "The Comic" (lecture of 1839), *CWE,* VIII, 158–59, 161.

46 H. Melville, "Authentic Anecdotes of 'Old Zack,'" *PIPCUB,* p. 1140.

47 Quoted in Phineas T. Barnum, *Struggles and Triumphs; or, The Life of P. T. Barnum, Written by Himself,* ed. George S. Bryan (New York: Alfred A. Knopf, 1927), p. xliv. The subsequent quotation in this paragraph is on p. xvi.

48 See M. M. Bakhtin, *Rabelais and His World* (Cambridge, Mass.: MIT Press, 1968), and *Problems of Dostoevski's Poetics* (New York: Ardis, 1973).

49 *The New York Picayune,* July 12, 1856.

50 Quoted in George F. Whicher, *This Was a Poet: A Critical Biography of Emily Dickinson,* p. 176.

51 *The New York Picayune,* August 23, 1856.

52 W. H. Levison, *Black Diamonds; or, Humor, Satire, and Sentiment, Treated Scientifically by Professor Julius Caesar Hannibal. A Series of Burlesque Lectures, Darkly Colored. Originally Published in "The New York Picayune"* (New York: A Ranney, 1855), pp. 25, 27. The quotations in the next paragraph are on pp. 199, 245.

53 *Diogenes, hys Lantern,* April 17, 1852.

54 *The Yankee Doodle* (New York), October 31, 1846.

55 M. N. Thompson, *Doesticks' Letters: and What He Says* (Philadelphia: T. B. Peterson, 1855), p. 21.

56 *The New York Picayune,* November 1, 1856.

57 *Diogenes, hys Lantern,* February 19, 1853.

58 *The New York Picayune,* February 9, 1856.

59 *The John-Donkey* (New York and Philadelphia), March 18, 1848. The burlesque cited in the following sentence appeared in the May 6, 1848, issue.

60 *EDL,* I, 264.

61 *Diogenes, hys Lantern,* May 14, 1853.

62 *The Yankee Doodle,* December 19, 1846. The article cited in the following sentence is in the March 27, 1847, issue.

63 *The John-Donkey,* January 1, 1848.

64 *Holden's Dollar Magazine,* II (July 1848), 422, 423.

65 M. N. Thompson, *Doesticks' Letters,* p. 232.

66 G. Foster, *New York in Slices,* p. 91.

67 *De Darkie's Comic All-Me-Nig* (Philadelphia: Colon and Adriance, 1846).

68 *The New York Picayune,* June 14, 1856.

69 *Diogenes, hys Lantern,* April 24, 1852.

70 *The New York Picayune,* June 14, 1856.

71 *Young America* (New York), I (1856), 165.

72 *Diogenes, hys Lantern,* April 17, 1852.

73 *Diogenes, hys Lantern,* May 29, 1852.

74 *Diogenes, hys Lantern,* June 12, 1852.

75 M. N. Thompson, *Plu-Ri-Bus-Tah. A Song that's by No Author; A Deed without a Name* (Philadelphia: T. B. Peterson, 1856), pp. 203–60.

76 Fred Folio, *Lucy Boston; or, Woman's Rights and Spiritualism: Illustrating the Follies and Delusions of the Nineteenth Century* (Auburn and Rochester: Alsen and Beardsley, 1855), p. 403.

77 *The Yankee Doodle,* November 28, 1846, and July 17, 1847.

78 *The New York Picayune,* March 20, 1858.

79 *Diogenes, hys Lantern,* October 16, 1852.

80 *The New York Picayune,* December 6, 1856. The *Picayune* piece mentioned in the next sentence is in the July 24, 1852, issue.

81 *The John-Donkey,* February 19, 1848.

82 *The John-Donkey,* March 18, 1848.

83 *The New York Picayune,* July 12, 1856.

84 M. N. Thompson, *Plu-Ri-Bus-Tah,* pp. ix–x.

85 *The New York Picayune,* August 2, 1856.
86 G. Hugnet quoted in J. H. Matthews, *An Introduction to Surrealism* (Philadelphia: Pennsylvania State University Press, 1965), p. 64.
87 M. N. Thompson, *Doesticks' Letters,* p. 30.
88 *The John-Donkey,* March 25, 1848.

CHAPTER 16

1 "The American Scholar," *EL,* p. 68.
2 *The Journals of Bronson Alcott,* ed. Odell Shepard (Boston: Little, Brown, 1938), p. 68.
3 *EJ,* p. 6. The subsequent quotation in this paragraph is on p. 58.
4 *Journals of Bronson Alcott,* p. 60. The subsequent quotations in this paragraph are on pp. 81, 82, 24.
5 *Emerson Among His Contemporaries: A Harvest of Estimates, Insights, and Anecdotes from the Victorian Literary World,* ed. Kenneth Walter Cameron (Hartford: Transcendental Books, 1967), p. 106. The subsequent quotation in this paragraph is on p. 115.
6 *EJ,* pp. 158, 340.
7 "Power," *EL,* p. 980.
8 *LecE,* I, 224. The subsequent quotation in this paragraph is also on p. 224.
9 "Europe and European Books," *EL,* p. 1250.
10 *JE,* IV, 297.
11 *EJ,* 240–41, 218.
12 James Russell Lowell, *Literary Essays* (Boston and New York: Houghton Mifflin, 1892), p. 353, and *The Correspondence of Emerson and Carlyle,* ed. Joseph Locke Slater (New York: Columbia University Press, 1964), p. 371.
13 *Emerson Among His Contemporaries,* pp. 28, 43.
14 *EJ,* p. 372.
15 *LecE,* II, 186.
16 *EL,* p. 10.
17 *EL,* p. 22. The subsequent quotations in this paragraph are on pp. 22, 23.
18 *EL,* p. 32.
19 "The American Scholar," *EL,* pp. 68–69. The indented quotations at the end of this paragraph are, successively, on pp. 54, 64, 66 (two), 68.
20 "The American Scholar," *EL,* p. 69.
21 The Divinity School Address, *EL,* pp. 75, 79, 81. The next quotation in this paragraph is on p. 80.
22 "Self-Reliance," *EL,* p. 265.
23 "The Comic," *CWE,* VIII, 158–59, 161–62.
24 "Success," *CWE,* VII, 290.
25 "The Fortune of the Republic" (address of 1878), *CWE,* XI, 537.
26 *EJ,* p. 372.
27 "The Tragic" (1844), *EL,* p. 1289. The subsequent quotation in this paragraph is on p. 1295.
28 "The Poet," *EL,* pp. 454–55.
29 "Self-Reliance," *EL,* p. 262.
30 "The Transcendentalist," *EL,* p. 194.
31 "Experience," *EL,* p. 478.
32 Letter to Thomas Carlyle, May 10, 1838, in *Norton Anthology of American Literature,* I, 859.
33 *Christian Register,* August 26, 1854.
34 *Graham's Magazine,* XLV (September 1854), 299.

35 *Knickerbocker Magazine,* March 1855.
36 *JHDT,* VII, 7–8.
37 *JHDT,* VI, 238; I, 301; X, 191; III, 327.
38 *JHDT,* II, 179.
39 H. D. Thoreau, *A Week* [. . .], *Walden* [. . .], *Cape Cod* (New York: Library of America, 1985), p. 151.
40 *JHDT,* IV, 267.
41 *JHDT,* VII, 89.
42 *HDT,* II *(Walden),* 363. The next quotation in this paragraph is on p. 9.
43 *TEM,* pp. 236–37.
44 *Salem Observer,* November 25, 1848.
45 *Salem Observer,* March 3, 1849.
46 *JHDT,* VII, 89.
47 For a representative sampling of reprinted Thoreau passages, see *Literary Comment in American Renaissance Newspapers: Fresh Discoveries Concerning Emerson, Thoreau, Alcott and Transcendentalism,* ed. Kenneth Walter Cameron (Hartford: Transcendental Books, 1977), pp. 37–49.
48 This and other comparisons between the early drafts of *Walden* and the final version are based on my analysis of parallel texts of successive drafts reprinted in J. Lyndon Shanley, *The Making of Walden, with the Text of the First Edition* (Chicago: University of Chicago Press, 1957).
49 *JHDT,* VII, 103.
50 *HDT,* II *(Walden),* 94.
51 R. M. Bird, *Nick of the Woods, or the Jibbenainosay: A Tale of Kentucky* (1837; rpt., New York: Vanguard, 1928), p. 49.
52 *HDT,* II *(Walden),* 2.
53 *HDT,* II *(Walden,)* 65. The subsequent quotations in this paragraph are on pp. 15, 24, 28.
54 *HDT,* II *(Walden),* 58. The subsequent quotations in this paragraph are on pp. 77, 119.
55 *TEM,* p. 244.
56 *HDT,* II *(Walden),* 109. The quotation in the next paragraph is on p. 20.

CHAPTER 17

1 *WWC,* IV, 49.
2 This interchange between Schmidt and Whitman is reprinted in *WC,* II, 176.
3 W. Whitman, "The Sun-Down Papers," *WUP,* I, 44, 45.
4 *WEP,* p. 241.
5 *WUP,* I, 194.
6 *WUP,* I, 226.
7 *Brooklyn Daily Eagle,* January 9, 1847.
8 *NYD,* p. 21. The subsequent quotation in this paragraph is on p. 130.
9 G. Foster, *New York by Gas-Light,* p. 109.
10 W. D. Howells, *Criticism and Fiction and Other Essays* (New York: New York University Press, 1959), p. 271.
11 W. Whitman, "The Old Bowery," in *PW,* II, 595.
12 G. Foster, *New York Naked,* p. 44.
13 *PW,* I, 172.
14 *NUPM,* I, 333. The next quotation in this paragraph is on p. 199.
15 *WWC,* III, 582.
16 *WCP,* p. 83.
17 *LGV,* I, 189.

18 *LGV*, II, 307.
19 *WCP*, p. 50.
20 Review in *Putnam's Monthly* (September 1855), reprinted in *Leaves of Grass Imprints* (Boston: Thayer and Eldridge, 1860).
21 *PW*, I, 285.
22 *WWW*, p. 130.
23 *LGC*, p. 64.
24 *LGC*, p. 424.
25 G. Lippard, *The Midnight Queen;* passage reprinted in *George Lippard, Prophet of Protest*, ed. D. S. Reynolds, p. 299.
26 *LGC*, p. 424.
27 *LGC*, p. 426. The subsequent quotation in this paragraph is on p. 427. The quotations in the next paragraph are on pp. 431, 432.
28 *LGC*, p. 592.
29 *LGC*, pp. 162–63. The quotations in the next paragraph are both on p. 160.
30 *LGC*, p. 32.
31 *WC*, I, 41.
32 *LGC*, pp. 87, 59.

CHAPTER 18

1 *The Poe Log*, p. 576.
2 *PER*, p. 796.
3 *PER*, pp. 586–87.
4 *PER*, p. 587. The subsequent quotation in this paragraph is on p. 782.
5 "The Psyche Zenobia," *EAP*, II, 357.
6 "Never Bet the Devil Your Head," *EAP*, II, 631.
7 "The Angel of the Odd," *EAP*, III, 1101. The subsequent quotation in this paragraph is on p. 1104.
8 *PER*, p. 399. The next quotation in this paragraph is on p. 402.
9 "Diddling Considered as One of the Exact Sciences," *EAP*, III, 870.
10 T. D. English in *The Aristidean* (October 1845), quoted in T. O. Mabbott's prefatory note to "The Gold-Bug," *EAP*, III, 799. For Poe's boast about the wide circulation of "The Gold-Bug," see *LEAP*, I, 253.
11 *PER*, p. 611.
12 E. A. Poe, "The Gold-Bug," *EAP*, III, 835.
13 *American Claimant Manuscripts*, p. 292.
14 *The Yankee Blade* (Boston), September 29, 1849.
15 *The Literary World*, IX (November 29, 1851), 424.
16 "HawMoss," p. 538.
17 *Bakhtin: Essays and Dialogues on His Work*, ed. Gary Saul Morson (Chicago: University of Chicago Press, 1986), p. ix.
18 *American Claimant Manuscripts*, p. 58.
19 *SL*, p. 5.
20 *SL*, p. 17. The quotation in the next sentence is on p. 19.
21 "Preface to the Second Edition," *The Complete Novels and Selected Tales of Nathaniel Hawthorne*, ed. Norman Holmes Pearson (New York: Modern Library, 1937), p. 83.
22 *SL*, p. 18. The subsequent quotations in this paragraph are on pp. 8, 11, 10.
23 *SL*, p. 151.
24 H. James, *Hawthorne*, p. 94.
25 *The John-Donkey*, March 25, 1848.
26 *SL*, p. 56.

27 *ML*, p. 253.
28 *ML*, p. 264.
29 *New Monthly Magazine* (London), XCVII (July 1853), 307.
30 *Omoo*, p. 41.
31 The Black Sampson episode from Lippard's *Washington and His Generals* is reprinted in *George Lippard, Prophet of Protest*, ed. D. S. Reynolds, pp. 124–28.
32 G. Lippard, *Blanche of Brandywine* (1846); passage reprinted in *George Lippard, Prophet of Protest*, p. 286.
33 *MD*, p. 21. The subsequent quotations in this paragraph are on pp. 25, 31.
34 "HawMoss," p. 543.
35 *MD*, p. 14, The subsequent quotations in this paragraph are on pp. 15, 16.
36 *MD*, p. 52.
37 *MD*, p. 189.
38 *QC*, p. 34.
39 H. Melville, c. June 1, 1851, letter to N. Hawthorne, *HP*, pp. 558.
40 *MD*, p. 113. The subsequent quotations in this paragraph are on pp. 149, 360, 392, 115, 116.
41 *MD*, p. 149.
42 P. T. Barnum, *Struggles and Triumphs*, p. 317.
43 *MD*, p. 108.
44 W. H. Levison, *Black Diamonds*, p. 155.
45 *MD*, p. 170.
46 *MD*, p. 345.
47 W. H. Levison, *Black Diamonds*, p. 41.
48 *MD*, p. 362.
49 *MD*, p. 75.
50 "HawMoss," p. 545.
51 *MD*, p. 246.
52 *MD*, p. 188. The quotation in the next sentence is on p. 189.
53 *Mardi*, p. 597.
54 The quotations in this sentence are in *MD*, pp. 108, 105.
55 "HawMoss," p. 543.
56 November 17, 1851, letter to Hawthorne, *HP*, p. 566.
57 G. W. Harris, *The Sut Lovingood Papers*, p. 171.
58 M. N. Thompson, *Plu-Ri-Bus-Tah*, p. ix.
59 P. T. Barnum, *Struggles and Triumphs*, p. 408.
60 *PIPCUB*, p. 988.
61 *PIPCUB*, pp. 1098, 1097.
62 *PIPCUB*, p. 915.
63 *Diogenes, hys Lantern*, February 19, 1853.
64 *PIPCUB*, p. 874, and *The New York Picayune*, July 24, 1852.
65 *The New York Picayune*, June 14, 1856.
66 *PIPCUB*, p. 1037. The subsequent quotation in this paragraph is also on p. 1037.
67 C. W. Webber, *Spiritual Vampirism*, p. 257.
68 F. Folio, *Lucy Boston*, p. 403.
69 M. N. Thompson, *Plu-Ri-Bus-Tah*, p. ix.
70 *The New York Picayune*, November 1, 1856. The indented quotation at the end of this paragraph is also in this issue of the *Picayune*.
71 *PIPCUB*, p. 848.
72 *PIPCUB*, p. 846.

EPILOGUE

1 *WWC,* IV, 54.
2 *Writings of Margaret Fuller,* ed. M. Wade, p. 398.
3 H. James, letter to the Hon. Robert S. Rantoul, June 10, 1904, in H. James, *Literary Criticism,* p. 474. For further discussion of the relation between canon revision and literary artistry, see David S. Reynolds, "Revising the American Canon: The Question of Literariness," *Canadian Journal of Comparative Literature,* VIII (June 1986), 230–35.
4 H. James, *Literary Criticism,* p. 364. The subsequent quotation in this paragraph is on p. 473. The quotations in the next paragraph are both on p. 320.

INDEX

ILLUSTRATIONS CREDITS

Grateful acknowledgment is made to the following for permission to reproduce photographs and drawings that appear after page 340 and on the book jacket:

Photograph of Herman Melville by permission of the Houghton Library, Harvard University.

Daguerreotype portrait of Emily Dickinson by permission of the Trustees of Amherst College.

Daguerreotype of Edgar Allan Poe courtesy of Brown University Library. Photography: John Miller Documents.

Portrait of Nathaniel Hawthorne by Charles Osgood, 1840. Photograph © 1987 Mark Sexton. Courtesy of the Essex Institute, Salem, Massachusetts.

Photograph of Ralph Waldo Emerson courtesy of the Ralph Waldo Emerson Memorial Association, Boston.

Photograph of Walt Whitman by Frank Pearsall, 1869, from the Oscar Lion Collection of Walt Whitman, Rare Books and Manuscripts Division, The New York Public Library, Astor, Lenox and Tilden Foundations.

Daguerreotype of Henry David Thoreau by B. D. Maxham, 1856. Courtesy of the Concord Free Public Library, Concord, Massachusetts.

Detail from the frontispiece of the temperance work *Deacon Giles' Distillery,* by George B. Cheever. Courtesy of the American Antiquarian Society.

Engravings from the popular novel *The Doom of the Dolphin,* by Harry Halyard, 1848. Courtesy of the Houghton Library, Harvard University.

A NOTE ABOUT THE AUTHOR

David S. Reynolds is a literary scholar and professor of American litera-
ture who was born and raised in Rhode Island. He received his B.A. from
Amherst College and his Ph.D. from the University of California, Berke-
ley. Professor Reynolds is currently a member of the English Department
at Rutgers University at Camden, where he is Henry Rutgers Research
Fellow and Director of Whitman Studies. He has previously taught
American literature and American Studies at Northwestern University,
Barnard College, and New York University. His publications include
Faith in Fiction: The Emergence of Religious Literature in America (1981), *George
Lippard* (1982), and *George Lippard, Prophet of Protest: Writings of an American
Radical, 1822–1854* (anthology, 1986). He is also the author of numerous
articles and reviews in the field of American literature and culture.

A NOTE ON THE TYPE

The text of this book has been set in a digitized version of a typeface
called Baskerville. The face is a facsimile reproduction of types cast from
molds made for John Baskerville (1706–75) from his designs. The
punches for the revived Linotype Baskerville were cut under the supervi-
sion of the English printer George W. Jones. John Baskerville's original
face was one of the forerunners of the type style known as modern face
to printers: a "modern" of the period A.D. 1800. Composed by The
Haddon Craftsmen, Inc., Scranton, Pennsylvania. Printed and bound by
Fairfield Graphics, Fairfield, Pennsylvania.

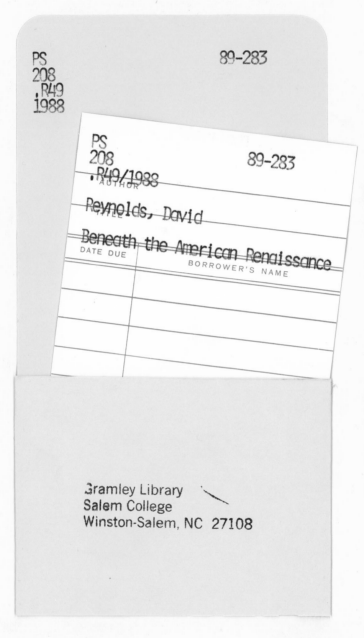